外教社学术阅读文库

语义学经典论文选读
Basic Readings in Semantics

束定芳 选编

上海外语教育出版社
外教社 SHANGHAI FOREIGN LANGUAGE EDUCATION PRESS

图书在版编目（CIP）数据

语义学经典论文选读／束定芳选编.
—上海：上海外语教育出版社，2014（2017重印）
（外教社学术阅读文库）
ISBN 978-7-5446-3816-6

Ⅰ.①语… Ⅱ.①束… Ⅲ.①语义学—文集 Ⅳ.①H030-53

中国版本图书馆CIP数据核字（2014）第217721号

出版发行：上海外语教育出版社
（上海外国语大学内） 邮编：200083
电　　话：021-65425300（总机）
电子邮箱：bookinfo@sflep.com.cn
网　　址：http://www.sflep.com.cn http://www.sflep.com
责任编辑：蒋浚浚

印　　刷：江苏凤凰数码印务有限公司
开　　本：700×1000 1/16 印张39.5 字数684千字
版　　次：2014年12月第1版 2017年12月第2次印刷

书　　号：ISBN 978-7-5446-3816-6 / H·1377
定　　价：78.00 元

本版图书如有印装质量问题，可向本社调换

目 录

第四部分：认知语义学

编者的话

　　欧美很多知名大学，在本科阶段许多课程就要求学生阅读经典，包括人文学科的一些名著，还有各学科领域的标志性著作，这既是通识教育的一部分，同时又是学科训练的要求。到了研究生阶段，学生则被要求大量阅读各学科领域最近发表的各类学术著作和论文，以尽快走到学术前沿并尝试去发现和解决目前研究中的一些问题。

　　但是，在中国，就外语学科而言，本科阶段主要还是学习语言本身，知识积累和学术训练则严重不足。以前的课程内容中所学语言中的文学经典阅读还是学生语言基本功训练的一部分（这对学生综合素质的提高非常关键），而现在很多学校已将文学内容改成经贸方面等选读课了，其他人文方面的经典——包括中国文化的经典，学生在本科阶段基本不可能接触到。

　　就语言学（主要指外国语言学与应用语言学）专业而言，很多人到了研究生阶段，不但没有读过语言学方向的经典著作，很有可能连《语言学导论》这样的教科书也没认真读过（如果所在学校研究生考试不考语言学的话）。多数学生到了研究生阶段，许多语言学的基本概念和基础理论还需要从头开始学起。毫无疑问，这对学生创新能力的培养、与国际同行的对话能力造成了几乎难以逾越的障碍。

　　"亡羊补牢，犹未为晚"，我们选编这部《语义学经典论文选读》，主要目的之一就是为了帮助语言学方向的研究生弥补知识结构上的这一缺憾。当然，语言学专业研究生能否提高自己的专业创新能力，能否与国际同行对话和交流，甚至能否走到学术前沿，还需要其他很多条件，并非读了这几十篇文章就能解决问题。但反过来说，如果我们的研究生同学根本没读过这些对语义学乃至语言学发展产生过重要影响的经典，那他今后即使在某一方向学有所成，仍然是一种遗憾，一种缺陷。

《语义学经典选读》安排了四大板块的经典论文，语言哲学、形式语义学、语用学和认知语义学。

语言哲学：

G. Frege: On sense and reference

B. Russell: Descriptions

P. Strawson: On referring

K. Donnellan: Reference and definite descriptions

S. Kripke: Lecture II of *Naming and Necessity*

形式语义学：

D. Davidson: Truth and meaning

D. Davidson: The logical form of action sentences

D. Kaplan: On the logic of demonstratives

I. Heim: File change semantics and the familiarity theory of definiteness

D. Lewis: Scorekeeping in a language game

语用学：

P. Grice: Logic and conversation

F. Recanati: The pragmatics of what is said

L. Horn: Toward a new taxonomy for pragmatic inference

S. Levinson: Three levels of meaning

I. Heim: On the projection problem of presuppositions

认知语义学：

D. Geeraerts: Prospects and problems of prototype theory

G. Lakoff: The contemporary theory of metaphor

W. Croft: The role of domains in the interpretation of metaphors and metonymies

C. Fillmore: Frame semantics

M. Tomasello: First steps toward a usage-based theory of language acquisition

我们这样安排的主要考虑是：

（1）现代语义学的源头主要在语言哲学，语义学领域涉及的基本理论问题，如"什么是意义？""语言与现实世界的关系是什么？"等问题都是哲学家们长期思考并有丰富成果的研究课题，现代语义理论，尤其是形式语义学理论在很大程度上是对语言哲学研究很多课题的继承和延伸，而认知语义学又是在批判和纠正形式语义学的过程中诞生的，因此，我们所选的论文，在大的方面来说，是按照一个大的线索来组织的，之间有一个承上启下和延伸的关系。

（2）语义学的发展，一方面是受到了哲学的影响，吸取了语言哲学的成果，另一方面当然也受到语言研究本身的影响，尤其是语用学和认知语言学的影响，所以我们这里也收录了相当数量的语言学家的论文。

（3）语言研究最早是语文学、修辞学等对语言的研究，包括对词语和表达效果的研究，后来的比较语言学、结构主义语言学、转换生成语法等都对语义学研究产生过影响，但这方面的研究往往都包含在一些专门著作中，我们建议大家通过阅读语言学领域相关的经典来了解这一传统。

在这里，我们需要指出的是，语言学方向的学生阅读语言哲学方面的经典，其目的和侧重点与哲学专业的学生读这些文章应该不一样。语言学方向的学生阅读这些经典时，主要是了解一下这些语言问题的哲学背景和哲学意义，看他们的讨论和达成的共识对构建语言学，特别是语义学理论有什么启发意义、产生了什么影响，而哲学家分析语言的方法和手段则不一定成为我们关注的重点。换句话说，语言学专业的学生阅读语言哲学经典，既要想办法钻进该学科体系内部以大概了解一些重要话题的来龙去脉和哲学意义，另一方面又要从中跳出来，不受哲学讨论的束缚和限制，而是应该用另一种眼光，即语言学家的眼光来打量原来被认为是纯粹哲学的问题。语言学家的任务，说到底，还是要解决语言本身的问题，说明语言是什么，语言是怎样实现其功能的，等等，而不是像哲学家一样主要关心语言与概念、世界的关系等宏观和抽象的问题。语言学研究者还是要从具体的语言现象入手，以小见大，从小到大。哲学的眼光可以帮助我们既见树，又见林，不至于在具体的语言事实中迷失了方向。

  阅读这些文章时，我们建议：

（1）同时翻阅一些语言哲学、语义学、语用学等方面的概论书，看它们之间的关联，看哪些概念是语言研究中的基本和核心概念；哲学讨论中是如何解释这些概念的；

（2）关注各个不同研究者讨论相同问题时的关联性，不同研究者对相同概念的理解的差异；

（3）读一些有关这些文章和讨论的中文介绍或翻译，一方面可以帮助理解原文，另一方面可注意看是否译文或自己阅读时有误解。

  为了帮助大家阅读理解，并抓住要点，我们每一单元提供了"内容简介"，对该单元的几篇文章的主要内容做一个提示和导读。我的几位博士研究生陈佳、黄洁、田臻和唐树华为此提供了帮助，特此致谢。

束定芳

2009 年 2 月

第一部分：
语言哲学

导　读

这一部分选了弗雷格（G. Frege）、罗素（B. Russell）、斯特劳森（P. F. Strawson）、唐奈兰（K. Donnellan）和克里普克（S. Kripke）所撰写的五篇文章，讨论的都是专有名词的意义，都跟词语的指称有关，或者说，都跟语言与世界之间的关系有关。

弗雷格是数学家、逻辑学家，是分析哲学的创始人之一。他对数理逻辑、数理哲学和语言哲学都做出了重要的贡献。《论意义与指称》（On Sense and Reference）是他语言哲学论文中的作表作，也是后来语言哲学家讨论语言哲学问题的出发点之一。

这篇论文的目的是要解决两个哲学问题。第一个问题是所谓的等式句（identity statements）；而第二个问题则是关于内涵语境（intensional context）的问题，即在命题态度动词如"相信"、"认为"之后出现的专名和摹状词的意义问题。

弗雷格首先提出，等式句并非关于事物之间的等同，而是代表事物的符号之间的等同。

弗雷格区分了一个符号的两种意义，指称义（reference）和表达义（sense），前者为符号所指的对象，而后者为表达的方式。某一所指对象可以有多个不同的符号来指称它，而同一表达义在不同语言，甚至在同一语言中又可以有不同的表达。

弗雷格用了"望远镜"的比喻来说明"想法"（idea）、表达义（sense）和指称义（reference）之间的区别。如果我们用望远镜来观察月亮，那么，"月亮"相等于"指称"，具有高度客观性；望远镜镜片上看到的月亮的影像相等于"表达"，而观察者视网膜上形成的月亮相等于"想法"，带有高度的主观性。

弗雷格指出，我们在使用任何专有名词的时候，一般都会"预设"它所指对象的存在。例如，当我们说"月亮"这个词时，我们不是指有关月亮的想法，也不是要谈论它的表达方式，而是预设它的存在。

弗雷格还谈论了陈述句的指称和表达义问题。弗雷格提出，陈述句表达一个思想（thought），该思想不是该句的指称义，而是该句的表达义。一个陈述句的指称义是该句的"真值"（truth value）。

按照莱布尼茨（G. W. Leibniz）定律，当一个句子中的某一部分被具有同样指称的词语替代时，该句子的意义应该保持不变。

弗雷格对一些不同句式中从句的意义进行了讨论，检验不同从句是否具有指称义。

弗雷格发现，含有"say"、"hear"这些词的句子中，其从句的指称是一个"思想"，因为不管它是否为真，它对整个句子的真值没有影响。

但是在所谓的"内涵语境"中，也就是含有"believe"一类动词的句子中，整个句子表达的是一个"思想"，它的真值不包括从句的真假。如：

(1) Copernicus believed that the planetary orbits are circles.

不管后面的内容是否为真，整个句子的真值不受影响。在这样的句子中，如果我们将一个具有相同指称的词替代从句中的某一个专有名词，整个句子表达的思想却完全不一样了。如：

(2) a. John believes that the Morning Star is the Morning Star.
    b. John believes that the Morning Star is the Evening Star.

虽然Morning Star和Evening Star具有同样的指称意义，按照莱布尼茨定律，两者互换，等式依然成立。然而，John可能相信Morning star is the Morning Star，但不一定相信The Morning Star is the Evening Star.

罗素的《摹状词》（Description）一文是其《数理哲学导论》（1919）一书的第十六章。在这篇文章中罗素讨论了语言和存在的关系问题，主要是限定摹状词的指称对象问题，是从语言哲学的"否定存在问题"、"同一问题"和"排中律问题"三大经典难题入手进行逻辑的严密论证的经典。所涉及的问题具体用例子来说就是解释"The unicorn does not exist." "Scott is the author of Waverly." 和 "The Present King of France is (not) bald." 这三类语句的限定摹状词指称和存在关系的语言哲学分析难题。也即，为什么现实中并不存在"the unicorn"（独角兽）这种动物，而我们却可以谈论它？为什么，根据同一律，"Scott is the author of Waverly."（司各特是写《威佛利》的作者）应该等同于"Scott is Scott."（司各特是司各特），而事实上并非如此？为什么"The Present King of France is (not) bald."（现在的"法国国王是/不是秃头"）的命题为假？罗素试图用他所提出的摹状词理论来解决这三个难题。

在本文中，罗素把摹状词（description）区分为不定摹状词（a so-and-so）和限定摹状词（the so-and-so）两类。"一个非限定的摹状词是一个这种形式的词组：'一个如此这般的某事物'，一个限定的摹状词是一个这种形式的词组：'这/那个如此这般的某事物'"。我们通常所说的摹状词，主要指限定摹状词。罗素关心的也是限定摹状词。罗素也对专名和摹状词作了严格的区分，罗素把知识分为亲知的知识和描述的知识，前者是个人直接感知和由经验所得到的，后者则是通过描述对象的属性来认识对象的间接知识。与这两种知识相对应，语言有两种不同的语义功能：命名和描述。专名就是具有命名功能的语词，我们之所以能够理解它，是因为我们能够直接亲知它所指的对象，这个对象构成了它的意义。摹状词则是具有描述功能的语词，我们之所以能理解它，是因为我们能够通过它对于一个对象的特征性质的描述去识别那个特定的对象。罗素指出专名和限定摹状词两者的语词结构不同。一个专名是"一个简单的符号，它的意义是只能作为主词出现的东西"。"所谓一个简单的符号就是其内容不再是符号的符号。"一个简单的符号虽然也有内容，如"司各特"（Scott）这个专名，它是一个简单符号，虽然它也有自己的组成内容如字母s-c-o-t-t，但是它的内容的意义与原来的意义无关；而一个限定摹状词则不是一个简单的符号，它是一个复合的符号，如"那个写《威弗利》的作者"、"the author of *Waverly*"就包含了定冠词"the"、"……的作者"、"author of"，以及"威弗利""*Waverly*"几个符号，它们都有各自的意义，且在句子中完全保留。"专名与描述不同，除非专名指示一件实有的事物，专名是没有意义的。""如果一个名称没有所指，它在一个命题里就没有意义，而一个描述却不受这种限制。"这又体现了罗素对弗雷格思想的继承，不过，他作了进一步的发挥。他指出，用"Scott"去替换"Scott is the author of *Waverly*"中的"the author of *Waverly*"所得到的命题和原命题是不一样的。原命题是一个分析命题，它教给人们知识。而新命题是一个综合判断，是一个一般的自明之理。另一方面，根据同一律a=a,将任何名字代入a，都会得到真命题。假定亚里士多德、柏拉图是名字，根据同一律，我们可以推出，亚里士多德是亚里士多德，柏拉图是柏拉图。但是以限定摹状词"那个写《威弗利》的作者"代入a，所得的命题就是"那个写《威弗利》的人是那个写《威弗利》的作者"。这个命题的真假是不能确定的，欲使其真必须要先假设"那个写《威弗利》的作者"存在。这一点摹状词不能保证，但专名却可以。

区分一个专名和一个限定的摹状词是重要的，罗素认为导致三大难题的原因就是因为这三个难题都认为限定摹状词和专名具有相同的属性。罗素认为限定摹状词和专名是不同的。在他看来，如果承认摹状词和专名是一回事，那么就会得出"Scott is the author of *Waverly*（司各特是《威弗利》的作者）"的意思不过是"Scott is Scott（司各特是司各特）"的意思。为了解决这个问题，罗素将"司各特是《威弗利》的作者"这样的句子扩展成"有一个X，那个X写了《威弗利》，那对所有的Y而言，如果Y写了《威弗利》，Y就等于X而且X也相等于司各特"。简单说来，罗素将"司各特是《威弗利》的作者"分析为"有且仅有一个实体写了《威弗利》，并且这个实体就是司各特"。显然，罗素的方法是将任何包含有限定摹状词作为它的语法主词的语句，改述为一个相等的语句，在后面这个语句中，原来的语法主词不出现了。如"《威弗利》的作者是司各特"被分析成："有一个人写了《威弗利》，而他就是司各特"。这样，在原句中"《威弗利》的作者"处于命题主词位置上，而分析后的句子中"写了《威弗利》"和"是司各特"同时处于谓词的位置上，它们需要由某个或某些主目来满足，或者，没有任何主目可以满足上述谓词，这种只有谓词而主目虚位以待的表达式即是命题函项，罗素称其为不完全符号。它们之所以是不完全的，就在于它们没有独立的意义，只有填上主目，变成命题，才具有意义。简单地说，也就是罗素将语句中作为语法的主词的限定摹状词通过三个逻辑语句进行改写，将限定摹状词置于逻辑谓词的位置，这样所有的问题都转变为存在的问题。对于任何The F is G.的语句，罗素认为都可以看成是改写自以下三个语句"at least there is an F, at most there is an F, whoever or whatever is F is G."至少一个F存在，至多有一个F存在，任何是F的就是G的情况。如果现实中并不存在一个F，那么这个语句即为假。例如"当今法国国王是秃头"一句，根据罗素的思路，可以改写分析为：至少有一个当今法国国王，至多有一个法国国王，任何是当今法国国王的人都是秃头。通过改写，罗素将语句中的主词转变为逻辑谓词，而逻辑分句中的谓词表述如果和现实世界存在不符则整个语句为假。

斯特劳森是以奥斯丁（Austin）为代表的"日常语言哲学家"群体当中的重要一员。斯特劳森在语言哲学当中最有影响的著作是关于逻辑和自然语言的关系，特别是他对"预设"的定义。

他的论文《论指称》（On Referring）（1951）是对将近五十多年未受挑战的罗素的摹状词理论进行的第一次批判，这篇论文的主要贡献是提出了指称的语用观。

罗素认为限定摹状词不是指称表达单位，而是只有在句子当中才具有意义的复杂语言标记。此外，罗素认为含有限定摹状词的句子的语法形式并不对应于句子的逻辑形式，因为句子的逻辑是有关存在和特殊性的复杂命题构成。例如"法国国王是秃头"这个句子并不是一个逻辑的主谓形式，并没有指向某个个体的性质，而必须被"翻译"成逻辑式，或者说必须将语法的主词通过改写换成逻辑的谓词。如以上句子可以改写成："存在这样的一个个体，这个个体是法国的国王，这个个体是唯一的，这个个体是秃头。"根据罗素的观点，如果现在并不存在一个唯一个体是法国国王，那么句子"法国国王是秃头"的真值为假。也就是说，按照罗素的观点，句子"The F is G."包含了一个逻辑概括：存在并且仅仅存在一个F。如果并不存在一个F，那么该语句为假。

斯特劳森在《论指称》的开篇就对罗素的这一观点提出了质疑。斯特劳森认为"我们经常使用某些表达来指称人、事物个体、或者事件、地点、过程"，并认为诸如"法国国王"这类限定摹状词也是属于这个类别。他坚持认为，哲学讨论必须关注说话人对言语表达的使用，而不应将语言孤立于其使用。此外他也认为限定摹状词可以进行指称。

而按照斯特劳森的观点，当"The F is G."（"F是G"）这样的语句说出时：

（1）如果有人说出"The F is G"，如果并没有F存在，那么他就没有作出一个为真或是为假的陈述。

（2）如果没有F存在，那么说话人没有指称任何事物。

（3）而因为他并没有指称任何事物，所以他没有说出任何为真或者为假的信息。

斯特劳森认为是否存在一个法国国王并不是"法国国王是秃头"这个语句的逻辑真值，而只是由说话人对该语句的使用来进行指称的。在《论指称》一文的结尾，他指出"亚里士多德或者是罗素的规则都不能对任何普通语言进行逻辑描写，因为普通语言并没有确切的逻辑"。

斯特劳森认为若没有正确指称the F，则the F is G.无真值，而说话人也没有指称任何东西。说话人所说的话非真非假，这是因为他没有成功地指称。

斯特劳森在后来的《逻辑理论导论》(*Introduction to Logical Theory*)（1952）当中将这种"法国国王是秃头"当中摹状词的用法称为"预设"。他认为一些命题是可以由肯定和否定陈述来预设的，而预设可以为真也可以为假。斯特劳森的观点成为此后语言哲学和语言学研究者对于"预设"的性质和作用讨论的基础。

唐奈兰试图综合罗素和斯特劳森等人相互对立的观点。他认为限定摹状词具有两种用法，分别是：归属性用法（attributive use）和指称性用法（referential use）。唐奈兰认为罗素没有看到限定摹状词的指称性用法；而斯特劳森则混淆了二者，只谈论了指称性用法。

按照罗素的思路，可以将语法的主词通过改写换成逻辑的谓词，如下所示：

At lease one person is Smith's murderer.

At most one person is Smith's murderer.

Whoever is Smith's murderer is insane.

If there is no Smith's murderer, the sentence is false.

至少有一个人是"杀害史密斯的凶手"，至多有一个人是"杀害史密斯的凶手"，任何是"杀害史密斯的凶手"的人都是"丧心病狂"的。如果并没有一个"杀害史密斯的凶手"，那么这句话为假。

斯特劳森的思路是，在这样的语境中，说话人和听众都知道谁是指称对象，并通过语境和语言规约规则的指引了解基于这个陈述的有关信息，这一陈述可能为真也可能为假，这取决于使用该限定摹状词的说话人是否用该限定摹状词指称在语境所在的现实中确实存在的指称对象。斯特劳森认为考虑语词或语句的意义必须考虑以下两个要素：

（1）语境（context）。也就是说话者在一定语境下意图表达的意义，即一定的时间地点人物事件。

（2）语言规约规则（Linguistic conventions）。也就是说话者正确地把它们用于指称或断定某事物时遵循的语言规则和规约。

唐奈兰的观点更接近于斯特劳森的语用观点，因为他也强调说话人使用专名来指称、指出或谈论事物。唐奈兰认为"杀害史密斯的凶手"这个限定摹状词有两种用法。对于"杀害史密斯的凶手"的归属性用法，这一用法与罗素的观点不矛盾：人们虽然不知道谁是凶手，但是限定摹状词从其语言意义上谈论的是任何符合这一描述的对象。"Whoever is Smith's murderer is insane." 而 "杀害史密斯的凶手" 还可以进行指称性使用：如果说话人在当时心里有一个对象，例如在法庭上一名名叫琼斯的男子被控告为凶手，该说话人在听过证词和看到琼斯的表情后说：Smith's murderer is insane. 那么他就是在指称方式下使用的该限定摹状词，用这个摹状词来指听众面前的琼斯，即使事实上琼斯并不是凶手，甚至根本没有凶手，听众也知道说话人所指的就是琼斯。这也就是说摹状词的归属性用法和指称性用法决定于说话人的意图和摹状词使用的语境。

《命名与必要性》（*Naming and Necessity*）（1980）是克里普克关于指称的论述。该书由克里普克的三个讲座组成，通过丰富有趣的例子和轻松的语言进行论述。在该书的 "讲座一" 部分中，他针对罗素的摹状理论以及弗雷格的意义决定指称的理论进行了讨论。

克里普克认为专名不是伪装的摹状词，他提出了三个论证：

（1）很多情况下名字并不与任何唯一的限定性摹状或者摹状特征集合相联系。

（2）一个人可以在不知道与某个专名相关的任何描述性特征的情况下使用该专名。说话人经常在不知道某个人或事物的特有属性和描述性特征的前提下使用专名来指称这些人或者事物。

（3）一些名称，专名或者其他自然类别都是固定指称词（rigid designators）。

克里普克提出固定指称词和非固定指称词之分。专名是固定指称词，也就是说在任何可能世界和时间当中这些专名都指称同样的对象。而大多数摹状词都是非固定指称词，因为这些摹状词可以在不同的可能世界当中指称不同的对象。克里普克的可能世界是指世界可能存在的方式。所以他认为可能存在这样的可能世界，其中 "亚里士多德" 不是亚历山大的老师；但是不可能存在这样的可能世界，其中 "亚里士多德" 不是由亚里士多德这个人构成的。

在 "讲座二" 当中，克里普克提出了指称的历史因果链条观。他认为事物以及人都是通过最早的命名过程获得各自的名称。这些名称通过一个说话人到另一个说话人的使用进行指称。如果一个人通过该名称对某一人或事物进行指称，而这个名称就是指称之前因果指称链条当中所指称的同一人或事物，那么这个说话人就成功地对该人或事物进行了指称。

举例来说：一个婴儿刚刚出生时，父母给他取名，然后用这个名字与朋友们谈论这个婴儿，于是其他来看婴儿的人用这个名字来谈论这个婴儿。经过各种对这个名字的谈论，很快这个名字就从一个人传到另外一个人，就仿佛通过链条传播使用一样。

克里普克将因果链条理论应用于专名和普通名词，例如一般的事物名词如"水""老虎""柠檬""金子"等等。一般的自然普通名词和专名一样是固定指称词，他们总是指称同一个事物，因为在指称因果链条当中这个名称和事物通过因果链条相联系。而不是通过与这个名称相关联的一系列摹状特征来关联的。

此外，这些自然普通名词的本质属性是微观结构的而非现象的。比如金子是由化学元素周期表上的元素79构成的，而不是由任何色泽硬度形状看上去像是金子的物质构成的。

克里普克对于普通名词、固定指称词和指称的观点也使他发展出了形而上学（metaphysics）理论框架。他认为一个事物的重要性质在于它的起源。如果不是亚里士多德的基因和物理属性构成的，就不是亚里士多德本人了。

On Sense and Reference

Gottlob Frege

Equality^{①} gives rise to challenging questions which are not altogether easy to answer. Is it a relation? A relation between objects, or between names or signs of objects? In my *Begriffsschrift*[1] I assumed the latter. The reasons which seem to favour this are the following: *a* = *a* and *a* = *b* are obviously statements of differing cognitive value; *a* = *a* holds *a priori* and, according to Kant, is to be labelled analytic, while statements of the form *a* = *b* often contain very valuable extensions of our knowledge and cannot always be established *a priori*. The discovery that the rising sun is not new every morning, but always the same, was one of the most fertile astronomical discoveries. Even to-day the identification of a small planet or a comet is not always a matter of course. Now if we were to regard equality as a relation between that which the names '*a*' and '*b*' designate, it would seem that *a* = *b* could not differ from *a* = *a* (i.e. provided *a* = *b* is true). A relation would thereby be expressed of a thing to itself, and indeed one in which each thing stands to itself but to no other thing. What is intended to be said by *a* = *b* seems to be that the signs or names '*a*' and '*b*' designate the same thing, so that those signs themselves would be under discussion; a relation between them would be asserted. But this relation would hold between the names or signs only in so far as they named or designated something. It would be mediated by the connexion of each of the two signs with the same designated thing. But this is arbitrary. Nobody can be forbidden to use any arbitrarily producible event or object as a sign for something. In that case the sentence *a* = *b* would no longer refer to the subject matter, but only to its mode of designation; we would express no proper knowledge by its means. But in many cases this is just what we want to do. If the sign 'a' is distinguished from the sign 'b' only as object (here, by means of its shape), not as sign (i.e. not by the manner in which it designates something), the cognitive value of $a = a$ becomes essentially equal to that of $a = b$, provided $a = b$ is true. A difference can arise only if the difference between the signs corresponds to a difference in the mode of presentation of that which is designated. Let a, b, c be the lines connecting the vertices of a triangle with the midpoints of the opposite sides. The point of intersection of a and b is then the same as the point of intersection of b and c. So we have different designations for the same point, and these names ('point of intersection of a and b,' 'point of intersection of b and c') likewise indicate the mode of presentation; and hence the statement contains actual knowledge.

It is natural, now, to think of there being connected with a sign (name, combination of words, letter), besides that to which the sign refers, which may be called the reference of the sign, also what I should like to call the *sense* of the sign, wherein the mode of presentation is contained. In our example, accordingly, the reference of the expressions 'the point of intersection of a and b' and 'the point of intersection of b and c' would be the same, but not their senses. The reference of 'evening star' would be the same as that of 'morning star,' but not the sense.

It is clear from the context that by 'sign' and 'name' I have here understood any designation representing a proper name, which thus has as its reference a definite object (this word taken in the widest range), but not a concept or a relation, which shall be discussed further in another article.[2] The designation of a single object can also consist of several words or other signs. For brevity, let every such designation be called a proper name.

The sense of a proper name is grasped by everybody who is sufficiently familiar with the language or totality of designations to which it belongs;[②] but this serves to illuminate only a single aspect of the reference, supposing it to have one. Comprehensive knowledge of the reference would require us to be able to say immediately whether any given sense belongs to it. To such knowledge we never attain.

The regular connexion between a sign, its sense, and its reference is of such a kind that to the sign there corresponds a definite sense and to that in turn a definite reference, while to a given reference (an object) there does not belong only a single sign. The same sense has different expressions in different languages or even in the same language. To be sure, exceptions to this regular behaviour occur. To every expression belonging to a complete totality of signs, there should certainly correspond a definite sense; but natural languages often do not satisfy this condition, and one must be content if the same word has the same sense in the same context. It may perhaps be granted that every grammatically well-formed expression representing a proper name always has a sense. But this is not to say that to the sense there also corresponds a reference. The words 'the celestial body most distant from the Earth' have a sense, but it is very doubtful if they also have a reference. The expression 'the least rapidly convergent series' has a sense but demonstrably has no reference, since for every given convergent series, another convergent, but less rapidly convergent, series can be found. In grasping a sense, one is not certainly assured of a reference.

If words are used in the ordinary way, what one intends to speak of is their reference. It can also happen, however, that one wishes to talk about the words themselves or their sense. This happens, for instance, when the words of another are quoted. One's own words then first designate words of the other speaker, and only the latter have their usual reference. We then have signs of signs. In writing, the words are in this case enclosed in quotation marks. Accordingly, a word standing between quotation marks must not be taken as having its ordinary reference.

In order to speak of the sense of an expression 'A' one may simply use the phrase 'the sense of the expression "A"'. In reported speech one talks about the sense, e.g., of another person's remarks. It is quite clear that in this way of speaking words do not have their customary reference but designate what is usually their sense. In order to have a short expression, we will say: In reported speech, words are used *indirectly* or have their *indirect* reference. We distinguish accordingly the *customary* from the *indirect* reference of a word; and its *customary* sense from its *indirect* sense. The indirect reference of a word is accordingly its customary sense. Such exceptions must always be borne in mind if the mode of connexion between sign, sense, and reference in particular cases is to be correctly understood.

The reference and sense of a sign are to be distinguished from the associated idea. If the reference of a sign is an object perceivable by the senses, my idea of it is an internal image,[3] arising from memories of sense impressions which I have had and acts, both internal and external, which I have performed. Such an idea is often saturated with feeling; the clarity of its separate parts varies and oscillates. The same sense is not always connected, even in the same man, with the same idea. The idea is subjective: one man's idea is not that of another. There result, as a matter of course, a variety of differences in the ideas associated with the same sense. A painter, a horseman, and a zoologist will probably connect different ideas with the name 'Bucephalus.' This constitutes an essential distinction between the idea and the sign's sense, which may be the common property of many and therefore is not a part or a mode of the individual mind. For one can hardly deny that mankind has a common store of thoughts which is transmitted from one generation to another.†

In the light of this, one need have no scruples in speaking simply of *the* sense, whereas in the case of an idea one must, strictly speaking, add to whom it belongs and at what time. It might perhaps be said: Just as one man connects this idea, and another that idea, with the same word, so also one man can associate this sense and another that sense. But there still remains a difference in the mode of connexion. They are not prevented from grasping the same sense; but they cannot have the same idea. *Si duo idem faciunt, non est idem.* If two persons picture the same thing, each still has his own idea. It is indeed sometimes possible to establish differences in the ideas, or even in the sensations, of different men; but an exact comparison is not possible, because we cannot have both ideas together in the same consciousness.

The reference of a proper name is the object itself which we designate by its means; the idea, which we have in that case, is wholly subjective; in between lies the sense, which is indeed no longer subjective like the idea, but is yet not the object itself. The following analogy will perhaps clarify these relationships. Somebody observes the Moon through a telescope. I compare the Moon itself to the reference; it is the object of the observation, mediated by the real image projected by the object glass in the interior of the telescope, and by the retinal image of the observer.

The former I compare to the sense, the latter is like the idea or experience. The optical image in the telescope is indeed one-sided and dependent upon the standpoint of observation; but it is still objective, inasmuch as it can be used by several observers. At any rate it could be arranged for several to use it simultaneously. But each one would have his own retinal image. On account of the diverse shapes of the observers' eyes, even a geometrical congruence could

---

† Hence it is inadvisable to use the word 'idea' to designate something so basically different.

hardly be achieved, and an actual coincidence would be out of the question. This analogy might be developed still further, by assuming A's retinal image made visible to B; or A might also see his own retinal image in a mirror. In this way we might perhaps show how an idea can itself be taken as an object, but as such is not for the observer what it directly is for the person having the idea. But to pursue this would take us too far afield.

We can now recognize three levels of difference between words, expressions, or whole sentences. The difference may concern at most the ideas, or the sense but not the reference, or, finally, the reference as well. With respect to the first level, it is to be noted that, on account of the uncertain connexion of ideas with words, a difference may hold for one person, which another does not find. The difference between a translation and the original text should properly not overstep the first level. To the possible differences here belong also the colouring and shading which poetic eloquence seeks to give to the sense. Such colouring and shading are not objective, and must be evoked by each hearer or reader according to the hints of the poet or the speaker. Without some affinity in human ideas art would certainly be impossible; but it can never be exactly determined how far the intentions of the poet are realized.

In what follows there will be no further discussion of ideas and experiences; they have been mentioned here only to ensure that the idea aroused in the hearer by a word shall not be confused with its sense or its reference.

To make short and exact expressions possible, let the following phraseology be established:

A proper name (word, sign, sign combination, expression) *expresses* its sense, *stands for* or *designates* its reference. By means of a sign we express its sense and designate its reference.

Idealists or sceptics will perhaps long since have objected: 'You talk, without further ado, of the Moon as an object; but how do you know that the name 'the Moon' has any reference? How do you know that anything whatsoever has a reference?' I reply that when we say 'the Moon,' we do not intend to speak of our idea of the Moon, nor are we satisfied with the sense alone, but we presuppose a reference. To assume that in the sentence 'The Moon is smaller than the Earth' the idea of the Moon is in question, would be flatly to misunderstand the sense. If this is what the speaker wanted, he would use the phrase 'my idea of the Moon.' Now we can of course be mistaken in the presupposition, and such mistakes have indeed occurred. But the question whether the presupposition is perhaps always mistaken need not be answered here; in order to justify mention of the reference of a sign it is enough, at first, to point out our intention in speaking or thinking. (We must then add the reservation: provided such reference exists.)

So far we have considered the sense and reference only of such expressions, words, or signs as we have called proper names. We now inquire concerning the sense and reference for an entire declarative sentence. Such a sentence contains a thought.[④] Is this thought, now, to be regarded as its sense or its reference? Let us assume for the time being that the sentence has reference. If we now replace one word of the sentence by another having the same reference, but a different sense, this can have no bearing upon the reference of the sentence. Yet we can see that in such a case the thought changes; since, e.g., the thought in the sentence 'The morning star is a body illuminated by the Sun' differs from that in the sentence 'The evening star is a body illuminated by the Sun.' Anybody who did not know that the evening star is the morning star might hold the one thought to be true, the other false. The thought, accordingly, cannot be the reference of the sentence, but must rather be considered as the sense. What is the position now with regard to the reference? Have we a right even to inquire about it? Is it possible that a sentence as a whole has only a sense, but no reference? At any rate, one might expect that such sentences occur, just as there are parts of sentences having sense but no reference. And sentences which contain proper names without reference will be of this kind. The sentence 'Odysseus was set ashore at Ithaca while sound asleep' obviously has a sense. But since it is doubtful whether the name 'Odysseus,' occurring therein, has reference, it is also doubtful whether the whole sentence has one. Yet it is certain, nevertheless, that anyone who seriously took the sentence to be true or false would ascribe to the name 'Odysseus' a reference, not merely a sense; for it is of the reference of the name that the predicate is affirmed or denied. Whoever does not admit the name has reference can neither apply nor withhold the predicate. But in that case it would be superfluous to advance to the reference of the name; one could be satisfied with the sense, if one wanted to go no further than the thought. If it were a question only of the sense of the sentence, the thought, it would be unnecessary to bother with the reference of a part of the sentence; only the sense, not the reference, of the part is relevant to the sense of the whole sentence. The thought remains the same whether 'Odysseus' has reference or not. The fact that we concern ourselves at all about the reference of a part of the sentence indicates that we generally recognize and expect a reference for the sentence itself. The thought loses value for us as soon as we recognize that the reference of one of its parts is missing. We are therefore justified in not being satisfied with the sense of a sentence, and in inquiring also as to its reference. But now why do we want every proper name to have not only a sense, but also a reference? Why is the thought not enough for us? Because, and to the extent that, we are concerned with its truth value. This is not always the case. In hearing an epic poem, for instance, apart from the euphony of the language we are interested only in the sense of the sentences and the images and feelings thereby aroused. The question of truth would cause us to abandon aesthetic delight for an attitude of scientific investigation. Hence it is a matter of no concern to us whether the name 'Odysseus,' for instance, has reference, so long as we accept the poem as a work of art.⑤ It is the striving for truth that drives us always to advance from the sense to the reference.

We have seen that the reference of a sentence may always be sought, whenever the reference of its components is involved; and that this is the case when and only when we are inquiring after the truth value.

We are therefore driven into accepting the *truth value* of a sentence as constituting its reference. By the truth value of a sentence I understand the circumstance that it is true or false. There are no further truth values. For brevity I call the one the True, the other the False. Every declarative sentence concerned with the reference of its words is therefore to be regarded as a proper name, and its reference, if it has one, is either the True or the False. These two objects are recognized, if only implicitly, by everybody who judges something to be true — and so even by a sceptic. The designation of the truth values as objects may appear to be an arbitrary fancy or perhaps a mere play upon words, from which no profound consequences could be drawn. What I mean by an object can be more exactly discussed only in connexion with concept and relation. I will reserve this for another article.[3] But so much should already be clear, that in every judgment,⑥ no matter how trivial, the step from the level of thoughts to the level of reference (the objective) has already been taken.

One might be tempted to regard the relation of the thought to the True not as that of sense to reference, but rather as that of subject to predicate. One can, indeed, say: 'The thought, that 5 is a prime number, is true.' But closer examination shows that nothing more has been said than in the simple sentence '5 is a prime number.' The truth claim arises in each case from the form of the declarative sentence, and when the latter lacks its usual force, e.g., in the mouth of an actor upon the stage, even the sentence 'The thought that 5 is a prime number is true' contains only a thought, and indeed the same thought as the simple '5 is a prime number.' It follows that the relation of the thought to the True may not be compared with that of subject to predicate.

Subject and predicate (understood in the logical sense) are indeed elements of thought; they stand on the same level for knowledge. By combining subject and predicate, one reaches only a thought, never passes from sense to reference, never from a thought to its truth value. One moves at the same level but never advances from one level to the next. A truth value cannot be a part of a thought, any more than, say, the Sun can, for it is not a sense but an object.

If our supposition that the reference of a sentence is its truth value is correct, the latter must remain unchanged when a part of the sentence is replaced by an expression having the same reference. And this is in fact the case. Leibniz gives the definition: *'Eadem sunt, quae sibi mutuo substitui possunt, salva veritate.'* What else but the truth value could be found, that belongs quite generally to every sentence if the reference of its components is relevant, and remains unchanged by substitutions of the kind in question?

If now the truth value of a sentence is its reference, then on the one hand all true sentences have the same reference and so, on the other hand, do all false sentences. From this we see that in the reference of the sentence all that is specific is obliterated. We can never be concerned only with the reference of a sentence; but again the mere thought alone yields no knowledge, but only the thought together with its reference, i.e. its truth value. Judgments can be regarded as advances from a thought to a truth value. Naturally this cannot be a definition. Judgment is something quite peculiar and incomparable. One might also say that judgments are distinctions of parts within truth values. Such distinction occurs by a return to the thought. To every sense belonging to a truth value there would correspond its own manner of analysis. However, I have here used the word 'part' in a special sense. I have in fact transferred the relation between the parts and the whole of the sentence to its reference, by calling the reference of a word part of the reference of the sentence, if the word itself is a part of the sentence. This way of speaking can certainly be attacked, because the whole reference and one part of it do not suffice to determine the remainder, and because the word 'part' is already used in another sense of bodies. A special term would need to be invented.

The supposition that the truth value of a sentence is its reference shall now be put to further test. We have found that the truth value of a sentence remains unchanged when an expression is replaced by another having the same reference: but we have not yet considered the case in which the expression to be replaced is itself a sentence. Now if our view is correct, the truth value of a sentence containing another as part must remain unchanged when the part is replaced by another sentence having the same truth value. Exceptions are to be expected when the whole sentence or its part is direct or indirect quotation; for in such cases, as we have seen, the words do not have their customary reference. In direct quotation, a sentence designates another sentence, and in indirect quotation a thought.

We are thus led to consider subordinate sentences or clauses. These occur as parts of a sentence complex, which is, from the logical standpoint, likewise a sentence — a main sentence. But here we meet the question whether it is also true of the subordinate sentence that its reference is a truth value. Of indirect quotation we already know the opposite. Grammarians view subordinate clauses as representatives of parts of sentences and divide them accordingly into noun clauses, adjective clauses, adverbial clauses. This might generate the supposition that the reference of a subordinate clause was not a truth value but rather of the same kind as the reference of a noun or adjective or adverb — in short, of a part of a sentence, whose sense was not a thought but only a part of a thought. Only a more thorough investigation can clarify the issue. In so doing, we shall not follow the grammatical categories strictly, but rather group together what is logically of the same kind. Let us first search for cases in which the sense of the subordinate clause, as we have just supposed, is not an independent thought.

The case of an abstract[4] noun clause, introduced by 'that,' includes the case of indirect quotation, in which we have seen the words to have their indirect reference coinciding with what is customarily their sense. In this case, then, the subordinate clause has for its reference a thought, not a truth value; as sense not a thought, but the sense of the words 'the thought, that ... ,' which is only a part of the thought in the entire complex sentence. This happens after 'say,' 'hear,' 'be of the opinion,' 'be convinced,' 'conclude,' and similar words.[7] There is a different, and indeed somewhat complicated, situation after words like 'perceive,' 'know,' 'fancy,' which are to be considered later.

That in the cases of the first kind the reference of the subordinate clause is in fact the thought can also be recognized by seeing that it is indifferent to the truth of the whole whether the subordinate clause is true or false. Let us compare, for instance, the two sentences 'Copernicus believed that the planetary orbits are circles' and 'Copernicus believed that the apparent motion of the sun is produced by the real motion of the Earth.' One subordinate clause can be substituted for the other without harm to the truth. The main clause and the subordinate clause together have as their sense only a single thought, and the truth of the whole includes neither the truth nor the untruth of the subordinate clause. In such cases it is not permissible to replace one expression in the subordinate clause by another having the same customary reference, but only by one having the same indirect reference, i.e. the same customary sense. If somebody were to conclude: The reference of a sentence is not its truth value, for in that case it could always be replaced by another sentence of the same truth value; he would prove too much; one might just as well claim that the reference of 'morning star' is not Venus, since one may not always say 'Venus' in place of 'morning star.' One has the right to conclude only that the reference of a sentence is not *always* its truth value, and that 'morning star' does not always stand for the planet Venus, viz. when the word has its indirect reference. An exception of such a kind occurs in the subordinate clause just considered which has a thought as its reference.

If one says 'It seems that ...' one means 'It seems to me that ...' or 'I think that ...' We therefore have the same case again. The situation is similar in the case of expressions such as 'to be pleased,' 'to regret,' 'to approve,' 'to blame,' 'to hope,' 'to fear.' If, toward the end of the battle of Waterloo,[5] Wellington was glad that the Prussians were coming, the basis for his joy was a conviction. Had he been deceived, he would have been no less pleased so long as his illusion lasted; and before he became so convinced he could not have been pleased that the Prussians were coming — even though in fact they might have been already approaching.

Just as a conviction or a belief is the ground of a feeling, it can, as in inference, also be the ground of a conviction. In the sentence: 'Columbus inferred from the roundness of the Earth that he could reach India by travelling towards the west,' we have as the reference of the parts two thoughts, that the Earth is round, and that Columbus by travelling to the west could reach India. All that is relevant here is that Columbus was convinced of both, and that the one conviction was a ground for the other. Whether the Earth is really round and Columbus could really reach India by travelling west, as he thought, is immaterial to the truth of our sentence; but it is not immaterial whether we replace 'the Earth' by 'the planet which is accompanied by a moon whose diameter is greater than the fourth part of its own.' Here also we have the indirect reference of the words.

Adverbial final clauses beginning 'in order that' also belong here; for obviously the purpose is a thought; therefore: indirect reference for the words, subjunctive mood.

A subordinate clause with 'that' after 'command,' 'ask,' 'forbid,' would appear in direct speech as an imperative. Such a clause has no reference but only a sense. A command, a request, are indeed not thoughts, yet they stand on the same level as thoughts. Hence in subordinate clauses depending upon 'command,' 'ask,' etc., words have their indirect reference. The reference of such a clause is therefore not a truth value but a command, a request, and so forth.

The case is similar for the dependent question in phrases such as 'doubt whether,' 'not to know what.' It is easy to see that here also the words are to be taken to have their indirect reference. Dependent clauses expressing questions and beginning, with 'who,' 'what,' 'where,' 'when,' 'how,' 'by what means,' etc., seem at times to approximate very closely to adverbial clauses in which words have their customary references. These cases are distinguished linguistically [in German] by the mood of the verb. With the subjunctive, we have a dependent question and indirect reference of the words, so that a proper name cannot in general be replaced by another name of the same object.

In the cases so far considered the words of the subordinate clauses had their indirect reference, and this made it clear that the reference of the subordinate clause itself was indirect, i.e. not a truth value but a thought, a command, a request, a question. The subordinate clause could be regarded as a noun, indeed one could say: as a proper name of that thought, that command, etc., which it represented in the context of the sentence structure.

We now come to other subordinate clauses, in which the words do have their customary reference without however a thought occurring as sense and a truth value as reference. How this is possible is best made clear by examples.

Whoever discovered the elliptic form of the planetary orbits died in misery.

If the sense of the subordinate clause were here a thought, it would have to be possible to express it also in a separate sentence. But this does not work, because the grammatical subject 'whoever' has no independent sense and only mediates the relation with the consequent clause 'died in misery.' For this reason the sense of the subordinate clause is not a complete thought, and its reference is Kepler, not a truth value. One might object that the sense of the whole does contain a thought as part, viz. that there was somebody who first discovered the elliptic form of the planetary orbits; for whoever takes the whole to be true cannot deny this part. This is undoubtedly so; but only because otherwise the dependent clause 'whoever discovered the elliptic form of the planetary orbits' would have no reference. If anything is asserted there is always an obvious presupposition that the simple or compound proper names used have reference. If one therefore asserts 'Kepler died in misery,' there is a presupposition that the name 'Kepler' designates something; but it does not follow that the sense of the sentence 'Kepler died in misery' contains the thought that the name 'Kepler' designates something. If this were the case the negation would have to run not

Kepler did not die in misery

but

Kepler did not die in misery, or the name 'Kepler' has no reference.

That the name 'Kepler' designates something is just as much a presupposition for the assertion

Kepler died in misery

as for the contrary assertion. Now languages have the fault of containing expressions which fail to designate an object (although their grammatical form seems to qualify them for that purpose) because the truth of some sentence is a prerequisite. Thus it depends on the truth of the sentence:

There was someone who discovered the elliptic form of the planetary orbits whether the subordinate clause

Whoever discovered the elliptic form of the planetary orbits

really designates an object or only seems to do so while having in fact no reference. And thus it may appear as if our subordinate clause contained as a part of its sense the thought that there was somebody who discovered the elliptic form of the planetary orbits. If this were right the negation would run:

Either whoever discovered the elliptic form of the planetary orbits did not die in misery or there was nobody who discovered the elliptic form of the planetary orbits.

This arises from an imperfection of language, from which even the symbolic language of mathematical analysis is not altogether free; even there combinations of symbols can occur that seem to stand for something but have (at least so far) no reference, e.g. divergent infinite series. This can be avoided, e.g., by means of the special stipulation that divergent infinite series shall stand for the number 0. A logically perfect language (*Begriffsschrift*) should satisfy the conditions, that every expression grammatically well constructed as a proper name out of signs already introduced shall in fact designate an object, and that no new sign shall be introduced as a proper name without being secured a reference. The logic books contain warnings against logical mistakes arising from the ambiguity of expressions. I regard as no less pertinent a warning against apparent proper names having no reference. The history of mathematics supplies errors which have arisen in this way. This lends itself to demagogic abuse as easily as ambiguity — perhaps more easily. 'The will of the people' can serve as an example; for it is easy to establish that there is at any rate no generally accepted reference for this expression. It is therefore by no means unimportant to eliminate the source of these mistakes, at least in science, once and for all. Then such objections as the one discussed above would become impossible, because it could never depend upon the truth of a thought whether a proper name had a reference.

With the consideration of these noun clauses may be coupled that of types of adjective and adverbial clauses which are logically in close relation to them.

Adjective clauses also serve to construct compound proper names, though, unlike noun clauses, they are not sufficient by themselves for this purpose. These adjective clauses are to be regarded as equivalent to adjectives. Instead of 'the square root of 4 which is smaller than 0,' one can also say 'the negative square root of 4.' We have here the case of a compound proper name constructed from the expression for a concept with the help of the singular definite article. This is at any rate permissible if the concept applies to one and only one single object.[8]

Expressions for concepts can be so constructed that marks of a concept are given by adjective clauses as, in our example, by the clause 'which is smaller than 0.' It is evident that such an adjective clause cannot have a thought as sense or a truth value as reference, any more than the noun clause could. Its sense, which can also be expressed in many cases by a single adjective, is only a part of a thought. Here, as in the case of the noun clause, there is no independent subject and therefore no possibility of reproducing the sense of the subordinate clause in an independent sentence.

Places, instants, stretches of time, are, logically considered, objects; hence the linguistic designation of a definite place, a definite instant, or a stretch of time is to be regarded as a proper name. Now adverbial clauses of place and time can be used for the construction of such a proper name in a manner similar to that which we have seen in the case of noun and adjective clauses. In the same way, expressions for concepts bringing in places, etc., can be constructed. It is to be noted here also that the sense of these subordinate clauses cannot be reproduced in an independent sentence, since an essential component, viz. the determination of place or time, is missing and is only indicated by a relative pronoun or a conjunction.[†]

---

† In the case of these sentences, various interpretations are easily possible. The sense of the sentence, 'After Schleswig-Holstein was separated from Denmark, Prussia and Austria quarrelled' can also be rendered in the form 'After the separation of Schleswig-Holstein from Denmark, Prussia and Austria quarrelled'. In this version, it is surely sufficiently clear that the sense is not to be taken as having as a part the thought that Schleswig-Holstein was once separated from Denmark, but that this is the necessary presupposition in order for the expression 'after the separation of Schleswig-Holstein from Denmark' to have any reference at all. To be sure, our sentence can also be interpreted as saying that Schleswig-Holstein was once separated from Denmark. We then have a case which is to be considered later. In order to understand the difference more clearly, let us project ourselves into the mind of a Chinese who, having little knowledge of European history, believes it to be false that Schleswig-Holstein was ever separated from Denmark. He will take our sentence, in the first version, to be neither true nor false but will deny it to have any reference, on the ground of absence of reference for its subordinate clause. This clause would only apparently determine a time. If (转下页注)

In conditional clauses, also, there may usually be recognized to occur an indefinite indicator, having a similar correlate in the dependent clause. (We have already seen this occur in noun, adjective, and adverbial clauses.) In so far as each indicator refers to the other, both clauses together form a connected whole, which as a rule expresses only a single thought. In the sentence

If a number is less than 1 and greater than 0, its square is less than 1 and greater than 0

the component in question is 'a number' in the conditional clause and 'its' in the dependent clause. It is by means of this very indefiniteness that the sense acquires the generality expected of a law. It is this which is responsible for the fact that the antecedent clause alone has no complete thought as its sense and in combination with the consequent clause expresses one and only one thought, whose parts are no longer thoughts. It is, in general, incorrect to say that in the hypothetical judgment two judgments are put in reciprocal relationship. If this or something similar is said, the word 'judgment' is used in the same sense as I have connected with the word 'thought,' so that I would use the formulation: 'A hypothetical thought establishes a reciprocal relationship between two thoughts.' This could be true only if an indefinite indicator is absent;[9] but in such a case there would also be no generality.

If an instant of time is to be indefinitely indicated in both conditional and dependent clauses, this is often achieved merely by using the present tense of the verb, which in such a case however does not indicate the temporal present. This grammatical form is then the indefinite indicator in the main and subordinate clauses. An example of this is: 'When the Sun is in the tropic of Cancer, the longest day in the northern hemisphere occurs.' Here, also, it is impossible to express the sense of the subordinate clause in a full sentence, because this sense is not a complete thought. If we say: 'The Sun is in the tropic of Cancer,' this would refer to our present time and thereby change the sense. Just as little is the sense of the main clause a thought; only the whole, composed of main and subordinate clauses, has such a sense. It may be added that several common components in the antecedent and consequent clauses may be indefinitely indicated.

(接上页注) he interpreted our sentence in the second way, however, he would find a thought expressed in it which he would take to be false, beside a part which would be without reference for him.

It is clear that noun clauses with 'who' or 'what' and adverbial clauses with 'where,' 'when,' 'wherever,' 'whenever' are often to be interpreted as having the sense of conditional clauses, e.g. 'who touches pitch, defiles himself.'

Adjective clauses can also take the place of conditional clauses. Thus the sense of the sentence previously used can be given in the form 'The square of a number which is less than 1 and greater than 0 is less than 1 and greater than 0.'

The situation is quite different if the common component of the two clauses is designated by a proper name. In the sentence:

Napoleon, who recognized the danger to his right flank, himself led his guards against the enemy position

two thoughts are expressed:

1   Napoleon recognized the danger to his right flank
2   Napoleon himself led his guards against the enemy position.

When and where this happened is to be fixed only by the context, but is nevertheless to be taken as definitely determined thereby. If the entire sentence is uttered as an assertion, we thereby simultaneously assert both component sentences. If one of the parts is false, the whole is false. Here we have the case that the subordinate clause by itself has a complete thought as sense (if we complete it by indication of place and time). The reference of the subordinate clause is accordingly a truth value. We can therefore expect that it may be replaced, without harm to the truth value of the whole, by a sentence having the same truth value. This is indeed the case; but it is to be noticed that for purely grammatical reasons, its subject must be 'Napoleon,' for only then can it be brought into the form of an adjective clause belonging to 'Napoleon.' But if the demand that it be expressed in this form be waived, and the connexion be shown by 'and,' this restriction disappears.

Subsidiary clauses beginning with 'although' also express complete thoughts. This conjunction actually has no sense and does not change the sense of the clause but only illuminates it in a peculiar fashion.[10] We could indeed replace the concessive clause without harm to the truth of the whole by another of the same truth value; but the light in which the clause is placed by the conjunction might then easily appear unsuitable, as if a song with a sad subject were to be sung in a lively fashion.

In the last cases the truth of the whole included the truth of the component clauses. The case is different if a conditional clause expresses a complete thought by containing, in place of an indefinite indicator, a proper name or something which is to be regarded as equivalent. In the sentence

If the Sun has already risen, the sky is very cloudy

the time is the present, that is to say, definite. And the place is also to be thought of as definite. Here it can be said that a relation between the truth values of conditional and dependent clauses has been asserted, viz. such that the case does not occur in which the antecedent stands for the True and the consequent for the False. Accordingly, our sentence is true if the Sun has not yet risen, whether the sky is very cloudy or not, and also if the Sun has risen and the sky is very cloudy. Since only truth values are here in question, each component clause can be replaced by another of the same truth value without changing the truth value of the whole. To be sure, the light in which the subject then appears would usually be unsuitable; the thought might easily seem distorted; but this has nothing to do with its truth value. One must always take care not to clash with the subsidiary thoughts, which are however not explicitly expressed and therefore should not be reckoned in the sense. Hence, also, no account need be taken of their truth values.[†]

The simple cases have now been discussed. Let us review what we have learned.

The subordinate clause usually has for its sense not a thought, but only a part of one, and consequently no truth value as reference. The reason for this is either that the words in the subordinate clause have indirect reference, so that the reference, not the sense, of the subordinate clause is a thought; or else that, on account of the presence of an indefinite indicator, the subordinate clause is incomplete and expresses a thought only when combined with the main clause.

---

† The thought of our sentence might also be expressed thus: 'Either the Sun has not risen yet or the sky is very cloudy' — which shows how this kind of sentence connexion is to be understood.

It may happen, however, that the sense of the subsidiary clause is a complete thought, in which case it can be replaced by another of the same truth value without harm to the truth of the whole — provided there are no grammatical obstacles.

An examination of all the subordinate clauses which one may encounter will soon provide some which do not fit well into these categories. The reason, so far as I can see, is that these subordinate clauses have no such simple sense. Almost always, it seems, we connect with the main thoughts expressed by us subsidiary thoughts which, although not expressed, are associated with our words, in accordance with psychological laws, by the hearer. And since the subsidiary thought appears to be connected with our words of its own accord, almost like the main thought itself, we want it also to be expressed. The sense of the sentence is thereby enriched, and it may well happen that we have more simple thoughts than clauses. In many cases the sentence must be understood in this way, in others it may be doubtful whether the subsidiary thought belongs to the sense of the sentence or only accompanies it.[11] One might perhaps find that the sentence

> Napoleon, who recognized the danger to his right flank, himself led his guards against the enemy position

expresses not only the two thoughts shown above, but also the thought that the knowledge of the danger was the reason why he led the guards against the enemy position. One may in fact doubt whether this thought is merely slightly suggested or really expressed. Let the question be considered whether our sentence be false if Napoleon's decision had already been made before he recognized the danger. If our sentence could be true in spite of this, the subsidiary thought should not be understood as part of the sense. One would probably decide in favour of this. The alternative would make for a quite complicated situation: We would have more simple thoughts than clauses. If the sentence

> Napoleon recognized the danger to his right flank

were now to be replaced by another having the same truth value, e.g.

> Napoleon was already more than 45 years old

not only would our first thought be changed, but also our third one. Hence the truth value of the latter might change — viz. if his age was not the reason for the decision to lead the guards against the enemy. This shows why clauses of equal truth value cannot always be substituted for one another in such cases. The clause expresses more through its connexion with another than it does in isolation.

Let us now consider cases where this regularly happens. In the sentence:

Bebel fancies that the return of Alsace-Lorraine would appease France's desire for revenge

two thoughts are expressed, which are not however shown by means of antecedent and consequent clauses, viz.:

(1)   Bebel believes that the return of Alsace-Lorraine would appease France's desire for revenge
(2)   the return of Alsace-Lorraine would not appease France's desire for revenge.

In the expression of the first thought, the words of the subordinate clause have their indirect reference, while the same words have their customary reference in the expression of the second thought. This shows that the subordinate clause in our original complex sentence is to be taken twice over, with different reference, standing once for a thought, once for a truth value. Since the truth value is not the whole reference of the subordinate clause, we cannot simply replace the latter by another of equal truth value. Similar considerations apply to expressions such as 'know,' 'discover,' 'it is known that.'

By means of a subordinate causal clause and the associated main clause we express several thoughts, which however do not correspond separately to the original clauses. In the sentence: 'Because ice is less dense than water, it floats on water' we have

(1)   Ice is less dense than water;
(2)   If anything is less dense than water, it floats on water;
(3)   Ice floats on water.

The third thought, however, need not be explicitly introduced, since it is contained in the remaining two. On the other hand, neither the first and third nor the second and third combined would furnish the sense of our sentence. It can now be seen that our subordinate clause

because ice is less dense than water

expresses our first thought, as well as a part of our second. This is how it comes to pass that our subsidiary clause cannot be simply replaced by another of equal truth value; for this would alter our second thought and thereby might well alter its truth value.

The situation is similar in the sentence

If iron were less dense than water, it would float on water.

Here we have the two thoughts that iron is not less dense than water, and that something floats on water if it is less dense than water. The subsidiary clause again expresses one thought and a part of the other.

If we interpret the sentence already considered

After Schleswig-Holstein was separated from Denmark, Prussia and Austria quarrelled

in such a way that it expresses the thought that Schleswig-Holstein was once separated from Denmark, we have first this thought, and secondly the thought that at a time, more closely determined by the subordinate clause, Prussia and Austria quarrelled. Here also the subordinate clause expresses not only one thought but also a part of another. Therefore it may not in general be replaced by another of the same truth value.

It is hard to exhaust all the possibilities given by language; but I hope to have brought to light at least the essential reasons why a subordinate clause may not always be replaced by another of equal truth value without harm to the truth of the whole sentence structure. These reasons arise:

(1) when the subordinate clause does not stand for a truth value, inasmuch as it expresses only a part of a thought;

(2)　when the subordinate clause does stand for a truth value but is not restricted to so doing, inasmuch as its sense includes one thought and part of another.

The first case arises:

(a)　in indirect reference of words

(b)　if a part of the sentence is only an indefinite indicator instead of a proper name.

In the second case, the subsidiary clause may have to be taken twice over, viz. once in its customary reference, and the other time in indirect reference; or the sense of a part of the subordinate clause may likewise be a component of another thought, which, taken together with the thought directly expressed by the subordinate clause, makes up the sense of the whole sentence.

It follows with sufficient probability from the foregoing that the cases where a subordinate clause is not replaceable by another of the same value cannot be brought in disproof of our view that a truth value is the reference of a sentence having a thought as its sense.

Let us return to our starting point.

When we found '$a = a$' and '$a = b$' to have different cognitive values, the explanation is that for the purpose of knowledge, the sense of the sentence, viz., the thought expressed by it, is no less relevant than its reference, i.e. its truth value. If now $a = b$, then indeed the reference of 'b' is the same as that of 'a,' and hence the truth value of '$a = b$' is the same as that of '$a = a$.' In spite of this, the sense of 'b' may differ from that of 'a,' and thereby the thought expressed in '$a = b$' differs from that of '$a = a$.' In that case the two sentences do not have the same cognitive value. If we understand by 'judgment' the advance from the thought to its truth value, as in the above paper, we can also say that the judgments are different.

Translator's Notes

1　The reference is to Frege's *Begriffsschrift, eine der arithmetischen nachgebildete Formelsprache des reinen Denkens* (Halle, 1879).

2   See his 'Über Begriff und Gegenstand' *(Vierteljahrsschrift für wissenschaftliche Philosophie* XVI [1892], 192–205).

3   See his 'Über Begriff und Gegenstand' *(Vierteljahrsschrift für wissenschaftliche Philosophie* XVI [1892], 192–205).

4   A literal translation of Frege's 'abstracten Nennsätzen' whose meaning eludes me.

5   Frege uses the Prussian name for the battle — 'Belle Alliance.'

①   I use this word in the sense of identity, and understand '$a = b$' to have the sense of 'a is the same as b' or 'a and b coincide.'

②   In the case of an actual proper name such as 'Aristotle' opinions as to the sense may differ. It might, for instance, be taken to be the following: the pupil of Plato and teacher of Alexander the Great. Anybody who does this will attach another sense to the sentence 'Aristotle was born in Stagira' than will a man who takes as the sense of the name: the teacher of Alexander the Great who was born in Stagira. So long as the reference remains the same, such variations of sense may be tolerated, although they are to be avoided in the theoretical structure of a demonstrative science and ought not to occur in a perfect language.

③   We can include with ideas the direct experiences in which sense-impressions and acts themselves take the place of the traces which they have left in the mind. The distinction is unimportant for our purpose, especially since memories of sense-impressions and acts always go along with such impressions and acts themselves to complete the perceptual image. One may on the other hand understand direct experience as including any object, in so far as it is sensibly perceptible or spatial.

④   By a thought I understand not the subjective performance of thinking but its objective content, which is capable of being the common property of several thinkers.

⑤   It would be desirable to have a special term for signs having only sense. If we name them, say, representations, the words of the actors on the stage would be representations; indeed the actor himself would be a representation.

⑥   A judgment, for me, is not the mere comprehension of a thought, but the admission of its truth.

⑦   In 'A lied in saying he had seen B,' the subordinate clause designates a thought which is said (1) to have been asserted by A (2) while A was convinced of its falsity.

⑧ In accordance with what was said above, an expression of the kind in question must actually always be assured of reference, by means of a special stipulation, e.g. by the convention that 0 shall count as its reference, when the concept applies to no object or to more than one.

⑨ At times an explicit linguistic indication is missing and must be read off from the entire context.

⑩ Similarly in the case of 'but,' 'yet.'

⑪ This may be important for the question whether an assertion is a lie, or an oath a perjury.

Descriptions

Bertrand Russell

We dealt in the preceding chapter with the words *all* and *some*; in this chapter we shall consider the word *the* in the singular, and in the next chapter we shall consider the word *the* in the plural. It may be thought excessive to devote two chapters to one word, but to the philosophical mathematician it is a word of very great importance: like Browning's Grammarian with the enclitic δε, I would give the doctrine of this word if I were "dead from the waist down" and not merely in a prison.

We have already had occasion to mention "descriptive functions," i.e. such expressions as "the father of *x*" or "the sine of *x*." These are to be defined by first defining "descriptions."

A "description" may be of two sorts, definite and indefinite (or ambiguous). An indefinite description is a phrase of the form "a so-and-so," and a definite description is a phrase of the form "the so-and-so" (in the singular). Let us begin with the former.

"Who did you meet?" "I met a man." "That is a very indefinite description." We are therefore not departing from usage in our terminology. Our question is: What do I really assert when I assert "I met a man"? Let us assume, for the moment, that my assertion is true, and that in fact I met Jones. It is clear that what I assert is *not* "I met Jones." I may say "I met a man, but it was not Jones"; in that case, though I lie, I do not contradict myself, as I should do if when I say[①] I met a man I really mean that I met Jones. It is clear also that the person to whom I am speaking can understand what I say, even if he is a foreigner and has never heard of Jones.

But we may go further: not only Jones, but no actual man, enters into my statement. This becomes obvious when the statement is false, since then there is no more reason why Jones should be supposed to enter into the proposition than why anyone else should. Indeed the statement would remain significant, though it could not possibly be true, even if there were no man at all. "I met a unicorn" or "1 met a sea-serpent" is a perfectly significant assertion, if we know what it would be to be a unicorn or a sea-serpent, i.e. what is the definition of these fabulous monsters. Thus it is only what we may call the *concept* that enters into the proposition. In the case of "unicorn," for example, there is only the concept: there is not also, somewhere among the shades, something unreal which may be called "a unicorn." Therefore, since it is significant (though false) to say "I met a unicorn," it is clear that this proposition, rightly analyzed, does not contain a constituent "a unicorn," though it does contain the concept "unicorn."

The question of "unreality," which confronts us at this point, is a very important one. Misled by grammar, the great majority of those logicians who have dealt with this question have dealt with it on mistaken lines. They have regarded grammatical form as a surer guide in analysis than, in fact, it is. And they have not known what differences in grammatical form are important. "I met Jones" and "I met a man" would count traditionally as propositions of the same form, but in actual fact they are of quite different forms: the first names an actual person, Jones; while the second involves a propositional function, and becomes, when made explicit: "The function '1 met x and x is human' is sometimes true." (It will be remembered that we adopted the convention of using "sometimes" as not implying more than once.) This proposition is obviously not of the form "I met x" which accounts for the existence of the proposition "I met a unicorn" in spite of the fact that there is no such thing as "a unicorn."

For want of the apparatus of propositional functions, many logicians have been driven to the conclusion that there are unreal objects. It is argued, e.g. by Meinong,[1] that we can speak about "the golden mountain," "the round square," and so on; we can make true propositions of which these are the subjects; hence they must have some kind of logical being, since otherwise the propositions in which they occur would be meaningless. In such theories, it seems to me, there is a failure of that feeling for reality which ought to be preserved even in the most abstract studies. Logic, I should maintain, must no more admit a unicorn than zoology can; for logic is concerned with the real world just as truly as zoology, though with its more abstract and general features. To say that unicorns have an existence in heraldry, or in literature, or in imagination, is a most pitiful and paltry evasion. What exists in heraldry is not an animal, made of flesh and blood, moving and breathing of its own initiative. What exists is a picture, or a description in words. Similarly, to maintain that Hamlet, for example, exists in his own world, namely, in the world of Shakespeare's imagination, just as truly as (say) Napoleon existed in the ordinary world, is to say something deliberately confusing, or else confused to a degree which is scarcely credible. There is only one world, the "real" world: Shakespeare's imagination is part of it, and the thoughts that he had in writing Hamlet are real. So are the thoughts that we have in reading the play. But it is of the very essence of fiction that only the thoughts, feelings, etc., in Shakespeare and his readers are real, and that there is not, in addition to them, an objective Hamlet. When you have taken account of all the feelings roused by Napoleon in writers and readers of history, you have not touched the actual man; but in the case of Hamlet you have come to the end of him. If no one thought about Hamlet, there would be nothing left of him; if no one had thought about Napoleon, he would have soon seen to it that some one did. The sense of reality is vital in logic, and whoever juggles with it by pretending that Hamlet has another kind of reality is doing a disservice to thought. A robust sense of reality is very necessary in framing a correct analysis of propositions about unicorns, golden mountains, round squares, and other such pseudo-objects.

In obedience to the feeling of reality, we shall insist that, in the analysis of propositions, nothing "unreal" is to be admitted. But, after all, if there *is* nothing unreal, how, it may be asked, *could* we admit anything unreal? The reply is that, in dealing with propositions, we are dealing in the first instance with symbols, and if we attribute significance to groups of symbols which have no significance, we shall fall into the error of admitting unrealities, in the only sense in which this is possible, namely, as objects described. In the proposition "I met a unicorn," the whole four words together make a significant proposition, and the word "unicorn" by itself is significant, in just the same sense as the word "man." But the *two* words "a unicorn" do not form a subordinate group having a meaning of its own. Thus if we falsely attribute meaning to these two words, we find ourselves saddled with "a unicorn," and with the problem how there can be such a thing in a world where there are no unicorns. "A unicorn" is an indefinite description which describes nothing. It is not an indefinite description which describes something unreal. Such a proposition as "*x* is unreal" only has meaning when "*x*" is a description, definite or indefinite; in that case the proposition will be true if "*x*" is a description which describes nothing. But whether the description "*x*" describes something or describes nothing, it is in any case not a constituent of the proposition in which it occurs; like "a unicorn" just now, it is not a subordinate group having a meaning of its own. All this results from the fact that, when "*x*" is a description, "*x* is unreal" or "*x* does not exist" is not nonsense, but is always significant and sometimes true.

We may now proceed to define generally the meaning of propositions which contain ambiguous descriptions. Suppose we wish to make some statement about "a so-and-so," where "so-and-so's" are those objects that have a certain property ϕ, i.e. those objects *x* for which the propositional function ϕx is true. (E.g. if we take "a man" as our instance of "a so-and-so," ϕx will be "*x* is human.") Let us now wish to assert the property ψ of "a so-and-so," i.e. we wish to assert that "a so-and-so" has that property which *x* has when ψx is true. (E.g. in the case of "I met a man," ψx will be "I met *x*.") Now the proposition that "a so-and-so" has the property ψ is *not* a proposition of the form "ψx." If it were, "a so-and-so" would have to be identical with *x* for a suitable *x*; and although (in a sense) this may be true in some cases, it is certainly not true in such a case as "a unicorn." It is just this fact, that the statement that a so-and-so has the property ψ is not of the form ψx, which makes it possible for "a so-and-so" to be, in a certain clearly definable sense, "unreal." The definition is as follows:

The statement that "an object having the property ϕ has the property ψ"

means:

"The joint assertion of ϕx and ψx is not always false."

So far as logic goes, this is the same proposition as might be expressed by "some ϕ's are ψ's"; but rhetorically there is a difference, because in the one case there is a suggestion of singularity, and in the other case of plurality. This, however, is not the important point. The important point is that, when rightly analyzed, propositions verbally about "a so-and-so" are found to contain no constituent represented by this phrase. And that is why such propositions can be significant even when there is no such thing as a so-and-so.

The definition of *existence,* as applied to ambiguous descriptions, results from what was said at the end of the preceding chapter [chapter 15 of *Introduction to Mathematical Philosophy*]. We say that "men exist" or "a man exists" if the propositional function "x is human" is sometimes true; and generally "a so-and-so" exists if "x is so-and-so" is sometimes true. We may put this in other language. The proposition "Socrates is a man" is no doubt *equivalent* to "Socrates is human," but it is not the very same proposition. The *is* of "Socrates is human" expresses the relation of subject and predicate; the *is* of "Socrates is a man" expresses identity. It is a disgrace to the human race that it has chosen to employ the same word "is" for these two entirely different ideas — a disgrace which a symbolic logical language of course remedies. The identity in "Socrates is a man" is identity between an object named (accepting "Socrates" as a name, subject to qualifications explained later) and an object ambiguously described. An object ambiguously described will "exist" when at least one such proposition is true, i.e. when there is at least one true proposition of the form "x is a so-and-so," where "x" is a name. It is characteristic of ambiguous (as opposed to definite) descriptions that there may be any number of true propositions of the above form — Socrates is a man, Plato is a man, etc. Thus "a man exists" follows from Socrates, or Plato, or anyone else. With definite descriptions, on the other hand, the corresponding form of proposition, namely, "x is the so-and-so" (where "x" is a name), can only be true for one value of x at most. This brings us to the subject of definite descriptions, which are to be defined in a way analogous to that employed for ambiguous descriptions, but rather more complicated.

We come now to the main subject of the present chapter, namely, the definition of the word *the* (in the singular). One very important point about the definition of "a so-and-so" applies equally to "the so-and-so"; the definition to be sought is a definition of propositions in which this phrase occurs, not a definition of the phrase itself in isolation. In the case of "a so-and-so," this is fairly obvious: no one could suppose that "a man" was a definite object, which could be defined by itself. Socrates is a man, Plato is a man, Aristotle is a man, but we cannot infer that "a man" means the same as "Socrates" means and also the same as "Plato" means and also the same as "Aristotle" means, since these three names have different meanings. Nevertheless, when we have enumerated all the men in the world, there is nothing left of which we can say, "This is a man, and not only so, but it is *the* 'a man,' the quintessential entity that is just an indefinite man without being anybody in particular." It is of course quite clear that whatever there is in the world is definite: if it is a man it is one definite man and not any other. Thus there cannot be such an entity as "a man" to be found in the world, as opposed to specific men. And accordingly it is natural that we do not define "a man" itself, but only the propositions in which it occurs.

In the case of "the so-and-so" this is equally true, though at first sight less obvious. We may demonstrate that this must be the case, by a consideration of the difference between a *name* and a *definite description.* Take the proposition, "Scott is the author of *Waverley.*" We have here a name, "Scott," and a description, "the author of *Waverley*," which are asserted to apply to the same person. The distinction between a name and all other symbols may be explained as follows:

A name is a simple symbol whose meaning is something that can only occur as subject, i.e. something of the kind that we defined as an "individual" or a "particular." And a "simple" symbol is one which has no parts that are symbols. Thus "Scott" is a simple symbol, because, though it has parts (namely, separate letters), these parts are not symbols. On the other hand, "the author of *Waverley*" is not a simple symbol, because the separate words that compose the phrase are parts which are symbols. If, as may be the case, whatever *seems* to be an "individual" is really capable of further analysis, we shall have to content ourselves with what may be called "relative individuals," which will be terms that, throughout the context in question, are never analyzed and never occur otherwise than as subjects. And in that case we shall have correspondingly to content ourselves with "relative names." From the standpoint of our present problem, namely, the definition of descriptions, this problem, whether these are absolute names or only relative names, may be ignored, since it concerns different stages in the hierarchy of "types," whereas we have to compare such couples as "Scott" and "the author of *Waverley*," which both apply to the same object, and do not raise the problem of types. We may, therefore, for the moment, treat names as capable of being absolute; nothing that we shall have to say will depend upon this assumption, but the wording may be a little shortened by it.

We have, then, two things to compare: (1) a *name,* which is a simple symbol, directly designating an individual which is its meaning, and having this meaning in its own right, independently of the meanings of all other words; (2) a *description,* which consists of several words, whose meanings are already fixed, and from which results whatever is to be taken as the "meaning" of the description.

A proposition containing a description is not identical with what that proposition becomes when a name is substituted, even if the name names the same object as the description describes. "Scott is the author of *Waverley*" is obviously a different proposition from "Scott is Scott": the first is a fact in literary history, the second a trivial truism. And if we put anyone other than Scott in place of "the author of *Waverley,*" our proposition would become false, and would therefore certainly no longer be the same proposition. But, it may be said, our proposition is essentially of the same form as (say) "Scott is Sir Walter," in which two names are said to apply to the same person. The reply is that, if "Scott is Sir Walter" really means "the person named 'Scott' is the person named 'Sir Walter,'" then the names are being used as descriptions: i.e. the individual, instead of being named, is being described as the person having that name. This is a way in which names are frequently used in practice, and there will, as a rule, be nothing in the phraseology to show whether they are being used in this way or *as* names. When a name is used directly, merely to indicate what we are speaking about, it is no part of the *fact* asserted, or of the falsehood if our assertion happens to be false: it is merely part of the symbolism by which we express our thought. What we want to express is something which might (for example) be translated into a foreign language; it is something for which the actual words are a vehicle, but of which they are no part. On the other hand, when we make a proposition about "the person called 'Scott,'" the actual name "Scott" enters into what we are asserting, and not merely into the language used in making the assertion. Our proposition will now be a different one if we substitute "the person called 'Sir Walter.'" But so long as we are using names *as* names, whether we say "Scott" or whether we say "Sir Walter" is as irrelevant to what we are asserting as whether we speak English or French. Thus so long as names are used *as* names, "Scott is Sir Walter" is the same trivial proposition as "Scott is Scott." This completes the proof that "Scott is the author of *Waverley*" is not the same proposition as results from substituting a name for "the author of *Waverley,*" no matter what name may be substituted.

When we use a variable, and speak of a propositional function, ϕx say, the process of applying general statements about x to particular cases will consist in substituting a name for the letter "x," assuming that ϕ is a function which has individuals for its arguments. Suppose, for example, that ϕx is "always true"; let it be, say, the "law of identity," $x=x$. Then we may substitute for "x" any name we choose, and we shall obtain a true proposition. Assuming for the moment that "Socrates," "Plato," and "Aristotle" are names (a very rash assumption), we can infer from the law of identity that Socrates is Socrates, Plato is Plato, and Aristotle is Aristotle. But we shall commit a fallacy if we attempt to infer, without further premisses, that the author of *Waverley* is the author of *Waverley*. This results from what we have just proved, that, if we substitute a name for "the author of *Waverley*" in a proposition, the proposition we obtain is a different one. That is to say, applying the result to our present case: If "x" is a name, "$x=x$" is not the same proposition as "the author of *Waverley* is the author of *Waverley*," no matter what name "x" may be. Thus from the fact that all propositions of the form "$x=x$" are true we cannot infer, without more ado, that the author of *Waverley* is the author of *Waverley*. In fact, propositions of the form "the so-and-so is the so-and-so" are not always true: it is necessary that the so-and-so should *exist* (a term which will be explained shortly). It is false that the present King of France is the present King of France, or that the round square is the round square. When we substitute a description for a name, propositional functions which are "always true" may become false, if the description describes nothing. There is no mystery in this as soon as we realize (what was proved in the preceding paragraph) that when we substitute a description the result is not a value of the propositional function in question.

We are now in a position to define propositions in which a definite description occurs. The only thing that distinguishes "the so-and-so" from "a so-and-so" is the implication of uniqueness. We cannot speak of "*the* inhabitant of London," because inhabiting London is an attribute which is not unique. We cannot speak about "the present King of France," because there is none; but we can speak about "the present King of England." Thus propositions about "the so-and-so" always imply the corresponding propositions about "a so-and-so," with the addendum that there is not more than one so-and-so. Such a proposition as "Scott is the author of Waverley" could not be true if *Waverley* had never been written, or if several people had written it; and no more could any other proposition resulting from a propositional function x by the substitution of "the author of *Waverley*" for "x." We may say that "the author of *Waverley*" means "the value of x for which 'x wrote *Waverley*' is true." Thus the proposition "the author of *Waverley* was Scotch," for example, involves:

(1)   "x wrote *Waverley*" is not always false
(2)   "if x and y wrote *Waverley*, x and y are identical" is always true
(3)   "if x wrote *Waverley*, x was Scotch" is always true

These three propositions, translated into ordinary language, state:

(1)   at least one person wrote *Waverley*
(2)   at most one person wrote *Waverley*
(3)   whoever wrote *Waverley* was Scotch

All these three are implied by "the author of *Waverley* was Scotch." Conversely, the three together (but no two of them) imply that the author of *Waverley* was Scotch. Hence the three together may be taken as defining what is meant by the proposition "the author of *Waverley* was Scotch."

We may somewhat simplify these three propositions. The first and second together are equivalent to: "There is a term c such that 'x wrote *Waverley*' is true when x is c and is false when x is not c." In other words, "There is a term c such that 'x wrote *Waverley*' is always equivalent to 'x is c.'" (Two propositions are "equivalent" when both are true or both are false.) We have here, to begin with, two functions of x, "x wrote *Waverley*" and "x is c," and we form a function of c by considering the equivalence of these two functions of x for all values of x; we then proceed to assert that the resulting function of c is "sometimes true," i.e. that it is true for at least one value of c. (It obviously cannot be true for more than one value of c.) These two conditions together are defined as giving the meaning of "the author of *Waverley* exists."

We may now define "the term satisfying the function ϕx exists." This is the general form of which the above is a particular case. "The author of *Waverley*" is "the term satisfying the function 'x wrote *Waverley*.'" And "the so-and-so" will always involve reference to some propositional function, namely, that which defines the property that makes a thing a so-and-so. Our definition is as follows:

"The term satisfying the function ϕx exists"

means:

"There is a term c such that ϕx is always equivalent to 'x is c.'"

In order to define "the author of *Waverley* was Scotch," we have still to take account of the third of our three propositions, namely, "Whoever wrote *Waverley* was Scotch." This will be satisfied by merely adding that the c in question is to be Scotch. Thus "the author of *Waverley* was Scotch" is:

"There is a term c such that (1) 'x wrote *Waverley*' is always equivalent to 'x is c,' (2) c is Scotch."

And generally: "the term satisfying ϕx satisfies ψx" is defined as meaning:

"There is a term c such that (1) ϕx is always equivalent to 'x is c,' (2) ψx is true."

This is the definition of propositions in which descriptions occur.

It is possible to have much knowledge concerning a term described, i.e. to know many propositions concerning "the so-and-so," without actually knowing what the so-and-so is, i.e. without knowing any proposition of the form "x is the so-and-so," where "x" is a name. In a detective story propositions about "the man who did the deed" are accumulated, in the hope that ultimately they will suffice to demonstrate that it was A who did the deed. We may even go so far as to say that, in all such knowledge as can be expressed in words — with the exception of "this" and "that" and a few other words of which the meaning varies on different occasions — no names, in the strict sense, occur, but what seem like names are really descriptions. We may inquire significantly whether Homer existed, which we could not do if "Homer" were a name. The proposition "the so-and-so exists" is significant, whether true or false; but if a is the so-and-so (where "a" is a name), the words "a exists" are meaningless. It is only of descriptions — definite or indefinite — that existence can be significantly asserted; for, if "a" is a name, it *must* name something: what does not name anything is not a name, and therefore, if intended to be a name, is a symbol devoid of meaning, whereas a description, like "the present King of France," does not become incapable of occurring significantly merely on the ground that it describes nothing, the reason being that it is a *complex* symbol, of which the meaning is derived from that of its constituent symbols. And so, when we ask whether Homer existed, we are using the word "Homer" as an abbreviated description: we may replace it by (say) "the author of the *Iliad* and the *Odyssey*." The same considerations apply to almost all uses of what look like proper names.

When descriptions occur in propositions, it is necessary to distinguish what may be called "primary" and "secondary" occurrences. The abstract distinction is as follows. A description has a "primary" occurrence when the proposition in which it occurs results from substituting the description for "x" in some propositional function ϕx; a description has a "secondary" occurrence when the result of substituting the description for x in ϕx gives only *part* of the proposition concerned. An instance will make this clearer. Consider "the present King of France is bald." Here "the present King of France" has a primary occurrence, and the proposition is false. Every proposition in which a description which describes nothing has a primary occurrence is false. But now consider "the present King of France is not bald." This is ambiguous. If we are first to take "x is bald," then substitute "the present King of France" for "x," and then deny the result, the occurrence of "the present King of France" is secondary and our proposition is true; but if we are to take "x is not bald" and substitute "the present King of France" for "x," then "the present King of France" has a primary occurrence and the proposition is false. Confusion of primary and secondary occurrences is a ready source of fallacies where descriptions are concerned.

Descriptions occur in mathematics chiefly in the form of *descriptive functions*, i.e. "the term having the relation R to y," or "the R of y" as we may say, on the analogy of "the father of y" and similar phrases. To say "the father of y is rich," for example, is to say that the following propositional function of c: "c is rich, and 'x begat y' is always equivalent to 'x is c,'" is "sometimes true," i.e. is true for at least one value of c. It obviously cannot be true for more than one value.

The theory of descriptions, briefly outlined in the present chapter, is of the utmost importance both in logic and in theory of knowledge. But for purposes of mathematics, the more philosophical parts of the theory are not essential, and have therefore been omitted in the above account, which has confined itself to the barest mathematical requisites.

References

1   *Untersuchungen zur Gegenstandstheorie und Psychologie,* 1904.
①   From *Introduction to Mathematical Philosophy* (London: George Allen and Unwin Ltd., 1919), pp. 167–180.

On Referring

P. F. Strawson

I

WE very commonly use expressions of certain kinds to mention or refer to some individual person or single object or particular event or place or process, in the course of doing what we should normally describe as making a statement about that person, object, place, event, or process. I shall call this way of using expressions the "uniquely referring use". The classes of expressions which are most commonly used in this way are: singular demonstrative pronouns ("this" and "that"); proper names (*e.g.* "Venice", "Napoleon", "John"); singular personal and impersonal pronouns ("he", "she", "I", "you", "it"); and phrases beginning with the definite article followed by a noun, qualified or unqualified, in the singular (*e.g.* "the table", "the old man", "the king of France")· Any expression of any of these classes can occur as the subject of what would traditionally be regarded as a singular subject-predicate sentence; and would, so occurring, exemplify the use I wish to discuss.

I do not want to say that expressions belonging to these classes never have any other use than the one I want to discuss. On the contrary, it is obvious that they do. It is obvious that anyone who uttered the sentence, "The whale is a mammal", would be using the expression "the whale" in a way quite different from the way it would be used by anyone who had occasion seriously to utter the sentence, "The whale struck the ship". In the first sentence one is obviously *not* mentioning, and in the second sentence one obviously *is* mentioning, a particular whale. Again if I said, "Napoleon was the greatest French soldier", I should be using the word "Napoleon" to mention a certain individual, but I should not be using the phrase, "the greatest French soldier", to mention an individual, but to say something about an individual I had already mentioned. It would be natural to say that in using this sentence I was talking *about* Napoleon and that what I was *saying* about him was that he was the greatest French soldier. But of course I *could* use the expression, "the greatest French soldier", to mention an individual; for example, by saying: "The greatest French soldier died in exile". So it is obvious that at least some expressions belonging to the classes I mentioned *can* have uses other than the use I am anxious to discuss. Another thing I do not want to say is that in any given sentence there is never more than one expression used in the way I propose to discuss. On the contrary, it is obvious that there may be more than one. For example, it would be natural to say that, in seriously using the sentence, "The whale struck the ship", I was saying something about both a certain whale and a certain ship, that I was using each of the expressions "the whale" and "the ship" to mention a particular object; or, in other words, that I was using each of these expressions in the uniquely referring way. In general, however, I shall confine my attention to cases where an expression used in this way occurs as the grammatical subject of a sentence.

I think it is true to say that Russell's Theory of Descriptions, which is concerned with the last of the four classes of expressions I mentioned above (*i.e.* with expressions of the form "the so-and-so") is still widely accepted among logicians as giving a correct account of the use of such expressions in ordinary language. I want to show, in the first place, that this theory, so regarded, embodies some fundamental mistakes.

What question or questions about phrases of the form "the so-and-so" was the Theory of Descriptions designed to answer? I think that at least one of the questions may be illustrated as follows. Suppose some one were now to utter the sentence, "The king of France is wise". No one would say that the sentence which had been uttered was meaningless. Everyone would agree that it was significant. But everyone knows that there is not at present a king of France. One of the questions the Theory of Descriptions was designed to answer was the question: how can such a sentence as "The king of France is wise" be significant even when there is nothing which answers to the description it contains, *i.e.*, in this case, nothing which answers to the description "The king of France"? And one of the reasons why Russell thought it important to give a correct answer to this question was that he thought it important to show that another answer which might be given was wrong. The answer that he thought was wrong, and to which he was anxious to supply an alternative, might be exhibited as the conclusion of either of the following two fallacious arguments. Let us call the sentence "The king of France is wise" the sentence S. Then the first argument is as follows:

(1) The phrase, "the king of France", is the subject of the sentence S.

Therefore (2) if S is a significant sentence, S is a sentence *about* the king of France.

But (3) if there in no sense exists a king of France, the sentence is not about anything, and hence not about the king of France.

Therefore (4) since S is significant, there must in some sense (in some world) exist (or subsist) the king of France.

And the second argument is as follows:

(1) If S is significant, it is either true or false.

(2) S is true if the king of France is wise and false if the king of France is not wise.

(3) But the statement tkat the king of France is wise and the statement that the king of France is not wise are alike true only if there is (in some sense, in some world) something which is the king of France.

Hence (4) since S is significant, there follows the same conclusion as before.

These are fairly obviously bad arguments, and, as we should expect, Russell rejects them. The postulation of a world of strange entities, to which the king of France belongs, offends, he says, against "that feeling for reality which ought to be preserved even in the most abstract studies". The fact that Russell rejects these arguments is, however, less interesting than the extent to which, in rejecting their conclusion, he concedes the more important of their principles. Let me refer to the phrase, "the king of France", as the phrase D. Then I think Russell's reasons for rejecting these two arguments can be summarised as follows. The mistake arises, he says, from thinking that D, which is certainly the *grammatical* subject of S, is also the *logical* subject of S. But D is not the logical subject of S. In fact S, although grammatically it has a singular subject and a predicate, is not logically a subject-predicate sentence at all. The proposition it expresses is a complex kind of *existential* proposition, part of which might be described as a "uniquely existential" proposition. To exhibit the logical form of the proposition, we should re-write the sentence in a logically appropriate grammatical form; in such a way that the deceptive similarity of S to a sentence expressing a subject-predicate proposition would disappear, and we should be safeguarded against arguments such as the bad ones I outlined above. Before recalling the details of Russell's analysis of S, let us notice what his answer, as I have so far given it, seems to imply. His answer seems to imply that in the case of a sentence which is similar to S in that (1) it is grammatically of the snbject-predicate form and (2) its grammatical subject does not refer to anything, then the only alternative to its being meaningless is that it should not really (*i.e.* logically) be of the snbject-predicate form at all, but of some quite different form. And this in its turn seems to imply that if there are any sentences which are genuinely of the subject-predicate form, then the very fact of their being significant, having a meaning, guarantees that there *is* something referred to by the logical (and grammatical) subject. Moreover, Russell's answer seems to imply that there are such sentences. For if it is true that one may be misled by the grammatical similarity of S to other sentences into thinking that it is logically of the subject-predicate form, then surely there must be other sentences grammatically similar to S, which *are* of the subject-predicate form. To show not only that Russell's answer seems to imply these conclusions, but that he accepted at least the first two of them, it is enough to consider what he says about a class of expressions which he calls "logically proper names" and contrasts with expressions, like D, which he calls "definite descriptions". Of logically proper names Russell says or implies the following things:

(1) That they and they alone can occur as subjects of sentences which are genuinely of the subject-predicate form;

(2) that an expression intended to be a logically proper name is *meaningless* unless there is some single object for which it stands: for the *meaning* of such an expression just is the individual object which the expression designates. To be a name at all, therefore, it *must* designate something.

It is easy to see that if anyone believes these two propositions, then the only way for him to save the significance of the sentence S is to deny that it is a logically subject-predicate sentence. Generally, we may say that Russell recognises only two ways in which sentences which seem, from their grammatical structure, to be about some particular person or individual object or event, can be significant:

(1) The first is that their grammatical form should be misleading as to their

logical form, and that they should be analysable, like S, as a special kind of existential sentence;

(2) The second is that their grammatical subject should be a logically proper name, of which the meaning is the individual thing it designates.

I think that Russell is unquestionably wrong in this, and that sentences which are significant, and which begin with an expression used in the uniquely referring way fall into neither of these two classes. Expressions used in the uniquely referring way are never either logically proper names or descriptions, if what is meant by calling them "descriptions" is that they are to be analysed in accordance with the model provided by Russell's Theory of Descriptions.

There are no logically proper names and there are no descriptions (in this sense).

Let us now consider the details of Russell's analysis. According to Russell, anyone who asserted S would be asserting that:

(1)　There is a king of France.
(2)　There is not more than one king of France.
(3)　There is nothing which is king of France and is not wise.

It is easy to see both how Russell arrived at this analysis, and how it enables him to answer the question with which we began, *viz.* the question: How can the sentence S be significant when there is no king of France? The way in which he arrived at the analysis was clearly by asking himself what would be the circumstances in which we would say that anyone who uttered the sentence S had made a true assertion. And it does seem pretty clear, and I have no wish to dispute, that the sentences (1)–(3) above do describe circumstances which are at least *necessary* conditions of anyone making a true assertion by uttering the sentence S. But, as I hope to show, to say this is not at all the same thing as to say that Russell has given a correct account of the use of the sentence S or even that he has given an account which, though incomplete, is correct as far as it goes; and is certainly not at all the same thing as to say that the model translation provided is a correct model for all (or for any) singular sentences beginning with a phrase of the form "the so-and-so".

It is also easy to see how this analysis enables Russell to answer the question of how the sentence S can be significant, even when there is no king of France.

For, if this analysis is correct, anyone who utters the sentence S to-day would be jointly asserting three propositions, one of which *(viz.* that there is a king of France) would be false; and since the conjunction of three propositions, of which one is false, is itself false, the assertion as a whole would be significant, but false. So neither of the bad arguments for subsistent entities would apply to such an assertion.

II

As a step towards showing that Russell's solution of his problem is mistaken, and towards providing the correct solution, I want now to draw certain distinctions. For this purpose I shall, for the remainder of this section, refer to an expression which has a uniquely referring use as "an expression" for short; and to a sentence beginning with such an expression as "a sentence" for short. The distinctions I shall draw are rather rough and ready, and, no doubt, difficult cases could be produced which would call for their refinement. But I think they will serve my purpose. The distinctions are between:

(Al) a sentence,
(A2) a use of a sentence,
(A3) an utterance of a sentence,

and, correspondingly, between:

(Bl) an expression,
(B2) a use of an expression,
(B3) an utterance of an expression.

Consider again the sentence, "The king of France is wise". It is easy to imagine that this sentence was uttered at various times from, say, the beginning of the seventeenth century onwards, during the reigns of each successive French monarch; and easy to imagine that it was also uttered during the subsequent periods in which France was not a monarchy. Notice that it was natural for me to speak of "the sentence" or "this sentence" being uttered at various times during this period; or, in other words, that it would be natural and correct to speak of *one and the same* sentence being uttered on all these various occasions. It is in the sense in which it would be correct to speak of one and the same sentence being uttered on all these various occasions that I want to use the expression (Al) "a sentence". There are, however, obvious differences between different *occasions of the use* of this sentence. For instance, if one man uttered it in the reign of Louis XIV and another man uttered it in the reign of Louis XV, it would be natural to say (to assume) that they were respectively talking about different people; and it might be held that the first man, in using the sentence, made a true assertion, while the second man, in using the same sentence, made a false assertion. If on the other hand two different men simultaneously uttered the sentence (*e.g.* if one wrote it and the other spoke it) during the reign of Louis XIV, it would be natural to say (assume) that they were both talking about the same person, and, in that case, in using the sentence, they *must* either both have made a true assertion or both have made a false assertion. And this illustrates what I mean by *a use* of a sentence. The two men who uttered the sentence, one in the reign of Louis XV and one in the reign of Louis XIV, each made a different use of the same sentence; whereas the two men who uttered the sentence simultaneously in the reign of Louis XIV, made the same use[1] of the same sentence. Obviously in the case of this sentence, and equally obviously in the case of many others, we cannot talk of *the sentence* being true or false, but only of its being used to make a true or false assertion, or (if this is preferred) to express a true or a false proposition. And equally obviously we cannot talk of *the sentence* being *about* a particular person, for the same sentence may be used at different times to talk about quite different particular persons, but only of *a use* of the sentence to talk about a particular person. Finally it will make sufficiently clear what I mean by an utterance of a sentence if I say that the two men who simultaneously uttered the sentence in the reign of Louis XIV made two different utterances of the same sentence, though they made the same *use* of the sentence.

If we now consider not the whole sentence, "The king of France is wise", but that part of it which is the expression, "the king of France", it is obvious that we can make analogous, though not identical distinctions between (1) the expression, (2) a use of the expression and (3) an utterance of the expression. The distinctions will not be identical; we obviously cannot correctly talk of the expression "the king of France" being used to express a true or false proposition, since in general only sentences can be used truly or falsely; and similarly it is only by using a sentence and not by using an expression alone, that you can talk about a particular person. Instead, we shall say in this case that you *use* the expression to *mention* or *refer to* a particular person in the course of using the sentence to talk about him. But obviously in this case, and a great many others, the *expression* (Bl) cannot be said to mention, or refer to, anything, any more than the *sentence* can be said to be true or false. The same expression can have different mentioning-uses, as the same sentence can be used to make statements with different truth-values. "Mentioning", or "referring", is not something an expression does; it is something that some one can use an expression to do. Mentioning, or referring to, something is a characteristic of *a use* of an expression, just as "being about" something, and truth-or-falsity, are characteristics of *a use* of a sentence.

A very different example may help to make these distinctions clearer. Consider another case of an expression winch has a uniquely referring use, *viz·* the expression "I"; and consider the sentence, "I am hot". Countless people may use this same sentence; but it is logically impossible for two different people to make *the same use* of this sentence: or, if this is preferred, to use it to express the same proposition. The expression "I" may correctly be used by (and only by) any one of innumerable people to refer to himself. To say this is to say something about the expression "I": it is, in a sense, to give its meaning. This is the sort of thing that can be said about *expressions*. But it makes no sense to say of the *expression* "I" that it refers to a particular person. This is the sort of thing that can be said only of a particular use of the expression.

Let me use "type" as an abbreviation for "sentence or expression". Then I am not saying that there are sentences and expression (types), *and* uses of them, *and* utterances of them, as there are ships *and* shoes *and* sealing-wax. I am saying that we cannot say *the same things* about types, uses of types, and utterances of types. And the fact is that we do talk about types; and that confusion is apt to result from the failure to notice the differences between what we can say about these and what we can say only about the *uses* of types. We are apt to fancy we are talking about sentences and expressions when we are talking about the uses of sentences and expressions.

This is what Russell does. Generally, as against Russell, I shall say this. Meaning (in at least one important sense) is a function of the sentence or expression; mentioning and referring and truth or falsity, are functions of the use of the sentence or expression. To give the meaning of an expression (in the sense in which I am using the word) is to give *general directions* for its use to refer to or mention particular objects or persons; to give the meaning of a sentence is to give *general directions* for its use in making true or false assertions. It is not to talk about any particular occasion of the use of the sentence or expression. The meaning of an expression cannot be identified with the object it is used, on a particular occasion, to refer to. The meaning of a sentence cannot be identified with the assertion it is used, on a particular occasion, to make. For to talk about the meaning of an expression or sentence is not to talk about its use on a particular occasion, but about the rules, habits, conventions governing its correct use, on all occasions, to refer or to assert. So the question of whether a sentence or expression *is significant or not* has nothing whatever to do with the question of whether the sentence, *uttered on a particular occasion,* is, on that occasion, being used to make a true-or-false assertion or not, or of whether the expression is, on that occasion, being used to refer to, or mention, anything at all.

The source of Russell's mistake was that he thought that referring or mentioning, if it occurred at all, must be meaning. He did not distinguish Bl from B2; he confused expressions with their use in a particular context; and so confused meaning with mentioning, with referring. If I talk about my handkerchief, I can, perhaps, produce the object I am referring to out of my pocket. I can't produce the meaning of the expression, "my handkerchief", out of my pocket. Because Russell confused meaning with mentioning, he thought that if there were any expressions having a uniquely referring use, which were what they seemed (*i.e.* logical subjects) and not something else in disguise, their meaning must *be* the particular object which they were used to refer to. Hence the troublesome mythology of the logically proper name. But if some one asks me the meaning of the expression "this" — once Russell's favourite candidate for this status — I do not hand him the object I have just used the expression to refer to, adding at the same time that the meaning of the word changes every time it is used. Nor do I hand him all the objects it ever has been, or might be, used to refer to. I explain and illustrate the conventions governing the use of the expression. This *is* giving the meaning of the expression. It is quite different from giving (in any sense of giving) the object to which it refers; for the expression itself does not refer to anything; though it can be used, on different occasions, to refer to innumerable things. Now as a matter of fact there is, in English, a sense of the word "mean" in which this word does approximate to "indicate, mention or refer to"; *e.g.* when somebody (unpleasantly) says, "I mean yon"; or when I point and say, "That's the one I mean". But *the one I meant* is quite different from *the meaning of the expression* I used to talk of it. In this special sense of "mean", it is people who mean, not expressions. People use expressions to refer to particular things. But the meaning of an expression is not the set of things or the single thing it may correctly be used to refer to: the meaning is the set of rules, habits, conventions for its use in referring.

It is the same with sentences: even more obviously so. Every one knows that the sentence, "The table is covered with books", is significant, and every one knows what it means. But if I ask, "What object is that sentence about?" I am asking an absurd question — a question which cannot be asked about the sentence, but only about some use of the sentence: and in this case the sentence hasn't been used, it has only been taken as an example. In knowing what it means, you are knowing how it could correctly be used to talk about things: so knowing the meaning hasn't anything to do with knowing about any particular use of the sentence to talk about anything. Similarly, if I ask: "Is the sentence true or false?" I am asking an absurd question, which becomes no less absurd if I add, "It must be one or the other since it's significant". The question is absurd, because the *sentence* is neither true nor false any more than it's *about* some object. Of course the fact that it's significant is the same as the fact that it *can* correctly be used to talk about something and that, in so using it, some one will be making a true or false assertion. And I will add that it will be used to make a true or false assertion *only* if the person using it *is* talking about something. If, when he utters it, he is not talking about anything, then his use is not a genuine one, but a spurious or pseudo-use: he is not making either a true or a false assertion, though he may think he is. And this points the way to the correct answer to the puzzle to which the Theory of Descriptions gives a fatally incorrect answer. The important point is that the question of whether the sentence is significant or not is quite independent of the question that can be raised about a particular use of it, *viz.* the question whether it is a genuine or a spurious use, whether it is being used to talk about something, or in make-believe, or as an example in philosophy. The question whether the sentence is significant or not is the question whether there exist such language habits, conventions or rules that the sentence logically could be used to talk about something; and is hence quite independent of the question whether it is being so used on a particular occasion.

III

Consider again the sentence, "The king of France is wise", and the true and false things Russell says about it.

There are at least two true things which Russell would say about the sentence:

(1) The first is that it is significant; that if anyone were now to utter it, he would be uttering a significant sentence.

(2) The second is that anyone now uttering the sentence would be making a true assertion only if there in fact at present existed one and only one king of France, and if he were wise.

What are the false things which Russell would say about the sentence? They are:

(1) That anyone now uttering it would be making a true assertion or a false assertion;

(2) That part of what he would be asserting would be that there at present existed one and only one king of France.

I have already given some reasons for thinking that these two statements are incorrect. Now suppose some one were in fact to say to you with a perfectly serious air: "The king of France is wise". Would you say, "That's untrue"? I think it's quite certain that you wouldn't· But suppose he went on to *ask* you whether you thought that what he had just said was true, or was false; whether you agreed or disagreed with what he had just said. I think you would be inclined, with some hesitation, to say that you didn't do either; that the question of whether his statement was true or false simply *didn't arise,* because there was no such person as the king of France.[2] You might, if he were obviously serious (had a dazed astray-in-the-centuries look), say something like: "I'm afraid you must be under a misapprehension. France is not a monarchy. There is no king of France." And this brings out the point that if a man seriously uttered the sentence, his uttering it would in some sense be *evidence* that he *believed* that there was a king of France. It would not be evidence for his believing this simply in the way in which a man's reaching for his raincoat is evidence for his believing that it is raining. But nor would it be evidence for his believing this in the way in which a man's saying, "It's raining" is evidence for his believing that it is raining. We might put it as follows. To say, "The king of France is wise" is, in some sense of "imply", to *imply* that there is a king of France. But this is a very special and odd sense of "imply". "Implies" in this sense is certainly not equivalent to "entails" (or "logically implies"). And this comes out from the fact that when, in response to his statement, we say (as we should) "There is no king of France", we should certainly *not* say we were *contradicting* the statement that the king of France is wise. We are certainly not saying that it's false. We are, rather, giving a reason for saying that the question of whether it's true or false simply doesn't arise.

And this is where the distinction I drew earlier can help us. The sentence, "The king of France is wise", is certainly significant; but this does not mean that any particular use of it is true or false. We use it truly or falsely when we use it to talk about some one; when, in using the expression, "The king of France", we are in fact mentioning some one. The fact that the sentence and the expression, respectively, are significant just is the fact that the sentence *could* be used, in certain circumstances, to say something true or false, that the expression *could* be used, in certain circumstances to mention a particular person; and to know their meaning is to know what sort of circumstances these are. So when we utter the sentence without in fact mentioning anybody by the use of the pkrase, "The king of France", the sentence doesn't cease to be significant: we simply *fail* to say anytliing true or false because we simply fail to mention anybody by this particular use of that perfectly significant phrase. It is, if you like, a spurious use of the sentence, and a spurious use of the expression; though we may (or may not) mistakenly think it a genuine use.

And such spurious uses are very familiar. Sophisticated romancing, sophisticated fiction,[3] depend upon them. If I began, "The king of France is wise", and went on, "and he lives in a golden castle and has a hundred wives", and so on, a hearer would understand me perfectly well, without supposing *either* that I was talking about a particular person, *or* that I was making a false statement to the effect that there existed such a person as my words described. (It is worth adding that where the use of sentences and expressions is overtly fictional, the sense of the word "about" may change. As Moore said, it is perfectly natural and correct to say that some of the statements in *Pickwick Papers* are *about* Mr. Pickwick. But where the use of sentences and expressions is not overtly fictional, this use of "about" seems less correct; *i.e.* it would not *in general* be correct to say that a statement was about Mr. X or the so-and-so, unless there were such a person or thing. So it is where the romancing is in danger of being taken seriously that we might answer the question, "Who is he talking about?"

with "He's not talking about anybody"; but, in saying this, we are not saying that what he is saying is either false or nonsense.)

Overtly fictional uses apart, however, I said just now that to use such an expression as "The king of France" at the beginning of a sentence was, in some sense of "imply", to imply that there was a king of France. When a man uses such an expression, he does not *assert*, nor does what he says *entail*, a uniquely existential proposition. But one of the conventional functions of the definite article is to act as a *signal* that a unique reference is being made — a signal, not a disguised assertion. When we begin a sentence with "the such-and-such" the use of "the" shows, but does not state, that we are, or intend to be, referring to one particular individual of the species "such-and-such". *Which* particular individual is a matter to be determined from context, time, place and any other features of the situation of utterance. Now, whenever a man uses any expression, the presumption is that he thinks he is using it correctly: so when he uses the expression, "the such-and-such", in a uniquely referring way, the presumption is that he thinks both that there is *some* individual of that species, and that the context of use will sufficiently determine which one he has in mind. To use the word "the" in this way is then to imply (in the relevant sense of "imply") that the existential conditions described by Russell are fulfilled. But to use "the" in this way is not to *state* that those conditions are fulfilled. If I begin a sentence with an expression of the form, "the so-and-so", and then am prevented from saying more, I have made no statement of any kind; but I may have succeeded in mentioning some one or something.

The uniquely existential assertion supposed by Russell to be part of any assertion in which a uniquely referring use is made of an expression of the form "the so-and-so" is, he observes, a compound of two assertions. To say that there is a ϕ is to say something compatible with there being several ϕS; to say there is not more than one ϕ is to say something compatible with there being none. To say there is one ϕ and one only is to compound these two assertions. I have so far been concerned mostly with the alleged assertion of existence and less with the alleged assertion of uniqueness. An example which throws the emphasis on to the latter will serve to bring out more clearly the sense of "implied" in which a uniquely existential assertion is implied, but not entailed, by the use of expressions in the uniquely referring way. Consider the sentence, "The table is covered with books". It is quite certain that in any normal use of this sentence, the expression "the table" would be used to make a unique reference, *i.e.* to refer to some one table. It is a quite strict use of the definite article, in the sense in which Russell talks on p. 30 of *Princi/pia Mathematical* of using the article "*strictly*, so as to imply uniqueness"· On the same page Russell says that a phrase of the form "the so-and-so", used strictly, "will only have an application in the event of there being one so-and-so and no more". Now it is obviously quite false that the phrase "the table" in the sentence "the table is covered with books", used normally, will "only have an application in the event of there being one table and no more". It is indeed tautologically true that, in such a use, the phrase will have an application only in the event of there being one table and no more *which is being referred to,* and that it will be understood to have an application only in the event of there being one table and no more which it is understood as being used to refer to. To use the sentence is not to assert, but it is (in the special sense discussed) to imply, that there is only one thing which is *both* of the kind specified (*i.e.* a table) *and is being referred to* by the speaker. It is obviously not to assert this. To refer is not to say you are referring. To say there is *some table or other* to which you are referring is not the same as referring to a particular table. We should have no use for such phrases as "the individual I referred to" unless there were something which counted as referring. (It would make no sense to say you had pointed if there were nothing which counted as pointing.) So once more I draw the conclusion that referring to or mentioning a particular thing cannot be dissolved into any kind of assertion. To refer is not to assert, though you refer in order to go on to assert.

Let me now take an example of the uniquely referring use of an expression not of the form, "the so-and-so". Suppose I advance my hands, cautiously cupped, towards someone, saying, as I do so, "This is a fine red one". He, looking into my hands and seeing nothing there, may say: "What is? What are you talking about?" Or perhaps, "But there's nothing in your hands"· Of course it would be absurd to say that in saying "But you've got nothing in your hands", he was *denying* or *contradicting* what I said. So "this" is not a disguised description in Russell's sense. Nor is it a logically proper name. For one must know what the sentence means in order to react in that way to the utterance of it. It is precisely because the significance of the word "this" is independent of any particular reference it may be used to make, though not independent of the way it may be used to refer, that I can, as in this example, use it to *pretend* to be referring to something.

The general moral of all this is that communication is much less a matter of explicit or disguised assertion than logicians used to suppose. The particular application of this general moral in which I am interested is its application to the case of making a unique reference. It is a part of the significance of expressions of the kind I am discussing that they can be used, in an immense variety of contexts, to make unique references. It is no part of their significance to assert that they are being so used or that the conditions of their being so used are fulfilled. So the wholly important distinction we are required to draw is between:

(1) using an expression to make a unique reference; and

(2) asserting that there is one and only one individual which has certain characteristics (*e.g.* is of a certain kind, or stands in a certain relation to the speaker, or both).

This is, in other words, the distinction between

(1) sentences containing an expression used to indicate or mention or refer to a particular person or thing; and

(2) uniquely existential sentences.

What Russell does is progressively to assimilate more and more sentences of class (1) to sentences of class (2), and consequently to involve himself in insuperable difficulties about logical subjects, and about values for individual variables generally: difficulties which have led him finally to the logically disastrous theory of names developed in the *Enquiry* and in *Human Knowledge*. That view of the meaning of logical-subject-expressions which provides the whole incentive to the Theory of Descriptions at the same time precludes the possibility of Russell's ever finding any satisfactory substitutes for those expressions which, beginning with substantival phrases, he progressively degrades from the status of logical subjects.[4] It is not simply, as is sometimes said, the fascination of the relation between a name and its bearer, that is the root of the trouble. Not even names come up to the impossible standard set. It is rather the combination of two more radical misconceptions: first, the failure to grasp the importance of the distinction (section II above) between what may be said of an expression and what may be said of a particular use of it; second, a failure to recognise the uniquely referring use of expressions for the harmless, necessary thing it is, distinct from, but complementary to, the predicative or ascriptive use of expressions. The expressions which can in fact occur as singular logical subjects are expressions of the class I listed at the outset (demonstratives, substantival phrases, proper names, pronouns): to say this is to say that these expressions, together with context (in the widest sense) are what one uses to make unique references. The point of the conventions governing the uses of such expressions is, along with the situation of utterance, to secure uniqueness of reference. But to do this, enough is enough. We do not, and we cannot, while referring, attain the point of complete explicitness at which the referring function is no longer performed. The actual unique reference made, if any, is a matter of the particular use in the particular context; the significance of the expression used is the set of rules or conventions which permit such references to be made. Hence we can, using significant expressions, pretend to refer, in make-believe or in fiction, or mistakenly think we are referring when we are not referring to anything.

This shows the need for distinguishing two kinds (among many others) of linguistic conventions or rules: rules for referring, and rules for attributing and ascribing; and for an investigation of the former. If we recognise this distinction of use for what it is, we are on the way to solving a number of ancient logical and metaphysical puzzles.

My last two sections are concerned, but only in the barest outline, with these questions.

IV

One of the main purposes for which we use language is the purpose of stating facts about things and persons and events. If we want to fulfil this purpose, we must have some way of forestalling the question, "What (who, which one) are you talking about?" as well as the question, "What are you saying about it (him, her)?" The task of forestalling the first question is the referring (or identifying) task. The task of forestalling the second is the attributive (or descriptive or classificatory or ascriptive) task. In the conventional English sentence which is used to state, or to claim to state, a fact about an individual thing or person or event, the performance of these two tasks can be roughly and approximately assigned to separable expressions.[5] And in such a sentence, this assigning of expressions to their separate roles corresponds to the conventional grammatical classification of subject and predicate. There is nothing sacrosanct about the employment of separable expressions for these two tasks. Other methods could be, and are, employed. There is, for instance, the method of uttering a single word or attributive phrase in the conspicuous presence of the object referred to; or that analogous method exemplified by, *e.g.* the painting of the words "unsafe for lorries" on a bridge, or the tying of a label reading "first prize" on a vegetable marrow. Or one can imagine an elaborate game in which one never used an expression in the uniquely referring way at all, but uttered only uniquely existential sentences, trying to enable the hearer to identify what was being talked of by means of an accumulation of relative clauses. (This description of the purposes of the game shows in what sense it would be a game: this is not the normal use we make of existential sentences.) Two points require emphasis. The first is that the necessity of performing these two tasks in order to state particular facts requires no transcendental explanation: to call attention to it is partly to elucidate the meaning of the phrase, "stating a fact". The second is that even this elucidation is made in terms derivative from the grammar of the conventional singular sentence; that even the overtly functional, linguistic distinction between the identifying and attributive roles that words may play in language is prompted by the fact that ordinary speech offers us separable expressions to which the different functions may be plausibly and approximately assigned. And this functional distinction has cast long philosoplncal shadows. The distinctions between particular and universal, between substance and quality, are such pseudomaterial shadows, cast by the grammar of the conventional sentence, in which separable expressions play distinguishable roles.

To use a separate expression to perform the first of these tasks is to use an expression in the uniquely referring way. I want now to say something in general about the conventions of use for expressions used in this way, and to contrast them with conventions of ascriptive use. I then proceed to the brief illustration of these general remarks and to some further applications of them.

What in general is required for making a unique reference is, obviously, some device, or devices, for showing both *that* a unique reference is intended and *what* unique reference it is; some device requiring and enabling the hearer or reader to identify what is being talked about. In securing this result, the context of utterance is of an importance which it is almost impossible to exaggerate; and by "context" I mean, at least, the time, the place, the situation, the identity of the speaker, the subjects which form the immediate focus of interest, and the personal histories of both the speaker and those he is addressing. Besides context, there is, of course, convention; — linguistic convention. But, except in the case of genuine proper names, of which I shall have more to say later, the fulfilment of more or less precisely stateable contextual conditions is *conventionally* (or, in a wide sense of the word, *logically*) required for the correct referring use of expressions in a sense in which this is not true of correct ascriptive uses. The requirement for the correct application of an expression in its ascriptive use to a certain thing is simply that the thing should be of a certain kind, have certain characteristics. The requirement for the correct application of an expression in its referring use to a certain thing is something over and above any requirement derived from such ascriptive meaning as the expression may have; it is, namely, the requirement that the thing should be in a certain relation to the speaker and to the context of utterance. Let me call this the contextual requirement. Thus, for example, in the limiting case of the word "I" the contextual requirement is that the thing should be identical with the speaker; but in the case of most expressions which have a referring use this requirement cannot be so precisely specified. A further, and perfectly general, difference between conventions for referring and conventions for describing is one we have already encountered, *viz.* that the fulfilment of the conditions for a correct ascriptive use of an expression is a part of what is stated by such a use; but the fulfilment of the conditions for a correct referring use of an expression is never part of what is stated, though it is (in the relevant sense of "implied") implied by such a use.

Conventions for referring have been neglected or misinterpreted by logicians. The reasons for this neglect are not hard to see, though they are hard to state briefly. Two of them are, roughly: (1) the preoccupation of most logicians with definitions; (2) the preoccupation of some logicians with formal systems. (1) A definition, in the most familiar sense, is a specification of the conditions of the correct ascriptive or classificatory use of an expression. Definitions take no account of contextual requirements. So that in so far as the search for the meaning or the search for the analysis of an expression is conceived as the search for a definition, the neglect or misinterpretation of conventions other than ascriptive is inevitable. Perhaps it would be better to say (for I do not wish to legislate about "meaning" or "analysis") that logicians have failed to notice that problems of use are wider than problems of analysis and meaning. (2) The influence of the preoccupation with mathematics and formal logic is most clearly seen (to take no more recent examples) in the cases of Leibniz and Russell. The constructor of calculuses, not concerned or required to make factual statements, approaches applied logic with a prejudice. It is natural that he should assume that the types of convention with whose adequacy in one field he is familiar should be really adequate, if only one could see how, in a quite different field — that of statements of fact. Thus we have Leibniz striving desperately to make the uniqueness of unique references a matter of logic in the narrow sense, and Russell striving desperately to do the same thing, in a different way, both for the implication of uniqueness and for that of existence.

It should be clear that the distinction I am trying to draw is primarily one between different rôles or parts that expressions may play in language, and not primarily one between different groups of expressions; for some expressions may appear in either rôle. Some of the kinds of words I shall speak of have predominantly, if not exclusively, a referring rôle. This is most obviously true of pronouns and ordinary proper names. Some can occur as wholes or parts of expressions which have a predominantly referring use, and as wholes or parts of expressions which have a predominantly ascriptive or classificatory use. The obvious cases are common nouns; or common nouns preceded by adjectives, including participial adjectives; or, less obviously, adjectives or participial adjectives alone. Expressions capable of having a referring use also differ from one another in at least the three following, not mutually independent, ways:

(1) They differ in the extent to which the reference they are used to make is dependent on the context of their utterance. Words like "I" and "it" stand at one end of this scale — the end of maximum dependence — and phrases like "the author of Waverley" and "the eighteenth king of France" at the other.

(2) They differ in the degree of "descriptive meaning" they possess: by "descriptive meaning" I intend "conventional limitation, in application, to things of a certain general kind, or possessing certain general characteristics". At one end of this scale stand the proper names we most commonly use in ordinary discourse; men, dogs and motorbicycles may be called "Horace". The pure name has no descriptive meaning (except such as it may acquire *as a result of* some one of its uses as a name). A word like "he" has minimal descriptive meaning, but has some. Substantival phrases like "the round table" have the maximum descriptive meaning. An interesting intermediate position is

occupied by 'impure' proper names like "The Round Table" — substantival phrases which have grown capital letters.

(3)   Finally, they may be divided into the following two classes: (i) those of which the correct referring use is regulated by some *general* referring-cum-ascriptive conventions. To this class belong both pronouns, which have the least descriptive meaning, and substantival phrases which have the most; (ii) those of which the correct referring use is regulated by no general conventions, either of the contextual or the ascriptive kind, but by conventions which are *ad hoc* for each particular use (though not for each particular utterance). Roughly speaking, the most familiar kind of proper names belong to this class. Ignorance of a man's name is not ignorance of the language. This is why we do not speak of the meaning of proper names. (But it won't do to say they are meaningless.) Again an intermediate position is occupied by such phrases as "The Old Pretender". Only an old pretender may be so referred to; but to know which old pretender is not to know a general, but an *ad hoc,* convention.

In the case of phrases of the form "the so-and-so" used referringly, the use of "the" together with the position of the phrase in the sentence *(i.e.* at the beginning, or following a transitive verb or preposition) acts as a signal *that* a unique reference is being made; and the following noun, or noun and adjective, together with the context of utterance, shows *what* unique reference is being made. In general the functional difference between common nouns and adjectives is that the former are naturally and commonly used referringly, while the latter are not commonly, or so naturally, used in this way, except as qualifying nouns; though they can be and are, so used alone. And of course this functional difference is not independent of the descriptive force peculiar to each word. In general we should expect the descriptive force of nouns to be such that they are more efficient tools for the job of showing what unique reference is intended when such a reference is signalised; and we should also expect the descriptive force of the words we naturally and commonly use to make unique reference to mirror our interest in the salient, relatively permanent and behavioural characteristics of things. These two expectations are not independent of one another; and, if we look at the differences between the commoner sort of common nouns and the commoner sort of adjectives, we find them both fulfilled. These are differences of the kind that Locke quaintly reports, when he speaks of our ideas of substances being *collections* of simple ideas; when he says that "powers make up a great part of our ideas of substances"; and when he goes on to contrast the identity of real and nominal essence in the case of simple ideas with their lack of identity and the shiftingness of the nominal essence in the case of substances. "Substance" itself is the troublesome tribute Locke pays to his dim awareness of the difference in predominant linguistic function that lingered even when the noun had been expanded into a more or less indefinite string of adjectives. Russell repeats Locke's mistake with a difference when, admitting the inference from syntax to reality to the extent of feeling that he can get rid of this metaphysical unknown only if he can purify language of the referring function altogether, he draws up his programme for "abolishing particulars"; a programme, in fact, for abolishing the distinction of logical use which I am here at pains to emphasise.

The contextual requirement for the referring use of pronouns may be stated with the greatest precision in some cases (*e.g.* "I" and "you") and only with the greatest vagueness in others ("it" and "this"). I propose to say nothing further about pronouns, except to point to an additional symptom of the failure to recognise the uniquely referring use for what it is; the fact, namely, that certain logicians have actually sought to elucidate the nature of a variable by offering such *sentences* as "he is sick", "it is green", as examples of something in ordinary speech like a *sentential function*. Now of course it is true that the word "he" may be used on different occasions to refer to different people or different animals: so may the word "John" and the phrase "the cat". What deters such logicians from treating these two expressions as quasi-variables is, in the first case, the lingering superstition that a name is logically tied to a single individual, and, in the second case, the descriptive meaning of the word "cat". But "he", which has a wide range of applications and minimal descriptive force, only acquires a use as a referring word. It is this fact, together with the failure to accord to expressions used referringly, the place in logic which belongs to them (the place held open for the mythical logically proper name), that accounts for the misleading attempt to elucidate the nature of the variable by reference to such words as "he", "she", "it".

Of ordinary proper names it is sometimes said that they are essentially words each of which is used to refer to just one individual. This is obviously false. Many ordinary personal names — names par excellence — are correctly used to refer to numbers of people. An ordinary personal name, is, roughly, a word, used referringly, of which the use is *not* dictated by any descriptive meaning the word may have, and is *not* prescribed by any such general rule for use as a referring expression (or a part of a referring expression) as we find in the case of such words as "I", "this" and "the", but is governed by *ad hoc* conventions for each particular set of applications of the word to a given person. The important point is that the correctness of such applications does not follow from any *general* rule or convention for the use of the word as such. (The limit of absurdity and obvious circularity is reached in the attempt to treat names as disguised description in Russell's sense; for what is in the special sense implied, but not entailed, by my now referring to some one by name is simply the existence of some one, *now being referred to*, who is *conventionally referred to* by that name.) Even this feature of names, however, is only a symptom of the purpose for which they are employed. At present our choice of names is partly arbitrary, partly dependent on legal and social observances. It would be perfectly possible to have a thorough-going *system* of names, based *e.g.* on dates of birth, or on a minute classification of physiological and anatomical differences. But the success of any such system would depend entirely on the convenience of the resulting name-allotments for the purpose of making unique references; and this would depend on the multiplicity of the classifications used and the degree to which they cut haphazard across normal social groupings. Given a sufficient degree of both, the selectivity supplied by context would do the rest; just as is the case with our present naming habits. Had we such a system, we could use name-words descriptively (as we do at present, to a limited extent and in a different way, with some famous names) as well as referringly. But it is by criteria derived from consideration of the requirements of the referring task that we should assess the adequacy of any system of naming. From the naming point of view, no kind of classification would be better or worse than any other simply because of the kind of classification — natal or anatomical — that it was.

I have already mentioned the class of quasi-names, of substantival phrases which grow capital letters, and of which such phrases as "the Glorious Revolution", "the Great War", "the Annunciation", "the Round Table" are examples. While the descriptive meaning of the words which follow the definite article is still relevant to their referring role, the capital letters are a sign of that extra-logical selectivity in their referring use, which is characteristic of pure names. Such phrases are found in print or in writing when one member of some class of events or things is of quite outstanding interest in a certain society. These phrases are embryonic names. A phrase may, for obvious reasons, pass into, and out of, this class (*e.g.* "the Great War").

V

I want to conclude by considering, all too briefly, three further problems about referring uses.

(*a*) *Indefinite references.* Not all referring uses of singular expressions forestall the question "What (who, which one) are you talking about?" There are some which either invite this question, or disclaim the intention or ability to answer it. Examples are such sentence-beginnings as "A man told me that ...", "Some one told me that. ..." The orthodox (Russellian) doctrine is that such sentences are existential, but not uniquely existential. This seems wrong in several ways. It is ludicrous to suggest that part of what is asserted is that the class of men or persons is not empty. Certainly this is *implied* in the by now familiar sense of implication; but the implication is also as much an implication of the *uniqueness* of the particular object of reference as when I begin a sentence with such a phrase as "the table". The difference between the use of the definite and indefinite articles is, very roughly, as follows. We use "the" either when a previous reference has been made, and when "the" signalises that the same reference is being made; or when, in the absence of a previous indefinite reference, the context (including the hear's assumed knowledge) is expected to enable the hearer to tell *what* reference is being made. We use "a" either when these conditions are not fulfilled, or when, although a definite reference *could* be made, we wish to keep dark the identity of the individual to whom, or to which, we are referring. This is the *arch* use of such a phrase as "a certain person" or "some one"; where it could be expanded, not into "some one, but you wouldn't (or I don't) know who" but into "some one, but I'm not telling you who."

(*b*) *Identification statements.* By this label I intend statements like the following:

(i*a*)   That is the man who swam the channel twice on one day.

(ii*a*) Napoleon was the man who ordered the execution of the Due D'Enghien.

The puzzle about these statements is that their grammatical predicates do not seem to be used in a straightforwardly ascriptive way as are the grammatical predicates of the statements:

(i*b*) That man swam the channel twice in one day.
(ii*b*) Napoleon ordered the execution of the Due D'Enghien.

But if, in order to avoid blurring the difference between (i*a*) and (i*b*) and (ii*a*) and *(ii*b*)*, one says that the phrases which form the grammatical complements of (i*a*) and (ii*a*) are being used referringly, one becomes puzzled about what is being said in these sentences. We seem then to be referring to the same person twice over and either saying nothing about him and thus making no statement, or identifying him with himself and thus producing a trivial identity.

The bogey of triviality can be dismissed. This only arises for those who think of the object referred to by the use of an expression as its meaning, and thus think of the subject and complement of these sentences as meaning the same because they could be used to refer to the same person.

I think the differences between sentences in the *(a)* group and sentences in the *(b)* group can best be understood by considering the differences between the circumstances in winch, you would say (i*a*) and the circumstances in which you would say (i*b*). You would say (i*a*) instead of (i*b*) if you knew or believed that your hearer knew or believed that *some one* had swum the channel twice in one day. You say (i*a*) when you take your hearer to be in the position of one who can ask: "Who swam the channel twice in one day?" (And in asking this, he is not saying that anyone did, though, his asking it implies — in the relevant sense — that some one did.) Such sentences are like answers to such questions. They are better called "identification-statements" than "identities". Sentence (i*a*) does not assert more or less than sentence (i*b*). It is just that you say (i*a*) to a man whom you take to know certain things that you take to be unknown to the man to whom you say (i*b*).

This is, in the barest essentials, the solution to Russell's puzzle about "denoting phrases" joining by "is"; one of the puzzles which he claims for the Theory of Descriptions the merit of solving.

(*c*) *The logic of subjects and predicates.* Much of what I have said of the uniquely referring use of expressions can be extended, with suitable modifications, to the non-uniquely referring use of expressions; *i.e.* to some uses of expressions consisting of "the" "all the", "all", "some", "some of the", etc. followed by a noun, qualified or unqualified, in the *plural*; to some uses of "they", "them", "those", "these"; and to conjunctions of names. Expressions of the first kind have a special interest. Roughly speaking, orthodox modern criticism, inspired by mathematical logic, of such traditional doctrines as that of the Square of Opposition and of some of the forms of the syllogism traditionally recognised as valid, rests on the familiar failure to recognise the special sense in which existential assertions may be implied by the referring use of expressions. The universal propositions of the fourfold schedule, it is said, must *either* be given a negatively existential interpretation (*e.g.,* for A, "there are no Xs which are not Ys") *or* they must be interpreted as conjunctions of negatively and positively existential statements of, *e.g.,* the form (for A) "there are no Xs which are not Ys, and there are Xs". The I and O forms are normally given a positively existential interpretation. It is then seen that, whichever of the above alternatives is selected, some of the traditional laws have to be abandoned. The dilemma, however, is a bogus one. If we interpret the propositions of the schedule as neither positively, nor negatively, nor positively *and* negatively, existential, but as sentences such that *the question of whether they are being used to make true or false assertions does not arise except when the existential condition is fulfilled for the subject term,* then all the traditional laws hold good together. And this interpretation is far closer to the most common uses of expressions beginning with "all" and "some" that is any Russellian alternative. For these expressions are most commonly used in the referring way. A literal-minded and childless man asked whether all his children are asleep will certainly not answer "Yes" on the ground that he has none; but nor will he answer "No" on this ground. Since he has no children, the question does not arise. To say this is not to say that I may not use the sentence, "All my children are asleep", with the intention of letting some one know that I have children, or of deceiving him into thinking that I have. Nor is it any weakening of my thesis to concede that singular phrases of the form "the so-and-so" may sometimes be used with a similar purpose. Neither Aristotelian nor Russellian rules give the exact logic of any expression of ordinary language; for ordinary language has no exact logic.

1   This usage of 'use' is, of course, different from (*a*) the current usage in which 'use' (of a particular word, phrase, sentence) = (roughly) 'rules for using' = (roughly) 'meaning'; and from (*b*) my own usage in the phrase "uniquely referring use of expressions" in which 'use' = (roughly) 'way of using'.

2   Since this article was written, there has appeared a clear statement of this point by Mr Geach in *Analysis* Vol. 10, No. 4, March, 1950.

3   The unsophisticated kind begins: "Once upon time there was ...".

4   And this in spite of the danger-signal of that phrase, "*misleading* grammatical form".

5   I neglect relational sentences; for these require, not a modification in the principle of what I say, but a complication of the detail.

Reference and Definite Descriptions[1]

Keith S. Donnellan

外教社学术阅读文库——语义学经典论文选读

I

Definite descriptions, I shall argue, have two possible functions. They are used to refer to what a speaker wishes to talk about, but they are also used quite differently. Moreover, a definite description occurring in one and the same sentence may, on different occasions of its use, function in either way. The failure to deal with this duality of function obscures the genuine referring use of definite descriptions. The best-known theories of definite descriptions, those of Russell and Strawson, I shall suggest, are both guilty of this. Before discussing this distinction in use, I will mention some features of these theories to which it is especially relevant.

On Russell's view a definite description may denote an entity: "if 'C' is a denoting phrase [as definite descriptions are by definition], it may happen that there is one entity x (there cannot be more than one) for which the proposition 'x is identical with C' is true. ... We may then say that the entity x is the denotation of the phrase 'C.'"[2] In using a definite description, then, a speaker may use an expression which denotes some entity, but this is the only relationship between that entity and the use of the definite description recognized by Russell. I shall argue, however, that there are two uses of definite descriptions. The definition of denotation given by Russell is applicable to both, but in one of these the definite description serves to do something more. I shall say that in this use the speaker uses the definite description to *refer* to something, and call this use the "referential use" of a definite description. Thus, if I am right, referring is not the same as denoting and the referential use of definite descriptions is not recognized on Russell's view.

Furthermore, on Russell's view the type of expression that comes closest to performing the function of the referential use of definite descriptions turns out, as one might suspect, to be a proper name (in "the narrow logical sense"). Many of the things said about proper names by Russell can, I think, be said about the referential use of definite descriptions without straining senses unduly. Thus the gulf Russell thought he saw between names and definite descriptions is narrower than he thought.

Strawson, on the other hand, certainly does recognize a referential use of definite definitions. But what I think he did not see is that a definite description may have a quite different role — may be used nonreferentially, even as it occurs in one and the same sentence. Strawson, it is true, points out nonreferential uses of definite descriptions,[3] but which use a definite description has seems to be for him a function of the kind of sentence in which it occurs; whereas, if I am right, there can be two possible uses of a definite description in the same sentence. Thus, in "On Referring," he says, speaking of expressions used to refer, "Any expression of any of these classes [one being that of definite descriptions] can occur as the subject of what would traditionally be regarded as a singular subject-predicate sentence; and would, so occurring, exemplify the use I wish to discuss."[4] So the definite description in, say, the sentence "The Republican candidate for president in 1968 will be a conservative" presumably exemplifies the referential use. But if I am right, we could not say this of the sentence in isolation from some particular occasion on which it is used to state something; and then it might or might not turn out that the definite description has a referential use.

Strawson and Russell seem to me to make a common assumption here about the question of how definite descriptions function: that we can ask how a definite description functions in some sentence independently of a particular occasion upon which it is used. This assumption is not really rejected in Strawson's arguments against Russell. Although he can sum up his position by saying, "'Mentioning' or 'referring' is not something an expression does; it is something that someone can use an expression to do,"[5] he means by this to deny the radical view that a "genuine" referring expression *has* a referent, functions to refer, independent of the context of some use of the expression. The denial of this view, however, does not entail that definite descriptions cannot be identified as referring expressions in a sentence unless the sentence is being used. Just as we can speak of a function of a tool that is not at the moment performing its function, Strawson's view, I believe, allows us to speak of the referential function of a definite description in a sentence even when it is not being used. This, I hope to show, is a mistake.

A second assumption shared by Russell's and Strawson's account of definite descriptions is this. In many cases a person who uses a definite description can be said (in some sense) to presuppose or imply that something fits the description.[6] If I state that the king is on his throne, I presuppose or imply that there is a king. (At any rate, this would be a natural thing to say for anyone who doubted that there is a king.) Both Russell and Strawson assume that where the presupposition or implication is false, the truth value of what the speaker says is affected. For Russell the statement made is false; for Strawson it has no truth value. Now if there are two uses of definite descriptions, it may be that the truth value is affected differently in each case by the falsity of the presupposition or implication. This is what I shall in fact argue. It will turn out, I believe, that one or the other of the two views, Russell's or Strawson's, may be correct about the nonreferential use of definite descriptions, but neither fits the referential use. This is not so surprising about Russell's view, since he did not recognize this use in any case, but it is surprising about Strawson's since the referential use is what he tries to explain and defend. Furthermore, on Strawson's account, the result of there being nothing which fits the description is a failure of reference.[7] This too, I believe, turns out not to be true about the referential use of definite descriptions.

II

There are some uses of definite descriptions which carry neither any hint of a referential use nor any presupposition or implication that something fits the description. In general, it seems, these are recognizable from the sentence frame in which the description occurs. These uses will not interest us, but it is necessary to point them out if only to set them aside.

An obvious example would be the sentence "The present king of France does not exist," used, say, to correct someone's mistaken impression that de Gaulle is the king of France.

A more interesting example is this. Suppose someone were to ask, "Is de

Gaulle the king of France?" This is the natural form of words for a person to use who is in doubt as to whether de Gaulle is king or president of France. Given this background to the question, there seems to be no presupposition or implication that someone is the king of France. Nor is the person attempting to refer to someone by using the definite description. On the other hand, reverse the name and description in the question and the speaker probably would be thought to presuppose or imply this. "Is the king of France de Gaulle?" is the natural question for one to ask who wonders whether it is de Gaulle rather than someone else who occupies the throne of France.[8]

Many times, however, the use of a definite description does carry a presupposition or implication that something fits the description. If definite descriptions do have a referring role, it will be here. But it is a mistake, I think, to try, as I believe both Russell and Strawson do, to settle this matter without further ado. What is needed, I believe, is the distinction I will now discuss.

III

I will call the two uses of definite descriptions I have in mind the attributive use and the referential use. A speaker who uses a definite description attributively in an assertion states something about whoever or whatever is the so-and-so. A speaker who uses a definite description referentially in an assertion, on the other hand, uses the description to enable his audience to pick out whom or what he is talking about and states something about that person or thing. In the first case the definite description might be said to occur essentially, for the speaker wishes to assert something about whatever or whoever fits that description; but in the referential use the definite description is merely one tool for doing a certain job — calling attention to a person or thing — and in general any other device for doing the same job, another description or a name, would do as well. In the attributive use, the attribute of being the so-and-so is all important, while it is not in the referential use.

To illustrate this distinction, in the case of a single sentence, consider the sentence, "Smith's murderer is insane." Suppose first that we come upon poor Smith foully murdered. From the brutal manner of the killing and the fact that Smith was the most lovable person in the world, we might exclaim, "Smith's murderer is insane." I will assume, to make it a simpler case, that in a quite ordinary sense we do not know who murdered Smith (though this is not in the end essential to the case). This, I shall say, is an attributive use of the definite description.

The contrast with such a use of the sentence is one of those situations in which we expect and intend our audience to realize whom we have in mind when we speak of Smith's murderer and, most importantly, to know that it is this person about whom we are going to say something.

For example, suppose that Jones has been charged with Smith's murder and has been placed on trial. Imagine that there is a discussion of Jones's odd behavior at his trial. We might sum up our impression of his behavior by saying, "Smith's murderer is insane." If someone asks to whom we are referring, by using this description, the answer here is "Jones." This, I shall say, is a referential use of the definite description.

That these two uses of the definite description in the same sentence are really quite different can perhaps best be brought out by considering the consequences of the assumption that Smith had no murderer (for example, he in fact committed suicide). In both situations, in using the definite description "Smith's murderer," the speaker in some sense presupposes or implies that there is a murderer. But when we hypothesize that the presupposition or implication is false, there are different results for the two uses. In both cases we have used the predicate "is insane," but in the first case, if there is no murderer, there is no person of whom it could be correctly said that we attributed insanity to him. Such a person could be identified (correctly) only in case someone fitted the description used. But in the second case, where the definite description is simply a means of identifying the person we want to talk about, it is quite possible for the correct identification to be made even though no one fits the description we used.[9] We were speaking about Jones even though he is not in fact Smith's murderer and, in the circumstances imagined, it was his behavior we were commenting upon. Jones might, for example, accuse us of saying false things of him in calling him insane and it would be no defense, I should think, that our description, "the murderer of Smith," failed to fit him.

It is, moreover, perfectly possible for our audience to know to whom we refer, in the second situation, even though they do not share our presupposition. A person hearing our comment in the context imagined might know we are talking about Jones even though he does not think Jones guilty.

Generalizing from this case, we can say, I think, that there are two uses of sentences of the form, "The ϕ is ψ." In the first, if nothing is the ϕ then nothing has been said to be ψ. In the second, the fact that nothing is the ϕ does not have this consequence.

With suitable changes the same difference in use can be formulated for uses of language other than assertions. Suppose one is at a party and, seeing an interesting-looking person holding a martini glass, one asks, "Who is the man drinking a martini?" If it should turn out that there is only water in the glass, one has nevertheless asked a question about a particular person, a question that it is possible for someone to answer. Contrast this with the use of the same question by the chairman of the local Teetotalers Union. He has just been informed that a man is drinking a martini at their annual party. He responds by asking his informant, "Who is the man drinking a martini?" In asking the question the chairman does not have some particular person in mind about whom he asks the question; if no one is drinking a martini, if the information is wrong, no person can be singled out as the person about whom the question was asked. Unlike the first case, the attribute of being the man drinking a martini is all-important, because if it is the attribute of no one, the chairman's question has no straightforward answer.

This illustrates also another difference between the referential and the attributive use of definite descriptions. In the one case we have asked a question about a particular person or thing even though nothing fits the description we used; in the other this is not so. But also in the one case our question can be answered; in the other it cannot be. In the referential use of a definite description we may succeed in picking out a person or thing to ask a question about even though he or it does not really fit the description; but in the attributive use if nothing fits the description, no straightforward answer to the question can be given.

This further difference is also illustrated by commands or orders containing definite descriptions. Consider the order, "Bring me the book on the table." If "the book on the table" is being used referentially, it is possible to fulfill the order even though there is no book on the table. If, for example, there is a book *beside* the table, though there is none *on* it, one might bring that book back and ask the issuer of the order whether this is "the book you meant." And it may be. But imagine we are told that someone has laid a book on our prize antique table, where nothing should be put. The order, "Bring me the book on the table" cannot now be obeyed unless there is a book that has been placed on the table. There is no possibility of bringing back a book which was never on the table and having it be the one that was meant, because there is no book that in that sense was "meant." In the one case the definite description was a device for getting the other person to pick the right book; if he is able to pick the right book even though it does not satisfy the description, one still succeeds in his purpose. In the other case, there is, antecedently, no "right book" except one which fits the description; the attribute of being the book on the table is essential. Not only is there no book about which an order was issued, if there is no book on the table, but the order itself cannot be obeyed. When a definite description is used attributively in a command or question and nothing fits the description, the command cannot be obeyed and the question cannot be answered. This suggests some analogous consequence for assertions containing definite descriptions used attributively. Perhaps the analogous result is that the assertion is neither true nor false: this is Strawson's view of what happens when the presupposition of the use of a definite description is false. But if so, Strawson's view works not for definite descriptions used referentially, but for the quite different use, which I have called the attributive use.

I have tried to bring out the two uses of definite descriptions by pointing out the different consequences of supposing that nothing fits the description used. There are still other differences. One is this: when a definite description is used referentially, not only is there in some sense a presupposition or implication that someone or something fits the description, as there is also in the attributive use, but there is a quite different presupposition; the speaker presupposes of some *particular* someone or something that he or it fits the description. In asking, for example, "Who is the man drinking a martini?" where we mean to ask a question about that man over there, we are presupposing that that man over there is drinking a martini — not just that *someone* is a man drinking a martini. When we say, in a context where it is clear we are referring to Jones, "Smith's murderer is insane," we are presupposing that Jones is Smith's murderer. No such presupposition is present in the attributive use of definite descriptions. There is, of course, the presupposition that someone *or other* did the murder, but the speaker does not presuppose of someone in particular — Jones or Robinson, say — that he did it. What I mean by this second kind of presupposition that someone or something in particular fits the description — which is present in a referential use but not in an attributive use — can perhaps be seen more clearly by considering a member of the speaker's audience who believes that Smith was not murdered at all. Now in the case of the referential use of the description, "Smith's murderer," he could accuse the speaker of mistakenly presupposing both that someone or other is the murderer and that also Jones is the murderer, for even though he believes Jones not to have done the deed, he knows that the speaker was referring to Jones. But in the case of the attributive use, he can accuse the speaker of having only the first, less specific presupposition; he cannot pick out some person and claim that the speaker is presupposing that that person is Smith's murderer. Now the more particular presuppositions that we find present in referential uses are clearly not ones we can assign to a definite description in some particular sentence in isolation from a context of use. In order to know that a person presupposes that Jones is Smith's murderer in using the sentence "Smith's murderer is insane," we have to know that he is using the description referentially and also to whom he is referring. The sentence by itself does not tell us any of this.

IV

From the way in which I set up each of the previous examples it might be supposed that the important difference between the referential and the attributive use lies in the beliefs of the speaker. Does he believe of some particular person or thing that he or it fits the description used? In the Smith murder example, for instance, there was in the one case no belief as to who did the deed, whereas in the contrasting case it was believed that Jones did it. But this is, in fact, not an essential difference. It is possible for a definite description to be used attributively even though the speaker (and his audience) believes that a certain person or thing fits the description. And it is possible for a definite description to be used referentially where the speaker believes that nothing fits the description. It is true — and this is why, for simplicity, I set up the examples the way I did — that if a speaker does not believe that anything fits the description or does not believe that he is in a position to pick out what does fit the description, it is likely that he is not using it referentially. It is also true that if he and his audience would pick out some particular thing or person as fitting the description, then a use of the definite description is very likely referential. But these are only presumptions and not entailments.

To use the Smith murder case again, suppose that Jones is on trial for the murder and I and everyone else believe him guilty. Suppose that I comment that the murderer of Smith is insane, but instead of backing this up, as in the example previously used, by citing Jones's behavior in the dock, I go on to outline reasons for thinking that *anyone* who murdered poor Smith in that particularly horrible way must be insane. If now it turns out that Jones was not the murderer after all, but someone else was, I think I can claim to have been right if the true murderer is after all insane. Here, I think, I would be using the definite description attributively, even though I believe that a particular person fits the description.

It is also possible to think of cases in which the speaker does not believe that what he means to refer to by using the definite description fits the description, or to imagine cases in which the definite description is used referentially even though the speaker believes *nothing* fits the description. Admittedly, these cases may be parasitic on a more normal use; nevertheless, they are sufficient to show that such beliefs of the speaker are not decisive as to which use is made of a definite description.

Suppose the throne is occupied by a man I firmly believe to be not the king, but a usurper. Imagine also that his followers as firmly believe that he is the king. Suppose I wish to see this man. I might say to his minions, "Is the king in his countinghouse?" I succeed in referring to the man I wish to refer to without myself believing that he fits the description. It is not even necessary, moreover, to suppose that his followers believe him to be the king. If they are cynical about the whole thing, know he is not the king, I may still succeed in referring to the man I wish to refer to. Similarly, neither I nor the people I speak to may suppose that *anyone* is the king and, finally, each party may know that the other does not so suppose and yet the reference may go through.

V

Both the attributive and the referential use of definite descriptions seem to carry a presupposition or implication that there is something which fits the description. But the reasons for the existence of the presupposition or implication are different in the two cases.

There is a presumption that a person who uses a definite description referentially believes that what he wishes to refer to fits the description. Because the purpose of using the description is to get the audience to pick out or think of the right thing or person, one would normally choose a description that he believes the thing or person fits. Normally a misdescription of that to which one wants to refer would mislead the audience. Hence, there is a presumption that the speaker believes *something* fits the description — namely, that to which he refers.

When a definite description is used attributively, however, there is not the same possibility of misdescription. In the example of "Smith's murderer" used attributively, there was not the possibility of misdescribing Jones or anyone else; we were not referring to Jones nor to anyone else by using the description. The presumption that the speaker believes *someone* is Smith's murderer does not arise here from a more specific presumption that he believes Jones or Robinson or someone else whom he can name or identify is Smith's murderer.

The presupposition or implication is borne by a definite description used attributively because if nothing fits the description the linguistic purpose of the speech act will be thwarted. That is, the speaker will not succeed in saying something true, if he makes an assertion; he will not succeed in asking a question that can be answered, if he has asked a question; he will not succeed in issuing an order that can be obeyed, if he has issued an order. If one states that Smith's murderer is insane, when Smith has no murderer, and uses the definite description nonreferentially, then one fails to say anything *true*. If one issues the order "Bring me Smith's murderer" under similar circumstances, the order cannot be obeyed; nothing would count as obeying it.

When the definite description is used referentially, on the other hand, the presupposition or implication stems simply from the fact that normally a person tries to describe correctly what he wants to refer to because normally this is the best way to get his audience to recognize what he is referring to. As we have seen, it is possible for the linguistic purpose of the speech act to be accomplished in such a case even though nothing fits the description; it is possible to say something true or to ask a question that gets answered or to issue a command that gets obeyed. For when the definite description is used referentially, one's audience may succeed in seeing to what one refers even though neither it nor anything else fits the description.

VI

The result of the last section shows something to be wrong with the theories of both Russell and Strawson; for though they give differing accounts of the implication or presupposition involved, each gives only one. Yet, as I have argued, the presupposition or implication is present for a quite different reason, depending upon whether the definite description is used attributively or referentially, and exactly what presuppositions or implications are involved is also different. Moreover, neither theory seems a correct characterization of the referential use. On Russell's there is a logical entailment: "The ϕ is ψ" entails "There exists one and only one ϕ." Whether or not this is so for the attributive use, it does not seem true of the referential use of the definite description. The "implication" that something is the ϕ, as I have argued, does not amount to an entailment; it is more like a presumption based on what is *usually* true of the use of a definite description to refer. In any case, of course, Russell's theory does not show — what is true of the referential use — that the implication that *something* is the ϕ comes from the more specific implication that *what is being referred* to is the ϕ. Hence, as a theory of definite descriptions, Russell's view seems to apply, if at all, to the attributive use only.

Russell's definition of denoting (a definite description denotes an entity if that entity fits the description uniquely) is clearly applicable to either use of definite descriptions. Thus whether or not a definite description is used referentially or attributively, it may have a denotation. Hence, denoting and referring, as I have explicated the latter notion, are distinct and Russell's view recognizes only the former. It seems to me, moreover, that this is a welcome result, that denoting and referring should not be confused. If one tried to maintain that they are the same notion, one result would be that a speaker might be referring to something without knowing it. If someone said, for example, in 1960 before he had any idea that Mr. Goldwater would be the Republican nominee in 1964, "The Republican candidate for president in 1964 will be a conservative," (perhaps on the basis of an analysis of the views of party leaders) the definite description here would *denote* Mr. Goldwater. But would we wish to say that the speaker had referred to, mentioned, or talked about Mr. Goldwater?

I feel these terms would be out of place. Yet if we identify referring and denoting, it ought to be possible for it to turn out (after the Republican Convention) that the speaker had, unknown to himself, referred in 1960 to Mr. Goldwater. On my view, however, while the definite description used did *denote* Mr. Goldwater (using Russell's definition), the speaker used it *attributively* and did not *refer* to Mr. Goldwater.

Turning to Strawson's theory, it was supposed to demonstrate how definite descriptions are referential. But it goes too far in this direction. For there are nonreferential uses of definite descriptions also, even as they occur in one and the same sentence. I believe that Strawson's theory involves the following propositions:

(1)　If someone asserts that the ϕ is ψ he has not made a true or false statement if there is no ϕ.[10]

(2)　If there is no ϕ then the speaker has failed to refer to anything.[11]

(3)　The reason he has said nothing true or false is that he has failed to refer.

Each of these propositions is either false or, at best, applies to only one of the two uses of definite descriptions.

Proposition (1) is possibly true of the attributive use. In the example in which "Smith's murderer is insane" was said when Smith's body was first discovered, an attributive use of the definite description, there was no person to whom the speaker referred. If Smith had no murderer, nothing true was said. It is quite tempting to conclude, following Strawson, that nothing true *or* false was said. But where the definite description is used referentially, something true may well have been said. It is possible that something true was said of the person or thing referred to.[12]

Proposition (2) is, as we have seen, simply false. Where a definite description is used referentially it is perfectly possible to refer to something though nothing fits the description used.

The situation with proposition (3) is a bit more complicated. It ties together, on Strawson's view, the two strands given in (1) and (2). As an account of why, when the presupposition is false, nothing true or false has been stated, it clearly cannot work for the attributive use of definite descriptions, for the reason it supplies is that reference has failed. It does not then give the reason why, if indeed this is so, a speaker using a definite description attributively fails to say anything true or false if nothing fits the description. It does, however, raise a question about the referential use. Can reference fail when a definite description is used referentially?

I do not fail to refer merely because my audience does not correctly pick out what I am referring to. I can be referring to a particular man when I use the description "the man drinking a martini," even though the people to whom I speak fail to pick out the right person or any person at all. Nor, as we have stressed, do I fail to refer when nothing fits the description. But perhaps I fail to refer in some extreme circumstances, when there is nothing that *I* am willing to pick out as that to which I referred.

Suppose that I think I see at some distance a man walking and ask, "Is the man carrying a walking stick the professor of history?" We should perhaps distinguish four cases at this point, (a) There is a man carrying a walking stick; I have then referred to a person and asked a question about him that can be answered if my audience has the information, (b) The man over there is not carrying a walking stick, but an umbrella; I have still referred to someone and asked a question that can be answered, though if my audience sees that it is an umbrella and not a walking stick, they may also correct my apparently mistaken impression, (c) It is not a man at all, but a rock that looks like one; in this case, I think I still have referred to something, to the thing over there that happens to be a rock but that I took to be a man. But in this case it is not clear that my question can be answered correctly. This, I think, is not because I have failed to refer, but rather because, given the true nature of what I referred to, my question is not appropriate. A simple "No, that is not the professor of history" is at least a bit misleading if said by someone who realizes that I mistook a rock for a person. It may, therefore, be plausible to conclude that in such a case I have not asked a question to which there is a straightforwardly correct answer. But if this is true, it is not because nothing fits the description I used, but rather because what I referred to is a rock and my question has no correct answer when asked of a rock, (d) There is finally the case in which there is nothing at all where I thought there was a man with a walking stick; and perhaps here we have a genuine failure to refer at all, even though the description was used for the purpose of referring. There is no rock, nor anything else, to which I meant to refer; it was, perhaps, a trick of light that made me think there was a man there. I cannot say of anything,

"That is what I was referring to, though I now see that it's not a man carrying a walking stick." This failure of reference, however, requires circumstances much more radical than the mere nonexistence of anything fitting the description used. It requires that there be nothing of which it can be said, "That is what he was referring to." Now perhaps also in such cases, if the speaker has asserted something, he fails to state anything true or false if there is nothing that can be identified as that to which he referred. But if so, the failure of reference and truth value does not come about merely because nothing fits the description he used. So (3) may be true of some cases of the referential use of definite descriptions; it may be true that a failure of reference results in a lack of truth value. But these cases are of a much more extreme sort than Strawson's theory implies.

I conclude, then, that neither Russell's nor Strawson's theory represents a correct account of the use of definite descriptions — Russell's because it ignores altogether the referential use, Strawson's because it fails to make the distinction between the referential and the attributive and mixes together truths about each (together with some things that are false).

VII

It does not seem possible to say categorically of a definite description in a particular sentence that it is a referring expression (of course, one could say this if he meant that it *might* be used to refer). In general, whether or not a definite description is used referentially or attributively is a function of the speaker's intentions in a particular case. "The murderer of Smith" may be used either way in the sentence "The murderer of Smith is insane." It does not appear plausible to account for this, either, as an ambiguity in the sentence. The grammatical structure of the sentence seems to me to be the same whether the description is used referentially or attributively: that is, it is not syntactically ambiguous. Nor does it seem at all attractive to suppose an ambiguity in the meaning of the words; it does not appear to be semantically ambiguous. (Perhaps we could say that the sentence is pragmatically ambiguous: the distinction between roles that the description plays is a function of the speaker's intentions.) These, of course, are intuitions; I do not have an argument for these conclusions. Nevertheless, the burden of proof is surely on the other side.

This, I think, means that the view, for example, that sentences can be divided up into predicates, logical operators, and referring expressions is not generally true. In the case of definite descriptions one cannot always assign the referential function in isolation from a particular occasion on which it is used.

There may be sentences in which a definite description can be used only attributively or only referentially. A sentence in which it seems that the definite description could be used only attributively would be "Point out the man who is drinking my martini," I am not so certain that any can be found in which the definite description can be used only referentially. Even if there are such sentences, it does not spoil the point that there are many sentences, apparently not ambiguous either syntactically or semantically, containing definite descriptions that can be used either way.

If it could be shown that the dual use of definite descriptions can be accounted for by the presence of an ambiguity, there is still a point to be made against the theories of Strawson and Russell. For neither, so far as I can see, has anything to say about the possibility of such an ambiguity and, in fact, neither seems compatible with such a possibility. Russell's does not recognize the possibility of the referring use, and Strawson's, as I have tried to show in the last section, combines elements from each use into one unitary account. Thus the view that there is an ambiguity in such sentences does not seem any more attractive to these positions.

VIII

Using a definite description referentially, a speaker may say something true even though the description correctly applies to nothing. The sense in which he may say something true is the sense in which he may say something true about someone or something. This sense is, I think, an interesting one that needs investigation. Isolating it is one of the by-products of the distinction between the attributive and referential uses of definite descriptions.

For one thing, it raises questions about the notion of a statement. This is brought out by considering a passage in a paper by Leonard Linsky in which he rightly makes the point that one can refer to someone although the definite description used does not correctly describe the person:

... said of a spinster that "Her husband is kind to her" is neither true nor false. But a speaker might very well be referring to someone using these words, for he may think that someone is the husband of the lady (who in fact is a spinster). Still, the statement is neither true nor false, for it presupposes that the lady has a husband, which she has not. This last refutes Strawson's thesis that if the presupposition of existence is not satisfied, the speaker has failed to refer.[13]

There is much that is right in this passage. But because Linsky does not make the distinction between the referential and the attributive uses of definite descriptions, it does not represent a wholly adequate account of the situation. A perhaps minor point about this passage is that Linsky apparently thinks it sufficient to establish that the speaker in his example is referring to someone by using the definite description "her husband," that he *believe* that someone is her husband. This will only approximate the truth provided that the "someone" in the description of the belief means "someone in particular" and is not merely the existential quantifier, "there is someone or other." For in both the attributive and the referential use the belief that someone *or other* is the husband of the lady is very likely to be present. If, for example, the speaker has just met the lady and, noticing her cheerfulness and radiant good health, makes his remark from his conviction that these attributes are always the result of having good husbands, he would be using the definite description attributively. Since she has no husband, there is no one to pick out as the person to whom he was referring. Nevertheless, the speaker believed that *someone or other* was her husband. On the other hand, if the use of "her husband" was simply a way of referring to a man the speaker has just met whom he assumed to be the lady's husband, he would have referred to that man even though neither he nor anyone else fits the description. I think it is likely that in this passage Linsky did mean by "someone," in his description of the belief, "someone in particular." But even then, as we have seen, we have neither a sufficient nor a necessary condition for a referential use of the definite description. A definite description can be used attributively even when the speaker believes that some particular thing or person fits the description, and it can be used referentially in the absence of this belief.

My main point, here, however, has to do with Linsky's view that because the presupposition is not satisfied, the *statement* is neither true nor false. This seems to me possibly correct *if* the definite description is thought of as being used attributively (depending upon whether we go with Strawson or Russell). But when we consider it as used referentially, this categorical assertion is no longer clearly correct. For the man the speaker referred to may indeed be kind to the spinster; the speaker may have said something true about that man. Now the difficulty is in the notion of "the statement." Suppose that we know that the lady is a spinster, but nevertheless know that the man referred to by the speaker is kind to her. It seems to me that we shall, on the one hand, want to hold that the speaker said something true, but be reluctant to express this by "It is true that her husband is kind to her."

This shows, I think, a difficulty in speaking simply about "the statement" when definite descriptions are used referentially. For the speaker stated something, in this example, about a particular person, and his statement, we may suppose, was true. Nevertheless, we should not like to agree with his statement by using the sentence he used; we should not like to identify the true statement via the speaker's words. The reason for this is not so hard to find. If we say, in this example, "It is true that her husband is kind to her," *we* are now using the definite description either attributively or referentially. But we should not be subscribing to what the original speaker truly said if we use the description attributively, for it was only in its function as referring to a particular person that the definite description yields the possibility of saying something true (since the lady has no husband). Our reluctance, however, to endorse the original speaker's statement by using the definite description referentially to refer to the same person stems from quite a different consideration. For if we too were laboring under the mistaken belief that this man was the lady's husband, we could agree with the original speaker using his exact words. (Moreover, it is possible, as we have seen, deliberately to use a definite description to refer to someone we believe not to fit the description.) Hence, our reluctance to use the original speaker's words does not arise from the fact that if we did we should not succeed in stating anything true or false. It rather stems from the fact that when a definite description is used referentially there is a presumption that the speaker believes that what he refers to fits the description. Since we, who know the lady to be a spinster, would not normally want to give the impression that we believe otherwise, we would not like to use the original speaker's way of referring to the man in question.

How then would we express agreement with the original speaker without involving ourselves in unwanted impressions about our beliefs? The answer shows another difference between the referential and attributive uses of definite descriptions and brings out an important point about genuine referring.

When a speaker says, "The ϕ is ψ," where "the ϕ" is used attributively, if there is no ϕ, we cannot correctly report the speaker as having said *of* this or that person or thing that it is ψ. But if the definite description is used referentially we can report the speaker as having attributed ψ to something. And *we* may refer to what the speaker referred to, using whatever description or name suits our purpose. Thus, if a speaker says, "Her husband is kind to her," referring to the man he was just talking to, and if that man is Jones, we may report him as having said *of Jones* that he is kind to her. If Jones is also the president of the college, we may report the speaker as having said *of the president of the college* that he is kind to her. And finally, if we are talking to Jones, we may say, referring to the original speaker, "He said of you that *you* are kind to her." It does not matter here whether or not the woman has a husband or whether, if she does, Jones is her husband. If the original speaker referred to Jones, he said of him that he is kind to her. Thus where the definite description is used referentially, but does not fit what was referred to, we can report what a speaker said and agree with him by using a description or name which does fit. In doing so we need not, it is important to note, choose a description or name which the original speaker would agree fits what he was referring to. That is, we can report the speaker in the above case to have said truly of Jones that he is kind to her even if the original speaker did not know that the man he was referring to is named Jones or even if he thinks he is not named Jones.

Returning to what Linsky said in the passage quoted, he claimed that, were someone to say "Her husband is kind to her," when she has no husband, *the statement* would be neither true nor false. As I have said, this is a likely view to hold if the definite description is being used attributively. But if it is being used referentially it is not clear what is meant by "the statement." If we think about what the speaker said about the person he referred to, then there is no reason to suppose he has not said something true or false about him, even though he is not the lady's husband. And Linsky's claim would be wrong. On the other hand, if we do not identify the statement in this way, what is the statement that the speaker made? To say that the statement he made was that her husband is kind to her lands us in difficulties. For we have to decide whether in using the definite description here in the identification of the statement, we are using it attributively or referentially. If the former, then we misrepresent the linguistic performance of the speaker; if the latter, then we are ourselves referring to someone and reporting the speaker to have said something of that person, in which case we are back to the possibility that he did say something true or false of that person.

I am thus drawn to the conclusion that when a speaker uses a definite description referentially he may have stated something true or false even if nothing fits the description, and that there is not a clear sense in which he has made a statement which is neither true nor false.

IX

I want to end by a brief examination of a picture of what a genuine referring expression is that one might derive from Russell's views. I want to suggest that this picture is not so far wrong as one might suppose and that strange as this may seem, some of the things we have said about the referential use of definite descriptions are not foreign to this picture.

Genuine proper names, in Russell's sense, would refer to something without ascribing any properties to it. They would, one might say, refer to the thing itself, not simply the thing in so far as it falls under a certain description.[14] Now this would seem to Russell something a definite description could not do, for he assumed that if definite descriptions were capable of referring at all, they would refer to something only in so far as that thing satisfied the description. Not only have we seen this assumption to be false, however, but in the last section we saw something more. We saw that when a definite description is used referentially, a speaker can be reported as having said something *of* something. And in reporting what it was of which he said something we are not restricted to the description he used, or synonyms of it; we may ourselves refer to it using any descriptions, names, and so forth, that will do the job. Now this seems to give a sense in which we are concerned with the thing itself and not just the thing under a certain description, when we report the linguistic act of a speaker using a definite description referentially. That is, such a definite description comes closer to performing the function of Russell's proper names than certainly he supposed.

Secondly, Russell thought, I believe, that whenever we use descriptions, as opposed to proper names, we introduce an element of generality which ought to be absent if what we are doing is referring to some particular thing. This is clear from his analysis of sentences containing definite descriptions. One of the conclusions we are supposed to draw from that analysis is that such sentences express what are in reality completely general propositions: there is a ϕ and only one such and any ϕ is ψ. We might put this in a slightly different way. If there is anything which might be identified as reference here, it is reference in a very weak sense — namely, reference to *whatever* is the one and only one ϕ, if there is any such. Now this is something we might well say about the attributive use of definite descriptions, as should be evident from the previous discussion. But this lack of particularity is absent from the referential use of definite descriptions precisely because the description is here merely a device for getting one's audience to pick out or think of the thing to be spoken about, a device which may serve its function even if the description is incorrect. More importantly perhaps, in the referential use as opposed to the attributive, there is a *right* thing to be picked out by the audience and its being the right thing is not simply a function of its fitting the description.

1   I should like to thank my colleagues, John Canfield, Sydney Shoemaker, and Timothy Smiley, who read an earlier draft and gave me helpful suggestions. I also had the benefit of the valuable and detailed comments of the referee for the paper, to whom I wish to express my gratitude.

2   "On Denoting," reprinted in *Logic and Knowledge*, ed. by Robert C. Marsh (London, 1956), p. 51.

3   "On Referring," reprinted in *Philosophy and Ordinary Language*, ed. by Charles C. Caton (Urbana, 1963), pp. 162–163.

4   *Ibid.*, p. 162.

5   *Ibid.*, p. 170.

6   Here and elsewhere I use the disjunction "presuppose or imply" to avoid taking a stand that would side me with Russell or Strawson on the issue of what the relationship involved is. To take a stand here would be beside my main point as well as being misleading, since later on I shall argue that the presupposition or implication arises in a different way depending upon the use to which the definite description is put. This last also accounts for my use of the vagueness indicator, "in some sense."

7   In a footnote added to the original version of "On Referring" (*op. cit.*, p. 181) Strawson seems to imply that where the presupposition is false, we

still succeed in referring in a "secondary" way, which seems to mean "as we could be said to refer to fictional or make-believe things." But his view is still that we cannot refer in such a case in the "primary" way. This is, I believe, wrong. For a discussion of this modification of Strawson's view see Charles C. Caton, "Strawson on Referring," *Mind*, LXVIII (1959), 539–544.

8 This is an adaptation of an example (used for a somewhat different purpose) given by Leonard Linsky in "Reference and Referents," in *Philosophy and Ordinary Language*, p. 80.

9 In "Reference and Referents" (pp. 74–75, 80), Linsky correctly points out that one does not fail to refer simply because the description used does not in fact fit anything (or fits more than one thing). Thus he pinpoints one of the difficulties in Strawson's view. Here, however, I use this fact about referring to make a distinction I believe he does not draw, between two uses of definite descriptions. I later discuss the second passage from Linsky's paper.

10 In "A Reply to Mr. Sellars," *Philosophical Review*, LXIII (1954), 216–231, Strawson admits that we do not always refuse to ascribe truth to what a person says when the definite description he uses fails to fit anything (or fits more than one thing). To cite one of his examples, a person who said, "The United States Chamber of Deputies contains representatives of two major parties," would be allowed to have said something true even though he had used the wrong title. Strawson thinks this does not constitute a genuine problem for his view. He thinks that what we do in such cases, "where the speaker's intended reference is pretty clear, is simply to amend his statement in accordance with his guessed intentions and assess the amended statement for truth or falsity; we are not awarding a truth value at all to the original statement" (p. 230).

The notion of an "amended statement," however, will not do. We may note, first of all, that the sort of case Strawson has in mind could arise only when a definite description is used referentially. For the "amendment" is made by seeing the speaker's intended reference. But this could happen only if the speaker had an intended reference, a particular person or thing in mind, independent of the description he used. The cases Strawson has in mind are presumably not cases of slips of the tongue or the like; presumably they are cases in which a definite description is used because the speaker believes, though he is mistaken, that he is describing correctly what he wants to refer to. We supposedly amend the statement by knowing to what he intends to refer. But what description is to be used in the amended statement? In the example, perhaps, we could use "the United States Congress." But this description might be one the speaker would not even accept as correctly describing what he wants to refer to, because he is misinformed about the correct title. Hence, this is not a case of deciding what the speaker meant to say as opposed to what he in fact said, for the speaker did not mean to say "the United States Congress." If this is so, then there is no bar to the "amended" statement containing any description that does correctly pick out what the speaker intended to refer to. It could be, e.g., "The lower house of the United States Congress." But this means that there is no one unique "amended" statement to be assessed for truth value. And, in fact, it should now be clear that the notion of the amended statement really plays no role anyway. For if we can arrive at the amended statement only by first knowing to what the speaker intended to refer, we can assess the truth of what he said simply by deciding whether what he intended to refer to has the properties he ascribed to it.

11 As noted earlier (n. 7), Strawson may allow that one has possibly referred in a "secondary" way, but, if I am right, the fact that there is no ϕ does not preclude one from having referred in the same way one does if there is a ϕ.

12 For a further discussion of the notion of saying something true *of* someone or something, see sec. VIII.

13 "Reference and Referents," p. 80. It should be clear that I agree with Linsky in holding that a speaker may refer even though the "presupposition of existence" is not satisfied. And I agree in thinking this an objection to Strawson's view. I think, however, that this point, among others, can be used to define two distinct uses of definite descriptions which, in turn, yields a more general criticism of Strawson. So, while I develop here a point of difference, which grows out of the distinction I want to make, I find myself in agreement with much of Linsky's article.

14 Cf. "The Philosophy of Logical Atomism," reprinted in *Logic and Knowledge*, p. 200.

Naming and Necessity: Lecture II

Saul A. Kripke

Last time we ended up talking about a theory of naming which is given by a number of theses here on the board.

(1) To every name or designating expression 'X', there corresponds a cluster of properties, namely the family of those properties φ such that A believes 'φX'.

(2) One of the properties, or some conjointly, are believed by A to pick out some individual uniquely.

(3) If most, or a weighted most, of the φ's are satisfied by one unique object y, then y is the referent of 'X'.

(4) If the vote yields no unique object, 'X' does not refer.

(5) The statement, 'If X exists, then X has most of the φ' s' is known *a priori* by the speaker.

(6) The statement, 'If X exists, then X has most of the φ' s' expresses a necessary truth (in the idiolect of the speaker).

(C) For any successful theory, the account must not be circular. The properties which are used in the vote must not themselves involve the notion of reference in such a way that it is ultimately impossible to eliminate.

(C) is not a thesis but a condition on the satisfaction of the other theses. In other words, Theses (1)–(6) cannot be satisfied in a way which leads to a circle, in a way which does not lead to any independent determination of reference. The example I gave last time of a blatantly circular attempt to satisfy these conditions was a theory of names mentioned by William Kneale. I was a little surprised at the statement of the theory when I was reading what I had copied down, so I looked it up again. I looked it up in the book to see if I'd copied it down accurately. Kneale *did* use the past tense. He said that though it is not trifling to be told that Socrates was the greatest philosopher of ancient Greece, it is trifling to be told that Socrates was called 'Socrates'. Therefore, he concludes, the name 'Socrates' must simply mean 'the individual called "Socrates"'. Russell, as I've said, in some places gives a similar analysis. Anyway, as stated using the past tense, the condition wouldn't be circular, because one certainly could decide to use the term 'Socrates' to refer to whoever was called 'Socrates' by the Greeks. But, of course, in that sense it's not at all trifling to be told that Socrates was called 'Socrates'. If this is any kind of fact, it might be false. Perhaps we know that *we* call him 'Socrates'; that hardly shows that the Greeks did so. In fact, of course, they may have pronounced the name differently. It may be, in the case of this particular name, that transliteration from the Greek is so good that the English version is not pronounced *very* differently from the Greek. But that won't be so in the general case. Certainly it is not trifling to be told that Isaiah was called 'Isaiah'. In fact, it is false to be told that Isaiah was called 'Isaiah'; the prophet wouldn't have recognized this name at all. And of course the Greeks didn't call their country anything like 'Greece'. Suppose we amend the thesis so that it reads: it's trifling to be told that Socrates is called 'Socrates' by us, or at least, by me, the speaker. Then in some sense this is fairly trifling. I don't think it is necessary or analytic. In the same way, it is trifling to be told that horses are called 'horses', without this leading to the conclusion that the word 'horse' simply *means* 'the animal called a "horse"'. As a theory of the reference of the name 'Socrates' it will lead immediately to a vicious circle. If one was determining the referent of a name like 'Glunk' to himself and made the following decision, 'I shall use the term "Glunk" to refer to the man that I call "Glunk"', this would get one nowhere. One had better have some independent determination of the referent of 'Glunk'. This is a good example of a blatantly circular determination. Actually sentences like 'Socrates is called "Socrates"' are very interesting and one can spend, strange as it may seem, hours talking about their analysis. I actually did, once, do that. I won't do that, however, on this occasion. (See how high the seas of language can rise. And at the lowest points too.) Anyway this is a useful example of a violation of the noncircularity condition. The theory will satisfy all of these statements, perhaps, but it satisfies them only because there is some independent way of determining the reference independently of the particular condition: being the man called 'Socrates'.

I have already talked about, in the last lecture, Thesis (6). Theses (5) and (6), by the way, have converses. What I said for Thesis (5) is that the statement that if X exists, X has most of the φ's, is *a priori* true for the speaker. It will also be true under the given theory that certain converses of this statement hold true also *a priori* for the speaker, namely: if any unique thing has most of the properties φ in the properly weighted sense, it is X. Similarly a certain converse to this will be *necessarily* true, namely: if anything has most of the properties φ in the properly weighted sense, it is X. So really one can say that it is both *a priori* and necessary that something is X if and only if it uniquely has most of the properties φ. This really comes from the previous Theses (1)–(4), I suppose. And (5) and (6) really just say that a sufficiently reflective speaker grasps this theory of proper names. Knowing this, he therefore sees that (5) and (6) are true. The objections to Theses (5) and (6) will *not* be that some speakers are unaware of this theory and therefore don't know these things.

What I talked about in the last lecture is Thesis (6). It's been observed by many philosophers that, if the cluster of properties associated with a proper name is taken in a very narrow sense, so that only one property is given any weight at all, let's say one definite description to pick out the referent — for example, Aristotle was the philosopher who taught Alexander the Great — then certain things will seem to turn out to be necessary truths which are not necessary truths — in this case, for example, that Aristotle taught Alexander the Great. But as Searle said, it is not a necessary truth but a contingent one that Aristotle ever went into pedagogy. Therefore, he concludes that one must drop the original paradigm of a single description and turn to that of a cluster of descriptions.

To summarize some things that I argued last time, this is not the correct answer (whatever it may be) to this problem about necessity. For Searle goes on to say,

> Suppose we agree to drop 'Aristotle' and use, say, 'the teacher of Alexander', then it is a necessary truth that the man referred to is Alexander's teacher — but it is a contingent fact that Aristotle ever went into pedagogy, though I am suggesting that it is a necessary fact that Aristotle has the logical sum,

inclusive disjunction, of properties commonly attributed to him. ...[1]

This is what is not so. It just is not, in any intuitive sense of necessity, a necessary truth that Aristotle had the properties commonly attributed to him. There is a certain theory, perhaps popular in some views of the philosophy of history, which might both be deterministic and yet at the same time assign a great role to the individual in history. Perhaps Carlyle would associate with the meaning of the name of a great man his achievements. According to such a view it will be necessary, once a certain individual is born, that he is destined to perform various great tasks and so it will be part of the very nature of Aristotle that he should have produced ideas which had a great influence on the western world. Whatever the merits of such a view may be as a view of history or the nature of great men, it does not seem that it should be trivially true on the basis of a theory of proper names. It would seem that it's a contingent fact that Aristotle ever did *any* of the things commonly attributed to him today, *any* of these great achievements that we so much admire. I must say that there is *something* to this feeling of Searle's. When I hear the name 'Hitler', I do get an illusory 'gut feeling' that it's sort of analytic that that man was evil. But really, probably not. Hitler might have spent all his days in quiet in Linz. In that case we would not say that then this man would not have been Hitler, for we use the name 'Hitler' just as the name of that man, even in describing other possible worlds. (This is the notion which I called a *rigid designator* in the previous talk.) Suppose we do decide to pick out the reference of 'Hitler', as the man who succeeded in having more Jews killed than anyone else managed to do in history. That is the way we pick out the reference of the name; but in another counterfactual situation where some one else would have gained this discredit, we wouldn't say that in that case that other man would have been Hitler. If Hitler had never come to power, Hitler would not have had the property which I am supposing we use to fix the reference of his name. Similarly, even if we define what a meter is by reference to the standard meter stick, it will be a contingent truth and not a necessary one that that particular stick is one meter long. If it had been stretched, it would have been longer than one meter. And that is because we use the term 'one meter' rigidly to designate a certain length. Even though we fix what length we are designating by an accidental property of that length, just as in the case of the name of the man we may pick the man out by an accidental property of the man, still we use the name to designate that man or that length in all possible worlds. The property we use need not be one which is regarded in any way as necessary or essential. In the case of a yard, the original way this length was picked out was, I think, the distance when the arm of King Henry I of England was outstretched from the tip of his finger to his nose. If this was the length of a yard, it nevertheless will not be a necessary truth that the distance between the tip of his finger and his nose should be a yard. Maybe an accident might have happened to foreshorten his arm; that would be possible. And the reason that it's not a necessary truth is not that there might be other criteria in a 'cluster concept' of yardhood. Even a man who strictly uses King Henry's arm as his one standard of length can say, counterfactually, that if certain things had happened to the King, the exact distance between the end of one of his fingers and his nose would not have been exactly a yard. He need not be using a cluster as long as he uses the term 'yard' to pick out a certain fixed reference to be that length in all possible worlds.

These remarks show, I think, the intuitive bizarreness of a good deal of the literature on 'transworld identification' and 'counterpart theory'. For many theorists of these sorts, believing, as they do, that a 'possible world' is given to us only qualitatively, argue that Aristotle is to be 'identified in other possible worlds', or alternatively that his counterparts are to be identified, with those things in other possible worlds who most closely resemble Aristotle in his most important properties. (Lewis, for example, says: 'Your counterparts ... resemble you ... in important respects ... more closely than do the other things in their worlds ... weighted by the importance of the various respects and by the degrees of the similarities.'[2]) Some may equate the important properties with those properties used to identify the object in the actual world.

Surely these notions are incorrect. To me Aristotle's most important properties consist in his philosophical work, and Hitler's in his murderous political role; both, as I have said, might have lacked these properties altogether. Surely there was no logical fate hanging over either Aristotle or Hitler which made it in any sense inevitable that they should have possessed the properties we regard as important to them; they could have had careers completely different from their actual ones. *Important* properties of an object need not be essential, unless 'importance' is used as a synonym for essence; and an object could have had properties very different from its most striking actual properties, or from the properties we use to identify it.

To clear up one thing which some people have asked me: When I say that a designator is rigid, and designates the same thing in all possible worlds, I mean that, as used in *our* language, it stands for that thing, when *we* talk about counterfactual situations. I don't mean, of course, that there mightn't be counterfactual situations in which in the other possible worlds people actually spoke a different language. One doesn't say that 'two plus two equals four' is contingent because people might have spoken a language in which 'two plus two equals four' meant that seven is even. Similarly, when we speak of a counterfactual situation, we speak of it in English, even if it is part of the description of that counterfactual situation that we were all speaking German in that counterfactual situation. We say, 'suppose we had all been speaking German' or 'suppose we had been using English in a nonstandard way'. Then we are describing a possible world or counterfactual situation in which people, including ourselves, did speak in a certain way different from the way we speak. But still, in describing that world, we use *English* with *our* meanings and *our* references. It is in this sense that I speak of a rigid designator as having the same reference in all possible worlds. I also don't mean to imply that the thing designated exists in all possible worlds, just that the name refers rigidly to that thing. If you say 'suppose Hitler had never been born' then 'Hitler' refers here, still rigidly, to something that would not exist in the counterfactual situation described.

Given these remarks, this means we must cross off Thesis (6) as incorrect. The other theses have nothing to do with necessity and can survive. In particular Thesis (5) has nothing to do with necessity and it can survive. If I use the name 'Hesperus' to refer to a certain planetary body when seen in a certain celestial position in the evening, it will not therefore be a necessary truth that Hesperus is ever seen in the evening. That depends on various contingent facts about people being there to see and things like that. So even if I should say to myself that I will use 'Hesperus' to name the heavenly body I see in the evening in yonder position of the sky, it will not be necessary that Hesperus was ever seen in the evening. But it may be *a priori* in that this is how I have determined the referent. If I have determined that Hesperus is the thing that I saw in the evening over there, then I will know, just from making that determination of the referent, that if there is any Hesperus at all it's the thing I saw in the evening. This at least survives as far as the arguments we have given up to now go.

How about a theory where Thesis (6) is eliminated? Theses (2), (3), and (4) turn out to have a large class of counterinstances. Even when Theses (2)–(4) are true, Thesis (5) is usually false; the truth of Theses (3) and (4) is an empirical 'accident', which the speaker hardly knows *a priori*. That is to say, other principles really determine the speaker's reference, and the fact that the referent coincides with that determined by (2)–(4) is an 'accident', which we were in no position to know *a priori*. Only in a rare class of cases, usually initial baptisms, are all of (2)–(5) true.

What picture of naming do these Theses ((1)–(5)) give you? The picture is this. I want to name an object. I think of some way of describing it uniquely and then I go through, so to speak, a sort of mental ceremony: By 'Cicero' I shall mean the man who denounced Catiline; and that's what the reference of 'Cicero' will be. I will use 'Cicero' to designate rigidly the man who (in fact) denounced Catiline, so I can speak of possible worlds in which he did not. But still my intentions are given by first, giving some condition which uniquely determines an object, then using a certain word as a name for the object determined by this condition. Now there may be some cases in which we actually do this. Maybe, if you want to stretch and call it description, when you say: I shall call that heavenly body over there 'Hesperus'.[3] That is really a case where the theses not only are true but really even give a correct picture of how the reference is determined. Another case, if you want to call this a name, might be when the police in London use the name 'Jack' or 'Jack the Ripper' to refer to the man, whoever he is, who committed all these murders, or most of them. Then they are giving the reference of the name by a description.[4] But in many or most cases, I think the theses are false. So let's look at them.[5]

Thesis (1), as I say, is a definition. Thesis (2) says that one of the properties believed by *A* of the object, or some conjointly, are believed to pick out some individual uniquely. A sort of example people have in mind is just what I said: I shall use the term 'Cicero' to denote the man who denounced Catiline (or first denounced him in public, to make it unique). This picks out an object uniquely in this particular reference. Even some writers such as Ziff in *Semantic Analysis,* who don't believe that names have meaning in any sense, think that this is a good picture of the way reference can be determined.

Let's see if Thesis (2) is true. It seems, in some *a priori* way, that it's got to be true, because if you don't think that the properties you have in mind pick out anyone uniquely — let's say they're all satisfied by two people — then how can you say which one of them you're talking about? There seem to be no grounds for saying you're talking about the one rather than about the other. Usually the properties in question are supposed to be some famous deeds of the person in question. For example, Cicero was the man who denounced Catiline. The average person, according to this, when he refers to Cicero, is saying something like 'the man who denounced Catiline' and thus has picked out a certain man uniquely. It is a tribute to the education of philosophers that they have held this thesis for such a long time. In fact, most people, when they think of Cicero, just think of *a famous Roman orator,* without any pretension to think either that there was only one famous Roman orator or that one must know something else about Cicero to have a referent for the name. Consider Richard Feynman, to whom many of us are able to refer. He is a leading contemporary theoretical physicist. Everyone *here* (I'm sure!) can state the contents of one of Feynman's theories so as to differentiate him from Gell-Mann. However, the man in the street, not possessing these abilities, may still use the name 'Feynman'. When asked he will say: well he's a physicist or something. He may not think that this picks out anyone uniquely. I still think he uses the name 'Feynman' as a name for Feynman.

But let's look at some of the cases where we do have a description to pick out someone uniquely. Let's say, for example, that we know that Cicero was the man who first denounced Catiline. Well, that's good. That really picks someone out uniquely. However, there is a problem, because this description contains another name, namely 'Catiline'. We must be sure that we satisfy the conditions in such a way as to avoid violating the noncircularity condition here. In particular, we must not say that Catiline was the man denounced by Cicero. If we do this, we will really not be picking out anything uniquely, we will simply be picking out a pair of objects A and B, such that A denounced B. We do not think that this was the only pair where such denunciations ever occurred; so we had better add some other conditions in order to satisfy the uniqueness condition.

If we say Einstein was the man who discovered the theory of relativity, that certainly picks out someone uniquely. One can be sure, as I said, that everyone *here* can make a compact and independent statement of this theory and so pick out Einstein uniquely; but many people actually don't know enough about this stuff, so when asked what the theory of relativity is, they will say: 'Einstein's theory', and thus be led into the most straightforward sort of vicious circle.

So Thesis (2), in a straightforward way, fails to be satisfied when we say Feynman is a famous physicist without attributing anything else to Feynman. In another way it may not be satisfied in the proper way even when it is satisfied: If we say Einstein was 'the man who discovered relativity theory', that does pick someone out uniquely; but it may not pick him out in such a way as to satisfy the noncircularity condition, because the theory of relativity may in turn be picked out as 'Einstein's theory'. So Thesis (2) seems to be false.

By changing the conditions φ from those usually associated with names by philosophers, one could try to improve the theory. There have been various ways I've heard; maybe I'll discuss these later on. Usually they think of famous achievements of the man named. Certainly in the case of famous achievements, the theory doesn't work. Some student of mine once said, 'Well, Einstein discovered the theory of relativity'; and he determined the reference of 'the theory of relativity' independently by referring to an encyclopedia which would give the details of the theory. (This is what is called a transcendental deduction of the existence of encyclopedias.) But it seems to me that, even if someone has heard of encyclopedias, it really is not essential for his reference that he should know whether this theory is given in detail in any encyclopedia. The reference might work even if there had been no encyclopedias at all.

Let's go on to Thesis (3): If most of the φ's, suitably weighted, are satisfied by a unique object *y*, then *y* is the referent of the name for the speaker. Now, since we have already established that Thesis (2) is wrong, why should any of the rest work? The whole theory depended on always being able to specify unique conditions which are satisfied. But still we can look at the other theses. The picture associated with the theory is that only by giving some unique properties can you know who someone is and thus know what the reference of your name is. Well, I won't go into the question of knowing who someone is. It's really very puzzling. I think you *do* know who Cicero is if you just can answer that he's a famous Roman orator. Strangely enough, if you know that Einstein discovered the theory of relativity and nothing about that theory, you can both know who Einstein is, namely the discoverer of the theory of relativity, and who discovered the theory of relativity, namely Einstein, on the basis of this knowledge. This seems to be a blatant violation of some sort of noncircularity condition; but it is the way we talk. It therefore would seem that a picture which suggests this condition must be the wrong picture.

Suppose most of the φ's are in fact satisfied by a unique object. Is that object necessarily the referent of 'X' for A? Let's suppose someone says that Gödel is the man who proved the incompleteness of arithmetic, and this man is suitably well educated and is even able to give an independent account of the incompleteness theorem. He doesn't just say, 'Well, that's Gödel's theorem', or whatever. He actually states a certain theorem, which he attributes to Gödel as the discoverer. Is it the case, then, that if most of the φ's are satisfied by a unique object y, then y is the referent of the name 'X' for A? Let's take a simple case. In the case of Gödel that's practically the only thing many people have heard about him — that he discovered the incompleteness of arithmetic. Does it follow that whoever discovered the incompleteness of arithmetic is the referent of 'Gödel'?

Imagine the following blatantly fictional situation. (I hope Professor Gödel is not present.) Suppose that Gödel was not in fact the author of this theorem. A man named 'Schmidt', whose body was found in Vienna under mysterious circumstances many years ago, actually did the work in question. His friend Gödel somehow got hold of the manuscript and it was thereafter attributed to Gödel. On the view in question, then, when our ordinary man uses the name 'Gödel', he really means to refer to Schmidt, because Schmidt is the unique person satisfying the description, 'the man who discovered the incompleteness of arithmetic'. Of course you might try changing it to 'the man who *published* the discovery of the incompleteness of arithmetic'. By changing the story a little further one can make even this formulation false. Anyway, most people might not even know whether the thing was published or got around by word of mouth. Let's stick to 'the man who discovered the incompleteness of arithmetic'. So, since the man who discovered the incompleteness of arithmetic is in fact Schmidt, we, when we talk about 'Gödel', are in fact always referring to Schmidt. But it seems to me that we are not. We simply are not. One reply, which I will discuss later, might be: You should say instead, 'the man to whom the incompleteness of arithmetic is commonly attributed', or something like that. Let's see what we can do with that later.

But it may seem to many of you that this is a very odd example, or that such a situation occurs rarely. This also is a tribute to the education of philosophers. Very often we use a name on the basis of considerable misinformation. The case of mathematics used in the fictive example is a good case in point. What do we know about Peano? What many people in this room may 'know' about Peano is that he was the discoverer of certain axioms which characterize the sequence of natural numbers, the so-called 'Peano axioms'. Probably some people can even state them. I have been told that these axioms were not first discovered by Peano but by Dedekind. Peano was of course not a dishonest man. I am told that his footnotes include a credit to Dedekind. Somehow the footnote has been ignored. So on the theory in question the term 'Peano', as we use it, really refers to — now that you've heard it you see that you were really all the time talking about — Dedekind. But you were not. Such illustrations could be multiplied indefinitely.

Even worse misconceptions, of course, occur to the layman. In a previous example I supposed people to identify Einstein by reference to his work on relativity. Actually, I often used to hear that Einstein's most famous achievement was the invention of the atomic bomb. So when we refer to Einstein, we refer to the inventor of the atomic bomb. But this is not so. Columbus was the first man to realize that the earth was round. He was also the first European to land in the western hemisphere. Probably none of these things are true, and therefore, when people use the term 'Columbus' they really refer to some Greek if they use the roundness of the earth, or to some Norseman, perhaps, if they use the 'discovery of America'. But they don't. So it does not seem that if most of the φ's are satisfied by a unique object y, then y is the referent of the name. This seems simply to be false.[6]

Thesis (4): If the vote yields no unique object the name does not refer. Really this case has been covered before — has been covered in my previous examples. First, the vote may not yield a *unique* object, as in the case of Cicero or Feynman. Secondly, suppose it yields *no* object, that nothing satisfies most, or even any, substantial number, of the φ's. Does that mean the name doesn't refer? No: in the same way that you may have false beliefs about a person which may actually be true of someone else, so you may have false beliefs which are true of absolutely no one. And these may constitute the totality of your beliefs. Suppose, to vary the example about Gödel, no one had discovered the incompleteness of arithmetic — perhaps the proof simply materialized by a random scattering of atoms on a piece of paper — the man Gödel being lucky enough to have been present when this improbable event occurred. Further, suppose arithmetic is in fact complete. One wouldn't really expect a random scattering of atoms to produce a correct proof. A subtle error, unknown through the decades, has still been unnoticed — or perhaps not actually unnoticed, but the friends of Gödel. ... So even if the conditions are not satisfied by a unique object the name may still refer. I gave you the case of Jonah last week. Biblical scholars, as I said, think that Jonah really existed. It isn't because they think that someone ever was swallowed by a big fish or even went to Nineveh to preach. These conditions may be true of no one whatsoever and yet the name 'Jonah' really has a referent. In the case above of Einstein's invention of the bomb, possibly no one really deserves to be called the 'inventor' of the device.

Thesis 5 says that the statement 'If X exists, then X has most of the φ's', is *a priori* true for *A*. Notice that even in a case where (3) and (4) *happen* to be true, a typical speaker hardly knows *a priori* that they are, as required by the theory. I *think* that my belief about Gödel *is* in fact correct and that the 'Schmidt' story is just a fantasy. But the belief hardly constitutes *a priori* knowledge.

What's going on here? Can we rescue the theory?[7] First, one may try and vary these descriptions — not think of the famous achievements of a man but, let's say, of something else, and try and use that as our description. Maybe by enough futzing around someone might eventually get something out of this;[8] however, most of the attempts that one tries are open to counterexamples or other objections. Let me give an example of this. In the case of Gödel one may say, 'Well, "Gödel" doesn't mean "the man who proved the incompleteness of arithmetic"'. Look, all we really know is that most people *think* that Gödel proved the incompleteness of arithmetic, that Gödel is the man to whom the incompleteness of arithmetic is commonly attributed. So when I determine the referent of the name 'Gödel', I don't say to myself, 'by "Gödel" I shall mean "the man who proved the incompleteness of arithmetic, whoever he is"'. That might turn out to be Schmidt or Post. But instead I shall mean 'the man who most people *think* proved the incompleteness of arithmetic'.

Is this right? First, it seems to me that it's open to counterexamples of the same type as I gave before, though the counterexamples may be more recherché. Suppose, in the case of Peano mentioned previously, unbeknownst to the speaker, most people (at least by now) thoroughly realize that the nuniber-theoretic axioms should not be attributed to him. Most people don't credit them to Peano but now correctly ascribe them to Dedekind. So then even the man to whom this thing is commonly attributed will still be Dedekind and not Peano. Still, the speaker, having picked up the old outmoded belief, may still be referring to Peano, and hold a false belief about Peano, not a true belief about Dedekind.

But second, and perhaps more significantly, such a criterion violates the noncircularity condition. How is this? It is true that most of us think that Gödel proved the incompleteness of arithmetic. Why is this so? We certainly say, and sincerely, 'Gödel proved the incompleteness of arithmetic'. Does it follow from that that we believe that Gödel proved the incompleteness of arithmetic — that we attribute the incompleteness of arithmetic to this man? No. Not just from that. We have to be *referring to Gödel* when we say 'Gödel proved the incompleteness of arithmetic'. If, in fact, we were always referring to Schmidt, then we would be attributing the incompleteness of arithmetic to Schmidt and not to Gödel — if we used the sound 'Gödel' as the name of the man whom I am calling 'Schmidt'.

But we do in fact refer to Gödel. How do we do this? Well, not by saying to ourselves, 'By "Gödel" I shall mean the man to whom the incompleteness of arithmetic is commonly attributed'. If we did that we would run into a circle. Here we are all in this room. Actually in this institution[9] some people have met the man, but in many institutions this is not so. All of us in the community are trying to determine the reference by saying 'Gödel is to be the man to whom the incompleteness of arithmetic is commonly attributed'. None of us will get started with any attribution unless there is some independent criterion for the reference of the name other than 'the man to whom the incompleteness of arithmetic is commonly attributed'. Otherwise all we will be saying is, 'We attribute this achievement to the man to whom we attribute it', without saying who that man is, without giving any independent criterion of the reference, and so the determination will be circular. This then is a violation of the condition I have marked 'C', and cannot be used in any theory of reference.

Of course you might try to avoid circularity by passing the buck. This is mentioned by Strawson, who says in his footnote on these matters that one man's reference may derive from another's.

The identifying description, though it must not include a reference to the speaker's own reference to the particular in question, may include a reference to another's reference to that particular. If a putatively identifying description is of this latter kind, then, indeed, the question, whether it is a genuinely identifying description, turns on the question, whether the reference it refers to is itself a genuinely identifying reference. So one reference may borrow its credentials, as a genuinely identifying reference, from another; and that from another. But this regress is not infinite.[10]

I may then say, 'Look, by "Gödel" I shall mean the man Joe thinks proved the incompleteness of arithmetic'. Joe may then pass the thing over to Harry. One has to be very careful that this doesn't come round in a circle. Is one really sure that this won't happen? If you could be sure yourself of knowing such a chain, and that everyone else in the chain is using the proper conditions and so is not getting out of it, then maybe you could get back to the man by referring to such a chain in that way, borrowing the references one by one. However, although in general such chains do exist for a living man, you won't know what the chain is. You won't be sure what descriptions the other man is using, so the thing won't go into a circle, or whether by appealing to Joe you won't get back to the right man at all. So you cannot use this as your identifying description with any confidence. You may not even remember from whom you heard of Gödel.

What is the true picture of what's going on? May be reference doesn't really take place at all! After all, we don't really know that any of the properties we use to identify the man are right. We don't know that they pick out a unique object. So what *does* make my use of 'Cicero' into a name of *him*? The picture which leads to the cluster-of-descriptions theory is something like this: One is isolated in a room; the entire community of other speakers, everything else, could disappear; and one determines the reference for himself by saying — 'By "Gödel" I shall mean the man, whoever he is, who proved the incompleteness of arithmetic'. Now you can do this if you want to. There's nothing really preventing it. You can just stick to that determination. If that's what you do, then if Schmidt discovered the incompleteness of arithmetic you *do* refer to him when you say 'Gödel did such and such'.

But that's not what most of us do. Someone, let's say, a baby, is born; his parents call him by a certain name. They talk about him to their friends. Other people meet him. Through various sorts of talk the name is spread from link to link as if by a chain. A speaker who is on the far end of this chain, who has heard about, say Richard Feynman, in the market place or elsewhere, may be referring to Richard Feynman even though he can't remember from whom he first heard of Feynman or from whom he ever heard of Feynman. He knows that Feynman is a famous physicist. A certain passage of commumcation reaching ultimately to the man himself does reach the speaker. He then is referring to Feynman even though he can't identify him uniquely. He doesn't know what a Feynman diagram is, he doesn't know what the Feynman theory of pair production and annihilation is. Not only that: he'd have trouble distinguishing between Gell-Mann and Feynman. So he doesn't have to know these things, but, instead, a chain of communication going back to Feynman himself has been established, by virtue of his membership in a community which passed the name on from link to link, not by a ceremony that he makes in private in his study: 'By "Feynman" I shall mean the man who did such and such and such and such'.

How does this view differ from Strawson's suggestion, mentioned before, that one identifying reference may borrow its credentials from another? Certainly Strawson had a good insight in the passage quoted; on the other hand, he certainly shows a difference at least in emphasis from the picture I advocate, since he confines the remark to a footnote. The main text advocates the cluster-of-descriptions theory. Just because Strawson makes his remark in the context of a description theory, his view therefore differs from mine in one important respect. Strawson apparently requires that the speaker must *know* from whom he got his reference, so that he can say: 'By "Gödel" I mean the man *Jones* calls "Gödel"'. If he does not remember how he picked up the reference, he cannot give such a description. The present theory sets no such requirement. As I said, I may well not remember from whom I heard of Gödel, and I may think I remember from which people I heard the name, but wrongly.

These considerations show that the view advocated here can lead to consequences which actually *diverge* from those of Strawson's footnote. Suppose that the speaker has heard the name 'Cicero' from Smith and others, who use the name to refer to a famous Roman orator. He later thinks, however, that he picked up the name from Jones, who (unknown to the speaker) uses 'Cicero' as the name of a notorious German spy and has never heard of any orators of the ancient world. Then, according to Strawson's paradigm, the speaker must determine his reference by the resolution, 'I shall use "Cicero" to refer to the man whom Jones calls by that name', while on the present view, the referent will be the orator in spite of the speaker's false impression about where he picked up the name. The point is that Strawson, trying to fit the chain of communication view into the description theory, relies on what the speaker *thinks* was the source of his reference. If the speaker has forgotten his source, the description Strawson uses is unavailable to him; if he misremembers it, Strawson's paradigm can give the wrong results. On our view, it is not how the speaker thinks he got the reference, but the actual chain of communication, which is relevant.

I think I said the other time that philosophical theories are in danger of being false, and so I wasn't going to present an alternative theory. Have I just done so? Well, in a way; but my characterization has been far less specific than a real set of necessary and sufficient conditions for reference would be. Obviously the name is passed on from link to link. But of course not every sort of causal chain reaching from me to a certain man will do for me to make a reference. There may be a causal chain from our use of the term 'Santa Claus' to a certain historical saint, but still the children, when they use this, by this time probably do not refer to that saint. So other conditions must be satisfied in order to make this into a really rigorous theory of reference. I don't know that I'm going to do this because, first, I'm sort of too lazy at the moment; secondly, rather than giving a set of necessary and sufficient conditions which will work for a term like reference, I want to present just a *better picture* than the picture presented by the received views.

Haven't I been very unfair to the description theory? Here I have stated it very precisely — more precisely, perhaps, than it has been stated by any of its advocates. So then it's easy to refute. Maybe if I tried to state mine with sufficient precision in the form of six or seven or eight theses, it would also turn out that when you examine the theses one by one, they will all be false. That might even be so, but the difference is this. What I think the examples I've given show is not simply that there's some technical error here or some mistake there, but that the whole picture given by this theory of how reference is determined seems to be wrong from the fundamentals. It seems to be wrong to think that we give ourselves some properties which somehow qualitatively uniquely pick out an object and determine our reference in that manner. What I am trying to present is a better picture — a picture which, if more details were to be filled in, might be refined so as to give more exact conditions for reference to take place.

One might never reach a set of necessary and sufficient conditions. I don't know, I'm always sympathetic to Bishop Butler's 'Everything is what it is and not another thing' — in the nontrivial sense that philosophical analyses of some concept like reference, in completely different terms which make no mention of reference, are very apt to fail. Of course in any particular case when one is given an analysis one has to look at it and see whether it is true or false. One can't just cite this maxim to oneself and then turn the page. But more cautiously, I want to present a better picture without giving a set of necessary and sufficient conditions for reference. Such conditions would be very complicated, but what is true is that it's in virtue of our connection with other speakers in the community, going back to the referent himself, that we refer to a certain man.

There may be some cases where the description picture is true, where some man really gives a name by going into the privacy of his room and saying that the referent is to be the unique thing with certain identifying properties. 'Jack the Ripper' was a possible example which I gave. Another was 'Hesperus'. Yet another case which can be forced into this description is that of meeting someone and being told his name. Except for a belief in the description theory, in its importance in other cases, one probably wouldn't think that that was a case of giving oneself a description, i.e., 'the guy I'm just meeting now'. But one can put it in these terms if one wishes, and if one has never heard the name in any other way. Of course, if you're introduced to a man and told, 'That's Einstein', you've heard of him before, it may be wrong, and so on. But maybe in some cases such a paradigm works — especially for the man who first gives someone or something a name. Or he points to a star and says, 'That is to be Alpha Centauri'. So he can really make himself this ceremony: 'By "Alpha Centauri" I shall mean the star right over there with such and such coordinates'. But in general this picture fails. In general our reference depends not just on what we think ourselves, but on other people in the community, the history of how the name reached one, and things like that. It is by following such a history that one gets to the reference.

More exact conditions are very complicated to give. They seem in a way somehow different in the case of a famous man and one who isn't so famous. For example, a teacher tells his class that Newton was famous for being the first man to think there's a force pulling things to the earth; I think that's what little kids think Newton's greatest achievement was. I won't say what the merits of such an achievement would be, but, anyway, we may suppose that just being told that this was the sole content of Newton's discovery gives the students a false belief *about Newton,* even though they have never heard of him before. If, on the other hand,[11] the teacher uses the name 'George Smith' — a man by that name is actually his next door neighbor — and says that George Smith first squared the circle, does it follow from this that the students have a false belief about the teacher's neighbor? The teacher doesn't tell them that Smith is his neighbor, nor does he believe Smith first squared the circle. He isn't particularly trying to get any belief *about the neighbor* into the students' heads. He tries to inculcate the belief that there was a man who squared the circle, but not a belief about any particular man—he just pulls out the first name that occurs to him — as it happens, he uses his neighbor's name. It doesn't seem clear in that case that the students have a false belief about the neighbor, even though there is a causal chain going back to the neighbor. I am not sure about this. At any rate more refinements need to be added to make this even begin to be a set of necessary and sufficient conditions. In that sense it's not a theory, but is supposed to give a better picture of what is actually going on.

A rough statement of a theory might be the following: An initial 'baptism' takes place. Here the object may be named by ostension, or the reference of the name may be fixed by a description.[12] When the name is 'passed from link to link', the receiver of the name must, I think, intend when he learns it to use it with the same reference as the man from whom he heard it. If I hear the name 'Napoleon' and decide it would be a nice name for my pet aardvark, I do not satisfy this condition[13] (Perhaps it is some such failure to keep the reference fixed which accounts for the divergence of present uses of 'Santa Claus' from the alleged original use.)

Notice that the preceding outline hardly *eliminates* the notion of reference; on the contrary, it takes the notion of intending to use the same reference as a given. There is also an appeal to an initial baptism which is explained in terms either of fixing a reference by a description, or ostension (if ostension is not to be subsumed under the other category).[14] (Perhaps there are other possibilities for initial baptisms.) Further, the George Smith case casts some doubt as to the sufficiency of the conditions. Even if the teacher does refer to his neighbor, is it clear that he has passed on his reference to the pupils? Why shouldn't their belief be about any other man named 'George Smith'? If he says that Newton was hit by an apple, somehow his task of transmitting a reference is easier, since he has communicated a common misconception about Newton.

To repeat, I may not have presented a theory, but I do think that I have presented a better picture than that given by description theorists.

I think the next topic I shall want to talk about is that of statements of identity. Are these necessary or contingent? The matter has been in some dispute in recent philosophy. First, everyone agrees that descriptions can be used to make contingent identity statements. If it is true that the man who in vented bifocals was the first Postmaster General of the United States — that these were one and the same — it's contingently true. That is, it might have been the case that one man invented bifocals and another was the first Postmaster General of the United States. So certainly when you make identity statements using descriptions — when you say 'the x such that φx and the x such that ψ/x are one and the same' — that can be a contingent fact. But philosophers have been interested also in the question of identity statements between names. When we say 'Hesperus is Phosphorus' or 'Cicero is Tully', is what we are saying necessary or contingent? Further, they've been interested in another type of identity statement, which comes from scientific theory. We identify, for example, light with electromagnetic radiation between certain limits of wavelengths, or with a stream of photons. We identify heat with the motion of molecules; sound with a certain sort of wave disturbance in the air; and so on. Concerning such statements the following thesis is commonly held. First, that these are obviously contingent identities: we've found out that light is a stream of photons, but of course it might not have been a stream of photons. Heat is in fact the motion of molecules; we found that out, but heat might not have been the motion of molecules. Secondly, many philosophers feel damned lucky that these examples are around. Now, why? These philosophers, whose views are expounded in a vast literature, hold to a thesis called 'the identity thesis' with respect to some psychological concepts. They think, say, that pain is just a certain material state of the brain or of the body, or what have you — say the stimulation of C-fibers. (It doesn't matter what.) Some people have then objected, 'Well, look, there's perhaps a *correlation* between pain and these states of the body; but this must just be a contingent correlation between two different things, because it was an empirical discovery that this correlation ever held. Therefore, by "pain" we must mean something different from this state of the body or brain; and, therefore, they must be two different things.'

Then it's said, 'Ah, but you see, this is wrong! Everyone knows that there can be contingent identities.' First, as in the bifocals and Postmaster General case, which I have mentioned before. Second, in the case, believed closer to the present paradigm, of theoretical identifications, such as light and a stream of photons, or water and a certain compound of hydrogen and oxygen. These are all contingent identities. They might have been false. It's no surprise, therefore, that it can be true as a matter of contingent fact and not of any necessity that feeling pain, or seeing red, is just a certain state of the human body. Such psychophysical identifications can be contingent facts just as the other identities are contingent facts. And of course there are widespread motivations — ideological, or just not wanting to have the 'nomological dangler' of mysterious connections not accounted for by the laws of physics, one to one correlations between two different kinds of thing, material states, and things of an entirely different kind, which lead people to want to believe this thesis.

I guess the main thing I'll talk about first is identity statements between names. But I hold the following about the general case. First, that characteristic theoretical identifications like 'Heat is the motion of molecules', are not contingent truths but necessary truths, and here of course I don't mean just physically necessary, but necessary in the highest degree — whatever that means. (Physical necessity, *might* turn out to be necessity in the highest degree. But that's a question which I don't wish to prejudge. At least for this sort of example, it might be that when something's physically necessary, it always is necessary *tout court.*) Second, that the way in which these have turned out to be necessary truths does not seem to me to be a way in which the mind-brain identities could turn out to be either necessary or contingently true. So this analogy has to go. It's hard to see what to put in its place. It's hard to see therefore how to avoid concluding that the two are actually different.

Let me go back to the more mundane case about proper names. This is already mysterious enough. There's a dispute about this between Quine and Ruth Barcan Marcus.[15] Marcus says that identities between names are necessary. If someone thinks that Cicero is Tully, and really uses 'Cicero' and 'Tully' as names, he is thereby committed to holding that his belief is a necessary truth. She uses the term 'mere tag'. Quine replies as follows, 'We may tag the planet Venus, some fine evening, with the proper name "Hesperus". We may tag the same planet again, some day before sunrise, with the proper name "Phosphorus". When we discover that we have tagged the same planet twice our discovery is empirical. And not because the proper names were descriptions.'[16] First, as Quine says when we discovered that we tagged the same planet twice, our discovery was empirical. Another example I think Quine gives in another book is that the same mountain seen from Nepal and from Tibet, or something like that, is from one angle called 'Mt. Everest' (you've heard of that); from another it's supposed to be called 'Gaurisanker'. It can actually be an empirical discovery that Gaurisanker is Everest. (Quine says that the example is actually false. He got the example from Erwin Schrödinger. You wouldn't think the inventor of wave mechanics got things that wrong. I don't know where the mistake is supposed to come from. One could certainly imagine this situation as having been the case; and it's another good illustration of the sort of thing that Quine has in mind.)

What about it? I wanted to find a good quote on the other side from Marcus in this book but I am having trouble locating one. Being present at that discussion, I remember[17] that she advocated the view that if you really have names, a good dictionary should be able to tell you whether they have the same reference. So someone should be able, by looking in the dictionary, to say that Hesperus and Phosphorus are the same. Now this does not seem to be true. It does seem, to many people, to be a consequence of the view that identities between names are necessary. Therefore the view that identity statements between names are necessary has usually been rejected. Russell's conclusion was somewhat different. He did think there should never be any empirical question whether two names have the same reference. This isn't satisfied for ordinary names, but it is satisfied when you're naming your own sense datum, or something like that. You say, 'Here, this, and that (designating the same sense datum by both demonstratives).' So you can tell without empirical investigation that you're naming the same thing twice; the conditions are satisfied. Since this won't apply to ordinary cases of naming, ordinary 'names' cannot be genuine names.

What should we think about this? First, it's true that someone can use the name 'Cicero' to refer to Cicero and the name 'Tully' to refer to Cicero also, and not know that Cicero is Tully. So it seems that we do not necessarily know *a priori* that an identity statement between names is true. It doesn't follow from this that the statement so expressed is a contingent one if true. This is what I've emphasized in my first lecture. There is a very strong feeling that leads one to think that, if you can't know something by *a priori* ratiocination, then it's got to be contingent: it might have turned out otherwise; but nevertheless I think this feeling is wrong.

Let's suppose we refer to the same heavenly body twice, as 'Hesperus' and 'Phosphorus'. We say: Hesperus is that star over there in the evening; Phosphorus is that star over there in the morning. Actually, Hesperus is Phosphorus. Are there really circumstances under which Hesperus wouldn't have been Phosphorus? Supposing that Hesperus is Phosphorus, let's try to describe a possible situation in which it would not have been. Well, it's easy. Someone goes by and he calls two *different* stars 'Hesperus' and 'Phosphorus'. It may even be under the same conditions as prevailed when we introduced the names 'Hesperus' and 'Phosphorus'. But are those circumstances in which Hesperus is not Phosphorus or would not have been Phosphorus? It seems to me that they are not.

Now, of course I'm committed to saying that they're not, by saying that such terms as 'Hesperus' and 'Phosphorus', when used as names, are rigid designators. They refer in every possible world to the planet Venus. Therefore, in that possible world too, the planet Venus is the planet Venus and it doesn't matter what any other person has said in this other possible world. How should *we* describe this situation? He can't have pointed to Venus twice, and in the one case called it 'Hesperus' and in the other 'Phosphorus', as we did. If he did so, then 'Hesperus is Phosphorus' would have been true in that situation too. He pointed maybe neither time to the planet Venus — at least one time he didn't point to the planet Venus, let's say when he pointed to the body he called 'Phosphorus'. Then in that case we can certainly say that the name 'Phosphorus' might not have referred to Phosphorus. We can even say that in the very position when viewed in the morning that we found Phosphorus, it might have been the case that Phosphorus was not there — that something else was there, and that even, under certain circumstances it would have been *called* 'Phosphorus'. But that still is not a case in which Phosphorus was not Hesperus. There might be a possible world in which, a possible counterfactual situation in which, 'Hesperus' and 'Phosphorus' weren't names of the things they in fact are names of. Someone, if he did determine their reference by identifying descriptions, might even have used the very identifying descriptions we used. But still that's not a case in which Hesperus wasn't Phosphorus. For there couldn't have been such a case, given that Hesperus is Phosphorus.

Now this seems very strange because in advance, we are inclined to say, the answer to the question whether Hesperus is Phosphorus might have turned out either way. So aren't there really two possible worlds — one in which Hesperus was Phosphorus, the other in which Hesperus wasn't Phosphorus — in advance of our discovering that these were the same? First, there's one sense in which things might turn out either way, in which it's clear that that doesn't imply that the way it finally turns out isn't necessary. For example, the four color theorem might turn out to be true and might turn out to be false. It might turn out either way. It still doesn't mean that the way it turns out is not necessary. Obviously, the 'might' here is purely 'epistemic' — it merely expresses our present state of ignorance, or uncertainty.

But it seems that in the Hesperus-Phosphorus case, something even stronger is true. The evidence I have before I know that Hesperus is Phosphorus is that I see a certain star or a certain heavenly body in the evening and call it 'Hesperus', and in the morning and call it 'Phosphorus'. I know these things. There certainly is a possible world in which a man should have seen a certain star at a certain position in the evening and called it 'Hesperus' and a certain star in the morning and called it 'Phosphorus'; and should have concluded — should have found out by empirical investigation — that he names two different stars, or two different heavenly bodies. At least one of these stars or heavenly bodies was not Phosphorus, otherwise it couldn't have come out that way. But that's true. And so it's true that given the evidence that someone has antecedent to his empirical investigation, he can be placed in a sense in exactly the same situation, that is a qualitatively identical epistemic situation, and call two heavenly bodies 'Hesperus' and 'Phosphorus', without their being identical. So in that sense we can say that it might have turned out either way. Not that it might have turned out either way as to Hesperus's being Phosphorus. Though for all we knew in advance, Hesperus wasn't Phosphorus, that couldn't have turned out any other way, in a sense. But being put in a situation where we have exactly the same evidence, qualitatively speaking, it could have turned out that Hesperus was not Phosphorus; that is, in a counterfactual world in which 'Hesperus' and 'Phosphorus' were not used in the way that we use them, as names of this planet, but as names of some other objects, one could have had qualitatively identical evidence and concluded that 'Hesperus' and 'Phosphorus' named two different objects.[18] But we, using the names as we do right now, can say in advance, that if Hesperus and Phosphorus are one and the same, then in no other possible world can they be different. We use 'Hesperus' as the name of a certain body and 'Phosphorus' as the name of a certain body. We use them as names of those bodies in all possible worlds. If, in fact, they are the *same* body, then in any other possible world we have to use them as a name of that object. And so in any other possible world it will be true that Hesperus is Phosphorus. So two things are true: first, that we do not know *a priori* that Hesperus is Phosphorus, and are in no position to find out the answer except empirically. Second, this is so because we could have evidence qualitatively indistinguishable from the evidence we have and determine the reference of the two names by the positions of two planets in the sky, without the planets being the same.

Of course, it is only a contingent truth (not true in every other possible world) that the star seen over there in the evening is the star seen over there in the morning, because there are possible worlds in which Phosphorus was not visible in the morning. But that contingent truth shouldn't be identified with the statement that Hesperus is Phosphorus. It could only be so identified if you thought that it was a necessary truth that Hesperus is visible over there in the evening or that Phosphorus is visible over there in the morning. But neither of those are necessary truths even if that's the way we pick out the planet. These are the contingent marks by which we identify a certain planet and give it a name.

1   Searle, 'Proper Names', in Caton, op. cit., p. 160.

2   D. Lewis, op. cit., pp. 114–15.

3   An even better case of determining the reference of a name by description, as opposed to ostension, is the discovery of the planet Neptune. Neptune was hypothesized as the planet which caused such and such discrepancies in the orbits of certain other planets. If Leverrier indeed gave the name 'Neptune' to the planet before it was ever seen, then he fixed the reference of 'Neptune' by means of the description just mentioned. At that time he was unable to see the planet even through a telescope. At this stage, an *a priori* material equivalence held between the statements 'Neptune exists' and 'some one planet perturbing the orbit of such and such other planets exists in such and such a position', and also such statements as 'if such and such perturbations are caused by a planet, they are caused by Neptune' had the status of *a priori* truths. Nevertheless, they were not *necessary* truths, since 'Neptune' was introduced as a name rigidly designating a certain planet. Leverrier could well have believed that if Neptune had been knocked off its course one million years earlier, it would have caused no such perturbations and even that some other object might have caused the perturbations in its place.

4   Following Donnellan's remarks on definite descriptions, we should add

that in some cases, an object may be identified, and the reference of a name fixed, using a description which may turn out to be false of its object. The case where the reference of 'Phosphorus' is determined as the 'morning star', which later turns out not to be a star, is an obvious example. In such cases, the description which fixes the reference clearly is in no sense known *a priori* to hold of the object, though a more cautious substitute may be. If such a more cautious substitute is available, it is really the substitute which fixes the reference in the sense intended in the text.

5 Some of the theses are sloppily stated in respect of fussy matters like use of quotation marks and related details. (For example, Theses (5) and (6), as stated, presuppose that the speaker's language is English.) Since the purport of the theses is clear, and they are false anyway, I have not bothered to set these things straight.

6 The cluster-of-descriptions theory of naming would make 'Peano discovered the axioms for number theory' express a trivial truth, not a misconception, and similarly for other misconceptions about the history of science. Some who have conceded such cases to me have argued that there are *other* uses of the same proper names satisfying the cluster theory. For example, it is argued, if we say, 'Gödel proved the incompleteness of arithmetic,' we are, of course, referring to Gödel, not to Schmidt. But, if we say, 'Gödel relied on a diagonal argument in this step of the proof,' don't we here, perhaps, refer to *whoever proved the theorem*? Similarly, if someone asks, 'What did Aristotle (or Shakespeare) have in mind here?', isn't he talking about the author of the passage in question, whoever he is? By analogy to Donnellan's usage for descriptions, this might be called an "attributive" use of proper names. If this is so, then assuming the Gödel-Schmidt story, the sentence 'Gödel proved the incompleteness theorem' is false, but 'Gödel used a diagonal argument in the proof' is (at least in some contexts) true, and the reference of the name 'Gödel' is ambiguous. Since some counterexamples remain, the cluster-of-descriptions theory would still, in general, be false, which was my main point in the text; but it would be applicable in a wider class of cases than I thought. I think, however, that no such ambiguity need be postulated. It is, perhaps, true that sometimes when someone uses the name 'Gödel', his main interest is in whoever proved the theorem, and *perhaps,* in some sense, he 'refers' to him. I do not think that this case is

different from the case of Smith and Jones in n. 3, p. 25. If I mistakeJones for Smith, I may *refer* (in an appropriate sense) to Jones when I say that Smith is raking the leaves; nevertheless I do not use 'Smith' ambiguously, as a name sometimes of Smith and sometimes of Jones, but univocally as a name of Smith. Similarly, if I erroneously think that Aristotle wrote such-and-such passage, I may perhaps sometimes use 'Aristotle' to *refer* to the actual author of the passage, even though there is no ambiguity in my use of the name. In both cases, I will withdraw my original statement, and my original use of the name, if apprised of the facts. Recall that, in these lectures, 'referent' is used in the technical sense of the thing named by a name (or uniquely satisfying a description), and there should be no confusion.

7   It has been suggested to me that someone might argue that a name is associated with a 'referential' use of a description in Donnellan's sense. For example, although we identify Gödel as the author of the incompleteness theorem, we are talking about him even if he turns out not to have proved the theorem. Theses (2)–(6) could then fail; but nevertheless each name would abbreviate a description, though the role of description in naming would differ radically from that imagined by Frege and Russell. As I have said above, I am inclined to reject Donnellan's formulation of the notion of referential definite description. Even if Donnellan's analysis is accepted, however, it is clear that the present proposal should not be. For a referential definite description, such as 'the man drinking champagne', is typically withdrawn when the speaker realizes that it does not apply to its object. If a Gödelian fraud were exposed, Gödel would no longer be called 'the author of the incompleteness theorem' but he would still be called 'Gödel'. The name, therefore, does not abbreviate the description.

8   As Robert Nozick pointed out to me, there is a sense in which a description theory must be trivially true if any theory of the reference of names, spelled out in terms independent of the notion of reference, is available. For if such a theory gives conditions under which an object is to be the referent of a name, then it of course uniquely satisfies these conditions. Since I am not pretending to give any theory which eliminates the notion of reference in this sense, I am not aware of any such trivial fulfillment of the description theory and doubt that one exists. (A description using the

notion of the reference of a name is easily available but circular, as we saw in our discussion of Kneale.) If any such trivial fulfillment were available, however, the arguments I have given show that the description must be one of a completely different sort from that supposed by Frege, Russell, Searle, Strawson and other advocates of the description theory.

9   Princeton University.

10   Strawson, op. cit., p. 182 n.

11   The essential points of this example were suggested by Richard Miller.

12   A good example of a baptism whose reference was fixed by means of a description was that of naming Neptune in n. 33, p. 79. The case of a baptism by ostension can perhaps be subsumed under the description concept also. Thus the primary applicability of the description theory is to cases of initial baptism. Descriptions are also used to fix a reference in cases of designation which are similar to naming except that the terms introduced are not usually called 'names'. The terms 'one meter', '100 degrees Centigrade', have already been given as examples, and other examples will be given later in these lectures. Two things should be emphasized concerning the case of introducing a name via a description in an initial baptism. First, the description used is not synonymous with the name it introduces but rather fixes its reference. Here we differ from the usual description theorists. Second, most cases of initial baptism are far from those which originally inspired the description theory. Usually a baptizer is acquainted in some sense with the object he names and is able to name it ostensively. Now the inspiration of the description theory lay in the fact that we can often use names of famous figures of the past who are long dead and with whom no living person is acquainted; and it is precisely these cases which, on our view, cannot be correctly explained by a description theory.

13   I can transmit the name of the aardvark to other people. For each of these people, as for me, there will be a certain sort of causal or historical connection between my use of the name and the Emperor of the French, but not one of the required type.

14   Once we realize that the description used to fix the reference of a name is not synonymous with it, then the description theory can be regarded as presupposing the notion of naming or reference. The requirement I made

that the description used not itself involve the notion of reference in a circular way is something else and is crucial if the description theory is to have any value at all. The reason is that the description theorist supposes that each speaker essentially uses the description he gives in an initial act of naming to determine his reference. Clearly, if he introduces the name 'Cicero' by the determination, 'By "Cicero" I shall refer to the man I call "Cicero",' he has by this ceremony determined no reference at all.

Not all description theorists thought that they were eliminating the notion of reference altogether. Perhaps some realized that some notion of ostension, or primitive reference, is required to back it up. Certainly Russell did.

15 Ruth Barcan Marcus, 'Modalities and Intensional Languages' (comments by W. V. Quine, plus discussion) *Boston Studies in the Philosophy of Science,* volume I, Reidel, Dordrecht, Holland, 1963, pp. 77–116.

16 p. 101.

17 p. 115.

18 There is a more elaborate discussion of this point in the third lecture, where its relation to a certain sort of counterpart theory is also mentioned.

第二部分：
形式语义学

　　形式语义学是在逻辑学、哲学和语言学等学科的共同影响下产生的语义学流派，它的核心思想是用形式化的方法描写自然语言的意义。本章选取的五篇章均是形式语义学的名篇，讨论的主题有意义和真值的关系，句子意义的形式化表征、指示语的形式化表征等问题。

　　第一篇文章是戴维森（D. Davidson）的《真理和意义》（Truth and Meaning）（1967），该文主要关注意义和真理的关系，关注的焦点是句子的意义问题。戴维森指出，一个好的意义理论应该能够说明句子的意义如何依赖于词语的意义。作者在对四种意义观逐一进行批判的基础上提出了意义的真理论。

　　指称论是针对句子意义和词语意义关系问题的一种理论。根据指称论，给句子中的每个词语指派（assign）实体（entity）作为词语的意义，我们就可以由此获得句子的意义。例如，对于*Theaetetus flies.*这个句子，我们可以给词语*Theaetetus*指派 "Theaetetus" 这个实体，给*flies*指派 "飞" 这个属性。

　　戴维森指出，这样处理的问题在于，当我们把Theatetus和flies这两个词语连接为句子*Theatetus flies*这个句子时，我们还要指派 "连接"（concatenation）这种句法关系作为它的意义。因此，这个句子就有三个句子成分，即*Theatetus*、*flies*和句法关系 "连接"。如果要把一个句子的成分连接起来构成一个句子，就需要再给每两个句子成分指派某种连接关系，这样 "指派" 关系的行为就会数不胜数。

　　针对这个问题，弗雷格曾经提出，与名称（names）对应的实体不同的是，与谓词对应的实体是不饱和（unsaturated）或不完全的（incomplete）。戴维森认为，弗雷格的处理在面对复合名称（complex singular terms）时又会出现问题。例如，*the father of t*的意义如何依赖于这个句子的成分呢？根据弗雷格的观点，这个句子指t所指称的人的父亲。这样，就没有实体对应于*the father of*。弗雷格区分了指称和意义。他提出，句子的指称就是其真值，句子的意义就是命题。据此，所有具有相同真值的句子具有相同的指称。如果所有为真的句子都有相同的指称，所有为假的句子也都有相同的指称，这样的结论难以令人接受。戴维森认为，弗雷格对指称和意义的区分并不能很好地解释句子的意义如何依赖于词语的意义。

另一种意义理论认为，假设我们已有一种满意的句法理论，它就能够确定任何一个表达式是否有独立的意义，同时假定构成句子的成分均来自一个固定的、有限的原子句法成分库，而句子正是以一种合理的方式由这些成分构成。理想的情况是，如果我们有一本字典来说明每个原子句法成分的意义，我们就能根据句法理论来建构语义理论。戴维森认为这仅仅是一种理想。因为仅依赖句子成分之间的句法关系和原子成分的意义并不能获得句子的意义。例如，对于信念句（belief sentences），仅依赖句法关系和词语的意义很难知道其真值。戴维森提出，语义学的中心任务是对每个句子作出语义解释，而句法学的主要任务是说明句子的有意义性（meaningfulness）或句子身份（sentencehood）。

戴维森反驳的第四种意义观是意义的整体观（a holistic view）。根据这一理论，句子成分只有在其所在语境中才有意义。句子的意义依赖于它的结构，而结构中的每个成分的意义又是从作为整体的句子中抽象出来的。因此，要给出任何一个句子（或词语）意义，只有通过给出语言中的每个句子（或词语）的意义才能实现。戴维森指出，整体观同样存在问题。因为根据整体观，一个合适的意义理论必须能够衍推（entail）所有具有"s意谓（means that）p"形式的句子。这里的p是一个句子。问题在于，句子不能命名意义，因为句子没有命名的作用。可见"意谓"这个概念使意义的整体观陷入了困境。

戴维森对意义问题的认识受到了塔斯基真理理论中T约定（T Convention）思想的影响。塔斯基真理理论的核心思想是用对象语言（object language）和元语言（metalanguage）这两种语言来定义真理，即"s为真，当且仅当p"。s是对象语言，是被讨论的语言；p是元语言，是讨论对象语言时所使用的语言。例如，语句"雪是白的"为真，当且仅当雪是白的。根据塔斯基的定义，在一定条件下，可由对象语言中的句子获得"s为真，当且仅当p"这种形式的句子。这就是塔斯基的T约定。

戴维森指出，塔斯基的真理理论表明如何建构真理定义和意义概念之间的明显联系。"这种联系是，塔斯基的定义是靠给出每个句子成真的必要充分条件而生效的，而给出成真条件是给出句子意义的一种方式。认识一种语言的真理的语义概念就是认识什么叫做一个句子为真"。虽然句子的意义和句子为真不是同一个概念，但根据塔斯基的真理理论，判断一个句子为真需说明它成真的条件，而了解句子成真的条件就了解了句子的意义。

戴维森认为，获得一个语句意义的途径是陈述其成真条件。在他看来，真理和意义是密切相关的，可将句子的意义描述为"s为真当且仅当p"。s是被描写的对象语言，是提及（mention）；p是用于解释的元语言，是使用（use）。例如，"雪是白的"的意义是"雪是白的当且仅当雪是白的"。由此可见，意义和真理密切相关。塔斯基在意义概念的基础上定义真理，戴维森在真理概念的基础上定义意义。

戴维森指出，"为真"不是句子的属性，而是语句、言语行为、人和时间的属性。可以将真值看作是句子、人和时间的关系。例如，当说话者p在时间t说出*I am tired*，当且仅当p在t时是累的，*I am tired*这个语句为真。

这篇论文的价值在于，戴维森尝试建立自然语言的形式语义学，用形式化的方法描述自然语言的意义，这种句义真值观对形式语义学的发展具有深远影响。在《英语是形式语言》（English as a Formal Language）（1970）的经典论文中，蒙太古（Montague）否认传统逻辑学家和语言学家提出的自然语言和形式语言存在差别的观点，用一阶谓词逻辑（first-order logic）的形式翻译英语，在戴维森的基础上，蒙太古将自然语言形式化推进了一步。不过，戴维森还是留下了待解决的问题，例如，用他的方法不能获得信念句（belief sentences）、疑问句、祈使句等句子的意义，因为这类句子没有真值。

第二篇论文《动作句的逻辑形式》（The Logical Form of Action Sentences）（1967）是戴维森的代表作，是事件语义学（event-based semantics）发展的基石，对巴威斯和佩里（Barwise & Perry, 1983）的境况语义学（situational semantics）以及帕森斯（Parsons）、希金博特姆（Higginbotham）、罗特施泰因（Rothstein）等为代表的新戴维森理论、梅因伯恩（Meinborn）等反新戴维森理论等流派思想的形成和发展均产生了重大影响。

针对例（1）这类动作句（action sentences）的逻辑表达式问题，赖欣巴哈（Reichenbach）、肯尼（Kenny）、冯·赖特（von Wright）、奇斯霍姆（Chisholm）等提出不同看法，戴维森认为他们的方案均存在问题。

(1) Jones buttered the toast in the bathroom with a knife at midnight.

按照传统的逻辑表达方式，这个句子的逻辑形式是（1'）：

(1') butter (Jones, the toast, the bathroom, a knife, midnight).

从（1'）可以看出，butter是个五元谓词，五个论元分别是Jones, the toast, the bathroom, a knife, midnight。

再看句（2）：

(2) Jones buttered the toast in the bathroom with a knife.

这个句子的逻辑形式是（2'）：

(2') butter (Jones, the toast, the bathroom, a knife).

（1）和（2）是衍推关系，但是（1'）和（2'）并不能展现这两个句子的衍推关系。

赖欣巴哈（Reichenbach, 1947）将动作句的逻辑形式描述为*x is an event that consist in the fact that ...*。例如，（3）的逻辑形式是（3'）：

(3) Amundsen flew to the North Pole.
(3') (∃x) (x consists in the fact that Amundsen flew to the North Pole).

戴维森认为这样的描述不能解释*I flew my spaceship to the Morning Star*和*I flew my spaceship to the Evening Star*这类句子之间的衍推关系。

肯尼（Kenny, 1963）将动作句的逻辑形式表述为*x brought it about that p*。肯尼旨在通过三个要素来表征动作句的逻辑形式，即（1）施事者；（2）导致某种状态；（3）是施事者导致了这种结果。据此，句（1）的逻辑形式是（1"）：

(1") Jones brought it about that the toast was buttered in the bathroom with a knife at midnight.

代替*x brought it about that p*中p的句子描述的是施事者行为的结果，用现在时。例如，（4）的逻辑形式是（4'）：

(4) Cass walked to the store.

(4') Cass brought it about that Cass is at the store.

这样处理的问题在于，（4）和（4'）的意义不同，后者没有描述动作的方式*walking*。除了这个问题之外，戴维森还认为，许多动作句并非描述由施事导致的动作，肯尼的处理对非施事行为句无能为力。例如，*I sleep, I catch cold*这类句子就不涉及施事性（agency）。

冯·赖特认为动作句的逻辑形式是*x brings it about that a state where p changes into a state where q*。和肯尼不同，他除了描述动作的结果之外，还描述了动作的起始状态。戴维森指出，许多动作句并不涉及对动作起始状态的描写。例如，*He circled the field, He recited the Odyssey*等。

奇斯霍姆（Chishlom, 1964）认为动作句的逻辑形式是"x makes p happen"。他指出、取代p的表达式描述的是事件的状态（state of affairs），它可以是变化（changes）、事件（events）或者非变化（unchanges）。戴维森（1967）指出，*make something happen* 说明动作是意向性的，不同于"致使某事发生"。奇斯霍姆提出的逻辑式不能处理*He fell down*这类不涉及受事的句子，也不能处理涉及动作意图（intentionality）的句子，像*Jones raised his arm*。另一个问题是，无论我们用什么取代p，它都是描述某个事件，而整个句子*x makes p happen*也是描述事件，难于确定二者关系是否是同一关系。

在此基础上，戴维森提出了针对动作句逻辑形式这一问题的解决方案。戴维森的核心思想是，对于动作句，事件论元x是谓词的必带论元之一。例如，（5）的逻辑形式是（5'）：

(5) Shem kicked Shaun.

(5') (∃x) (kicked (Shem, Shaun, x)),)

和（1'）所示的传统逻辑形式处理不同，在（5'）中，kick被看作一个三元谓词，事件论元x是kick的论元之一。（5'）表达的意思是，有一个事件x，x是Shem踢Shaun这一事件。

句子中的状语是事件的述谓，而非动词的述谓。据此，动作句*John buttered the toast*的逻辑形式是（ ∃x）（buttered（John, the toast, x）），表达的是"有一个事件x，即约翰给面包涂黄油"。这样的处理能解决赖欣巴哈所不能解决的（6）和（7）这两个句子的衍推关系。

(6)　I flew my spaceship to the Morning Star.

(7)　I flew my spaceship to the Evening Star.

　　根据戴维森的处理，（6）和（7）的逻辑形式分别为（6'）和（7'）：

(6')　($\exists$x) (Flew (I, my spaceship, x)) & To (the Morning Star, x))

(7')　($\exists$x) (Flew (I, my spaceship, x)) & To (the Evening Star, x))
　　　the Morning Star = the Evening Star

　　因此，（6'）和（7'）能展现两个句子的衍推关系。

　　戴维森进一步论述了表达具有施事性特征句子的逻辑形式问题。施事性有两个要素。一个是施事者主动地发出动作，而不是被动地接受动作的发生。例如，*Others are insulted by me/struck by me/admired by me*不是表达具有施事性特征的句子，因为*others*被动地接受动作的发生。另一个要素是动作具有意向性。例如，*I insulted him*是表达具有施事性特征的句子，而*I caught cold, I had my thirteenth birthday*则不是，因为它们不具有意向性。戴维森指出，意向性与人关联，而不是与动作动词关联，表意向性的句子表达的是*It was intentional of x that p*，其中x是施事者，p是描述施事者做某事的句子。

　　戴维森的处理与先前其他学者的处理相比，主要有两大优点：

　　第一，可以很好地解决动词是几元谓词的不确定性问题。例如，

(8)　John buttered the toast.

(9)　John buttered the toast with a knife.

　　按照前人的处理，（8）中*butter*是带*John*和*the toast*这两个论元的二元谓词，而若将句子加上状语，变为（9）时，*butter*则变为带有*John, the toast, a knife*这三个论元的三元谓词。这样处理带来的问题是，如果无限制地添加句子的状语，动词所带论元的数量就具有不确定性。

　　戴维森的处理则将事件论元e看作动词的必带论元之一，而将句子中时间、地点、工具等状语看作对事件的描述，由此，以上两句的逻辑

形式分别为（8'）和（9'）。这样处理就保持了动词所带论元数量的一致性。

(8')　(∃x) (buttered (John, the toast, x)).

(9')　(∃x)(buttered (John, the toast, x) & with (knife, x))

第二，可以很好地展示句子之间的衍推关系。因为状语被看作是对事件的述谓，一个不带状语的句子、带一个或几个状语的句子之间的衍推关系可以通过逻辑式清晰体现，例如（8）和（9）的衍推关系可由它们的逻辑式体现。

第三篇论文是卡普兰（D. Kaplan）的《论指示语的逻辑》（On the Logic of Demonstratives）。作者认为，指示语（例如，*I, you, here, now, that, actual, present*）的外延（extension）和内涵（intension）都由语境决定。本文旨在解决如何用形式的方法表征指示语的问题。

根据传统逻辑，一个陈述（statement）的真值是不固定的，它依赖于时间。一个句子为真的条件是w, t, p, a等均为真，其中w是世界，t是时间，p =（x, y, z）是世界的一个三维处所，a是施事。

传统逻辑不能处理情态、时间、地点等指示语，例如，

(1)　I am here now.

（1）是个典型的含指示语的句子，涉及人*I*、地点*here*和时间*now*三个指示语。只有在世界w中，x在时间t位于处所p，（1）为真。如果我们将这三个指示语换掉，将此句改写为

(2)　David Kaplan is in Los Angeles on April, 21, 1973.

可以发现这两个句子的区别：前句总是为真，后句则不一定为真。

在克里普克的先验性（the a-priori）和必然性（the necessary）的区分，以及Strawson的句子意义性（meaning fulness）和命题之区分的基础上，Kaplan区分了内容（content）和特质（character）这两个意义的变体（varieties of sense）。一个表达式的内容是针对它在一个具体语境中的使用而言的，因此同一个表达式不仅会在不同语境中产生不同的真

值，而且表达不同的命题。以（3）为例：

(3) I was insulted yesterday.

当我说这句话时，我所说的就是内容。你说同样的话，或者我在另外一天说同样的话，表达的是不同的内容。也就是说，在这三种情况下，不仅真值会变，而且所说的内容也不同。

(4) David Kaplan is insulted on April 20, 1973.

当卡普兰今天说（4）时，（3）和（4）有相同的内容，但是，因为（4）不含指示语，不论说话者是谁，它表达的内容都相同。换句话说，（4）的内容在任何语境中都是一样的。

一个表达式的特质决定内容如何由语境决定。例如，讲英语的人知道 *I* 的特质是说话者，例（1）的特质决定：

a) 在不同的语境中，语句（1）表达不同的内容。

b) 在大部分语境中，语句（1）表达的命题都是视具体情况而定的。

c) 在所有语境中，语句（1）表达为真的命题。

内容是必然的（necessary），特质是分析性的（analytic），因为特质可以通过分析词义获得。"内容由从可能世界到外延（extension）的函项表征（function），特质由从语境到内容的函项表征"。可见，就一个句子而言，内容是它表达的命题，特质是相对稳定的意义。对于不含指示语的句子，内容和特质的区分并不显得十分重要。因为这类句子有固定的特质，且在每个语境中表达的都是相同的内容。而对于含指示语的句子，区分内容和特质十分必要，这样就能区分句子在不同语境中所表达的内容的差异。

因此，回归到句子（1）和（2）的关系问题，卡普兰认为，句子的特质决定了同一个句子在不同语境下表达内容不同的、但总为真的命题。在此基础上，他引入时间、地点、人物等变量，将指示语引入内涵逻辑（intensional logics），从而为解决指示语难于形式化的问题提供了一种可行的思路。

卡普兰使用一些初始符号（primitive symbols），用形式化的方法定义并处理指示语。这些符号包括：

个体变项(individual variables): v_i

位置变项(position variables): v_p

1—0元谓词(the 1-0-place predicate): Exist

1—1元谓词(the 1-1-place predicate): Located

个体常项(an individual constant): I

位置常项(a position constant): Here

一元命题算子(one-place sentential operators): N（表示现在的情况）

A（表示实际的情况）

Y（表示昨天的情况）

一元算符：dthat

……

卡普兰据此提出，合适的表达式（well-formed expressions）有三种类型：个体词项（i-terms）、位置词项（p-terms）和公式（formulas）。卡普兰对它们做出如下规定：

如果$\alpha \in v_i$，则α是个体词项；

如果$\alpha \in v_p$，则α是位置词项；

如果π是m-n元谓词（m-n-place predicate），$\alpha_1 \ldots \alpha_m$是个体词项，$\beta_1 \ldots \beta_n$是位置词项，那么$\pi\alpha_1 \ldots \alpha_m \beta \ldots \beta_n$是公式；

如果Φ是公式，且$\alpha \in v_i$，或$\alpha \in v_p$，则$\forall\alpha\Phi$和$\exists\alpha\Phi$都是公式；

如果α是个体词项，则dthat是α个体词项；

如果α是位置词项，则dthat是α位置词项。

……

卡普兰进一步对它们做出语义解释。当且仅当存在CWUPT$\mathscr{J}$，$\mathscr{Q}$是一个LD结构，即：

$\mathscr{Q}$=<CWUPT$\mathscr{J}$>

其中，C是语境集，W是可能世界集，U是个体集，P是空间集，T是时间集，$\mathscr{J}$是功能，它赋予每个谓词和算符合适的内涵。

若C是语境集C的成员，当且仅当C_A在时间C_T时在世界C_W中位于C_P，$\mathscr{Q}$是一个LD结构。C_A、C_T、C_P和C_W分别表示C的施事者（agent）、时间、空间位置和世界。

卡普兰区分语境（context）和情境（circumstance）。情境由世界和时间组成，可表示为<w, t>。在此基础上，卡普兰提出"真"的定义：

给定一个语句Φ和语境C，语句是否为真是参照可能世界w和时间t来确定的。

本章的第四篇论文《档案变化语义学》（File Change Semantics）

以名词短语的指称为切入点，从信息建立与更新的角度讨论句子之间的信息关联以及名词短语的回指问题。针对句子中限定名词短语（definite noun phrases，简称限定NP）和非限定NP（indefinite noun phrases）的意义差别，克里斯托弗森Christophersen，叶斯泊森Jespersen 等传统语法学家提出"关于限定性的熟悉理论（the Familiarity Theory of Definiteness）"，认为限定NP指称一个已知的事物，非限定NP引入新事物。根据这一理论，限定NP和非限定NP都是指称表达式（referring expressions）。但是自然语言中存在NP无指称对象的情况，这一理论无法解决限定和非限定NP的非指称性用法问题。以（1）和（2）为例：

(1) Every cat ate its food.

(2) John didn't see a cat.

在（1）中，*its*并不指某只猫。在（2）中，非限定NP *a cat*没有指称对象。

针对这一问题，卡尔图宁（Karttunen, 1968, 1976）提出"语篇所指（discourse referent）"的概念，认为限定NP选择一个已知语篇所指，非限定NP引入一个新的语篇所指。这样的处理避免考虑一个NP是否在现实中有指称对象的问题，"语篇所指"概念的提出能解决一个NP即使没有指称对象也会有语篇所指的情况，由此避免了熟悉理论关于指称性（referentiality）的问题。

海姆（Heim）将语篇所指的思想引入对限定和非限定NP以及回指（anaphor）等语言与世界关系问题的研究，并提出与其具有类似性质的概念"档案卡片（file cards）"，由此发展为"File Change Semantics（档案变化语义学）"。其核心思想是，语言理解是一个"档案夹"的建立和更新的过程，一个更新的"档案夹"是由已知档案夹受新信息影响而变化的结果。非限定NP引入一个新的档案卡片，限定NP使我们更新（update）一个已知的档案卡片。例如：

(3) a. A woman was bitten by a dog.

　　　b. She hit it.

　　　c. It jumped over a fence.

在话语开始之前，听话者只拥有一个空档案夹F_0，里面没有卡片。

当说话者说出（3a）时，听话者把两张卡片放入档案夹内，并给这两张卡片分别编号为1和2。卡片1和卡片2上的内容如下图所示。这个包含两张卡片的档案夹叫F₁。

当说话者说出（3b）时，听话者分别在F₁的两张卡片上增加内容，更新的档案夹叫F₂。如下图所示：

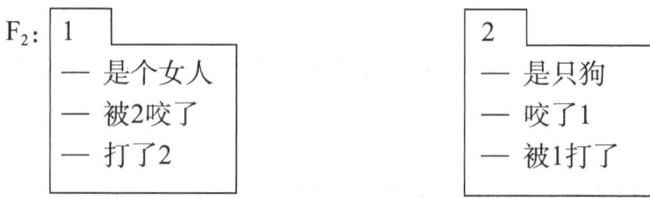

当说话者说出（3c）时，听话者更新卡片2的内容，且建立一张新卡片，并编号为3，这个包含三张卡片的档案夹叫F₃。如图所示：

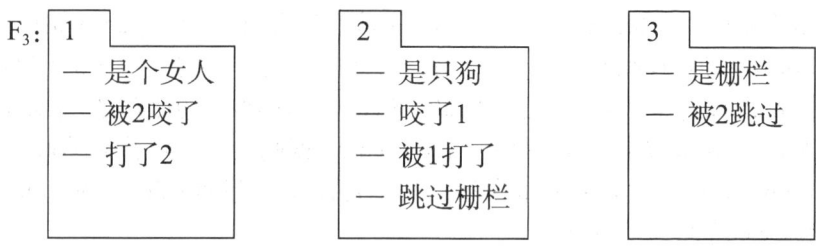

由此可以看出，限定NP和非限定NP的区别在于他们作用于档案夹内容建立或更新。如例（3）所示，话语中出现*a woman*、*a dog*、*a fence*这类非限定NP时，听话者要建立一个新的卡片。话语中出现*she*、*it*这类限定NP时，听话者要更新已有的卡片。

与传统的熟悉理论不同的是，在档案变化语义学中，与"已知"和"新"对立的不是所指，而是档案卡片。档案卡片可以没有描述的指称对象，两张档案卡片也可描述同一个事物，档案卡片还可以建立或删除。和"语篇所指"相比，档案卡片的这种灵活性特征显示出优点，由此避免了熟悉理论遇到的指称问题。

海姆进一步讨论了句法表征、逻辑形式、档案变化潜势以及成真条件之间的关系，如原文中（8）所示。句法表征和句子的逻辑形式是一个对应多个的关系（a one-to-many relation）。逻辑形式被赋予档案变化潜势，档案夹和成真条件相关。

如果一个档案夹和事实相符，则这个档案夹为真。使一个档案夹的内容为真的条件是，档案夹中的个体序列和与之相关的档案卡片的描述相符。例如，对于例（3a），成真条件可表述为：

$<a_1, a_2>$ satisfies F_1 iff a_1 is a woman, a_2 is a dog, and a_2 bite a_1.

当且仅当a_1是个女人，a_2是只狗，且a_2咬了a_1，个体a_1和a_2满足F_1的描述。

由此可见，一个档案夹为真，当且仅当总存在满足（satisfy）档案卡片描述的个体序列，即：

F is true iff Sat (F) $\neq \Phi$ (and false otherwise)

海姆将命题分为不同类型的原子命题（atomic propositions）。一种原子命题是由动词和主语（以及补语）构成，例如 *She hit it* 涉及的命题$[_s$ she$_1$ hit it$_2]$, *A cat arrived* 涉及的命题之一$[_s$ e$_1$ arrived], *Every cat died* 涉及的命题之一$[_s$ e$_1$ died]。另一种原子命题是关于名词性谓词（nominal predicates）的。例如，*A cat arrived* 涉及的命题之一$[_{NP1}$ a cat], *Every cat died* 涉及的命题之一$[_{NP1}$ _ cat]。据此，可将分子命题(molecular propositions) *A cat arrived* 分解为两个直接成分（immediate constituents）$[_{NP1}$ a cat]和$[_s$ e$_1$ arrived]。

逻辑形式被赋予档案变化潜势，它使一个档案夹由F更新为F'，这个档案变化的过程可描述为：

F+p=F'

"+"表示改变档案的操作（the file change operation）。以 *A cat arrived* 为例，改变档案的操作过程是，以一个空档案夹F_0为起点，句子 *A cat arrived* 使我们建立一个包含一种卡片的档案夹，包含一个个体的序列满足这张卡片的描述，即这个个体是 *a cat*，且它 *arrived*。可表示为：

Sat (F_0+p^1) =

= Sat $(F_0 + [_{NP1}$ a cat]$) + [_s$ e_1 arrived]$)$ =

= $\{<b_1>:b_1 \in$ Ext ("cat") and $b_1 \in$ Ext ("arrived")$\}$

海姆由此提出了真值的判断标准：

F是为真的档案夹，P是逻辑形式，如果F+p为真，则相对于F而言p为真；如果F+p为假，则相对于F而言p为假；如果F+p的真值是不明确的，则p无真值。

以建立和更新档案的思想为基础，针对含有不具有照应关系的名词和代词的句子，海姆分析了其档案建立与更新的过程。试比较（4）和（5）：

(4)　Every man who likes a donkey buys it.

(5)　Every man who likes it buys it

与（4）相关的档案建立与更新的过程包含三个步骤。在初始档案夹F的基础上，先要进行两次档案建立和更新的操作，即F'=F+p和F"=F'+q，分别如下所示：

(4a)　Sat (F')=$\{a_{N}\cup b_{(1, 2)}: a_N \in$ Sat (F), b_1 is a man, b_2 is a donkey, and b_1 likes $b_2\}$

(4b)　Sat (F")=$\{a_N\cup b_{(1, 2)}: a_N \in$ Sat (F), b_1 is a man, b_2 is a donkey, b_1 likes b_2, and b_1 buys $b_2\}$

在以上两步的基础上，进行第三步档案更新操作，如下所示：

(4c)　Sat $(F+P^2)=\begin{cases} \text{Sat (F), if every man who likes a donkey buys it.} \\ \Phi, \text{otherwise} \end{cases}$

与（5）相关的档案建立与更新的过程也包含三个步骤。在初始档案夹F的基础上，先要进行两次档案建立和更新的操作，即F'=F+p和F"=F'+q，分别如下所示：

(5a)　Sat (F')=$\{a_N\cup b_{(1, 2)} \in A^{NU(1, 2)}: a_N \in$ Sat (F), b_1 is a man, and b_1 likes $b_2\}$

(5b) Sat (F'')={ $a_N \cup b_{(1, 2)}$: $a_N \in$ Sat (F), b_1 is a man, b_1 likes b_2, and b_1 buys b_2}

在以上两步的基础上，进行第三步档案更新操作，如下所示：

(5c) Sat (F+p^3)={ $a_N \in$ Sat (F): for every b_1, if b_1 is a man and b_1 likes a_2, then b_1 buys a_2}.

比较（4a）（4b）（4c）和（5a）（5b）（5c），可以看出（4）和（5）的区别。对于（4）的初始档案夹F，1和2不在F的域（原文用DomF表示）内，更新的档案夹F'则包含1和2，即*a man*和*a donkey he likes*。第二次更新的档案夹F''则包含"每个""人"和"驴"的对子，即"每个喜欢驴的人"就是"每个买驴的人"。对于（5）的初始档案夹F，1不在F的域内，但2在F的域内。更新的档案夹F'包含1和2，即*a man*和*it*。因为a_2属于原始档案夹F，即2∈Dom（F），a_N包含成员a_2 F'和F''中的a_N都包含a_2，第二次更新的档案夹F''则包含"每个""人"和"a_2"的对子，即"喜欢a_2的人"就是"买a_2的人"。由此可见，（4）涉及对"人—驴"对子的全称量化，而（5）量化的是喜欢某个"固定的"个体的人。

海姆的理论关注的是涉及词语照应关系的句子之间的意义关系问题，它与坎普（Kamp, 1993）的话语表征理论（Discourse Representation Theory）之间的共性在于，对句子的语义分析采用信息更新的动态方法，都强调语境对句子意义的影响，特别是非限定NP和代词的所指都依赖于语境。

第五篇文章是刘易斯（Lewis, 1979）的《语言游戏中的记分》（Scorekeeping in a Language Game），作者讨论言语交际过程中判断句子真值和可接受性需要遵循的"适应规则（the rule of accommodation）"。

例如，在言语交际过程中，存在听话者建立、修改、取消等调整预设的情况，预设（presupposition）是有规则的（rule-governed）。作者指出，语句的可接受性和预设相关。例如：

(1) The king of France is bald.

(2) Even George Lakoff could win.

(3) *All Fred's children are asleep, and Fred has children.

(4) Fred has children, and all Fred's children are asleep.

（1）预设法国有且仅有一个国王。（2）预设George Lakoff不是有优势的选手。（3）之所以不可接受，是因为前半句预设Fred有孩子，所以后半句是冗余的。颠倒一下顺序，（4）就变得可以接受。

刘易斯提出预设的适应规则（the rule of accommodation for presupposition）：

如果在某个时间t说出话语需要预设p，且p在t之前并不存在，p便在t成为新的预设。

刘易斯认为，一个陈述的真值和判断的相对标准有关，要在某个时间使陈述为真，有时需调整在此之前提出的判断标准。作者提出，句子的可接受性和一个奴隶被允许和不被允许做的行为的规定具有相似性，由此提出允许性的适应规则（the rule of accommodation for permissibility）。例如，一个奴隶主规定奴隶的行为有的是被允许的，有的是不被允许的。在不同时间，允许和不允许的界限有可能会发生改变。如果奴隶主在时间t改变允许和不允许行为之间的界限，奴隶主在时间t关于允许行为陈述的真假就依赖于调整后允许和不允许行为之间的界限在哪里。允许性的适应规则是：

在时间t奴隶主陈述允许的行为，如果根据在t之前的允许与不允许行为之间的界限，奴隶主的陈述为假，需调整t之前允许与不允许行为之间的界限，以使奴隶主在t的陈述为真。

句子可接受性不是一个静态的概念，而是在具体言语事件中动态认识的。为了使语句具有真值或可接受性，言语交际要遵循如下"适应规则"：

在时间t，要使语句可被接受或为真，且这个语句在t之前在r范围内没有值，在其他条件不变的情况下，在时间t和在r范围内语句需获得真值。

除了以上论述的预设的适应规则和允许性的适应规则以外，言语交际的"适应规则"还包括其他六种情况：

[1]描述语所指事物在语篇中的显著度（salience）是不固定的，为了使句子可被接受或为真，语言使用者在言语交际过程中需调整事物的显著度。对于涉及限定描述语（definite descriptions）的句子，限定描述语的凸显度通过语篇和话语手段体现。罗素认为"the F"表达的是有且仅有F。例如，当且仅当"法国国王"是唯一存在的符合句（1）描述的人，*the king of France*指法国国王。

刘易斯认为，"the F"指语篇中最显著的F。例如：

(5)　The pig is grunting, but the pig with floppy ears is not grunting.

(6)　The dog got in a fight with another dog.

（5）中的*the pig*指语篇中两头猪中的一头，（6）中的*the dog*指语篇中两条狗中的一条，*the pig*和*the dog*都不具有罗素所说的唯一性。（5）表示，*the pig*凸显度最高，它在发出呼噜声，而*the pig with floppy ear*凸显度则相对低些，这头猪没有发出呼噜声。（6）表示，*the dog*的凸显度最高，*another dog*的凸显度则相对较低。

　　某一事物在语篇中的凸显度是相对的，且不是固定的，听话者会为了句子的可接受性（acceptability），通过一些会话手段（conversational means）调整其在语篇中的凸显度。相对凸显度的适应规则是：

　　　　如果在话语的某个时间t，需要x比y显著度高，且在t之前x并不比y显著度高，那么，在其他条件不变的情况下，在时间t，x比y的显著度高。

　　[2]指称角度（point of reference）不是固定不变的，为了使句子可被接受或为真，语言使用者在言语交际过程中需调整指称的角度。指称角度不同，预设不同，"来"和"去"，"这里"和"那里"等表达触发（trigger）不同的预设。例如：

(7)　The beggars are coming to town.

　　句（7）预设指称的角度是在镇上，否则就不会用*coming*。
　　指称的角度不是固定的，听话者会为了句子的可接受性，调整指称的角度。例如：

(8)　When the beggars came to town, the rich folk went to the shore. But soon the beggars came after them, so they went home.

　　句（8）的指称角度就是从一个地方转移到另一个地方。
　　而且，指称的角度也有可能不是完全确定的地点。例如：

(9)　After the beggars came to town, they held a meeting. All of them came

外教社学术阅读文库——语义学经典论文选读

to the square. Afterwards they went to another part of town.

句（9）中第一个句子的指称角度是镇上，但没有具体的位置。相比之下，第二个句子的指称角度就比较确定，是在市镇广场。

[3]判断的标准不是固定的，为了使句子可被接受或为真，语言使用者在言语交际过程中需调整判断的标准。同一种表达在具有不同精确标准（standards of precision）的语境中可接受度不同，也就是说，精确的标准不同，句子的可接受度不同。例如，如果Fred处于"秃"与"不秃"的界点，（10）为真还是为假？

(10) Fred is bald.

句（10）没有绝对确定的真值。它的真值取决于我们怎样界定"秃顶"，取决于我们怎样划分"秃顶"和"非秃顶"的界限。如果采取严格的划分标准，则句（10）为真，如果采取宽松的划分标准，句（10）为假。

由此可见，判断语句的可接受性和我们在具体语境中采取的判断标准的精确程度有关，真值和预设相关。例如：

(11) The pavement is flat.
(12) The desk is flatter than the pavement.

如果采取宽松的判断标准，句（11）为真。如果采取比句（11）严格的判断标准，句（12）为真。但是，句（12）为真并不改变句（11）在其所处语境中为真的事实。

[4]情态词表达的可能性程度是不固定的，为了使句子可被接受或为真，语言使用者在言语交际过程中需调整可能性的程度。must、can等可表达绝对可能性，也可表达相对可能性。因相关的可能性和被忽略的可能性之间的界限不同，含情态词的句子在不同情况下真值不同。例如，在一般情况下，某个语句为真。而当考虑到被忽略的某种可能的情况时，这个语句则为假。

[5]我们也可将行为句看作和非行为句一样，即都看作是具有真值条件的句子。例如：

(13) I hereby name this ship the Generalissimo Stalin.

这个行为句在合适的条件下为真。合适的条件包括：说话者通过口头宣布的方式给船命名，在说话者说出这句话之前这条船没有这个名字等。

[6]计划（planning）和预设一样，也有"适应规则"。言语交流中，语句需要合适的预设。同样，为了语句的可接受性，说话者说出计划时也需要提供合适的条件。"如果……那么……然后"等表达计划的结构往往涉及预设，但计划和预设有别，前者往往涉及人为的努力，后者涉及先决条件。例如，我们计划从加工场偷钵，我们说出以下语句：

(14) Then you drive the getaway car up to the side gate.

对于句（14），"车"是计划的，"门"是预设的。

综上所述，刘易斯在本文中主要关注存在性预设（例如，*The present king of France is bald*）和由某些词语或结构（例如，限定描述语、情态词、"如果……"等）触发的预设，讨论言语交际过程中判断句子真值或可接受性所遵循的规则，指出真值具有动态性，和预设、视角、标准等诸多因素相关。

1   p是A cat arrived的逻辑形式，如原文（12b）所标。
2   p是句子Every man who likes a donkey buys it的逻辑形式，如原文(31')所示。
3   p'是句子Every man who likes it buys it的逻辑形式，如原文(32')所示。

Truth and Meaning

Donald Davidson

It is conceded by most philosophers of language, and recently even by some linguists, that a satisfactory theory of meaning must give an account of how the meanings of sentences depend upon the meanings of words. Unless such an account could be supplied for a particular language, it is argued, there would be no explaining the fact that we can learn the language: no explaining the fact that, on mastering a finite vocabulary and a finitely stated set of rules, we are prepared to produce and to understand any of a potential infinitude of sentences. I do not dispute these vague claims, in which I sense more than a kernel of truth.[1] Instead I want to ask what it is for a theory to give an account of the kind adumbrated.

One proposal is to begin by assigning some entity as meaning to each word (or other significant syntactical feature) of the sentence; thus we might assign Theaetetus to 'Theaetetus' and the property of flying to 'flies' in the sentence 'Theaetetus flies'. The problem then arises how the meaning of the sentence is generated from these meanings. Viewing concatenation as a significant piece of syntax, we may assign to it the relation of participating in or instantiating; however, it is obvious that we have here the start of an infinite regress. Frege sought to avoid the regress by saying that the entities corresponding to predicates (for example) are 'unsaturated' or 'incomplete' in contrast to the entities that correspond to names, but this doctrine seems to label a difficulty rather than solve it.

The point will emerge if we think for a moment of complex singular terms, to which Frege's theory applies along with sentences. Consider the expression 'the father of Annette'; how does the meaning of the whole depend on the meaning

143

of the parts? The answer would seem to be that the meaning of 'the father of' is such that when this expression is prefixed to a singular term the result refers to the father of the person to whom the singular term refers. What part is played, in this account, by the unsaturated or incomplete entity for which 'the father of' stands? All we can think to say is that this entity 'yields' or 'gives' the father of x as value when the argument is x, or perhaps that this entity maps people onto their fathers. It may not be clear whether the entity for which 'the father of' is said to stand performs any genuine explanatory function as long as we stick to individual expressions; so think instead of the infinite class of expressions formed by writing 'the father of' zero or more times in front of 'Annette'. It is easy to supply a theory that tells, for an arbitrary one of these singular terms, what it refers to: if the term is 'Annette' it refers to Annette, while if the term is complex, consisting of 'the father of' prefixed to a singular term t, then it refers to the father of the person to whom t refers. It is obvious that no entity corresponding to 'the father of' is, or needs to be, mentioned in stating this theory.

It would be inappropriate to complain that this little theory *uses* the words 'the father of' in giving the reference of expressions containing those words. For the task was to give the meaning of all expressions in a certain infinite set on the basis of the meaning of the parts; it was not in the bargain also to give the meanings of the atomic parts. On the other hand, it is now evident that a satisfactory theory of the meanings of complex expressions may not require entities as meanings of all the parts. It behooves us then to rephrase our demand on a satisfactory theory of meaning so as not to suggest that individual words must have meanings at all, in any sense that transcends the fact that they have a systematic effect on the meanings of the sentences in which they occur. Actually, for the case at hand we can do better still in stating the criterion of success: what we wanted, and what we got, is a theory that entails every sentence of the form 't refers to x' where 't' is replaced by a structural description[2] of a singular term, and 'x' is replaced by that term itself. Further, our theory accomplishes this without appeal to any semantical concepts beyond the basic 'refers to'. Finally, the theory clearly suggests an effective procedure for determining, for any singular term in its universe, what that term refers to.

A theory with such evident merits deserves wider application. The device proposed by Frege to this end has a brilliant simplicity: count predicates as a special case of functional expressions, and sentences as a special case of complex singular terms. Now, however, a difficulty looms if we want to continue in our present (implicit) course of identifying the meaning of a singular term with its reference. The difficulty follows upon making two reasonable assumptions: that logically equivalent singular terms have the same reference; and that a singular term does not change its reference if a contained singular term is replaced by another with the same reference. But now suppose that 'R' and 'S' abbreviate any two sentences alike in truth value. Then the following four sentences have the same reference:

(1) R
(2) $\hat{x}(x = x.R) = \hat{x}(x = x)$
(3) $\hat{x}(x = x.S) = \hat{x}(x = x)$
(4) S

For (1) and (2) are logically equivalent, as are (3) and (4), while (3) differs from (2) only in containing the singular term '$\hat{x}(x = x.S)$' where (2) contains '$\hat{x}(x = x.R)$' and these refer to the same thing if S and R are alike in truth value. Hence any two sentences have the same reference if they have the same truth value.[3] And if the meaning of a sentence is what it refers to, all sentences alike in truth value must be synonymous — an intolerable result.

Apparently we must abandon the present approach as leading to a theory of meaning. This is the natural point at which to turn for help to the distinction between meaning and reference. The trouble, we are told, is that questions of reference are, in general, settled by extra-linguistic facts, questions of meaning not, and the facts can conflate the references of expressions that are not synonymous. If we want a theory that gives the meaning (as distinct from reference) of each sentence, we must start with the meaning (as distinct from reference) of the parts.

Up to here we have been following in Frege's footsteps; thanks to him, the path is well known and even well worn. But now, I would like to suggest, we have reached an impasse: the switch from reference to meaning leads to no useful account of how the meanings of sentences depend upon the meanings of the words (or other structural features) that compose them. Ask, for example, for the meaning of 'Theaetetus flies'. A Fregean answer might go something like this: given the meaning of 'Theaetetus' as argument, the meaning of 'flies' yields the meaning of 'Theaetetus flies' as value. The vacuity of this answer is obvious. We wanted to know what the meaning of 'Theaetetus flies' is; it is no progress to be told that it is the meaning of 'Theaetetus flies'. This much we knew before any theory was in sight. In the bogus account just given, talk of the structure of the sentence and of the meanings of words was idle, for it played no role in producing the given description of the meaning of the sentence.

The contrast here between a real and pretended account will be plainer still if we ask for a theory, analogous to the miniature theory of reference of singular terms just sketched, but different in dealing with meanings in place of references. What analogy demands is a theory that has as consequences all sentences of the form 's means m' where 's' is replaced by a structural description of a sentence and 'm' is replaced by a singular term that refers to the meaning of that sentence; a theory, moreover, that provides an effective method for arriving at the meaning of an arbitrary sentence structurally described. Clearly some more articulate way of referring to meanings than any we have seen is essential if these criteria are to be met.[4] Meanings as entities, or the related concept of synonymy, allow us to formulate the following rule relating sentences and their parts: sentences are synonymous whose corresponding parts are synonymous ('corresponding' here needs spelling out of course). And meanings as entitles may, in theories such as Frege's, do duty, on occasion as references, thus losing their status as entities distinct from references. Paradoxically, the one thing meanings do not seem to do is oil the wheels of a theory of meaning — at least as long as we require of such a theory that it non-trivially give the meaning of every sentence in the language. My objection to meanings in the theory of meaning is not that they are abstract or that their identity conditions are obscure, but that they have no demonstrated use.

This is the place to scotch another hopeful thought. Suppose we have a satisfactory theory of syntax for our language, consisting of an effective method of telling, for an arbitrary expression, whether or not it is independently meaningful (i.e., a sentence), and assume as usual that this involves viewing each sentence as composed, in allowable ways, out of elements drawn from a fixed finite stock of atomic syntactical elements (roughly, words). The hopeful thought is that syntax, so conceived, will yield semantics when a dictionary giving the meaning of each syntactic atom is added. Hopes will be dashed, however, if semantics is to comprise a theory of meaning in our sense, for knowledge of the structural characteristics that make for meaningfulness in a sentence, plus knowledge of the meanings of the ultimate parts, does not add up to knowledge of what a sentence means. The point is easily illustrated by belief sentences. Their syntax is relatively unproblematic. Yet, adding a dictionary does not touch the standard semantic problem, which is that we cannot account for even as much as the truth conditions of such sentences on the basis of what we know of the meanings of the words in them. The situation is not radically altered by refining the dictionary to indicate which meaning or meanings an ambiguous expression bears in each of its possible contexts; the problem of belief sentences persists after ambiguities are resolved.

The fact that recursive syntax with dictionary added is not necessarily recursive semantics has been obscured in some recent writing on linguistics by the intrusion of semantic criteria into the discussion of purportedly syntactic theories. The matter would boil down to a harmless difference over terminology if the semantic criteria were clear; but they are not. While there is agreement that it is the central task of semantics to give the semantic interpretation (the meaning) of every sentence in the language, nowhere in the linguistic literature will one find, so far as I know, a straightforward account of how a theory performs this task, or how to tell when it has been accomplished. The contrast with syntax is striking. The main job of a modest syntax is to characterize *meaningfulness* (or sentencehood). We may have as much confidence in the correctness of such a characterization as we have in the representativeness of our sample and our ability to say when particular expressions are meaningful (sentences). What clear and analogous task and test exist for semantics?[5]

We decided a while back not to assume that parts of sentences have meanings except in the ontologically neutral sense of making a systematic contribution to the meaning of the sentences in which they occur. Since postulating meanings has netted nothing, let us return to that insight. One direction in which it points is a certain holistic view of meaning. If sentences depend for their meaning on their structure, and we understand the meaning of each item in the structure only as an abstraction from the totality of sentences in which it features, then we can give the meaning of any sentence (or word) only by giving the meaning of every sentence (and word) in the language. Frege said that only in the context of a sentence does a word have meaning; in the same vein he might have added that only in the context of the language does a sentence (and therefore a word) have meaning.

This degree of holism was already implicit in the suggestion that an adequate theory of meaning must entail *all* sentences of the form 's means m'. But now, having found no more help in meanings of sentences than in meanings of words, let us ask whether we can get rid of the troublesome singular terms supposed to replace 'm' and to refer to meanings. In a way, nothing could be easier: just write 's means that p', and imagine 'p' replaced by a sentence. Sentences, as we have seen, cannot name meanings, and sentences with 'that' prefixed are not names at all, unless we decide so. It looks as though we are in trouble on another count, however, for it is reasonable to expect that in wrestling with the logic of the apparently non-extensional 'means that' we will encounter problems as hard as, or perhaps identical with, the problems our theory is out to solve.

The only way I know to deal with this difficulty is simple, and radical. Anxiety that we are enmeshed in the intensional springs from using the words 'means that' as filling between description of sentence and sentence, but it may be that the success of our venture depends not on the filling but on what it fills. The theory will have done its work if it provides, for every sentence *s* in the language under study, a matching sentence (to replace '*p*') that, in some way yet to be made clear, 'gives the meaning' of *s*. One obvious candidate for matching sentence is just *s* itself, if the object language is contained in the metalanguage; otherwise a translation of *s* in the metalanguage. As a final bold step, let us try treating the position occupied by '*p*' extensionally: to implement this, sweep away the obscure 'means that', provide the sentence that replaces '*p*' with a proper sentential connective, and supply the description that replaces '*s*' with its own predicate. The plausible result is

(T)   *s* is *T* if and only if *p*.

What we require of a theory of meaning for a language *L* is that without appeal to any (further) semantical notions it place enough restrictions on the predicate 'is *T*' to entail all sentences got from schema *T* when '*s*' is replaced by a structural description of a sentence of *L* and '*p*' by that sentence.

Any two predicates satisfying this condition have the same extension[6], so if the metalanguage is rich enough, nothing stands in the way of putting what I am calling a theory of meaning into the form of an explicit definition of a predicate 'is

T. But whether explicitly defined or recursively characterized, it is clear that the sentences to which the predicate 'is *T*' applies will be just the true sentences of *L*, for the condition we have placed on satisfactory theories of meaning is in essence Tarski's Convention *T* that tests the adequacy of a formal semantical definition of truth.[7]

The path to this point has been tortuous, but the conclusion may be stated simply: a theory of meaning for a language *L* shows "how the meanings of sentences depend upon the meanings of words" if it contains a (recursive) definition of truth-in-*L*. And, so far at least, we have no other idea how to turn the trick. It is worth emphasizing that the concept of truth played no ostensible role in stating our original problem. That problem, upon refinement, led to the view that an adequate theory of meaning must characterize a predicate meeting certain conditions. It was in the nature of a discovery that such a predicate would apply exactly to the true sentences. I hope that what I am doing may be described in part as defending the philosophical importance of Tarski's semantical concept of truth. But my defense is only distantly related, if at all, to the question whether the concept Tarski has shown how to define is the (or a) philosophically interesting conception of truth, or the question whether Tarski has cast any light on the ordinary use of such words as 'true' and 'truth'. It is a misfortune that dust from futile and confused battles over these questions has prevented those with a theoretical interest in language — philosophers, logicians, psychologists, and linguists alike — from recognizing in the semantical concept of truth (under whatever name) the sophisticated and powerful foundation of a competent theory of meaning.

There is no need to suppress, of course, the obvious connection between a definition of truth of the kind Tarski has shown how to construct, and the concept of meaning. It is this: the definition works by giving necessary and sufficient conditions for the truth of every sentence, and to give truth conditions is a way of giving the meaning of a sentence. To know the semantic concept of truth for a language is to know what it is for a sentence — any sentence — to be true, and this amounts, in one good sense we can give to the phrase, to understanding the language. This at any rate is my excuse for a feature of the present discussion that is apt to shock old hands: my freewheeling use of the word 'meaning', for what I call a theory of meaning has after all turned out to make no use of meanings, whether of sentences or of words. Indeed, since a Tarski-type truth definition supplies all we have asked so far of a theory of meaning, it is clear that such a theory falls comfortably within what Quine terms the 'theory of reference' as distinguished from what he terms the 'theory of meaning'. So much to the good for what I call a theory of meaning, and so much, perhaps, against my so calling it.[8]

A theory of meaning (in my mildly perverse sense) is an empirical theory, and its ambition is to account for the workings of a natural language. Like any theory, it may be tested by comparing some of its consequences with the facts. In the present case this is easy, for the theory has been characterized as issuing in an infinite flood of sentences each giving the truth conditions of a sentence; we only need to ask, in selected cases, whether what the theory avers to be the truth conditions for a sentence really are. A typical test case might involve deciding whether the sentence 'Snow is white' *is* true if and only if snow is white. Not all cases will be so simple (for reasons to be sketched), but it is evident that this sort of test does not invite counting noses. A sharp conception of what constitutes a theory in this domain furnishes an exciting context for raising deep questions about when a theory of language is correct and how it is to be tried. But the difficulties are theoretical, not practical. In application, the trouble is to get a theory that comes close to working; anyone can tell whether it is right.[9] One can see why this is so. The theory reveals nothing new about the conditions under which an individual sentence is true; it does not make those conditions any clearer than the sentence itself does. The work of the theory is in relating the known truth conditions of each sentence to those aspects ('words') of the sentence that recur in other sentences, and can be assigned identical roles in other sentences. Empirical power in such a theory depends on success in recovering the structure of a very complicated ability — the ability to speak and understand a language. We can tell easily enough when particular pronouncements of the theory comport with our understanding of the language; this is consistent with a feeble insight into the design of the machinery of our linguistic accomplishments.

The remarks of the last paragraph apply directly only to the special case where it is assumed that the language for which truth is being characterized is part of the language used and understood by the characterizer. Under these circumstances, the framer of a theory will as a matter of course avail himself when he can of the built-in convenience of a metalanguage with a sentence guaranteed equivalent to each sentence in the object language. Still, this fact ought not to con us into thinking a theory any more correct that entails "'Snow is white' is true if and only if snow is white" than one that entails instead:

(S) 'Snow is white' is true if and only if grass is green,

provided, of course, we are as sure of the truth of (S) as we are of that of its more celebrated predecessor. Yet (S) may not encourage the same confidence that a theory that entails it deserves to be called a theory of meaning.

The threatened failure of nerve may be counteracted as follows. The grotesqueness of (S) is in itself nothing against a theory of which it is a consequence, provided the theory gives the correct results for every sentence (on the basis of its structure, there being no other way). It is not easy to see how (S) could be party to such an enterprise, but if it were — if, that is, (S) followed from a characterization of the predicate 'is true' that led to the invariable pairing of truths with truths and falsehoods with falsehoods — then there would not, I think, be anything essential to the idea of meaning that remained to be captured.

What appears to the right of the biconditional in sentences of the form '*s* is true if and only if *p*' when such sentences are consequences of a theory of truth plays its role in determining the meaning of s not by pretending synonymy but by adding one more brush-stroke to the picture which, taken as a whole, tells what there is to know of the meaning of *s*; this stroke is added by virtue of the fact that the sentence that replaces '*p*' is true if and only if *s* is.

It may help to reflect that (S) is acceptable, if it is, because we are independently sure of the truth of 'Snow is white' and 'Grass is green'; but in cases where we are unsure of the truth of a sentence, we can have confidence in a characterization of the truth predicate only if it pairs that sentence with one we have good reason to believe equivalent. It would be ill advised for someone who had any doubts about the color of snow or grass to accept a theory that yielded (S), even if his doubts were of equal degree, unless he thought the color of the one was tied to the color of the other. Omniscience can obviously afford more bizarre theories of meaning than ignorance; but then, omniscience has less need of communication.

It must be possible, of course, for the speaker of one language to construct a theory of meaning for the speaker of another, though in this case the empirical test of the correctness of the theory will no longer be trivial. As before, the aim of theory will he an infinite correlation of sentences alike in truth. But this time the theory-builder must not be assumed to have direct insight into likely equivalences between his own tongue and the alien. What he must do is find out, however he can, what sentences the alien holds true in his own tongue (or better, to what degree he holds them true). The linguist then will attempt to construct a characterization of truth-for-the-alien which yields, so far as possible, a mapping of sentences held true (or false) by the alien onto sentences held true (or false) by the linguist. Supposing no perfect fit is found, the residue of sentences held true translated by sentences held false (and vice versa) is the margin for error (foreign or domestic). Charity in interpreting the words and thoughts of others is unavoidable in another direction as well: just as we must maximize agreement, or risk not making sense of what the alien is talking about, so we must maximize the self-consistency we attribute to him, on pain of not understanding *him*. No single principle of optimum charity emerges; the constraints therefore determine no single theory. In a theory of radical translation (as Quine calls it) there is no completely disentangling questions of what the alien means from questions of what he believes. We do not know what someone means unless we know what he believes; we do not know what someone believes unless we know what he means. In radical translation we are able to break into this circle, if only incompletely, because we can sometimes tell that a person accedes to a sentence we do not understand.[10]

In the past few pages I have been asking how a theory of meaning that takes the form of a truth definition can be empirically tested, and have blithely ignored the prior question whether there is any serious chance such a theory can be given for a natural language. What are the prospects for a formal semantical theory of a natural language? Very poor, according to Tarski; and I believe most logicians, philosophers of language and linguists agree.[11] Let me do what I can to dispel the pessimism. What I can in a general and programmatic way, of course; for here the proof of the pudding will certainly be in the proof of the right theorems.

Tarski concludes the first section of his classic essay on the concept of truth in formalized languages with the following remarks, which he italicizes:

> *The very possibility of a consistent use of the expression 'true sentence' which is in harmony with the laws of logic and the spirit of everyday language seems to be very questionable, and consequently the same doubt attaches to the possibility of*

constructing a correct definition of this expression.[12]

Late in the same essay, he returns to the subject:

> The concept of truth (as well as other semantical concepts) when applied
> to colloquial language in conjunction with the normal laws of logic leads
> inevitably to confusions and contradictions. Whoever wishes, in spite of all
> difficulties, to pursue the semantics of colloquial language with the help of
> exact methods will be driven first to undertake the thankless task of a reform
> of this language. He will find it necessary to define its structure, to overcome
> the ambiguity of the terms which occur in it, and finally to split the language
> into a series of languages of greater and greater extent, each of which stands
> in the same relation to the next in which a formalized language stands to its
> metalanguage. It may, however be doubted whether the language of everyday
> life, after being 'rationalized' in this way, would still preserve its naturalness
> and whether it would not rather take on the characteristic features of the
> formalized languages.[13]

Two themes emerge: that the universal character of natural languages leads
to contradiction (the semantic paradoxes), and that natural languages are too
confused and amorphous to permit the direct application of formal methods.
The first point deserves a serious answer, and I wish I had one. As it is, I will say
only why I think we are justified in carrying on without having disinfected this
particular source of conceptual anxiety. The semantic paradoxes arise when the
range of the quantifiers in the object language is too generous in certain ways.
But it is not really clear how unfair to Urdu or to Hindi it would be to view
the range of their quantifiers as insufficient to yield an explicit definition of
'true-in-Urdu' or 'true-in-Hindi'. Or, to put the matter in another, if not more
serious way, there may in the nature of the case always be something we grasp
in understanding the language of another (the concept of truth) that we cannot
communicate to him. In any case, most of the problems of general philosophical
interest arise within a fragment of the relevant natural language that may be
conceived as containing very little set theory. Of course, these comments do not
meet the claim that natural languages are universal. But it seems to me this claim,
now that we know such universality leads to paradox, is suspect.

Tarski's second point is that we would have to reform a natural language out of all recognition before we could apply formal semantical methods. If this is true, it is fatal to my project, for the task of a theory of meaning as I conceive it is not to change, improve or reform a language, but to describe and understand it. Let us look at the positive side. Tarski has shown the way to giving a theory for interpreted formal languages of various kinds; pick one as much like English as possible. Since this new language has been explained in English and contains much English we not only may, but I think must, view it as part of English for those who understand it. For this fragment of English we have, ex hypothesi, a theory of the required sort. Not only that, but in interpreting this adjunct of English in old English we necessarily gave hints connecting old and new. Wherever there are sentences of old English with the same truth conditions as sentences in the adjunct we may extend the theory to cover them. Much of what is called for is just to mechanize as far as possible what we now do by art when we put ordinary English into one or another canonical notation. The point is not that canonical notation is better than the rough original idiom, but rather that if we know what idiom the canonical notation is canonical *for*, we have as good a theory for the idiom as for its kept companion.

Philosophers have long been at the hard work of applying theory to ordinary language by the device of matching sentences in the vernacular with sentences for which they have a theory. Frege's massive contribution was to show how 'all', 'some', 'every', 'each', 'none', and associated pronouns, in some of their uses, could be tamed; for the first time, it was possible to dream of a formal semantics for a significant part of a natural language. This dream came true in a sharp way with the work of Tarski. It would be a shame to miss the fact that as a result of these two magnificent achievements, Frege's and Tarski's, we have gained a deep insight into the structure of our mother tongues. Philosophers of a logical bent have tended to start where the theory was and work out toward the complications of natural language. Contemporary linguists, with an aim that cannot easily be seen to be different, start with the ordinary and work toward a general theory. If either party is successful, there must be a meeting. Recent work by Chomsky and others is doing much to bring the complexities of natural languages within the scope of serious semantic theory. To give an example: suppose success in giving the truth conditions for some significant range of sentences in the active voice. Then with a formal procedure for transforming each such sentence into a corresponding sentence in the passive voice, the theory of truth could be extended in an obvious way to this new set of sentences.[14]

One problem touched on in passing by Tarski does not, at least in all its manifestations, have to be solved to get ahead with theory: the existence in natural languages of 'ambiguous terms'. As long as ambiguity does not affect grammatical form, and can be translated, ambiguity for ambiguity, into the metalanguage, a truth definition will not tell us any lies. The trouble, for systematic semantics, with the phrase 'believes that' in English is not its vagueness, ambiguity, or unsuitability for incorporation in a serious science: let our metalanguage be English, and all *these* problems will be translated without loss or gain into the metalanguage. But the central problem of the logical grammar of 'believes that' will remain to haunt us.

The example is suited to illustrating another, and related, point, for the discussion of belief sentences has been plagued by failure to observe a fundamental distinction between tasks: uncovering the logical grammar or form of sentences (which is in the province of a theory of meaning as I construe it), and the analysis of individual words or expressions (which are treated as primitive by the theory). Thus Carnap, in the first edition of *Meaning and Necessity*, suggested we render 'John believes that the earth is round' as 'John responds affirmatively to "the earth is round" as an English sentence'. He gave this up when Mates pointed out that John might respond affirmatively to one sentence and not to another, no matter how close in meaning. But there is a confusion here from the start. The semantic structure of a belief sentence, according to this idea of Carnap's, is given by a three-place predicate with places reserved for expressions referring to a person, a sentence, and a language. It is a different sort of problem entirely to attempt an analysis of this predicate, perhaps along behavioristic lines. Not least among the merits of Tarski's conception of a theory of truth is that the purity of method it demands of us follows from the formulation of the problem itself, not from the self-imposed restraint of some adventitious philosophical puritanism.

I think it is hard to exaggerate the advantages to philosophy of language of bearing in mind this distinction between questions of logical form or grammar, and the analysis of individual concepts. Another example may help advertise the point.

If we suppose questions of logical grammar settled, sentences like 'Bardot is good' raise no special problems for a truth definition. The deep differences between descriptive and evaluative (emotive, expressive, etc.) terms do not show here. Even if we hold there is some important sense in which moral or evaluative sentences do not have a truth value (for example, because they cannot be 'verified'), we ought not to boggle at "'Bardot is good' is true if and only if Bardot is good"; in a theory of truth, this consequence should follow with the rest, keeping track, as must be done, of the semantic location of such sentences in the language as a whole — of their relation to generalizations, their role in such compound sentences as 'Bardot is good and Bardot is foolish', and so on. What is special to evaluative words is simply not touched: the mystery is transferred from the word 'good' in the object language to its translation in the metalanguage.

But 'good' as it features in 'Bardot is a good actress' is another matter. The problem is not that the translation of this sentence is not in the metalanguage — let us suppose it is. The problem is to frame a truth definition such that "'Bardot is a good actress' is true if and only if Bardot is a good actress" — and all other sentences like it — are consequences. Obviously 'good actress' does not mean 'good and an actress'. We might think of taking 'is a good actress' as an unanalyzed predicate. This would obliterate all connection between 'is a good actress' and 'is a good mother', and it would give us no excuse to think of 'good', in these uses, as a word or semantic element. But worse, it would bar us from framing a truth definition at all, for there is no end to the predicates we would have to treat as logically simple (and hence accommodate in separate clauses in the definition of satisfaction): 'is a good companion to dogs', 'is a good twenty-eight-year-old conversationalist', and so forth. The problem is not peculiar to the case: it is the problem of attributive adjectives generally.

It is consistent with the attitude taken here to deem it usually a strategic error to undertake philosophical analysis of words or expressions which is not preceded by or at any rate accompanied by the attempt to get the logical grammar straight. For how can we have any confidence in our analyses of words like 'right', 'ought', 'can', and 'obliged', or the phrases we use to talk of actions, events, and causes, when we do not know what (logical, semantical) parts of speech we have to deal with? I would say much the same about studies of the "logic" of these and other words, and the sentences containing them. Whether the effort and ingenuity that has gone into the study of deontic logics, modal logics, imperative and erotetic logics has been largely futile or not cannot be known until we have acceptable semantic analyses of the sentences such systems purport to treat. Philosophers and logicians sometimes talk or work as if they were free to choose between, say, the truth-functional conditional and others, or free to introduce non-truth-functional sentential operators like 'Let it be the case that' or 'It ought to be the case that'. But in fact the decision is crucial. When we depart from idioms we can accomodate in a truth definition, we lapse into (or create) language for which we have no coherent semantical account — that is, no account at all of how such talk can be integrated into the language as a whole.

To return to our main theme: we have recognized that a theory of the kind proposed leaves the whole matter of what individual words mean exactly where it was. Even when the metalanguage is different from the object language, the theory exerts no pressure for improvement, clarification or analysis of individual words, except when, by accident of vocabulary, straightforward translation fails. Just as synonomy, as between expressions, goes generally untreated, so also synonomy of sentences, and analyticity. Even such sentences as 'A vixen is a female fox' bear no special tag unless it is our pleasure to provide it. A truth definition does not distinguish between analytic sentences and others, except for sentences that owe their truth to the presence alone of the constants that give the theory its grip on structure: the theory entails not only that these sentences are true but that they will remain true under all significant rewritings of their non-logical parts. A notion of logical truth thus given limited application, related notions of logical equivalence and entailment will tag along. It is hard to imagine how a theory of meaning could fail to read a logic into its object language to this degree; and to the extent that it does, our intuitions of logical truth, equivalence and entailment may he called upon in constructing and testing the theory.

I turn now to one more, and very large, fly in the ointment: the fact that the same sentence may at one time or in one mouth be true and at another time or in another mouth be false. Both logicians and those critical of formal methods here seem largely (though by no means universally) agreed that formal semantics and logic are incompetent to deal with the disturbances caused by demonstratives. Logicians have often reacted by downgrading natural language and trying to show how to get along without demonstratives; their critics react by downgrading logic and formal semantics. None of this can make me happy: clearly demonstratives cannot be eliminated from a natural language without loss or radical change, so there is no choice but to accommodate theory to them.

No logical errors result if we simply treat demonstratives as constants;[15] neither do any problems arise for giving a semantic truth definition. "'I am wise' is true if and only if I am wise," with its bland ignoring of the demonstrative element in 'I' comes off the assembly line along with "'Socrates is wise' is true if and only if Socrates is wise" with *its* bland indifference to the demonstrative element in 'is wise' (the tense).

What suffers in this treatment of demonstratives is not the definition of a truth predicate but the plausibility of the claim that what has been defined is truth. For this claim is acceptable only if the speaker and circumstances of utterance of each sentence mentioned in the definition is matched by the speaker and circumstances of utterance of the truth definition itself. It could also be fairly pointed out that part of understanding demonstratives is knowing the rules by which they adjust their reference to circumstance; assimilating demonstratives to constant terms obliterates this feature. These complaints can be met, I think, though only by a fairly far-reaching revision in the theory of truth. I shall barely suggest how this could be done, but bare suggestion is all that is needed: the idea is technically trivial, and quite in line with work being done on the logic of the tenses.[16]

We could take truth to be a property, not of sentences, but of utterances, or speech acts, or ordered triples of sentences, times and persons; but it is simplest just to view truth as a relation between a sentence, a person, and a time. Under such treatment, ordinary logic as now read applies as usual, but only to sets of sentences relativized to the same speaker and time; further logical relations between sentences spoken at different times and by different speakers may be articulated by new axioms. Such is not my concern. The theory of meaning undergoes a systematic but not puzzling change: corresponding to each expression with a demonstrative element there must in the theory be a phrase that relates the truth conditions of sentences in which the expression occurs to changing times and speakers. Thus the theory will entail sentences like the following:

'I am tired' is true as (potentially) spoken by p at t if and only if p is tired at t.

'That book was stolen' is true as (potentially) spoken by p at t if and only if the book demonstrated by p at t is stolen prior to t.[17]

Plainly, this course does not show how to eliminate demonstratives; for example, there is no suggestion that 'the book demonstrated by the speaker' can be substituted ubiquitously for 'that book' *salva veritate*. The fact that demonstratives are amenable to formal treatment ought greatly to improve hopes for a serious semantics of natural language, for it is likely that many outstanding puzzles, such as the analysis of quotations or sentences about propositional attitudes, can be solved if we recognize a concealed demonstrative construction.

Now that we have relativized truth to times and speakers, it is appropriate to glance back at the problem of empirically testing a theory of meaning for an alien tongue. The essence of the method was, it will be remembered, to correlate held-true sentences with held-true sentences by way of a truth definition, and within the bounds of intelligible error. Now the picture must be elaborated to allow for the fact that sentences are true, and held true, only relative to a speaker and a time. The real task is therefore to translate each sentence by another that is true for the same speakers at the same times. Sentences with demonstratives obviously yield a very sensitive test of the correctness of a theory of meaning, and constitute the most direct link between language and the recurrent macroscopic objects of human interest and attention.[18]

In this paper I have assumed that the speakers of a language can effectively determine the meaning or meanings of an arbitrary expression (if it has a meaning), and that it is the central task of a theory of meaning to show how this is possible. I have argued that a characterization of a truth predicate describes the required kind of structure, and provides a clear and testable criterion of an adequate semantics for a natural language. No doubt there are other reasonable demands that may be put on a theory of meaning. But a theory that does no more than define truth for a language comes far closer to constituting a complete theory of meaning than superficial analysis might suggest; so, at least, I have urged.

Since I think there is no alternative, I have taken an optimistic and programmatic view of the possibilities for a formal characterization of a truth predicate for a natural language. But it must be allowed that a staggering list of difficulties and conundrums remains. To name a few: we do not know the logical form of counterfactual or subjunctive sentences, nor of sentences about probabilities and about causal relations; we have no good idea what the logical role of adverbs is, nor the role of attributive adjectives; we have no theory for mass terms like 'fire', 'water', and 'snow', nor for sentences about belief, perception, and intention, nor for verbs of action that imply purpose. And finally, there are all the sentences that seem not to have truth values at all: the imperatives, optatives, interrogatives, and a host more. A comprehensive theory of meaning for a natural language must cope successfully with each of these problems.

Notes

An earlier version of this paper was read at the Eastern Division meeting of the American Philosophical Association in December, 1966; the main theme traces back to an unpublished paper delivered to the Pacific Division of the American Philosophical Association in 1953. Present formulations owe much to John Wallace, with whom I have discussed these matters since 1962. My research was supported by the National Science Foundation.

1   Elsewhere I have urged that it is a necessary condition, if a language is to be learnable, that it have only a finite number of semanticat primitives: see "Theories of Meaning and Learnable Languages," in *Proceeding of the 1964 International Congress for Logic, Methodology and Philosophy of Science* (North-Holland Publishing Company, Amsterdam, 1965), pp. 383–394.

2   A 'structural description' of an expression describes the expression as a concatenation of elements drawn from a fixed finite list (for example of words or letters).

3   The argument is essentially Frege's. See A. Church, *Introduction to Mathematical Logic,* Vol. 1 (Princeton 1956), pp. 24–25. It is perhaps worth mentioning that the argument does not depend on any particular identification of the entities to which sentences are supposed to refer.

4   It may be thought that Church, in "A Formulation of the Logic of Sense and Denotation," in *Structure, Method and Meaning: Essays in Honor of H. M. Sheffer,* ed. Henle, Kallen and Langer (Liberal Arts Press, New York, 1951), pp. 3–24, has given a theory of meaning that makes essential use of meanings as entities. But this is not the case: Church's logics of sense and denotation are interpreted as being about meanings, but they do not mention expressions and so cannot of course be theories of meaning in the sense now under discussion.

5   For a recent and instructive statement of the role of semantics in linguistics, see Noam Chomsky, "Topics in the Theory of Generative Grammar," in

Current Trends in Linguistics, ed. Thomas A. Sebeok, Vol. 3 (The Hague, 1966). In this article, Chomsky (1) emphasizes the central importance of semantics in linguistic theory, (2) argues for the superiority of transformational grammars over phrase structure grammars largely on the grounds that, although phrase structure grammars may be adequate to define sentence-hood for (at least) some natural languages, they are inadequate as a foundation for semantics, and (3) comments repeatedly on the "rather primitive state" of the concepts of semantics and remarks that the notion of semantic interpretation "still resists any deep analysis."

6 Assuming, of course, that the extension of these predicates is limited to the sentences of *L.*

7 Alfred Tarski, "The Concept of Truth in Formalized Language," in *Logic, Semantics, Metamathematics* (Oxford, 1956), pp. 152–278.

8 But Quine may be quoted in support of my usage: "in point of *meaning* ... a word may be said to be determined to whatever extent the truth or falsehood of its contexts is determined." "Truth by Convention," first published in 1936; now in *The Ways of Paradox* (New York, 1966), p. 82. Since a truth definition determines the truth value of every sentence in the object language (relative to a sentence in the metalanguage), it determines the meaning of every word and sentence. This would seem to justify the title "Theory of Meaning."

9 To give a single example: it is clearly a count in favor of a theory that it entails "'Snow is white' is true if and only if snow is white." But to contrive a theory that entails this (and works for all related sentences) is not trivial. I do not know a theory that succeeds with this very case (the problem of "mass terms").

10 This sketch of how a theory of meaning for an alien tongue can be tested obviously owes its inspiration to Quine's account of radical translation in chapter 2 of *Word and Object* (New York, 1960). In suggesting that an acceptable theory of radical translation take the form of a recursive characterization of truth, I go beyond anything explicit in Quine. Toward the end of this paper, in the discussion of demonstratives, another strong point of agreement will turn up.

11 So far as I am aware, there has been very little discussion of whether a formal truth definition can be given for a natural language. But in

a more general vein, several people have urged that the concepts of formal semantics be applied to natural language. See, for example, the contributions of Yehoshua Bar-Hillel and Evert Beth to *The Philosophy of Rudolph Carnap* (ed. by Paul A. Schilpp), La Salle, Ill., 1963, and Bar-Hillel's (1964) "Logical Syntax and Semantics," *Language* 30: 230–237.

12   Tarski, ibid., p. 165.

13   Ibid., p. 267.

14   The rapprochement I prospectively imagine between transformational grammar and a sound theory of meaning has been much advanced by a recent change in the conception of transformational grammar described in Chomsky in (1966). The structures generated by the phrase-structure part of the grammar, it has been realized for some time, are those suited to semantic interpretation; but this view is inconsistent with the idea, held by Chomsky until recently, that recursive operations are introduced only by the transformation rules. Chomsky now believes the phrase-structure rules are recursive. Since languages to which formal semantic methods directly and naturally apply are ones for which a (recursive) phrase-structure grammar is appropriate, it is clear that Chomsky's present picture of the relation between the structures generated by the phrase-structure part of the grammar, and the sentences of the language, is very much like the picture many logicians and philosophers have had of the relation between the richer formalized languages and ordinary language. (In these remarks I am indebted to Bruce Vermazen.)

15   Quine has good things to say about this in *Methods of Logic* (New York, 1950), § 8.

16   For an up-to-date bibliography, and discussion, see A. N. Prior, *Past, Present, and Future* (Oxford, 1967).

17   There is more than an intimation of this approach to demonstratives and truth in Austin's 1950 article "Truth", reprinted in *Philosophical Papers* (Oxford, 1961). See pp. 89–90.

18   These remarks clearly derive from Quine's idea that "occasion sentences" (those with a demonstrative element) must play a central role in constructing a translation manual.

The Logical Form of Action Sentences

Donald Davidson

Strange goings on! Jones did it slowly, deliberately, in the bathroom, with a knife, at midnight. What he did was butter a piece of toast. We are too familiar with the language of action to notice at first an anomaly: the 'it' of 'Jones did it slowly, deliberately, ...' seems to refer to some entity, presumably an action, that is then characterized in a number of ways. Asked for the logical form of this sentence, we might volunteer something like, 'There is an action x such that Jones did x slowly and Jones did x deliberately and Jones did x in the bathroom, ...' and so on. But then we need an appropriate singular term to substitute for 'x'. In fact we know Jones buttered a piece of toast. And, allowing a little slack, we can substitute for 'x' and get 'Jones buttered a piece of toast slowly and Jones buttered a piece of toast deliberately and Jones buttered a piece of toast in the bathroom ...' and so on. The trouble is that we have nothing here we would ordinarily recognize as a singular term. Another sign that we have not caught the logical form of the sentence is that in this last version there is no implication that any one action was slow, deliberate, and in the bathroom, though this is clearly part of what is meant by the original.

The present Essay is devoted to trying to get the logical form of simple sentences about actions straight. I would like to give an account of the logical or grammatical role of the parts or words of such sentences that is consistent with the entailment relations between such sentences and with what is known of the role of those same parts or words in other (non-action) sentences. I take this enterprise to be the same as showing how the meanings of action sentences depend on their structure. I am not concerned with the meaning analysis of logically simple expressions in so far as this goes beyond the question of logical form. Applied to the case at hand, for example, I am not concerned with the meaning of 'deliberately' as opposed, perhaps, to 'voluntary'; but I am interested in the logical role of both these words. To give another illustration of the distinction I have in mind: we need not view the difference between 'Joe believes that there is life on Mars' and 'Joe knows that there is life on Mars' as a difference in logical form. That the second, but not the first, entails 'There is life on Mars' is plausibly a logical truth; but it is a truth that emerges only when we consider the meaning analysis of 'believes' and 'knows'. Admittedly there is something arbitrary in how much of logic to pin on logical form. But limits are set if our interest is in giving a coherent and constructive account of meaning: we must uncover enough structure to make it possible to state, for an arbitrary sentence, how its meaning depends on that structure, and we must not attribute more structure than such a theory of meaning can accommodate. Consider the sentence:

(1)　Jones buttered the toast slowly, deliberately, in the bathroom, with a knife, at midnight.

Despite the superficial grammar we cannot, I shall argue later, treat the 'deliberately' on a par with the other modifying clauses. It alone imputes intention, for of course Jones may have buttered the toast slowly, in the bathroom, with a knife, at midnight, and quite unintentionally, having mistaken the toast for his hairbrush which was what he intended to butter. Let us, therefore, postpone discussion of the 'deliberately' and its intentional kindred.

'Slowly', unlike the other adverbial clauses, fails to introduce a new entity (a place, an instrument, a time), and also may involve a special difficulty. For suppose we take 'Jones buttered the toast slowly' as saying that Jones's buttering of the toast was slow; is it clear that we can equally well say of Jones's action, no matter how we describe it, that it was slow? A change in the example will help. Susan says, 'I crossed the Channel in fifteen hours.' 'Good grief, that was slow.' (Notice how much more naturally we say 'slow' here than 'slowly'. But what was slow, what does 'that' refer to? No appropriate singular term appears in 'I crossed the Channel in fifteen hours.') Now Susan adds, 'But I swam.' 'Good grief, that was fast.' We do not withdraw the claim that it was a slow crossing;

this is consistent with its being a fast swimming. Here we have enough to show, I think, that we cannot construe 'It was a slow crossing' as 'It was slow and it was a crossing' since the crossing may also be a swimming that was not slow, in which case we would have 'It was slow and it was a crossing and it was a swimming and it was not slow.' The problem is not peculiar to talk of actions, however. It appears equally when we try to explain the logical role of the attributive adjectives in 'Grundy was a short basketball player, but a tall man', and 'This is a good memento of the murder, but a poor steak knife.' The problem of attributives is indeed a problem about logical form, but it may be put to one side here because it is not a problem for action sentences alone.

We have decided to ignore, for the moment at least, the first two adverbial modifiers in

(1)   and may now deal with the problem of the logical form of:
(2)   Jones buttered the toast in the bathroom with a knife at midnight.

Anthony Kenny, who deserves the credit for calling explicit attention to this problem,[1] points out that most philosophers today would, as a start, analyse this sentence as containing a five-place predicate with the argument places filled in the obvious ways with singular terms or bound variables. If we go on to analyse 'Jones buttered the toast' as containing a two-place predicate, 'Jones buttered the toast in the bathroom' as containing a three-place predicate, and so forth, we obliterate the logical relations between these sentences, namely that (2) entails the others. Or, to put the objection another way, the original sentences contain a common syntactic element ('buttered') which we intuitively recognize as relevant to the meaning relations of the sentences. But the proposed analyses show no such common element.

Kenny rejects the suggestion that 'Jones buttered the toast' be considered as elliptical for 'Jones buttered the toast somewhere with something at some time', which would restore the wanted entailments, on the ground that we could never be sure how many standby positions to provide in each predicate of action. For example, couldn't we add to (2) the phrase 'by holding it between the toes of his left foot'? Still, this adds a place to the predicate only if it differs in meaning from, 'while holding it between the toes of his left foot', and it is not quite clear that this is so. I am inclined to agree with Kenny that we cannot view verbs of action as usually containing a large number of standby positions, but I do not have what I consider a knock-down argument. (A knock-down argument would consist in a method for increasing the number of places indefinitely.)[2] Kenny proposes that we may exhibit the logical form of (2) in somewhat the following manner:

(3)   Jones brought it about that the toast was buttered in the bathroom with a
       knife at midnight.

Whatever the other merits in this proposal (I shall consider some of them presently) it is clear that it does not solve the problem Kenny raises. For it is, if anything, even more obscure how (3) entails 'Jones brought it about that the toast was buttered' or 'The toast was buttered' then how (2) entails 'Jones buttered the toast.' Kenny seems to have confused two different problems. One is the problem of how to represent the idea of agency: it is this that prompts Kenny to assign 'Jones' a logically distinguished role in

(3)   The other is the problem of the 'variable polyadicity' (as Kenny calls it) of
       action verbs. And it is clear that this problem is independent of the first,
       since it arises with respect to the sentences that replace 'p' in 'x brings it
       about that p'.

If I say I bought a house downtown that has four bedrooms, two fireplaces, and a glass chandelier in the kitchen, it's obvious that I can go on forever adding details. Yet the logical form of the sentences I use presents no problem (in this respect). It is something like, 'There is a house such that I bought it, it is downtown, it has four bedrooms, ...' and so forth. We can tack on a new clause at will because the iterated relative pronoun will carry the reference back to the same entity as often as desired. (Of course we know how to state this much more precisely.) Much of our talk of action suggests the same idea: that there are such things as actions, and that a sentence like (2) describes the action in a number of ways. 'Jones did it with a knife.' 'Please tell me more about it.' The 'it' here doesn't refer to Jones or the knife, but to what Jones did — or so it seems.

    '... it is in principle always open to us, along various lines, to describe or refer to "what I did" in so many ways,' writes Austin.[3] Austin is obviously leery of the apparent singular term, which he puts in scare quotes; yet the grammar of his sentence requires a singular term. Austin would have had little sympathy, I imagine, for the investigation into logical form I am undertaking here, though the demand that underlies it, for an intuitively acceptable and constructive theory of meaning, is one that begins to appear in the closing chapters of How to Do Things with Words. But in any case, Austin's discussion of excuses illustrates over and over the fact that our common talk and reasoning about actions is most naturally analysed by supposing that there are such entities.

'I didn't know it was loaded' belongs to one standard pattern of excuse. I do not deny that I pointed the gun and pulled the trigger, nor that I shot the victim. My ignorance explains how it happened that I pointed the gun and pulled the trigger intentionally, but did not shoot the victim intentionally. That the bullet pierced the victim was a consequence of my pointing the gun and pulling the trigger. It is clear that these are two different events, since one began slightly after the other. But what is the relation between my pointing the gun and pulling the trigger, and my shooting the victim? The natural and, I think, correct answer is that the relation is that of identity. The logic of this sort of excuse includes, it seems, at least this much structure: I am accused of doing b, which is deplorable. I admit I did a, which is excusable. My excuse for doing b rests upon my claim that I did not know that a = b.

Another pattern of excuse would have me allow that I shot the victim intentionally, but in self-defence. Now the structure includes something more. I am still accused of b (my shooting the victim), which is deplorable. I admit I did c (my shooting the victim in self-defence), which is excusable. My excuse for doing b rests upon my claim that I knew or believed that b = c.

The story can be given another twist. Again I shoot the victim, again intentionally. What I am asked to explain is my shooting of the bank president (d), for the victim was that distinguished gentleman. My excuse is that I shot the escaping murderer (e), and surprising and unpleasant as it is, my shooting the escaping murderer and my shooting of the bank president were one and the same action (e = d), since the bank president and the escaping murderer were one and the same person. To justify the 'since' we must presumably think of 'my shooting of x' as a functional expression that names an action when the 'x' is replaced by an appropriate singular term. The relevant reasoning would then be an application of the principle $x = y \rightarrow fx = fy$.

Excuses provide endless examples of cases where we seem compelled to take talk of 'alternative descriptions of the same action' seriously, i.e., literally. But there are plenty of other contexts in which the same need presses. Explaining an action by giving an intention with which it was done provides new descriptions of the action: I am writing my name on a piece of paper with the intention of writing a cheque with the intention of paying my gambling debt. List all the different descriptions of my action. Here are a few for a start: I am writing my name. I am writing my name on a piece of paper. I am writing my name on a piece of paper with the intention of writing a cheque. I am writing a cheque. I am paying my gambling debt. It is hard to imagine how we can have a coherent theory of action unless we are allowed to say that each of these sentences is made true by the same action. Redescription may supply the motive ('I was getting my revenge'), place the action in the context of a rule ('I am castling'), give the outcome ('I killed him'), or provide evaluation ('I did the right thing').

According to Kenny, as we just noted, action sentences have the form 'Jones brought it about that p.' The sentence that replaces 'p' is to be in the present tense, and it describes the result that the agent has wrought: it is a sentence 'newly true of the patient'.[4] Thus, 'The doctor removed the patient's appendix' must be rendered, 'The doctor brought it about that the patient has no appendix.' By insisting that the sentence that replaces 'p' describe a terminal state rather than an event, it may be thought that Kenny can avoid the criticism made above that the problem of the logical form of action sentences turns up within the sentence that replaces 'p': we may allow that 'The patient has no appendix' presents no relevant problem. The difficulty is that neither will the analysis stand in its present form. The doctor may bring it about that the patient has no appendix by turning the patient over to another doctor who performs the operation; or by running the patient down with his Lincoln Continental. In neither case would we say the doctor removed the patient's appendix. Closer approximations to a correct analysis might be, 'The doctor brought it about that the doctor has removed the patient's appendix' or perhaps, 'The doctor brought it about that the patient has had his appendix removed by the doctor.' One may still have a few doubts, I think, as to whether these sentences have the same truth conditions as 'The doctor removed the patient's appendix.' But in any case it is plain that in these versions, the problem of the logical form of action sentences does turn up in the sentences that replace 'p': 'The patient has had his appendix removed by the doctor' or 'The doctor has removed the patient's appendix' are surely no easier to analyse than 'The doctor removed the patient's appendix.' By the same token, 'Cass walked to the store' can't be given as 'Cass brought it about that Cass is at the store', since this drops the idea of walking. Nor is it clear that 'Cass brought it about that Cass is at the store and is there through having walked' will serve; but in any case, the contained sentence is again worse than what we started with.

It is not easy to decide what to do with 'Smith coughed.' Should we say 'Smith brought it about that Smith is in a state of just having coughed'? At best this would be correct only if Smith coughed on purpose.

The difficulty in Kenny's proposal that we have been discussing may perhaps be put this way: he wants to represent every (completed) action in terms only of the agent, the notion of bringing it about that a state of affairs obtains, and the state of affairs brought about by the agent. But many action sentences yield no description of the state of affairs brought about by the action except that it is the state of affairs brought about by that action. A natural move, then, is to allow that the sentence that replaces 'p' in 'x brings it about that p' may (or perhaps must) describe an event.

If I am not mistaken, Chisholm has suggested an analysis that at least permits the sentence that replaces 'p' to describe (as we are allowing ourselves to say) an event.[5] His favoured locution is 'x makes p happen', though he uses such variants as 'x brings it about that p' or 'x makes it true that p'. Chisholm speaks of the entities to which the expressions that replace 'p' refer as 'states of affairs', and explicitly adds that states of affairs may be changes or events (as well as 'unchanges'). An example Chisholm provides is this: if a man raises his arm, then we may say he makes it happen that his arm goes up. I do not know whether Chisholm would propose 'Jones made it happen that Jones's arm went up' as an analysis of 'Jones raised his arm', but I think the proposal would be wrong because although the second of these sentences does perhaps entail the first, the first does not entail the second. The point is even clearer if we take as our example 'Jones made it happen that Jones batted an eyelash' (or some trivialvariant), and this cannot be called progress in uncovering the logical form of 'Jones batted an eyelash.'

There is something else that may puzzle us about Chisholm's analysis of action sentences, and it is independent of the question what sentence we substitute for 'p'. Whatever we put for 'p', we are to interpret it as describing some event. It is natural to say, I think, that whole sentences of the form 'x makes it happen that p' also describe events. Should we say that these events are the same event, or that they are different? If they are the same event, as many people would claim (perhaps including Chisholm), then no matter what we put for 'p', we cannot have solved the general problem of the logical form of sentences about actions until we have dealt with the sentences that can replace 'p'. If they are different events, we must ask how the element of agency has been introduced into the larger sentence though it is lacking in the sentence for which 'p' stands; for each has the agent as its subject. The answer Chisholm gives, I think, is that the special notion of making it happen that he has in mind is intentional, and thus to be distinguished from simply causing something to happen. Suppose we want to say that Alice broke the mirror without implying that she did it intentionally. Then Chisholm's special idiom is not called for; but we could say, 'Alice caused it to happen that the mirror broke.' Suppose we now want to add that she did it intentionally. Then the Chisholm-sentence would be: 'Alice made it happen that Alice caused it to happen that the mirror broke.' And now we want to know, what is the event that the whole sentence reports, and that the contained sentence does not? It is, apparently, just what used to be called an act of the will. I will not dredge up the standard objections to the view that acts of the will are special events distinct from, say, our bodily movements, and perhaps the causes of them. But even if Chisholm is willing to accept such a view, the problem of the logical form of the sentences that can replace 'p' remains, and these describe the things people do as we describe them when we do not impute intention.

A somewhat different view has been developed with care and precision by von Wright.[6] In effect, von Wright puts action sentences into the following form: 'x brings it about that a state where p changes into a state where q'. Thus the important relevant difference between von Wright's analysis and the ones we have been considering is the more complex structure of the description of the change or event the agent brings about: where Kenny and Chisholm were content to describe the result of the change, von Wright includes also a description of the initial state.

Von Wright is interested in exploring the logic of change and action and not, at least primarily, in giving the logical form of our common sentences about acts or events. For the purposes of his study, it may be very fruitful to think of events as ordered pairs of states. But I think it is also fairly obvious that this does not give us a standard way of translating or representing the form of most sentences about acts and events. If I walk from San Francisco to Pittsburgh, for example, my initial state is that I am in San Francisco and my terminal state is that I am in Pittsburgh; but the same is more pleasantly true if I fly. Of course, we may describe the terminal state as my having walked to Pittsburgh from San Francisco, but then we no longer need the separate statement of the initial state. Indeed, viewed as an analysis of ordinary sentences about actions, von Wright's proposal seems subject to all the difficulties I have already outlined plus the extra one that most action sentences do not yield a non-trivial description of the initial state (try 'He circled the field', 'He recited the Odyssey', 'He flirted with Olga').

In two matters, however, it seems to me von Wright suggests important and valuable changes in the pattern of analysis we have been considering, or at least in our interpretation of it. First, he says that an action is not an event, but rather the bringing about of an event. I do not think this can be correct. If I fall down, this is an event whether I do it intentionally or not. If you thought my falling was an accident and later discovered I did it on purpose, you would not be tempted to withdraw your claim that you had witnessed an event. I take von Wright's refusal to call an action an event to reflect the embarrassment we found to follow if we say that an act is an event, taking agency to be introduced by a phrase like 'brings it about that'. The solution lies, however, not in distinguishing acts from events, but in finding a different logical form for action sentences. The second important idea von Wright introduces comes in the context of his distinction between generic and individual propositions about events.[7]

The distinction, as von Wright makes it, is not quite clear, for he says both: that an individual proposition differs from a generic one in having a uniquely determined truth value, while a generic proposition has a truth value only when coupled with an occasion; and that, that Brutus killed Caesar is an individual proposition while that Brutus kissed Caesar is a generic proposition, because 'a person can be kissed by another on more than one occasion'. In fact the proposition that Brutus kissed Caesar seems to have a uniquely determined truth value in the same sense that the proposition that Brutus killed Caesar does. But it is, I believe, a very important observation that 'Brutus kissed Caesar' does not, by virtue of its meaning alone, describe a single act.

It is easy to see that the proposals we have been considering concerning the logical form of action sentences do not yield solutions to the problems with which we began. I have already pointed out that Kenny's problem, that verbs of action apparently have 'variable polyadicity', arises within the sentences that can replace 'p' in such formulas as 'x brought it about that p'. An analogous remark goes for von Wright's more elaborate formula. The other main problem may be put as that of assigning a logical form to action sentences that will justify claims that two sentences describe 'the same action'.

Our study of some of the ways in which we excuse, or attempt to excuse, acts shows that we want to make inferences such as this: I flew my spaceship to the Morning Star, the Morning Star is identical with the Evening Star; so, I flew my spaceship to the Evening Star. (My leader told me not to go the Evening Star; I headed for the Morning Star not knowing.) But suppose we translate the action sentences along the lines suggested by Kenny or Chisholm or von Wright. Then we have something like, 'I brought it about that my spaceship is on the Morning Star.' How can we infer, given the well-known identity, 'I brought it about that my spaceship is on the Evening Star'? We know that if we replace 'the Morning Star' by 'the Evening Star' in, 'My spaceship is on the Morning Star' the truth-value will not be disturbed; and so if the occurrence of this sentence in, 'I brought it about that my spaceship is on the Morning Star' is truth-functional, the inference is justified. But of course the occurrence can't be truth-functional: otherwise, from the fact that I brought about one actual state of affairs it would follow that I brought about every actual state of affairs. It is no good saying that after the words 'bring it about that' sentences describe something between truth-values and propositions, say states of affairs. Such a claim must be backed by a semantic theory telling us how each sentence determines the state of affairs it does; otherwise the claim is empty.

Israel Scheffler has put forward an analysis of sentences about choice that can be applied without serious modification to sentences about intentional acts.[8] Scheffler makes no suggestion concerning action sentences that do not impute intention, and so has no solution to the chief problems I am discussing. Nevertheless, his analysis has a feature I should like to mention. Scheffler would have us render, 'Jones intentionally buttered the toast' as, 'Jones made-true a that Jones-buttered-the-toast inscription.' This cannot, for reasons I have urged in detail elsewhere,[9] be considered a finally satisfying form for such sentences because it contains the logically unstructured predicate 'is a that Jones-buttered-the-toast inscription', and there are an infinite number of such semantical primitives in the language. But in one respect, I believe Scheffler's analysis is clearly superior to the others, for it implies that introducing the element of intentionality does not call for a reduction in the content of the sentence that expresses what was done intentionally. This brings out a fact otherwise suppressed, that, to use our example, 'Jones' turns up twice, once inside and once outside the scope of the intensional operator. I shall return to this point.

A discussion of the logical form of action sentences in ordinary language is to be found in the justly famed Chapter VII of Reichenbach's Elements of Symbolic Logic.[10] According to Reichenbach's doctrine, we may transform a sentence like

(4)   Amundsen flew to the North pole

into:

(5) (x) (x consists in the fact that Amundsen flew to the North Pole).

The expression 'is an event that consists in the fact that' is to be viewed as an operator which, when prefixed to a sentence, forms a predicate of events. Reichenbach does not think of (5) as showing or revealing the logical form of (4), for he thinks (4) is unproblematic. Rather he says (5) is logically equivalent to (4). (5) has its counterpart in a more ordinary idiom:

(6)   A flight by Amundsen to the North Pole took place.

Thus Reichenbach seems to hold that we have two ways of expressing the same idea, (4) and (6); they have quite different logical forms, but they are logically equivalent; one speaks literally of events while the other does not. I believe this view spoils much of the merit in Reichenbach's proposal, and that we must abandon the idea that (4) has an unproblematic logical form distinct from that of (5) or (6). Following Reichenbach's formula for putting any action sentence into the form of (5) we translate

(7)   Amunsden flew to the North Pole in May 1926

into:

(8)　(x) (x consists in the fact that Amundsen flew to the North Pole in May 1926).

The fact that (8) entails (5) is no more obvious than that (7) entails (4); what was obscure remains obscure. The correct way to render (7) is:

(9)　(x) (x consists in the fact that Amundsen flew to the North Pole and x took place in May 1926).

But (9) does not bear the simple relation to the standard way of interpreting (7) that (8) does. We do not know of any logical operation on (7) as it would usually be formalised (with a three-place predicate) that would make it logically equivalent to (9). This is why I suggest that we treat (9) alone as giving the logical form of (7). If we follow this strategy, Kenny's problem of the 'variable polyadicity' of action verbs is on the way to solution; there is, of course, no variable polyadicity. The problem is solved in the natural way, by introducing events as entities about which an indefinite number of things can be said.

Reichenbach's proposal has another attractive feature: it eliminates a peculiar confusion that seemed to attach to the idea that sentences like (7) 'describe an event'. The difficulty was that one wavered between thinking of the sentence as describing or referring to that one flight Amundsen made in May 1926, or as describing a kind of event, or perhaps as describing (potentially?) several. As von Wright pointed out, any number of events might be described by a sentence like 'Brutus kissed Caesar.' This fog is dispelled in a way I find entirely persuasive by Reichenbach's proposal that ordinary action sentences have, in effect, an existential quantifier binding the action-variable. When we were tempted into thinking a sentence like (7) describes a single event we were misled: it does not describe any event at all. But if (7) is true, then there is an event that makes it true. (This unrecognized element of generality in action sentences is, I think, of the utmost importance in understanding the relation between actions and desires.)

There are two objections to Reichenbach's analysis of action sentences. The first may not be fatal. It is that as matters stand the analysis may be applied to any sentence whatsoever, whether it deals with actions, events, or anything else. Even '2 + 3 = 5' becomes '(x) (x consists in the fact that 2 + 3 = 5)'. Why not say '2 + 3 = 5' does not show its true colours until put through the machine? For that matter, are we finished when we get to the first step? Shouldn't we go on to '(y) (y consists in the fact that (x) (x consists in the fact that 2 + 3 = 5)'? And so on. It isn't clear on what principle the decision to apply the analysis is based.

The second objection is worse. We have:

(10) (x) (x consists in the fact that I flew my spaceship to the Morning Star)

and

(11) the Morning Star = the Evening Star

and we want to make the inference to

(12) (x) (x consists in the fact that I flew my spaceship to the Evening Star).

The likely principle to justify the inference would be:

(13) (x) (x consists in the fact that S $\longleftrightarrow$ x consists in the fact that S')

where 'S' is obtained from 'S' by substituting, in one or more places, a co-referring singular term. It is plausible to add that (13) holds if 'S' and 'S' are logically equivalent. But (13) and the last assumption lead to trouble. For observing that 'S' is logically equivalent to '$\hat{y}(y = y \ \& \ S) = \hat{y}(y = y)$' we get

(14) (x) (x consists in the fact that S $\longleftrightarrow$ x consists in the fact that ($\hat{y}(y = y \ \& \ S) = (\hat{y}(y = y))$).

Now suppose 'R' is any sentence materially equivalent to 'S': then '$\hat{y}(y = y \ \& \ S)$' and '$\hat{y}(y = y \ \& \ R)$' will refer to the same thing. Substituting in (14) we obtain

(15) (x) (x consists in the fact that S $\longleftrightarrow$ x consists in the fact that ($\hat{y}(y = y \ \& \ R) = \hat{y}(y = y)$),

175

which leads to

(16) (x) (x consists in the fact that S $\longleftrightarrow$ x consists in the fact that R)

when we observe the logical equivalence of 'R' and '$\hat{y}(y = y$ & $R) = \hat{y}(y = y)$'. (16) may be interpreted as saying (considering that the sole assumption is that 'R' and 'S' are materially equivalent) that all events that occur (= all events) are identical. This demonstrates, I think, that Reichenbach's analysis is radically defective.

Now I would like to put forward an analysis of action sentences that seems to me to combine most of the merits of the alternatives already discussed, and to avoid the difficulties. The basic idea is that verbs of action — verbs that say 'what someone did' — should be construed as containing a place, for singular terms or variables, that they do not appear to. For example, we would normally suppose that 'Shem kicked Shaun' consisted in two names and a two-place predicate. I suggest, though, that we think of 'kicked' as a three-place predicate, and that the sentence to be given in this form:

(17) (x) (Kicked (Shem, Shaun, x)).

If we try for an English sentence that directly reflects this form, we run into difficulties. 'There is an event x such that x is a kicking of Shaun by Shem' is about the best I can do, but we must remember 'a kicking' is not a singular term. Given this English reading, my proposal may sound very like Reichenbach's; but of course it has quite different logical properties. The sentence 'Shem kicked Shaun' nowhere appears inside my analytic sentence, and this makes it differ from all the theories we have considered.

The principles that license the Morning Star-Evening Star inference now make no trouble: they are the usual principles of extensionality. As a result, nothing now stands in the way of giving a standard theory of meaning for action sentences, in the form of a Tarski-type truth definition; nothing stands in the way, that is, of giving a coherent and constructive account of how the meanings (truth conditions) of these sentences depend upon their structure. To see how one of the troublesome inferences now goes through, consider (10) rewritten as

外教社学术阅读文库 ｜ 语义学经典论文选读

(18) (*x*) (Flew (I, my spaceship, *x*) & To (the Morning Star, *x*)).

which, along with (11), entails

(19) (*x*) (Flew (I, my spaceship, *x*) & To (the Evening Star, *x*)).

It is not necessary, in representing this argument, to separate off the To-relation; instead we could have taken, 'Flew' as a four-place predicate. But that would have obscured another inference, namely that from (19) to

(20) (*x*) (Flew (I, my spaceship, *x*)).

In general, we conceal logical structure when we treat prepositions as integral parts of verbs; it is a merit of the present proposal that it suggests a way of treating prepositions as contributing structure. Not only is it good to have the inference from (19) to (20); it is also good to be able to keep track of the common element in 'fly to' and 'fly away from' and this of course we cannot do if we treat these as unstructured predicates.

The problem that threatened in Reichenbach's analysis, that there seemed no clear principle on which to refrain from applying the analysis to every sentence, has a natural solution if my suggestion is accepted. Part of what we must learn when we learn the meaning of any predicate is how many places it has, and what sorts of entities the variables that hold these places range over. Some predicates have an event-place, some do not.

In general, what kinds of predicates do have event-places? Without pursuing this question very far, I think it is evident that if action predicates do, many predicates that have little relation to action do. Indeed, the problems we have been mainly concerned with are not at all unique to talk of actions: they are common to talk of events of any kind. An action of flying to the Morning Star is identical with an action of flying to the Evening Star; but equally, an eclipse of the Morning Star is an eclipse of the Evening Star. Our ordinary talk of events, of causes and effects, requires constant use of the idea of different descriptions of the same event. When it is pointed out that striking the match was not sufficient to light it, what is not sufficient is not the event, but the description of it — it was a dry match, and so on.[11] And of course Kenny's problem of 'variable polyadicity', though he takes it to be a mark of verbs of action, is common to all verbs that describe events.

It may now appear that the apparent success of the analysis proposed here is due to the fact that it has simply omitted what is peculiar to action sentences as contrasted with other sentences about events. But I do not think so. The concept of agency contains two elements, and when we separate them clearly, I think we shall see that the present analysis has not left anything out. The first of these two elements we try, rather feebly, to elicit by saying that the agent acts, or does something, instead of being acted upon, or having something happen to him. Or we say that the agent is active rather than passive; and perhaps try to make use of the moods of the verb as a grammatical clue. And we may try to depend upon some fixed phrase like 'brings it about that' or 'makes it the case that'. But only a little thought will make it clear that there is no satisfactory grammatical test for verbs where we want to say there is agency. Perhaps it is a necessary condition of attributing agency that one argument-place in the verb is filled with a reference to the agent as a person; it will not do to refer to his body, or his members, or to anyone else. But beyond that it is hard to go. I sleep, I snore, I push buttons, I recite verses, I catch cold. Also others are insulted by me, struck by me, admired by me, and so on. No grammatical test I know of, in terms of the things we may be said to do, of active or passive mood, or of any other sort, will separate out the cases here where we want to speak of agency. Perhaps it is true that 'brings it about that' guarantees agency; but as we have seen, many sentences that do attribute agency cannot be cast in this grammatical form.

I believe the correct thing to say about this element in the concept of agency is that it is simply introduced by certain verbs and not by others; when we understand the verb we recognize whether or not it includes the idea of an agent. Thus, 'I fought' and 'I insulted him' do impute agency to the person referred to by the first singular term, 'I caught cold' and, 'I had my thirteenth birthday' do not. In these cases, we do seem to have the following test: we impute agency only where it makes sense to ask whether the agent acted intentionally. But there are other cases, or so it seems to me, where we impute agency only when the answer to the question whether the agent acted intentionally is 'yes'. If a man falls down by accident or because a truck knocks him down, we do not impute agency; but we do if he fell down on purpose.[12]

This introduces the second element in the concept of agency, for we surely impute agency when we say or imply that the act is intentional. Instead of speaking of two elements in the concept of agency, perhaps it would be better to say there are two ways we can imply that a person acted as an agent: we may use a verb that implies it directly, or we may use a verb that is non-committal, and add that the act was intentional. But when we take the second course, it is important not to think of the intentionality as adding an extra doing of the agent; we must not make the expression that introduces intention a verb of action. In particular, we cannot use 'intentionally brings it about that' as the expression that introduces intention, for 'brings it about that' is in itself a verb of action, and imputes agency, but it is neutral with respect to the question whether the action was intentional as described.

This leaves the question what logical form the expression that introduces intention should have. It is obvious, I hope, that the adverbial form must be in some way deceptive; intentional actions are not a class of actions, or, to put the point a little differently, doing something intentionally is not a manner of doing it. To say someone did something intentionally is to describe the action in a way that bears a special relation to the beliefs and attitudes of the agent; and perhaps further to describe the action as having been caused by those beliefs and attitudes.[13] But of course to describe the action of the agent as having been caused in a certain way does not mean that the agent is described as performing any further action.

1   Anthony Kenny, Action, Emotion and Will, Ch. VII.
2   Kenny seems to think there is such a method, for he writes, 'If we cast our net widely enough, we can make "Brutus killed Caesar" into a sentence which describes, with a certain lack of specification, the whole history of the world, (op. cit., 160). But he does not show how to make each addition to the sentence one that irreducibly modifies the killing as opposed, say, to Brutus or Caesar, or the place or the time.
3   J. L. Austin, 'A Plea for Excuses', 148.
4   Kenny, op. cit., 181.
5   Roderick Chisholm, 'The Descriptive Element in the Concept of Action'. Also see Chisholm, 'The Ethics of Requirement'.
6   Georg Henrik von Wright, Norm and Action.
7   Op. cit., 23.

8   Israel Scheffler, The Anatomy of Inquiry, 104–5.

9   Donald Davidson, 'Theories of Meaning and Learnable Languages', 390–1.

10   Hans Reichenbach, Elements of Symbolic Logic, sect. 48.

11   See Essay 7 for more on this topic.

12   See Essay 3.

13   See Essay 1.

On the Logic of Demonstratives

David Kaplan

In this paper, I propose to outline briefly a few results of my investigations into the theory of demonstratives: words and phrases whose intension is determined by the contexts of their use. Familiar examples of demonstratives are the nouns 'I', 'you', 'here', 'now', 'that', and the adjectives 'actual' and 'present'. It is, of course, clear that the extension of 'I' is determined by the context — if you and I both say 'I' we refer to different persons. But I would now claim that the intension is also so determined. The intension of an 'eternal' term (like 'The Queen of England in 1973') has generally been taken to be represented by a function which assigns to each possible world the Queen of England in 1973 of that world. Such functions would have been called *individual concepts* by Camap. It has been thought by some — myself among others — that by analogy, the intension of "I" could be represented by a function from speakers to individuals (in fact, the identity function). And similarly, that the intensions of 'here' and 'now' would be represented by (identity) functions on places and times. The role of contextual factors in determining the extension (with respect to such factors) of a demonstrative was thought of as analogous to that of a possible world in determining the extension of 'The Queen of England in 1973' (with respect to that possible world). Thus an enlarged view of an intension was derived. The intension of an expression was to be represented by a function from certain factors to the extension of the expression (with respect to those factors). Originally such factors were simply possible worlds, but as it was noticed that the so-called tense operators exhibited a structure highly analogous to that of the modal operators, the factors with respect to which an extension was to be determined were enlarged to include moments of time. When it was noticed that contextual factors were required to determine the extension of sentences containing demonstratives, a still more general notion was developed and called an 'index'. The extension of an expression was to be determined with respect to an index. The intension of an expression was that function which assigned to every index, the extension at that index. Here is a typical passage.

The above example supplies us with a statement whose truth-value is not constant but varies as a function of $i \in I$. This situation is easily appreciated in the context of time-dependent statements; that is, in the case where I represents the instants of time. Obviously the same statement can be true at one moment and false at another. For more general situations one must not think of the $i \in I$ as anything as simple as instants of time or even possible worlds. In general we will have

$$i = (w, t, p, a, ...)$$

where the index i has many *coordinates:* for example, w is a *world,* t is a *time, p* = (x, y, z) is a (3-dimensional) *position* in the world, a is an *agent,* etc. All these coordinates can be varied, possibly independently, and thus affect the truth values of statements which have indirect reference to these coordinates. (From the Advice of a prominent logician.)

A sentence ϕ was taken to be logically true if true at every index (in every 'structure'), and $\Box\phi$ was taken to be true at a given index (in a given structure) just in case ϕ was true at every index (in that structure).[1] Thus the familiar principle of modal generalization: if $\models\phi$, then $\models\Box\phi$, is validated.

This view, in its treatment of demonstratives, now seems to me to have been technically wrong (though perhaps correctable by minor modification) and, more importantly, conceptually misguided.

Consider the sentence

(1) I am here now.

It is obvious that for many choices of index — i.e. for many quadruples $<w, x, p, t>$ where w is a possible world, x is a person, p is a place, and t is a time —

(1) will be false. In fact, (1) is true only with respect to those indices $<w, x, p, t>$ which are such that in the world w, x is located at p at the time t. Thus (1) fares about on a par with

(2)   David Kaplan is in Los Angeles on April 21,1973.

(2)   is contingent, and so is (1).

But here we have missed something essential to our understanding of demonstratives. Intuitively, (1) is deeply, and in some sense universally, true. One need only understand the meaning of (1) to know that it cannot be uttered falsely. No such guarantees apply to (2). A *Logic of Demonstratives* which does not reflect this intuitive difference between (1) and (2) has bypassed something essential to the logic of demonstratives.

Here is a proposed correction. Let the class of indices be narrowed to include only the *proper* ones — namely, those $<w, x, p, t>$ *such that in the world w, x is located at p at the time t*. Such a move may have been intended originally since improper indices are like impossible worlds; no such contexts *could* exist and thus there is no interest in evaluating the extensions of expressions with respect to them. Our reform has the consequence that (1) comes out, correctly, to be logically true. Now consider

(3)   □I am here now.

Since the contained sentence (namely (1)) is true at every proper index, (3) also is true at every proper index and thus also is logically true. (As would be expected by the aforementioned principle of modal generalization.)

But (3) should not be *logically* true, since it is false. It is certainly *not* necessary that I be here now. But for several contingencies, I would be working in my garden now, or even writing this in a location outside of Los Angeles.

Perhaps enough has now been said to indicate that there are difficulties in the attempt to assimilate the role of a *context* in a logic of demonstratives to that of a *possible world* in the familiar modal logics or a *moment of time* in the familiar tense logics.

I believe that the source of the difficulty lies in a conceptual confusion between two kinds of meaning. Ramifying Frege's distinction between sense and denotation, I would add two varieties of sense: content and character. The content of an expression is always taken *with respect to* a given context of use. Thus when I say

(4)   I was insulted yesterday.

a specific content — *what I said* — is expressed. Your utterance of the same sentence, or mine on another day, would not express the same content. What is important to note is that it is not just the truth value that may change; what is said is itself different. Speaking today, my utterance of (4) will have a content roughly equivalent to that which

(5)   David Kaplan is insulted on April 20,1973.

would have been spoken by you or anyone at any time. Since (5) contains no demonstratives, its content is the same with respect to all contexts. This content is what Carnap called an 'intension' and what, I believe, has been often referred to as a 'proposition'. So my theory is that different contexts for (4) produce not just different truth values, but different propositions.

Turning now to character, I call that component of the sense of an expression which determines how the content is determined by the context, the 'character' of an expression. Just as contents (or intensions) can be represented by functions from possible worlds to extensions, so characters can be represented by functions from contexts to contents. The character of 'I' would then be represented by *the function (or rule, if you prefer) which assigns to each context that content which is represented by the constant function from possible worlds to the agent of the context.* The latter function has been called an 'individual concept'. Note that the character of 'I' is represented by a function from contexts to individual *concepts*, not from contexts to individuals. It was the idea that a function from contexts to individuals could represent the intension of 'I' which lead to the difficulties discussed earlier.

Now what is it that a competent speaker of English knows about the word 'I'? Is it the content with respect to some particular occasion of use? No. It is the character of 'I': the rule italicized above. Competent speakers recognize that the proper use of 'I' is — loosely speaking — to refer to the speaker. Thus, that component of sense which I call 'character' is best identified with what might naturally be called 'meaning'.

To return, for a moment, to (1). The character (meaning) of (1) determines each of the following:

(a)   In different contexts, an utterance of (1) expresses different contents (propositions).

(b)   In most (if not all) contexts, an utterance of (1) expresses a contingent proposition.

(c)   In all contexts, an utterance of (1) expresses a true proposition (i.e. a proposition which is true at the world of the context).

On the basis of (c), we might claim that (1) is analytic (i.e. it is true solely in virtue of its meaning). Although as we see from (b), (1) rarely or never expresses a necessary proposition. This separation of analyticity and necessity is made possible — even, I hope, plausible — by distinguishing the kinds of entities of which 'is analytic' and 'is necessary' are properly predicated: characters (meanings) are analytic, contents (propositions) are necessary.

The distinction between character and content was unlikely to be noticed before demonstratives came under consideration, because demonstrative-free expressions have a constant character, i.e. they express the same content in every context. Thus, character becomes an uninteresting complication in the theory.

Though I have spoken above of contexts of utterance, my primary theoretical notion of *content with respect to a context* does not require that the agent of the context utter the expression in question. I believe that there are good reasons for taking this more general notion as fundamental.

I believe that my distinction between character and content can be used to throw light on Kripke's distinction between the *a-priori* and the necessary. Although my distinction lies more purely within logic and semantics, and Kripke's distinction is of a more general epistemic metaphysical character, both seem to me to be of the same *structure*. (I leave this remark in a rather cryptic state.)

The distinction between content and character and the related analysis of demonstratives have certainly been foreshadowed in the literature (though they are original-with-me, in the sense that I did not consciously extract them from prior sources). But to my knowledge they have not previously been cultivated to meet the standards for logical and semantical theories which currently prevail. In particular, Strawson's distinction between the significance (meaningfulness) of a sentence and the statement (proposition) which is expressed in a given use is clearly related. Strawson recognizes that such sentences as 'The *present* King of France is *now* bald' may express different propositions in different utterances, and he identifies the meaningfulness of the sentence with its potential for expressing a true or false proposition in some possible utterance. Though he does not explicitly discuss *the* meaning of the sentence, it is clear that he would not identify such a meaning with any of the propositions expressed by particular utterances. Unfortunately Strawson seems to regard the fact that sentences containing demonstratives can be used to express different propositions as immunizing such sentences against treatment by 'the logician'.

In order to convince myself that it is possible to carry out a consistent analysis of the semantics of demonstratives along the above lines, I have attempted to carry through the program for a version of first order predicate logic. The result is the following Logic of Demonstratives.

If my views are correct, the introduction of demonstratives into intensional logics will require more extensive reformulation than was thought to be the case.

THE LOGIC OF DEMONSTRATIVES

The *Language* LD is based on first-order predicate logic with identity and descriptions. We deviate slightly from standard formulations in using two sorts of variables, one sort for positions and a second sort for individuals other than positions (hereafter called simply 'individuals').

Primitive Symbols for Two Sorted Predicate Logic

0.   Punctuation: (,)
1.   (i) An infinite set of individual variables: $\mathcal{V}_i$
     (ii) An infinite set of position variables: $\mathcal{V}_p$
2.   (i) An infinite number of *m-n*-place predicates, for all natural numbers *m, n*
     (ii) The 1-0-place predicate: Exist
     (iii) The 1-1-place predicate: Located
3.   (i) An infinite number of *m-n*-place *i*-functors (functors which form terms

denoting individuals)

(ii) An infinite number of *m-n*-place *p*-functors (functors which form terms denoting positions)

4. Sentential Connectives: $\wedge, \vee, \neg, \rightarrow, \leftrightarrow$
5. Quantifiers: $\forall, \exists$
6. Definite Description Operator: the
7. Identity: =

Primitive Symbols for Modal and Tense Logic

8. Modal Operators: $\square, \diamondsuit$
9. Tense Operators: *F* (it will be the case that)

　　　　　　　　　　　P (it has been the case that)

　　　　　　　　　　　G (one day ago, it was the case that)

Primitive Symbols for the Logic of Demonstratives

10. Three one place sentential operators:

　　　　　　N (it is now the case that)

　　　　　　A (it is actually the case that)

　　　　　　Y (yesterday, it was the case that)

11. A one place functor: dthat
12. An individual constant (0-0-place *i*-functor): I
13. A position constant (0-0-place *p*-functor): Here

The *well formed expressions* are of three kinds: formulas, position terms (*p*-terms) and individual terms (*i*-terms).

1. (i) If $\alpha \in \mathcal{V}_i$, then α is an *i*-term

　　(ii) If $\alpha \in \mathcal{V}_p$, then α is a *p*-term

2. If π is an *m-n*-place predicate, $\alpha_1 \dots \alpha_m$ are *i*-terms, and $\beta_1 \dots \beta_n$ are *p*-terms, then $\pi\alpha_1 \dots \alpha_m\beta_1 \dots \beta_n$ is a formula.

3. (i) If η is an *m-n*-place *i*-functor, $\alpha_1 \dots \alpha_m, \beta_1 \dots \beta_n$ as in 2., then $\eta\alpha_1 \dots \alpha_m\beta_1 \dots \beta_n$ is an *i*-term.

　　(ii) If η is an *m-n*-place *p*-functor, $\alpha_1 \dots \alpha_m, \beta_1 \dots \beta_n$ as in 2., then $\eta\alpha_1 \dots \alpha_m\beta_1 \dots$

β_n is a p-term.

4. If ϕ, ψ are formulas, then $(\phi \wedge \psi)$, $(\phi \vee \psi)$, $\neg \phi$, $(\phi \rightarrow \psi)$, $(\phi \leftrightarrow \psi)$ are formulas.

5. If ϕ is a formula and $\alpha \in \mathcal{V}_i^\circ \cup \mathcal{V}_p$, then $\forall \alpha \phi$, $\exists \alpha \phi$ are formulas.

6. If ϕ is a formula, then

   (i) if $\alpha \in \mathcal{V}_i^\circ$, then the $\alpha \phi$ is an i-term.

   (ii) if $\alpha \in \mathcal{V}_p$, then the $\alpha \phi$ is a p-term.

7. If both α, β are either i-terms or p-terms, then $\alpha = \beta$ is a formula.

8. If ϕ is a formula, then $\Box \phi$, $\Diamond \phi$ are formulas.

9. If ϕ is a formula, then $F\phi$, $P\phi$, $G\phi$ are formulas.

10. If ϕ is a formula, then $N\phi$, $A\phi$, $Y\phi$ are formulas.

11. (i) If α is an i-term, then dthat α is an i-term.

    (ii) If α is a p-term, then dthat α is a p-term.

Semantics for LD

DEFINITION. $\mathfrak{A}$ *is an LD Structure* iff there are $\mathcal{C}\,\mathcal{W}^\circ\mathcal{U}\,\mathcal{P}\mathcal{T}\mathcal{J}$ such that

1. $\mathfrak{A} = \langle \mathcal{C}\,\mathcal{W}^\circ\mathcal{U}\,\mathcal{P}\mathcal{T}\mathcal{J} \rangle$.

2. $\mathcal{C}$ is a non-empty set (the set of *contexts*, see 10 below).

3. If $c \in \mathcal{C}$, then   (i) $c_A \in \mathcal{U}$ (the *agent* of c).

       (ii) $c_T \in \mathcal{T}$ (the *time* of c).

       (iii) $c_P \in \mathcal{P}$ (the *position* of c).

       (iv) $c_W \in \mathcal{W}^\circ$ (the *world* of c).

4. $\mathcal{W}^\circ$ is a non-empty set (the set of *worlds*).

5. $\mathcal{U}$ is a non-empty set (the set of all *individuals*, see 9 below).

6. $\mathcal{P}$ is a non-empty set (the set of *positions*; common to all worlds).

7. $\mathcal{T}$ is the set of integers (thought of as the *times*; common to all worlds).

8. $\mathcal{J}$ is a function which assigns to each predicate and functor an appropriate *intension* as follows:

   (i) If π is an m-n-place predicate, $\mathcal{J}_\pi$ is a function such that for each $t \in \mathcal{T}$ and $w \in \mathcal{W}^\circ$, $\mathcal{J}_\pi (tw) \subseteq (\mathcal{U}^m \times \mathcal{P}^n)$.

   (ii) If η is an m-n-place i-functor, $\mathcal{J}_\pi$ is a function such that for each $t \in \mathcal{T}$ and $w \in \mathcal{W}^\circ$,

   $$\mathcal{J}_\eta(tw) \in (\mathcal{U} \cup \{\dagger\})^{(\mathcal{U}^m \times \mathcal{P}^n)}.$$

(*Note*: † is a completely alien entity, in neither $\mathcal{U}$ nor $\mathcal{P}$, which represents an 'undefined' value of the function. In a normal set theory we can take † to be $\{\mathcal{U}, \mathcal{P}\}$.)

(iii) If η is an *m-n*-place *p*-functor, $\mathcal{I}_\eta$ is a function such that for each $t \in \mathcal{I}$ and $w \in \mathcal{W}$, $\mathcal{I}_\eta\,(tw) \in (\mathcal{P} \cup \{\dagger\})^{(\mathcal{U}^m \times \mathcal{P}^n)}$

9. $i \in \mathcal{U}$ iff $\exists t \in \mathcal{I}\ \exists w \in \mathcal{W}\ <i> \in \mathcal{I}_{\text{Exists}}(tw)$.

10.   If $c \in \mathcal{C}$, then $<c_A\,c_P> \in \mathcal{I}_{\text{Located}}(c_T c_W)$.

11.   If $<i\,p> \in \mathcal{I}_{\text{Located}}(tw)$, then $<i> \in \mathcal{I}_{\text{Exists}}(tw)$.

Truth and Denotation in a Context

We write: $\overset{\mathfrak{A}}{\underset{cftw}{\vDash}}$ ϕ for ϕ when taken in the context c (under the assignment f and in the structure $\mathfrak{A}$) *is true with respect to* the time t and the world w.

We write: $|\alpha|^{\mathfrak{A}}_{cftw}$ for   *The denotation of* α when taken in the context c (under the assignment f and in the structure $\mathfrak{A}$) *with respect to* the time t and the world w.

In general we will omit the superscript '$\mathfrak{A}$', and we will assume that the structure $\mathfrak{A}$ is $<\mathcal{C}\,\mathcal{W}\,\mathcal{U}\,\mathcal{P}\,\mathcal{I}\,\mathcal{I}>$.

DEFINITION, *f is an assignment* (with respect to $<\mathcal{C}\,\mathcal{W}\,\mathcal{U}\,\mathcal{P}\,\mathcal{I}\,\mathcal{I}>$) iff $\exists f_1 f_2$ ($f_1 \in \mathcal{U}^{V_i}\ \&\ f_2 \in \mathcal{P}^{V_p}\ \&\ f = f_1 \cup f_2$).

DEFINITION, $f^\alpha_x = (f \sim \{<\alpha\,f(\alpha)>\}) \cup \{<\alpha x>\}$ (i.e. the assignment which is just like f except that it assigns x to α).

For the following recursive definitions, assume that $c \in \mathcal{C}$, f is an assignment, $t \in \mathcal{I}$, and $w \in \mathcal{W}$.

1.   If α is a variable, $|\alpha|_{cftw} = f(\alpha)$.

2. $\underset{cftw}{\vDash} \pi\alpha_1...\alpha_m\beta_1...\beta_n$ iff
$<|\alpha_1|_{cftw}...|\beta_n|_{cftw}> \in \mathcal{I}_\pi(tw)$.

3.   If η is neither I nor Here (see 12,13 below), then
$|\eta\alpha_1...\,\alpha_m\beta_1...\beta_n|_{cftw}$

$$= \begin{cases} \mathcal{I}_{\eta}(tw)(<|\alpha_1|_{cftw} \ldots |\beta_n|_{cftw})), \text{ if none of} \\ |\alpha_i|_{cftw} |\beta_k|_{cftw} \text{ are } \dagger \\ \dagger, \text{ otherwise.} \end{cases}$$

4.   (i) $\models_{cftw} (\phi \wedge \psi)$ iff $\models_{cftw} \phi$ & $\models_{cftw} \psi$.

      (ii) $\models_{cftw} \neg \phi$ iff $\sim \models_{cftw} \phi$.

        etc.

5.   (i)   If $\alpha \in \mathcal{V}_i$,   then $\models_{cftw} \forall \alpha \phi$ iff $\forall_i \in \mathcal{U} \models_{cf_i^{\alpha};tw} \phi$.

      (ii)   If $\alpha \in \mathcal{V}_p$,   then $\models_{cftw} \forall \alpha \phi$ iff $\forall_p \in \mathcal{P} \models_{cf_i^{\alpha};tw} \phi$.

        Similarly for $\exists \alpha \phi$.

6.   (i)   If $\alpha \in \mathcal{V}_i$,   then $|\text{the } \alpha \phi|_{cftw}$

       $= \begin{cases} \text{the unique } i \in \mathcal{U} \text{ such that } \models_{cf_i^{\alpha};tw} \phi, \text{ if there is such} \\ \dagger \text{ otherwise.} \end{cases}$

      (ii)   Similarly for $\alpha \in \mathcal{V}_p$.

7. $\models_{cftw} \alpha = \beta$ iff $|\alpha|_{cftw} = |\beta|_{cftw}$.

8.   (i) $\models_{cftw} \Box \phi$ iff $\forall w' \in \mathcal{W}^o \models_{cftw'} \phi$.

      (ii) $\models_{cftw} \Diamond \phi$ iff $\exists t' \in \mathcal{W}^o \models_{cftw'} \phi$.

9.   (i) $\models_{cftw} F\phi$ iff $\exists t' \in \mathcal{I}$ such that $t' > t$ and $\models_{cft'w} \phi$.

      (ii) $\models_{cftw} P\phi$ iff $\exists t' \in \mathcal{I}$ such that $t' < t$ and $\models_{cft'w} \phi$.

      (iii) $\models_{cftw} G\phi$ iff $\models_{cf(t-1)w} \phi$.

10.   (i) $\models_{cftw} N\phi$ iff $\models_{cfc_T w} \phi$.

      (ii) $\models_{cftw} A\phi$ iff $\models_{cftc_W} \phi$.

      (iii) $\models_{cftw} Y\phi$ iff $\models_{cf(c_T-1)w} \phi$.

11. $|\text{dthat } \alpha|_{cftw} = |\alpha|_{cfc_T c_W}$.

12. $|I|_{cftw} = c_A$.

13. $|\text{Here}|_{cftw} = c_P$.

Remark 1. Expressions containing demonstratives will, in general, express different concepts in different contexts. We call the concept expressed in a given context, the *Content* of the expression in that context. The Content of a sentence in a context is, roughly, the proposition the sentence would express if uttered in that context. This description is not quite accurate on two counts. First, it is important to distinguish an *utterance* from a *sentence-in-a-context*. The former notion is from the theory of speech acts, the latter from semantics. Utterances take time, and utterances of distinct sentences can not be simultaneous (i.e. in the same context). But in order to develop a logic of demonstratives it seems most natural to be able to evaluate several premisses and a conclusion all in the same context. Thus, the notion of ϕ being true in c and $\mathfrak{A}$ does not require an utterance of ϕ. In particular, c_A need not be uttering ϕ in c_W at c_T. Second, the truth of a proposition is not usually thought of as dependent on a time as well as a possible world. The time is thought of as fixed by the context. If ϕ is a sentence, the more usual notion of the proposition expressed by ϕ-in-c is what is here called the Content of $N\phi$ in c.

Where Γ is either a term or a formula, we write: $\{\Gamma\}_{cf}^{\mathfrak{A}}$ for
>the Content of Γ in the context c (under the assignment f and in the structure $\mathfrak{A}$).

DEFINITION. (i) If ϕ is a formula, $\{\phi\}_{cf}$ = that function which assigns to each $t \in \mathscr{T}$ and $w \in \mathscr{W}^{o}$, Truth if $\vDash_{\overline{cf}tw}^{\mathfrak{A}} \phi$, and Falsehood otherwise.

       (ii) If α is a term, $\{\alpha\}_{cf}$ = that function which assigns to each $t \in \mathscr{T}$ and $w \in \mathscr{W}^{o}$, $|\alpha|_{\overline{cf}tw}^{\mathfrak{A}}$.

Remark 2. $\vDash_{\overline{cf}tw}^{\mathfrak{A}} \phi$ iff $\{\phi\}_{cf}^{\mathfrak{A}}(tw)$ = Truth. Roughly speaking, the sentence ϕ taken in the context c is *true with respect to* t and w iff the proposition expressed by ϕ-in-the-context-c would be true at the time t if w were the actual world. In the formal development of pages 89 and 90 it was smoother to ignore the conceptual break marked by the notion of *Content in a context* and to directly define *truth in a context with respect to a possible time and world*. The important conceptual role of the notion of Content is partially indicated by the following two definitions.

DEFINITION. ϕ *is true in the context* c (in the structure $\mathfrak{A}$) iff for every assignment f, $\{\phi\}_{cf}^{\mathfrak{A}}(c_T, c_W)$ = Truth.

DEFINITION. ϕ *is valid in LD* ($\vDash\phi$) iff for every LD structure $\mathfrak{A}$, and every context c of $\mathfrak{A}$, ϕ is true in c (in $\mathfrak{A}$).

Remark 3. $\vDash(\alpha = \text{dthat } \alpha)$, $\vDash N$ (Located I, Here), $\vDash$Exist I, $\sim \vDash \Box(\alpha = \text{dthat } \alpha)$, $\sim \vDash \Box N$ (Located I, Here), $\sim \vDash \Box$(Exist I). In the converse direction we have the usual results in view of the fact that $\vDash (\Box\phi \rightarrow \phi)$.

DEFINITION. If $\alpha_1 \ldots \alpha_n$ are all the free variables of ϕ in alphabetical order, then *the closure of* $\phi = AN\forall\alpha_1 \ldots \alpha_n\phi$.

DEFINITION. ϕ *is closed* iff ϕ is equivalent to its closure (in the sense of Remark 12, below).

Remark 4. If ϕ is closed, then ϕ is true in c (and $\mathfrak{A}$) iff for every assignment f, time t, and world $w \models^{\mathfrak{A}}_{cftw} \phi$.

DEFINITION. Where Γ is either a term or a formula, *the Content of* Γ *in the context c (in the structure $\mathfrak{A}$) is stable* iff for every assignment f, $\{\Gamma\}^{\mathfrak{A}}_{cf}$ is a constant function, (i.e., $\{\Gamma\}^{\mathfrak{A}}_{cf}(tw) = \{\Gamma\}^{\mathfrak{A}}_{cf}(t'w')$, for all t, t', w, w' in $\mathfrak{A}$).

Remark 5. Where ϕ is a formula, α is a term, and β is a variable, each of the following has a stable Content in every context (in every structure): $AN\phi$, dthat α, β, I, Here.

If we were to extend the notion of Content to apply to operators, we would see that all demonstratives have a stable Content in every context. The same is true of the familiar logical constants although it does not hold for the modal and tense operators (not, at least, according to the foregoing development).

Remark 6. That aspect of the meaning of an expression which determines what its Content will be in each context, we call the *Character* of the expression. Although a lack of knowledge about the context (or perhaps about the structure) may cause one to mistake the Content of a given utterance, the Character of each well formed expression is determined by rules of the language (such as 1–13 pages 89–91 above) which are presumably known to all competent speakers. Our notation '$\{\phi\}^{\mathfrak{A}}_{cf}$' for the Content of an expression gives a natural notation for the Character of an expression, namely '$\{\phi\}$'.

DEFINITION. Where Γ is either a term or a formula the *Character of* Γ is that function which assigns to each structure $\mathfrak{A}$, assignment f, and context c of $\mathfrak{A}$, $\{\Gamma\}^{\mathfrak{A}}_{cf}$.

DEFINITION. Where Γ is either a term or a formula, *the Character of* Γ *is stable* iff for every structure $\mathfrak{A}$, and assignment f the Character of Γ (under f in $\mathfrak{A}$) is a constant function. (i.e. $\{\Gamma\}^{\mathfrak{A}}_{cf} = \{\Gamma\}^{\mathfrak{A}}_{c'f}$ for all c, c' in $\mathfrak{A}$).

Remark 7. A formula or term has a stable Character iff it has the same Content in every context (for each $\mathfrak{A}$, f).

Remark 8. A formula or term has a stable Character iff it contains no essential occurrence of a demonstrative.

Remark 9. The logic of demonstratives determines a sub-logic of those formulas of LD which contain no demonstratives. These formulas (and their equivalents which contain inessential occurrences of demonstratives) are exactly the formulas with a stable Character. The logic of demonstratives brings a new perspective even to formulas such as these. The sub-logic of LD which concerns only formulas of stable Character is not identical with traditional logic. Even for such formulas, the familiar Principle of Necessitation: if $|=\phi$, then $|=\Box\phi$, fails. And so does its tense logic counterpart: if $|=\phi$, then $|=(\neg P \neg \phi \wedge \neg F \neg \phi \wedge \phi)$. From the perspective of LD, validity is truth in every possible *context*. For traditional logic, validity is truth in every possible *circumstance*. Each possible context determines a possible circumstance, but, it is not the case that each possible circumstance is part of a possible context. In particular, the fact that each possible context has an agent implies that any possible circumstance in which no individuals exist will not form a part of any possible context. Within LD, a possible context is represented by $<\mathfrak{A}, c>$ and a possible circumstance by $<\mathfrak{A}, t, w>$. To any $<\mathfrak{A}, c>$, there corresponds $<\mathfrak{A}, c_T, c_w>$. But it is not the case that to every $<\mathfrak{A}, t, w>$ there exists a context c of $\mathfrak{A}$ such that $t = c_T$ and $w = c_w$. The result is that in LD such sentences as $\exists x$ Exist x, and $\exists x \exists p$ Located x, p are valid, although they would not be so regarded in traditional logic. At least not in the neo-traditional logic that countenances empty worlds. Using the semantical developments of pages 88–91, we can define this traditional sense of validity (for formulas which do not contain demonstratives) as follows. First note that by Remark 7, if ϕ has a stable Character

$$\models^{\mathfrak{A}}_{\overline{cf}tw} \phi \quad \text{iff} \quad \models^{\mathfrak{A}}_{\overline{c}ftw} \phi.$$

Thus for such formulas we can define,

ϕ *is true at tw (in* $\mathfrak{A}$*)*   iff   for every assignment f and every context c

$$\underset{c f t w}{\overset{\mathfrak{A}}{\models}} \phi.$$

The neo-traditional sense of validity is now definable as follows, $\underset{T}{\models} \phi$. iff for all structures $\mathfrak{A}$, times t, and worlds w, ϕ is true at tw (in $\mathfrak{A}$). (Properly speaking, what I have called the neo-traditional sense of validity is the notion of validity now common for a quantified SS modal tense logic with individual variables ranging over possible individuals and a predicate of existence.) Adding the subscript 'LD' for explidtness, we can now state some results.

(i)   If ϕ contains no demonstratives, if $\underset{T}{\models} \phi$,   then $\underset{LD}{\models} \phi$.

(ii) $\underset{LD}{\models} \exists x$ Exist x, but ~ $\underset{T}{\models} \exists x$ Exist x.

Of course $\square \exists x$ Exist x is not valid even in LD. Nor are its counterparts, $\neg F \neg \exists x$ Exist x and $\neg P \neg \exists x$ Exist x.

This suggests that we can transcend the context oriented perspective of LD by generalizing over times and worlds so as to capture those possible circumstances $<\mathfrak{A}, t, w>$ which do not correspond to any possible contexts $<\mathfrak{A}, c>$. We have the following result.

(iii)   If ϕ contains no demonstratives

$\underset{T}{\models} \phi$,   iff $\underset{LD}{\models} \square (\neg P \neg \phi \wedge \neg F \neg \phi \wedge \phi)$.

Although our definition of the neo-traditional sense of validity was motivated by consideration of demonstrative-free formulas, we could apply it also to formulas containing essential occurrences of demonstratives.

To do so would nullify the most interesting features of the logic of demonstratives. But it raises the question, can we express our new sense of validity in terms of the neo-traditional sense. This can be done:

(iv) $\underset{LD}{\models} \phi$ iff $\underset{T}{\models} AN\phi$.

Remark 10. Rigid designators (in the sense of Kripke) are terms with a stable Content. Since Kripke does not discuss demonstratives, his examples all have, in addition, a stable Character (by Remark 8). Kripke claims that for proper names α,

β it may happen that $\alpha = \beta$, though not *a-priori*, is nevertheless necessary. This, in spite of the fact that the names α, β may be introduced by means of descriptions α', β' for which $\alpha' = \beta'$ is not necessary. An analogous situation holds in LD. Let α', β' be definite descriptions (without free variables) such that $\alpha' = \beta'$ is not *a-priori*, and consider the rigid terms dthat α' and dthat β' which are formed from them. We know that $\models$ (dthat α' = dthat $\beta' \leftrightarrow \alpha' = \beta'$). Thus, if $\alpha' = \beta'$ is not *a-priori*, neither is dthat α' = dthat β'. But, since $\models$ [dthat α' = dthat $\beta' \rightarrow \square$ (dthat α' = dthat β')], it may happen that dthat α' = dthat β' is necessary. The converse situation can also be illustrated in LD. Since (α = dthat α) is valid (see Remark 3), it is surely capable of being known *a-priori*. But if α lacks a stable Content (in some context c), $\square$(α = dthat α) will be false.

Remark 11. Our *o-o*-place *i*-functors are not proper names, in the sense of Kripke, since they do not have a stable Content. But they can easily be converted by means of the stabilizing influence of dthat. Even dthat α lacks a stable Character. The process by which such expressions are converted into expressions with a stable Character is 'dubbing' — a form of definition in which context may play an essential role. The means to deal with such context indexed definitions is not available in our object language.

There would, of course, be no difficulty in supplementing our language with a syntactically distinctive set of *o-o*-place *i*-functors whose semantics requires them to have both a stable Character and a stable Content in every context. Variables already behave this way, what is wanted is a class of constants that behave, in these respects, like variables.

The difficulty comes in expressing the definition. My thought is that when a name, like 'Bozo', is introduced by someone saying, in some context c^*, 'Let's call the Governor, "Bozo"', we have a context indexed definition of the form: $A =_{c^*} \alpha$, where A is a new constant (here, 'Bozo') and α is some term whose denotation depends on context (here, 'the Governor'). The intention of such a dubbing is, presumably, to induce the semantical clause: for all c, $\{A\}_{cf}^{\mathfrak{A}} = \{\alpha\}_{c^*f}^{\mathfrak{A}}$. Such a clause gives A a stable Character. The context indexing is required by the fact that the Content of α (the 'definiens') may vary from context to context. Thus the same semantical clause is not induced by taking either $A = \alpha$ or even A = dthat α as an axiom;

I think it likely that such definitions play a practically (and perhaps theoretically) indispensable role in the growth of language, allowing us to introduce a vast stock of names on the basis of a meager stock of demonstratives and some ingenuity in the staging of demonstrations.

Perhaps such introductions should not be called 'definitions' at all, since they essentially enrich the expressive power of the language. What a nameless man may express by 'I am hungry' may be inexpressible in remote contexts. But once he says 'Let's call me "Bozo" ' his Content is accessible to us all.

Remark 12. The strongest form of logical equivalence between two formulas ϕ and ϕ' is sameness of Character, $\{\phi\} = \{\phi'\}$. This form of synonymy is expressible in terms of validity.

$$\{\phi\} = \{\phi'\} \quad \text{iff} \quad |=\Box[\neg P \neg (\phi \leftrightarrow \phi') \wedge \neg F \neg (\phi \leftrightarrow \phi') \wedge (\phi \leftrightarrow \phi')].$$

[Using Remark 9 (iii) and dropping the condition, which was stated only to express the intended range of applicability of $|\overline{\overline{T}}$, we have: $\{\phi\} = \{\phi'\}$ iff $|\overline{\overline{T}} (\phi \leftrightarrow \phi')$.] Since definitions of the usual kind (as opposed to dubbings) are intended to introduce a short expression as a mere abbreviation of a longer one, the Character of the defined sign should be the same as the Character of the definiens. Thus, with LD, definitional axioms must take the form indicated above.

Remark 13. If β is a variable of the same sort as the term α but is not free in α, then $\{$dthat $\alpha\} = \{$the β AN $(\beta = \alpha)\}$. Thus for every formula ϕ, there can be constructed a formula ϕ' such that ϕ' contains no occurrence of dthat and $\{\phi\} = \{\phi'\}$.

Remark 14. Y (yesterday) and G (one day ago) superficially resemble one another in view of the fact that $|= (Y\phi \leftrightarrow G\phi)$. But the former is a demonstrative whereas the latter is an iterative temporal operator. 'One day ago it was the case that one day ago it was the case that John yawned' means that John yawned the day before yesterday. But 'Yesterday it was the case that yesterday it was the case that John yawned' is only a stutter.

POSSIBLE REFINEMENTS

(1) The primitive predicates and functors of first-order predicate logic are all taken to be extensional. Alternatives are possible.

(2) Many conditions might be added on $\mathcal{J}$; many alternatives might be chosen for $\mathcal{J}$. If the elements of $\mathcal{J}$ do not have a natural relation to play the role of $<$, such a relation must be added to the structure.

(3) When K is a set of LD formulas, $K\models\phi$ is easily defined in any of the usual ways.

(4) Aspects of the contexts other than c_A, c_P, c_T, and c_W would be used if new demonstratives (e.g. pointings, 'You', etc.) were added to the language. (Note that the subscripts A, P, T, W are external parameters. They may be thought of as functions applying to contexts, with c_A being the value of A for the context c.

(5) Special continuity conditions through time might be added for the predicate Exists.

(6) If individuals lacking positions are admitted as agents of contexts, 3(iii) of page 88 should be weakened to $c_P \in \mathscr{P} \cup \{\dagger\}$. It would no longer be the case that $\models$ Located I, Here. If individuals also lacking temporal location (disembodied minds?) are admitted as agents of contexts, a similar weakening is required of 3(ii). In any case it would still be true that $\models$ Exist I.

Notes

1   This paper was originally composed in two parts. The formal Logic of Demonstratives was first presented at the Irvine Summer Institute on the Philosophy of Language in 1971. It was expanded in 1973. The initial discursive material was written on April 20,1973 as part of a research proposal. This paper was intended as a companion piece to and progress report on the material in 'Dthat'. A more extensive presentation occurs in my manuscript *Demonstratives*. This work was supported by the National Science Foundation.

2   Or possibly, just in case ϕ was true at every index *which differed from the given index only in possible world coordinate.*

Bibliography

Kaplan, D., 'Dthat', in Peter Cole (ed.), *Syntax and Semantics,* Vol. 9; *Pragmatics,* Academic Press, New York, 1978, pp. 221–243. Also reprinted in *Contemporary Perspectives in the Philosophy of Language,* ed. by Wettstein *et al.,* The University of Minnesota, Morris, forthcoming.

Kaplan, D., *Demonstratives* (Draft #2) mimeographed, UCLA Philosophy Department, 1977.

Kripke, S., 'Naming and Necessity', in Donald Davidson and Gilbert Harman (eds.), *Semantics of Natural Language,* Reidel Publishing Co., Dordrecht-Holland, 1972, pp. 253–355; Addenda, pp. 763–69.

Strawson, P., *Introduction to Logical Theory,* John Wiley & Sons, New York, 1952.

File Change Semantics and the Familiarity Theory of Definiteness

Irene Heim

1 Introduction

What is the difference in meaning between definite noun phrases and indefinite ones? Traditional grammarians, in particular Christophersen and Jespersen, worked on this question and came up with an answer that nowadays finds little favor with semanticists trained in twentieth century logic. It amounts to the following, in a nutshell:

(1)   A definite is used to refer to something that is already *familiar* at the current stage of the conversation. An indefinite is used to introduce a *new* referent.

This has been labeled the "familiarity theory of definiteness."[1]

When confronted with (1), the logically minded semanticist will notice immediately that it presumes something very objectionable: that definites and indefinites are referring expressions. For only if there is a referent at all can there be any question of its familiarity or novelty. Advocates of (1) cannot happily admit that there are nonreferring uses of definites or indefinites (or both), because that would be tantamount to admitting that their theory leaves the definite-indefinite-contrast in a significant subset of NP uses unaccounted for.

But the existence of nonreferential uses of definite and indefinite NPs can hardly be denied, and I will take it for granted without repeating the familiar arguments.[2] Just think of examples like (2) and (3).

199

(2) Every cat ate its food.

(3) John didn't see a cat.

(2) has a reading where "its", a personal pronoun, i.e. a type of definite NP, functions as a so-called "bound variable pronoun" and doesn't refer to any particular cat. Under the preferred reading of (3), with negation taking widest scope, the indefinite "a cat" fails to refer.

So the cards appear to be stacked against the familiarity theory of definiteness. Nevertheless, I will try to revive and defend it, or a theory very much like it. The version I will defend is just different enough from (1) to avoid the problematic presumption of referentiality. Otherwise it agrees with (1) — and accordingly deviates from standard assumptions in logical semantics — in fundamental respects: It involves familiarity and novelty as a central pair of notions, and it takes neither definites nor indefinites to be quantifiers.

What is the point of rehabilitating a problem-ridden traditional approach when much more sophisticated alternatives have become available through the work of logical semanticists from Russell to the present? — I would like to argue that a familiarity theory of definiteness, if construed along the lines of this article, enables us to make better predictions than competing theories about the behavior of definites and indefinites in natural languages, in particular about their participation in anaphora relationships. I return to this point in section 7 below, but first I must lay out the theory I am proposing.

2 Karttunen's "Discourse Referents"

Mine is not the first attempt to rehabilitate the familiarity theory of definiteness by dissociating it from the problematic presumption that definites and indefinites are referring expressions. In the late 1960s, Karttunen wrote some papers[3] directed at the same goal. In order to avoid untenable claims about reference, Karttunen reformulates the familiarity theory by using a new notion, that of "discourse reference", in place of "reference". So instead of principle (1), he has a requirement that a definite NP has to pick out an already familiar *discourse* referent, whereas an indefinite NP always introduces a new *discourse* referent. Since discourse reference is distinct from reference, and since, in particular, an NP may have a discourse referent even when it has no referent, this reformulation makes the familiarity theory immune to the objections encountered by its traditional version (1).

Let me illustrate with two examples how the distinction between discourse reference and genuine reference can be exploited in evading dilemmata that the traditional familiarity theorist must find fatal. Consider the text under (4).

(4)   John came, and so did Mary. *One of them* brought a cake.

The underlined NP "one of them" is indefinite, therefore (1) would seem to predict that it must refer to an as yet "unfamiliar" person, i.e. a person not already introduced in the previous discourse. Now the first sentence of (4) mentions both John and Mary, hence both of them are familiar when "one of them" gets uttered and should consequently be excluded as potential referents for "one of them". But that is counterintuitive, since (4) is naturally read as saying that one of John and Mary, not some third person, brought a cake. "One of them" — if we are to admit that it refers to anything at all — clearly can refer to John or Mary here, in apparent violation of the familiarity theory. — But now suppose we have replaced (1) by Karttunen's version in terms of discourse referents. Then the prediction about "one of them" will be that, since it is indefinite, its discourse referent must be new and must be distinct from the discourse referents of "John" and "Mary" in particular. There is no prediction about the referents of these three NPs, and we may consistently hold any assumption we please about those. In particular, we may assume that NPs with distinct discourse reference sometimes happen to coincide in reference, and that (4), being a case of this kind, involves three discourse referents, but only two referents.

Next, consider (5).

(5)   (a) Everybody found a cat and kept *it*. (b) *It* ran away.

The relevant facts here are that the "it" in (5a), but not the "it" in (5b), can be interpreted as anaphoric to "a cat", (the intended reading being one with "everybody" taking wider scope than "a cat"). Since the first "it" and its antecedent "a cat" both fail to refer, the traditional version of the familiarity theory cannot really be applied to them at all. Talking in terms of discourse referents, however, we can describe what is going on in (5) as follows: The indefinite "a cat" introduces a discourse referent. The first "it" picks up that same discourse referent, which — having just been introduced — is familiar, as required. At the end of (5a), this discourse referent ceases to exist and is no longer available when the second "it" comes along. Therefore that second "it" must find the familiar discourse referent it requires elsewhere, or the text is inacceptable. — Note that this way of talking about (5) implies that discourse referents behave in ways which it wouldn't make any sense to attribute to real referents: not only are there discourse referents for NPs that have no referents, but moreover, discourse referents may suddenly go out of existence, depending on certain properties of the utterance. In this case, the relevant generalization is that if a discourse referent gets first introduced inside the scope of a quantifier (here: "everybody"), then its lifespan cannot extend beyond the scope of that quantifier.

But what are discourse referents? We have seen that for this new concept to be useful we must dissociate it from certain properties inherent in the notion of a referent. But a merely negative characterization is of course not enough if we don't want to be reduced to vacuity. Karttunen (in the papers cited) formulates a number of generalizations about discourse referents, i.e. about the conditions under which they get introduced and the factors that determine their lifespan, such as for instance the generalization about quantifier scope limiting the lifespan of discourse referents that I just alluded to above. Taken together, these generalizations combine with Karttunen's version of the familiarity theory into a theory that yields empirical predictions and in the context of which "discourse reference" is a non-vacuous theoretical concept. In this sense, the question what discourse referents are has a satisfactory answer implicit in Karttunen's work, although there is no explicit definition.

Still, it has remained puzzling in many ways just what discourse referents are and where they fit into semantic theory. It seems appropriate to say that we are describing some aspect of the meaning of a word or construction of English when we talk about its capacity for introducing, picking up, or influencing the lifespan of, discourse referents. But is that an entirely separate aspect of meaning, or is it dependent upon other aspects of meaning, such as the referential and truth-conditional aspect? — Questions of this sort I hope to shed light on by suggesting that Karttunen's discourse referents be identified with what I will call "file cards", i.e. elements of a so-called "file", a theoretical construct which mediates in a way to be made precise between language and the world.

3 Conversation and File-keeping

A listener's task of understanding what is being said in the course of a conversation bears relevant similarities to a file clerk's task. Speaking metaphorically, let me say that to understand an utterance is to keep a file which, at every time in the course of the utterance, contains the information that has so far been conveyed by the utterance.[4] Suppose, for instance, someone is listening to an utterance of the following three-sentence-text.

(6)　(a) A woman was bitten by a dog. (b) She hit it. (c) It jumped over a fence.

Before the utterance starts, the listener has an empty file, i.e. a collection of zero file cards. Call that empty file "F_0". As soon as (6a) has been uttered, the listener puts two cards into the file, gives each card a number — say "1" and "2", and writes the following entries on them: on card 1, he writes "is a woman" and "was bitten by 2", and on card 2, "is a dog" and "bit 1". He now has a two card file, call it "F_1", which looks like this:

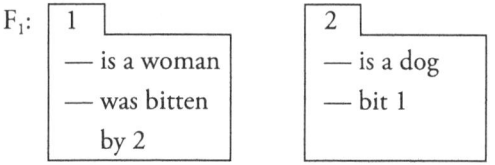

Next, (6b) gets uttered, which prompts the listener to update card 1 by adding the entry "hit 2", and to update card 2 by adding "was hit by 1". He now has F_2, still a two card file, but a different one:

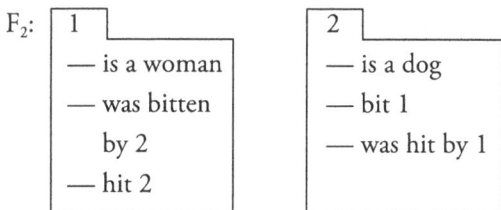

Now comes the utterance of (6c). The listener takes a new card, numbers it "3", writes on it "is a fence" and "was jumped over by 2", and also updates card 2 by adding on it "jumped over 3". This leaves him with F_3, a three card file:

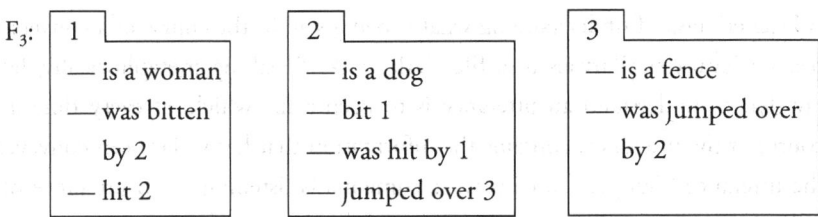

F_3:

1	2	3
— is a woman	— is a dog	— is a fence
— was bitten by 2	— bit 1	— was jumped over by 2
— hit 2	— was hit by 1	
	— jumped over 3	

With this illustration in mind, let us repeat our initial question: How do definites differ from indefinites? We may now answer: They differ in the way they influence the development of the file; the listener treats them differently, apparently following an instruction like (7) in his file keeping.

(7)   For every indefinite, start a new card. For every definite, update an old card.

For instance, cards 1 and 2 were newly introduced in response to the indefinites "a woman" and "a dog" that occurred in (6a). Only definites, namely "she" and "it", occurred in (6b), therefore F_2 only contained the same cards that were already in F_1, albeit updated. (6c) had both an indefinite ("a fence") and a definite ("it") in it, hence it prompted both introduction of a new card (card 3) and updating of an old one (card 2). All of this conformed to (7).

Instruction (7) is reminiscent of principle (1) above and can in fact be seen as incorporating a version of the familiarity theory of definiteness: Like (1), (7) links definiteness to familiarity (= "oldness") and indefiniteness to novelty. The only difference of (7) from (1) is that not referents are supposed to be old or new, but rather file cards. By substituting file cards for referents in the formulation of the familiarity theory of definiteness, I have made basically the same move as Karttunen, who substituted discourse referents for referents, and like in Karttunen's case, this move enables me to avoid the presumption of referentiality which caused such problems for the traditional version (1) of the familiarity theory. Examples like (4) and (5) are easily accommodated, once we think of file cards instead of referents, since it is quite conceivable for there to be a file card that fails to describe a referent, or for two different file cards to happen to describe the same thing, or for file cards to be introduced into and be removed from the file, depending on what is getting uttered. In short, just the properties we have found it necessary to attribute to Karttunen's discourse referents are properties that fit right into the file card metaphor. This is why I would like to suggest that Karttunen's talk about "discourse referents" be rephrased by substituting "file card" for "discourse referent": once we realize that discourse referents are essentially like file cards, their identity criteria and their relation to referents come to look much less mysterious.

In this section, I have introduced the file metaphor and have applied it informally to examples. Now it remains to give a more precise account of the theoretically relevant properties of files and of the role they play in the semantic interpretation of natural language. Roughly, the model of semantics that I am going to present will embody the following assumptions. The grammar of a language generates sentences with representations on various levels of analysis, among them a level of "logical form". Each logical form is assigned a "file change potential", i.e. a function from files into files. Given an utterance with a certain logical form, this function will determine how you get from the file that obtains prior to the utterance to the file that comes to obtain as a result of the utterance. The system moreover includes an assignment of truth conditions to files. Note that logical forms themselves are not assigned truth conditions, only files are. Only in an indirect way, i.e. via the files they affect, will logical forms be associated with truth conditions. The diagram under (8) shows how this model of semantic interpretation is organized. I will elaborate on its various components in the next few sections, starting with the association of files with their truth conditions.

(8)

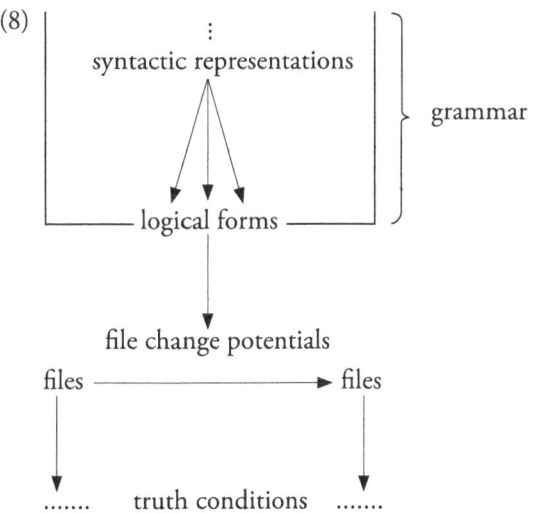

4 Files and the World

A file can be evaluated as to whether it corresponds to the actual facts or misrepresents them. Take e.g. the file F_1 of our example above. If it so happens that among all the women and dogs that there are there is not a woman-and-dog-pair such that the dog bit the woman, then F_1 obviously misrepresents the facts. I will speak of a "false" file in such a case, and correspondingly will call a file "true" if it fits the facts.

What does it take for a file to be true? To establish the truth of a file, we have to, so to speak, line up the sequence of cards in the file with a sequence of actual individuals, such that each individual fits the description on the corresponding card. Or, as I will put it, we have to find a sequence of individuals that *satisfies* the file. For file F_1, for instance, we have to find a two-membered sequence, i.e. a pair, that consists of a 1st member a_1 and a 2nd member a_2 such that a_1 fits card 1, and a_2 fits card 2 of F_1. Any such pair will satisfy F_1, i.e. we have:

$\langle a_1, a_2 \rangle$ satisfies F_1 iff a_1 is a woman, a_2 is a dog, and a_2 bit a_1.

Depending on how many cards a file contains, it will take pairs, triples, quadruples, or what not to satisfy it, therefore I speak generally of "sequences". Technically, a sequence is a function from some subset of N (the natural numbers) into A (the domain of all individuals). The pair $\langle a_1, a_2 \rangle$, for instance, is the function which maps 1 to a_1 and 2 to a_2. (Notice that I also admit sequences whose domains are not initial segments of N. E.g. a function that assigns an individual each to the numbers 2 and 7, but is not defined for any other numbers, also qualifies as a sequence. This would be the sort of sequence to satisfy a file whose only two cards are numbered "2" and "7".) A degenerate sort of sequence is the one whose domain is the empty set ϕ and which is therefore ϕ itself, ϕ is the only sequence that satisfies file F_0, the file of zero cards in our example above.

I will often want to refer to the set of all sequences that satisfy a given file, therefore I introduce a piece of notation, "Sat(F)" (read: "the satisfaction set of F").

(9) $\text{Sat}(F) =_{def} \{a_N : a_N \text{ satisfies } F\}$.

(Here and elsewhere, "a_N", "b_M", and the like range over sequences, where the subscripts "N", "M", etc. stand for each sequence's domain.) I also need a short way of referring to all the card-numbers that are used in a given file, so I use the notation "Dom(F)" (read: "the domain of F").

(10) Dom(F) = $_{def}$ {n $\in$ N: F contains a card with number n}.

As I said before, a file is to count as true if some satisfying sequence for it can be found. Definition (11) expresses this.

(11) F is true iff Sat(F) $\neq$ ϕ (and false otherwise).

In the remainder of this article, I will often describe a file solely in terms of its domain and satisfaction set. It should be clear that that does not suffice to pick out a unique file. There are always many distinct files that happen to have the same domain and satisfaction set. To give an extreme example, any two false files which happen to employ the same set of card numbers are indistinguishable if you look only at domains and satisfaction sets, the satisfaction sets being empty for all false files. Yet, two such files may have completely different entries on their cards. So by specifying only the domains and satisfaction sets, I am leaving the files I am talking about grossly underspecified. Nevertheless, for certain selected purposes, such as those of the present article, it is possible to abstract away from all the ways in which files with identical domains and satisfaction sets may differ, and to still formulate the relevant principles.

5 Semantic Categories and Logical Forms

I will now turn to the upper part of diagram (8) and highlight some of the assumptions about logical forms that I need to rely on. Following standard practice, I assume that logical forms differ from surface structures and other syntactic levels of representation in that they are disambiguated in two respects: scope, and anaphoric relations. Scope is marked configurationally, with an element c-commanding its scope, and anaphoric relatedness is marked by coindexing, with two anaphorically related elements bearing identical numerical subscripts. The relation between sentences and their logical forms, generally a one-to-many relation, is defined by a set of transformational rules that derive logical forms from syntactic representations and by wellformedness constraints on the output of those rules.[5]

Both the rules that derive logical forms and the rules that interpret them by assigning them file change potentials appear to discriminate between elements of different semantic categories, such as variables, operators, and the like. Here I will not go into such questions as how many and which semantic categories there are, and to what extent the syntactic category of an element determines its semantic category. I just assume that there are at least the following semantic categories and they include at least the kinds of things listed, whether as a matter of stipulation or of principle.

> *variables:* pronouns, empty NPs, indices on NPs with predicate heads (see below for illustration of the latter);
> *predicates:* verbs, nouns;
> *operators:* "every", negation.

As for the rules and constraints that define the relation between the syntactic representation of a sentence and its logical forms, I will be very informal and incomplete here. Consider the structures in (12), each of which represents one of the logical forms that the English sentence below it can have.

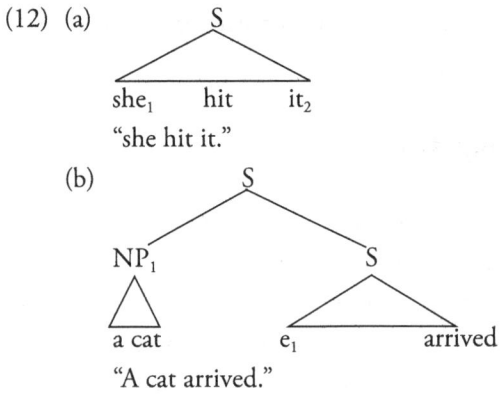

(12) (a)

she₁　hit　it₂
"she hit it."

(b)

a cat　　e₁　　arrived
"A cat arrived."

(c)

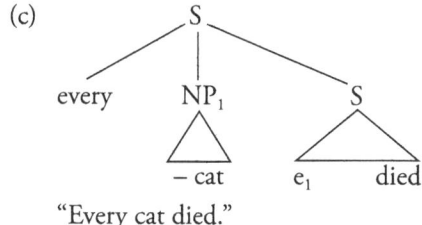

"Every cat died."

("e" marks an empty NP-position; the blank before "cat" in (12c) indicates an empty determiner-position.) These three examples may serve to illustrate a few general assumptions about logical forms:

- Every NP in logical form carries a numerical index.
- Only variables occur in the argument positions of predicates.[6]
- NPs that are not variables, i.e. those headed by predicates, are adjoined to their scopes and coindexed with the argument position they originate from.[7]
- Operators are adjoined as sisters to their argument(s). (Most operators are 2-place operators, in particular the quantifiers; some may be 1-place, e.g. negation.)

There is more to be said about how these assumptions follow from the way in which rules of logical-form-construction, wellformedness constraints on logical forms, and limitations on semantic interpretability interact with each other.

Note the contrast between structures (12b) and (12c), which is due to an assumption whose significance I will have more to say about, viz. the assumption that the articles "a" and "the" are not operators, whereas certain other determiners, e.g. "every", are. What then is the semantic category of articles? None at all. They are treated as though they weren't there at all when it comes to semantic interpretation.

What I have so far said about semantic categorization applies only to lexical items and other basic units, but fails to specify a semantic category for the complex building blocks of logical forms, such as S-constituents and predicate-headed NP-constituents. With some simplification, we may assume that all complex constituents that are of any semantic category at all are *propositions*. These subdivide into atomic propositions, which consist of a predicate and its arguments, and molecular propositions, which are made up of other propositions and may or may not involve an operator. One kind of atomic proposition is dominated by S and made up of a verb and its subject and complements (if any), where the verb is the predicate and the variables in the subject and complement positions are its arguments. In (12), $[_s she_1 hit\ it_2]$, $[_s e_1 arrived]$, and $[_s e_1 died]$ exemplify this kind of atomic proposition. The other option for an atomic proposition is to have a noun as the predicate, in which case the dominating node is NP. (12) contains the examples $[_{NP_1} a\ cat]$ and $[_{NP_1\_} cat]$. Nominal predicates always have one of their arguments realized as a mere numerical index which appears on the dominating NP-node. "Cat", for instance, is a 1-place predicate, and its argument in the examples just cited is the index 1. This is why I included "indices on NPs with predicate heads" in the above list of variables.

6 Logical Forms and their File Change Potentials

We can now proceed to the heart of the system diagrammed in (8), the assignment of file change potentials to logical forms. It will be useful to have another piece of notation, the symbol "+", which stands for the file change operation. Suppose we have a logical form p that determines a file change from F to F'. We express this by writing:

$$F + p = F'$$

(read: "the result of updating F on account of p is F'"). The task of assigning file change potentials to logical forms can now be seen as amounting to the task of defining "F + p" for files F and logical forms p of arbitrary composition and complexity. Actually, I will limit my efforts to a more modest task than that: Instead of committing myself to a full specification of the formal properties of files and the changes they undergo, I will characterize only one aspect of file change, namely how the satisfaction set is affected. As I noted earlier, this means that I am leaving a lot about the files I am talking about wide open. What I will define, thus, is not actually "F + p", but rather "Sat (F + p)".

A standard way of assigning interpretations to a language with expressions of unlimited complexity is by means of a recursive definition. Following this format, I will begin by specifying the file changes induced by atomic propositions and then characterize the file changes that molecular propositions bring about in terms of the file change potentials of their parts.

Consider (12a), repeated below, one of the logical forms of the simple sentence "She hit it."

(12) (a)

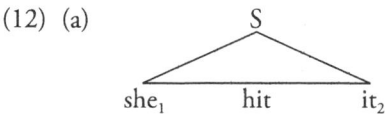

In the informal introduction of the file metaphor in section 3, I had the file clerk react to this sentence by changing a certain file F_1 into a certain file F_2. Recall what F_1 and F_2 were supposed to look like. Using the terminology I have since made available, they can now be described as follows:

$Dom(F_1) = Dom(F_2) = \{1,2\}$
$Sat(F_1)$ = $\{<a_1, a_2>: a_1$ is a woman, a_2 is a dog, and a_2 bit $a_1\}$
$Sat(F_2)$ = $\{<a_1, a_2>: a_1$ is a woman, a_2 is a dog, a_2 bit a_1, and a_1 hit $a_2\}$

It is apparent that the transition from Sat (F_1) to Sat (F_2) consists in eliminating from Sat (F_1) all those pairs which fail to satisfy the sentence being processed, i.e. those pairs which fail to stand in the relation that the predicate of the sentence denotes, in this case the relation of hitting. Put formally:

$Sat(F_2) = \{<a_1, a_2>: <a_1, a_2> \in Sat(F_1)$ and $<a_1, a_2> \in Ext("hit")\}$

(I write "Ext" for "the extension of".) The general rule under which this transition falls may be given as follows (subject to later revision):

(13) Let F be a file, and let p be an atomic proposition that consists of an n-place predicate R and an n-tuple of variables whose indices are i_1, ..., and i_n respectively. Then:
$Sat(F + p) = \{a_N: a_N \in Sat(F)$ and $<a_{i_1}, ..., a_{i_n}> \in Ext(R)\}$.
Applied to the file F_1 and the logical form (12a), (13) gives us:
$Sat(F_1 + (12a)) = Sat(F_2)$,

as intended.

We just focussed on a particular logical form that grammar provides for the sentence "She hit it", namely (12a). But there are infinitely many others, since the choice of indices is supposed to be free. So (12a) represents really only one of many readings that the sentence may be uttered with, and we have yet to talk about the others. We also have to say something to explain the puzzling fact that despite the infinity of distinct logical forms assigned to each sentence by the grammar, most real-life utterances can be immediately understood in an unambiguous way. To appreciate the problem, put yourself once more into the imaginary file clerk's shoes. You have so far constructed the file F_1, and now you hear the speaker say: "She hit it". How do you guess that the intended reading is "She$_1$ hit it$_2$", and not, say, one of the following?

(14) (a) She$_1$ hit it$_1$.

　　 (b) She$_3$ hit it$_7$.

　　 (c) She$_2$ hit it$_1$.

(14a) is pretty easy to exclude: there is a well-known constraint, called "Disjoint Reference", which we may think of as a wellformedness condition on some level of representation in the grammar (logical form or one of the levels it is derived from). By this constraint, coindexings like the one in (14a) are ruled out, so (14a) doesn't count as a welformed logical form and thus doesn't represent an available reading for any utterance of the sentence "She hit it" whatsoever.

With (14b), it's a rather different matter. No known constraint on indexing applies here, and it would quite clearly be wrong-headed to expect that anything would rule (14b) an ill-formed logical form. It can't be ill-formed, because we can imagine utterances of "She hit it" where (14b) would be precisely the logical form that represents the intended reading. Suppose, for instance, the preceding conversation had taken its course in such a way that you, the file clerk, had come up with a file F4, which, unlike F_1, is characterized by the domain Dom $(F_4) = \{3, 7\}$ and the satisfaction set Sat $(F_4) = \{<a_3, a_7>: a_3$ is a woman, a_7 is a dog, and a_7 bit $a_3\}$. If at this point you were confronted with an utterance of "She hit it", (14b) rather than (12a) would be the reading to construe it with. — What this shows is that in order to disambiguate the uttered sentence as (12a) as opposed to (14b), the file clerk must take into account what his current file looks like. What is at work here is thus not a constraint on logical forms considered in isolation, but rather a principle that constrains the choice of logical form *relative to a given file.* I want to propose that a principle of this sort, and in fact just the right principle to help us rule out (14b) when given F_1, is suggested to us by the familiarity theory of definiteness. The principle, which I call the "Novelty/Familiarity Condition", is this:

(15) Let F be a file, p an atomic proposition. Then p is appropriate with respect to F only if, for every noun phrase NP_i with index i that p contains:
if NP_i is definite, then $i \notin Dom(F)$,
and if NP_i is indefinite, then $i \notin Dom(F)$.

With respect to the file F_1, for instance, (14b) is inappropriate because it contains two definite NPs, "she_3" and "it_7", whose indices fail to be in Dom (F_1). (12a), on the other hand, with the definites "she_1" and "it_2", meets (15)'s requirement for appropriateness w.r.t. F_1. Note that for (15) to be applicable in the intended way, we must generally assume that NPs in logical form are marked for the feature [± definite].

(15) is presumably only one among other conditions on when a logical form is appropriate w.r.t. a file. Much of what has been discussed under the name of "presupposition" seems to be a matter of conditions of this sort.[8] From the point of view of the task of assigning file change potentials to logical forms, we may take appropriateness conditions as delimiting the range of pairs <F, p> for which the file change operation F + p is at all defined. Unless p is appropriate w.r.t. F, there is no file change result F + p determined. — As you will come to see shortly (once I have discussed indefinites), (15) interacts with the rules for file change in such a way that files will in effect always develop in accordance with instruction (7), which I formulated in section 3 as a first informal way of incorporating the familiarity theory of definiteness into a file-based semantics.

Returning to the file clerk's problem of eliminating all but the intended one among the infinity of logical forms for a given sentence, the Novelty/ Familiarity Condition (15) will certainly help to rule out a lot of unwanted options, but it will still let through some. (14c) above is a case in point: Given the file F_1, the indexing "she_2"/"it_1" violates (15) no more than "she_1"/"it_2" (and (14c) is of course not ill-formed as a logical from either). In order to predict the inappropriateness of (14c) w.r.t. F_1, we need some account of gender, which I will not provide here. Another problem whose solution I must leave for another occasion[9] is the fact that different kinds of definites, e.g. personal pronouns in comparison with definite descriptions, differ in their appropriateness conditions in a way that the Novelty/Familiarity Condition, which is sensitive only to the distinction between definites and indefinites, is incapable of predicting.

Let us now turn to an example with an indefinite, such as the sentence "A cat arrived", one of whose logical forms is (12b), repeated from above, this time with the definiteness features filled in.

(12) (b)

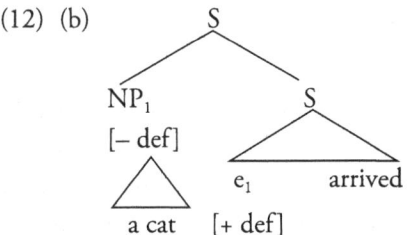

To determine the file change that (12b) induces, we will have to consider two questions: First, since (12b) is a molecular proposition, we have to ask ourselves how its overall effect on the file may be calculated on the basis of the file changes that each of its two parts would induce. Second, which rules of file change pertain to each of those parts?

The answer to the first question is as simple as it could be: We compute the file change of (12b) as a whole by subjecting the file first to the change that the left constituent dictates, and subsequently to the file change that the right constituent dictates. The general rule for this successive left-to-right mode of file change is this:

(16) Let F be a file, and let p be a molecular proposition whose immediate constituents are the propositions q and r (in that order). Then:
Sat (F + p) = Sat ((F + q) + r).

Applied to (12b), this means that we get from a given file F with satisfaction set Sat (F) to Sat (F + (12b)) by first calculating Sat (F + [$_{NP_1}$ a cat]) and then, from that, Sat((F + [$_{NP}$ a cat]) + [$_s e_1$ arrived]).

$[_{NP_1}$ a cat] is an atomic proposition. Before we try to determine Sat (F + $[_{NP_1}$ a cat]), we have to make sure that it is even welldefined, i.e. that $[_{NP_1}$ a cat] is appropriate w.r.t. F in the sense of the Novelty/Familiarity Condition (15). Since $[_{NP_1}$ a cat] contains (in this case, exhaustively contains) an indefinite with index 1, (15) requires that $1 \notin \text{Dom}(F)$. Let's assume F meets that requirement. Then Sat(F + $[_{NP_1}$ a cat]) is defined and should, by rule (13) above, equal the set:

(17) $\{a_N: a_N \in \text{Sat (F) and } a_1 \in \text{Ext ("cat")}\}$

That doesn't seem right, however. The problem is that if, as we are assuming, $1 \notin$ Dom (F), then no element $a_N \in$ Sat (F) will have a first member a_1 at all, let alone one that is in the extension of "cat". So the set described in (17) would of necessity be empty. This is not consistent with our intuition that "A cat arrived" is a contingent statement and should, at least sometimes, lead to a non-empty, i.e. true, file. We have to fix up rule (13) accordingly. The revised version under (18) is more adequately equipped to handle the example under consideration, while it still works just like (13) in cases of the sort that made us first design (13).

(18) Let F be a file, and let p be an atomic proposition that consists of an n-place predicate R and an n-tuple of variables whose indices are i_1, ..., i_n respectively. Then:
Sat (F + p) = $\{a_N \cup b_M \in A^{\text{NUM}}: a_N \in \text{Sat (F), M} = \{i_1, ..., i_n\}$,
and $<b_{i_1}, ..., b_{i_n}> \in \text{Ext (R)}\}$.

In contrast with (13), (18) allows for cases where F + p has a larger domain than F, i.e. where the sequences in Sat (F + p) have to be longer than those in Sat (F). Put informally, (18) says that every sequence in Sat (F + p) has to include as subsequences a sequence a_N satisfying F and a sequence b_M satisfying the proposition p. Whenever you can find an a_N satisfying F and a b_M satisfying p, where a_N and b_M agree on the intersection of their domains, link them together and the result, $a_N \cup b_M$, will be a member of Sat (F + p). (That a_N and b_M have to agree on the common part of their domains is expressed in (18) by requiring "$a_N \cup b_M \in A^{\text{NUM}}$". A^{NUM} denotes the set of functions from N ∪ M into A, and the union of two sequences is itself a sequence (i.e. a function) just in case they coincide on their common domain.) (18) reduces to (13) whenever $\{i_1, ..., i_n\}$

happens to be a subset of Dom (F).

Returning to our example, assume for concreteness that we start out with the empty file F_0, i.e. the one which has Dom $(F_0) = \phi$ and Sat $(F_0) = \{\phi\}$. F_0 is of course among those files w.r.t. which $[_{NP_1}$ a cat] is appropriate in the sense of (15). What, then, does (18) tell us about the file-change result $F_0 + [_{NP_1}$ a cat]? We calculate:

(19) Sat $(F_0 + [_{NP_1}$ a cat]) = {<b_1>: $b_1 \in$ Ext ("cat")}.

It is now easy to compute Sat(F_0 + (12b)) by applying (16) and, once more, (18).

(20) Sat $(F_0 + (12b)) =$
  = Sat ($(F_0 + [_{NP_1}$ a cat]) + $[_,e_1$ arrived]) =
  = {<b_1>: $b_1 \in$ Ext ("cat") and $b_1 \in$ Ext ("arrived")}.

This result is in line with our earlier, metaphorical, characterization of file change: Starting from a zero-card file, the sentence "A cat arrived" has brought us to a one-card file which is satisfied by any one-membered sequence whose one member is a cat and arrived.

Before I conclude this section, let me substantiate a remark that I made at the end of section 3. There I said that, although logical forms are not directly mapped onto truth conditions in a semantics that is organized along the lines of diagram (8), they still receive truth conditions indirectly, via the files they affect. I had in mind the following truth criterion for logical forms:

(21) Let F be a true file and p a logical form. Then p is true w.r.t. F if F + p is true, false w.r.t. F if F + p is false, and truth-value-less w.r.t. F if F + p is undefined.

(21) makes reference to the notion of truth that I defined for files in (11) above, and it basically equates the truth conditions of what is being said with the truth conditions of the resulting file. However, the applicability of this truth criterion is limited to cases where we can assume the truth of the file we start out with. If we have a false file to begin with, then we will always end up with another false

file, however "true", in an intuitive sense, the utterance under consideration may be.

7 The Non-quantificational Analysis of Indefinites

I am only half way through with my recursive set of rules for assigning file change potentials to logical forms. But this is a good point to take a break and have a critical look at the present analysis of indefinite NPs and how it compares with the widely accepted Russellian analysis. Russell[10] argued that intuitively correct truth-conditions for sentences with indefinites result when the indefinite article is treated as an existential quantifier and sentences of the form (22) are assigned logical analyses of roughly the form (23).

(22) $[_S X[_{NP} a Y]Z]$
(23) $\exists x (Y(x) \& (X x Z))$.

"A cat arrived", for instance, would be logically analyzed as: "$\exists x$ (cat (x) & x arrived)". This "quantificational analysis of indefinites", as I will call it, is nowadays accepted in one variant or another by the vast majority of philosophers and linguists.

This paper contains what I will call, by contrast, a "non-quantificational analysis of indefinites". The logical analysis of an indefinite, as presented above, is just a proposition with a variable free in it. E.g. "a cat" corresponds to something like "cat(x)". When an indefinite occurs in a sentence, as in schema (22), the logical analysis of that sentence is again a proposition with a variable free in it:

(24) $Y(x) \& (X x Z)$

The free variable in the indefinite remains free in the sentence as a whole. An existential quantifier is not part of the indefinite or of the sentence that contains it, neither is a quantifier of some other force than existential.[11] This section is intended to bring to bear some linguistic evidence on the choice between a quantificational and a non-quantificational analysis of indefinites. But first let me clarify to what extent the two analyses agree in their empirical predictions.

Despite the absence of an existential quantifier in the logical forms of sentences with indefinites, my theory predicts what are, in effect, existential truth-conditions for such sentences. Consider again "A cat arrived" with the logical form (12b). By the truth criterion (21) for logical forms, we know that (12b) is true w.r.t. a true file F if and only if F + (12b) is true. For F + (12b) to be true, in turn, means two things: First, (12b) must be appropriate w.r.t. F, in particular, Dom(F) must not contain 1, for F + (12b) to be defined. Second, Sat(F + (12b)) must be non-empty. Rules (16) and (18) determine that Sat (F + (12b)) = $\{a_N \cup b_{\{1\}} \in A^{N \cup \{1\}}: a_N \in$ Sat (F), b_1 is a cat, and b_1 arrived$\}$. Given that Sat(F) is non-empty (since F is true), this set is non-empty just in case there is at least one cat that arrived. What we have just shown is that (12b) is true w.r.t. F if and only if at least one cat arrived. Since the proof did not depend on any particular properties of F other than that it be true and that (12b) be appropriate w.r.t. it, we may suppress relativization to F and simply say that (12b) is true if and only if at least one cat arrived. Moreover, since an analogous proof would have gone through for any other wellformed logical form of the sentence that (12b) represents, we can say that we have shown that the sentence "A cat arrived" is true if and only if at least one cat arrived. This prediction coincides of course with the familiar existential truth-condition that a quantificational analysis would have predicted as well.

At first sight, one might have thought it impossible that an existential truth-condition can be predicted while assuming a quantifier-free logical form like (12b) or (24). But there was of course no magic involved in the proof I just gave. The truth-condition came out existential because the notion of truth of a file has, so to speak, existential quantification built into it: truth of a file was defined as *there being at least one* satisfying sequence. So my disagreement with the quantificational analysis of indefinites is not a disagreement about whether or not we understand statements with indefinites in them as existentially quantified. It is rather a disagreement as to what is to be held responsible for the existential force of such statements: the indefinite article itself, or rather the way in which files generally relate to the facts that verify them? If we are to find any empirical evidence that will discriminate between these two points of view, it won't help to simply examine our intuitions about what sentences like "A cat arrived" mean. We will have to resort to considerations based on relatively indirect evidence like the following.

It is well-known of certain undebatable cases of quantifying NPs in natural language that they are subject to tighter restrictions on anaphora than certain other NPs. I have in mind contrasts like this one:

(25) Every soldier is armed. He will shoot.
(26) He is armed. He will shoot.

The two "he"'s can be anaphorically related in (26), but no anaphoric relation is possible between "every soldier" and "he" in (25). Why should this be so? — An explanation suggests itself if we assume that "every" is a quantifier, pronouns are variables, and (25) and (26) have logical analyses of essentially these forms:

(25') $\forall x_i$ (soldier (x_i) → armed (x_i)) & $(x_j$ will shoot)
(26') armed (x_i) & $(x_j$ will shoot)

Is $i = j$ or $i \neq j$? Let us try to get away with the simplest possible assumption, i.e. that both texts permit readings with any arbitrary choice of i and j, and in particular readings with $i = j$ as well as readings with $i \neq j$. Now look at the satisfaction conditions that formulas like (25') and (26') receive under standard interpretations of predicate calculus. If (26') has two different variables $x_i \neq x_j$, then a sequence satisfying it will have to contain an armed person and a (possibly distinct) person that will shoot. If the variables are the same in (26'), then a satisfying sequence has to include a person that is both armed and will shoot. So in the case of $i = j$, we have a substantially different satisfaction condition than in the case of $i \neq j$.

Now take (25') and compare the satisfaction conditions that we get with $i = j$ to those we get with $i \neq j$. It turns out that it makes no difference: A sequence that satisfies (25') must contain a person that will shoot, and provided it does, will satisfy (25') only if every soldier is armed. This same satisfaction condition applies regardless of whether x_i and x_j are different variables or the same. This seems to be what is behind our judgment that (25) has no reading where "every soldier" and "he" are "anaphorically related": Even if we make a point of coindexing "every soldier" with "he", i.e. of picking identical variables in the logical analysis of (25), the coindexing is of necessity a semantically "vacuous" coindexing.[12]

What we have just observed about (25') falls under a general law, so to speak a design feature of quantificational logic:

(27) If x_i is bound by a quantifier whose scope does not include x_j, then coindexing between x_i and x_j can only be vacuous.

(27) makes explicit what it is about the logical analysis of (25) that makes it different from the logical analysis of (26) in such a way that (25) will permit only vacuous coindexing where (26) permits the sort of non-vacuous coindexing that we perceive as an anaphoric reading. The crucial point is that "every soldier" was analyzed as a quantifying NP, whereas there was no quantifier assumed to occur in the corresponding position in (26).

What does all this have to do with the choice between a quantificational and a non-quantificational analysis of indefinites? Well, since (27) makes reference to quantifiers, we might try to exploit it as a diagnostic test for quantifyingness: If indefinites turn out to bear non-vacuous coindexing relations to variables outside their scope, then that ought to show they are not quantifiers. Unfortunately, this test is not as foolproof in application as one might hope. But let's try it first.

Consider (28).

(28) A soldier will accompany us. He will shoot.

Presumably, (28) would be analyzed as (28') under a quantificational treatment of indefinites, but as (28") under a non-quantificational treatment.

(28') $\exists x_i$ (soldier (x_i) & $(x_i$ will accompany us)) & $(x_j$ will shoot)
(28") (soldier (x_i) & $(x_i$ will accompany us)) & $(x_j$ will shoot)

By (27), the coindexing $i = j$ in (28') is bound to be vacuous, while (28") contains no obstacle to non-vacuous coindexing. Our intuitive judgment is that anaphora is possible in (28), just like in (26), and unlike in (25). We can straightforwardly predict the anaphoric reading by assuming a logical form along the lines of (28"), with $i = j$, a non-vacuous coindexing. (28'), on the other hand, would seem to preclude an anaphoric reading. This is prima facie evidence in favor of the non-quantificational analysis of indefinites.

There are various ways in which the conclusion just drawn can be, and has been, challenged. First, one might call into question a tacit assumption I have been making about the scope-options for quantifying NPs. With both (25) and (28), I took it for granted that a quantifying NP that occurred in the first sentence of each text could take scope at most over that sentence, not over the entire bisentential text. Had I permitted the quantifying NP "every soldier" in (25) and the putatively quantifying NP "a soldier" in (28) to take wider scope than the sentence, then the variable x_j in (25') and (28') could have come under the scope of $\forall$ or $\exists$, in which case $i = j$ would have been a non-vacuous coindexing. (Cf. (27).) This suggests that the quantificational analysis of indefinites could be saved if one were to maintain that indefinites, unlike certain other quantifying NPs, can take scope across several sentences.[13]

A second way of undermining my use of (28) as evidence against a quantificational analysis of indefinites goes like this: What we customarily describe as "anaphoric relations" may not be one and the same kind of logical relation in all cases, and in particular, need not always be non-vacuous identity of variables. So even if the logical analysis of (28) is (28') (with either $i = j$ or $i \neq j$, it doesn't matter), we may still use (28) with the intention that x_j refer to whatever individual is responsible for the truth of "$\exists x_i$ (soldier(x_i) & (x_i will accompany us))". Viewed in this way, the so-called "anaphoric" use of the pronoun in (28) has really a lot more in common with deictic pronoun uses than with bound-variable anaphora: The pronoun is here taken to refer to a contextually salient individual, just like deictic pronouns do, except that in this case the crucial factor in making the intended referent salient is the fact that it verifies a piece of immediately preceding discourse.[14]

Both of these objections deserve serious consideration before we can be sure that the ability of indefinites to serve as antecedents for anaphoric pronouns beyond their scope is indeed a symptom of the non-quantificational nature of indefinites. I will have to be brief here.[15] My answer to both objections is that the alternative accounts they give of the anaphoric relation between "a soldier" and "he" in (28) do not carry over to certain other examples of an analogous nature. Consider (29).

(29) Every time a soldier accompanies us he shoots.

Under a quantificational analysis of indefinites, (29) ought to get the following logical analysis:

(29') $\forall t\ (\exists x_i\ (\text{soldier}\ (x_i)\ \&\ (x_i\ \text{accompanies us at } t))\ \rightarrow\ (x_j\ \text{shoots at } t)).$

Unlike in the case of (28), the truth-conditions of (29) are clearly inconsistent with an alternative analysis under which "a soldier" takes wide enough scope to include x_j.[16] This shows that if a quantificational analysis of indefinites is to be reconciled with their behavior w.r.t. anaphora, it will not suffice to appeal to their unconstrained scope options.

But (29) also doesn't lend itself to an account in terms of the sort of quasi-deictic use of "he" that had some plausibility for examples like (28). The problem is that the "he" in (29) fails to refer, and that deixis without reference is a contradiction in terms by all available explications of the concept.

So (29), more compellingly than (28), shows that indefinites enter into anaphoric relations where this is not to be expected from the point of view of a quantificational analysis. I have yet to show that the non-quantificational alternative that I am developing in this article covers examples like (29) in a natural way. This leads us to the topic of quantification.

8 File Change Rules for Quantified Sentences

Before I give the file change potentials for operator-headed logical forms, in particular universally quantified and negated ones, I should say something about "closed" propositions (i.e. propositions without free variables) in general. Take a simple sentence with a 0-place predicate:

(30) It is raining.

In the context of the file metaphor, one doesn't quite know how to deal with (30): As an informative sentence, it ought to call for an updating of the file somehow; but what exactly is the file clerk supposed to do? The information that it is raining does not belong on any particular file card, it seems, since each file card is a description of an individual, but (30) is not about any individual. Should the file clerk perhaps write on some arbitrary card: "is such that it is raining"? Or should he write that on all cards? And what if the file so far doesn't contain any cards yet? — Fortunately, we can leave these questions unanswered here. Recall that we have already resigned ourselves to characterizing file change only as far as the domain and satisfaction set are concerned. So we need not specify anything else about the file change potential of (30) than its impact on domain and satisfaction set. And that is already taken care of by rule (18) above. We only need to assume that the extension of a 0-place predicate is empty if the corresponding state of affairs fails to obtain, and is the unit set of the empty sequence if it does obtain. E.g. we have Ext ("rain") = $\{\phi\}$ if it rains, Ext ("rain") = ϕ otherwise. This way we can apply (18) to give us:

$$\text{Sat } (F + (30)) = \begin{cases} \text{Sat } (F), \text{ if Ext ("rain")} = \{\phi\}, \\ \phi, \text{ otherwise.} \end{cases}$$

This amounts to the correct truth conditions for such sentences. The reason why I dwelled on this point is that quantified and negated propositions are similarly puzzling if we are so ambitious as to want to say what exactly the file clerk does in response to them. Under the modest aspect of domain and satisfaction set change, however, they pose no problem.

An example of a universally quantified logical form is (12c), repeated from above.

(12) (c)

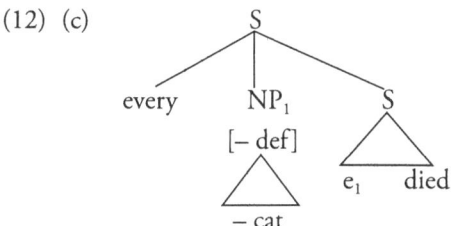

Note that I have here marked the determinerless NP [_ cat] as indefinite. I assume that NPs which have had their determiners moved out generally qualify as [— definite].

Unlike in the case of operator-free molecular propositions, the file change induced by (12c) cannot be broken down into a simple, so to speak "linear", succession of smaller steps that correspond to each of the sub-propositions. The presence of an operator makes considerably higher demands on the file clerk's memory and computational abilities. We may think of the evaluation of (12c) as proceeding in three steps as follows:

Step 1: Tentatively update the original file F by incorporating $[_{NP_1}-$ cat] into it. This gets you to F' = F + $[_{NP_1}$ cat] with the following satisfaction set, as determined by rule (18):

$$\text{Sat(F')} = \{a_N \cup b_{\{1\}} \in A^{N \cup \{1\}} : a_N \in \text{Sat (F) and } b_1 \text{ is a cat}\}.$$

The change from F to F' is only "tentative" insofar as the file clerk retains F in his memory and is prepared to make his next actions depend not only on F', but also on F.

Step 2: Tentatively update F' by incorporating $[_s e_i$ died] into it. This results in F", determined by rule (18) as follows:

$$\text{Sat (F'')} = \{a_N \cup b_{\{1\}} \in A^{N \cup \{1\}} : a_N \in \text{Sat (F), and } b_1 \text{ is a cat, and } b_1 \text{ died}\}.$$

Again, F' is retained in memory, which now contains both F and F'.

Step 3: For each sequence a_N in Sat (F), do the following: Determine whether all "continuations" of a_N that are in Sat (F') are also in Sat (F"). (By a "continuation" of a_N I mean a sequence that includes a_N as a subsequence.) If yes, carry a_N along into the satisfaction set of the new file F + (12c); if no, eliminate a_N. After you have done this for each $a_N \in$ Sat (F), you will thus have:

$$\text{Sat(F + (12c))} = \{a_N \in \text{Sat (F): for every } b_M \supseteq a_N,$$
$$\text{if } b_M \in \text{Sat (F') then } b_M \in \text{Sat (F'')}\}.$$

You may now clear the memory of F, F', and F".

Step 3 is obviously the one which takes into account the specific force of the operator involved, here universal quantification. The preceding two steps serve only to set up the auxiliary files on which the calculation in step 3 is based. These two steps are the same for all two-place operators.

Let us figure out the result of this three-step procedure for a concrete choice of initial file, the empty file F_0. Starting from F_0, the outcomes of steps 1 and 2 will look like this:

Sat $(F_0 + [_{NP_1\_} \text{cat}]) = \{b_{\{1\}}: b_1 \text{ is a cat}\}$.

Sat $((F_0 + [_{NP_1\_} \text{cat}]) + [_s e_1 \text{ died}]) = \{b_{\{1\}}: b_1 \text{ is a cat and } b_1 \text{ died}\}$.

The result of step 3 is then the following:

$$\text{Sat } (F_0 + (12c)) = \begin{cases} \text{Sat } (F_0), \text{ if every cat died;} \\ \phi, \text{ otherwise.} \end{cases}$$

In view of the truth criterion (21) above, this implies that (12c) is true w.r.t. F_0 just in case every cat died, an intuitively adequate prediction. However, we still have to show that equally adequate predictions are generated with choices other than F_0 for the initial file.

At first glance, there seems to be a problem with initial files F that already contain a card number 1. For instance, if we assumed $\text{Dom}(F) = \{1\}$ and $\text{Sat}(F) = \{a_{\{1\}}: a_1 \text{ is a pet}\}$, then each sequence in Sat(F) could have at most one continuation in Sat $(F + [_{NP_1\_} \text{cat}])$, namely the trivial continuation, which is itself. The result of step 3 would then be this:

Sat $(F + (12c)) = \{a_{\{1\}}: a_1 \text{ is a pet, and if } a_i \text{ is a cat, then } a_i \text{ died}\}$.

This conflicts with the intuitive truth conditions of (12c) and in particular with its universal force.

However, we have no reason to worry about this result, because it only arises if we neglect the constraints which the Novelty/Familiarity Condition imposes on the choice of F. Recall that the Novelty/Familiarity Condition (= (15) above) has to be met each time an atomic proposition is incorporated into the file, or else there won't be a file change result defined at all. Applied to the evaluation of (12 c), this means in particular that step 1 cannot be carried out unless $[_{NP_1\_} \text{cat}]$ is appropriate w.r.t. the initial file F. According to (15), F is therefore not permitted to contain the number 1 in its domain, "_ cat$_1$" being indefinite. In particular, the choice of F which in the example above seemed to lead to inadequate predictions about the truth conditions of (12c) was inconsistent with the Novelty/Familiarity Condition, and we should have realized that neither F+ (12c) nor, consequently, the truth of (12c) w.r.t. F is at all defined for such choices of F.

Turning to examples of greater complexity than (12c), we find that the three step procedure that I have proposed applies analogously, and that it interacts with the Novelty/Familiarity Condition in such a way as to predict the contrast between definites and indefinites when they appear inside a universally quantifying NP. Compare (31) and (32).

(31) Every man who likes a donkey buys it.

(32) Every man who likes it buys it.

(31) expresses a generalization about man-donkey-pairs; it is as though the universal quantifier "every" was here binding the donkey-variable along with the man-variable. (32), by contrast, is read as generalizing over all men that like a fixed object. The variable corresponding to the "it" in "every man who likes it" may refer to a contextually supplied object, or may be anaphoric to an antecedent in the larger text in which (32) appears. Either way, it is not understood as bound to "every" in the way that "a donkey" in (31) is. Let me briefly show how this contrast is derived from the assumptions I have introduced.

(31) is represented on the logical form level roughly as follows.

Starting from an initial file F, steps 1 and 2, in analogy to the specifications given above, provide us with auxiliary files $F' = F + p$ and $F'' = F' + q$. These have the following satisfaction sets, according to rules (16) and (18).

$$\text{Sat}(F') = \{a_N \cup b_{\{1,2\}}: a_N \in \text{Sat}(F), b_1 \text{ is a man}, b_2 \text{ is a donkey, and } b_1 \text{ likes } b_2\}.$$

$$\text{Sat}(F'') = \{a_N \cup b_{\{1,2\}}: a_N \in \text{Sat}(F), b_1 \text{ is a man}, b_2 \text{ is a donkey}, b_1 \text{ likes } b_2,$$
$$\text{and } b_1 \text{ buys } b_2\}.$$

Concerning F, we must assume that Dom (F) contains neither 1 nor 2, because otherwise the Novelty/Familiarity Condition would not let F' be defined. We now proceed to step 3, in which we consider one by one the members a_N of Sat (F). For each such a_N, we form every continuation of a_N that is in Sat (F') and determine whether it is also in Sat (F''). To satisfy F', a continuation of a_N has to contain two members, number 1 and number 2, which are a man and a donkey he likes, respectively. Every man/donkey-pair of this sort will figure in some continuation of a_N, because a_N itself does not contain any members number 1 and number 2. Therefore the requirement that every continuation of a_N that

(31')

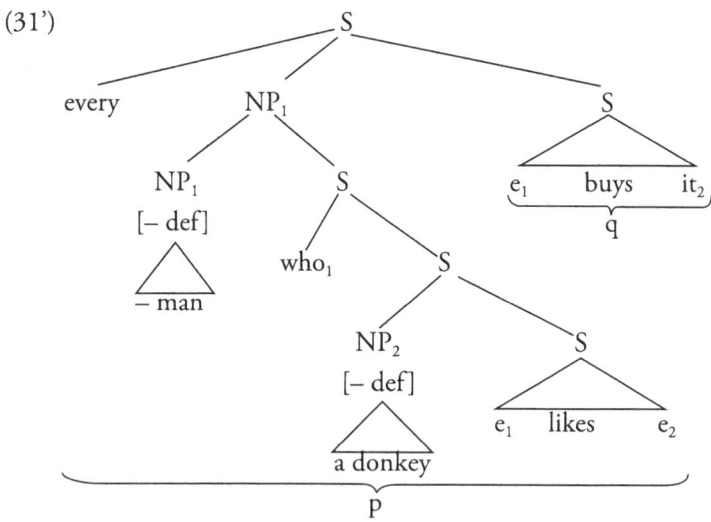

satisfies F' must also satisfy F" amounts to the requirement that every man-donkey pair in which the man likes the donkey is also such that the man buys the donkey. The result of step 3 is therefore:

$$\text{Sat (F + (30'))} = \begin{cases} \text{Sat (F), if every man who likes a donkey buys it,} \\ \phi, \text{ otherwise.} \end{cases}$$

The logical form of (32) differs from that of (31) in that it has the definite "it" instead of the indefinite "a donkey":

(32')

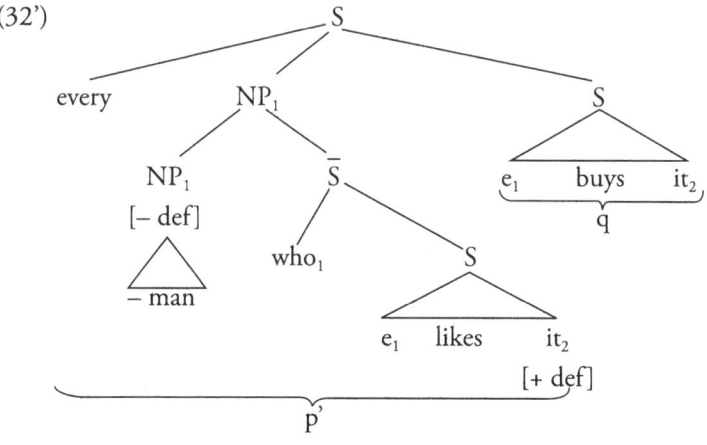

This time, steps 1 and 2 will produce the auxiliary files F' = F +p' and F" = F' + q (where F stands again for the initial file):

$$\text{Sat (F')} = \{a_N \cup b_{\{1,2\}} \in A^{N \cup \{1,2\}}: a_N \in \text{Sat (F)}, b_1 \text{ is a man, and } b_1 \text{ likes } b_2\}.$$
$$\text{Sat (F")} = \{a_N \cup b_{\{1,2\}}: a_N \in \text{Sat (F)}, b_1 \text{ is a man, } b_1 \text{ likes } b_2, \text{ and } b_1 \text{ buys } b_2\}.$$

Unlike in the previous example, the Novelty/Familiarity Condition this time requires that Dom (F) doesn't contain 1, but does contain 2. This has important consequences for how step 3 applies. In step 3, we look at each $a_N \in$ Sat (F) and form all continuations of a_N that satisfy F'. Because $2 \in$ Dom (F), a_N includes a member a_2, and every continuation of a_N has that same a_2 as its member number 2 as well. Therefore, not every pair of a man and an individual he likes will necessarily be part of a continuation of a_N, but rather, only those pairs where the individual the man likes is none other than a_2. The predicted result of step 3 is a file with the following satisfaction set:

$$\text{Sat (F + (32'))} = \{a_N \in \text{Sat (F)}: \text{ for every } b_1, \text{ if } b_1 \text{ is a man and } b_1 \text{ likes } a_2,$$
$$\text{then } b_1 \text{ buys } a_2\}.$$

The difference between this and Sat (F + (31')) above reflects the intuition that (31) involves universal quantification over pairs, whereas (32) quantifies over men which like a "fixed" individual.

It remains to write up explicitly the file change rule which dictates the three step procedure I have described. We want this rule to be general enough to work not only for examples like (12c), (31), and (32), but also for examples like (33):[17]

(33) Every man who owns a donkey sells it to a merchant.

(33) contains an indefinite ("a merchant") in the right-hand argument of the quantifier, and this creates complications for step 3 as I have specified it so far. The problem is that in a case like this, F" will contain more cards than F', and it will therefore be impossible in principle for any sequence that satisfies F' to also satisfy F". The following formulation of the file change rule for universally quantified propositions is designed to deal with this additional complication. This is why it doesn't simply require that every continuation of a given a_N that satisfies F'

also satisfy F", but rather that a further continuation of the continuation satisfy F".

(34) Let F be a file, and let p be a molecular proposition whose immediate constituents are a universal quantifier and the propositions q and r (in that order). Then: Sat $(F + p)$ = $\{a_N \in$ Sat (F): for every $b_M \supseteq a_N$ such that $b_M \in$ Sat $(F + q)$, there is a $c_L \supseteq b_M$ such that $c_L \in$ Sat $((F + q) + r)\}$.

I leave it to the reader to verify that (34) applies satisfactorily to example (33).

I complete this section by formulating the file change rule for negated propositions, trusting that the reader can come up with his or her own illustrations.

(35) Let F be a file, and let p be a molecular proposition whose immediate constituents are a negation operator and the proposition q. Then:
Sat $(F + p)$ = $\{a_N \in$ Sat (F): there is no $b_M \supseteq a_N$ such that $b_M \in$ Sat $(F + q)\}$.

Notes

The ideas contained in this article are elaborated more fully in my Ph. D. thesis (Heim 1982). All the people whose help I acknowledge there should also be mentioned here, in particular Angelika Kratzer and my thesis advisor Barbara Partee.

1   The label is due to Hawkins (1978).

2   See in particular Russell (1919, Ch. 16), Quine (1960), Kaplan (1972), and Geach (1962).

3   Karttunen (1968a, b, 1976).

4   The file metaphor was first suggested to me by Angelika Kratzer, in response to an earlier attempt of mine to modify Grice's and Stalnaker's notion of "common ground" (cf. especially Stalnaker 1979) in such a way as to impose on common grounds an essentially file-like structure. I subsequently found uses of the file metaphor for more or less similar purposes elsewhere in the literature, e.g. in Karttunen (1976). With respect to their role in a model of semantics, my files are closely related not only to Stalnaker's "common grounds", but particularly to the "discourse representation structures" of Kamp (1981).

5   These assumptions about logical form are taken over from Chomsky's

work and other work in the framework of the "Revised Extended Standard Theory", see in particular May (1977) and Reinhart (1976).

6   This is similar to the "predication condition" of May (1977).

7   May (1977) makes this assumption only for quantifying NPs, whereas I extend it to all predicate-headed NPs, quantifying or not.

8   Heim (1983) argues that this view of what presuppositions are throws light on the behavior of presuppositions with respect to the so-called "projection problem".

9   See Heim (1982).

10   Russell (1919, Ch. 6).

11   When I say (here and elsewhere in this article) that the indefinite is not a quantifier, I am of course not using "quantifier" in the sense of Barwise and Cooper (1981). In their sense of "quantifier", anything that denotes a function from predicate-meanings to proposition-meanings is a quantifier, and every kind of NP, even proper names and pronouns, can therefore be construed as quantifiers.

12   The relevant notion of "vacuity" could be defined as follows:

Def.: Let p be a formula, x a variable, and A the set of all occurrences of x in p. Suppose B and C are two disjoint subsets of A, with $A = B \cup C$. Then the members of B are *vacuously coindexed* with the members of C iff for some variable $y = x$, p and p' have identical satisfaction conditions; where p' results from p by substituting y for every occurrence of x that is in C.

Note that the "law" under (27) in the text is not a definition of vacuity, but rather a theorem that follows from the definition above, given the standard interpretation of quantifiers. This is why one could not simply choose to replace (27) by a stipulation that permits certain quantifiers to be coindexed non-vacuously with variables beyond their scope — unless one were to use logic as an uninterpreted formalism altogether.

13   This is basically what Geach (1962) suggests.

14   This line is taken by Kripke (1977), Lewis (1979), and elsewhere.

15   For more careful argumentation, see Heim (1982, Ch. 1), where I also address a third way of undermining the use of (28) as evidence against the quantificational analysis of indefinites, advocated by Evans (1977) and Cooper (1979), among others.

16 Unless one assumes, moreover, that the wide-scope taking indefinite switches its quantificational force from existential to universal. That assumption has been pursued in Egli (1979) and Smaby (1979), whose proposals are discussed in depth in Heim (1982, Ch. 1).

17 The example is from Kamp (1981), whose treatment of quantification (designed to go with his version of the non-quantificational analysis of indefinites) made me aware that I had overlooked cases like (33) in a earlier version of my theory.

References

Barwise, Jon and Robin Cooper. 1981. Generalized quantifiers and natural language. *Linguistics and Philosophy* 4: 159–219.

Christophersen, Paul. 1939. *The Articles: A Study of their Theory and Use in English.* Copenhagen: Munksgaard.

Cooper, Robin. 1979. The interpretation of pronouns. In F. Heny and H. Schnelle (eds), *Selections from the Third Groningen Round Table (Syntax and Semantics,* vol. 10), New York: Academic Press.

Egli, U. 1979. The Stoic concept of anaphora. In Rainer Bäuerle, Urs Egli, and Arnim von Stechow (eds), *Semantics from Different Points of View,* Berlin: Springer-Verlag.

Evans, Gareth. 1977. Pronouns, quantifiers, and relative clauses. *Canadian Journal of Philosophy 7:* 467–536.

Geach, Peter. 1962. *Reference and Generality; An Examination of Some Medieval and Modern Theories.* Ithaca, N.Y.: Cornell University Press.

Hawkins, John A. 1978. *Definiteness and Indefiniteness: A Study in Reference and Grammaticality Prediction.* London: Croom Helm.

Heim, Irene. 1982. The Semantics of Definite and Indefinite Noun Phrases. Doctoral dissertation, University of Massachusetts, Amherst.

Heim, Irene. 1983. On the projection problem for presuppositions. In M. Barlow, D. Flickinger, and M. Wescoat (eds), *WCCFL 2: Second Annual West Coast Conference on Formal Linguistics,* Stanford, Calif.: Stanford University.

Jespersen, Otto. 1949. *A Modern English Grammar on Historical Principles,* part VII, completed and published by N. Haislund. Copenhagen: Munksgaard.

Kamp, Hans. 1981. A theory of truth and semantic representation. In J. A. G.

Groenendijk, T. M. V. Janssen, and M. B. J. Stokhof (eds), *Formal Methods in the Study of Language,* Amsterdam: Mathematisch Centrum, University of Amsterdam.

Kaplan, David. 1972. What is Russell's theory of definite descriptions?. In D. Davidson and G. Harman (eds), *The Logic of Grammar,* Encino, Calif.: Dickenson.

Karttunen, Lauri. 1968a. What Makes Definite Noun Phrases Definite?, RAND Corporation report P3871, unpublished.

Karttunen, Lauri. 1968b. What Do Referential Indices Refer To?, RAND Corporation report P3854, unpublished.

Karttunen, Lauri. 1976. Discourse referents. In J. McCawley (ed.), *Notes from the Linguistic Underground (Syntax and Semantics,* vol. 7), New York: Academic Press.

Kripke, Saul. 1977. Speaker reference and semantic reference. In P. A. French, T. E. Uehling, Jr., and H. K. Wettstein (eds), *Midwest Studies in Philosophy,* vol. 2, *Studies in the Philosophy of Language.* Minneapolis, Minn.: University of Minnesota Press, 6–27.

Lewis, David. 1979. Scorekeeping in a language game. In Rainer Bäuerle, Urs Egli, and Arnim von Stechow (eds), *Semantics from Different Points of View,* Berlin: Springer-Verlag.

May, Robert. 1977. The Grammar of Quantification. Ph.D. dissertation, MIT.

Quine, Willard Van Orman. 1960. *Word and Object.* Cambridge, Mass.: MIT Press.

Reinhart, T. 1976. The Syntactic Domain of Anaphora. Ph.D. dissertation, MIT.

Russell, Bertrand. 1919. *Introduction to Mathematical Philosophy.* London.

Smaby, R. 1979. Ambiguous coreference with quantifiers. In F. Günthner and S. J. Schmidt (eds), *Formal Semantics and Pragmatics for Natural Languages,* Dordrecht: D. Reidel.

Stalnaker, Robert C. 1978. Assertion. In Peter Cole (ed.), *Pragmatics (Syntax and Semantics,* vol. 9), New York: Academic Press, 315–22.

Scorekeeping in a Language Game

David Lewis

EXAMPLE 1: PRESUPPOSITION[1]

At any stage in a well-run conversation, a certain amount is presupposed. The parties to the conversation take it for granted; or at least they purport to, whether sincerely or just "for the sake of the argument". Presuppositions can be created or destroyed in the course of a conversation. This change is rule-governed, at least up to a point. The presuppositions at time t' depend, in a way about which at least some general principles can be laid down, on the presuppositions at an earlier time t and on the course of the conversation (and nearby events) between t and t'.

Some things that might be said require suitable presuppositions. They are acceptable if the required presuppositions are present; not otherwise. "The king of France is bald" requires the presupposition that France has one king, and one only; "Even George Lakoff could win" requires the presupposition that George is not a leading candidate; and so on.

We need not ask just what sort of unacceptability results when a required presupposition is lacking. Some say falsehood, some say lack of truth value, some just say that it's the kind of unacceptability that results when a required presupposition is lacking, and some say it might vary from case to case.

Be that as it may, it's not as easy as you might think to say something that will be unacceptable for lack of required presuppositions. Say something that requires a missing presupposition, and straightway that presupposition springs

233

into existence, making what you said acceptable after all. (Or at least, that is what happens if your conversational partners tacitly acquiesce — if no one says "But France has *three* kings!" or "Whadda ya mean, '*even* George'?") That is why it is peculiar to say, out of the blue, "All Fred's children are asleep, and Fred has children." The first part requires and thereby creates a presupposition that Fred has children; so the second part adds nothing to what is already presupposed when it is said; so the second part has no conversational point. It would not have been peculiar to say instead "Fred has children, and all Fred's children are asleep."

I said that presupposition evolves in a more or less rule-governed way during a conversation. Now we can formulate one important governing rule: call it the *rule of accommodation for presupposition.*

> If at time *t* something is said that requires presupposition *P* to be acceptable, and if *P* is not presupposed just before *t*, then — *ceteris paribus* and within certain limits — presupposition *P* comes into existence at *t*.

This rule has not yet been very well stated, nor is it the only rule governing the kinematics of presupposition. But let us bear it in mind nevertheless, and move on to other things.

EXAMPLE 2: PERMISSIBILITY[2]

For some reason — coercion, deference, common purpose — two people are both willing that one of them should be under the control of the other. (At least within certain limits, in a certain sphere of action, so long as certain conditions prevail.) Call one the *slave,* the other the *master.* The control is exercised verbally, as follows.

At any stage in the enslavement, there is a boundary between some courses of action for the slave that are permissible, and others that are not. The range of permissible conduct may expand or contract. The master shifts the boundary by saying things to the slave. Since the slave does his best to see to it that his course of action is a permissible one, the master can control the slave by controlling what is permissible.

Here is how the master shifts the boundary. From time to time he says to the slave that such-and-such courses of action are impermissible. Any such statement depends for its truth value on the boundary between what is permissible and what isn't. But if the master says that something is impermissible, and if that would be false if the boundary remained stationary, then straightway the boundary moves inward. The permissible range contracts so that what the master says is true after all. Thereby the master makes courses of action impermissible that used to be permissible. But from time to time also the master relents, and says to the slave that such-and-such courses of action are permissible. Or perhaps he says that some of such-and-such courses of action are permissible, but doesn't say just which ones. Then the boundary moves outward. The permissible range expands, if need be (and if possible), so that what the master says is true. Thereby the master makes courses of action permissible that used to be impermissible.

The truth of the master's statements about permissibility — one aspect of their acceptability — depends on the location of the boundary. The boundary shifts in a rule-governed way. The rule is as follows; call it the *rule of accommodation for permissibility.*

If at time *t* something is said about permissibility by the master to the slave that requires for its truth the permissibility or impermissibility of certain courses of action, and if just before *t* the boundary is such as to make the master's statement false, then — *ceteris paribus* and within certain limits — the boundary shifts at *t* so as to make the master's statement true.

Again, this is not a very satisfactory formulation. For one thing, the limits and qualifications are left unspecified. But more important, the rule as stated does not say exactly how the boundary is to shift.

What if the master says that some of such-and-such courses of actions are permissible, when none of them were permissible before he spoke. By the rule, some of them must straightway become permissible. Some — but which ones? The ones that were closest to permissibility beforehand, perhaps. Well and good, but now we have a new problem. At every state there is not only a boundary between the permissible and the impermissible, but also a relation of comparative near-permissibility between the courses of action on the impermissible side. Not only do we need rules governing the shifting boundary, but also we need rules to govern the changing relation of comparative near-permissibility. Not only must we say how this relation evolves when the master says something about absolute permissibility, but also we must say how it evolves when he says something — as he might — about comparative near-permissibility. He might say, for instance, that the most nearly permissible courses of action in a class A are those in a subclass A'; or that some courses of action in class B are more nearly permissible than any in class C. Again the rule is a rule of accommodation. The relation of comparative near-permissibility changes, if need be, so that what the master says to the slave is true. But again, to say that is not enough. It does not suffice to determine just what the change is.

Those were Examples 1 and 2. Examples of what? I'll say shortly; but first, a digression.

SCOREKEEPING IN A BASEBALL GAME

At any stage in a well-run baseball game, there is a septuple of numbers $<r_v, r_h, h, i,$ $s, b, o>$ which I shall call the *score* of that game at that stage. We recite the score as follows: the visiting team has r_v runs, the home team has r_h runs, it is the hth half (h being 1 or 2) of the ith inning; there are s strikes, b balls, and o outs. (In another terminology, the score is only the initial pair $<r_v, r_h>$, but I need a word for the entire septuple.) A possible codification of the rules of baseball would consist of rules of four different sorts.

(1) *Specifications of the kinematics of score.* Initially, the score is $<0, 0, 1, 1, 0,$ $0, 0>$. Thereafter, if at time t the score is s, and if between time t and time t' the players behave in manner m, then at time t' the score is s', where s' is determined in a certain way by s and m.

(2) *Specifications of correct play.* If at time t the score is s, and if between time t and time t' the players behave in manner m, then the players have behaved incorrectly. (Correctness depends on score: what is correct play after two strikes differs from what is correct play after three.) What is not incorrect play according to these rules is correct.

(3) *Directive requiring correct play.* All players are to behave, throughout the game, in such a way that play is correct.

(4) *Directives concerning score.* Players are to strive to make the score evolve in certain directions. Members of the visiting team try to make r_v large and r_h small, members of the home team try to do the opposite.

(We could dispense with roles of sorts (2) and (3) by adding an eighth component to the score which, at any stage of the game, measures the amount of incorrect play up to that stage. Specifications of correct play are then included among the specifications of the kinematics of score, and the directive requiring correct play becomes one of the directives concerning score.)

Rules of sorts (1) and (2) are sometimes called *constitutive rules*. They are said to be akin to definitions, though they do not have the form of definitions. Rules of sorts (3) and (4) are called *regulative rules*. They are akin to the straightforward directives "No smoking!" or "Keep left!".

We could explain this more fully, as follows. Specifications of sorts (1) and (2) are not themselves definitions of "score" and "correct play". But they are consequences of reasonable definitions. Further, there is a systematic way to construct the definitions, given the specifications. Suppose we wish to define the *score function*: the function from game-stages to septuples of numbers that gives the score at every stage. The specifications of the kinematics of score, taken together, tell us that the score function evolves in such-and-such way. We may then simply define the score function as that function which evolves in such-and-such way. If the kinematics of score are well specified, then there is one function, and one only, that evolves in the proper way; and if so, then the score function evolves in the proper way if and only if the suggested definition of it is correct. Once we have defined the score function, we have thereby defined the score and all its components at any stage. There are two outs at a certain stage of a game, for instance, if and only if the score function assigns to that game-stage a septuple whose seventh component is the number 2.

Turn next to the specifications of correct play. Taken together, they tell us that correct play occurs at a game-stage if and only if the players' behavior at that stage bears such-and-such relation to score at that stage. This has the form of an explicit definition of correct play in terms of current behavior. If current score has already been defined in terms of the history of the players' behavior up to now, in the way just suggested, then we have defined correct play in terms of current and previous behavior.

Once score and correct play are defined in terms of the players' behavior, then we may eliminate the defined terms in the directive requiring correct play and the directives concerning score. Thanks to the definitions constructed from the constitutive rules, the regulative rules become simply directives to strive to see to it that one's present behavior bears a certain rather complicated relation to the history of the players' behavior in previous stages of the game. A player might attempt to conform to such a directive for various reasons: contractual obligation, perhaps, or a conventional understanding with his fellow players based on their common interest in enjoying a proper game.

The rules of baseball could in principle be formulated as straighforward directives concerning behavior, without the aid of definable terms for score and its components. Or they could be formulated as explicit definitions of the score function, the components of score, and correct play, followed by directives in which the newly defined terms appear. It is easy to see why neither of these methods of formulation has found favor. The first method would pack the entire rulebook into each directive; the second would pack the entire rulebook into a single preliminary explicit definition. Understandably averse to very long sentences, we do better to proceed in our more devious way.

There is an alternative analysis — the baseball equivalent of operationalism or legal realism. Instead of appealing to constitutive rules, we might instead claim that the score is, by definition, whatever some scoreboard says it is. Which scoreboard? Various answers are defensible: maybe the visible scoreboard with its arrays of light bulbs, maybe the invisible scoreboard in the head umpire's head, maybe the many scoreboards in many heads to the extent that they agree. No matter. On any such view, the specifications of the kinematics of score have a changed status. No longer are they constitutive rules akin to definitions. Rather, they are empirical generalizations, subject to exceptions, about the ways in which the players' behavior tends to cause changes on the authoritative scoreboard. Under this analysis, it is impossible that this scoreboard fails to give the score. What is possible is that the score is in an abnormal and undesired relation to its causes, for which someone may perhaps be blamed.

I do not care to say which analysis is right for baseball as it is actually played. Perhaps the question has no determinate answer, or perhaps it has different answers for formal and informal baseball. I only wish to distinguish the two alternatives, noting that both are live options.

This ends the digression. Now want to propose some general theses about language — theses that were examplified by Examples 1 and 2, and that will be exemplified also by several other examples.

CONVERSATIONAL SCORE

With any stage in a well-run conversation, or other process of linguistic interaction, there are associated many things analogous to the components of a baseball score. I shall therefore speak of them collectively as the *score* of that conversation at that stage. The points of analogy are as follows.

(1) Like the components of a baseball score, the components of a consational score at a given stage are abstract entities. They may not be numbers, but they are other set-theoretic constructs: sets of presupposed propositions, boundaries between permissible and impermissible courses of action, or the like.

(2) What play is correct depends on the score. Sentences depend for their truth value, or for their acceptability in other respects, on the components of conversational score at the stage of conversation when they are uttered. Not only aspects of acceptability of an uttered sentence may depend on score. So may other semantic properties that play a role in determining aspects of acceptability. For instance, the constituents of an uttered sentence — subsentences, names, predicates, etc. — may depend on the score for their intension or extension.

(3) Score evolves in a more-or-less rule-governed way. There are rules that specify the kinematics of score:

If at time t the conversational score is s, and if between time t and time t' the course of conversation is c, then at time t' the score is s', where s' is determined in a certain way by s and c.

Or at least:

... then at time t' the score is some member of the class S of possible scores, where S is determined in a certain way by s and c.

(4) The conversationalists may conform to directives, or may simply desire, that they strive to steer certain components of the conversational score in certain directions. Their efforts may be cooperative, as when all participants in a discussion try to increase the amount that all of them willingly presuppose. Or there may be conflict, as when each of two debaters tries to get his opponent to grant him — to join with him in presupposing — parts of his case, and to give

239

away parts of the contrary case.

(5) To the extent that conversational score is determined, given the history of the conversation and the rules that specify its kinematics, these rules can be regarded as constitutive rules akin to definitions. Again, constitutive rules could be traded in for explicit definitions: the conversational score function could be defined as that function from conversation-stages to n-tuples of suitable entities that evolves in the specified way.

Alternatively, conversational score might be operationally defined in terms of mental scoreboards — some suitable attitudes — of the parties to the conversation. The rules specifying the kinematics of conversational score then become empirical generalizations, subject to exceptions, about the causal dependence of what the scoreboards register on the history of the conversation.

In the case of baseball score, either approach to the definition of score and the status of the rules seems satisfactory. In the case of conversational score, on the other hand, both approaches seem to meet with difficulties. If, as seems likely, the rules specifying the kinematics of conversational score are seriously incomplete, then often there may be many candidates for the score function, different but all evolving in the specified way. But also it seems difficult to say, without risk of circularity, what are the mental representations that comprise the conversationalists' scoreboards.

It may be best to adopt a third approach — a middle way, drawing on both the alternatives previously considered. Conversational score is, by definition, whatever the mental scoreboards say it is; but we refrain from trying to say just what the conversationalists' mental scoreboards are. We assume that some or other mental representations are present that play the role of a scoreboard, in the following sense: what they register depends on the history of the conversation in the way that score should according to the rules. The rules specifying the kinematics of score thereby specify the role of a scoreboard; the scoreboard is whatever best fills this role; and the score is whatever this scoreboard registers. The rules specifying the kinematics of score are to some extent constitutive, but on this third approach they enter only in a roundabout way into the definition of score. It is no harm if they underdetermine the evolution of score, and it is possible that score sometimes evolves in a way that violates the rules.

RULES OF ACCOMMODATION

There is one big difference between baseball score and conversational score. Suppose the batter walks to first base after only three balls. His behavior would be correct play if there were four balls rather than three. That's just too bad — his behavior does not at all make it the case that there *are* four balls and his behavior *is* correct. Baseball has no rule of accommodation to the effect that if a fourth ball is required to make correct the play that occurs, then that very fact suffices to change the score so that straightway there are four balls.

Language games are different. As I hope my examples will show, conversational score does tend to evolve in such a way as is required in order to make whatever occurs count as correct play. Granted, that is not invariable but only a tendency. Granted also, conversational score changes for other reasons as well. (As when something conspicuous happens at the scene of a conversation, and straightway it is presupposed that it happened.) Still, I suggest that many components of conversational score obey rules of accommodation, and that these rules figure prominently among the rules governing the kinematics of conversational score.

Recall our examples. Example 1: presupposition evolves according to a rule of accommodation specifying that any presuppositions that are required by what is said straightway come into existence, provided that nobody objects. Example 2: permissibility evolves according to a rule of accommodation specifying that the boundaries of the permissible range of conduct shift to make true whatever is said about them, provided that what is said is said by the master to the slave, and provided that there does exist some shift that would make what he says true. Here is a general scheme for rules of accommodation for conversational score.

> If at time t something is said that requires component s_n of conversational score to have a value in the range r if what is said is to be true, or otherwise acceptable; and if s_n does not have a value in the range r just before t; and if such-and-such further conditions hold; then at t the score-component s_n takes some value in the range r.

Once we have this scheme in mind, I think we will find many instances of it. In the rest of this paper I shall consider some further examples. I shall have little that is new to say about the individual examples. My interest is in the common pattern that they exhibit.

EXAMPLE 3: DEFINITE DESCRIPTIONS[3]

It is not true that a definite description "the F" denotes x if and only if x is the one and only F in existence. Neither is it true that "the F" denotes x if and only if x is the one and only F in some contextually determined domain of discourse. For consider this sentence: "The pig is grunting, but the pig with floppy ears is not grunting" (Lewis). And this: "The dog got in a fight with another dog" (McCawley). They could be true. But for them to be true, "the pig" or "the dog" must denote one of two pigs or dogs, both of which belong to the domain of discourse.

The proper treatment of descriptions must be more like this: "the F" denotes x if and only if x is the most salient F in the domain of discourse, according to some contextually determined salience ranking. The first of our two sentences means that the most salient pig is grunting but the most salient pig with floppy ears is not. The second means that the most salient dog got in a fight with some less salient dog.

(I shall pass over some complications. Never mind what happens if two F's are tied for maximum salience, or if no F is at all salient. More important, I shall ignore the possibility that something might be highly salient in one of its guises, but less salient in another. Possibly we really need to appeal to a salience ranking not of individuals but rather of individuals-in-guises — that is, of individual concepts.)

There are various ways for something to gain salience. Some have to do with the course of conversation, others do not. Imagine yourself with me as I write these words. In the room is a cat, Bruce, who has been making himself very salient by dashing madly about. He is the only cat in the room, or in sight, or in earshot. I start to speak to you:

The cat is in the carton. The cat will never meet our other cat, because our other cat lives in New Zealand. Our New Zealand cat lives with the Cresswells. And there he'll stay, because Miriam would be sad if the cat went away.

At first, "the cat" denotes Bruce, he being the most salient cat for reasons having nothing to do with the course of conversation. If I want to talk about Albert, our New Zealand cat, I have to say "our other cat" or "our New Zealand cat". But as I talk more and more about Albert, and not any more about Bruce, I raise Albert's salience by conversational means. Finally, in the last sentence of my monologue, I am in a position to say "the cat" and thereby denote not Bruce but rather the newly-most-salient cat Albert.

The ranking of comparative salience, I take it, is another component of conversational score. Denotation of definite descriptions is score-dependent. Hence so is the truth of sentences containing such descriptions, which is one aspect of the acceptability of those sentences. Other aspects of acceptability in turn are score-dependent: non-triviality, for one, and possibility of warranted assertion, for another.

One rule, among others, that governs the kinematics of salience is a rule of accommodation. Suppose my monologue has left Albert more salient than Bruce; but the next thing I say is "The cat is going to pounce on you!" If Albert remains most salient and "the cat" denotes the most salient cat, then what I say is patently false: Albert cannot pounce all the way from New Zealand to Princeton. What I have said requires for its acceptability that "the cat" denote Bruce, and hence that Bruce be once again more salient than Albert. If what I say requires that, then straightway it is so. By saying what I did, I have made Bruce more salient than Albert. If next I say "The cat prefers moist food", that is true if Bruce prefers moist food, even if Albert doesn't.

The same thing would have happened if instead I had said "The cat is out of the carton" or "The cat has gone upstairs". Again what I say is unacceptable unless the salience ranking shifts so that Bruce rises above Albert, and hence so that 'the cat' again denotes Bruce. The difference is in the type of unacceptability that would ensue without the shift. It is trivially true, hence not worth saying, that Albert is out of the carton. ("The carton" denotes the same carton as before; nothing has been done to raise the salience of any carton in New Zealand.) It may be true or it may be false that Albert has gone upstairs in the Cresswells' house in New Zealand. But I have no way of knowing, so I have no business saying that he has.

We can formulate a *rule of accommodation for comparative salience* more or less as follows. It is best to speak simply of unacceptability, since it may well be that the three sorts of unacceptability I have mentioned are not the only sorts that can give rise to a shift in salience.

> If at time *t* something is said that requires, if it is to be acceptable, that *x* be more salient than *y*; and if, just before *t*, *x* is no more salient than *y*; then — *ceteris paribus* and within certain limits — at *t*,*x* becomes more salient than *y*.

Although a rule of accommodation, such as this one, states that shifts of score take place when they are needed to preserve acceptability, we may note that the preservation is imperfect. It is not good conversational practice to rely too heavily on rules of accommodation. The monologue just considered illustrates this. Because "the cat" denotes first Bruce, then Albert, then Bruce again, what I say is to some extent confusing and hard to follow. But even if my monologue is not perfectly acceptable, its flaws are much less serious than the flaws that are averted by shifts of salience in accordance with our rule of accommodation. Confusing shifts of salience and reference are not as bad as falsity, trivial truth, or unwarranted assertion.

(It is worth mentioning another way to shift comparative salience by conversational means. I may say "A cat is on the lawn" under circumstances in which it is apparent to all parties to the conversation that there is some one particular cat that is responsible for the truth of what I say, and for my saying it. Perhaps I am looking out the window, and you rightly presume that I said what I did because I saw a cat; and further (since I spoke in the singular) that I saw only one. What I said was an existential quantification; hence, strictly speaking, it involves no reference to any particular cat. Nevertheless it raises the salience of the cat that made me say it. Hence this newly-most-salient cat may be denoted by brief definite descriptions, or by pronouns, in subsequent dialogue: "No, it's on the sidewalk." "Has Bruce noticed the cat?" As illustrated, this may happen even if the speaker contradicts my initial existential statement. Thus although indefinite descriptions — that is, idioms of existential quantification — are not themselves referring expressions, they may raise the salience of particular individuals in such a way as to pave the way for referring expressions that follow.)

EXAMPLE 4: COMING AND GOING[4]

Coming is a movement toward a point of reference. Going is movement away from it. Sometimes the point of reference is fixed by the location of speaker and hearer, at the time of conversation or the time under discussion. But sometimes not. In third-person narrative, whether fact or fiction, the chosen point of reference may have nothing to do with the speaker's or the hearer's location.

One way to fix the point of reference at the beginning of a narrative, or to shift it later, is by means of a sentence that describes the direction of some movement both with respect to the point of reference and in some other way. "The beggars are coming to town" requires for its acceptability, and perhaps even for its truth, that the point of reference be in town. Else the beggars' townward movement is not properly called "coming". This sentence can be used to fix or to shift the point of reference. When it is said, straightway the point of reference is in town where it is required to be. Thereafter, unless something is done to shift it elsewhere, coming is movement toward town and going is movement away. If later we are told that when the soldiers came the beggars went, we know who ended up in town and who did not.

Thus the point of reference in narrative is a component of conversational score, governed by a rule of accommodation. Note that the rule must provide for two sorts of changes. The point of reference may simply go from one place to another, as is required by the following text:

> When the beggars came to town, the rich folk went to the shore. But soon the beggars came after them, so they went home.

But also the point of reference is usually not fully determinate in its location. It may become more or less determinate, as is required by the following:

> After the beggars came to town, they held a meeting. All of them came to the square. Afterwards they went to another part of town.

The first sentence puts the point of reference in town, but not in any determinate part of town. The second sentence increases its determinacy by putting it in the square. The initial fixing of the point of reference is likewise an increase in determinacy — the point of reference starts out completely indeterminate and becomes at least somewhat more definitely located.

EXAMPLE 5: VAGUENESS[5]

If Fred is a borderline case of baldness, the sentence "Fred is bald" may have no determinate truth value. Whether it is true depends on where you draw the line. Relative to some perfectly reasonable ways of drawing a precise boundary between bald and not-bald, the sentence is true. Relative to other delineations, no less reasonable, it is false. Nothing in our use of language makes one of these delineations right and all the others wrong. We cannot pick a delineation once and for all (not if we are interested in ordinary language), but must consider the entire range of reasonable delineations.

If a sentence is true over the entire range, true no matter how we draw the line, surely we are entitled to treat it simply as true. But also we treat a sentence more or less as if it is simply true, if it is true over a large enough part of the range of delineations of its vagueness. (For short: if it is *true enough*.) If a sentence is true enough (according to our beliefs) we are willing to assert it, assent to it without qualification, file it away among our stocks of beliefs, and so forth. Mostly we do not get into any trouble this way. (But sometimes we do, as witness the paradoxes that arise because truth-preserving reasoning does not always preserve the property of being true enough.)

When is a sentence true enough? Which are the "large enough" parts of the range of delineations of its vagueness? This is itself a vague matter. More important for our present purposes, it is something that depends on context. What is true enough on one occasion is not true enough on another. The standards of precision in force are different from one conversation to another, and may change in the course of a single conversation. Austin's "France is hexagonal" is a good example of a sentence that is true enough for many contexts, but not true enough for many others. Under low standards of precision it is acceptable. Raise the standards and it loses its acceptability.

Taking standards of precision as a component of conversational score, we once more find a rule of accommodation at work. One way to change the standards is to say something that would be unacceptable if the standards remained unchanged. If you say "Italy is boot-shaped" and get away with it, low standards are required and the standards fall if need be; thereafter "France is hexagonal" is true enough. But if you deny that Italy is bootshaped, pointing out the differences, what you have said requires high standards under which "France is hexagonal" is far from true enough.

I take it that the rule of accommodation can go both ways. But for some reason raising of standards goes more smoothly than lowering. If the standards have been high, and something is said that is true enough only under lowered standards, and nobody objects, then indeed the standards are shifted down. But what is said, although true enough under the lowered standards, may still seem imperfectly acceptable. Raising of standards, on the other hand, manages to seem commendable even when we know that it interferes with our conversational purpose. Because of this asymmetry, a player of language games who is so inclined may get away with it if he tries to raise the standards of precision as high as possible — so high, perhaps, that no material object whatever is hexagonal.

Peter Unger has argued that hardly anything is flat. Take something you claim is flat; he will find something else and get you to agree that it is even flatter. You think the pavement is flat — but how can you deny that your desk is flatter? But "flat" is an *absolute term:* it is inconsistent to say that something is flatter than something that is flat. Having agreed that your desk is flatter than the pavement, you must concede that the pavement is not flat after all. Perhaps you now claim that your desk is flat; but doubtless Unger can think of something that you will agree is even flatter than your desk. And so it goes.

Some might dispute Unger's premise that "flat" is an absolute term; but on that score it seems to me that Unger is right. What he says is inconsistent does indeed sound that way. I take this to mean that on no delineation of the correlative vagueness of "flatter" and "flat" is it true that something is flatter than something that is flat.

The right response to Unger, I suggest, is that he is changing the score on you. When he says that the desk is flatter than the pavement, what he says is acceptable only under raised standards of precision. Under the original standards the bumps on the pavement were too small to be relevant either to the question whether the pavement is flat or to the question whether the pavement is flatter than the desk. Since what he says requires raised standards, the standards accommodatingly rise. Then it is no longer true enough that the pavement is flat. That does not alter the fact that it *was* true enough *in its original context.* "The desk is flatter than the pavement" said under raised standards does not contradict "The pavement is flat" said under unraised standards, any more than "It is morning" said in the morning contradicts "It is afternoon" said in the afternoon. Nor has Unger shown in any way that the new context is more legitimate than the old one. He can indeed create an unusual context in which hardly anything can acceptably be called "flat", but he has not thereby cast any discredit on the more usual contexts in which lower standards of precision are in force.

In parallel fashion Unger observes, I think correctly, that "certain" is an absolute term; from this he argues that hardly ever is anyone certain of anything. A parallel response is in order. Indeed the rule of accommodation permits Unger to create a context in which all that he says is true, but that does not show that there is anything whatever wrong with the claims to certainty that we make in more ordinary contexts. It is no fault in a context that we can move out of it.

EXAMPLE 6: RELATIVE MODALITY[6]

The "can" and "must" of ordinary language do not often express absolute ("logical" or "metaphysical") possibility. Usually they express various relative modalities. Not all the possibilities there are enter into consideration. If we ignore those possibilities that violate laws of nature, we get the physical modalities; if we ignore those that are known not to obtain, we get the epistemic modalities; if we ignore those that ought not to obtain — doubtless including actuality — we get the deontic modalities; and so on. That suggests that "can" and "must" are ambiguous. But on that hypothesis, as Kratzer has convincingly argued, the alleged senses are altogether too numerous. We do better to think of our modal verbs as unambiguous but relative. Sometimes the relativity is made explicit. Modifying phrases like "in view of what is known" or "in view of what custom requires" may be present to indicate just which possibilities should be ignored.

But sometimes no such phrase is present. Then context must be our guide. The boundary between the relevant possibilities and the ignored ones (formally, the accessibility relation) is a component of conversational score, which enters into the truth conditions of sentences with "can" or "must" or other modal verbs. It may change in the course of conversation. A modifying phrase "in view of such-and-such" does not only affect the sentence in which it appears, but also remains in force until further notice to govern the interpretation of modal verbs in subsequent sentences.

This boundary may also shift in accordance with a rule of accommodation. Suppose I am talking with some elected official about the ways he might deal with an embarassment. So far, we have been ignoring those possibilities that would be political suicide for him. He says: "You see, I must either destroy the evidence or else claim that I did it to stop Communism. What else can I do?" I rudely reply: "There is one other possibility — you can put the public interest first for once!" That would be false if the boundary between relevant and ignored possibilities remained stationary. But it is not false in its context, for hitherto ignored possibilities come into consideration and make it true. And the boundary, once shifted outward, stays shifted. If he protests "I can't do that", he is mistaken.

Take another example. The commonsensical epistemologist says: "I *know* the cat is in the carton — there he is before my eyes — I just *can't* be wrong about that!" The sceptic replies: "You might be the victim of a deceiving demon". Thereby he brings into consideration possibilities hitherto ignored, else what he says would be false. The boundary shifts outward so that what he says is true. Once the boundary is shifted, the commonsensical epistemologist must concede defeat. And yet he was not in any way wrong when he laid claim to infallible knowledge. What he said was true with respect to the score as it then was.

We get the impression that the sceptic, or the rude critic of the elected official, has the last word. Again this is because the rule of accommodation is not fully reversible. For some reason, I know not what, the boundary readily shifts outward if what is said requires it, but does not so readily shift inward if what is said requires that. Because of this asymmetry, we may think that what is true with respect to the outward-shifted boundary must be somehow more true than what is true with respect to the original boundary. I see no reason to respect this impression. Let us hope, by all means, that the advance toward truth is irreversible. That is no reason to think that just any change that resists reversal is an advance toward truth.

EXAMPLE 7: PERFORMATIVES[7]

Suppose we are unpersuaded by Austin's contention that explicit performatives have no truth value. Suppose also that we wish to respect the seeming parallelism of form between a performative like "I hereby name this ship the *Generalissimo Stalin*" and such non-performative statements as "Fred thereby named that ship the *President Nixon*". Then we shall find it natural to treat the performative, like the non-performative, as a sentence with truth conditions. It is true, on a given occasion of its utterance, if and only if the speaker brings it about, by means of that very utterance, that the indicated ship begins to bear the name "Generalissimo Stalin". If the circumstances are felicitous, then the speaker does indeed bring it about, by means of his utterance, that the ship begins to bear the name. The performative sentence is therefore true on any occasion of its felicitous utterance. In Lemmon's phrase, it is a sentence verifiable by its (felicitous) use.

When the ship gets its name and the performative is verified by its use, what happens may be described as a change in conversational score governed by a rule of accommodation. The relevant component of score is the relation that pairs ships with their names. The rule of accommodation is roughly as follows.

If at time *t* something is said that requires for its truth that ship *s* bear name *n*; and if *s* does not bear *n* just before *t*; and if the form and circumstances of what is said satisfy certain conditions of felicity; then *s* begins at *t* to bear *n*.

Our performative sentence does indeed require for its truth that the indicated ship bear the name "Generalissimo Stalin" at the time of utterance. Therefore, when the sentence is felicitously uttered, straightway the ship bears the name.

The sentence has other necessary conditions of truth: the ship must not have borne the name beforehand, the speaker must bring it about that the ship begins to bear the name, and he must bring it about by uttering the sentence. On any felicitous occasion of utterance, these further conditions take care of themselves. Our rule of accommodation is enough to explain why the sentence is verified by its felicitous use, despite the fact that the rule deals only with part of what it takes to make the sentence true.

A similar treatment could be given of many other performatives. In some cases the proposal may seem surprising. "With this ring I thee wed" is verified by its felicitous use, since the marriage relation is a component of conversational score governed by a rule of accommodation. Is marriage then a *linguistic* phenomenon? Of course not, but that was not implied. The lesson of performatives, on any theory, is that use of language blends into other social practices. We should not assume that a change of conversational score has its impact only within, or by way of, the realm of language. Indeed, we have already seen another counterexample: the case of permissibility, considered as Example 2.

EXAMPLE 8: PLANNING

Suppose that you and I are making a plan — let us say, a plan to steal some plutonium from a reprocessing plant and make a bomb of it. As we talk, our plan evolves. Mostly it grows more and more complete. Sometimes, however, parts that had been definite are revised, or at least opened for reconsideration.

Much as some things said in ordinary conversation require suitable presuppositions, so some things we say in the course of our planning require, for their acceptability, that the plan contain suitable provisions. If I say "Then you drive the getaway car up to the side gate", that is acceptable only if the plan includes provision for a getaway car. That might or might not have been part of the plan already. If not, it may become part of the plan just because it is required by what I said. (As usual the process is defeasible. You can keep the getaway car out of the plan, for the time being at least, by saying "Wouldn't we do better with mopeds?") The plan is a component of conversational score. The rules governing its evolution parallel the rules governing the kinematics of presupposition, and they include a rule of accommodation.

So good is the parallel between plan and presupposition that we might well ask if our plan simply *is* part of what we presuppose. Call it that if you like, but there is a distinction to be made. We might take for granted, or purport to take for granted, that our plan will be carried out. Then we would both plan and presuppose that we are going to steal the plutonium. But we might not. We might be making our plan not in order to carry it out, but rather in order to show that the plant needs better security. Then plan and presupposition might well conflict. We plan to steal the plutonium, all the while presupposing that we will not. And indeed our planning may be interspersed with commentary that requires presuppositions contradicting the plan. "Then I'll shoot the guard (I'm glad I won't really do that) while you smash the floodlights." Unless we distinguish plan from presupposition (or distinguish two levels of presupposition) we must think of presuppositions as constantly disappearing and reappearing throughout such a conversation.

The distinction between plan and presupposition is not the distinction between what we purport to take for granted and what we really do. While planning that we will steal the plutonium and presupposing that we will not, we might take for granted neither that we will nor that we won't. Each of us might secretly hope to recruit the other to the terrorist cause and carry out the plan after all.

One and the same sentence may require, and if need be create, both provisions of the plan and presuppositions. "Then you drive the getaway car up to the side gate" requires both a getaway car and a side gate. The car is planned for. The gate is more likely presupposed.

Notes

* I am doubly grateful to Robert Stalnaker: first, for his treatment of presupposition, here summarized as Example 1, which I have taken as the prototype for parallel treatments of other topics; and second, for valuable comments on a previous version of this paper. I am also much indebted to Stephen Isard, who discusses many of the phenomena that I consider here in his 'Changing the Context' in Edward L. Keenan, ed., *Formal Semantics of Natural Language* (Cambridge University Press, 1974). Proposals along somewhat the same lines as mine are to be found in Thomas T. Ballmer, 'Einführung und Kontrolle von Diskurswelten', in Dieter Wunderlich, ed., *Linguistische Pragmatik* (Athenäum-Verlag, 1972), and Ballmer, *Logical Grammar: with Special Consideration of Topics in Context Change* (North-Holland, 1978).

An early version of this paper was presented to the Vacation School in Logic at Victoria University of Wellington in August 1976; I thank the New Zealand-United States Educational Foundation for research support on that occasion. The paper also was presented at a workshop on pragmatics and conditionals at the University of Western Ontario in May 1978, and at a colloquium on semantics at Konstanz University in September 1978.

1 This treatment of presupposition is taken from two papers of Robert Stalnaker: 'Presuppositions', *Journal of Philosophical Logic* 2 (1973), 447–457, and 'Pragmatic Presuppositions', in Milton K. Munitz and Peter K. Unger, eds., *Semantics and Philosophy* (New York University Press, 1974).

2   This treatment of permissibility is discussed more fully in my paper 'A Problem about Permission', in Esa Saarinen *et al.*, eds., *Essays in Honour of Jaakko Hintikka* (Reidel).

3   Definite descriptions governed by salience are discussed in my *Counterfactuals* (Blackwell, 1973), pp. 111–117; and in James McCawley, 'Presupposition and Discourse Structure', in David Dinneen and Choon-Kyu Oh, eds., *Syntax and Semantics*, Vol. 11 (Academic Press, 1979). A similar treatment of demonstratives is found in Isard, *op. cit.*

     Manfred Pinkal, 'How to Refer with Vague Descriptions' (presented at the Konstanz colloquium on semantics, September 1978) notes a further complication: if some highly salient things are borderline cases of *F*-hood, degree of *F*-hood and salience may trade off.

     Indefinite descriptions that pave the way for referring expressions are discussed in Charles Chastain, 'Reference and Context', *Minnesota Studies in the Philosophy of Science* 7 (1975), 194-269, and in Saul Kripke, 'Speaker's Reference and Semantic Reference', *Midwest Studies in Philosophy* 2 (1977), 255–276.

4   See Charles Fillmore, 'How to Know Whether You're Coming or Going', in Karl Hyldgaard-Jensen, ed., *Linguistik 1971* (Athenäum-Verlag, 1972), and 'Pragmatics and the Description of Discourse', in Siegfried J. Schmidt, ed., *Pragmatik/Pragmatics II* (Wilhelm Fink Verlag, 1976).

5   See the treatment of vagueness in my 'General Semantics', *Synthese* 22 (1970), 18–67. For arguments that hardly anything is flat or certain, see Peter Unger, *Ignorance* (Oxford University Press, 1975), pp. 65–68. For another example of accommodating shifts in resolution of vagueness, see the discussion of back-tracking counterfactuals in my 'Counterfactual Dependence and Time's Arrow', *Noûs* 13 (1979).

6   See Angelika Kratzer, 'What "Must" and "Can" Must and Can Mean', *Linguistics and Philosophy* 1 (1977), 337–355. The accessibility semantics considered here is equivalent to a slightly restricted form of Kratzer's semantics for relative modality.

     Knowledge and irrelevant possibilities of error are discussed in Alvin I. Goldman, 'Discrimination and Perceptual Knowledge', *Journal of Philosophy* 73 (1976), 771–791.

7   See J. L. Austin, 'Performative Utterances', in his *Philosophical Papers*

(Oxford University Press, 1961) for the original discussion of performatives. For treatments along the lines here preferred, see E. J. Lemmon 'On Sentences Verifiable by Their Use' *Analysis* 22 (1962), 86–89; Ingemar Hedenius, 'Performatives', *Theoria* 29 (1963), 1–22; and Lennart Aqvist, *Performatives and Verifiability by the Use of Language* (Filosofiska Studier, Uppsala University, 1972). Isard (*op. cit.*) suggests as I do that performative utterances are akin to other utterances that 'change the context'.

第三部分：
语用学

┌─────────────────────────┐
│   导　读   │
└─────────────────────────┘

　　本部分选的文章涉及语用学领域的核心，从合作原则及会话含义的提出与讨论，到话语意义的三个层面、预设映射问题等，这些都是语用学中的重要课题。

　　第一篇文章（Grice, 1975）是会话含义理论（conversational implicature）及其核心——合作原则（Cooperative Principle）的发源之作。该论文奠定了推理语用学（inferential pragmatics）的基础，从此，言语理解的推理特性得到了广泛的认同。

　　该文首先指出了哲学逻辑语言与自然语言在意义理解和推导上的偏离，虽然前者被认为更系统、更科学、更具有形式的可推导性和精确性，但是自然语言中仍然有很多推断和意义，即使不能用逻辑和形式的方式表达出来，仍是有效的（valid）。

　　格赖斯接下来区分了规约性意义（conventional meaning）和非规约性意义（non-conventional meaning）或会话含义（conversational implicature）。会话的字面和隐含义都由规约意义决定，但会话含义通常需要在语境中，通过会话参与者遵守合作原则来明确，具有可取消性（cancellability）、不可分离性（non-detachability）、可推导性（calculability）和非规约性（non-conventionality）等特征。

　　会话含义的产生源于现实交际中，人们对于彼此合作默契的期待以及期待被接受或违反的程度。人们期待彼此遵守普遍会话原则即合作原则（Cooperative Principle），该原则是指人们在交谈中参与会话的程度，应以谈话双方所能接受的意图或方向的要求为准。在合作原则的大前提下，格赖斯套用德国哲学家康德（Kant）的量、质、关系和方式四大哲学范畴体系，提出了质的准则、量的准则、关联准则和方式准则：

　　量的准则——所说的话尽量包含当前交谈目的所需要的信息（不多也不少）。

　　质的准则——尽量使说的话为真：不说自认为假的话；不说缺少证据的话。

　　关联准则——使所说的话有关联。

　　方式准则——使所说的话清晰、明确；避免歧义；避免含糊；简洁；有序。

"合作原则"作为一个假设，要解释发话者的意图是如何传递和领会的，即如何通过语码——推理达到相互理解，主要是如何通过推导获得会话含义。它是语言研究史上试图解开人之所以能传递和理解同语句字面意义、不同交际意向的秘密的第一次认真的理论尝试。一般认为，正是言语行为理论和会话含义理论这两个理论使语用学从概念发展为语言学的一个分支学科，并成为语用学的理论支柱。

格赖斯会话含义理论的出现，在语言学内部局部地出现了研究范式的转换，即从语码模型研究范式转换为语码——推理模型研究范式，从而促成语言学研究内部局部地出现了一些新趋势：从单纯研究语言客体走向重视主客体结合并使客体趋向于主体的研究，研究的对象从句子走向话语，从句子命题真值条件的逻辑——语义分析研究走向话语有效性条件的研究，从语形研究和语义研究走向语形、语义、语用研究的统一。

第二篇文章是雷卡那提（F. Recanati）的《所言内容语用学》（The Pragmatics of What is Said）。雷卡那提承认格赖斯理论在区分所言、会话含义和句子意义之间的联系与互动方面的影响力和解释性，但认为将所递分为所言和所含的做法不符合对语言的直觉，从而将一些本质完全不同的语言现象统统牵强地用所含（会话含义）来解释，见句（1）和（2）：

(1) John has three children.
(2) I've had no breakfast today.

格赖斯理论认为例（1）表达了"John has at least three children"，从而暗含了"John has no more than three children"。可是明显例（2）与例（1）的暗含方式不同，因为例（2）可能暗含了"说话人很饿，想要吃的"。这里的暗含明显属于所言之外的内容（external to what is said），这才是我们直觉感受到的会话含义。而例（1）的所言（John至少有三个孩子）与所含（John至多有三个孩子）从直觉来说却不是那么容易分离，我们只是意识到二者结合后的结果，就是"John有三个孩子"。

作者认为，从以上例子的分析来看，格赖斯理论上区分的命题表达与会话含义同我们直觉感受到的所言与所含的区分并不吻合。因此，作者提出了另外一层他认为重要的理论区分，即会话含义（genuine implicatures）和命题语用成分（pragmatic constituents of the proposition expressed）。雷卡那提考察了这对区分的三个可能标准：最小原则、可及原则和独立原则。他最终只保留了可及原则，并提出了范畴原则，认为这两个原则就可以对绝大多数的会话含义和所言语用成分作出有效的区分。

雷卡那提首先质疑了规约性意义与所言之间的紧密联系，认为所言在很大程度上是语用决定（pragmatically determined）而非语义决定（semantically determined）的。那么如何区分所言的语用因素与会话含义呢？作者首先讨论了三个标准。

一、最小原则（Minimalist Principle）：某些意义通过语用因素决定，当且仅当该意义的语用决定对于话语表达一个完整命题必须时，此语用决定的意义成分才属于所言。

最小原则蕴含了卡斯特（Carston, 1988）提出的"语言指向原则"。任何所言中通过语用因素决定的意义成分，必然用以填充句子意义的一定缺口以使其具有真值可评估性。对于语境敏感的表达式如"he"即形成这样的缺口，需要通过语境才能确定其所指。根据最小原则，在句子"He has bought John's book"中，对于"he"以及"John"和"the book"之间关系的语用决定构成了所言的一部分，帮助决定句子的真值。而对比之下，会话含义并非所言的一部分，因为即使不确定具体会话含义的情形下，该句子表达的命题仍然完整。

第二个标准是可及性原则（The Availability Principle）：要判断句子意义中的语用成分是否是所言的一部分，应该尽量服从先于理论的直觉。按照格赖斯的理论，可以推知如图1的树形图：

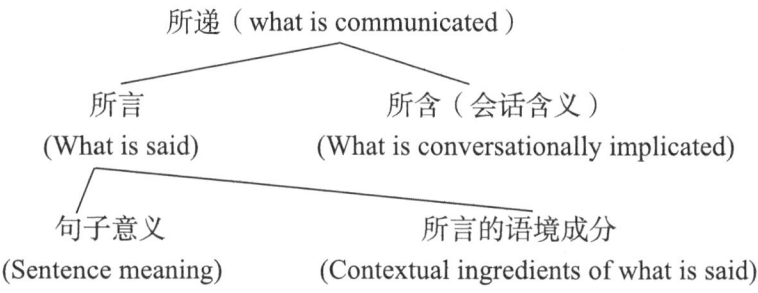

图1　格赖斯理论图示（Recanati, 1989: 106）

正如图1所显示的，格赖斯的理论预设了如下几点：即所递是语用理解过程中意识可及的输出，所言和所含共同成为其下级输入成分。下级内容相对上级更为抽象和更不可及。比如处于底层的句子意义，要比所言更抽象、更具理论性。

但是雷卡那提认为这违反了我们的直觉，并对图1提出了修订：所递由所言和所含组成（consists of），而非处于所言和所含之上；所递只是所言和所含这一层次的名称（name）而已，它们共同处于顶层，并且对于说话人都是可及的，如图2所示：

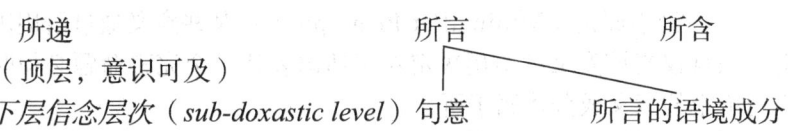

图2　雷卡那提对格赖斯理论修订后的图示（Recanati, 1989: 107）

雷卡那提用可及性原则反驳了巴哈（Bach）等人之前对一些句子的分析，如例（3）中：

(3)　Everybody went to Paris.

通常情况下，说话人此时并非是说世界上每个人都去了巴黎，而是指特定圈子里的人都去了巴黎。对该句的分析一般有两种方式：一是直接将说话人所说对应于其话语意义，即特定圈子的人去了巴黎；另外一种方式是首先按字面意义理解所说，再进一步发现字面意义与实际意义不符，说明说话人是通过非字面方式，如隐喻等来表达的。可及性原则反驳了第二种方式，认为对所说的判定是理论家的分析，但是违反了说话人的直觉，即当说话人说这句话时，并不会首先预设"世界上的每个人都去了巴黎"。

第三个标准是独立性原则（The Independence Principle）：所含在功能上是独立于所言的，彼此之间没有蕴含关系，否则，所含就非所含，而是所言的一部分。雷卡那提认为此原则并不成立，因为卡斯特虽然反复强调功能独立（functional independence），可是实际却是依赖形式独立（formal independence）来判定隐含义与所言语用成分之间的区分，作者认为这是典型的语用"形式谬误"（formal fallacy）。对隐含义的界定并非通过形式特征，尤其并非通过使所表达的命题实现逻辑独立的形式特征，因为极有可能通过语用推导的方式获得的隐含义结果却蕴含了最小命题，从而被看作是所言而非隐含义。

最后作者提出范围原则，与可及性原则共同作为评判所含与所言语用成分区别的标准：当且仅当语用决定的意义部分属于否定、条件等逻辑算子的范围时，该部分属于所言而非所含。范围原则以人们对与逻辑算子相关的会话含义的考察为基础，这些考察可以提供依据，用来区别两种陈述的隐含义：一种属于逻辑算子范围，另一种则不属于,见句（4）和（5）：

(4) The old king has died of a heart attack and a republic has been declared.
(5) A republic has been declared and the old king has died of a heart attack.

同样的事件用不同的顺序来表达，具有不同的隐含义：暗含了前半句的命题是后半句的诱因。如何解释这里的隐含义呢？格莱斯认为这里时间暗示只是纯粹的会话含义，而非所言的部分，对句子的真值没有影响，因此严格字面来讲，两句表达的是同样的内容。可是，如果说这样解释上句4）和5）还能够说得过去的话，那么句6）和7）就很难说通了。

(6) If the old king has died of a heart attack and a republic has been declared, then Tom will be quite content.
(7) If a republic has been declared and the old king has died of a heart attack, then Tom will be quite content.

假如我们坚持说句（6）和（7）具有同样的真值条件，我们如何解释直觉上二者的差别呢？作者的解决办法就是进一步将这逻辑算子能够决定的语用成分作为所言的部分，而非隐含的部分，即范围原则。

第三篇和第四篇文章都与格赖斯会话含义理论有关，都是试图对合作原则中具体原则做出修订，这在语用学理论研究中被称为"新格赖斯理论"。

在《语用推理的新分类：Q为基础和R为基础的含义》（Toward a new Taxonomy for Pragmatic Inference: Q-based and R-based Implicature）一文中，霍恩提出，要理解语言变迁的原因和方式，语言学家必须牢记两方面交织并对立的因素，即一方面交际的需要要求发话者尽量传递他的信息，另一方面最小努力原则使发话者在实现交际目的的前提下将自己的能量（精神的和身体的）输出限制到最低。据此，霍恩提出了数量原则（Q-Principle）和关系原则（R-Principle），力图展示这两方面相互对立竞争的力量以及二者之间的互动如何更系统地解释格赖斯提出的会话四准则以及相应的语用推导图式。

（a）数量原则（或Q原则，基于受话者）：要使话语充分，能说多少就尽量说多少（以关系原则为条件）；

（b）关系原则（或R原则，基于发话者）：要使话语只是必需的，不说多于所要求说的话（以数量原则为条件）。

从受话者角度出发的数量原则是一个充分条件，因为所传递的信息是发话者能够提供的最大量信息。霍恩将其称作底界原则（lower-bounding principle），意味着与这一原则相符的信息已经满足了最低标准。相对应的从发话者角度出发的关系原则促使受话者根据有限的语言形式推测出超越话语本身的意义，霍恩将其称作上限原则（upper-bounding principle）。

第四篇文章是莱文森的《意义的三个层次》（Three Levels of Meaning）。莱文森主张把意义划分为三个层次：句子意义（sentence meaning）、话语类型意义（utterance type meaning）和话语实例意义（utterance token），并强调了把话语类型意义作为意义中间层次的必要性和重要性。句子意义研究的是语码内容，话语类型意义研究的是一般性谈话隐含，话语实例意义研究的是特殊性谈话隐含。作者提出的GCI理论所要研究的是意义系统中的话语类型意义。构成GCI理论主体的是三条原则或三个交谈策略（heuristics）：

（1）Q1（量原则）：假如没有这么说，就没有这个意思，适用范围限于可以互换的表达式；例如：如果说了"X是G"，而G和F是形成对比的表达，那么就隐含了"X不是F"。举例来说，如果一个人说了"花儿是红的"，就隐含了"花儿不是白的，不是黄的……"等。

（2）Q2（信息原则）：简单描述的就是常规的或具体的情况。简单来说，就是虽然没有这么说，但是有这个意思。

（3）M（方式原则）：有标记的描述提示"有标记的情形"的存在。也就是说：既然这么说就有这个意思，或，只有这么说才有这个意思。相当于"方式准则"中的"要避免含糊和歧义"。

莱文森（1995）将推导的隐含义明确地分为两类，即"一般会话含义（Generalized Conversational Implicature，简称 GCI）"和"特殊会话含义（Particularized Conversational Implicature，简称 PCI）"，他又把前者叫做"类含义"，把后者叫做"例含义"，前者不随语境的改变而改变，后者随语境的改变而改变。

GCI理论与PCI理论同等重要，它不仅在语用学研究内部具有重要的地位，在整个意义理论的宏观体系中，该理论也占有一个独立的层次。首先，从整个意义理论的体系来看，一般性会话含义不同于语义学研究的各种意义，尤其不同于规约含义。二者区分的关键之处在于，一般性会话含义是可取消的，而规约含义却是不可取消的。其次，从语用学研究的内部来看，一般性会话含义不同于特殊性会话含义。前者是由语段本身的形式和内容所引发的，它不需要通过语境就能够获得。GCI理论和PCI理论对于语义演变，尤其是语法化等现象具有很强的解释力。一种十分重要的语义演变过程就是PCI → GCI → SM。也就是说，词义引申是从"特殊含义"开始的，用例不多，要靠语境来逐步推导，后来这样的推导反复进行并扩散开来，不需要靠语境和逐步的推导就可以直接得出相关的隐含义，其地位也就变成了"一般含义"。"一般含义"再进一步固化，就变为语词的"固有义"。

最后一篇文章是海姆对预设问题的讨论。预设是语义学和语用学中的一个重要话题。对预设问题的讨论涉及预设的定义、预设的触发机制、预设的映射等问题。

卡尔图宁和彼得斯（Karttunen & Peters）从语用预设的角度来解决问题，他们认为英语语法词汇意义涉及三方面的信息：第一层信息纯粹涉及真值条件；第二层信息指明词汇在预设实现过程中的作用，比如特指冠词"the"往往预设了其所共现的名词集合非空集；第三层信息只和算符相关，涉及算符引起的预设继承性。

以上三类信息可以称为内容特征（content property）、预设特征（presupposition property）和继承特征（heritage property）。继承特征的功能就是控制隐含表达中预设的投射。这样，对通启算子、阻断算子和启断算子的功能就有了新的解释。当一个内嵌成分是阻断算子时，它会有个继承表达，该继承表达会阻挡隐含表达中的预设上升成为整个句子的预设。对启断算子来说，每一个连接词都有一个继承表达,它们会按照启断条件允许子句的预设上升为整个句子的预设。对通启算子来说，继承表达会允许隐含表达上升为整个句子的预设。按照这个理论，预设实际上并没有取消，它们只是在句子转换过程中被阻挡,不能成为整个句子的预设。

　　盖茨达（Gazdar）反对卡尔图宁和彼得斯的理论（以下简称K&P理论）。他指出，首先，不应当将内容特征（content property）、预设特征（presupposition property）和继承特征（inheritage property）看作是彼此孤立（mutually independent）的方面；其次，K&P理论仅仅描述了预设映射事实而没有解释预设映射现象。他提出了自认为更具有解释力的预设映射理论。他的理论重点在于揭示话语如何改变其所在的语境。以if the king has a son, the king's son is bald.为例，该句有着如下的隐含信息：即所有的说话人都知道，国王可能没有儿子。那么其中的一个存在预设"国王有儿子"（the king must have a son）因为与该会话含义冲突而被取消。映射取消源于要在语境变化的同时保持信息一致这一大的原则，既不是因为所谓的"继承特征"，也非因为"if"的任何独特的启断特征。

　　盖茨达认为，在特定的语境中，只有一部分预设能够生存下来，能生存下来的预设就是实际预设。会话参与者每说一句话，或者每表达一个命题，都是在扩展语境。语境在扩展过程中，一个命题能否加入进去还要看跟语境中原来的命题是否一致，如果不一致的话就会被取消。

　　海姆整合了盖茨达和K&P理论，提出了著名的语境变化潜势理论（Context Change Potentials），力求在保持K&P理论的覆盖面（descriptive coverage）的同时，具有盖茨达理论的解释充分性（explanatory adequacy）。海姆认为，预设作为语用推理展开，如果φ是一个句子，并且在所有语境中都允许φ蕴涵ψ，那么ψ就是它的预设。真值条件和语境变化的关系可以表达为：a.如果一个语境c为真（该语境为一组命题，或各个成分的合取），并且在该语境中句子φ被接受，同时如果c + φ（即由φ所增加的语境）为真的话，φ相对于c就为真。b. 如果在语境c中φ不被接受，听话者就会将语境c调整到c'，c'与c相似但是与φ一致（Heim, 1983: 117）。这样，海姆的投射理论就结合了斯托纳克（Stalnaker）和刘易斯的纳入理论（即在一个句子的预设不能被满足的情况下仍然可以有效地交流），然后动态地结合格赖斯的会话合作原则以产生语用推理。按照海姆和索姆斯（Soames）的观点，预设纳入可以和预设取消联系起来。在说话者说出某个话语时，它的语境会使听话者明白，对预设要求的公然违反的问题不能通过改变语境以蕴涵预设陈述，而是通过重新解读该陈述，调整预设要求以便与事实相吻合（Soames, 1989: 577）。海姆把这些过程区分为整体纳入和局部纳入。这样也可以解释盖茨达的潜在预设可以被隐含取消的问题。

Logic and Conversation

H. P. Grice

It is a commonplace of philosophical logic that there are, or appear to be, divergences in meaning between, on the one hand, at least some of what I shall call the FORMAL devices — $\sim$, $\wedge$, $\vee$, $\supset$, (x), $\exists(x)$, $\int x$ (when these are given a standard two-valued interpretation) — and, on the other, what are taken to be their analogs or counterparts in natural language — such expressions as *not, and, or, if, all, some* (or *at least one*), *the*. Some logicians may at some time have wanted to claim that there are in fact no such divergences; but such claims, if made at all, have been somewhat rashly made, and those suspected of making them have been subjected to some pretty rough handling.

Those who concede that such divergences exist adhere, in the main, to one or the other of two rival groups, which for the purposes of this article I shall call the formalist and the informalist groups. An outline of a not uncharacteristic formalist position may be given as follows: Insofar as logicians are concerned with the formulation of very general patterns of valid inference, the formal devices possess a decisive advantage over their natural counterparts. For it will be possible to construct in terms of the formal devices a system of very general formulas, a considerable number of which can be regarded as, or are closely related to, patterns of inferences the expression of which involves some or all of the devices: Such a system may consist of a certain set of simple formulas that must be acceptable if the devices have the meaning that has been assigned to them, and an indefinite number of further formulas, many of them less obviously acceptable, each of which can be shown to be acceptable if the members of the original set are acceptable. We have, thus, a way of handling dubiously acceptable

265

patterns of inference, and if, as is sometimes possible, we can apply a decision procedure, we have an even better way. Furthermore, from a philosophical point of view, the possession by the natural counterparts of those elements in their meaning, which they do not share with the corresponding formal devices, is to be regarded as an imperfection of natural languages; the elements in question are undesirable excrescences. For the presence of these elements has the result that the concepts within which they appear cannot be precisely/clearly defined, and that at least some statements involving them cannot, in some circumstances, be assigned a definite truth value; and the indefiniteness of these concepts is not only objectionable in itself but leaves open the way to metaphysics — we cannot be certain that none of these natural language expressions is metaphysically 'loaded'. For these reasons, the expressions, as used in natural speech, cannot be regarded as finally acceptable, and may turn out to be, finally, not fully intelligible. The proper course is to conceive and begin to construct an ideal language, incorporating the formal devices, the sentences of which will be clear, determinate in truth value, and certifiably free from metaphysical implications; the foundations of science will now be philosophically secure, since the statements of the scientist will be expressible (though not necessarily actually expressed) within this ideal language. (I do not wish to suggest that all formalists would accept the whole of this outline, but I think that all would accept at least some part of it.)

To this, an informalist might reply in the following vein. The philosophical demand for an ideal language rests on certain assumptions that should not be conceded; these are, that the primary yardstick by which to judge the adequacy of a language is its ability to serve the needs of science, that an expression cannot be guaranteed as fully intelligible unless an explication or analysis of its meaning has been provided, and that every explication or analysis must take the form of a precise definition that is the expression/assertion of a logical equivalence. Language serves many important purposes besides those of scientific inquiry; we can know perfectly well what an expression means (and so a fortiori that it is intelligible) without knowing its analysis, and the provision of an analysis may (and usually does) consist in the specification, as generalized as possible, of the conditions that count for or against the applicability of the expression being analyzed. Moreover, while it is no doubt true that the formal devices are especially amenable to systematic treatment by the logician, it remains the case that there are very many inferences and arguments, expressed in natural language and not in terms of these devices, that are nevertheless recognizably valid. So there must be a place for an unsimplified, and so more or less unsystematic, logic of the natural counterparts of these devices; this logic may be aided and guided by the simplified logic of the formal devices but cannot be supplanted by it; indeed, not only do the two logics differ, but sometimes they come into conflict; rules that hold for a formal device may not hold for its natural counterpart.

Now, on the general question of the place in philosophy of the reformation of natural language, I shall, in this article, have nothing to say. I shall confine myself to the dispute in its relation to the alleged divergences mentioned at the outset. I have, moreover, no intention of entering the fray on behalf of either contestant. I wish, rather, to maintain that the common assumption of the contestants that the divergences do in fact exist is (broadly speaking) a common mistake, and that the mistake arises from an inadequate attention to the nature and importance of the conditions governing conversation. I shall, therefore, proceed at once to inquire into the general conditions that, in one way or another, apply to conversation as such, irrespective of its subject matter.

IMPLICATURE

Suppose that A and B are talking about a mutual friend, C, who is now working in a bank. A asks B how C is getting on in his job, and B replies, *Oh quite well, I think; he likes his colleagues, and he hasn't been to prison yet.* At this point, A might well inquire what B was implying, what he was suggesting, or even what he meant by saying that C had not yet been to prison. The answer might be any one of such things as that C is the sort of person likely to yield to the temptation provided by his occupation, that C's colleagues are really very unpleasant and treacherous people, and so forth. It might, of course, be quite unnecessary for A to make such an inquiry of B, the answer to it being, in the context, clear in advance. I think it is clear that whatever B implied, suggested, meant, etc., in this example, is distinct from what B said, which was simply that C had not been to prison yet. I wish to introduce, as terms of art, the verl *implicate* and the related nouns *implicature* (cf. *implying*) and *implicatum* (cf. *what is implied*). The point of this maneuver is to avoid having, on each occasion, to choose between this or that member of the family of verbs for which *implicate* is to do general duty.

I shall, for the time being at least, have to assume to a considerable extent an intuitive understanding of the meaning of *say* in such contexts, and an ability to recognize particular verbs as members of the family with which *implicate* is associated. I can, however, make one or two remarks that may help to clarify the more problematic of these assumptions, namely, that connected with the meaning of the word *say*.

In the sense in which I am using the word *say*, I intend what someone has said to be closely related to the conventional meaning of the words (the sentence) he has uttered. Suppose someone to have uttered the sentence *He is in the grip of a vice*. Given a knowledge of the English language, but no knowledge of the circumstances of the utterance, one would know something about what the speaker had said, on the assumption that he was speaking standard English, and speaking literally. One would know that he had said, about some particular male person or animal *x,* that at the time of the utterance (whatever that was), either (1) *x* was unable to rid himself of a certain kind of bad character trait or (2) some part of *x*'s person was caught in a certain kind of tool or instrument (approximate account, of course). But for a full identification of what the speaker had said, one would need to know (a) the identity of *x,* (b) the time of utterance, and (c) the meaning, on the particular occasion of utterance, of the phrase *in the grip of a vice* [a decision between (1) and (2)]. This brief indication of my use of *say* leaves it open whether a man who says (today) *Harold Wilson is a great man* and another who says (also today) *The British Prime Minister is a great man* would, if each knew that the two singular terms had the same reference, have said the same thing. But whatever decision is made about this question, the apparatus that I am about to provide will be capable of accounting for any implicatures that might depend on the presence of one rather than another of these singular terms in the sentence uttered. Such implicatures would merely be related to different maxims.

In some cases the conventional meaning of the words used will determine what is implicated, besides helping to determine what is said. If I say (smugly), *He is an Englishman; he is, therefore, brave,* I have certainly committed myself, by virtue of the meaning of my words, to its being the case that his being brave is a consequence of (follows from) his being an Englishman. But while I have said that he is an Englishman, and said that he is brave, I do not want to say that I have SAID (in the favored sense) that it follows from his being an Englishman that he is brave, though I have certainly indicated, and so implicated, that this is so. I do not want to say that my utterance of this sentence would be, STRICTLY SPEAKING, false should the consequence in question fail to hold. So SOME implicatures are conventional, unlike the one with which I introduced this discussion of implicature.

I wish to represent a certain subclass of nonconventional implicatures, which I shall call CONVERSATIONAL implicatures, as being essentially connected with certain general features of discourse; so my next step is to try to say what these features are.

The following may provide a first approximation to a general principle. Our talk exchanges do not normally consist of a succession of disconnected remarks, and would not be rational if they did. They are characteristically, to some degree at least, cooperative efforts; and each participant recognizes in them, to some extent, a common purpose or set of purposes, or at least a mutually accepted direction. This purpose or direction may be fixed from the start (e.g., by an initial proposal of a question for discussion), or it may evolve during the exchange; it may be fairly definite, or it may be so indefinite as to leave very considerable latitude to the participants (as in a casual conversation). But at each stage, SOME possible conversational moves would be excluded as conversationally unsuitable. We might then formulate a rough general principle which participants will be expected (ceteris paribus) to observe, namely: Make your conversational contribution such as is required, at the stage at which it occurs, by the accepted purpose or direction of the talk exchange in which you are engaged. One might label this the COOPERATIVE PRINCIPLE.

On the assumption that some such general principle as this is acceptable, one may perhaps distinguish four categories under one or another of which will fall certain more specific maxims and submaxims, the following of which will, in general, yield results in accordance with the Cooperative Principle. Echoing Kant, I call these categories Quantity, Quality, Relation, and Manner. The category of QUANTITY relates to the quantity of information to be provided, and under it fall the following maxims:

1. Make your contribution as informative as is required (for the current purposes of the exchange).
2. Do not make your contribution more informative than is required.

(The second maxim is disputable; it might be said that to be overinformative is not a transgression of the CP but merely a waste of time. However, it might be answered that such overinformativeness may be confusing in that it is liable to raise side issues; and there may also be an indirect effect, in that the hearers may be misled as a result of thinking that there is some particular POINT in the provision of the excess of information. However this may be, there is perhaps a different reason for doubt about the admission of this second maxim, namely, that its effect will be secured by a later maxim, which concerns relevance.)

Under the category of QUALITY falls a supermaxim — 'Try to make your contribution one that is true' — and two more specific maxims:

1. Do not say what you believe to be false.
2. Do not say that for which you lack adequate evidence.

Under the category of RELATION I place a single maxim, namely, 'Be relevant.' Though the maxim itself is terse, its formulation conceals a number of problems that exercise me a good deal: questions about what different kinds and focuses of relevance there may be, how these shift in the course of a talk exchange, how to allow for the fact that subjects of conversation are legitimately changed, and so on. I find the treatment of such questions exceedingly difficult, and I hope to revert to them in a later work.

Finally, under the category of MANNER, which I understand as relating not (like the previous categories) to what is said but, rather, to HOW what is said is to be said, I include the supermaxim — 'Be perspicuous' — and various maxims such as:

1. Avoid obscurity of expression.
2. Avoid ambiguity.
3. Be brief (avoid unnecessary prolixity).
4. Be orderly.

And one might need others.

It is obvious that the observance of some of these maxims is a matter of less urgency than is the observance of others; a man who has expressed himself with undue prolixity would, in general, be open to milder comment than would a man who has said something he believes to be false. Indeed, it might be felt that die importance of at least the first maxim of Quality is such that it should not be included in a scheme of the kind I am constructing; other maxims come into operation only on the assumption that this maxim of Quality is satisfied. While this may be correct, so far as the generation of implicatures is concerned it seems to play a role not totally different from the other maxims, and it will be convenient, for the present at least, to treat it as a member of the list of maxims.

There are, of course, all sorts of other maxims (aesthetic, social, or moral in character), such as 'Be polite', that are also normally observed by participants in talk exchanges, and these may also generate nonconventional implicatures. The conversational maxims, however, and the conversational implicatures connected with them, are specially connected (I hope) with the particular purposes that talk (and so, talk exchange) is adapted to serve and is primarily employed to serve. I have stated my maxims as if this purpose were a maximally effective exchange of information; this specification is, of course, too narrow, and the scheme needs to be generalized to allow for such general purposes as influencing or directing the actions of others.

As one of my avowed aims is to see talking as a special case or variety of purposive, indeed rational, behavior, it may be worth noting that the specific expectations or presumptions connected with at least some of the foregoing maxims have their analogues in the sphere of transactions that are not talk exchanges. I list briefly one such analog for each conversational category.

1. **Quantity.** If you are assisting me to mend a car, I expect your contribution to be neither more nor less than is required; if, for example, at a particular stage I need four screws, I expect you to hand me four, rather than two or six.
2. **Quality.** I expect your contributions to be genuine and not spurious. If I need sugar as an ingredient in the cake you are assisting me to make, I do not expect you to hand me salt; if I need a spoon, I do not expect a trick spoon made of rubber.
3. **Relation.** I expect a partner's contribution to be appropriate to immediate needs at each stage of the transaction; if I am mixing ingredients for a cake, I do not expect to be handed a good book, or even an oven cloth (though this might be an appropriate contribution at a later stage).

4. **Manner.** I expect a partner to make it clear what contribution he is making, and to execute his performance with reasonable dispatch.

These analogies are relevant to what I regard as a fundamental question about the CP and its attendant maxims, namely, what the basis is for the assumption which we seem to make, and on which (I hope) it will appear that a great range of implicatures depend, that talkers will in general (ceteris paribus and in the absence of indications to the contrary) proceed in the manner that these principles prescribe. A dull but, no doubt at a certain level, adequate answer is that it is just a well-recognized empirical fact that people DO behave in these ways; they have learned to do so in childhood and not lost the habit of doing so; and, indeed, it would involve a good deal of effort to make a radical departure from the habit. It is much easier, for example, to tell the truth than to invent lies.

I am, however, enough of a rationalist to want to find a basis that underlies these facts, undeniable though they may be; I would like to be able to think of the standard type of conversational practice not merely as something that all or most do IN FACT follow but as something that it is REASONABLE for us to follow, that we SHOULD NOT abandon. For a time, I was attracted by the idea that observance of the CP and the maxims, in a talk exchange, could be thought of as a quasi-contractual matter, with parallels outside the realm of discourse. If you pass by when I am struggling with my stranded car, I no doubt have some degree of expectation that you will offer help, but once you join me in tinkering under the hood, my expectations become stronger and take more specific forms (in the absence of indications that you are merely an incompetent meddler); and talk exchanges seemed to me to exhibit, characteristically, certain features that jointly distinguish cooperative transactions:

1. The participants have some common immediate aim, like getting a car mended; their ultimate aims may, of course, be independent and even in conflict — each may want to get the car mended in order to drive off, leaving the other stranded. In characteristic talk exchanges, there is a common aim even if, as in an over-the-wall chat, it is a second-order one, namely, that each party should, for the time being, identify himself with the transitory conversational interests of the other.

2. The contributions of the participants should be dovetailed, mutually dependent.

3. There is some sort of understanding (which may be explicit but which is often tacit) that, other things being equal, the transaction should continue in appropriate style unless both parties are agreeable that it should terminate. You do not just shove off or start doing something else.

But while some such quasi-contractual basis as this may apply to some cases, there are too many types of exchange, like quarreling and letter writing, that it fails to fit comfortably. In any case, one feels that the talker who is irrelevant or obscure has primarily let down not his audience but himself. So I would like to be able to show that observance of the CP and maxims is reasonable (rational) along the following lines: that any one who cares about the goals that are central to conversation/communication (e.g., giving and receiving information, influencing and being influenced by others) must be expected to have an interest, given suitable circumstances, in participation in talk exchanges that will be profitable only on the assumption that they are conducted in general accordance with the CP and the maxims. Whether any such conclusion can be reached, I am uncertain; in any case, I am fairly sure that I cannot reach it until I am a good deal clearer about the nature of relevance and of the circumstances in which it is required.

It is now time to show the connection between the CP and maxims, on the one hand, and conversational implicature on the other.

A participant in a talk exchange may fail to fulfill a maxim in various ways, which include the following:

1. He may quietly and unostentatiously VIOLATE a maxim; if so, in some cases he will be liable to mislead.

2. He may OPT OUT from the operation both of the maxim and of the CP; he may say, indicate, or allow it to become plain that he is unwilling to cooperate in the way the maxim requires. He may say, for example, *I cannot say more; my lips are sealed.*

3. He may be faced by a CLASH: He may be unable, for example, to fulfill the first maxim of Quantity (Be as informative as is required) without violating the second maxim of Quality (Have adequate evidence for what you say).

4. He may FLOUT a maxim; that is, he may BLATANTLY fail to fulfill it. On the assumption that the speaker is able to fulfill the maxim and to do so without violating another maxim (because of a clash), is not opting out, and is not, in view of the blatancy of his performance, trying to mislead, the hearer is faced with a minor problem: How can his saying what he did say be reconciled with the supposition that he is observing the overall CP? This situation is one that characteristically gives rise to a conversational implicature; and when a conversational implicature is generated in this way, I shall say that a maxim is being EXPLOITED.

I am now in a position to characterize the notion of conversational implicature. A man who, by (in, when) saying (or making as if to say) that p has implicated that q, may be said to have conversationally implicated that q, PROVIDED THAT (1) he is to be presumed to be observing the conversational maxims, or at least the cooperative principle; (2) the supposition that he is aware that, or thinks that, q is required in order to make his saying or making as if to say p (or doing so in THOSE terms) consistent with this presumption; and (3) the speaker thinks (and would expect the hearer to think that the speaker thinks) that it is within the competence of the hearer to work out, or grasp intuitively, that the supposition mentioned in (2) IS required. Apply this to my initial example, to B's remark that C has not yet been to prison. In a suitable setting A might reason as follows: '(1) B has apparently violated the maxim 'Be relevant' and so may be regarded as having flouted one of the maxims conjoining perspicuity, yet I have no reason to suppose that he is opting out from the operation of the CP; (2) given the circumstances, I can regard his irrelevance as only apparent if, and only if, I suppose him to think that C is potentially dishonest; (3) B knows that I am capable of working out step (2). So B implicates that C is potentially dishonest.'

The presence of a conversational implicature must be capable of being worked out; for even if it can in fact be intuitively grasped, unless the intuition is replaceable by an argument, the implicature (if present at all) will not count as a CONVERSATIONAL implicature; it will be a CONVENTIONAL implicature. To work out that a particular conversational implicature is present, the hearer will reply on the following data: (1) the conventional meaning of the words used, together with the identity of any references that may be involved; (2) the CP and its maxims; (3) the context, linguistic or otherwise, of the utterance; (4) other items of background knowledge; and (5) the fact (or supposed fact) that all relevant items falling under the previous headings are available to both participants and both participants know or assume this to be the case. A general pattern for the working out of a conversational implicature might be given as follows: 'He has said that p; there is no reason to suppose that he is not observing the maxims, or at least the CP; he could not be doing this unless he thought that q; he knows (and knows that I know that he knows) that I can see that the supposition that he thinks that q is required; he has done nothing to stop me thinking that q; he intends me to think, or is at least willing to allow me to think, that q; and so he has implicated that q.'

Examples of Conversational Implicature

I shall now offer a number of examples, which I shall divide into three groups.

GROUP A: *Examples in which no maxim is violated, or at least in which it is not clear that any maxim is violated*

A is standing by an obviously immobilized car and is approached by B; the following exchange takes place:

(1) A: *I am out of petrol.*
    B: *There is a garage round the corner.* (Gloss: B would be infringing the maxim 'Be relevant' unless he thinks, or thinks it possible, that the garage is open, and has petrol to sell; so he implicates that the garage is, or at least may be open, etc.)

In this example, unlike the case of the remark *He hasn't been to prison yet,* the unstated connection between B's remark and A's remark is so obvious that, even if one interprets the supermaxim of Manner, 'Be perspicuous,' as applying not only to the expression of what is said but also to the connection of what is said with adjacent remarks, there seems to be no case for regarding that supermaxim as infringed in this example. The next example is perhaps a little less clear in this respect:

(2) A: *Smith doesn't seem to have a girlfriend these days.*

B: *He has been paying a lot of visits to New York lately.*

B implicates that Smith has, or may have, a girlfriend in New York. (A gloss is unnecessary in view of that given for the previous example.)

In both examples, the speaker implicates that which he must be assumed to believe in order to preserve the assumption that he is observing the maxim of relation.

GROUP B: *An example in which a maxim is violated, but its violation is to be explained by the supposition of a clash with another maxim*

A is planning with B an itinerary for a holiday in France. Both know that A wants to see his friend C, if to do so would not involve too great a prolongation of his journey:

(3)   A: *Where does C live?*

　　　B: *Somewhere in the South of France.* (Gloss: There is no reason to suppose that B is opting out; his answer is, as he well knows, less informative than is required to meet A's needs. This infringement of the first maxim of Quantity can be explained only by the supposition that B is aware that to be more informative would be to say something that infringed the maxim of Quality, 'Don't say what you lack adequate evidence for', so B implicates that he does not know in which town C lives.)

GROUP C: *Examples that involve exploitation, that is, a procedure by which a maxim is flouted for the purpose of getting in a conversational implicature by means of something of the nature of a figure of speech*

In these examples, though some maxim is violated at the level of what is said, the hearer is entitled to assume that that maxim, or at least the overall Cooperative Principle, is observed at the level of what is implicated.

(1a) *A flouting of the first maxim of Quantity*

A is writing a testimonial about a pupil who is a candidate for a philosophy job, and his letter reads as follows: 'Dear Sir, Mr. X's command of English is excellent, and his attendance at tutorials has been regular. Yours, etc.' (Gloss: A cannot be opting out, since if he wished to be uncooperative, why write at all? He cannot be unable, through ignorance, to say more, since the man is his pupil; moreover, he knows that more information than this is wanted. He must, therefore, be wishing to impart information that he is reluctant to write down. This supposition is tenable only on the assumption that he thinks Mr. X is no good at philosophy. This, then, is what he is implicating.)

Extreme examples of a flouting of the first maxim of Quantity are provided by utterances of patent tautologies like *Women are women* and *War is war*. I would wish to maintain that at the level of what is said, in my favored sense, such remarks are totally noninformative and so, at that level, cannot but infringe the first maxim of Quantity in any conversational context. They are, of course, informative at the level of what is implicated, and the hearer's identification of their informative content at this level is dependent on his ability to explain the speaker's selection of this PARTICULAR patent tautology.

(3b) *An infringement of the second maxim of Quantity, 'Do not give more information than is required', on the assumption that the existence of such a maxim should be admitted*

A wants to know whether p, and B volunteers not only the information that p, but information to the effect that it is certain that p, and that the evidence for its being the case that p is so-and-so and such-and-such.

B's volubility may be undesigned, and if it is so regarded by A it may raise in A's mind a doubt as to whether B is as certain as he says he is ('Methinks the lady doth protest too much'). But if it is thought of as designed, it would be an oblique way of conveying that it is to some degree controversial whether or not p. It is, however, arguable that such an implicature could be explained by reference to the maxim of Relation without invoking an alleged second maxim of Quantity.

(2a) *Examples in which the first maxim of Quality is flouted*

1. *Irony.* X, with whom A has been on close terms until now, has betrayed a secret of A's to a business rival. A and his audience both know this. A says '*X is a fine friend*'. (Gloss: It is perfectly obvious to A and his audience that

what A has said or has made as it to say is something he does not believe, and the audience knows that A knows that this is obvious to the audience. So, unless A's utterance is entirely pointless, A must be trying to get across some other proposition than the one he purports to be putting forward. This must be some obviously related proposition; the most obviously related proposition is the contradictory of the one he purports to be putting forward.)

2. *Metaphor.* Examples like *You are the cream in my coffee* characteristically involve categorial falsity, so the contradictory of what the speaker has made as it to say will, strictly speaking, be a truism; so it cannot be THAT that such a speaker is trying to get across. The most likely supposition is that the speaker is attributing to his audience some feature or features in respect of which the audience resembles (more or less fancifully) the mentioned substance.

It is possible to combine metaphor and irony by imposing on the hearer two stages of interpretation. I say *You are the cream in my coffee,* intending the hearer to reach first the metaphor interpretant 'You are my pride and joy' and then the irony interpretant 'You are my bane.'

3. *Meiosis.* Of a man known to have broken up all the furniture, one says *He was a little intoxicated.*

4. *Hyperbole.* Every nice girl loves a sailor.

(2b) Examples in which the second maxim of Quality 'Do not say that for which you lack adequate evidence', is flouted are perhaps not easy to find, but the following seems to be a specimen. I say of X's wife, *She is probably deceiving him this evening.* In a suitable context, or with a suitable gesture or tone of voice, it may be clear that I have no adequate reason for supposing this to be the case. My partner, to preserve the assumption that the conversational game is still being played, assumes that I am getting at some related proposition for the acceptance of which I DO have a reasonable basis. The related proposition might well be that she is given to deceiving her husband, or possibly that she is the sort of person who would not stop short of such conduct.

(3) *Examples in which an implicature is achieved by real, as distinct from apparent, violation of the maxim of Relation* are perhaps rare, but the following seems

to be a good candidate. At a genteel tea party, A says *Mrs. X is an old bag.* There is a moment of appalled silence, and then B says *The weather has been quite delightful this summer, hasn't it?* B has blatantly refused to make what HE says relevant to A's preceding remark. He thereby implicates that A's remark should not be discussed and, perhaps more specifically, that A has committed a social gaffe.

(4) *Examples in which various maxims falling under the supermaxim 'Be perspicuous' are flouted*

1. *Ambiguity.* We must remember that we are concerned only with ambiguity that is deliberate, and that the speaker intends or expects to be recognized by his hearer. The problem the hearer has to solve is why a speaker should, when still playing the conversational game, go out of his way to choose an ambiguous utterance. There are two types of cases:

(a) Examples in which there is no difference, or no striking difference, between two interpretations of an utterance with respect to straightforwardness; neither interpretation is notably more sophisticated, less standard, more recondite or more far-fetched than the other. We might consider Blake's lines: 'Never seek to tell thy love, Love that never told can be.' To avoid the complications introduced by the presence of the imperative mood, I shall consider the related sentence, *I sought to tell my love, love that never told can be.* There may be a double ambiguity here. *My love* may refer to either a state of emotion or an object of emotion, and *love that never told can be* may mean either 'Love that cannot be told' or 'love that if told cannot continue to exist.' Partly because of the sophistication of the poet and partly because of internal evidence (that the ambiguity is kept up), there seems to be no alternative to supposing that the ambiguities are deliberate and that the poet is conveying both what he would be saying if one interpretation were intended rather than the other, and vice versa; though no doubt the poet is not explicitly SAYING any one of these things but only conveying or suggesting them (cf. 'Since she [nature] pricked thee out of women's pleasure, mine be thy love, and thy love's use their treasure.)

(b) Examples in which one interpretation is notably less straightforward than another. Take the complex example of the British General who captured the town of Sind and sent back the message *Peccavi*. The ambiguity involved ('I have Sind'/'I have sinned') is phonemic, not morphemic; and the expression actually used is unambiguous, but since it is in a language foreign to speaker and hearer, translation is called for, and the ambiguity resides in the standard translation into native English.

Whether or not the straightforward interpretant ('I have sinned') is being conveyed, it seems that the nonstraightforward must be. There might be stylistic reasons for conveying by a sentence merely its nonstraightforward interpretant, but it would be pointless, and perhaps also stylistically objectionable, to go to the trouble of finding an expression that nonstraightforwardly conveys that *p*, thus imposing on an audience the effort involved in finding this interpretant, if this interpretant were otiose so far as communication was concerned. Whether the straightforward interpretant is also being conveyed seems to depend on whether such a supposition would conflict with other conversational requirements, for example, would it be relevant, would it be something the speaker could be supposed to accept, and so on. If such requirements are not satisfied, then the straightforward interpretant is not being conveyed. If they are, it is. If the author of *Peccavi* could naturally be supposed to think that he had committed some kind of transgression, for example, had disobeyed his orders in capturing Sind, and if reference to such a transgression would be relevant to the presumed interests of the audience, then he would have been conveying both interpretants; otherwise he would be conveying only the nonstraightforward one.

2. *Obscurity.* How do I exploit, for the purposes of communication, a deliberate and overt violation of the requirement that I should avoid obscurity? Obviously, if the Cooperative Principle is to operate, I must intend my partner to understand what I am saying despite the obscurity I import into my utterance. Suppose that A and B are having a conversation in the presence of a third party, for example, a child, then A might be deliberately obscure, though not too obscure, in the hope that B would understand and the third party not. Furthermore, if A expects B to see that A is being deliberately obscure, it seems reasonable to suppose that, in making his conversational contribution in this way, A is implicating that

the contents of his communication should not be imparted to the third party.

3. *Failure to be brief or succinct.* Compare the remarks:

(a) *Miss X sang 'Home sweet home.'*
(b) *Miss X produced a series of sounds that corresponded closely with the score of 'Home sweet home'.*

Suppose that a reviewer has chosen to utter (b) rather than (a). (Gloss: Why has he selected that rigmarole in place of the concise and nearly synonymous *sang?* Presumably, to indicate some striking difference between Miss X's performance and those to which the word *singing* is usually applied. The most obvious supposition is that Miss X's performance suffered from some hideous defect. The reviewer knows that this supposition is what is likely to spring to mind, so that is what he is implicating.)

Generalized Conversational Implicature

I have so far considered only cases of what I might call particularized conversational implicature — that is to say, cases in which an implicature is carried by saying that *p* on a particular occasion in virtue of special features of the context, cases in which there is no room for the idea that an implicature of this sort is NORMALLY carried by saying that *p*. But there are cases of generalized conversational implicature. Sometimes one can say that the use of a certain form of words in an utterance would normally (in the ABSENCE of special circumstances) carry such-and-such an implicature or type of implicature. Noncontroversial examples are perhaps hard to find, since it is all too easy to treat a generalized conversational implicature as if it were a conventional implicature. I offer an example that I hope may be fairly noncontroversial.

Anyone who uses a sentence of the form *X is meeting a woman this evening* would normally implicate that the person to be met was someone other than X's wife, mother, sister, or perhaps even close platonic friend. Similarly, if I were to say *X went into a house yesterday and found a tortoise inside the front door,* my hearer would normally be surprised if some time later I revealed that the house was X's own. I could produce similar linguistic phenomena involving the expressions *a garden, a car, a college,* and so on. Sometimes, however, there would normally be no such implicature ('I have been sitting in a car all morning'), and sometimes a reverse implicature ('I broke a finger yesterday'). I am inclined to think that one would not lend a sympathetic ear to a philosopher who suggested that there are three senses of the form of expression *an X:* one in which it means roughly 'something that satisfies the conditions defining the word *X*,' another in which it means approximately 'an X (in the first sense) that is only remotely related in a certain way to some person indicated by the context,' and yet another in which it means 'an X (in the first sense) that is closely related in a certain way to some person indicated by the context.' Would we not much prefer an account on the following lines (which, of course, may be incorrect in detail): When someone, by using the form of expression *an X,* implicates that the X does not belong to or is not otherwise closely connected with some identifiable person, the implicature is present because the speaker has failed to be specific in a way in which he might have been expected to be specific, with the consequence that it is likely to be assumed that he is not in a position to be specific. This is a familiar implicature situation and is classifiable as a failure, for one reason or another, to fulfill the first maxim of Quantity. The only difficult question is why it should, in certain cases, be presumed, independently of information about particular contexts of utterance, that specification of the closeness or remoteness of the connection between a particular person or object and a further person who is mentioned or indicated by the utterance should be likely to be of interest. The answer must lie in the following region: Transactions between a person and other persons or things closely connected with him are liable to be very different as regards their concomitants and results from the same sort of transactions involving only remotely connected persons or things; the concomitants and results, for instance, of my finding a hole in MY roof are likely to be very different from the concomitants and results of my finding a hole in someone else's roof. Information, like money, is often given without the giver's knowing to just what use the recipient will want to put it. If someone to whom a transaction is mentioned gives it further consideration, he is likely to find himself wanting the answers to further questions that the speaker may not be able to identify in advance; if the appropriate specification will be likely to enable the hearer to answer a considerable variety of such questions for himself, then there is a presumption that the speaker should include it in his remark; if not, then there is no such presumption.

Finally, we can now show that, conversational implicature being what it is, it must possess certain features:

1. Since, to assume the presence of a conversational implicature, we have to assume that at least the Cooperative Principle is being observed, and since it is possible to opt out of the observation of this principle, it follows that a generalized conversational implicature can be canceled in a particular case. It may be explicitly canceled, by the addition of a clause that states or implies that the speaker has opted out, or it may be contextually canceled, if the form of utterance that usually carries it is used in a context that makes it clear that the speaker IS opting out.

2. Insofar as the calculation that a particular conversational implicature is present requires, besides contextual and background information, only a knowledge of what has been said (or of the conventional commitment of the utterance), and insofar as the manner of expression plays no role in the calculation, it will not be possible to find another way of saying the same thing, which simply lacks the implicature in question, except where some special feature of the substituted version is itself relevant to the determination of an implicature (in virtue of one of the maxims of Manner). If we call this feature NONDETACHABILITY, one may expect a generalized conversational implicature that is carried by a familiar, nonspecial locution to have a high degree of nondetachability.

3. To speak approximately, since the calculation of the presence of a conversational implicature presupposes an initial knowledge of the conventional force of the expression the utterance of which carries the implicature, a conversational implicatum will be a condition that is not included in the original specification of the expression's conventional force. Though it may not be impossible for what starts life, so to speak, as a conversational implicature to become conventionalized, to suppose that this is so in a given case would require special justification. So, initially at least, conversational implicata are not part of the meaning of the expressions to the employment of which they attach.

4. Since the truth of a conversational implicatum is not required by the truth of what is said (what is said may be true — what is implicated may be

false), the implicature is not carried by what is said, but only by the saying of what is said, or by 'putting it that way.'

5. Since, to calculate a conversational implicature is to calculate what has to be supposed in order to preserve the supposition that the Cooperative Principle is being observed, and since there may be various possible specific explanations, a list of which may be open, the conversational implicatum in such cases will be disjunction of such specific explanations; and if the list of these is open, the implicatum will have just the kind of indeterminacy that many actual implicata do in fact seem to possess.

The Pragmatics of What is Said

François Recanati

1. The Gricean Picture

According to Paul Grice, the meaning of a sentence conventionally determines, or helps to determine, what is literally said by uttering the sentence (the literal truth-conditions of the utterance); for example, the meaning of the sentence 'I have not had breakfast today' determines that, if S utters the sentence on a certain day, what he thereby says is that he has had no breakfast on that day. The meaning of the sentence also determines other, non-truth-conditional aspects of utterance meaning, like those responsible for the difference between 'and' and 'but'. In this paper, I will not be concerned with these 'conventional implicatures', as Grice calls them, but only with Grice's distinction between what is said and the 'conversational' implicatures of the utterance. Conversational implicatures are part of what the utterance communicates, but they are not conventionally determined by the meaning of the sentence; they are pragmatically rather than semantically determined. For example, in saying that he has had no breakfast, S may convey to his audience that he is hungry and wishes to be fed. As Grice pointed out, the generation of conversational implicatures can be accounted for by connecting them with certain general principles or 'maxims' of conversation that participants in a talk-exchange are mutually expected to observe. In the Gricean framework, conversational implicatures are contextual implications of the utterance act — they are the assumptions that follow from the speaker's saying what he says together with the presumption that he is observing the maxims of conversation.

Since what is communicated includes a pragmatic, nonconventional element, *viz.* the conversational implicatures, the fact that a given expression receives different interpretations in different contexts does not imply that it is semantically ambiguous. The intuitive difference in meaning can be accounted for at the semantic level, by positing two different literal meanings, but it can also be accounted for at the pragmatic level, by positing a conversational implicature which in some contexts combines with what is literally said. Take, for example, the sentence ⌜P or Q⌝. It can receive an inclusive or an exclusive interpretation. Instead of saying that 'or' is ambiguous in English, we may consider it as unambiguously inclusive, and account for the exclusive reading by saying that in some contexts the utterance conversationally implicates that ⌜P⌝ and ⌜Q⌝ are not both true. When there is such a conversational implicature, the overall meaning of the utterance is clearly exclusive, even though what is strictly and literally said corresponds to the logical formula ⌜P ∨ Q⌝.

When an intuitive 'ambiguity' can be accounted for either at the semantic level, by positing two different literal meanings, or at the pragmatic level, by positing a conversational implicature, the pragmatic account is to be preferred, according to Grice. This is the substance of the methodological principle he called 'Modified Occam's Razor': *Senses are not to be multiplied beyond necessity* (Grice 1978, pp. 118–9). This is a principle of theoretical parsimony, like Occam's Razor. Pragmatic explanations, when available, are to be preferred because they are economical, in the sense that the principles and assumptions they appeal to are very general and independently motivated. By contrast, positing a semantic ambiguity is an *ad hoc,* costly move — a move which the possibility of a pragmatic analysis makes entirely superfluous.

The Gricean picture which I have just presented has been enormously influential, and rightly so; but it raises a problem which has been recognized only recently. The problem is connected with the notion that sentence meaning conventionally determines what is said. It must be noted from the outset that Grice is rather cautious in his formulation. Vaguely enough, he ascribes to what is said the property of being 'closely related to the conventional meaning of words' (Grice 1975, p. 44). But how closely? Recent work in pragmatics has shown that the gap between the conventional meaning of the words and what is said by uttering them is wider than was previously acknowledged. As a result, it is no longer possible to contrast 'what is said' with those aspects of the interpretation of utterances that are pragmatically rather than semantically determined; for what is said turns out to be, in a large measure, pragmatically determined. Besides the conversational implicatures, which are external to (and combine with) what is said, there are other nonconventional, pragmatic aspects of utterance meaning, which are constitutive of what is said. The specific issue I want to address in this paper is that of the criteria that can be used to distinguish conversational implicatures from pragmatic constituents of what is said; in particular, I want to discuss a proposal made by Robyn Carston in a recent paper (Carston 1988). Before doing so, however, I shall briefly identify those aspects of the Gricean picture that are inconsistent with due recognition of the pragmatic determination of what is said.

2. Pragmatic Determinants of What is Said

Grice is aware that what is said depends not only on the conventional meaning of the words but also on the context of utterance. What is said by uttering 'I have not had breakfast today' depends on who is speaking and when. This is why there is a difference between the conventional meaning of words and what is said by uttering the words. The conventional meaning of the words determines, or helps to determine, what is said, but it cannot be identified with what is said.

But what does it mean to say that sentence meaning conventionally determines what is said? A common answer is that sentence meaning is a 'function' from context onto propositions; it is a rule which determines, for every context, what is said by uttering the sentence in that context. Similarly, the meaning of a word like 'I' is a function that takes us from a context of utterance to the semantic value of the word in that context, this semantic value (the reference of 'I') being what the word contributes to the proposition expressed by the utterance. On this view, made popular by David Kaplan's work on the logic of demonstratives (Kaplan 1977), what is said by an utterance depends not only on the conventional meaning of the words but also on the context of utterance; however, recourse to the context of utterance is guided and controlled by the conventional meaning of the words. The meaning of 'I' tells us what to look for in the context of utterance for a full identification of what is said; once the context is given, what is said can be automatically decoded.

Neat and attractive though it is, this view of the matter is quite unrealistic. In general, even if we know who is speaking, when, to whom, and so forth, the conventional meaning of the words falls short of supplying enough information to exploit this knowledge of the context so as to secure understanding of what is said. Consider a simple example, 'He has bought John's book'. To understand what is said, one must identify the intended referent of 'he'. At most, the conventional meaning of 'he' imposes that the referent be male, but this allegedly necessary condition is certainly not sufficient and does not uniquely identify the referent in the context of utterance. The meaning of the word 'he' provides no 'rule', no criterion enabling one to identify the reference. The meaning of the sentence, in this case as in many others, seriously underdetermines what is said. Nor is this underdetermination limited to the reference of referring expressions. To understand what is said by 'He has bought John's book', one must identify the referent of 'he', of 'John' and (perhaps) of 'John's book'. But one must also identify the relation that is supposed to hold between John and the book. According to Kay and Zimmer 1976, p. 29, 'genitive locutions present the hearer with two nouns and a metalinguistic instruction that there is a relation between these two nouns that the hearer must supply'. 'John's book' therefore means something like 'the book that bears relation x to John'. To understand what is said by means of a sentence in which the expression 'John's book' occurs, this meaning must be contextually enriched by instantiating the variable 'x'. In other words, not only the reference but the descriptive sense of the expression 'John's book' is context-dependent. Moreover, as in the case of 'he', there is no rule or function taking us from the context to the relevant semantic value. The only constraint linguistically imposed on the relation between John and the book is that it be a relation between John and the book.

The purpose of this paper not being to review the literature on context-dependence, I will not proceed with further examples. I will simply assume (1) that context-dependence extends far beyond reference assignment, and (2) that it is generally 'free' rather than 'controlled', in the sense that the linguistic meaning of a context-sensitive expression constrains its possible semantic values but does not consist in a 'rule' or 'function' taking us from context to semantic value.

Up to this point we need not depart from the Gricean picture, but simply enrich it. We have three levels of meaning: sentence meaning, what is said, and what is communicated. What is communicated includes not only what is said but also the conversational implicatures of the utterance.[1] The mechanism of implicature generation suggested by Grice is intended to account for the step from what is said to what is communicated. But how are we to account for the step from sentence meaning to what is said? What bridges the gap instituted by there being a 'free' type of context-dependence pervasive in natural language? Grice does not address this issue. However, as many people have suggested (*e.g.* Wilson and Sperber 1981, p. 156), the pragmatic apparatus by means of which Grice accounts for conversational implicatures can also be used to account for the determination of what is said on the basis of sentence meaning. In the interpretation process, the referent of 'he' and the relation between John and the book in 'He has bought John's book' are selected so as to make what the speaker says consistent with the presumption that he is observing the maxims of conversation. The speaker might have meant that Jim has bought the book written by John or that Bob has bought the book sought by John. The hearer will select the interpretation that makes the speaker's utterance consistent with the presumption that he is trying to say something true and relevant.

Once the Gricean picture is enriched in the manner indicated, a problem arises. Implicit in the Gricean picture is the assumption that there are two, *and only two,* ways of accounting for *prima facie* ambiguities: the semantic approach, which posits a multiplicity of literal meanings, and the pragmatic approach, which posits a conversational implicature. Modified Occam's Razor provides a reason to prefer the latter approach, when it can be implemented, to the former. These two approaches correspond to the two basic levels of meaning that are distinguished in the Gricean picture: sentence meaning, which determines what is literally said, and the utterance's overall meaning, which comprises not only what is said but everything that happens to be communicated, including the conversational implicatures. The semantic approach locates the ambiguity at the level of sentence meaning, while the pragmatic approach considers that it is generated only at the level of what is communicated. But in the enriched Gricean picture, there are three basic levels of meaning rather than two: sentence meaning, what is said, and what is communicated. A pragmatic process is involved not only to get from what is said to what is communicated but also to get from sentence meaning to what is said. It follows that there are three ways of accounting for *prima facie* ambiguities rather than just two. Besides the semantic approach, which locates the ambiguity at the first level, that of sentence meaning, there are two pragmatic approaches, corresponding to the second and third levels of meaning (what is said and what is communicated). The classical Gricean

289

approach considers that what is said is the same on all readings of the 'ambiguous' utterance, the difference between the readings being due to a conversational implicature which, in some contexts, combines with what is literally said. The other pragmatic approach considers that the difference is a difference in what is said, even though the sentence itself is not ambiguous; this is possible owing to the semantic underdetermination of what is said.[2]

The important point is that Modified Occam's Razor does not support the approach in terms of conversational implicature as against the other pragmatic approach; it only says that a pragmatic approach is to be preferred, *ceteris paribus,* to a semantic approach. Hence, enriching the Gricean picture in the manner indicated has the result that the classical Gricean approach to multiple readings in terms of conversational implicature can no longer be justified by appealing to Modified Occam's Razor, as it could when it was assumed to be the only pragmatic alternative to a semantic approach. The classical Gricean approach is threatened by the appearance of a pragmatic rival.

Consider, as an example, Donnellan's distinction between two uses of definite descriptions. Donnellan held that what is said by an utterance of 'Smith's murderer is insane' is different according to whether the description 'Smith's murderer' is used attributively or referentially. On the attributive interpretation, what is said is true if and only if there is one and only one person who murdered Smith and he is insane. But if the description 'Smith's murderer' is used to refer to a certain person, Jones, who is known to have murdered Smith, rather than in general to whomever murdered Smith, then the utterance is true if and only if *Jones* is insane: Jones's being the murderer of Smith is no more part of the truth-condition of what is said, on this 'referential' interpretation, than my being the speaker is part of the truth-condition of what I say when I utter the sentence 'I am insane'. This was Donnellan's view. Now a large number of competent philosophers have used the Gricean picture to argue against it. In doing so, they have taken for granted that there are only two possible approaches to Donnellan's distinction: a semantic approach, according to which the literal meaning of the sentence and, therefore, what is said, is different on the referential and the attributive reading, and a pragmatic approach, according to which what is said on both readings is the same (*viz.* that there is a unique murderer of Smith and he is insane), the referential reading being only distinguished at the level of what is communicated. Using Modified Occam's Razor as an argument for the pragmatic approach, they concluded that Donnellan was wrong to locate the difference between the two readings at the level of what is said. This argument against Donnellan's view is clearly fallacious; it relies on the mistaken assumption that there are only two possible accounts, a semantic account and a pragmatic account in terms of conversational implicature. But this is not so: another type of pragmatic account is possible, which incorporates Donnellan's view, according to which the difference between the referential and the attributive reading is a difference in what is said. On this approach, which I have developed elsewhere (Recanati 1989), the sentence 'Smith's murderer is insane' is not ambiguous, yet it can be used to express either a general or a singular proposition, depending on the context of utterance. Modified Occam's Razor provides no reason to prefer to this account an account in terms of conversational implicature; on the contrary, as I try to show in the paper referred to above, considerations of theoretical economy tend to favour the pragmatic account that incorporates Donnellan's view.

Another example is provided by Carston's pragmatic analysis of conjoined utterances (Carston 1988). In some contexts, a conjunctive utterance ⌜P and Q⌝ conveys the notion that the event described in the second conjunct occurred after the event described in the first conjunct; thus 'They got married and had many children' is not intuitively synonymous with 'They had many children and got married'. However, what is strictly and literally said is in both cases the same thing, according to Grice; the temporal ordering, which is responsible for the intuitive difference between the two examples, is conversationally implicated rather than part of what is said. Modified Occam's Razor dictates that this approach be preferred to a semantic approach ascribing to 'and' a temporal sense to account for this type of use and a non-temporal sense to account for other uses (such as 'Jane had three children and Mary two', in which no temporal ordering is suggested). However, as Robyn Carston has shown, another pragmatic account is possible, according to which the temporal ordering is part of what is said by means of 'They got married and had many children', even though 'and' is ascribed a single, non-temporal sense at the semantic level.[3] Modified Occam's Razor provides no reason to prefer to this account the classical Gricean account in terms of conversational implicature.[4]

To sum up: Enriching the Gricean picture to take into account the semantic underdetermination of what is said implies rejecting an assumption implicit in the Gricean picture, namely the assumption that there are two, and only two, possible approaches to *prima facie* ambiguities, the semantic approach and the pragmatic approach in terms of implicature. Once this assumption is abandoned, the classical Gricean treatment of *prima facie* ambiguities in terms of implicature is considerably weakened; instead of enjoying the privileges of monopoly, it has to compete with another pragmatic approach. This raises a central issue, which is the main topic of this paper: that of the criteria that can be used in adjudicating between the different pragmatic approaches. When should a pragmatically determined aspect of utterance meaning be considered as a conversational implicature, and when should it be considered as constitutive of what is said? In what follows, I shall consider four possible answers to this question, i.e. four criteria that could be used to decide whether a given aspect of meaning is a conversational implicature or a pragmatic constituent of what is said.

3. The Minimalist Principle

The first possible criterion, the Minimalist Principle, can be stated as follows:

> *Minimalist Principle*: A pragmatically determined aspect of meaning is part of what is said if and only if its determination is necessary for the utterance to express a complete proposition.

The Minimalist Principle entails what Carston (1988) calls the 'linguistic direction principle'. To every pragmatically determined aspect of meaning that is part of what is said, there corresponds a slot in the meaning of the sentence which must be filled for the utterance to be truth-evaluable. Context-sensitive expressions, such as 'he' or the genitive, set up such slots, which in some cases at least can be represented as variables in need of contextual instantiation. It follows, by the Minimalist Principle, that the pragmatic determination of the referent of 'he' and of the relation between John and the book contributes to determining what is said by uttering the sentence 'He has bought John's book'. By contrast, conversational implicatures are not part of what is said, because the utterance expresses a complete proposition without them. (Since conversational implicatures follow from the speaker's saying what he says, the generation of a conversational implicature presupposes that something has been said.)

Most theorists assume that to get from the meaning of the sentence to the proposition expressed, one has only to disambiguate the sentence, i.e. to select one of its possible readings, and to instantiate a few indexical variables. That semantic underdetermination goes beyond mere indexicality is often neglected, as is the fact that the contextual instantiation of many variables is 'free' rather than 'controlled'. In other words, the gap between sentence meaning and what is said is generally underestimated. But the Minimalist Principle itself might be considered as a manifestation of the general tendency to underestimate this gap. Once it is recognized that there are more variables than just indexical variables, and that the contextual instantiation of variables is not always linguistically controlled, why not go one step further and reject the Minimalist Principle itself? Why not question the claim that nothing more is needed to go from sentence meaning to what is said than just disambiguation and variable instantiation?

Following Sperber & Wilson, but more explicitly, Robyn Carston has taken this step (Carston 1988). She thinks that the Minimalist Principle must be rejected: what it presents as a necessary and sufficient condition is only sufficient, according to her. Consider sentences (1) and (2):

(1)　It will take us some time to get there.
(2)　I have had breakfast.

Once the identity of the speaker and hearer, the time of utterance and the reference of 'there' is determined, no further slot needs to be filled for an utterance of (1) to express a complete proposition. The proposition we get at this point is the truistic proposition that there is a lapse of time (of some length or other) between our departure, or some other point of reference, and our arrival at a certain place. But, according to Carston, who borrows this example from Sperber and Wilson 1986, pp. 186–90, this is not the proposition actually expressed; to get the latter, we need to go beyond the minimal proposition expressible by the sentence and enrich it by pragmatically specifying the relevant lapse of time as rather long (longer than expected, perhaps). This contextual specification is constitutive of what is said, yet it is not necessary for the sentence to express a definite proposition. It follows that the Minimalist Principle must be rejected. In the same way, according to Sperber and Wilson, once the identity of the speaker and the time of utterance has been fixed, (2) expresses a proposition, viz. the proposition that the speaker has had breakfast at least once before the time of utterance. This proposition, which would be true if the speaker had had breakfast twenty years earlier and never since, does not correspond to what the speaker means to say when he utters 'I have had breakfast'. What the speaker says goes beyond the minimal proposition expressible, contrary to what the Minimalist Principle predicts.

In Sperber and Wilson's framework, three processes are involved in getting from sentence meaning to what is said: disambiguation, fixation of reference and enrichment. The notion of enrichment, for them, covers things as different as the determination of the relation between John and the book in 'He has bought John's book' and the determination of the length of the lapse of time mentioned in 'It will take us some time to get there'. In the first case, the meaning of the sentence sets up a slot (representable as a variable: 'He has bought the book that bears relation x to John') that must be contextually filled for the utterance to express a complete proposition. This type of enrichment I shall call 'saturation'; it is not essentially different from the fixation of reference, but rather includes it as a particular case, since referential expressions themselves set up slots to be contextually filled for the utterance to express a complete proposition. In the other case, the enrichment of 'some time' into something more specific is not needed for the utterance to express a complete proposition, but for the proposition expressed to correspond to what the speaker means by his utterance. The input to this second type of enrichment is a complete proposition, and the output is a richer proposition, i.e. one that entails the input proposition. I shall refer to this type of enrichment as 'strengthening'. Sperber and Wilson's claim that the proposition expressed is obtained from the disambiguated meaning of the sentence not only by saturation but also by strengthening is inconsistent with the Minimalist Principle, according to which the proposition expressed — what is said — just is the minimal proposition expressible by the utterance, i.e. what results from simply saturating the disambiguated meaning of the sentence.

I find Sperber and Wilson's proposal very interesting. The Minimalist Principle seems arbitrary, and there may be good reasons to get rid of it. (One such reason, perhaps, is that the Minimalist Principle leads to implausible semantic hypotheses when taken in conjunction with two principles I shall introduce later — the Availability Principle and the Scope Principle.) Still, the matter is controversial, and I think caution is called for; the Minimalist Principle should not be dropped too lightly.

The examples given by Sperber and Wilson do not, in my opinion, require giving up the traditional framework: it is easy to handle these examples without dropping the Minimalist Principle. One obvious way to do so is to adopt the analysis in terms of conversational implicature, according to which the person who utters (2) 'says' that he has had breakfast at least once, and 'implicates' that this happened on the very day of utterance. (On this analysis, the proposition expressed — what is said — *is* the 'minimal' proposition expressible.) Sperber and Wilson do not agree with this analysis; neither do I. The reason why it seems inacceptable will be spelled out in the next section. What matters for my present purposes is that the analysis in terms of conversational implicature is not the only way to handle the examples without dropping the Minimalist Principle. Sperber and Wilson reject it because they believe that a pragmatically determined aspect of the meaning of (1) and (2) is such that:

(a)   it is constitutive of what is said, and

(b)   its determination is not necessary for the utterance to express a complete proposition.

This conjunction of (a) and (b) is inconsistent with the Minimalist Principle, which says that a pragmatically determined aspect of the meaning of an utterance is part of what is said if and only if its contextual determination is necessary for the utterance to express a complete proposition. However, the Minimalist Principle is not inconsistent with (a) or (b) taken separately. Defenders of the implicature analysis accept (b) but reject (a); they are thus able to maintain the Minimalist Principle. But there is another treatment, consistent with the Minimalist Principle: one may accept (a) but reject (b), i.e. consider that the relevant aspect of the meaning of (1) and (2) is constitutive of what is said (and therefore not a conversational implicature), while insisting that its contextual determination *is* necessary for the utterance to express a complete proposition. Let me briefly sketch this minimalist treatment of examples (1) and (2).

Both (1) and (2) can be analysed in terms of quantification. (1) quantifies over durations (it says that there is a duration t such that it will take us t to get there) and (2) quantifies over events (it says that there is a past event which is the speaker's having breakfast). Now, quantification involves a certain amount of context-dependence, because, in general, the domain of quantification has to be contextually specified. For example, it can be argued that the sentence 'Everybody went to Paris', by itself, does not express a complete proposition — not even the proposition that everybody in the world went to Paris: what it says is that everybody in some domain x went to Paris, and the context helps to instantiate the variable 'x'. (On this view, the variable 'x' may be contextually instantiated so as to make 'everybody in the world' the right interpretation, but this interpretation is no less contextual than any other interpretation.[5]) Suppose we accept this view. Then, in the case of (1), (2) and other utterances involving quantification, there is a slot to be filled, corresponding to the domain of quantification. It follows that the specific interpretations of (1) and (2), which Carston and Sperber and Wilson present as counterexamples to the Minimalist Principle, are perfectly consistent with the latter — one merely has to define the domain of quantification in an appropriate way. In the case of (1), we might say that the domain of quantification is a set of durations, contextually restricted to those that are long enough to be worth mentioning in connection with the process of our going there. (In this framework, the interpretation of (1) which corresponds to the so-called 'minimal proposition' expressible — the proposition that it will take us 'some time or other' to get there — is just the unlikely interpretation in which the domain of quantification is contextually identified with the set of all possible durations, including milliseconds.) In the case of (2), we might say that the domain of quantification is a time interval, or rather a set of happenings defined by a time interval. This allows us to account for the intuitive difference between 'I've had breakfast' and 'I've been to Tibet' (Sperber and Wilson 1986, pp. 189–90). In both cases, what is conveyed by virtue of linguistic meaning alone is that, in some temporal domain x prior to the time of utterance, there is a certain event, viz. the speaker's having breakfast or his going to Tibet; but in the first case, the time interval is contextually restricted to the day of utterance, while in the second case the relevant interval is more extended and covers the speaker's life (up to the time of utterance).

According to the view I have just outlined, it is a mistake to believe that (1) and (2) express complete propositions once the obvious indexical variables (identity of the speaker and hearer, time of utterance, reference of 'there') have been instantiated; a slot remains to be filled, which corresponds to the domain of quantification. It follows that the Minimalist Principle can be retained even though one accepts thesis (a) above, *i.e.* even though one considers that what is said by means of (1) and (2) is that it will take us a *long* time to get there or that the speaker has had breakfast *on the day of utterance.* Far from being added to an already complete proposition, the pragmatic specifications I have just italicized result from filling a slot, a slot that must be filled in some way or other for the utterance to express a complete proposition.

Not only is it the case that (1), (2) and similar 'counterexamples' to the Minimalist Principle *can* be handled in terms of saturation, without giving up minimalism, but I also believe that, in many such cases, a saturation-based account is actually preferable to an alternative account in terms of strengthening. Consider, for example, the sentence 'One boy came'. It can be used to say something quite specific, namely that *one of the boys in the class* came. This seems to be a typical case of strengthening: 'One boy came' might be said to express the 'minimal' proposition that at least one boy came, which minimal proposition is entailed by the richer proposition 'At least one of the boys in the class came' (if one of the boys in the class came, then one boy came); the notion of strengthening therefore applies in a straightforward manner. But this account is not general enough, as can be seen by considering other cases, which look very similar but are far more difficult to handle in terms of strengthening. Thus, the sentence 'Every boy came' can be used to say that every boy in the class came; the problem here is that the output proposition, *i.e.* the proposition that every boy in the class came, does not entail the input proposition, viz. the 'minimal' proposition that every boy (*i.e.* every boy in the world!) came. Because of this problem, the account in terms of strengthening seems less attractive than the minimalist account in terms of a contextually variable domain of quantification.

The same type of problem arises in connection with examples such as (2). 'I have had breakfast' can be used to say that the speaker has had breakfast on the day of utterance, even though, according to Sperber and Wilson, the minimal proposition expressible by this sentence is the proposition that the speaker has had breakfast at least once (but not necessarily on the day of utterance). This can be accounted for in terms of strengthening, because the proposition that the speaker has had breakfast on the day of utterance entails the proposition that he has had breakfast at least once in his life. But what about the similar utterance 'I have not had breakfast'? It can be used to say that the speaker has not had breakfast on the day of utterance, but this cannot be straightforwardly accounted for in terms of strengthening, because the proposition that the speaker has had no breakfast on the day of utterance does not entail the proposition that he has never eaten breakfast in his life. Here again, because of its greater generality, the minimalist account presented above looks more attractive than the alternative account in terms of strengthening.[6]

Shall we conclude from this discussion that the Minimalist Principle is to be retained after all? That would be excessive. With respect to examples other than those I have discussed, a strengthening-based account, inconsistent with the Minimalist Principle, may well seem more attractive or plausible than a saturation-based one. My discussion merely shows that the matter is not as a simple as one might think after reading Carston and Sperber and Wilson. Whether or not one should ultimately stick to the Minimalist Principle thus remains an open question.

In any event, I will now attempt to show that, even if there *were* decisive arguments in favour of the Minimalist Principle, the latter could not be used as a working criterion for distinguishing implicatures from the pragmatic aspects of what is said. In the next section, I will introduce another criterion, the Availability Principle, which is implicitly appealed to by those who reject the implicature analysis of (1) and (2). I will argue that this is the right criterion to use.

The Minimalist Principle states a biconditional: A pragmatically determined aspect of meaning is part of what is said if and only if its determination is necessary for the utterance to express a complete proposition. It follows that the Minimalist Principle can be used to decide whether a pragmatically determined aspect of utterance meaning is part of what is said, *provided* one knows whether or not the pragmatic determination of this aspect of meaning is necessary for the utterance to express a complete proposition. The qualification is important: the Minimalist Principle *per se* cannot be used to tell whether a pragmatically determined aspect of meaning is part of what is said; it can only be used to that effect if a decision has already been made concerning the variables that have to be contextually instantiated for the utterance to express a complete proposition. In other words:

(M) For any (pragmatically determined) aspect *a* of the meaning of an utterance, the Minimalist Principle can be used to decide whether *a* is a conversational implicature or an integral part of what is said only if one already knows whether or not the determination of *a* is necessary for the utterance to express a complete proposition, i.e. only if one already possesses a semantic analysis of the sentence uttered.

This immediately raises a problem. According to (M), the Minimalist Principle cannot be used to make a decision concerning what is said unless we already know precisely what the meaning of the sentence is. But this puts the cart before the horse: far from proceeding in that order, we generally start with some intuition concerning what is said (or, at least, what is communicated), and end up with a theory about what the sentence means. As I emphasize in the next section, sentence meaning is something more abstract and theoretical than what is said or what is communicated. For this reason, I believe that the Minimalist Principle does not actually provide a criterion for distinguishing implicatures from pragmatic aspects of what is said, because we do *not* possess a semantic analysis of the sentence ahead of any decision concerning what is said. The Minimalist Principle is more properly seen as providing a criterion for determining the semantic analysis of the sentence, on the basis of a prior, intuitive identification of what is said. For example, suppose that a theorist has decided in favour of (a) and believes, on an intuitive basis, that a certain pragmatically determined aspect of meaning is part of what is said. If he accepts the Minimalist Principle, he is led to posit a slot in the meaning of the sentence that must be filled for the utterance to express a complete proposition — a slot that corresponds to the pragmatically determined aspect of meaning which, by virtue of (a), he considers as part of what is said. Suppose, on the contrary, that he rejects (a). In this case, he must refrain from positing such a slot in the meaning of the sentence, for if there were one, the corresponding aspect of utterance meaning would be part of what is said, by virtue of the Minimalist Principle. Acceptance of the Minimalist Principle thus makes some semantic hypotheses look more attractive than others; it provides a criterion for choosing among alternative theories concerning the linguistic meaning of sentence. This is not the same thing as a criterion for determining what is said.

Considered as a criterion for selecting hypotheses about sentence meaning, the Minimalist Principle may well be retained, at least provisionally.[7] But it does not constitute an adequate criterion for determining what is said, and we must find something else to answer this purpose. I suggest that we take a closer look at a claim I have just made: that what is said is identified on an intuitive basis. This, I believe, leads us to the criterion we are looking for.

4. The Availability Principle

In the last part of section 3 I made two related claims: first, that sentence meaning is something more abstract and theoretical than what is said; second, that we have 'intuitions' concerning what is said that serve as a starting point in the process of determining what the linguistic meaning of the sentence is. Although obviously related, these two claims are to be distinguished; the second is stronger than the first. I shall argue that the stronger claim provides us with a criterion for telling implicatures apart from pragmatic aspects of what is said. This criterion, stated below, I shall refer to as the 'Availability Principle', because it presupposes that what is said by an utterance is available or accessible to the unsophisticated speaker-hearer. 'Available' must be understood here in a strong sense: what I mean is not that what is said by an utterance is tacitly identified at some sub-doxastic level, but that it is accessible to our ordinary, conscious intuitions. The Availability Principle just says that these intuitions are to be respected:

> *Availability Principle*: In deciding whether a pragmatically determined aspect of utterance meaning is part of what is said, that is, in making a decision concerning what is said, we should always try to preserve our pre-theoretic intuitions on the matter.

In this section, I will try to make more explicit the claim concerning the availability of what is said — the 'availability hypothesis', as I shall call it; I will then show how the Availability Principle works. I will conclude that some very common assumptions of Gricean pragmatics are to be rejected if we take the Availability Principle seriously.

Let us start with the claim that sentence meaning is something more abstract and theoretical than what is said. Consider the diagram labelled 'Figure 1'.

Starting at the top, it shows the various steps that lead, by analytical abstraction, from what is communicated to the meaning of the sentence. The analysis thus displayed is intended to mirror the actual process of understanding the utterance, this corresponding to a bottom-up reading of the diagram.

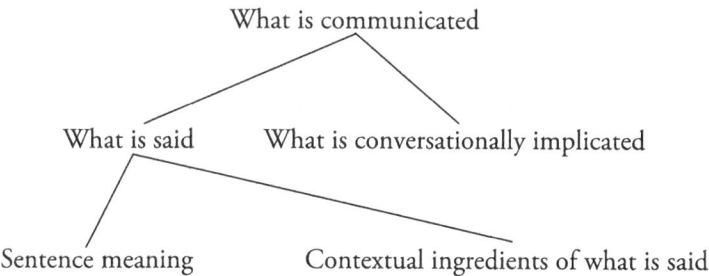

Figure 1

At the top (*i.e.* the root) of the inverted tree, 'what is communicated' is the intuitive datum we, as analysts, start from; it is also the consciously accessible output of the process of pragmatic understanding. Everything that occurs below the top level is more abstract, that is, farther from the starting point of the analysis. At the bottom of the tree, we find sentence meaning, a theoretical construct representing both the output of the process of semantic decoding and the input to the process of pragmatic understanding. To say that sentence meaning is something more abstract than what is said is just a way of putting sentence meaning closer to the bottom of the tree, while putting what is said closer to the top. In processing terms, sentence meaning is cognitively deeper and what is said shallower — they are respectively farther from and closer to the output of the process of pragmatic understanding.

In the case of sentence meaning, abstractness and cognitive depth go hand in hand with a further property, that of conscious unavailability. Of sentence meaning we can assume only tacit (unconscious) knowledge on the part of the speaker who utters the sentence. To be sure, users of the language claim to have intuitions concerning what the sentences in their language mean; but these intuitions are not directly about their purported objects — linguistic meanings. They do not bear on the linguistic meanings of sentences, which are very abstract and unaccessible to consciousness, but on what would be said or communicated

301

by the sentence were it uttered in a standard or easily accessible context.

Being located at an intermediate level in the diagram, what is said is cognitively shallower — less abstract — than sentence meaning. But we cannot conclude that it is more accessible to consciousness than the latter. We cannot infer, from the fact that what is said is shallower than sentence meaning, that there is between them a difference in nature such that the latter can only be cognized at the sub-doxastic level while the former is consciously accessible. The availability of what is said does not follow from its relative shallowness, *i.e.* from its proximity to the top level. *As an intermediate output, resulting from an advanced but nonfinal stage of unconscious pragmatic processing, what is said could be no less sub-doxastic than sentence meaning.* It is, therefore, a nontrivial hypothesis that I am making when I claim that what is said is consciously accessible. The availability hypothesis cannot be reduced to the claim that sentence meaning is more abstract and cognitively deeper than what is said.

To make sense of the availability hypothesis, I suggest a slight modification of the diagram in Figure 1. As it is, it implies that what is communicated — the object of our intuitions — is something over and above what is said and what is conversationally implicated: what is communicated is seen as the output of a specific cognitive process (the last step in the general process of pragmatic understanding) whose inputs are what is said and what is implicated. One way of understanding the claim concerning the availability of what is said is by rejecting this view altogether, considering that what is communicated *consists of* what is said and what is implicated, instead of being something *over and above* what is said and what is implicated. Instead of locating what is communicated at one level and what is said (as well as the implicatures) at another, I suggest that we consider 'what is communicated' as simply a *name* for the level at which we find both what is said and what is implicated — the top level, characterized by conscious accessibility (Figure 2). On this view, the conscious availability of what is said no longer is a mystery: if what is communicated, which is consciously accessible, consists of what is said and what is implicated, then what is said cannot but be consciously accessible.

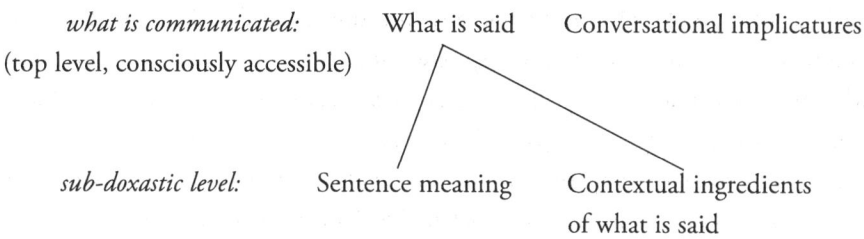

Figure 2

In the new diagram, it is no longer suggested that there is a specific process merging what is said and what is implicated. They constitute the final output of the general process of pragmatic understanding, not an intermediate output, as Figure 1 suggests. What is said and what is implicated thus remain distinct, and are consciously available as distinct.[8]

It is striking that the question of the availability of what is said has never been raised in the pragmatic literature.[9] I believe it is a very important issue. If we really have conscious access to what is said, then as theorists we have a very simple criterion for telling when a pragmatically determined aspect of meaning is part of what is said and when it is not: we merely have to check the proposal against our intuitions. This, I believe, is what most theorists have always done. Why, for example, do Sperber and Wilson claim that the proposition that the speaker has had breakfast at least once in his life is not the proposition actually expressed — what is said — by the speaker who utters (2)? Because *everybody knows* that this is not what the speaker says, under ordinary circumstances, when he utters (2). The appeal to common sense is perfectly justified once the availability hypothesis is made.

Perhaps we should consider the intuitions of the speaker instead of those of the theorist. According to the Availability Principle thus interpreted, a tentative identification of what is said has to be checked against the speaker's intuitions. In this framework, Sperber and Wilson's decision concerning example (2) can be justified as follows. We suppose that what is said by an utterance is known, at least, by the speaker (availability hypothesis). In the case of (2), if what the speaker says is that he has had breakfast at least once in his life, then the speaker does not know what he says, because he does not know that this is what he says (were he to be told, he would be very surprised); therefore, this is *not* what he says. Using the Availability Principle, we are thus able to reject the 'implicature analysis' of examples (1) and (2), because it assumes an identification of what is said which is inconsistent with the speaker's intuitions. The speaker believes that what he says is that he has had breakfast *on the day of utterance*; the Availability Principle dictates that we reject all pragmatic theories inconsistent with this belief, and, in particular, the implicature analysis, which identifies what the speaker says with the proposition that he has had breakfast at least once in his life.

Before proceeding, a caveat is in order. When I claim that we have intuitions concerning what is said, I do not wish to deny that these intuitions may be fuzzy, or that we may sometimes have conflicting intuitions. (The existence of a quotational concept of 'saying', to be mentioned in the next section, is but one factor among many that tend to make our intuitions fuzzy and conflicting.) What I am saying is that our intuitions are clear enough to rule out a number of analyses that are grossly inconsistent with them.

The Availability Principle can be appealed to in a number of cases to show that a tentative analysis is misguided. Consider an example mentioned earlier in this paper, the utterance 'Everybody went to Paris'. Under ordinary circumstances, what a speaker would mean by this is not that everybody in the absolute sense, *i.e.* every person in the world, went to Paris, but that everybody in some (contextually identifiable) group went to Paris. Suppose, for example, it is established that what the speaker means is that every member of the Johnson and Johnson staff went to Paris. Still, the utterance can be analyzed in two ways. The first analysis is quite straightforward: it identifies what the speaker says with what he means, *i.e.* with the proposition that every member of the Johnson and Johnson staff went to Paris. But there is another possible analysis. We may consider that what is literally said is that everybody in the world went to Paris, even though this is clearly not what the speaker means. A proponent of this analysis has only to assume that what the speaker says is different from what he means, i.e. that he speaks nonliterally, as in metaphor. Such an analysis has been put forward in Bach 1987 and extended to many examples, including the whole class of utterances in which an incomplete definite description occurs. Thus, Bach identifies the proposition literally expressed by the utterance 'The door is closed' with the Russellian proposition 'There is one and only one door in the world, and it is closed', this proposition not being what the speaker means to communicate when he utters the sentence. The Availability Principle militates against this type of analysis, which assumes a counter-intuitive identification of what is said. The difference with genuine cases of nonliterality should be apparent. When the speaker says to the hearer, 'You are the cream in my coffee', everybody would agree that what the speaker says is that the hearer is the cream in his coffee: this is clearly what he says, and it is no less clear that he is speaking nonliterally. But when the speaker says 'Everybody went to Paris', or 'The door is closed', it is counter-intuitive to identify what he says with the propositions that every person in the world went to Paris, or that the only door in the universe is closed. The speaker himself would not recognize those propositions as being what he said. The 'nonliteral' analysis must therefore be rejected, by virtue of the Availability Principle.[10]

One important consequence of the Availability Principle is that some of the most often cited examples of conversational implicatures turn out not to be conversational implicatures after all. So-called 'scalar implicatures' are a case in point. Suppose the speaker utters 'John has three children', thereby communicating that John has exactly three children. It is customary to say that the proposition literally expressed by 'John has three children' is the proposition that John has at least three children, even if what the speaker means to communicate by this utterance is that John has exactly three children. What is communicated (*viz.* that John has exactly three children) is classically accounted for by positing a conversational implicature that combines with the proposition allegedly expressed (*viz.* that John has at least three children). This proposal, however, does not pass the availability test, for the speaker himself would not recognize the latter proposition as being what he has said. Not being consciously available, the proposition which the classical account takes to be literally expressed cannot be identified with what is said, if we accept the Availability Principle. The latter dictates that we consider the aspect of meaning that is pragmatically determined (*viz.* the implicit restriction: no more than three children) as part of what is said rather than as a conversational implicature associated with what is said. The same remarks could be made with respect to other well-known examples, such as the exclusive reading of ⌜P or Q⌝, which are often presented as prototypical cases of conversational implicature.

5. The Independence Principle

In her aforementioned paper, Robyn Carston attempts to show that many cases that have been treated as typical examples of conversational implicature are better conceived of as pragmatic aspects of what is said. Not only is she right to hold this as a general thesis; I also believe she is right with respect to particular examples, in most cases at least. This should come as no surprise: Carston certainly relies on her intuitions when she decides that a particular aspect of meaning is to be considered as an integral part of what is said, and I have argued that we do have reliable intuitions concerning what is said. Carston, however, does not hold anything like the availability hypothesis, and thus she cannot be content to rely on her intuitions. What she wants — and what she offers — is an explicit criterion for telling implicatures apart from the pragmatic aspects of what is said. In this section, I shall consider the criterion she puts forward, and show that it does not work.

Those who, like Carston, reject the Minimalist Principle believe that the proposition expressed by an utterance — what is said — may be richer than what I called the 'minimal proposition' expressible by the utterance. Whether or not they are right is, as I said, an open question. But Carston goes further than merely rejecting the Minimalist Principle: she puts forward an alternative principle, which entails that every communicated assumption that is richer than the minimal proposition expressible by the utterance *must* be understood as part of what is said. This principle can be stated as follows:

> *Independence Principle*: Conversational implicatures are functionally independent of what is said; this means in particular that they do not entail, and are not entailed by, what is said. When an alleged implicature does not meet this condition, it must be considered as part of what is said.

It is not perfectly clear what Carston means by 'functional independence', but it is clear that, for her, functional independence entails logical independence: as she emphasizes in her paper, an implicature will not be functionally independent of the proposition expressed if it entails, or is entailed by, the latter. It is this feature of the Independence Principle that she uses as a criterion to distinguish genuine implicatures from pragmatic aspects of what is said. Owing to this criterion, it is not possible to consider that what is said by means of (2) is that the speaker has had breakfast at least once, the fact that he has had breakfast *on the day of utterance* being only implicated. For then the implicature would entail the proposition literally expressed, contrary to what the Independence Principle requires. (If the speaker has had breakfast on the day of utterance, then he has had breakfast at least once in his life.) In the same way, it is not possible to consider that the proposition expressed by (1) is the minimal proposition that it will take us some time or other to get there, the more specific proposition that it will take us a rather *long* time to get there being only implicated; for this alleged implicature would entail the proposition expressed, and thus would not be a genuine implicature. In general, when an alleged implicature entails the proposition allegedly expressed, it must be considered as part of what is said rather than as a genuine implicature.

Using this criterion, Carston is able to show that many pragmatically determined aspects of utterance meaning that have been classified as conversational implicatures in the Gricean tradition are better viewed as pragmatic aspects of the proposition expressed. For example, the utterance 'John has three children', used to communicate that John has exactly three children, cannot be said to express the proposition that John has at least three children, for if this were the proposition expressed, then the richer proposition — that John has exactly three children — would be an implicature, and we would have an implicature that entails the proposition expressed, in violation of the Independence Principle.[11] In this and related cases, I believe that Carston is right to say that the alleged implicature is not a genuine implicature but, rather, an aspect of the proposition expressed. However, I think the Independence Principle is to be rejected.

A first and obvious objection to the Independence Principle must be set aside. It might be argued that, in litotes, we have implicatures that entail what is said. (By saying that it is not bad, one implicates that it is excellent, and if it is excellent it cannot be bad.) This, however, is not a counterexample to Carston's Independence Principle, which is only intended to apply to literal assertions. But there are counterexamples even if we consider only literal assertions. Suppose that John says to Jim: 'Someone will come and see you today — someone you have been expecting for a long time. I am not permitted to reveal the identity of visitors in advance, but I take it that you see who I mean'. Suppose it is clear that

307

John means that Mrs Robertson is going to come and see Jim. Has John said that Mrs Robertson was going to come? No: he has said that *someone* was going to come, and has implied that it was Mrs Robertson. The implication is very clear, but the fact that it is an implication, and not something that is explicitly said, is no less clear: as John emphasizes, he is not entitled to *say* who is going to come. Carston's principle, however, predicts that John has said, rather than simply implicated, that Mrs Robertson was to come. For if this were an implicature, it would entail the proposition allegedly expressed (*viz.* that someone will come and see Jim), contrary to what the Independence Principle requires.

According to Ruth Kempson (personal communication), this is not really a counterexample to Carston's Independence Principle, because the concept of 'saying' which is involved when I deny that the speaker has 'said' that Mrs Robertson was to come is not the relevant one. Certainly, there is a concept of saying such that, when I utter 'I've had breakfast', I do not literally 'say' that I've had breakfast *today*, because I do not utter the word 'today'; what I 'say' is that I have had breakfast, but I do not 'say' when. In this sense of 'say', it is always possible to deny that something has been said, unless the word for that thing has been explicitly pronounced. This we may refer to as the 'quotational' sense of 'say'. The quotational sense of 'say', Kempson argues, is irrelevant to the issue we are discussing, but it is critical to the Robertson example; therefore, the latter is not a real counterexample.

I am not wholly convinced by Kempson's argument, although I agree with her that the existence of a quotational sense of 'say' has to be taken into account. In any event, I am willing to concede that the example is controversial. My case against the Independence Principle does not rest upon this particular example, but on general considerations to which I now turn. I shall first say what is wrong with Carston's proposal, and then use these general considerations to build up a better, and to my mind decisive, counterexample to the Independence Principle.

The problem with Carston's proposal is that, even though she constantly talks of 'functional' independence, the criterion she actually uses to distinguish conversational implicatures from pragmatic aspects of what is said is the relation of *logical* independence that must hold, she believes, between a genuine implicature and what is said: basically, an implicature must not entail what is said. Now, I believe that *any* formal principle of this sort is mistaken, and cannot but make wrong predictions. This point is very general, and before giving examples connected with the Independence Principle, I should like to mention two other instances of what we might call the 'formal fallacy' in pragmatics.

The first instance of the formal fallacy is a very common definition of direct and indirect speech acts. In speech-act theory sentences are taken to have a semantically determined 'illocutionary act potential'; that is, they are taken to be semantically associated with an illocutionary act type. An illocutionary act performed by uttering a sentence is commonly said to be direct if and only if it falls under the illocutionary act potential of the sentence, that is, if and only if it is an instance of the illocutionary act type semantically associated with the sentence. So, given that the sentence 'Can you pass the salt?' is semantically associated with the illocutionary act of asking the hearer whether he can pass the salt, an act of requesting the hearer to pass the salt, performed by uttering this sentence, can only be indirect. This same act will be direct when performed by means of the alternative sentence 'Please pass the salt', which is semantically associated with the act of requesting the hearer to pass the salt.

This 'formal' definition of direct and indirect illocutionary acts is seriously misguided, as the following counterexample shows. The sentence 'He has come' is semantically associated with the act of conveying the information, concerning someone, that he has come; any token of this act performed by means of this sentence must therefore be direct, in virtue of the formal definition. Now, suppose that by uttering 'He has come' the speaker says that John has come; and suppose a context in which, by saying that John has come, the speaker is able to communicate another piece of information, namely that Bill has come. (For example, it is mutually known that, whenever John comes, Bill comes too, and that the point of saying that John has come is, for the speaker, to convey indirectly that Bill has come.) This is a typical case of indirect speech act: by saying something, namely that John has come, the speaker conveys something else, namely that Bill has come. Nevertheless, this indirect speech act is to be treated as direct, according to the formal definition above, just because it happens to fall under the illocutionary act potential of the sentence uttered. The formal definition obliges us to consider that the speaker has directly asserted that Bill has come, just because he has conveyed this information by uttering a sentence that could have been (but was not!) used to say that. The formal definition must therefore be rejected: what defines a speech act as direct is the way it is peformed, not a formal relation of 'congruence' (Gardiner 1932, p. 142) between the speech act and the sentence uttered. To be sure, the fact that a speech act is directly performed implies that this relation holds, but it can hold also 'accidentally', even though the speech act performed is indirect.

The same type of counterexample can be brought against Sperber and Wilson's definition of explicitness, understood in a certain way. Clearly, what characterizes implicatures (implicitly communicated assumptions) and explicatures (explicitly commmunicated assumptions) is, for Sperber and Wilson, the way they are recovered in the interpretation process: explicatures are recovered by enriching and developing a logical form encoded in the sentence uttered, while implicatures are premises and conclusions in an inference process whose starting point is the explicature. It follows that an explicature necessarily bears a certain formal relation to the logical form of the sentence uttered: that of being a 'development' of that logical form, *i.e.* a generally richer and more complex form that incorporates it. But it is a mistake to use that formal property to define the explicature as opposed to the implicature, as Sperber and Wilson seem to do (Sperber and Wilson 1986, p. 182), for it is quite possible for an implicature to have this property accidentally. Suppose that by saying 'It will rain tomorrow' the speaker communicates the following explicature: that Mary believes that it will rain tomorrow. Suppose further that this explicature contextually implies that it is not the case that it will rain tomorrow, and that much of the relevance of the utterance predictably depends on this contextual implication. Then 'It is not the case that it will rain tomorrow' is an implicature, according to Sperber and Wilson's ordinary characterization. But it should be treated as an explicature according to the formal definition, because 'It is not the case that it will rain tomorrow' is formally a development of 'It will rain tomorrow'.[12]

Similar counterexamples can easily be found in connection with Carston's Independence Principle. Consider the following dialogue:

A: Was there anybody rich at the party, who might be asked to pay for the damages?
B: Jim is rich.
A: Yes, but did he go to the party?
B: I don't know, but I can tell you that if *anybody* was there, Jim was there.
A: *Somebody* was there — this I know for sure (I saw John going there). So it looks as if the damages will be paid for, after all.

The beginning of A's last reply, 'Somebody was there', clearly implicates (in virtue of the premiss provided by B's last reply: 'If anybody was there, Jim was there') that Jim was there and therefore (in virtue of the premiss provided by B's first reply: 'Jim is rich') that a rich man was there. This implicature is what links together the beginning ('Somebody was there') and the end ('The damages will be paid for') of A's last reply. Now, the implicature that Jim was there entails what is said, namely that somebody was there. So it should be considered as part of what is said rather than as a genuine implicature, according to the Independence Principle. But, clearly, by saying that somebody was there, A is not referring to Jim in any sense; if there is any reference here (which I doubt), it would be to the person of whom the speaker knows for sure that he went to the party, namely John. So there are three candidates for the status of what is said. The most plausible is the general proposition that there was at least one person at the party. Some people believe that there is a referential use of indefinites, and are therefore prepared to argue that A was referring to John when he said 'Somebody was there'; those people would perhaps conclude that A said of John that he was there. But who would accept the extraordinary conclusion, imposed by Carston's Independence Principle, that A, having John in mind and uttering 'Somebody was there', has actually said that Jim was there?

On this general pattern, we might construct as many counterexamples to the Independence Principle as we may wish. This type of counterexample shows that what defines a communicated assumption as an implicature is not a formal property, and in particular not the formal property of (logical) independence with respect to the proposition expressed, but the way it is recovered in the interpretation process — *i.e.* not by enriching and developing a logical form encoded in the sentence, but by an inference process the starting point of which is a proposition obtained by enriching and developing an encoded logical form. To be sure, when an assumption is reached through simply enriching an encoded logical form, it cannot but entail the minimal proposition expressible by the sentence; but it could easily occur that an implicature, *i.e.* an assumption obtained through a totally different process, turns out to entail this minimal proposition, by accident as it were; this is not a sufficient reason to consider it as part of what is said. I conclude that the Independence Principle must be rejected.[13]

6. The Scope Principle

I shall now consider a criterion which, I think, can be used in conjunction with the Availability Principle. I shall refer to this criterion as the Scope Principle. It is based on observations that various people have made on the behaviour of conversational implicatures in connection with logical operators. These observations tend to provide evidence for a distinction between two types of alleged implicatures: those that do and those that do not fall within the scope of logical operators. Carston devotes a section of her paper to some of these observations, showing that they can be accounted for in terms of the distinction between genuine implicatures and pragmatic aspects of what is said. Yet, when it comes to finding a criterion for deciding between the two alternative pragmatic approaches, she does not consider the Scope Principle, because of her misplaced confidence in the Independence Principle.

Consider the following pair of examples:

(3) The old king has died of a heart attack and a republic has been declared.

(4) A republic has been declared and the old king has died of a heart attack.

In (3), it is implied that the first event described (the death of the old king) occurred before the second one (the declaration of a republic). In (4) the same events are reported in a different order, and the implication is reversed; it is suggested that the death of the old king occurred after — and, perhaps, because of — the declaration of a republic. In both cases, the temporal suggestion is, for Grice, a conversational implicature, stemming from the presumption that the speaker is observing the maxim of manner: 'Be perspicuous'. In general, a narrative is more perspicuous if the events are reported in the order in which they occurred. The speaker's reporting a series of events in a certain order therefore implies that they occurred in that order, by virtue of the presumption that he is observing the maxim of manner. *Qua* conversational implicature, the temporal suggestion is not part of what is said and makes no contribution to the truth-condition of the utterance. Thus, according to Grice, what is strictly and literally said by means of (3) and (4) is the same thing, even though there is an important difference in (conveyed) meaning between these two utterances. The truth-functionality of 'and' can therefore be maintained.

Jonathan Cohen 1971 raised a serious objection to that view. He pointed out the following consequence of Grice's analysis: If (3) and (4) really have the same truth-conditions and differ only at the level of conversational implicatures, then, in Grice's framework, (5) and (6) also should have the same truth-conditions:

(5) If the old king has died of a heart attack and a republic has been declared, then Tom will be quite content.
(6) If a republic has been declared and the old king has died of a heart attack, then Tom will be quite content.

But, if (5) and (6) are ascribed the same truth-conditions, how are we to account for the intuitive difference in meaning between them? This difference is such that it is possible to assert (5) and to deny (6) in the same breath without contradiction. Again, we shall have to use the Gricean apparatus and say that (5) and (6) differ only at the level of conversational implicatures. This consequence is problematic, for it is unclear how the suggested Gricean analysis can be applied in the case of (5)–(6). While it may seem a good idea to say that (3) and (4) express the same proposition and differ only at the level of conversational implicatures, extending this type of analysis to (5) and (6) is hardly a credible move. It seems better to reject Grice's analysis, by admitting that (3) and (4) do not express the same proposition. This does not mean that one must follow Cohen in considering a semantic account of the temporal suggestion conveyed by $\ulcorner$P and Q$\urcorner$ as preferable to a pragmatic account. As Carston rightly emphasizes in her paper, Cohen's counterexample can be handled within the type of pragmatic account she advocates, according to which the temporal suggestion conveyed by $\ulcorner$P and Q$\urcorner$ is part of what is said even though it is not part of the linguistic meaning of 'and'. To dispose of Cohen's objection, one need only admit, as Carston does, that (3) and (4) do not express the same proposition.

Being counterexamples to the classical Gricean account but not to the other type of pragmatic account, examples such as (3)–(6) may be considered as providing a criterion for deciding between the two alternative pragmatic approaches, that is, for deciding whether a pragmatically determined aspect of utterance meaning must be considered as a conversational implicature or as an integral part of what is said. This criterion — the Scope Principle, stated below — is based on the behaviour of an alleged implicature when the utterance which gives rise to it is embedded in a larger utterance and dominated by a logical operator.

It has often been noticed that some *prima facie* implicatures fall within the scope of logical operators, while others do not. For example, when a seemingly implicature-bearing utterance is negated, sometimes the alleged implicature can be interpreted as (part of) what is negated and sometimes it cannot; when a seemingly implicature-bearing utterance is embedded as the antecedent of a conditional, sometimes the alleged implicature is an integral part of the antecedent, and sometimes it is not. (5) and (6) are evidence that the alleged implicatures conveyed by (3) and (4) belong to the first category. What (5) and (6) say is that Tom will be content if the following conditions obtain: the old king has died, a republic has been declared, *and there is a certain temporal relation between these two events.* The temporal relation allegedly implicated by (3) and (4) is an integral part of the antecedent of the conditional in (5) and (6); it falls within the scope of the conditional. In the same way, when (3) is negated, the alleged implicature falls within the scope of the negation. The negation of (3) is made true if one of the following conditions fails to be satisfied: the old king has died, a republic has been declared, *and the first event occurred before the second.* Thus, one can deny (3) and thereby mean, as in (7), that the suggested order of events does not correspond to the facts:

(7)   It is not the case that the old king has died and a republic has been declared; what is true is that a republic has been declared first and then the old king died of a heart attack.

The fact that some implicatures fall within the scope of logical operators has always been considered as raising a serious problem for pragmatics. From this fact, different theorists have drawn different conclusions. Some theorists (*e.g.* Anscombre and Ducrot 1978) have concluded that these 'implicatures' cannot be implicatures in the ordinary sense of the term. Their argument can be reconstructed as follows:

(a)   Conversational implicatures are pragmatic consequences of an act of saying something.

(b)   An act of saying something can be performed only be means of a complete utterance, not by means of an unasserted clause such as the antecedent of a conditional.

(c)   Hence, no implicature can be generated at the sub-locutionary level, *i.e.* at the level of an unasserted clause such as the antecedent of a conditional.

(d)   To say that an implicature falls within the scope of a logical operator is to say that it is generated at the sub-locutionary level, *viz.* at the level of the clause on which the logical operator operates.

(e)   Hence, no implicature can fall within the scope of a logical operator.

This argument is, I think, both sound and compelling. It shows that, when an alleged implicature seems to fall within the scope of a logical operator, either it is not really an implicature, or it does not really fall within the scope of the logical operator.[14]

From the fact that some implicatures apparently fall within the scope of logical operators, other theorists (*e.g.* Cornulier 1984, pp. 663–4) have concluded that it is a mistake to think that implicatures cannot fall within the scope of logical operators. As Carston points out in her paper, this position is based on the assumption that all pragmatically determined aspects of meaning are conversational implicatures. If this assumption is made, and one encounters a constituent of meaning that can fall within the scope of logical operators, one has no other choice but to conclude either that this aspect of meaning is not pragmatically determined (a conclusion which Anscombre and Ducrot, contrary to Cornulier, are willing to accept), or that implicatures can fall within the scope of logical operators. If one further assumes that the relevant aspect of meaning is pragmatically determined, one is led to deny the conclusion (e) of the argument above. This is what Cornulier does. But, as we know, the assumption that all pragmatically determined aspects of meaning are implicatures is unwarranted. Conclusion (e) can therefore be maintained, even though one admits that the relevant aspect of meaning (*i.e.* the alleged implicature) is pragmatically rather than semantically determined.

Once the assumption that all pragmatically determined aspects of meaning are implicatures is abandoned, it turns out that far from raising a problem, operator scope provides us with a criterion for distinguishing between conversational implicatures and pragmatically determined aspects of what is said. According to this criterion, genuine implicatures are external to the proposition expressed, and it is the latter that falls within the scope of logical operators. Thus, if the utterance which gives rise to an implicature is negated or made the antecedent of a conditional, the implicature itself cannot be considered as an integral part of what is negated or of the antecedent of the conditional. If it can — if the alleged implicature turns out to fall within the scope of logical operators such as negation (as in (7)) or conditionals (as in (5) and (6)) — then it is not a genuine implicature but a pragmatic constituent of what is said. Here is a tentative formulation of the criterion:

> *Scope Principle*: A pragmatically determined aspect of meaning is part of what is said (and, therefore, not a conversational implicature) if — and, perhaps, only if — it falls within the scope of logical operators such as negation and conditionals.

This could be tested, and weakened in various ways. I am sure that the matter is not as simple as the Scope Principle suggests, but at least it provides a starting point. Especially encouraging is the fact that the decisions it leads to concerning what is said seem to be consistent with those made by appealing to the Availability Principle. Thus the examples I mentioned earlier — 'I've had breakfast', 'Everybody went to Paris', 'John has three children', and so forth — are all treated in the same way whether one uses the Availability Principle or the Scope Principle.

7. Conclusion

Everybody would agree that the saying/implicating distinction is part of the ordinary, everyday picture of linguistic communication. We commonly talk of what is 'said' as opposed to what is only 'implied' by means of a certain utterance, and it is that distinction which Grice undertook to elaborate (Grice 1975, pp. 43-4). Being so closely related to the everyday picture of communication, Grice's theory of conversational implicatures has strong intuitive appeal. But on a certain view of the relation between theory and common sense, the intuitive appeal of Grice's theory does not constitute very strong evidence in its favour, because it can hardly be considered as a requirement of a theory that it match our ordinary intuitions. On this view, henceforth to be called the 'anti-prejudice view', there is nothing sacrosanct about our ordinary, folk concepts. If a theoretical account is consistent with our commonsensical intuitions, so much the better; if they conflict, so much the worse for common sense.

Because of this view, when the domain of Grice's theory of implicatures was extended far beyond our intuitive reach, this was hardly noticed, let alone considered to raise a problem. Not many people have observed that Grice's theory departs from our intuitions when it is applied to examples such as 'John has three children', which Griceans take to express the proposition that John has at least three children and to implicate that he has no more than three children. However, there is an important difference between this example and *e.g.* 'I've had no breakfast today', which implicates that the speaker is hungry and wishes to be fed. In the latter example, the implicature is intuitively felt to be external to what is said; it corresponds to something that we would ordinarily take to be 'implied', In the former case, we are not pre-theoretically able to distinguish between the alleged two components of the meaning of the utterance — the proposition expressed (that John has at least three children) and the implicature that he has at most three children). We are conscious only of the result of their combination, *i.e.* of the proposition that John has exactly three children. In this case as opposed to the other one, the theoretical distinction between the proposition expressed and the implicature does not correspond to the intuitive distinction between what is said and what is implied.

This difference between the two types of examples should have prompted the following questions: when, instead of considering intuitive examples of implied meaning, we extend the theory of implicatures to examples such as 'John has three children', are we not talking of something else? If really the same thing is involved in both cases, how are we to ccount for the difference?[15] These were interesting questions to raise, but, because of the anti-prejudice view, they were not raised. According to this view, it is a very good thing — not something to worry about — when a theory's domain of application is extended beyond its intuitive basis. As far as Grice's theory is concerned, the intuitive basis was the everyday distinction between what is said and what is implied. Starting with this distinction, Grice did two things. First, he outlined a mechanism accounting for the generation of implied meaning; second, he tried to show that the same mechanism was at work in examples which we would not ordinarily classify as cases of implied meaning. There seems to be nothing wrong with this. That some examples of implicatures do not fall under the folk concept of implied meaning merely shows that Grice's theory has augmented our knowledge not only of the *mechanism* responsible for the phenomenon he undertook to explore, but also of the *scope* of this phenomenon.

I agree that scientific theorizing is to be freed from, rather than impeded by, intuitions and common sense, which provide only a starting point. In particular, I agree that it was a good thing to go beyond our intuitions and to show, as Grice did, that in many cases the meaning of an utterance results from an unconscious process of 'meaning construction' (to use Fauconnier's suggestive phrase), an inferential process whose input is the linguistic meaning of the sentence uttered. In the case of 'John has three children', there is no doubt that what this utterance communicates (that John has exactly three children) is not to be identified with the meaning of the sentence, but results from inferentially combining the latter with the presumption that the speaker has given the strongest relevant information available to him. Still, I believe there was something to worry about when the theory of implicatures was extended to examples such as this, which we would not ordinarily consider as cases of implied meaning. This does not mean that I reject the anti-prejudice view. We may at the same time accept this view and recognize that human cognition is a very special field: in this field, our intuitions are not just a first shot at a theory — something like Wittgenstein's ladder, which may be thrown away after it has been climbed up — but also *part of what the theory is about,* and as such they cannot be neglected. In the case at hand, it was a mistake to ignore our intuitions, which tell us that there is a difference between standard cases of implied meaning and the other type of alleged implicatures. This difference pointed to an important theoretical distinction, between genuine implicatures and pragmatic constituents of the proposition expressed.

The theoretical distinction itself was attainable by another route. One only has to realize that sentence meaning largely underdetermines what is said, to be forced to the conclusion that a distinction must be made between genuine implicatures and pragmatic aspects of what is said. Note that, when this route is taken, one knows *that* there is a principled distinction to be made between implicatures and pragmatic aspects of what is said, but one does not know which pragmatic aspect of the meaning of an utterance is to be treated as an implicature, and which as a constituent of what is said. Grice's 'tests' for conversational implicature (cancellability, nondetachability, calculability, and so forth) test the presence of a pragmatically determined aspect of utterance meaning, but they do not tell us whether it is a genuine implicature or a constituent of what is said. New criteria have to be devised to make this decision possible.

In this paper, I have taken this route and considered various possible criteria for distinguishing implicatures from pragmatic constituents of what is said. I have considered four criteria in turn: the Minimalist Principle, the Availability Principle, the Independence Principle and the Scope Principle. I have shown that Carston's Independence Principle must be rejected, because it is an instance of a fallacy quite common in pragmatics (the 'formal fallacy'). As for the Minimalist Principle, Carston and Sperber and Wilson believe that it must be rejected; I have shown that the matter is not as simple as they seem to think, but I also pointed out that the Minimalist Principle could hardly be used as a working criterion. So we have to find something else. The solution I have suggested is very simple; it consists in going back to our intuitions, and using *them* as a criterion. This is the substance of the Availability Principle, which says that any decision concerning what is said and what is implicated must be consistent with our pretheoretic intuitions on the matter. (Again, the Availability Principle is not based on a rejection of the anti-prejudice view, but on a specific cognitive hypothesis, according to which what is said is consciously accessible.) Finally, I put forward another criterion, to be used in conjunction with the Availability Principle: the Scope Principle, which says that genuine conversational implicatures cannot fall within the scope of logical operators. I am confident that, using these two criteria, it will in most cases be possible to decide whether a given aspect of meaning is a conversational implicature or a pragmatic constituent of what is said.[16]

Notes

1   The opposition between what is said and the conversational implicatures survives the claim that what is said is conventionally determined by the meaning of the sentence. *Qua* assumptions following from the speaker's saying what he says, conversational implicatures are, by definition, external to what is said.

2   It may be argued that there are not only different pragmatic approaches

to *prima facie* ambiguities, but also different semantic approaches. Thus Cohen opposes to the standard 'insulationist' semantics an 'interactionist' semantics in terms of which, he says, those *prima facie* ambiguities which Grice handles within the implicature framework can be accounted for in a way that is immune to Modified Occam's Razor (Cohen 1971, p. 56; for a recent statement of the interactionist point of view, see Cohen 1986). I shall not address this issue in this paper; the Gricean picture will be questioned only as far as the pragmatic approach is concerned.

3   Carston's pragmatic account is, roughly, the following. To determine what is said by means of the sentence 'They got married and had many children', the hearer must assign a reference to each of the referring expressions, *including the past tense 'got married' and 'had'*. Just as pragmatic principles are employed in ascertaining the referent of 'they', so, Carston says, they are used in assigning temporal reference. The hearer goes beyond the strict semantic content of the sentence uttered, and on the basis of contextual assumptions and pragmatic principles recovers from 'They got married and had many children' a representation such as 'John and Mary got married at t and had many children at $t + n$'. 't is some more or less specific time prior to the time of utterance and $t + n$ is some more or less specific time, later than t. The temporal ordering of the events described in the conjuncts is thus treated as a by-product of the reference assignment process involved in determining "what is said"' (Carston 1988, p. 161). This suggested analysis raises some problems when the past tense is replaced by the present perfect, as in example (3) below, because the present perfect can hardly be considered as referring to a specific time. (In familiar terms, the present perfect is used to express general propositions of the type: 'There is a time t, prior to the time of utterance, such that blah blah', while it makes sense to say that the past tense is 'singular' and refers to a specific time t which must be contextually identified — with more or less precision — for the utterance to express a complete proposition.) I shall not discuss this issue in this paper; I am concerned only with the *type* of analysis Carston puts forward — a pragmatic analysis at the level of what is said. Whether or not the details of her analysis are correct is another matter.

4   In the light of Carston's suggestion concerning 'and' we may reconsider Grice's use of Modified Occam's Razor against ordinary language

philosophers, to whom he ascribed the semantic view, i.e. the notion that 'and', 'or', *etc.* are multiply ambiguous in English. The main reason why this view was ascribed to ordinary language philosophers like Strawson is the following: they held that what is said by uttering a sentence such as ⌜P or Q⌝ or ⌜P and Q⌝ varies according to the context of utterance; they considered that the truth conditions of an utterance of one of these sentences were not invariant under contextual change. Thus, ⌜P and Q⌝ is sometimes true if the event described in the second conjunct occurred before (or simultaneously with) that described in the first conjunct, and sometimes not; ⌜P or Q⌝ is sometimes true if ⌜P⌝ and ⌜Q⌝ are both true, and sometimes not. This way of putting the matter is certainly inconsistent with the classical Gricean approach, which assumes that what is said is the same on all readings, the difference being located at the level of implicatures. It was therefore natural to ascribe to ordinary philosophers the semantic approach, on the assumption that there are only two possible approaches, the semantic approach and the approach in terms of conversational implicature. However, this assumption must be abandoned, and the possibility of a pragmatic approach in terms of what is said acknowledged. Once this is done, Modified Occam's Razor no longer provides any reason to reject the claim that sentences such as ⌜P and Q⌝ can be used to say different things in different contexts; for this claim no longer implies that sentences such as ⌜P and Q⌝ are semantically ambiguous, and that 'and' has a range of different senses in English. (For a fuller defence of ordinary language philosophers along these lines, see Travis 1985.)

5   For further discussion of this example, see below, section 4.

6   To save the account in terms of strengthening, the notion of *local strengthening* could be introduced. For example, in the case of 'Every boy came', we might say that it is the predicate 'boy' that is strengthened into 'boy in the class', rather than the proposition 'Every boy came' into 'Every boy in the class came'. This seems to work because the predicate 'boy in the class' does entail the predicate 'boy'. In the same way, we might say that the strengthening in 'I have not had breakfast' applies not to the global proposition but, within the latter, to the proposition that is negated: 'I have had breakfast' is strengthened into 'I have had breakfast this morning', and

this is negated.

7　　I believe the Minimalist Principle has a methodological role to play, independent of its ultimate validity as a theoretical principle. In a recent paper (Recanati 1989, pp. 244–6), I called attention to a strategy that has dominated semantics to date and impedes the progress of pragmatics: the 'Anti-Contextualist Strategy', which consists in minimizing context-sensitivity. Whether true or false, the Minimalist Principle could certainly be used as part of an opposite, 'contextualist' strategy, intended to counterbalance the Anti-Contextualist Strategy in an effective way. [Footnote continues on next page.]

Since, for a defender of the Minimalist Principle, what is said departs from what the sentence means only insofar as there is in the meaning of the sentence a slot to be contextually filled, he is led to posit new slots, new dimensions of semantic indeterminacy, every time the following condition obtains: the traditional slots (identity of the speaker, time of utterance, etc.) have been filled, yet it seems that the meaning of the sentence still underdetermines what is said. Thus, a minimalist is led to postulate a hidden reference to a contextually variable domain of discourse in (1) and (2) — as well as in any quantificational utterance. It follows that there are more slots to be filled for a sentence to express a complete proposition, from the point of view of a minimalist, than there is from the point of view of someone who rejects the Minimalist Principle. Sperber and Wilson suggest that 'I've had breakfast' does express a complete proposition once the identity of the speaker and the time of utterance have been fixed, a proposition which is weaker than what the speaker means to say by his utterance. This move — distinguishing the minimal proposition expressed from what the speaker says — is not open to the minimalist; therefore he must deny that the sentence, once the traditional slots have been contextually filled, expresses a complete proposition: more slots need to be filled, according to him. I conclude that the Minimalist Principle is an incentive to maximize context-sensitivity; it leads its defenders to widen the gap between linguistic meaningfulness and full propositionality. From a contextualist point of view, this is a good reason for maintaining the Minimalist Principle as far as possible. *Even if Sperber and Wilson are right and the Minimalist Principle is ultimately to be dispensed with, it still has a methodological role to play within a contextualist strategy.* For example, a contextualist might observe the following maxim: Before supposing, in a particular case, that what is said is different from the minimal proposition expressible, always try to save the Minimalist Principle by exploring the various forms of semantic indeterminacy that may possibly affect the sentence.

What I have just said shows that it is controversial to claim, as Carston does, that the Minimalist Principle is partly responsible for the usual underrating of the gap between sentence meaning and what is said. Carston believes that partisans of the Minimalist Principle 'assume that the domain of grammar, sentences, and the domain of truth-conditional semantics, propositions, are essentially the same' (Carston 1988, p. 164). But this is not at all the case. Quite the contrary, defenders of the Minimalist Principle take the meaning of a sentence to be far less 'propositional', much more underdetermined as far as truth-conditions are concerned, than is ordinarily supposed.

8   For simplicity's sake, the fact that the derivation of implicatures presupposes the identification of what is said (and other things as well) has not been represented in the diagram. It could have been represented by distinguishing two sub-levels within 'what is communicated', what is said being input at the first sub-level and the implicatures output at the second one. (In fact, the matter is still more complicated than that, but there is no need to spell out the details here.)

9   There is an exception, though. According to Bach and Harnish (1979, p. 29), a correct account of linguistic communication 'should accord with how "said that" is commonly ascribed'. This is not very far from the Availability Principle, as Mike Harnish pointed out to me.

10   Bach, 1987, chapter 4 points out that the nonliteral use of sentences such as 'The door is closed' is their *standard* use; he speaks of 'standardized nonliterality'. He might therefore try to avoid the objection I have just raised by arguing as follows: The speaker is not conscious of having said something different from what he communicates because the sentence he uses is *standardly* used to communicate something different from the proposition literally expressed. After all, the same phenomenon occurs in cases of 'standardized indirection' (Bach and Harnish 1979, pp. 192ff):

when an indirect speech act is standardly performed by means of a certain type of sentence, the participants in the talk-exchange may not be conscious of the speech act directly performed (*e.g.* of the question in 'Can you pass me the salt?').

Another defence of Bach's account would run as follows. Bach does not speak of 'what is said'; he speaks of the proposition expressed by the sentence, as distinct from the proposition communicated. Despite Bach's use of the concept of 'nonliterality', this distinction might be equated with Sperber and Wilson's distinction between the minimal proposition expressible by the sentence and the proposition actually expressed (what is said), rather than with the distinction which applies to genuine cases of nonliterality, *viz.* that between what is said and what is communicated. Thus interpreted, Bach's view would be consistent with the Availability Principle, because it would no longer involve a counter-intuitive identification of what is said. The difference between Bach's position and that of Sperber and Wilson, on that interpretation, would be this: Sperber and Wilson require that the proposition actually expressed entail the minimal proposition expressible, while Bach believes that the minimal proposition literally expressed may be enriched ('expanded', he says) in a way that does not preserve its entailments. Thus, Bach's analysis applies not only to examples such as 'I've had breakfast' or 'John has three children' — which he calls 'nonliteral' because the proposition literally expressed by the sentence (that the speaker has had breakfast at least once, or that John has at least three children) is not identical with the proposition communicated (that the speaker has had breakfast this morning, or that John has exactly three children) — but also to examples such as 'Everybody came to Paris' or 'The door is closed', which Sperber and Wilson could not handle in terms of strengthening. 'Everybody from Johnson and Johnson came to Paris' is an 'expansion' of 'Everybody came to Paris' in Bach's framework, but it is not an 'enrichment' of the latter in Sperber and Wilson's framework. (Note that, when Sperber and Wilson first introduced their notion of enrichment, what they had in mind was probably something like Bach's expansion, rather than the more constrained concept of strengthening.) I would certainly object to Bach's position so interpreted, but I cannot discuss these problems here.

11   There is a difficulty here. Carston considers a series of cases in which an alleged implicature entails the proposition allegedly expressed and therefore cannot be a genuine implicature, by virtue of the Independence Principle. However, in many of those cases, the alleged implicature in question is not an implicature at all in the Gricean framework but rather the utterance's overall meaning, which includes what is said together with what is implicated. Thus, for a classical Gricean, 'John has three children' expresses the proposition that John has (at least) three children, and in many contexts implicates that he has at most three children. When this implicature is present, the utterance communicates that John has exactly three children. It is this overall communicated meaning that implies what is said, not the implicature. The same problem arises in connection with many other examples. For a Gricean, a conjunctive utterance ⌜P and Q⌝ says that ⌜P⌝ and ⌜Q⌝ are both true and, in many contexts, implicates that the event described in the second conjunct occurred later than the event described in the first conjunct. Does this alleged implicature entail the proposition allegedly expressed, as Carston suggests? It depends on how we formulate the implicature. Carston chooses the following formulation of what is said and implicated by means of ⌜P and Q⌝ in the classical Gricean framework:

what is said: P & Q.
implicature: P & then Q.

Thus formulated, the implicature does entail the proposition expressed. But the implicature need not be formulated that way. We may consider that what is implicated is that, *if* the event P (*i.e.* the event described in the first conjunct) occurred at a time t and the event Q (*i.e.* the event described in the second conjunct) occurred at a time t', *then* t' is later than t. In this formulation the implicature does not entail what is said, namely, that these events did occur — or, more explicitly: that there is a past time t and a past time t' such that P occurs at t and Q occurs at t'. In general, it seems that the classical Gricean approach can be saved from Carston's criticism in terms of the Independence Principle simply by changing the way the implicature is formulated. As Dan Sperber pointed out to me, Carston might reply to this objection as follows. We suppose that the proposition that John has exactly three children is being communicated (this much seems to be conceded by the classical Gricean.) Now, if it is communicated, either it is an implicature or it is part of what is said. The classical Gricean considers that it is not part of what is said; therefore, if it is communicated, it must be an implicature. In Sperber and Wilson's framework, it is an 'implicated conclusion', *i.e.* something that follows from an 'implicated premiss' (*viz.* the proposition that John has at most three children) together with the proposition expressed (*viz.* the proposition that John has at least three children). But this alleged implicature (that John has exactly three children) entails the proposition allegedly expressed (that John has at least three children). Therefore, by virtue of the Independence Principle, it is part of what is said. Now, if this proposition is part of what the speaker says, what a classical Gricean would consider as the implicature *stricto sensu*, namely the proposition that John has at most three children, cannot be an implicature either, for then it would be entailed by what is said. (The same argument would apply to the other examples.)

12   Sperber and Wilson could argue that, in their definition, 'development' must be understood as referring not to the formal property of incorporating as a sub-part a logical form, but to the process of developing a logical form into a more complex form that has the formal property. But then they should have defined the explicature as an assumption that *results from* a development of an encoded logical form, instead of saying that an assumption communicated by an utterance is an explicature if and only if it *is* a development of a logical form encoded by the utterance. In any case, what Sperber and Wilson *mean* by 'explicature' and 'implicature' is quite clear, despite the ambiguity of their definition.

13   Of course, Carston might try to reformulate the Independence Principle in purely 'functional' terms, with no reference whatsoever to *logical* independence. But it is not obvious that the Independence Principle, reformulated only in terms of the vague notion of functional independence, would still provide a working criterion enabling one to distinguish conversational implicatures from pragmatic aspects of what is said. In any case, when I say that the Independence Principle is to be rejected, I have in mind the criterion Carston actually uses in her paper, not an ideal reformulation of it.

14   This last remark may sound puzzling. What I have in mind is this.

Suppose a sentence S and a context C such that, when S is uttered in C, the utterance conversationally implicates that grass is green. (I shall call this the 'implicature of S', meaning: the implicature of an utterance of S in C.) Now, suppose that, without changing the context, S is embedded within a larger sentence S', where it is dominated by a logical operator D. For simplicity's sake, let us assume D is negation. Then, it may *seem* that the implicature of S falls within the scope of the negation: this will be so if part of what is communicated by uttering S' is that grass is *not* green. But this appearance may be accounted for without supposing that the implicature of S actually falls within the scope of D. It is logically possible that, just as the utterance of S implicates that grass is green, the utterance of S' (*i.e.* of the negation of S) *implicates* that grass is not green. In this case, despite appearances, the implicature that grass is green does not fall within the scope of the negation, because what is literally negated by S' is the proposition expressed by S, to the exclusion of the implicature. The latter is not literally negated — and therefore does not fall within the scope of D — but its negation happens to be conversationally implicated by uttering S'. Of course, the generation of this new implicature will have to be accounted for (it will have to be 'calculable', as Grice says), and the theoretical possibility I have just mentioned will not be considered seriously unless there is an easy way to do so.

15   My account of the difference between conscious and unconscious implicatures relies on the claim that the latter are not really implicatures, but something else (pragmatic aspects of what is said). However, there are other possible accounts. For example, one can use Grice's notion of 'generalized' implicatures, and argue that when an implicature is generalized (*i.e.* standardized, as Bach and Harnish would say), one is no longer conscious of its being external to what is said. This is a variant of the argument presented in footnote 10, p. 314.

16   I am indebted to Bob French, Mike Harnish, Larry Hirschfeld, Pierre Jacob, Sam Kerstein, and especially Ruth Kempson and Dan Sperber for their comments on an earlier version of this paper. Thanks are also due to members of the ESPRIT working group 3351 (Dialogue and Discourse).

References

Anscombre, J.-C. and Ducrot, O. 1978: Echelles argumentatives, échelles implicatives et lois de discours. *Semantikos*, 2, 43–67.

Bach, K. 1987: *Thought and Reference*. Oxford: Oxford University Press.

Bach, K. and Harnish, M. 1979: *Linguistic Communication and Speech Acts*. Cambridge, Mass.: MIT Press.

Carston, R. 1988: Implicature, Explicature, and Truth-Theoretic Semantics. In R. Kempson (ed.), *Mental Representations: The Interface between Language and Reality*. Cambridge: Cambridge University Press, 155–81.

Cohen, L. J. 1971: Some Remarks on Grice's Views about the Logical Particles of Natural Language. In Y. Bar-Hillel (ed.), *Pragmatics of Natural Language*. Dordrecht: Reidel, 50–68.

Cohen, L. J. 1986: How is Conceptual Innovation Possible? *Erkenntnis*, 25, 221–38.

Cornulier, B. de 1984: Pour l'analyse minimaliste de certaines expressions de quantité. *Journal of Pragmatics*, 8, 661–91.

Fauconnier, G. 1985: *Mental Spaces: Aspects of Meaning Construction in Natural Language*. Cambridge, Mass.: MIT Press.

Gardiner, A. 1932: *The Theory of Speech and Language*. Oxford: Oxford University Press.

Grice, P. 1975: Logic and Conversation. *Syntax and Semantics*, 3, 41–58.

Grice, P. 1978: Further Notes on Logic and Conversation. *Syntax and Semantics*, 9, 113–27.

Kaplan, D. 1977: Demonstratives. Mimeo, Department of Philosophy: UCLA.

Kay, P. and Zimmer, K. 1976: On the Semantics of Compounds and Genitives in English. In R. Underhill (ed.), *Sixth California Linguistics Association Conference Proceedings*. San Diego: Campanile, 29–35.

Recanati, F. 1989: Referential/Attributive: a Contextualist Proposal. *Philosophical Studies*, 56, 217–49.

Sperber, D. and Wilson, D. 1986: *Relevance: Communication and Cognition*. Oxford: Basil Blackwell.

Travis, C. 1985: On What is Strictly Speaking True. *Canadian Journal of Philosophy*, 15, 187–229.

Wilson, D. and Sperber, D. 1981: On Grice's Theory of Conversation. In P. Werth (ed.), *Conversation and Discourse*. London: Croom Helm, 155–78.

Toward a New Taxonomy for Pragmatic Inference: Q-based and R-based Implicature

Laurence R. Horn

1. The Principle of Least Effort (and the Principle of Sufficient Effort).

Thirty-five years ago, George Kingsley Zipf set out to explain all of natural language (along with almost everything else in the human universe, from dreams, art, and ritual to war, schizophrenia, and the incest taboo) in terms of an overarching Principle of Least Effort. In the linguistic realm, however, Zipf (1949: 20ff.) acknowledged two basic and competing forces. The Force of Unification, or Speaker's Economy, is a direct least effort correlate, a drive toward simplification which, operating unchecked, would result in the evolution of exactly one totally unmarked infinitely ambiguous vocable (presumably uhhhh). The antithetical Force of Diversification, or Auditor's Economy, is an antiambiguity principle leading toward the establishment of as many different expressions as there are messages to communicate. Given m meanings, the speaker's economy will tend toward 'a vocabulary of one word which will refer to all the m distinct meanings', while the hearer's economy will tend toward 'a vocabulary of m different words with one distinct meaning for each word'. As Zipf (1949: 21) (under)states, 'The two opposing economies are in extreme conflict.'

It is in the crucible of this conflict, argue Zipf, Martinet, and allied functionalists, that language change is forged. As Martinet notes (1962: 139):

In order to understand how and why a language changes, the linguist must keep in mind two ever-present and antinomic factors: first, the requirements of communication, the need for the speaker to convey his message, and second, the principle of least effort, which makes him restrict his output of energy, both mental and physical, to the minimum compatible with achieving his ends.

In this paper, I seek to demonstrate that these same two antinomic forces — and the interaction between them — are largely responsible for generating Grice's conversational maxims and the schema for pragmatic inference derived therefrom.

2. The Maxims of Conversation.

In his ground-breaking work on language use and the logic of conversation, Grice (1975) suggests a procedure whereby participants in a conversational context may compute what was meant (by a given speaker's contributing a given utterance at a given point in the interaction) based on what was said (by that speaker, in that utterance, at that point). The governing dictum is the Cooperative Principle: 'Make your conversational contribution such as is required, at the stage at which it occurs, by the accepted purpose or direction of the talk exchange' (1975: 45). Within this basic guideline, Grice establishes four specific subprinciples, the general, almost trivial-sounding, and presumably universal maxims of conversation which he takes to govern all rational interchange (Grice 1975: 45–46; cf. Levinson 1983: 100ff. for discussion).

Quality: Try to make your contribution one that is true.

    1. Do not say what you believe to be false.

    2. Do not say that for which you lack evidence.

Quantity:

    1. Make your contribution as informative as is required (for the current purposes of the exchange).

    2. Do not make your contribution more informative than is required.

Relation:

    Be relevant.

Manner:
1. Avoid obscurity of expression.
2. Avoid ambiguity.
3. Be brief. (Avoid unnecessary prolixity).
4. Be orderly.

The assumption that speaker and hearer are both observing the Cooperative Principle and its component maxims permits the exploitation of these maxims to generate conversational implicata, conveyed messages which are meant without being said.

The partial reductionist program I envision would retain the Maxim of Quality with its special character noted by Grice: unless Quality (or what Lewis 1969 has called a Convention of Truthfulness) obtains, the entire conversational and implicatural apparatus collapses. But the first Quantity maxim (henceforth Quantity$_1$, or simply Quantity) is essentially Zipf's Auditor's Economy, the need for the speaker to convey his message fully. Most if not all of the remaining Gricean rules respond to the Speaker's Economy, either directly (as consequences of the least effort principle) or indirectly (through the interaction of this principle with its antithesis). Notice in particular that the second quantity principle, as stated, is essentially akin to Relation (what would make a contribution more informative than required, except the inclusion of material not strictly relevant to and needed for the matter at hand?). Note also that Grice in effect builds in Relation when defining Quantity$_1$, and similarly builds in Quantity$_1$ in defining Quantity$_2$. In section 3, I have tentatively boiled down the maxims (leaving aside Quality) to two fundamental principles, echoing the two functional economies of Zipf and Martinet.

3. Minding our Qs and Rs.

(1a) The Q Principle (Hearer-based):
  MAKE YOUR CONTRIBUTION SUFFICIENT (cf. Quantity$_1$)
  SAY AS MUCH AS YOU CAN (given R)
  Lower-bounding principle, inducing upper-bounding implicata

(1b) The R Principle (Speaker-based):

MAKE YOUR CONTRIBUTION NECESSARY (cf. Relation, Quantity$_2$, Manner)

SAY NO MORE THAN YOU MUST (given Q)

Upper-bounding principle, inducing lower-bounding implicata

In the current coy style (cf. Chomsky 1982) which has given us D-structures and S-structures, LF and PF, R-expressions and A-binding (corresponding, more or less, to Deep and Surface structures, Logical and Phonetic form, Referring expressions, and Argument-binding, respectively), I am using Q and R to evoke Quantity (i.e. Quantity$_1$) and Relation while leaving open the extent to which my principles map onto these two maxims.

The hearer-based Q Principle is essentially a sufficiency condition. A lower-bounding law in terms of information structure, it may be (and systematically is) exploited to generate upper-bounding conversational implicata, as described by Grice (1975), Ducrot (1972), Horn (1972, 1973), and Gazdar (1979): a speaker, in saying '... p ...', implicates that (for all she knows) '... at most p ...'

The primary examples of generalized Q-based implicata arise from scalar predications. If I tell you that some of my friends are Buddhists, I license you to draw the inference that not all my friends are Buddhists. (If I knew they all were, and this knowledge was relevant to your interests, it would have been incumbent on me to obey the Q Principle and say so; the assumption that I am obeying Quantity allows you to infer that I did not know for a fact that the stronger predication — All of my friends are Buddhists — held.) Like all rules of pragmatic inference, Q-based implicature is context-dependent; as a generalized implicatum, the aforementioned inference goes through in unmarked contexts, but it may be cancelled — explicitly (cf. Some, {if not all/and perhaps all,} of my friends ...) or implicitly (by establishing the appropriate context, in which all that is relevant, or can be known, is the lower bound).

Examples of Q-based scalar implicature are legion. The following sentences all assert (or entail) a lower bound ('at least _____', their 'one-sided' reading as Aristotle dubbed it), and characteristically implicate an upper bound ('at most _____'); the conjunction of the assertion and implicatum results in conveying the corresponding 'two-sided' understanding ('exactly _____').

(2a) He ate 3 carrots
- 1-sided: 'at least 3'
- 2-sided: 'exactly 3'

(2b) You ate some of the cookies
- 1-sided: 'some if not all'
- 2-sided: 'some but not all'

(2c) It's possible she'll win
- 1-sided: 'possible if not certain'
- 2-sided: 'possible but not certain'

(2d) Maggie is patriotic or quixotic
- 1-sided = inclusive <u>or</u>
- 2-sided = exclusive <u>or</u>

(2e) I'm happy
- 1-sided: 'happy if not ecstatic'
- 2-sided: 'happy but not ecstatic'

(2f) It's warm
- 1-sided: 'at least warm'
- 2-sided: 'warm but not hot'

(cf. Horn 1972, 1973, to appear b for additional details)

This analysis, foreshadowed a century ago by DeMorgan (1847: 100) and Mill (1867: 501), allows us to preserve semantic parsimony by taking the infinitely many weak scalar predicates to be logically unambiguous while pragmatically ambivalent (cf. Hamilton 1860 and Kempson 1980 for alternative accounts in which the sentences of (2) are treated as logically ambiguous; these accounts are reviewed and rebutted in Horn 1973, to appear b).

If the Q-Principle corresponds to Quantity$_1$, the countervailing R-Principle collects not only Relation, but Quantity$_2$ and possibly all the manner maxims (although I shall not go through the arguments for that claim here). The R-Principle, mirroring the effect of the Q-Principle just discussed, is an upper-bounding principle which may be (and standardly is) exploited to generate lower-bounding implicata. A speaker who says '... p ...' may license the Q-inference that he meant '... at most p ...'; a speaker who says '... p ...' may license the R-inference that he meant '... more than p ...' The locus classicus here is the indirect speech act (Heringer 1972; Gordon and Lakoff 1975; Searle 1975): if I ask you whether you can pass me the salt, in a context where your abilities to do so are not in doubt, I license you to infer that I am doing something more that asking you whether you can pass the salt — I am in fact asking you to do it. (If I know for a fact that you can pass me the salt, the yes-no question is pointless; the assumption that I am obeying the Relation maxim allows you to infer that I mean something more than what I say.)

Grice notes that a speaker may 'quietly and unostentatiously violate a maxim' as well as exploit it to generate an implicature. Clark and Haviland (1977: 2) have suggested that intentional covert maxim violations result in lies, while unintentional violations are simply misleading. In fact, what is crucial is just which sort of maxim or pragmatic principle is violated: intentional quality violations result in lies (another reason for the special status of quality; cf. Coleman and Kay 1981 for additional factors in defining lie), intentional violations of the Q-based sufficiency principle result in a speaker's misleading the addressee, and intentional violations of the R-based least effort principle are often simply unhelpful or perverse. A courtroom witness must swear to tell the whole truth and nothing but the truth, i.e. to obey quantity and quality, while violations of relevance lead only to a possible lawyer's objection or judge's scolding.

4. Q-based vs. R-based Inference: Some Early Skirmishes.

Like the antinomic economies from which they derive, the Q-based and R-based principles just outlined often directly collide. A speaker obeying only Q would tend to say everything she knows on the off-chance that it might prove informative, while a speaker obeying only R would probably, to be on the safe side, not open her mouth. In fact, many of the maxim clashes Grice and others have discussed do involve $Quantity_1$ vs. Relation. In delineating the operation of quantity to generate upper-bounding scalar implicatures in my thesis (Horn 1972: Chapters 1 and 2), I was bothered by the contrast between (3a), where Quantity is in force, and (3b), where the principle of relevance is apparently responsible for the implicatum (as Karttunen 1970 suggests).

(3a) It is possible that John solved the problem $\longrightarrow$
      (For all S knows) John didn't solve the problem   (Q)
(3b) John was able to solve the problem $\longrightarrow$
      John solved the problem   (R)

An application of quantity in the latter case would generate the opposite implicatum, viz. that John didn't solve the problem. Similarly, in (4a) quantity leads to an upper bound on the information communicated, while in (4b) an

R-based inference renders the indefinite more informative than its logical form suggests (both examples from Grice 1975: 56; cf. Harnish 1976).

(4a) X is meeting a woman this evening ⎯⎯⎯⎯→
The woman in question is not X's wife, sister, or close platonic friend   (Q)

(4b) I broke a finger yesterday ⎯⎯⎯⎯→
The finger is mine   (R)

5. Politeness Rules, Pragmatic Competence, and Maxim Clashes.

A parallel to these clashes emerges from work by Robin Lakoff on the maxims of politeness outlined in (5), and by Brown and Levinson in their reformulation of Lakoff's maxims in terms of face wants and needs:

(5)   Rules of politeness (Lakoff 1973, Brown and Levinson 1979)

	Lakoff:	Brown and Levinson:
Rule 1.	Deference: 'don't impose', 'Keep aloof'	Negative politeness, polite formality
Rule 2.	Give options (special case of Rule 1, or derived as theorem from Rules 1 and 3?)	Respect 'negative face', i.e. freedom from imposition and freedom of action.
Rule 3.	Be friendly (Camaraderie)	Positive politeness, polite friendliness Respect 'positive face', i.e. positive consistent self-image and approval/ appreciation by others.

Crucially for us, the Deference or Aloofness maxim, Rule 1, is an upper-bounding R-based constraint on one's actions, while Friendliness, Rule 3, is a lower-bounding Q-based imperative.

Lakoff has noted several instances in which Rule 1 Politeness seems to clash with Rule 3, e.g. belching after a meal, which may signal appreciation (via Rule 3) or may simply be taken as offensive (by Rule 1). More systematically, when we look at languages like those in the Romance, Germanic, Slavic, and indic families of Indo-European, in which two different forms for the second person singular coexist but are associated with different presuppositions or conventional

335

implicata (cf. Levinson 1983: 128–29), we find that the use of a (familiar) T form rather than the more formal V form for the addressee may convey polite friendliness by Rule 3 or presumptuousness by Rule 1 (depending on the context and the interlocutors' assumptions and beliefs). Similarly, the use of a V form for the addressee may be polite by Rule 1, or aloof and unfriendly by Rule 3.

A particularly devastating kind of maxim clash which has been analyzed in similar terms is the communication mixup example from work by Tannen.

(6) Conversational breakdowns and marital breakups (Tannen 1975, 1979)
     First exchange:
     Wife: Bob's having a party. You wanna go?
     Husband: OK.
     Second exchange (later):
     Wife: Are you sure you want to go?
     Husband: OK. Let's not go. I'm tired anyway.
     Post-mortem:
     Wife: We didn't go to the party because you didn't want to.
     Husband: I wanted to. You didn't want to.

On Tannen's gloss of this canonical interchange, one partner (the wife) is operating on a direct strategy utilizing Rule 3 politeness: if one had meant more, s/he would (and should) have said it. Her partner (or opponent), on the other hand, is employing an indirect, hint-seeking strategy which emanates from Rule 1 politeness: avoid saying too much when you can get it across by hints. As Tannen observes, each strategy may link up with a different pragmatic competence, the difference involving not the set of operative rules but the relative strength of opposing rules within that set.

Notice that Tannen's account of the clash instantiated in (6) superimposes directly onto an alternative gloss utilizing Grice's Quantity and Relation maxims (or Quantity$_1$ and Quantity$_2$), respectively. Crucially, in either version we have to deal with Q-based vs. R-based inference patterns.

A closely related example of maxim clash is cited by Keenan (1976). As she reports and interprets the facts, the Malagasy-speaking culture of Madagascar is a speech community in which the Cooperative Principle, and in particular the maxim of Quantity, is not observed. Informativeness is apparently absent as a working principle in conversation, and the participants in a talk-exchange tend not to draw what we have been calling Q-based inferences in situations where such inferences would be drawn in Western communities.

> [Interlocutors] regularly provide less information than is required by their conversational partner, even though they have access to the necessary information. If A asks B, 'Where is your mother?' and B responds, 'she is either in the house or at the market', B's utterance is not usually taken to imply that B is unable to provide more specific information needed by the hearer. The implicature is not made, because the expectation that speakers will satisfy informational needs is not a basic norm. (Keenan 1976: 70)

In fact, however, as Keenan makes clear in her discussion, Quantity and Q-based inference do play a significant role in some conversational contexts. Where they do not, it is because Quantity is overridden by a countervailing R-based principle, in particular the imperative of avoiding tsiny (the responsibility, guilt, or other unpleasant consequences incurred by uttering claims which turn out to be false and/or offensive to other members of the society living or dead). Sex of speaker, and significance and accessibility of the information contributed, are other variables influencing the relative weights of Q-based and R-based principles and inference patterns in the Malagasy community. (Cf. Prince 1982 for a related critique of Keenan's conclusions.)

Both Tannen's and Keenan's cases involve situations in which different speakers practice different utilizations of essentially the same tools; pragmatic competence often differs across cultures — and across speakers within the same culture — in accordance with the assignment of relative weightings to different maxims or principles, and consequently with the inference patterns associated with the exploitation of those maxims.

6. Quantity vs. Informativeness.

The most detailed and careful discussion in the literature of Q vs. R clashes in English is due to Atlas and Levinson (1981) (cf. Levinson 1983: section 3.2 for related discussion). Atlas and Levinson begin by summarizing the evidence for the inference from Quantity for the scalar cases. Examples (after Horn 1972 and

337

Gazdar 1979) include the implicata in (7a); the general principle for the Q-based cases is given in (7b).

(7)   The inference from Quantity: What is communicated is more informative, more definite than what is said.

(7a)   some ↔ not all

     may ↔ may not

     3 → no more than 3

     p or q → not both p and q

     a believes that p → a does not know that p

     (cf. discussion of example (3).)

(7b)   'Given that there is available an expression of roughly equal length that is logically stronger and/or more informative, the failure to employ the stronger expression conveys that the speaker is not in a position to employ it.' (Atlas and Levinson 1981: 38)

But, Atlas and Levinson point out, there is a substantial class of (somewhat disparate) cases for which Quantity gives exactly the wrong results. For these cases, including those in (8a), they invoke a Principle of Informativeness, (8b).

(8)   The inference from Informativeness: What is communicated is more precise than (is a subcase of) what is said.

(8a)   if p then q → if -p then -q   (Geis and Zwicky's 1971 'invited inference' of conditional perfection)

     p and q → p preceded q   (cf. Grice 1975, Schmerling 1975 on

                $(\downarrow)$ 'asymmetric' conjunction)

          p caused q

     a and b VP'd → a and b VP'd together

     a ate the cake → a ate the whole cake   ⎱

     a ate the apples → a ate all the apples) ⎰ (cf. Harnish 1976)

     Do you know the time? → If you know the time, tell me what it is. (Indirect speech acts, cf. Cole and Morgan 1975)

     I don't think that p → (I think that) not-p (Neg-raising, cf. Horn 1978b)

     1 have a new car and the windows don't close → ... the windows of my new car .... (Bridging inferences, cf. Clark and Haviland 1976)

(8b) The Principle of Informativeness: 'Read as much into an utterance as is consistent with what you know about the world' (Levinson 1983: 146–47)

Atlas and Levinson (1981: 42) formulate their informativeness-based inference as an 'inference to the best interpretation'.

(8c) 'If a predicate Q is semantically nonspecific with respect to predicates P_i, $1 \leqslant i \leqslant n$, but for some j, $t \leqslant j \leqslant n$, P_j is stereotypical of Qs, then in saying ⌜Qt⌝ a speaker will convey ⌜P_jt⌝.'

The key notion here is the restriction of a more general predicate to a stereotypical instance. Two examples of this inference to a salient subset or exemplar cited by Atlas and Levinson are those in (8d).

(8d) The secretary smiled. → The female secretary smiled.
John had a drink. → John had an alcoholic drink.

The class of indefinite descriptions provides a major source of clashes between Quantity-based inference (cf. (9a)) and Informativeness-based inference (cf. (9b)).

(9) Quantity vs. informativeness (Atlas and Levinson 1981: 491f.; cf. Harnish 1976)

(9a) Quantity in force:	(9b) Informativeness in force:
I slept on a boat yesterday →	I lost a book yesterday →
The boat was not mine	The book was mine.
I slept in a car yesterday →	I broke a finger yesterday →
The car was not mine	The finger was mine.
Mort and David took a shower →	Mort and David bought a piano →
They took separate showers	They bought a piano together

A number of factors are involved in determining which principle takes precedence when the two are at odds; notice, for example, that the speaker in (9a) could have chosen the more precise genitive form (<u>I slept on my boat, in my</u>

car) but did not do so, while the use of the genitive in (9b) (my book, my finger) might suggest wrongly that I have but one book or one finger. Atlas and Levinson cite two additional factors which are relevant to the weighting of Quantity vs. Informativeness: if an entailment-based 'Horn scale' (cf. Horn 1972) can be constructed on which the predicates in question can be readily ranked, Quantity is more likely to win out; if the application of Quantity tends to contradict our assumed 'Conventions of Noncontroversiality', Informativeness takes precedence.

Within the framework being explored here, Atlas and Levinson's inference from Quantity corresponds directly to our Q Principle. There is an equally strong parallel between Atlas and Levinson's inference from Informativeness and our R Principle; my only objection to their formulation concerns their terminology. First of all, Informativeness suggests the Q Principle to me more strongly than, as intended, the R Principle (note the language of Grice's Quantity$_1$ maxim, which Keenan 1976 indeed glosses 'Be informative'). Furthermore, Ducrot (1972), who independently proposes a 'Loi d'exhaustivité' to do the work of Grice's maxim of Quantity, also invokes a 'Loi d'informativité' of a rather different nature from Atlas and Levinson's Principle of Informativeness (cf. Ducrot 1972: 132–34). Thus, I feel justified in taking Atlas and Levinson's so-called Informativeness as an instance of the R Principle.

7. Negation As Implicatum-canceffer: Q-based vs. R-based Inferences.

An opposition as fundamental as that between the Q Principle and the R Principle would be expected to have major linguistic consequences, and indeed this expectation is not disappointed. We begin by considering the effect of negation on conversational implicata. What we find is that Q-based implicata can be readily cancelled by a negation which does not affect what is said (through what I have elsewhere termed 'metalinguistic' negation: cf. Horn to appear a), but R-based implicata cannot be cancelled by negation at all.

This is illustrated in what follows. First, some instances of negated scalar implicata are given in (10a-f). That negation is being used in a marked way to deny the Q-implicated upper bound in these examples can best be seen by considering the well-formed affirmative counterparts of these sentences in (10a'-f') (cf. (2); also Horn to appear b, and references there).

(10a) He didn't eat 3 carrots — he ate 4 of them.

(10b) You didn't eat some of the cookies — you ate all of them.

(10c) It isn't possible she'll win — it's certain she will.

(10d) She isn't patriotic <u>or</u> quixotic — she's both.

(10e) I'm not happy — I'm ecstatic.

(10f) It isn't warm — it's downright hot.

(10a') He ate 3 carrots — in fact, he ate 4.

(10b') You ate some of the cookies — indeed, you ate all of them.

(10c') Not only is it possible she'll win — it's certain she will.

(10d') She's patriotic or quixotic — in fact, she's both.

(10e') I'm happy — indeed, I'm ecstatic.

(10f') It's warm — in fact, it's downright hot.

But now consider R-based implicata. To say that someone was able to solve the problem may R-implicate that she in fact solved it (Karttunen 1970). Similarly, to assert that someone was clever enough to do something generally implicates that he did it. As we have seen, my confiding to you that I broke a finger would normally be taken to refer to a finger of mine (given Atlas and Levinson's Conventions of Noncontroversiality) unless I knew you knew that 1 was an enforcer for the mob. And, as Wittgenstein and others have pointed out, an assertion of the form 'I believe that S' would normally be taken as an indirect assertion of S rather than merely a statement about my beliefs; this indirect speech act, too, works by R-inference. Yet none of these implicata can be cancelled by negation.

(11a) She wasn't able to solve the problem.

(≠ She was able to solve it, but didn't)

(11b) He wasn't clever enough to figure out the answer.

(≠ He was clever enough to do it, but he didn't)

(11c) 1 didn't break a finger yesterday.

(≠ I broke a finger, but it wasn't one of mine)

(11d) I don't believe the Yankees will win the pennant.

(≠ I believe they'll win the pennant, but I'm not [weakly] asserting that they will)

Why should this difference in cancellability exist? The answer lies in the logic of Q-based and R-based inference. Let S represent a given (stronger) proposition, and W the weaker proposition which it unilaterally entails and from which the relevant implicata are to be drawn. In the case of Q-based implicata, the assertion of 'W' Q-implicates-S. Where W is a scalar predicate truth-conditionally defined by its lower bound, the ordinary negation of W negates that lower bound, i.e. as 'less than W', and is hence incompatible with S; the assertion that he did not eat three carrots would be taken to amount to the assertion that he ate less than three (and hence not four, five, or more). But 'not W' uttered in a context where S is affirmed (as in (10a-f)) self-destructs on the unmarked 'less than W' understanding and must therefore be sent back through, in effect — whence the marked, metalinguistic quality of this variety of negation.

In the case of R-based implicata, the assertion of 'W' R-implicates not -S but S: the proposition that she solved the problem unilaterally entails the proposition that she was able to solve it (S entails W), but the assertion that she was able to solve it may implicate that she in fact solved it ('W' R-implicates S). Once again, 'not W' signifies 'less than W' and hence licenses the inference of -S (via modus tollens from the original S || W entailment). But crucially, there are no circumstances under which the implicatum S is cancelled and 'not W' cannot be interpreted consistently, as an ordinary descriptive negation. The negation in (11a-d) thus never gets sent back through to be interpreted metalinguistically, as an implicatum-canceller. Schematically, the situation we have is that in (12).

(12) Q-based implicata:
    S entails W
    'W' Q-implicates -S
    normally, 'not W' = 'less
    than W', incompatible with S
    'not W', asserted where S
    is given, reinterpreted as
    metalinguistic negation

    R-based implicata:
    S entails W
    'W' R-implicates S
    normally, 'not W' = 'less
    than W'
    'not W' || S (modus tollens)
    'not W' never gets reinter-
    preted, since it's always compatible
    with -S (the denial of W's implicatum)

Now, R-based implicata can be cancelled without negation, simply by assigning the contradiction contour (cf. Liberman and Sag 1974) and stressing the implicatum-inducing element.

(13) She was able to solve the problem (but she didn't solve it).

I believe the Yankees will win the pennant (but I'm not saying they will).

I broke a finger today (but not one of mine).

Notice that we tend to get the opposite, Q-based implicatum in these contexts; the contour which cancels the R-based inference sets up a strong expectation for the kind of continuations exemplified above.

When we appear to get cancellation of an R-based implicatum by negation, the implicatum in question has, in fact, become conventionalized as part of literal meaning (cf. Grice 1975:58 and Morgan 1978 on the gradual conventionalization of conversational implicata). Thus, for example, predicate expressions which denote various personal relationships may take on a narrowed symmetric sense (cf. X and Y are {married/friends/lovers/in love}) but need not (cf. X and Y are spouses). When the symmetric sense of these predicates is intended, negation may leave the more general sense unaffected.

(14) They aren't {married/friends/in love}. (i.e. with or to each other)

To confirm the claim that only conventionalized R-based implicata can be cancelled by negation, we need only reconsider the pair of examples from Atlas and Levinson (1981) cited in (8d). Both speakers' intuition and lexicographers' practice suggest that the implicatum associated with drink ('alcoholic drink') has become fossilized into conventional meaning, while the implicatum associated with secretary ('female secretary') has not. Thus, in the terms of Horn (to appear b), drink represents an autohyponymous lexical item while secretary does not. In this light, negation behaves precisely as predicted.

(15a) My secretary didn't smile — I have a male secretary.
(15b) John didn't have a drink — that was a Shirley Temple.

A male secretary is still a secretary (although not one of the salient variety), but a nonalcoholic beverage may or may not count as a drink.

8. The Division of Pragmatic Labor.

While the Q Principle and the R Principle are diametrically opposed forces in inference strategies and language change, it is perhaps in the resolution of the conflict between them that they play their major role in both 'langue' and 'parole'. The most general pattern for this resolution, the synthesis of the two antitheses, is summarized in (16) and derived more explicitly in (17a-f).

(16) The use of a marked (relatively complex and/or prolix) expression when a corresponding unmarked (simpler, less 'effortful') alternate expression is available tends to be interpreted as conveying a marked message (one which the unmarked alternative would not or could not have conveyed).

(17a) The speaker used marked expression E' containing 'extra' material (or otherwise less basic in form or distribution) when a corresponding unmarked expression E, essentially coextensive with it, was available.

(17b) Either (i) the 'extra' material was irrelevant and unnecessary, or (ii) it was necessary (i.e. E could not have been appropriately used).

(17c) (17b(i)) is in conflict with the R Principle and is thus (ceteris paribus) to be rejected.

(17d) Therefore, (17b(ii)), from (17b), (17c) by modus tollendo ponens.

(17e) The unmarked alternative E tends to become associated (by use or — through conventionalization — by meaning) with unmarked situation s, representing stereotype or salient member of extension of E/E'. (R-based inference; cf. Atlas and Levinson, (8b), (8c).)

(17f) The marked alternative E' tends to become associated with the complement of s with respect to the original extension of E/E'. (Q-based inference; cf. (6.12))

The key steps in the argument are those sketched in (17a), (17e), and (17f); they represent a characteristic shift which can be schematized as in (18):

(18)

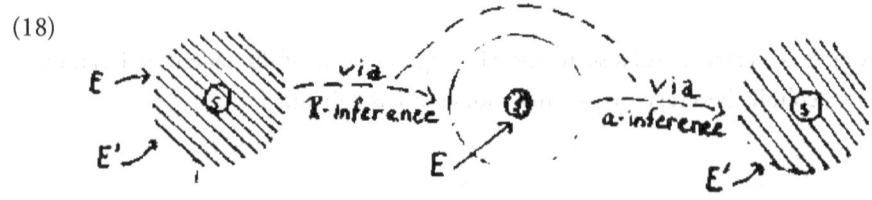

The result is an equilibrium which I shall call the division of pragmatic labor. (The equilibrium is, in fact, somewhat unstable; in particular, either the R-based inference represented in the second diagram or the Q-based inference in the third can become conventionalized, as we shall see later.) The remainder of this essay is devoted to rehearsing a number of instances of this pattern, varying in the details but essentially parallel in terms of the overall dynamics.

9. Avoid Pronoun (and Unavoidable Pronouns).

In considering the near-complementary distribution between his abstract, phonetically unrealized PRO element (which usurps many of the functions of Equi-deletion sites in the earlier Standard Theory) and overt pronominals, Chomsky (1982: 65) arrives at a general principle which he calls Avoid Pronoun, 'interpreted as imposing a choice of PRO over an overt pronoun where possible'. To illustrate, he cites the two cases of (19a-b).

(19a)   John would much prefer [his going to the movie]
(19b)   John would much prefer [his (own) book]

PRO may appear in the frame of (19a) in place of the pronoun (cf. <u>John would much prefer going to the movie</u>), and so <u>his</u> is taken here as non-coreferential with <u>John</u>; in (19b), PRO cannot appear and the overt pronominal <u>his</u> may be (and with <u>own</u> present must be) taken as coreferential with <u>John</u>. As Chomsky notes, the Avoid Pronoun principle

> might be regarded as a subcase of a conversational principle of not saying more than is required, or might be related to a principle of deletion-up-to-recoverability, but there is some reason to believe that it functions as a principle of grammar. (Chomsky 1982: 65)

Three important points emerge from this brief passage: the link between Avoid Pronoun and analogous principles applying to deletion, the grounding of the principle(s) in least effort (i.e. our R Principle), and the fossilization or grammaticization of the functional principle into conventional rules and constraints within particular grammars.

The transderivational nature of Avoid Pronoun is clear from Chomsky's discussion of (19a-b) and an analogous contrast in French (Chomsky 1982: 146).

(20a) Je veux qu'il vienne. 'I want him to come'
(20b) Il$_i$ veut qu'il$_i$ vienne. 'He$_i$ wants him$_j$ to come' (where i ≠ j)
(20c) *Il$_i$ veut qu'il$_i$ vienne. 'He$_i$ wants him(self)$_i$ to come'

Avoid Pronoun, in ruling out (20c), must refer to the availability of a corresponding derivation, that of (21).

(21) Il veut venir. 'He wants to come'

In (21) the subject of 'come' is realized as an abstract PRO argument of the embedded infinitive rather than an overt pronominal subject of an embedded subjunctive, as in (20a-c).

The applicability of Avoid Pronoun is also partially dependent on ambiguity avoidance, a fact not discussed by Chomsky. Thus, in the English versions of (20a-c) and similar sentences, coreference is ruled out totally only in third person cases (cf. Morgan 1970: 387).

(22a) *He$_i$ wants him$_i$ to win. (no coreference possible)
(22b) (?)I$_i$ want me to win. (coreference possible in contrastive contexts)
(22c) (?)You$_i$ want you$_i$ to win.

(Technically, Avoid Pronoun should be activated in (22c), since one can be speaking to different addressees within a single sentence, distinguishing them by pointing or eye gaze. This situation, however, is too marginal to trigger the ambiguity avoidance condition on Avoid Pronoun, and the second person case thus works like the first person case in (22b).)

The literature on reflexives offers further grist for a suitably upgraded Avoid Pronoun mill. As is well known, it is usually (although not always) the case that a nonreflexive pronoun can be interpreted as coreferential with a given antecedent just in case a reflexive (bound by that antecedent) could not have appeared in that position. Many instances of this pattern respond to the Disjoint Reference principle suggested in Postal (1974) and discussed further within the EST (cf.

Chomsky 1982). Thus, compare (23a) and (23b).

(23a) He$_i$ likes {himself$_i$/*him$_j$}.
(23b) He$_i$ said that she likes {*himself$_i$/him$_i$}.

Here again, as with the 'Equi' cases, ambiguity avoidance is relevant in the determination of when coreference is possible.

(24a) He's voting for him. (no coreference possible)
(24b) I'm voting for me. (OK contrastively)

In 'pro-drop' languages, PRO may appear in place of overt NPs freely in a wide range of positions, including subject and object; generally, verb agreement and/ or pragmatic context permits recoverability of the missing referent. As expected, the scope of the Avoid Pronoun principle is commensurately widened in these languages. In her analysis of one pro-drop language, Turkish, Enç (1982) shows that semantically redundant pronouns (i.e. those whose referent would be recoverable) tend to be interpreted as expressing contrast — including topic-change, which she argues is a subtype of contrast. (Notice that in English, too, the occurrence of an overt nonreflexive pronoun in a frame which permits a referentially equivalent gap or reflexive, e.g. (22b) or (24b), is likewise interpreted contrastively.) Enç argues that the interpretation of such marked pronouns, whose appearance seems to violate parsimony, is based on a conventionalization of a quantity-based inference — but she is referring here to Grice's Quantity$_2$ which we have previously subsumed under our R Principle (i.e. least effort).

In fact, while Avoid Pronoun, or whatever more general principle ultimately includes it, is basically a least effort correlate (as Chomsky observes), the division of labor we ultimately arrive at (in which abstract pronouns, i.e. PROs, are interpreted one way and real pronouns another) requires reference to both R and Q Principles, in the manner outlined in section 8.

A related instantiation of this division of pragmatic labor makes this clear. Chomsky proposes a 'general discourse principle' for R(eferring)-expressions, i.e. names and descriptions (1982: 227).

(25a) 'Avoid repetition of R(eferring)-expressions, except when conditions warrant.'

(25b) 'When conditions warrant, repeat.'

Note that this discourse principle comes in two parts, one (25a) R-based and one (25b) Q-based; furthermore, as with Grice's two submaxims of quantity, each of Chomsky's subprinciples is explicitly bounded in its applicability by the other (as the subordinate clause material indicates).

The choice among referentially equivalent referring expressions for picking out a given individual is also subject to R- and Q-based considerations, as Prince shows in working out her Scale of Assumed Familiarity (1981: 245). The matter is rather complex, however, and I shall not pursue it here.

One last example of the division of pragmatic labor emanating from the domain of reference is presented by Levinson (1983: 75):

The deictic words <u>yesterday</u>, <u>today</u>, and <u>tomorrow</u> pre-empt the calendric or absolute ways of referring to the relevant days. Thus the following, said on Thursday, can only be referring to next Thursday (or perhaps some more remote Thursday), otherwise the speaker should have said <u>today</u>:

I'll see you on Thursday.

The same holds if it is said on Wednesday, due to the pre-emptive <u>tomorrow</u>.

10. The division of pragmatic labor and the lexicon.

Aronoff has shown (1976: 43ff.) that the existence of a simple lexical item can block the formation of an otherwise expected affixally derived form synonymous with it. In particular, the existence of a simple abstract nominal underlying a given -<u>ous</u> adjective blocks or prevents the formation of an -<u>ity</u> nominalization based on that adjective.

(26a) fury   furious   *furiosity
       *cury curious   curiosity

(26b) fallacy   fallacious   *fallacity
       *tenacy   tenacious   tenacity

Aronoff's blocking phenomenon is the limiting case of a more general pattern independently observed and discussed by McCawley (1978), Kiparsky (1982), and indeed Bréal (1900); a pattern which directly reflects the division of pragmatic labor sketched in section 8 and exemplified in section 9: unmarked forms tend to be used for unmarked situations (via R) and marked forms for marked situations (via Q).

Kiparsky (1982) begins by noting that Aronoff's blocking paradigm is both too strong and too weak. Contrary to Aronoff's predictions, productive derivational processes are sometimes but not always blocked by the existence of a less productive corresponding form: <u>decency</u> and <u>aberrancy</u> block *<u>decentness</u> and *<u>aberrantness</u>, but <u>gloriousness</u> and <u>furiousness</u> survive alongside <u>glory</u> and <u>fury</u>. Blocking may also extend to inflectional processes as well, although again inconsistently: *<u>mans</u>/<u>men</u>, *<u>goed</u>/<u>went</u>, but <u>kneeled</u>/<u>knelt</u>, <u>dreamed</u>/<u>dreamt</u>. Aronoff's formulation of blocking, limited as it is to less than fully productive derivational processes, has nothing to say about these obviously related cases.

Kiparsky suggests a reformulation of Aronoff's blocking as a subcase of the (Pāṇini-Anderson-Kiparsky) Elsewhere Condition ('Special rules block general rules in their shared domain' — specifically, in morphology, irregular forms preclude regular forms). Kiparsky notes that 'blocking can be partial in that the special [less productive] affix occurs in some restricted meaning and the general [more productive] affix picks up the remaining meaning'. (These two components of the blocking process correspond to the second and third diagrams in our representation of the division of pragmatic labor, (18).) He cites as examples of partial blocking <u>refrigerant</u>/<u>refrigerator</u>, <u>informant</u>/<u>informer</u>, <u>contestant</u>/<u>contester</u>; full blocking results when there is no meaning 'left over' for the more productive form to pick up (*<u>borer</u>/<u>bore</u>$_N$, *<u>inhabiter</u>/<u>inhabitant</u>).

To handle these and other cases, Kiparsky formulates a general condition which he calls Avoid Synonymy.

(27) Avoid Synonymy: 'the output of a lexical rule may not be synonymous with an existing lexical item'.

This principle applies to both derivation and inflection, if we assume a level-ordered morphology. Its transderivational nature allows blocking between morphologically unrelated steins: <u>thief</u> blocks *<u>stealer</u> (but cf. <u>base-stealer</u>, with a noncoinpositional meaning), <u>cutter</u> ≠ knives, scissors, etc.

While there is something right about this principle, it is still too strong, as Kiparsky concedes. For one thing, we need to define a notion of 'corresponding item' relativized to a given speech level or register; words like <u>fridge</u> (underived), <u>icebox</u> (derived by compounding), and <u>refrigerator</u> (derived by affixation) can coexist within a single idiolect despite their referential equivalence. Indeed, the principle is almost self-falsifying: the doublets <u>synonymy</u> and <u>synonymity</u> strike me as perfect synonyms!

Working independently of the Aronoff-Kiparsky line, McCawley (1978) collects a number of examples where the appropriate use of a given expression formed by a relatively productive process (including syntactic formations) is restricted by the existence of a more 'lexicalized' alternative to this expression (i.e. one formed by a relatively nonproductive process). One case in point is originally due to Householder: the collocation <u>pale red</u> is (in the language of Aronoff and Kiparsky) fully or partially blocked by the lexical alternative <u>pink</u>. For some speakers <u>pale red</u> is simply anomalous (or at least nonoccurring); for others, it picks up whatever part of the 'pale' domain of 'red' <u>pink</u> has not preempted. In either case, <u>pale red</u> is limited in a way that <u>pale blue</u> and <u>pale green</u> are not.

In the same way, McCawley observes, the distribution of productive causatives (in English, Japanese, and other languages) is restricted by the existence of a corresponding lexical causative. Lexical causatives (e.g. (28a)) tend to be restricted in their distribution to the stereotypic causative situation: direct, unmediated causation through physical action.

(28a) Black Bart killed the sheriff.
(28b) Black Bart caused the sheriff to die.

This restriction can be viewed as a straightforward R-based conversational implicatum — an inference 'to the best interpretation', in the language of Atlas and Levinson (1981). The use of the relatively marked, morphologically more complex periphrastic causative (e.g. (28b)) will then Q-implicate that the unmarked situation does not obtain. Thus, (28b) suggests that (28a) could not have been used appropriately, possibly because Bart caused the sheriff's gun to backfire by stuffing it with cotton, or arranged for scorpions to be placed in the room of the sheriff (who is known to have a weak heart), etc. Similarly, the use of the unmarked lexical causative in (29a) R-implicates that the action was brought about in an unmarked way (presumably by stepping on the brake pedal), while the choice of the periphrastic (29b) correspondingly Q-implicates that some unusual method was employed (pulling the emergency brake, telekinesis, etc.).

(29a) Lee stopped the car.
(29b) Lee got the car to stop. (Lee made the car stop.)

McCawley's account of the division of labor between lexical and periphrastic causatives, like Chomsky's Avoid Pronoun and Kiparsky's Avoid Synonymy (or indeed, Grice's Avoid Prolixity maxim, which they all seem to reflect), is explicitly transderivational, and thus runs into some of the same problems of overgeneralization. Consider the data in (30a-d), which McCawley borrows from Heringer (1976: 207).

(30a) John made the plate move. (indirect)
(30b) John moved the plate. (direct)
(30c) John made the plate fall. (indirect or direct)
(30d) *John felled the plate.

Here, the periphrastic <u>make</u> versions, 'normally used only in a situation involving indirect causation', as in (30a) whose use is restricted (by the existence of (30b)) to situations involving some sort of supernatural power on John's part, may generalize (as in (30c)) to a wider domain of causative situations 'just in those cases where no lexical causative exists to express direct causation' (Heringer 1976: 207) (cf. (30d)). But, as Heringer and McCawley fail to notice, there is a simple lexical form corresponding to (30c), (30d), viz.

(30e) John dropped the plate.

If <u>drop</u> does not count as a corresponding form for <u>make ... fall</u> because it involves an unrelated stem, then we cannot legitimately invoke (28a) to predict the limited distribution of (28b).

Other problems for the analysis of McCawley (1978) are discussed in Horn (1978a), where it is argued that the general 'least effort' principle employed by McCawley is simply too powerful and, more specifically, that we need to develop a notion of 'corresponding item' which will take into account such variables as morphological relatedness, markedness, speech register, and inherent complexity. For example, lexical causative verbs may indeed be unmarked in English with respect to their periphrastic <u>make</u> or <u>cause</u> counterparts, but this is not the case for lexical causative adjectives. Thus, the distribution of the periphrastic forms in (31a-c) is not constrained by the existence of the corresponding 'simple' forms in (32a-c).

(31a) That sort of behavior really makes me angry.
(31b) I didn't know that teasing your dog would get you so upset.
(31c) Wild horses couldn't make me stay away.
(32a) That sort of behavior really angers me.
(32b) 1 didn't know that teasing your dog would upset you so (much).
(32c) Wild horses couldn't keep me away.

Similarly, as a variety of linguistic and psycholinguistic evidence demonstrates, incorporated negation remains relatively complex, and so the distribution of (33a-b) is not constrained by the existence of the superficially simpler examples of (34a-b).

(33a) I persuaded Bill not to date many girls.
(33b) It's not likely that your coin will land heads.
(34a) I dissuaded Bill from dating many girls.
(34b) It's unlikely that your coin wil land heads.

In particular, (33a) is neutral with respect to the (conventionalized) R-implicatum associated with the use of (34a), viz. that Bill had previously intended to date many girls, and (33b) is unspecitied for the implicatum associated with (34b), i.e. that it is likely your coin will not land heads (the so-called neg-raised interpretation). No Q-implicata are triggered in (31a-c) or (33a-b), and hence the working out of the division of pragmatic labor is not complete. (Cf. Horn 1978a for further examples and related discussion.)

While we must therefore refine and/or reevaluate the transderivational mechanisms invoked by Aronoff, McCawley, and Kiparsky for describing the division of labor between the use (or existence) of a simple lexical form and that of its more complex (lexical or phrasal) counterpart — in particular, by developing the tools to predict just when a given form counts as a counterpart to some other given form — the insight behind their various accounts is real, and it is essentially a single insight: the unmarked form is used for a stereotypical, unmarked situation (via R-implicature) and the marked counterpart for the situations 'left over' (via Q-implicature). This is the division of pragmatic labor outlined in section 8.

11. Division of Pragmatic Labor: Additional Cases.

Two more instances of the division of labor are worth mentioning here. First, consider the realm of indirect speech acts (cf. Searle 1975, Gordon and Lakoff 1975, and other articles in Cole and Morgan 1975). We find that modal auxiliaries which can be associated with indirect speech acts (ISAs) tend to become conventionally associated with the ISAs they convey. If (following Searle) we derive the ISA by an exploitation of the maxim of Relation (cf. section 3), we must nevertheless account for the fact that (35a-b) are conventionally used to convey the request in (36), while (35c-e) — which may (very indirectly) convey that request — are not conventionally used to do so.

(35a) Can you (please) close the window?
(35b) Could you (please) close the window?
(35c) Are you able to (?please) close the window?
(35d) Do you have the ability to (*please) close the window?
(35e) It's (*: please) cold in here.
(36)   (Please) close the window.

Searle observes (1975: 76) that 'there can be conventions of usage that are not meaning conventions' by which 'certain forms will tend to become conventionally established as the standard idiomatic forms for indirect speech acts', including the <u>can you/could you</u> forms of (35a-b) for indirect requests. Morgan (1978) takes these usage conventions to represent 'short-circuited conversational implicatures' which, though calculable, are no longer (after short-circuiting) actually calculated in normal conversation. It is this short-circuiting of the R-based implicatum which licenses the preverbal <u>please</u> in (35a-b); cf. (35c-e) where no short-circuiting has taken place. (A parallel account of the negraising phenomenon and the triggering of negative polarity items is offered in Horn and Bayer to appear.)

But if the modal auxiliaries, idiomatic and semantically versatile as they are, become associated through a convention of usage or short-circuited implicature with the ISAs they may be used to convey, their periphrastic counterparts tend (predictably) to be interpreted literally. Thus, compare the behavior of the modals in examples (37a), (38a), (39a), and (40a) (where the implicatum to the ISA is short-circuited) with that of their periphrastic equivalents in (37b), (38b), (39b), and (40b) (where the indirect reading is not a conventional use of the expression and may be totally unavailable).

(37a) Can you pass the salt? (request)
(37b) Are you able to pass the salt? (literal question)
(38a) Here, I can help you with that. (offer)
(38b) (?Here,) 1 am {able/allowed} to help you with that. (not an offer)
(39a) Will you join us? (invitation)
(39b) Are you going to join us? (literal question)
(40a) I will marry you. (promise)
(40b) I am {going to/willing} to marry you. (only very indirect promise)

Noting the tendency for the most colloquial expressions (typically, as we have seen, the modal auxiliaries) to serve as the conventional forms for conveying indirect speech acts, Searle invokes a new neo-Gricean maxim, 'Speak idiomatically unless there is some reason not to'. He observes (in language mutually intelligible with that spoken by Kiparsky 1982 and McCawley 1978),

> In general, if one speaks unidiomatically, hearers assume that there must be a special reason for it, and in consequence, ... the normal conversational assumptions on which the possibility of indirect speech acts rests are in large part suspended. (Searle 1975: 76–77)

The pattern discerned here by Searle responds not only to our division of pragmatic labor, but also to the set of statistical correlations at the core of Zipf's analysis of the Principle of Least Effort and its linguistic reflexes (Zipf 1949).

Zipf's Law of Abbreviation posits an inverse relation between the length of a word and the frequency of its tokens in an arbitrary text. His Principle of Economic Versatility stipulates a direct correlation between a word's frequency and its semantic versatility (i.e. the number of discrete senses or meanings it allows). The Principle of Economic Specialization states that the age of lexical item in the language correlates inversely with its size and directly with its frequency. By these measures, the relative simplicity of (35a), (35b) as against (35c) is directly confirmed: can and could are historically older than their periphrastic counterparts, phonologically simpler and shorter, more frequent in text tokens, and certainly more versatile semantically, as the contrasts in (41a-c) make clear.

(41a) I {can/am able to} stand on my nose.
       This knife {can/? is able to} cut the salami. (cf. ... is capable of cutting it)
       The salami {can be cut/*is able to be cut/is capable of being cut} by this knife.
(41b) Can it really be raining out?/Is it possible that it's raining out?
(41c) Can Billy come out and play?/Is Billy permitted to come out and play?

It is significant that modals, the constituents par excellence of least effort, figure so prominently among those forms conventionalized in English and other languages as conveyors of indirect speech acts, while their more expensive and complex counterparts do not.

Finally, we come to the case of logical double negation. What we find here is that the two negatives of the form not- (not-p) do not cancel out functionally even when they do semantically: they convey a positive which is characteristically weaker than the corresponding simple affirmative. In Jespersen's words,

> The two negatives [in not common, not infrequent] do not exactly cancel one another so that the result is identical with the simple common, frequent; the longer expression is always weaker; 'this is not unknown to me' or 'I am not ignorant of this' means 'I am to some extent aware of it', etc. The psychological reason for this is that the detour through the two mutually destructive negatives weakens the mental energy of the listener and implies ... a hesitation which is absent from the blunt, outspoken common or known. (Jespersen 1924: 332; cf. Horn 1978c: section 3.1 for discussion)

Rather than appealing, with Jespersen, to the metaphysical (and somewhat Victorian) notion of double negation sapping the listener's mental energy, we can more plausibly ascribe the weakening effect to the same general tendency we have already observed: the use of a marked expression when there is a shorter and less 'effortful' alternative available signals that the speaker felt s/he was not in a position to employ the simpler version felicitously.

With double negation, as with indirect speech acts, we see an especially clear correlation between the stylistic naturalness of a given form, its relative brevity and simplicity, and its use in stereotypic situations (via R-implicature). The corresponding periphrastic forms, stylistically less natural, longer and more complex, are restricted (via Q-implicature) to those situations outside the stereotype, for which the unmarked expression would have been inappropriate.

12. Q-based and R-based Processes in Language Change.

Perhaps the clearest lexical correlates of the clash and resolution of the R vs. Q conflict are in the area of diachrony. The most obvious R-based effects in language change are the reflexes in 'langue' of the well-known 'fast speech phenomena' in 'parole': contraction, clipping or truncation, assimilative shifts, and so on. Clipping (truncation) is a direct corollary of the aforementioned Law of Abbreviation: the more frequently a word or expression is used (within a given speech community), the shorter it will tend to become.

Among the contemporary examples of clipping cited by Stern (1931: 258) in his standard work on lexical change are pram (from perambulator), specs (<spectacles), rep (<repetition or reprobate); it is striking that the same clipped forms persist even when their conventional value has shifted — specs is now likely to abbreviate specifications, and rep would probably be taken to denote representative (or perhaps reputation, as in the somewhat dated bad rep). More clearly entered in our current lexicon are such conventional truncations as TV (or Brit. telly), phone, bus (<omnibus), and the conventionalized output of an extremely productive process of acronym formation (e.g. US(A), EST (with at least two senses for east-coast syntacticians), UCLA, OSU — 'Oregon State University', 'Oklahoma State University', or 'Ohio State University', depending on the shared assumptions of the members of the speech community).

In discussing the development of the truncated forms, Stern (1931: 257–58) warns that 'the demands of the speech functions must set a limit to the economic tendency' — i.e. the Q Principle constrains the power of the R Principle. (He also disparages 'the use of pronouns, or of generic words, to save mental effort' as 'especially characteristic of undeveloped minds, unintelligent or immature'. Avoid Pronoun or else!)

A more complex area of language change, involving the interaction of R-based and Q-based processes, is that of lexical shifts. Two traditional categories of lexical change (discussed by Paul 1909 and Brél 1900, inter alia) worth examining in this light are narrowing (or reduction) of meaning and broadening (or expansion) of meaning.

Narrowing generally involves an R-based shift from a set denotation to a subset (or member) of that set, representing the salient or stereotypical exemplar of the general category. Examples cited in the standard works (cf. Breal 1900, Stern 1931) which fit this definition include Greek <u>alogon</u> (lit. 'speechless one') for 'horse', Latin <u>fēnum</u> (orig. 'produce') for 'hay', and English <u>poison</u> (cognate with <u>potion</u>), <u>liquor</u> (cf. <u>liquid</u>), <u>undertaker</u> (from 'one who undertakes' to 'mortician'), and <u>corn</u> (used for whatever grain is the most important cereal crop of a particular region, e.g. wheat in England, oats in Scotland, maize in Australia or the New World).

In these instances, the shift has become virtually complete (although the original, broader extension may persist in marginal uses). Other cases manifest the intermediate stage of 'autohyponymy'[2] (Horn to appear b), in which the basic, general sense survives in privative opposition with a specific sense derived from it. Autohyponyms which have developed their specific meaning (indicated in parentheses) through R-based narrowing include the following:

(42) color (for 'hue', i.e. the range of colors excluding blacks, whites, and grays): in color, color TV

temperature (for 'fever'): The baby has a temperature number (for 'integer'): Pick a number from 1 to 10

drink (for 'drink alcohol'): I don't drink. Cf. the second example of (8d)

smell (for 'stink'): Something smells here

Frau (Ger.), femme (Fr.), mujer (Sp.) (for 'wife' as well as 'woman')

Dismissing a contemporary account of this variety of lexical shift in the evolution of <u>homo</u> 'man' from a source akin to humus 'earth', the first century grammarian Quintilian asks rhetorically, 'Are we to believe that <u>homo</u> comes from <u>humus</u>, because man is born of the earth, as if all animals had not the same origin?' (cited by Bréal 1900: 114). Yet the derivation is correct, as noted by Bréa), who points out that <u>alogon</u> can likewise designate 'horse' in modern Greek without implying that no other animal lacks the faculty of speech[3]. Like those logical fallacies based on real pragmatic inference patterns (e.g. 'denial of the antecedent', 'post hoc ergo propter hoc', and 'secundum quid' (Horn 1973: 212–13), all responding to the workings of the R Principle as exemplified in (8a)), the R-based inference from a set to a salient or stereotypical member is as linguistically plausible as it is logically invalid.

In other cases, lexical narrowing is Q-based, typically resulting is autohyponymy. Kempson (1980: 15–16) offers a characterization of the general process:

> If for some general term, representing a lexical field, there is a gap in the sub-parts of that field, with only one more narrowly specified lexical item, then the gap may be filled by a more specific use of the general term.

Thus, for example, the existence of <u>bitch</u> 'female dog', in the absence of a sex-specific mate, leads the general term <u>dog</u> to develop a hyponymic sense designating the male of the species.

The governing principle for such cases is given as follows (Kempson 1980:15):

> If a lexical item L_1 has as its extension a set S_1 which includes the set S_2 which a second lexical item [L_2] has as its extension ..., then the lexical item L_1 may be used to denote that subset of S_1 which excludes S_2.

We thus have a partial reconstruction of the division of pragmatic labor, in that the existence of a more informative, marked term (L_2), together with the choice by a (fully informed) speaker to employ a less informative, unmarked term (L_1) (in a context where the additional information would have been relevant), licenses the Q-inference that the speaker was not in a position to employ the more informative term. We can represent this state of affairs schematically as in (43).

(43)  (L₁ may be used to denote S_1-S_2, i.e. the complement of S_1 with respect to S_2)

Thus, we obtain a pragmatic resolution of the semantic asymmetry inherent in the original state diagram. At the same time, L_1 may (and usually does) retain its general application (so as to include S_2) in contexts where there is no contrast at issue with L_2: it is only when the sex of the beast is relevant that bitches do not count as dogs.

Noncanine examples of autohyponymy (i.e. private polysemy) deriving from Q-based narrowing include the following (cf. Kempson 1980, Horn to appear b):

(44) cow (excluding bulls)
rectangle (excluding squares)
finger (excluding thumbs)
gay (excluding lesbians)
player (excluding pitchers, in baseball)

I have argued elsewhere (Horn to appear b) that these cases are not homogeneous in nature, differing in degree of conventionalization of the relevant Q-based inference, and that (contra Kempson) they do not in any case represent the sole source of autohyponymy, given the examples of R-based narrowing cited earlier and those illustrating R-based broadening to be discussed further on.

The results of R-based and Q-based narrowing may be synchronically indistinguishable. As against the dog/bitch (and lion/lioness) variety, the narrowing of man seems to have preceded the development of its counterpart woman, and thus to represent an R-based rather than Q-based shift, males presumably being reckoned as the salient members of the species. More recent instances of what feminists have appropriately dubbed the masculine usurpation of the generic include mankind, chairman, and poet. Here, it is clearly the prior (R-based) specialization of the general term which created the perceived need for — and conscious innovation of — the corresponding feminine form; it is not the existence of sex-specific womankind, chairwoman, or poetess which led to a (Q-based) restriction on the extension of the general terms.

The specific L$_2$ term which triggers a Q-based restriction on the meaning or use of the general L$_1$ term must be sufficiently natural and stylistically unmarked, or (as we have observed in our earlier survey of Q-based restrictions) it will not count as a 'corresponding' item. Thus, Blackburn (1983: 495) observes that animal may (or may not) be used so as to exclude humans, and it may likewise be taken in the appropriate context to exclude birds and/or fish, but there is no use of animal which excludes mammals — despite the obvious fact that mammalia constitute just as valid a subgrouping of animals as do birds and fish. Crucially, however, mammal (unlike man, bird, fish) does not correspond to a basic level category in the sense of Rosch (1977) and so cannot trigger the division of pragmatic labor illustrated in (43).

We have seen that narrowing of a lexical item may be either R-based (the spontaneous delimitation of a general term to a sense representing a salient exemplar of the category denoted by that term) or Q-based (the motivated specialization of a general term triggered by the prior existence of a hyponyin of that term). The converse process — lexical broadening or expansion — is always R-based: the generalization of a term for a species to cover the encompassing genus, from genus to phylum, from subset to superset. Thus, Latin pecunia, originally denoting 'property or wealth in cattle' (cf. pecū 'livestock, cattle'), generalizes to signify 'wealth' and eventually 'money', a shift paralleled in the English cognate fee (<OE feoh 'cattle' → 'property'). As noted by Bréal (1900) and Ullman (1959), broadening is often accompanied by 'semantic impoverishment' resulting from the attrition of a qualifying context, as in the expansion of (assumed) Late Latin adripare, arripare, 'come to shore' into French arriver 'arrive (tout court)', or the generalization of panarium 'bread basket' into panier 'basket' (Ullman 1959: 209).

Broadening tends to apply regularly with place and origin names, as political entities grow and mutate; examples include the expansion of Lat. romanus (or Eng. New Yorker) to designate someone or something from the empire (state) at large, rather than specifically from its major city. An even more productive source of lexical broadening involves trade names which have lost their capital letters and become generics (cf. Mason and Pimm 1982, Horn to appear b), including those in (45).

(45) xerox   jello   good humor

| kleenex | thermos | toll-house cookies |
| scotch tape | vaseline | hoover (Br., 'vacuum cleaner') |

As in many of the instances of narrowing discussed earlier, the net result (or at least temporary equilibrium state) here is autohyponymy: the broadened term retains its original specific meaning in at least some contexts. We may even end up with multiple hyponymy, as in the case of the enthogeographic label Yankee, with its three semantically nested extensions cited by McCawley (1981: 9–10) and standard lexicographers[4], 'native or inhabitant of New England; or, more generally, of northern U.S.; or, more generally, of U.S.'

In these examples, broadening results when a specific term representing a salient exemplar (often the salient exemplar) of a wider class generalizes to denote that wider class; lexical expansion thus constitutes a perfect mirror image of R-based narrowing from a set to a salient exemplar of it. Once the new value for the term is entered in the lexicon — alongside or in place of the original specific value — semantic shifts (often culturally triggered) may ensue, obscuring the original set/salient member relation. It was the Romans' use of livestock as the medium of exchange which led to the broadening of pecūnia, a derivative of the term for 'livestock', into a term denoting 'property' — and it was the subsequent abandonment of barter in favor of a monetary system that led to the later loss of the etymological component altogether, to the point where pecūnia simply stood for 'wealth'.[5] So too, in Mayan languages studied by Lounsbury, a word referring to 'serpent' or 'jaguar' — animals with a particular ritual significance — became generalized as the standard term for 'animal', retaining its original specific meaning in compounds. The manufacturers of the items in (45) should therefore find a silver lining in the legal cloud of their copyright loss: their products obviously represent the prototypes or epitomes of their respective kind, even if this results in their brand name coming to stand for that kind.

Broadening and narrowing often operate in tandem within a given language, or in complementary fashion across related languages. Thus, German Tier has broadened from 'wild animal' to include domestic livestock and pets as well as man (especially in compounds like Tierwelt 'animal kingdom'). At the same time, its English cognate has turned autohyponymous (and eventually unambiguous once more) through narrowing. OE dēor, ME deer originally designated beasts in general, especially 'objects of chase' (Stern 1931: 416), then became restricted (initially in the lexicon of hunters) to single out the object of chase par excellence, fam. Cervidae. By the early modern period, the general use of <u>deer</u> had been largely supplanted by the Romance loans <u>beast</u>, <u>brute</u>, and <u>animal</u>, although it continued to retain a marginal application to the class of quadrupedal mammals, undifferentiated for species (as in Shakespeare's reference to <u>rats and mice and such small deer</u>). Eventually, only the specialized hyponyinic sense survived, spreading from hunters' use into the general speech community.

The adjustment in the extension of <u>deer</u> vis-à-vis <u>animal</u> reflects a general tendency in language insightfully described by Bréal (1900: 27ff.). Bréal's principle, in effect a diachronic precursor of Kiparsky's Avoid Synonymy, is the Law of Differentiation, governing

the intentional [1], ordered process by which words, apparently synonymous, and once synonyms, have nevertheless taken different meanings, and can no longer be used indiscriminately ... either they are differentiated, or else one of the two terms ceases to exist. (Bréal 1900: 27–28)

Typically, an older word for a given referent is retained, but limited to a specialized (often humble, 'degraded', or 'trivial') domain. Once again, the marked form is limited to a marked use.

Thus, Bréal informs us, the Swiss patois word for 'room', <u>païlé</u>, is restricted to the meaning 'garret' after standard French <u>chambre</u> is adopted as the unmarked term. The general use of Oscan <u>popina</u> 'kitchen', displaced by its Latin cognate <u>coquina,</u> eventually comes to denote 'tavern'. And now 'the Savoyard uses the names of <u>père</u> and <u>mère</u> for his parents, while he keeps for his cattle the old words pâré and mâré' (Bréal 1900: 29).

Among English examples of Béal's Law of Differentiation we might reckon <u>brethren</u> (whose restricted use is motivated by the adoption of the standard unmarked plural <u>brothers</u>), the <u>deer/animal</u> case already discussed, and the related and notorious <u>hound/dog</u> affair.

Once again, we find broadening and narrowing operating hand-in-hand (or paw-in-paw) until the eventual division of labor is arrived at. OE <u>dogca,</u> referring to a particular breed of dog (it is not entirely clear which one), represented a hyponym of the general term <u>hound,</u> then denoting the entire kind 'dog' (as its German littermate <u>Hund</u> continues to do). Sometime around the fourteenth century, when Chaucer's warning 'It is nought good a slepyng hound to wake' was turning into Heywood's 'It is evyll wakyng of a sleepyng dog', dog and hound were presumably both autohyponyms, with different specific understandings. Eventually, hound was totally displaces by dog in its general application but, in accordance with the Law of Differentiation, continued to retain its specialized use (originally developed via R-based narrowing in the vocabulary of hunters, for whom hounds were the salient representatives of the species, dogs par excellence).

Thus, narrowing and broadening, separately and in conjunction, reflect the centrality of R-based and Q-based shifts in the development of the lexicon. In R-based and Q-based narrowing, in R-based broadening, and in instantiations of Bréal's Law of Differentiation, as in the dynamics of use and meaning described by Chomsky (1982), Aronoff (1976), Kiparsky (1982), McCawley (1978), and Searle (1975), we descry the recurring patterns of our two general pragmatic principles and of the division of labor resulting from their interaction.

13. Varia and Concluding Remarks.

Other apparent reflexes of the R vs. Q dynamic cannot be discussed here in detail, but are worth mentioning as possible topics for further investigation. First, there is the class of rhetorical figures of speech, including synecdoche, metonymy, and litotes, representing the 'parole'-based equivalent of conventionalized narrowing (part for whole) and broadening (whole for part).

Second, there is the privative relation between the meanings (and uses) associated with nominative and ergative case marking for subjects of intransitive verbs in 'fluid' or 'active' systems (cf. Dixon 1979 and especially Holisky 1983). In Bats (a.k.a. Batsbiy and Tsova-Tush), a Caucasian language investigated by Holisky, the facts appear to be as follows:

(46) With intransitive verbs which are typically agentive and intentional (e.g. 'get dressed', 'wash', 'hide', 'run', 'bump into'), NOM(inative) case is semantically marked for nonagentivity and ERG(ative) is unmarked.

(47) With intransitives which are typically nonagentive (e.g. 'die', 'burn', 'become poor', 'forget', 'drown', 'go crazy'), ERG is marked as agentive and NOM is neutral.

(48) With intransitives which allow both agentive and nonagentive interpretations

equally freely (e.g. 'fall asleep', 'fall down', 'lose weight', 'be late'), ERG and NOM are equally natural and no markedness relation obtains.

In the first two sets of examples, we are dealing with a privative opposition (Zwicky and Sadock 1975, Horn to appear b), in which 'the marked member conveys its meaning truth-functionally, while the neutral member does so by implicature' (Holisky 1983: 5). The existence of the more informative, marked form, together with the speaker's choice of the unmarked, semantically neutral form, allows the addressee to construct a Q-based implicature: the inference from the use of ERG with the verbs of (46) that an agent was involved, and the corresponding inference from the use of NOM with the verbs in (47) that the nonagentive interpretation was intended. Once again, we arrive at a division of pragmatic labor, in which the marked form is used for the marked situation (relativized to the semantics of the verb in question), and the unmarked form for the unmarked situation.

Finally, one more possible locus of the dynamics and resolution of the R/Q conflict is the range of 'switch-reference' constructions (cf. e.g. Finer 1984). As I read the data, there seem to be some languages (including Seri and Washo) in which the presence of a DS (different-subject) marker indicates that an embedded clause has a different subject from the main clause, while the lack of a marker is semantically unspecified for same vs. different referent, but tends to be interpreted as indicating that the subject is the same in contexts where the distinction is relevant and no further disambiguating factors are available. The asymmetry involved here is apparently analogous to that just touched on in Bats case-marking (as well as other examples discussed earlier), and thus similarly reflective of the use of Q-based implicature to complete the division of labor, but further investigation is required to sharpen the account of switch-reference and situate it more clearly within the proposed framework.

We have surveyed (all too cursorily) a wide range of linguistic phenomena, both synchronic and diachronic, both lexical and syntactic, both 'parole'-based and 'langue'-based, from conversation implicature and politeness strategies to the interpretation of pronouns and gaps, from blocking and distributional constraints on lexical items to indirect speech acts, from lexical change to case marking. If I am right, these apparently diverse and unrelated domains are all motivated and governed by the same functional dynamic, the ongoing Zipfo-Gricean dialectic between the Q-based Sufficiency Principle and the R-based Principle of Least Effort.

Notes

1   Ducrot's model of pragmatic inference shares with Grice's the crucial feature of indeterminacy. Given an utterance like (i),

(i)   La situation n'est pas exceliente. 'The situation isn't excellent'

Ducrot notes (1972:132), an addressee may infer that the speaker intended to convey (ii),

(ii)   Elle est franchement mauvaise. 'It's pretty bad'

through the exploitation of the R-based 'Loi d'informativité' (the assumption that the hearer does not already know the information the speaker is conveying); since he has not said (ii), however, the speaker can always retreat to the literal meaning of what he has said, i.e. the weaker (i). On the other hand, given the Q-based 'Loi d'exhaustivité' (the principle which demands that the speaker provide the strongest possible information which he possesses and which he believes may interest the hearer; cf. Ducrot 1972:134), someone who utters (i) may, in the appropriate context, implicate that the situation is pretty good. This indeterminacy is perhaps more apparent when the negation applies to a semantically negative predication, as pointed out by Stern (1931: 312):

> Not bad, taken literally, leaves a large latitude, from indifferent to excellent, and may mean [sic] either, depending on the intonation used and the circumstances.

2   Following Lyons (1977: 9.4), A is called a 'hyponym' of B iff the extension of A is properly included in that of B: Labrador retriever is a hyponym of retriever, retriever of dog, dog of mammal, and so on. But some words are hyponyms of themselves: dog and bitch are (sex-differentiated) co-hyponyms of dog, lion and lioness of lion, etc. In these cases, we can call the unmarked term (dog or lion) an 'autohyponym'. Autohyponymy thus represents privative polysemy or ambiguity within a single lexical item (cf. Zwicky and Sadock 1975 on privative opposition).

3   Bréal (1900: 108) suggests that in fact alogon [aloro] came to stand for the

horse simply because 'the rider, speaking of his mount, was accustomed to say "the animal"'; similarly, <u>homines</u> were so-called not merely because of man's preeminent position among the creatures of earth, but because of the intended opposition between the earthbound human race as against 'the inhabitants of the sky <u>Dii</u> or <u>Superii</u>' (Bréal 1900: 114).

4   As noted in Horn (to appear b), there is an even more narrowly defined sense of <u>Yankee,</u> the sense in which the Kennedys are disqualified from true Yankee status by their Irish Catholic heritage. On this ultrarestrictive interpretation, a Yankee is someone from New England who approximates to a sufficient degree the prototype WASP of the Pepperidge Farm commercials. (We may need to invoke a Rosch (1977)- style prototype theory in any case to explain why a Vermont farmer or a Maine lobsterman is more of a Yankee than is a Greenwich stockbroker.)

5   The mirror image relation between R-based broadening (from salient subset to superset) and R-based narrowing (from superset to salient subset) is highlighted when we juxtapose the development of <u>pecūnia</u> with the opposite shift exemplified by <u>ktimata</u> in Greek, from the general 'possessions' to the specific 'cattle' (Bréal 1900:109).

References

Aronoff, M. 1976. Word formation in generative grammar. Cambridge, Mass.: MIT Press.

Atlas, J., and S. Levinson. 1981. <u>It</u>-cleits, informativeness, and logical form. In: Cole, ed. (1981: 1–61).

Blackburn, W. 1973. Ambiguity and non-specificity: A reply to Jay David Atlas. Linguistics and Philosophy 6.479–98.

Bréal, M. 1900. Semantics. Trans. Mrs. H. Cust. New York: Henry Holt.

Brown, P., and S. Levinson. 1979. Universals in language use: Politeness phenomena. In: Questions and politeness: Strategies in social interaction. Edited by E. Goody. Cambridge: Cambridge University Press. 56–311.

Chomsky, N. 1982. Lectures on government and binding, 2nd ed. Dordrecht: Foris.

Clark, H., and S. Haviland. 1977. Comprehension and the given-new contract. In: Discourse production and comprehension. Edited by R. Freedle. Hillside,

N.J.: Erlbaum. 1–40.

Cole, P., ed. 1978. Syntax and semantics 9: Pragmatics. New York: Academic Press.

Cole, P., ed. 1981. Radical pragmatics. New York: Academic Press.

Cole, P., and J. Morgan, eds. 1975. Syntax and semantics 3: Speech acts. New York: Academic Press.

Coleman, L., and P. Kay. 1981. Prototype semantics: The English word lie. Lg. 57.26–44.

DeMorgan, A. 1847. Formal logic. [Reprinted London: Open Court Co., 1926]

Dixon, R. M. W. 1979. Ergativity. Lg. 55.59–138.

Ducrot, O. 1972. Dire et ne pas dire. Paris: Hermann.

Enç, M. (to appear) Topic switching and pronominal subjects in Turkish. In: Studies in Turkish linguistics. Edited by K. Zimmer.

Finer, D. 1984. The formal grammar of switch reference. University of Massachusetts dissertation.

Gazdar, G. 1979. Pragmatics. New York: Academic Press.

Geis, M., and A. Zwicky. 1971. On invited inferences. Linguistic Inquiry 2.561–65.

Gordon, D., and G. Lakoff. 1975. Conversational postulates. In: Cole and Morgan, eds. (1975: 41–58).

Hamilton, Sir W. 1860. Lectures on logic. Edinburgh: Blackwood and Sons.

Harnish, R. M. 1976. Logical form and implicature. In: An integrated theory of linguistic ability. Edited by T. Bever, J. Katz, and D. T. Langendoen. New York: Crowell. 464–79.

Heringer, J. 1972. Some grammatical correlates of felicity conditions. Ohio State University dissertation. Distributed by Indiana University Linguistics Club.

Heringer, J. 1976. Idioms and lexicalization in English. In: Syntax and semantics 6: The grammar of causative constructions. Edited by M. Shibatani. New York: Academic Press. 205–16.

Holisky, D. 1983. The privative nature of agent-marking in Bats (and English). Paper presented at annual meeting of the Linguistic Society of America, Minneapolis.

Horn, L. 1972. On the semantic properties of logical operators in English. University of California at Los Angeles dissertation. Distributed by Indiana University Linguistics Club, 1976.

Horn, L. 1973. Greek Grice: A brief survey of proto-conversational rules in the

367

history of logic. In: Chicago Linguistic Society 9.205–14.

Horn, L. 1978a. Lexical incorporation, implicature, and the least effort hypothesis. In: Papers from the Parasession on the Lexicon. Chicago: Chicago Linguistic Society. 196–209.

Horn, L. 1978b. Remarks on neg-raising. In: Cole, ed. (1981: 129–220).

Horn, L. 1978c. Some aspects of negation. In: Universals of human language, vol. 4: Syntax. Stanford, Calif.: Stanford University Press. 127–210.

Horn, L. (to appear a) Metalinguistic negation and pragmatic ambiguity. Lg.

Horn, L. (to appear b) Ambiguity, negation, and the London School of Parsimony. In: Proceedings from New England Linguistic Society 14. Edited by C. Jones and P. Sells.

Horn, L., and S. Bayer. (to appear) Short-circuited implicature: A negative contribution. Linguistics and Philosophy.

Jespersen, O. 1924. The philosophy of grammar. [Reprinted New York: Norton, 1976.]

Karttunen, L. 1970. The logic of English predicate complement constructions. Unpublished MS, University of Texas.

Keenan, E. O. 1976. The universality of conversational postulates. Language in Society 5.67–80.

Kempson, R. 1980. Ambiguity and word meaning. In: Studies in English linguistics. Edited by S. Greenbaum, G. Leech, and J. Svartvik. London: Longmans. 7–16.

Kiparsky, P. 1982. Word-formation and the lexicon. In: Proceedings of the 1982 Mid-America Linguistic Conference, University of Kansas. Edited by F. Ingemann.

Lakoff, R. 1973. The logic of politeness; or, minding your P's and Q's. In: Chicago Linguistic Society 9.292–305.

Levinson, S. 1973. Pragmatics. Cambridge: Cambridge University Press.

Lewis, D. 1969. Convention. Cambridge, Mass.: Harvard University Press.

Liberman, M., and I. Sag. 1974. Prosodic form and discourse function. In: Chicago Linguistic Society 10.416–27.

Lyons, J. 1977. Semantics 1. Cambridge: Cambridge University Press.

McCawley, J. 1978. Conversational implicature and the lexicon. In: Cole, ed. (1978: 245–59).

McCawley, J. 1981. Everything that linguists have always wanted to know about logic. Chicago: University of Chicago Press.

Martinet, A. 1962. A functional view of language. Oxford: Clarendon Press.

Mason, J., and D. Pimm. 1982. Generic examples: Seeing the general in the particular. Unpublished MS, The Open University, Milton Keynes, England.

Mills, J. S. 1867. An examination of Sir William Hamilton's philosophy, 3rd ed. London: Longmans.

Morgan, J. 1970. On the criterion of identity for noun phrase deletion. In: Chicago Linguistic Society 6.380–89.

Morgan, J. 1978. Two types of convention in indirect speech acts. In: Cole, ed. (1978: 261–80).

Paul, H. 1909. Prinzipien der Sprachgeschichte, 4th ed. Halle: M. Niemeyer.

Postal, P. 1974. On raising. Cambridge, Mass.: MIT Press.

Prince, E. 1981. Toward a taxonomy of given-new information. In: Cole, ed. (1981: 223–55).

Prince, E. 1982. Grice and universality: A reappraisal. Unpublished MS, University of Pennsylvania.

Rosch, E. 1977. Human categorization. In: Advances in cross-cultural psychology. Edited by N. Warren. New York: Academic Press. 1–72.

Schmerling, S. 1975. Asymmetric conjuction and rules of conversation. In: Cole and Morgan, eds. (1975: 211–31).

Searle, J. 1975. Indirect speech acts. In: Cole and Morgan, eds. (1975: 59–82).

Stern, G. 1931. Meaning and change of meaning. Bloomington: Indiana University Press.

Tannen, D. 1975. Communication mix and mixup, or how linguistics can ruin a marriage. San Jose State Occasional Papers in Linguistics.

Tannen, D. 1979. Ethnicity as conversational style. Sociolinguistics Working Paper No. 55, Southwest Educational Development Laboratory, Austin, Texas.

Ullman, S. 1959. The principles of semantics, 2nd ed. Glasgow: Jackson, Son and Co.

Zipf, G. K. 1949. Human behavior and the principle of least effort. Cambridge: Addison-Wesley.

Zwicky, A., and J. Sadock. 1975. Ambiguity tests and how to fail them. In: Syntax and semantics 4. Edited by J. Kimball. New York: Academic Press. 1–36.

Three Levels of Meaning

Stephen C. Levinson

外
教
社
学
术
阅
读
文
库

语
义
学
经
典
论
文
选
读

1 Introduction

Many a student must have sighed when faced with what might seem the almost medieval casuistry of many of the distinctions in John Lyons' (1977) two-volume handbook, *Semantics*. Ambiguities and unclarities of every kind in our frail metalanguage for semantic analysis are there laid out for all to see; a formidable reef of difficult distinctions — types and tokens, acts and products, uses and mentions, originals and replicas, ambiguities of level, etc. — upon which we are all guaranteed sooner or later to founder. Introducing the type/token distinction in a straightforward manner, he goes on to tease us by showing how identifying different tokens of the same type can require a complex measure of similarity or identity of type, and then, having raised our anxieties, announces that it would be 'unnecessarily pedantic' to identify each such distinction (1977: 13–16).

One such distinction Lyons alludes to throughout the volumes may look particularly pedantic, the distinction between utterance-types and utterance-tokens, coming on top, as it does, of the distinctions between system-sentences and text-sentences, sentence-types and sentence-tokens, utterance-acts and -signals and so on. He himself seems to hint (1977: 570ff.) that the distinction may not be of any great utility (since utterance-tokens are rarely constrained to type, and such types could in any case be given formal definition, for example, in terms of sentence-types or forms).

In this chapter I want to suggest that this distinction between utterance-type meaning and utterance-token meaning, or something rather like it, may indeed prove to be an important division in levels of meaning. In finding utility in one of those obscure and seemingly pedantic distinctions, we can be thankful not only to John Lyons but to those generations of scholars in the western tradition, whose work Lyons has so usefully synthesised, who have laboured to hone these fundamental tools of semantic analysis.[1]

2 Levels of meaning

It has long been observed that we need a basic distinction between sentence-meaning and utterance-meaning, where sentence-meaning is understood as the overall meaning composed from the meanings of all the constituents together with the meaning of the constructions in which they occur, while utterance-meaning refers to the import of, say, the very same sentence when uttered in a particular context. (Utterances are thus often treated as pairings of sentences and contexts, namely the contexts in which they occur.) Thus a sentence with deictic elements like *I am sixty-three today* will clearly have different interpretations depending on who says it when, and mismatches between sentence-meaning and utterance-meaning are of course exploited in ironies and other tropes.

This observation is the foundation for the distinction between semantics and pragmatics however this is construed theoretically (see Levinson 1983: ch. 1 for a review; Lyons' *Semantics* of course encompassed both of these levels and the interactions between them).[2] That distinction established two fundamental explanatory levels in a theory of meaning, one responsible for the systematic process whereby the meaning of complex expressions can be built out of the meaning of their parts, and another responsible for explaining how the same expressions might have different meanings or interpretations in different contexts. Theoretical developments will tend to push the boundary one way or the other, but the distinction between the two levels, each with its different explanatory principles, seems certain to survive. It was partly the work of the speech act theorists (Austin and Searle in particular), but especially the work of Paul Grice, that opened up the prospect of a systematic pragmatics. Grice (1957) held that ultimately meaning could be reduced to matters of speaker's intentions, to meanting; but proximately, he held that meaning is a composite notion (see Grice 1989), He considered that the full import of an utterance could only be captured by distinguishing many different kinds of content — even the coded content (roughly, our sentence-meaning) was divided between 'the said' and

371

'the conventionally implicated' (and later he added 'the presupposed'), while the inferred content (our utterance-meaning) was divisible between particularised and generalised conversational implicatures and perhaps other kinds of inference altogether. (See Levinson, 1983: ch. 3, for an introductory exposition.)

It is this distinction between generalised and particularised implicatures that is the focus of this chapter. This distinction, I will argue, should force us to recognise not only the two major levels of a theory of meaning, semantics and pragmatics, but also a major distinction within pragmatics: a distinction between utterance-type meaning and utterance-token meaning. On general grounds of parsimony, this may be resisted; but I think that by recognising this further bifurcation, we will be greatly aided in understanding the relation of grammar to meaning.

Grice's (1975: 56f.; 1989: 37f.) distinction between particularised and generalised conversational implicatures needs a little exposition. A conversational implicature (henceforth 'implicature' for short), it will be recollected, is an inference that derives from what has been said in context taken together with some general background 'maxims of conversation', enjoining veracity, relevance, perspicacity and the provision of just the right amount of information. Because the inferences derive from both the linguistic expressions and these background assumptions, they are always *defeasible* (or cancellable) whenever the assumptions clearly do not hold. Now, Grice observed, some conversational implicatures seem context-bound, while others have a very general currency. Consider, for example, how a single utterance-form might suggest fundamentally different propositions (particularised conversational implicatures or PCIs) in two different contexts, while at the same time implicating something else (a generalised conversational implicature or GCI) in both these contexts and many others too:[3]

(1) Two possible contexts for B's utterance(-form):
     a. Context 1:
        A: "What time is it?"
        B: "Some of the guests are already leaving."
        PCI: '*It must be late.*'
        GCI: 'Not all of the guests are already leaving,'
     b. Context 2:
        A: "Where's John?"

B: "Some of the guests are already leaving."
PCI: 'Perhaps John is already leaving.'
GCI: 'Not all of the guests are already leaving.'

The inference labelled 'GCI' here is indeed one of very general currency: normally by stating "Some x are G", a speaker will implicate 'Not all x are G'. So general is the inference indeed that it might be mistaken for part of the meaning of *some* in English; but that it is a pragmatic inference is shown by (a) its predictability by general principle or maxim, (b) the semantic compatibility of its overt denial (as in *Some, in fact all, of the guests are already leaving*).

Some commentators (notably Sperber & Wilson, 1987: 748) have claimed that Grice attributed no real importance to this distinction,[4] but on the contrary the evidence is that he thought GCIs to be the source of many mistakes in the semantic analysis of, for example, the 'logical' connectives in English, Thus he was keen to point out that the inference from S's saying *"p or q"* to 'S doesn't know that p, or that q' is a regularity of interpretation not to be confused with the conventional or coded meaning of the disjunction. It is the regularity of association that makes the confusion so tempting.

In any case, since Grice much work has shown how useful the notion of a generalised conversational implicature is in linguistic analysis, even if it is not often so explicitly distinguished (see e.g. Gazdar & Pullum, 1976; Gazdar, 1979; Atlas & Levinson, 1981; Horn, 1989). Its utility lies precisely in the idea that certain linguistic expressions will tend to be associated with specific pragmatic inferences across a broad range of contexts, so that these associated inferences can be predicted in a systematic way, and play a systematic role in shaping patterns of lexicalisation and grammaticalisation.

The overall picture of a general theory of communication that then emerges is rather different from the standard picture. According to the standard line, there are just two levels to a theory of linguistic communication, a level of sentence-meaning (to be explicated by the theory of grammar in the broad sense) and a level of speaker-meaning (to be explicated by a theory of pragmatics, perhaps centrally employing Grice's notion of meaning-$_{nn}$). Speaker-meaning, or utterance-token-meaning, will be a matter of the actual 'nonce' or once-off inferences made in actual contexts by specific recipients with all of their rich particularities. This view, though parsimonious, is surely inadequate, indeed potentially pernicious, because it underestimates the regularity, recurrence and systematicity of many kinds of pragmatic inferences.

What it omits is a third layer, intermediate between coded meaning and nonce speaker-meaning, what we may call the level of *statement-* or *utterance-type-meaning.* This third layer is a level of systematic pragmatic inference based *not* on direct computations about speaker-intentions, but rather on *general expectations about how language is normally used.* These expectations give rise to presumptions, default inferences, about both content and force; and it is at this level (if at all) that we can sensibly talk about *speech acts, presuppositions, felicity conditions, conversational pre-sequences, preference organisation* and, of especial concern to us, *generalised conversational implicatures.* It is also at this level, naturally, that we can expect the systematicity of inference that might be deeply interconnected to linguistic structure and meaning, to the extent that it can become problematic to decide which phenomena should be rendered unto grammar and lexicon and which unto pragmatics (witness the long-standing disputes about the semantic or pragmatic status of illocutionary force and presupposition).

The supposition of this third, intermediate layer in a theory of communication is nothing new, Austin (1962), for example, clearly had something of this kind in mind when he proposed the three-way distinction between locutionary, illocutionary and perlocutionary acts; the cocutionary level corresponds to the level of sentence-meaning, the illocutionary to our intermediate layer formed of conventions or habits of use, and the perlocutionary to the level of speaker-intentions. Other theorists have energetically tried to defend the notion of a *convention of use* to be distinguished from a *convention of language*; for example, such a distinction seems essential if we are to retain the idea that indirect speech acts are both partially conventional and inferentially motivated (Searle, 1975). Without admitting the existence of such an intermediate layer, how are we to explain the use of routine formulae (like *Good luck, Bless you, See you later*) which, although meaning what they literally mean, simultaneously perform habitual everyday rituals (Morgan, 1978)? Why is it that I can introduce myself with *My name is Steve,* but not *I was given the name Steve;* that I can express sympathy with you with *I am really sorry* but not conventionally with *That really saddens me;* that I express outrage with *Really!* but not with *In truth!;* that I can say *I am delighted to meet you* but not idiomatically *I am gratified to meet you;* that I can choose a pastry by saying *I would like that one* but not *I would desire that one* and so on? And to every specification of proper usage there tends to be a restriction on interpretation (Levinson, 1992). There is a great body of language lore here, beyond knowledge of grammar and semantics, extensively studied of course by both ethnographers of speaking and students of second-language learning. That two ways of 'saying the same thing' might be unequal in their conversational import, or that one way of saying something might pre-empt another, these are surely not radical doctrines.

The theory of GCIs is not of course a theory of conventional idioms, clichés and formulae; but it is a *generative theory of idiomaticity*, that is to say a set of principles guiding the choice of the right expression to suggest a specific interpretation, and as a corollary, a theory accounting for preferred interpretations. GCI theory offers a systematic account of why, for example, saying "See you on Tuesday" when tomorrow is Tuesday would suggest not seeing you tomorrow, why saying "If you help, I'll finish it" suggests that otherwise I will not do so, or why saying "Some of my colleagues are competent" would suggest that not all of them are, and so on, matching a 'way of putting things' with a favoured interpretation in each case. The theory thus belongs to the intermediate level of a theory of communication, the level of utterance-type-meaning.

Nevertheless, that intermediate level is constantly under attack by reductionists seeking to assimilate it either to the level of sentence-meaning or to the level of speaker-meaning; thus, for example, in the case of the inferences we are here calling GCIs, many theorists (Kamp, Peters, Barwise and others) have suggested that they should be in effect semanticised, while Sperber and Wilson and some so-called local-pragmatics theorists have presumed that on the contrary they should be assimilated to matters of nonce-inference at the level of speaker-intention.[5] But generalised implica-tures are not going to reduce so easily in either direction, for they sit midway, systematically influencing grammar and semantics on the one hand and speaker-meaning on the other. I shall therefore presume that we do indeed need such a three-tiered theory of communication.

This presumption does not presuppose that the distinctions between the middle layer of utterance-type-meaning and the upper and lower levels is in any way cut and dried. Indeed, there is every reason to suppose that matters of utterance-type-meaning will shade into speaker-meaning at the one end and sentence-meaning at the other. This is in part because there is plenty of evidence that language use is the source for grammaticalised patterns, and that there is a diachronic path from speaker-meanings to utterance-type-meanings to sentence-meanings. Thus grey areas at the boundaries do not constitute evidence against the tripartite view, while evidence for it is the existence of preferred interpretations, default presumptions of the kind we shall illustrate in detail below.

3 Overcoming the bottleneck in human communication: Grice's maxims as heuristics

No student of language can fail to be awed by the intricacies and efficiency of human communication, and the underlying capacities that support it: the specialised physiology, the neurological pathways and the learning abilities that support the structural complexities of language, and above all the sheer miracle of the apparent speed and effortlessness whereby communicative intentions are encoded in articulatory gestures and acoustic signals converted into meanings. It may seem a bit like looking a gift horse in the mouth to point to one part of this miraculous process and identify it as a relatively slow and inefficient process, which acts as a bottleneck in the entire communicative procedure. still, if we do so, the finger points inevitably to the articulation process itself: we can think faster than we can speak (e.g. we can do other complex things at the same time, including planning speech ahead), and we can easily understand pitch-corrected speech at double speed, or scan a printed page far faster than it can be read aloud. In fact the psycholinguistic evidence seems to suggest that all the other processes in the entire complex chain of production and comprehension systems could run three to four times faster than the normal pace dictated by the articulation process.[6] Those with a technical turn of mind may like to ruminate on the fact that, even making optimistic assumptions, the transmission rate for human speech is still under 100 BAUD.[7]

The articulation bottleneck in human communication raises interesting questions from, as it were, a design perspective. We can see immediately that any trade-off from coded content to inferential meaning may greatly increase the speed of communication: it will pay to say little and infer much, provided of course the inferential content can be recovered (a) reliably, and (b) speedily. Although we may admire the rich monosyllables of husband-wife communication, the process of recovery of nonce speaker-meaning generally guarantees neither speed nor reliability: the process requires computation of indefinitely nested models of the other's train of thought — what the speaker intended the recipient would think the speaker intended, and so on (see Cohen, Morgan & Pollack, 1990). Even these considerations greatly underestimate the problem of the recovery (by the recipient) of speaker-meaning: there is what might be called the *logical* problem of reconstructed reasoning — since a single conclusion can be reached from an infinite series of different sets of premises, how can the recipient reconstruct the Gricean intentions that lay behind the utterance (Levinson, 1995)?

A much simpler solution would be the provision of some general *default heuristics,* frameworks of assumption that can be taken to amplify the coded content of messages in predictable ways unless there is an indication that they do not apply.

Those default heuristics, I will argue, can be identified with Grice's maxims, or at least a version of them. The heuristics have *default* application; that is, they are applied unless there are explicit indications (in the nature of the context or the content of the message) that they should not be. They then invoke and filter further information of two kinds: information about the structure of the world (or, rather, of stereotypical properties of the relevant domain) and metalinguistic knowledge, that is, information about semantically related expressions. This information, together with the heuristics and the content of the utterance, provide a set of premises yielding inferences that greatly enrich the informational content of the utterance.[8]

Let me exemplify with three such heuristics, which interact in an interesting way. The details are complex and lie beyond the scope of this chapter, and we must therefore treat them in the most informal way. Let us introduce the cast of characters loosely as follows:

(2) *Three heuristics*
Q1: 'What is not said is not the case'
    Constrained to expression-alternates; e.g.
    If "x is G" is said, and G and F form a contrast set of expressions, then 'x is not F' is implicated.
    Characteristics:

metalinguistic (makes reference to contrast sets e.g. {P, G}); negative (e.g. 'x is *not* F').

Q2: 'What is simply described is stereotypically and specifically exemplified'
(a) unmarked expressions warrant rich interpretations to the stereotype;
(b) minimal forms warrant maximal interpretations.
Constraint: only of unmarked, minimal expressions
Characteristics:
not fundamentally metalinguistic;
invokes world-knowledge of stereotypical relations;
positive inference to specific subcase.

M: 'Marked descriptions warn "marked situation"'
Constraint: only of marked, unusual or periphrastic expressions
Characteristics:
metalinguistic (marked compared to unmarked);
the inference is to the *complement* of the inference that would have been induced by the unmarked expression.

The idea is the following: suppose that the speaker and recipient each know that the other will use exactly these heuristics, then there are many things that will not need to be spelt out (i.e. coded in the linguistic expressions). So, for example, under the first heuristic, if I say "The flag is white", I will implicate (and you will understand) 'The flag is only white, not red, white and blue'. Under the second heuristic, if I say "He opened the door", I will suggest that he entered in the normal way, not using a crowbar or dynamite. Under the third heuristic, if I say "He turned the handle and pushed open the door" I will suggest that he opened the door in some non-stereotypical manner (e.g. with extra force or speed). In each of these cases, the inference is predictable and clear, and the speaker, knowing this, has — other things being equal — committed himself by a turn of phrase to an interpretation that he knows the recipient will make.

Of course these inferences are defeasible. There is no contradiction in saying "She was wearing a white dress. It had beautiful blue lace trim." Nor, when we are trying to decide whether we are looking at a British or a Russian warship does the observation "The flag is white" or "The flag is red" carry the suggestion 'wholly white' or 'wholly red'. And in complex sentences, the inferences in question may be cancelled by other inferences, as in "They're waving a white flag, even if it's stained red with blood". That is the nature of conversational implicature. Nevertheless, the striking fact is that *ceteris paribus* these inferences do go through by default.

These three heuristics each produce large families of defeasible inferences. By combining all three heuristics, and by presuming that both speaker and recipient will mutually expect them to be in operation, we can greatly amplify the content of what we say — thus overcoming the bottleneck provided by speech-encoding.

4 Default inferences under the three heuristics

The heuristic labels Q1, Q2 and M in (2) above are of course allusions to the corresponding Gricean maxims, the first and second maxim of Quantity and the maxim of Manner.[9] Let us take each of these in turn, and spell out how the heuristics work in a little more detail.

First, Q1, the heuristic that relies on contrast sets of expressions: what exactly is the character of these inferences and from which kinds of lexical sets do they arise? It is clear that there are different kinds of cases, and it is a matter for empirical investigation to find what different kinds of contrast set reliably yield inferences of this negative, complementary kind. Muchstudied prototypes are the entailment scales, where we may set up, for example, an ordered pair <S. W> where S is the 'strong' member, and W the 'weak' member, such that when S is substituted in an arbitrary declarative sentence it will entail the same sentence with W substituted for S. In these cases, assertion of the W sentence will carry a generalised implicature that the S variant does not hold, as illustrated below.[10]

(3) a. scale of contrastive expressions: <*all. some*>
   b. S-sentence: '*All of the students were in class.*'
   c. W-sentence: '*Some of the students were in class.*'
   d. scalar GCI from the assertion of c: 'Not all of the students were in class.'

These are the prototype cases, and there are many important scalar sets in natural-language vocabularies: all the quantifiers including the cardinal numbers, the truth-functional connectives (<*and, or*>), many gradable properties (e.g. English <*hot, warm*>), many kinds of closed sets of morphemes with so-called 'grammatical meaning' (e.g. English <*the*, a>), modal adjectives (e.g. <*necessary, possible>*) and much else besides. Closely related to the scalar sets, but yielding inferences of slightly different force, are subordinating connectives of various kinds, including, for example, *<since, if>*, as illustrated below (following Gazdar, 1979).

(4) a. clausal subordinators: *<since, if>*

b. S-sentence: *'since Ron saw my* manuscript, *he's a plagiarist.'*

c. W-sentence: *'If Ron saw my manuscript, he's a plagiarist.'*

d. clausal implicature from assertion of c:[11] 'Ron may or may not have seen my manuscript, and he may or may not be a plagiarist.'

Note that we now have Q1 default inferences attached to most of the 'logical' elements of the vocabulary: to the truth-functional connectives, conditionals, modals and quantifiers. If the systematic pragmatics of these crucial areas of the vocabulary were better appreciated by semanticists, semantic analyses might be rather different and simpler — in character.

In addition to these cases, there are many other kinds of contrast sets capable of yielding systematic Q1 inferences. For example, as illustrated above, the colour terms {*red, white, blue, green*, etc.} denote properties that are extensionally compatible; but asserting that something is red implies that it is not also green, etc., on the grounds typical of Q1 inferences — the speaker can be relied upon to provide enough information (see Harnish, 1976). Indeed, it is possible to plunder the rich observations in structural semantics (as e.g. in Lyons, 1977, or Cruse, 1986) about many different kinds of lexical sets, and explore all the kinds of inferences that may be associated with the employment of individual lexemes from these sets. Note, for example, how the assertion of a superordinate in a taxonomy suggests that the speaker does not know (or thinks irrelevant) which subordinate term or hyponym applies:

(5) a. "I saw an animal in the larder."

b. Q1 implicates: 'I don't know whether it was a mouse, a rat, a squirrel or what.'

There are probably many systematic patterns here yet to be properly explored. (See Hirschberg, 1985, Levinson, forthcoming, for more ideas here.) A cursory inspection suggests a novel idea. The kinds of semantic opposition between expressions in different kinds of sets can be very different in kind, as explored, for example, in Lyons (1977): as a result the Saussurean notion of *valeur* is then decomposed to the point of loss. Yet we should rightly grieve at the premature death by dissection of a fundamental tenet of structuralist thinking. We might attempt resuscitation by suggesting that *valeur* is not at root a semantic concept at all; perhaps the force is pragmatic, and can be attributed to the Q1 inference to the inapplicability of the contrastive alternate.[12]

Let us turn now to the much less well understood heuristic sketched as Q2 in (2) above ('What is simply described is stereotypically and specifically exemplified'). That there is some such heuristic is indubitable. Consider, for example, the English spatial preposition *in*, as in *in the box, in the garden, in the cup*. Clearly *in* has a wide range of application: to closed containers (boxes), open containers (cups), bounded spaces (gardens), etc. (see Hirsch-berg, 1985, for illuminating complexities). Yet when I say "The coffee is in the cup", you do not mistake the relationship between the coffee and the cup for the related but distinct relation indicated in "The pencil is in the cup": we expect partial projection for pencils but not for coffee. It would be more than pedantic to spell out "The coffee is entirely within the bowl of the cup" — more than pedantic because by so saying you would implicate by the third heuristic something other than normal coffee-to-cup relations.

Semantic generality, the large range of applicability of individual expressions, is typical of most of our (non-technical) vocabulary; it is what makes our lexicon of learnable size. Hence Barwise & Perry (1983) have dubbed this property the 'efficiency' of language, neglecting to note that the property would be inefficient indeed without the complementary property of pragmatic enrichment. Semantic generality is also typical of grammatical meaning. Take, for example, the fact that the compositional principles that compute the meaning of phrases specify the composite meaning in only the most general fashion. Thus nominal compounds like *bread knife, steel knife, murder knife, army knife* each have presumptive interpretations along different lines: bread knives are not made of bread, but steel knives are made of steel; murder knives are not made for murder, although army knives are of a type made for armies, and so on. Similarly for the possessive in English: the construction *X's Y* merely indicates that *some* relation holds between the two noun phrases, and we resolve the relation by pragmatic inference. Thus the phrases *Jupiter's moons, John's ideas, Anne's address, the building's condition, the encyclopedia's editor, the year's end,* are each understood to involve different relations (gravitational capture, ideational authorship, postal access, etc.). Note that all these phrases seem to have a default interpretation: *John's pens* will naturally be taken to mean the pens belonging to John, unless the context (e.g. talk between pen-designers) warrants another less stereotypical interpretation.

What is clear then is that, hearing an utterance, we imagine a specific instantiation, a stereotypical exemplification. But why should such a tendency, perhaps psychological in origin, constitute a heuristic? Arc we not confusing the private interaction between our individual knowledge of the world and our understanding of utterances with a theory of communication? The answers lie in the strange power of the reflexive reasoning that Grice introduced in his theory of meaning-$_{nn}$. The speaker, knowing the recipient's interpretation to tend in a particular direction, and knowing that the recipient knows the speaker so knows, can turn a good chance into a certainty: mutual awareness of the interpretation to the stereotype guarantees that this is what the speaker intends. The speaker *designs* his or her utterance accordingly. (The same principle holds, *mutatis mutandis,* for all the heuristics, of course.)

Closely allied to the inference to the stereotype is a class of other inferences to the more specific subcase. Many of these have to do with the maximisation of coherence, the minimisation of postulated entities and the presumptive enrichment of mentioned relations. For example, it has long been noted that conjunction, or in many languages paratactic adjunction, is presumptively enriched to suggest sequential occurrence of events and, further, intention and causality, as illustrated below, where the assertion of (a) will suggest (b), (c) and (d) even in the absence of stereotypical connections between bells and engines:

(6) *Conjunction-buttressing* (Atlas & Levinson, 1981)
   a. "Ann rang the bell and the engine started."
   b. 'Ann rang the bell and *then* the engine started.'
   c. 'Ann rang the bell and *therefore* the engine started.'
   d. 'Ann rang the bell, *thereby intending* the engine to start.'

A similar presumptive strengthening of content is typical of conditionals, as illustrated below, where the assertion of (a) will suggest (b) and thus jointly (c):[13]

(7) *Conditional perfection* (Geiss & Zwicky, 1971)
   a. "If you co-operate, there'll be no trouble."
   b. 'If you don't co-operate, there will be trouble.'
   c. 'If and only if you co-operate, will there be no trouble. '

Negative statements are of course informationlly weak: from the assertion that x is not F, one is left in the dark as to whether x is G or H, etc. They are thus ripe for pragmatic enrichments of many kinds (see Horn, 1989), but a genus that comes under the rubric of the Q2 heuristic includes the many cases where contradictories are routinely 'read as' contraries:

(8) a. "I don't like the new boss."
   b. "I positively dislike the new boss.'
(9) *Negative-raising*
   a. "I don't believe he will show up."
   b. 'I believe he will not show up.'

Another wide class of Q2 inferences involves interpretations that maximise cohesiveness — anaphoric linkages, for example, It is well known that anaphoric linkages are made partly on the basis of encyclopedic knowledge, but there are also clear preference patterns, for example for local (proximal) coreference which can be demonstrated in texts, as illustrated below:

(10) Then the thief$_1$ asks the butler$_2$, say, and the butler$_2$ confirms that. He$_2$ says, 'Yes the superintendent has only just left,'

   (from Agatha Christie, Hercule Poirot's Christmas)

The general heuristic seems to be: do not postulate more entities than necessary, and link locally by preference.

   No doubt rather specific mechanisms are involved in each of these preferences, including the inferences to the stereotype, that we currently do not fully understand; but that there are such preferences — and not just calculations of speaker-meaning — seems rather clear. Gathering them together under the rubric of the Q2 heuristic is not simply a matter of convenience, for the inferences share certain crucial properties. First, they are inferences to *more specific* interpretations, where what is implicated is a subcase, a specific instantiation, of what is said. The inferences are positive and non-metalinguistic in character, unlike Q1 or (as we shall see) M inferences. They are default inferences not all inferences to the subcase have this character. They are tied to the use of unmarked, 'minimal' or non-prolix, semantically general expressions (or even the absence of them as in parataxis or zero anaphora). Note, for example, the following interpretative contrasts between minimal expressions (italicised in the (i) examples) and more marked expressions (italicised in the paired (ii) examples) that might be thought to paraphrase their content:

(11) a. (i) John pushed the button *and* the motor started.
     (ii) John pushed the button. *In addition*, the motor started.
   b. (i) The detective came into the room and *he* sat down.
     (ii) The detective came into the room and *the man* sat down.
   c. (i) I *don't like* garlic.
     (ii) I *have no liking* for garlic.
   d. (i) The book is *on* the desk.
     (ii) The book is *in contact mth the upper surface of the desk*.
   e. (i) *John's picture* won critical acclaim.
     (ii) *The picture of John* won critical acclaim.

In addition to these shared properties, Q2 inferences share similar projection properties, to be noted below.

Any kind of inference from a general description to the special subcase clearly must be strictly constrained: we make no inference from the assertion "John drives a small car" to 'John drives a Honda Civic' even if the probabilities are so. Indeed, as discussed above, "I saw an animal in the larder" suggests that I do not know what animal I saw. How then are Q2 inferences constrained? Partly they are constrained with respect to depth; and here the notion of stereotype needs explication — as Putnam pointed out, a stereotype has nothing to do with statistical tendencies, or even with shared veracities. Fierce gorillas, gentle cows, absent-minded professors are stereotypes for which there is little evidence or even shared belief. There is no such stereotype from small cars to Honda Civics, and the speaker knows the addressee knows that the speaker will not presume so. But male surgeons are another matter, and there are many parlour puzzles of the sort "The patient went to see the surgeon. She described the problem to him and she decided at once to operate on him". Inferences to the stereotype are thus not 'generalised' in the sense that they are independent of shared beliefs (as Q1 and M inferences largely arc, since they are essentially based on metalinguistic considerations), but they are 'generalised' in the sense that they follow a general principle — restrict the interpretation to what by consensus constitutes the stereotypical, central extensions.

More importantly perhaps, Q2 inferences are constrained by the other heuristics. Any Q1 inference incompatible with a Q2 inference always takes precedence. Any M inference from a marked expression likewise defeats a Q2 inference, in ways that will be explained. The result is that a Q2 inference is induced by a certain kind of expression, especially expressions that are themselves brief and colloquial. Like the following heuristic that bounds it, Q2 is thus iconic: minimal expressions invite stereotypical, rich interpretations.

Finally, we turn to the third heuristic introduced in (2) above ('Marked descriptions warn "marked situation"'), labelled M after Grice's maxim of Manner.[14] Now, we have already seen from examples in (11) that marked or more prolix expressions do not give rise to the Q2 inferences that would have arisen from their unmarked or brief counterparts. In fact, there is a systematic complementarity between unmarked expressions and their associated Q2 inferences compared to marked expressions and their M inferences.[15] The relevant sense of 'markedness' is very broad, covering formal prolixity, infrequent expressions or those of unusual formation — the M-prindple is again iconic: 'non-stereotypical expressions invite interpretations to non-stereotypieal extensions'. Take, for example, the following lexical doublets, and the sort of denotation they might suggest in some arbitrary utterance (the symbol + > should be read 'implicates, *ceteris paribus*'):[16]

(12) a. unmarked: *drink* Q2 +> 'alcoholic drink'
      marked: *beverage* M +> 'non-alcoholic drink'
   b. unmarked: *chair (man)* Q2 + > 'male chair person'
      marked: *chairperson* M + > 'female chair person'
   c. unmarked: *knife* Q2 +> 'kitchen-type knife'
      marked: *cutter* M + > 'not a normal knife'
   d. unmarked: *missile* Q2 + > 'rocket with warhead'

         marked: *projectile* Q2 + > 'missile other than rocket'

  e. unmarked: *letter* Q2 + > 'personal letter'

         marked: *missive, dispatch, epistle* + > 'not a personal letter'

  f. unmarked: *house* Q2 + > 'normal family house'

         marked: *residence* M + > 'grander than normal family house'

  g. unmarked: *rare* Q2 + > 'unusual and valuable'

         marked: *scarce* M + > 'in short supply'

Similarly for word formation: derivations tend to sort into two classes, the usual, colloquial with a specialised stereotypical extension, and the more unusual or prolix derivation picking up (often now by convention) the complementary interpretation (see Horn, 1989: 273ff., for discussion):

(13) a. unmarked: *informer* Q2 +> 'supplier of information against someone'

         marked: *informant* M +> 'supplier of information for someone'

    b. unmarked: *unnatural, unscientific* Q2 + > 'and bad'

         marked: *nan-natural, non-scieniific* M +> '(no special evaluation)'

    c. unmarked: *imprecisefimmoral,* Q2 + > 'the opposite of precise/moral' (i.e. the contrary reading)

         marked: *unprecisefnm-* or *amoral* M + > 'just not precise or not moral' (i.e. the contradictory reading)

There is also an opposition between simplex lexemes and derived forms which might be thought to have the same meaning and use (e.g. *sad* vs. *unhappy*, or *rude* vs. *impolite*, where the lexicalised form invariably seems to denote a more extreme property; again, see Horn 1989: 279f., also Kiparsky, 1983).

    These sorts of pragmatic principles explain how specific kinds of word form may acquire specialisations of meaning: they are principles that may explain historical changes and semantic shifts. By the same token, the synchronic analysis of current lexical content is sometimes of course not so clear.

    Rather clearer cases of the Q2 vs. M opposition may therefore be found in periphrastic alternatives to simple lexicalisattons. Thus periphrastic modals, causatives and double negations contrast with their simpler counterparts:

(14) a. "John could solve the problem" Q2 + > 'and he did'

b. "John had the ability to solve the problem" M + > 'but be didn't'

(15) a. "James stopped the car" Q2 + > 'in the normal way, by using the foot pedal'

b. "James caused the car to stop" M + > 'in a nonstereotypical way, e.g. by using the hand-brake'

(16) a. "Sue moved the car" Q2 +> 'bydriving it'

b. "Sue made the car move" M + > 'e.g. by pushing it'

(17) a. "It's possible he will recover" Q2 + > some definite probability p

b. "It's not impossible that he will recover" M + > some probability less than p

c. "The mail is reliable" Q2 + > 'to degree *n*'

d. "The mail is not unreliable" M + > 'to degree less than *n*'

Repetition and reduplication also serve to deflect interpretation from Q2-directed extensions:

(18) a. "He ate" Q2 + > 'He ate the normal meal.'

b. "He ate and ate" M + > 'He ate more than the normal meal.'

In many languages, reduplication plays an important quasi-derivational role, and it is notable how such reduplications tend to pick out, not the central or prototypical extensions of the unreduplicated form, but their complements, the peripheral or non-stereotypical extensions.[17]

These three heuristics are each responsible for large families of inferences, each of a characteristic type. In certain ways the principles are quite clearly antagonistic: they encourage inferences in opposite directions. Thus whereas Q2 invites inferences to the more specific subcase (along the lines of 'The speaker hasn't said what is obvious'), Q1 forbids the inference to the more informative interpretation (along the lines 'If the speaker didn't say it, he didn't mean it'). Similarly, M1 inferences are specified as the complement of Q2 inferences. Contradictory premises would be fatal to any deductive device, and problematic for any inferential system. They must therefore be blocked at source, or filtered by simple rule or procedure. In fact, both mechanisms seem to be involved. For example, many apparently potential Q1 inferences do not in fact arise because there are strict criteria of both form and content on the sets that give rise to them

(Atlas & Levinson, 1981; Levinson, 1987a: 407). In addition, there are simple priority rules of the kind; Q1 and M inferences take precedence over inconsistent Q2 inferences; Q1 inferences take precedence over inconsistent M inferences (Levinson, 1987a: 409). Within each genus there also seem to be priorities; thus clausal Q1 inferences cancel inconsistent scalar Q1 inferences (as noted and formalised in Gazdar, 1979). In short, there is a serious projection problem for generalised implicatures, but fortunately we already have some understanding of how the problem is resolved.[18]

5 Grammar and meaning

The mechanisms reviewed here — a set of three general heuristics that induce default inferences — have completely general application across the vocabulary of a language; but they may yield inferences that are particularly precise, specific and recurrent where small closed sets of lexemes or morphemes yield contrast sets of the right kind to induce Q1 implicatures. Such sets are typical of the 'grammatical' or 'functor' words. For example, as noted above, early Gricean analyses pointed out that the English sentential connectives form a Q1 entailment set *<and, or>*, so that an utterance of the form "p or q" will generally implicate 'not p and q', while "p and q", unbounded by a Q1 inference, will (where p and q describe events) Q2 implicate 'p and then q' and so on. Such an analysis allows us to hang on to the simple underlying invariant meaning of the connectives, while explaining all the additional variable readings.

Exactly the same kind of analysis can now be applied to any grammatically closed class of morphemes, and should yield the same kind of harvest; invariant core meanings supplemented by preferred interpretations. Take, for example, the definite/indefinite articles in English. Simple accounts of the kind 'introduce a new referent under description Y with *a Y* and a previously mentioned one under description X with *the X*' or 'Use *the X* to refer to a unique entity, *a Y* to refer to a non-unique entity' run afoul of multitudinous counter-examples, as shown by Hawkins (1978, 1991). For example, it is quite normal to introduce some entities with *the X*:

(19) a. I just met the Mayor.

   b. I'm late because I missed the train.

    c. There's something wrong with the clutch (in my ear).

    d. She adores the man she met in Paris.

and indefinite articles can be used for previously introduced referents:

(20) a. All the members of the jury met for many hours because a *single member* was recalcitrant.

     b. His arms and legs were damaged in the blast, and in the end he lost a leg.

while some unique entities are happily referred to with an indefinite article:

(21) a. England has *a Queen* and Spain *a King*.

     b. There is *a dog* in that car.

Hawkins (1991) points out that if we adopt an account in terms of GCIs most of these puzzles evaporate. The articles form a Q1 entailment contrast set *<the, a>*, such that *the* X entails uniqueness, while *a* Y only implicates non-uniqueness, which may thus evaporate in contexts like those immediately above. Hawkins argues that *the* X conventionally (i.e. non-defeasibly) implicates that there is a mutually salient set in which X is unique, while *a* Y Q2-implicales (i.e. defeasibly) that there is a mutually salient set to which Y belongs (hence "He lost a leg" suggests one of his own).

    There are of course many other closed sets of grammatical contrasts, often notorious for their semantic subtleties, that could benefit from a pragmatic analysis of this kind, for example, deictic adverbs or determiners, tense and aspect markers and prepositions.[19]

    Further inroads into 'grammatical meaning' may be possible. There has been much speculation about whether a pragmatic analysis might undercut the purely grammatical analysis of anaphoric dependencies typical of modern grammatical theory (Reinhart, 1983; Levinson, 1989, 1991; Huang, 1994), For example, we can think of the opposition between non-reflexive and reflexive pronouns as similar to that between indefinite and definite pronouns: wherever *him* and *himself* can contrast, for example in direct-object position, we have a Q1 scale of the kind *<himself, him>* such that use of *him* will implicate 'not himself' — rather than be grammatically stipulated as non-coreferential by Binding Condition B in the Government-Binding framework of Chomsky (1981). The advantage of the pragmatic account is that, since GCIs are only default inferences, it allows the possibility of coreference between subject and a nonreflexive pronominal object in unusual cases (such as *Only Felix₁ voted for him₁* — see Reinhart, 1983). Given Binding Condition A (which stipulates that reflexives must find their antecedents in certain positions), the other Binding Conditions (Binding Condition B governing the non-coreferential interpretation of non-reflexive pronouns in certain positions and Binding Condition C stipulating the non-coreferential interpretation of full lexical NPs) are regularities at least partially predicted by the system of heuristics here outlined.[20] In sketch form, consider the following patterns:

(22) a. John₁ likes himself₁.

     (stipulated by Binding Condition A)

   b. John₁ likes him₂.

     (Q1 inference from the non-use of *himself*— pattern often attributed to Binding B)

   c. John₁ told her that he₁ would come.

     (Q2 inference to coreference, unblocked by Q1 inference since *himself* cannot occur in this position)

   d. John₁ told her that the man₂ would come.

     (M inference to an interpretation contrastive with that of unmarked, simpler form in (c); pattern often attributed to Binding C)

This is not the place to pursue this analysis, which can be refined — and of course countered — in various ways (see Levinson, 1987a, 1991). The point to be made here is that even if we decide that in fact these anaphoric patterns are grammaticalised in English, the very possibility of a (perhaps incomplete) pragmatic analysis undercuts Chomsky's view that the patterns in question must be specified by native 'universal grammar' because they are abstract and unpredictable from usage patterns, and thus in effect unlearnable.

    The pragmatic point of view seems to be supported by the facts from languages (like many Austronesisn ones, Biblical Hebrew, old Germanic languages, some Australian languages) which do not exhibit reflexives at all. In these languages a sentence glossing 'John hit him' may have a reflexive or nonreflexive reading, with the latter the default. The default reading presumably arises (as a Q2 inference) from the stereotypical agentive schema, in which an agent acts on another entity (Farmer & Harnish, 1987). To block this disjoint reading, the pronoun is normally marked by an emphatic particle or affix to indicate by M inference that the complementary interpretation is intended. Elsewhere, outside the clause, the pronoun tends to pick up coreferential readings as in English. Thus we have in schematic gloss the following pattern:

(23) a. 'John$_1$ likes him$_2$.'
          Q2 inference to stereotypical action
      b. 'John$_1$ likes him EMPHATIC$_1$.'
          M inference to complement of (a)
      c. 'John$_1$ told her that he$_1$ would come.'
          Q2 inference to minimal domain of discourse
      d. 'John$_1$ told her that the man$_2$ would come.'
          M inference to complement of (c)

This pattern in fact suggests a general diachronic source for true reflexives in marked, emphatic forms of a normally disjoint pronoun. Certainly the history of English reflexives has normally been analysed this way (see visser, 1963: 420–39), and in languages with continuous and ancient written traditions, like Japanese, Tamil and Chinese, there seems to be evidence in the same direction (see Faltz, 1985, and references in Levinson, 1991), while a swifter development of the same kind can perhaps be observed in creoles (Carden & Stewart, 1987, 1988).

Again, we cannot pursue these issues here (see Levinson, 1991), but the general point is that there are languages which have no reflexives, and a corresponding freedom of anaphoric interpretation (in part because they lack the strong Q1 inferences that play off the opposition between reflexive and non-reflexive pronoun). Such languages would seem to be anomalous to the Government-Binding framework, but the patterns of interpretation seem rather well predicted by our heuristics or something like them (see Huang (1991, 1994) for a developed account along similar lines of the flexible patterns of interpretation in Chinese).

In short, patterns of preferred interpretation may play an important role in the relation between grammar and meaning: grammatically or lexically stipulated meanings tend to generate a set of further default interpretations from the use of related but distinct forms. These in turn can become conventionalised or grammatically stipulated, yielding yet further default inferences. Given these diachronic tendencies, the analyst may easily mistake a default inference for a lexically or grammatically stipulated meaning, and of course vice versa (mistaking a conventionalised exinference for a live one).

6 Conclusion

This essay has argued for a fresh perspective on linguistic communication, where more attention is given to preferred ways of 'putting things', or the use of favoured construtions for conveying specific messages.[21] Instead of a bifurcation between grammatically and lexically specified meaning and nonce speaker-meaning, we need to develop a three-tiered theory of communication in which utterance-type meaning has a special place. The theory of utterance-type meaning should be a theory of default interpretation. This level of meaning may exhibit some relatively tight universal constraints, because (or so I have suggested) it is based on a set of heuristics that are designed to overcome an intrinsic bottleneck in the speed of communication, our slow articulation rate. Because this level of meaning sits midway between grammar and lexicon on the one hand and speaker-meaning on the other, most analysts attempt to reduce it in one or the other direction. This is a mistake, because it is a level with distinct properties — default, defeasible inferences based on the comparison of alternative linguistic expressions and on the presumption of stereotypical situations, which interact in specific ways. In addition, because these systematic mechanisms are so closely related to grammatical and lexical processes, they constrain them and, over the course of language history, feed them.[22] It is thus quite unlikely that we will have an adequate synchronic or diachronic theory of grammar and lexicon until we have a much deeper understanding of the level of utterance-type meaning.

Notes

1   This paper is a sketch of issues treated in more depth in Levinson (forthcoming: ch. 1). A prior, spirited defence of the idea of three levels of meaning may be found in Atlas (1989: 3–4 and *passim*).

2   Lyons thus uses the term 'semantics' in a pretheoretical way to denote the full range of linguistic meaning; I will use the term in the narrower sense, opposed to pragmatics. I will, however, continue to use the term 'meaning' in the wide sense, not restricting it to coded morpheme- or sentence-meaning. For the larger field, the study of meaning in this wide sense, I will use the phrases 'the theory of meaning' or, where the wide range might not be clear, 'the theory of (linguistic) communication'.

3   Let us adopt the typographical conventions that utterances (or rather utterance-types) are indicated by double quotes, interpretations or glosses by single quotes, linguistic expressions or sentences by italics. We will also use the symbol + > for '(generally) conversationally implicates', so that "Some boys are naughty" Q2 + > 'not all boys are naughty' is read as 'The uttering of the sentence *Some boys are naughty* will by default inference under the Q2 heuristic have the additional interpretation "not all boys are naughty".'

4   Sperber & Wilson (1987: 748) wish to abolish GCIs because their proposed account of how implicatures are calculated cannot accommodate the phenomenon (see Levinson, 1987b, 1989). For other kinds of problems with the distinction, see Hirschberg (1985: 42).

5   For a representative attempt to semanticise the phenomena, see, for example, Barwise (1986); for representative attempts to reduce GCIs to nonce inferences, see, for example, Hobbs (1987), Kempson (1986) and of course Sperber & Wilson (1986).

6   For the comparative speed of pre-articulation vs. articulation processes, see Wheeldon & Levelt (forthcoming). For the ability to parse and comprehend speeded speech, sec Mchler *et al.* (1993).

7   The calculation, kindly made for me by Bill Poser, assumes 7 syllables or 17.5 segments per second, and 5.5 bits per phoneme.

8   I will not here discuss the nature of the inference itself. With regard to the nature of implicature generally, there are divergent opinions: Sperber & Wilson (1986) maintain it is deductive, Grice (1973) explicitly likened it to inductive inference, while Atlas & Levinson (1981) suggested that some inferences have an abductive character. GCIs, though, are by hypothesis default inferences, both nonmonotonic and presumptive. There is now a large family of formal models for such systems of inference; see, for example, the collection in Ginsberg (1987).

9 The labels Q1, Q2 and M, adopted here in deference to Grice's maxims, refer respectively to the Principles Q, I and M (or Q/M) in Levinson (1987a, 1991). Comparison with Horn's (1989) system will be aided if it is noted that his R is my Q2 (or I), while he conflates my Q1 and M under a single rubric Q. All three of my principles are conflated into one R (or Relevance principle) in Sperber & Wilson's (1986) proposal. The profusion of proposals indicates of course that this is now an active research area.

10 For much further detail see Horn (1972, 1985, 1989), Gazdar (1979), Atlas &. Levinson (1981) and Hirschberg(1985). As Gazdar points out, the inferences are epistemically modified, in ways that are crucial to any formalisation, but which we ignore here.

11 That this inference is defeasible, therefore pragmatic, is shown by reasoning of the kind *He has AIDS, If he has AIDS, his wife has too.*

12 See also Clark (1993: ch. 5) for the view that *contrast* is a pragmatic strategy for language learning.

13 I have been loose about distinguishing what is implicated from what is said-and-implicated, although there is no particular problem in doing this. Incidentally, the 'conditional perfection' kind of inference is independent of the indirect illocutionary force of such utterances — promises, threats, predictions but also plain conditional assertions tend all to carry the inference.

14 The reference is particularly to Grice's first and fourth submaxims of Manner: 'avoid obscurity' and 'be brief'.

15 This observation is due to Horn (1985), who points, however, to a long tradition of essentially similar analyses in the study of morphology.

16 For reasons of space I have not spelt out the contexts of use in which the doublets might reasonably be claimed to have the same semantic content; obviously such lexical doublets are likely to have some divergence in use other than those explained by our pragmatic principles here.

17 For example, in Tamil there is a productive reduplication with rule-bound phonological alteration: thus *paittlyam* 'madness' becomes *paittlyam-giyttlyam* 'almost but not quite real insanity'. Moravcsik (1978) gives a partial account of some of these patterns. She points out that there are very different predictions where reduplication is the only signal available for some interpretation (as it is for plurality or repetition in many languages) —

M implicatures after all only function by contrast to another simpler way of 'saying the same thing'.

18   Gazdar's (1979) formal system might be adapted to handle many aspects of the observable cancellation properties of the different kinds of inferences. In effect, we would set up an incremental augmentation of the contextual assumptions in a specific order: entailments > Q1-clausal > Q1-scalar > M > Q2, etc., such that inferences arc added in that order only if they are consistent with what is already taken for granted. But certain problems remain: there are, for example, constraints beyond consistency.

19   Spatial prepositions in English are an interesting case: we can set up Q1 contrast sets of the kind <*at, near*>, such that "The train is near the station" suggests 'The train is not (yet) at the station', and so on. Q2 inferences from prepositions like *in* to the relevant stereotypical relations have been illustrated above, while M contrasts like {*on, on top of*} are also easy to find.

20   Much more needs to be said of course about c-command constraints on interpretation; see Levinson (1987) and discussion there of Reinhart's (1983) proposals.

21   I borrow here the emphasis on 'favoured constructions' from John Haviland.

22   For many insights into pragmatic constraints on lexicalisation, and diachronic processes, see Gazdar & Pullum (1976), McCawley (1978) and Horn (1985, 1989).

References

Atlas, J. D. (1989) *Philosophy without Ambiguity: a Logico-linguistic Essay.* Oxford: Clarendon Press.

Atlas, J. D. & S. C. Levinson (1981) It-clefts, informativeness and logical form. In P. Cole (ed.) *Radical Pragmatics.* New York: Academic Press, 1–61.

Austin, J. L. (1962) *How to Do Things with Words,* Oxford: Clarendon Press.

Barwise, J. (1986) Conditionals and conditional information. In E. Traugott. A. Ter Meulen, J. Reilly & C. Ferguson (eds.) *On Conditionals,* Cambridge University Press, 21–54.

Barwise, J. & J. Perry (1983) *Situations and Attitudes,* Cambridge, MA: MIT Press.

Carden, G. & W. Stewart (1987) Mauritian creole reflexives — an alternative historical scenario. MS, University of British Columbia.

(1987) Binding theory, bioprogram and creolization: evidence from Haitian creole. *Journal of Pidgin and Creole Linguistics* 3: 1–67.

Chomsky, N. (1981) *Lectures on Government and Binding.* Dordrecht: Foris.

Clark, E. (1993) *The Lexicon in Acquisition,* Cambridge University Press.

Cohen, L. J. (1971) The logical particles of natural language. In Y. Bar-Hillel (ed.), *Pragmatics of Natural Language,* Dordrecht: Reidel, 50–68.

Cohen, P., J. Morgan & M. Pollack (1990) *Intentions in Communication,* Cambridge, MA: MIT Press.

Cole, P. (1978) *Syntax and Semantics,* vol. IX: *Pragmatics,* New York; Academic Press.

Cole, P. & J. Morgan (1975) *Syntax and Semantics,* vol. III: *Speech Acts,* New York: Academic Press.

Cruse. D.A. (1986) *Lexical Semantics,* Cambridge University Press.

Faltz, L.M. (1985) *Reflexivization: a Study in Universal Grammar,* New York: Garland.

Farmer, A. & M. Harnish (1987) Communicative reference with pronouns. In M. Papi & J. Verschueren (eds.) *The Pragmatic Perspective,* Amsterdam: Benjamins, 000–00.

Gazdar, G. (1979) *Pragmatics,* New York: Academic Press.

Gazdar, G. & G. Pullum (1976) Truth-functional connectives in natural language. In *Papers from the thirteenth regional meeting of the Chicago Linguistic Society,* Chicago Linguistic Society, 137–46.

Geiss, M. & A. Zwicky (1971) On invited inferences. *Linguistic Inquiry* 2: 561–5.

Ginsberg, M. L. (ed.) (1987) *Readings in Non-monotonic Reasoning.* Los Altos: Morgan Kaufman.

Grice, H.P. (1957) Meaning. *Philosophical Review* 67: 377–88.

(1973) Probability, defeasibility and mood operators. MS, paper delivered to the Texas Conference on performatives, presuppositions and implicatures, 1973.

(1975) Logic and conversation, In P. Cole & J. Morgan (eds.) *Syntax and Semantics,* vol. III: *Speech Acts,* New York: Academic Press, 41–58.

(1989) *Studies in the Way of Words,* Cambridge, MA: Harvard University Press.

Harnish. R. (1976) Logical form and implicature. In T. Bever, J. J. Katz, & T. Langendoen (eds.) *An Integrated Theory of Linguistic Ability,* New York:

Crowell, 313–92.

Hawkins, J. (1978) *Definiteness and Indefiniteness: a Study in Reference and Grammaticality Prediction,* London: Croom Helm.

(1991) On (in) definite articles: implicatures and (un)grammaticality prediction. *Journal of Linguistics* 27: 405–42.

Hirschberg, J. (1985) *A Theory of Scalar Implicature,* Moore School of Electrical Engineering, University of Pennsylvania, MS-CIS-85–56.

Hobbs, J. (1987) *Implicature and Definite Reference,* Stanford; CSLI Report 87–99.

Horn, L. (1972) *On the Semantic Properties of the Logical Operators in English, Indiana University Linguistics Club mimeo.*

(1985) Toward a new taxonomy for pragmatic inference; Q- and R-based implicature, In D. Schiffrin (ed.) *Meaning, Form and Use in Context,* Washington: Georgetown University Press, 11–42.

(1989) *A Natural History of Negation.* Chicago University Press.

Huang, Y. (1991) A neo-Gricean pragmatic theory of anaphora. *Journal of Linguistics* 27: 301–35.

(1994) *The Syntax and Pragmatics of Anaphora: a Study with Special Reference to Chinese.* Cambridge University Press.

Kempson, R. (1986) Ambiguity and the semantics-pragmatics distinction. In C. Travis (ed.) *Meaning and Interpretation.* Oxford: Blackwell, 77–104.

Kiparsky, P. (1983) Word-formation and the lexicon. In *Proceedings of the 1982 Mid-America Linguistics Conference.* Lawrence: University of Kansas, Department of Linguistics, 47–78.

Levinson, S.C. (1983) *Pragmatics,* Cambridge University Press.

(1987a) Pragmatics and the grammar of anaphora: a partial pragmatic reduction of Binding and Control phenomena. *Journal of Linguistics* 23: 379–434.

(1987b) Implicature explicated? Commentary. *Behavioural and Brain Sciences,* 10 (4): 722–3.

(1989) A review of Relevance. *Journal of Linguistics* 25: 455–72.

(1991) Pragmatic reduction of the Binding Conditions revisited. *Journal of Linguistics* 27: 107–61.

(1992) Activity types and language. In P. Drew & J. Heritage (eds.) *Talk at Work.* Cambridge University Press, 66–100.

(1995) Interactional biases in human thinking. In E. Goody (ed.) *Social*

Intelligence and Interaction. Cambridge University Press, 221–60.

(forthcoming) *Generalized Conversational Implicature,* Cambridge University Press.

Lyons, J. (1977) *Semantics,* 2 vols., Cambridge University Press.

McCawley, J. (1978) Conversational implicature and the lexicon. In P. Cole (ed.), *Syntax and Semantics,* vol. IX: *Pragmatics,* New York: Academic Press, 245–59.

Mehler, J., N. Sebastlan, G. Altmann, E. Dupoux, A. Christophe & C. Pallier (1993) Understanding compressed sentences: the role of rhythm and meaning. In P. Tallal, A. M. Galaburda, R. Llinas & C. von Euler (eds.) *Temporal Information Processing in the Nervous System. Annals of the New York Academy of Sciences,* 682: 272–82.

Moravcsik, E. (1978) Reduplicative constructions. In J. Greenberg (ed.) *Universals of Human Language,* vol. III: *Word Structure.* Stanford University Press, 297–335.

Morgan, J. (1978) Two types of convention in indirect speech acts. In P. Cole (ed.) *Syntax and Semantics.* vol. IX: *Pragmatics,* New York: Academic Press. 261–80.

Papi, M. & J. Verschueren (1987) *The Pragmatic Perspective,* Amsterdam: Benjamins.

Reinhart, T. (1983) *Anaphora and Semantic Interpretation,* London: Croom Helm.

Searle, J. (1975) Indirect speech acts. In P. Cole & J. Morgan (eds.) *Syntax and Semantics,* vol. III: *Speech Acts,* New York: Academic Press, 59–82.

Sperber, D. & D. Wilson (1986) *Relevance,* Oxford: Black well.

(1987) Response to Peer review of Sperber & Wilson: *Relevance. Brain and Behavioural Sciences,* 10 (4): 697–754.

Visser, F.T. (1963) *An Historical Syntax of the English Language,* Part I, Leiden: Brill.

Wheeldon, L. & W. J. M. Levelt (forthcoming) Monitoring the time course of phonological encoding. *Journal of Memory and Language.*

On the Projection Problem for Presuppositions

Irene Heim

The projection problem is the problem of predicting the presuppositions of complex sentences in a compositional fashion from the presuppositions of their parts. A simple illustration is provided by the following three sentences.

(1)　The king has a son.
(2)　The king's son is bald.
(3)　If the king has a son, the king's son is bald.

Restricting our attention to existence presuppositions resulting from definite descriptions, we observe that (3) inherits the presupposition that there is a king, which both of its constituents carry, but doesn't inherit the presupposition that the king has a son, which its right constituent carries. The solution I will advocate was in some sense already arrived at by Karttunen (1974), but its full potential was not realized at the time, perhaps because an appropriately sophisticated view of context change and its relation to truthconditional meaning was not available then.

1. COMPLEMENTARY STRENGTHS AND WEAKNESSES OF TWO RECENT THEORIES

I start with a brief comparison between two well-known recent treatments of the problem, one due to Gazdar (henceforth G.), the other to Karttunen and Peters (henceforth K. & P.).

1.1 Explanation vs. Mere Description

G.'s strongest objection to K.&P.'s theory is that it merely describes the projection facts instead of explaining them. Recall what we just observed about (3). To predict this observation, K.&P. appeal to the assumption that the grammar of English supplies three pieces of information for each lexical item: The first piece pertains to the item's purely truthconditional content. For the word "if," let's say this is the information that "if" is material implication.[1] The second piece specifies what the item contributes in the way of presuppositions. E.g., for the word "the," this includes at least the information that "the" contributes the presupposition that the noun it combines with has a non-empty extension. (For "if," we presumably have the information that it contributes nothing.) The third piece of information becomes relevant only for items that are functors rather than arguments, and it concerns the item's permeability for the presuppositions of its arguments. E.g., for "if" (a functor taking two propositional arguments), this is the information that "if" lets through the full presupposition of its left argument, as well as as much of the presupposition of its right argument as doesn't follow from the left argument. In other words:

(4)   If A has p as its truthconditional content and p' as its presupposition, and B has content q and presupposition q', then the presupposition of "If A. B" is p' & (p → q').

Let's refer to these three pieces of information as the "content property," "presupposition property," and "heritage property" of the item in question. G.'s point of criticism is that the K.&P.-theory treats these three properties as mutually independent. None of them is derived from the other two. The theory thus implies — implausibly — that someone who learns the word "if" has to learn not only which truthfunction it denotes and that it contributes no presupposition, but moreover that it has the heritage property specified in (4). It also implies that there could well be a lexical item — presumably not attested as yet — whose content and presupposition properties are identical to those of "if," while its heritage property is different.[2] We have to agree with G. that a more explanatory theory would not simply stipulate (4) as a lexical idiosyncrasy of "if," but would somehow derive it on the basis of general principles and the other semantic properties of "if."

G. further claims that his own theory is explanatory in just this respect. While he, too, takes every basic expression to be lexically specified for a content and a presupposition property, he manages to get away without heritage properties. In their stead, he invokes a general and quite simple theory of how utterances change the context in which they occur. In the case of (3), for instance, G. assumes that one of the existence presuppositions of the consequent gets cancelled by a conflicting conversational implicature of (3): (3) implicates that, for all the speaker knows, the king may not have a son, which is not consistent with a presupposition to the effect that the king must have a son. The cancellation that ensues is dictated by a completely general strategy of maintaining consistency during context change; it does not depend upon a heritage property or other idiosyncratic property of "if."

1.2 Differing Predictions

It has been observed[3] that G. systematically makes inadequate predictions for examples of the following two types.

(5)　If John has children, then Mary will not like his twins.
(6)　If John has twins, then Mary will not like his children.

Intuitively, (6) as a whole presupposes nothing, in particular not that John has children. (5), by contrast, is slightly strange, at least out of context. It somehow suggests that it is a matter of course that someone with children will have twins among them. K.&P. predict just these judgments. But G. unfortunately predicts the opposite, i.e., that (5) presupposes nothing while (6) carries a substantial presupposition, viz. that John has children. These examples suggest to me that there is something fundamentally wrong with G.'s idea that presupposition projection in conditionals is a matter of cancellation.

The literature also contains a battery of examples designed to show that G.'s predictions are superior to those of K.&P. One group of such examples is supposed to discredit K.&P.'s assumption that conditionals presuppose the conditional p → q' (cf. (4) above) rather than q' simpliciter. I agree with Soames (1982) that none of these examples are convincing. The remaining

401

groups of genuine counterexamples to K.&P. are disjunctions whose disjuncts carry contradictory presuppositions (e.g., "He either just stopped or just started smoking.") and conditionals in which a presupposition of the antecedent fails to survive (e.g., "If I later realize I haven't told the truth, I will tell you.").

1.3 Subsentential Constituents and Quantification

In computing the presuppositions of sentences from the presuppositions of their parts, one must eventually attend to parts that are not complete sentences themselves. This presents no difficulty to K.&P., since their theory assigns presuppositions to expressions of any syntactic category and semantic type and employs projection rules above and below the sentence level that are not different in kind. G. remains silent about presupposition projection below the sentence level, and it is not obvious how he would handle it. Presumably, nonsentential phrases don't have presuppositions that are propositions; in the extended sense that they have any presuppositions at all, those are of other semantic types. But then G.'s mechanism of context change is not applicable to them: presuppositions that are not propositions are not the sort of thing that can get added to a context, at least not with contexts construed as sets of propositions. Given that G.'s main point is that presupposition projection is an epiphenomenon of the laws governing context change, his solution to the projection problem remains incomplete until this issue is addressed.

Quantified sentences provide a particularly interesting illustration of the task that G. faces here. Consider (7).

(7)   Every nation$_i$ cherishes its$_i$ king.

The parts of (7), at the relevant level of analysis (logical form), are something like the following three:

(8)   every x_i, x_i (is a) nation, x_i cherishes x_i's king

The third part of (8) contains the definite description "x_i's king," which one might want to say carries the existence presupposition expressed in (9).

(9)　x_i has a king

But whatever (9) expresses is not a proposition: the free variable in it makes it incomplete. Would G. say that (9) expresses a potential presupposition of a part of (7) and hence of (7) as a whole? If so, what would it mean for this presupposition to get added to the context?

2. THE CONCEPTUAL PRIORITY OF CONTEXT CHANGE

The following is an attempt to combine the descriptive coverage of the K.&P. -theory with the explanatory adequacy demanded by G.

2.1 Admittance Conditions

We start by reformulating the heritage property of "if," currently stated as in (4). As Karttunen (1974) has shown, a stipulation like (4) is reducible to a stipulation like (10) combined with a general principle along the lines of (11).

(10)　If "If A, B" is uttered in context c, then c is the local context for A, and c + A (read: "c incremented by A") is the local context for B.

(11)　A context c admits a sentence S just in case each of the constituent sentences of S is admitted by the corresponding local context.

A context is here construed more or less like in G.'s theory, i.e., as a set of propositions, or more simply, as a proposition, namely that proposition which is the conjunction of all the elements of the set. (See e.g., Stalnaker (1979).) (11) appeals to a relation of "admittance" which is to hold between contexts and sentences. This relation is taken to be inter-definable with the relation "presuppose" that relates sentences to the propositions they presuppose, under the following equivalence:

(12)　S presupposes p iff all contexts that admit S entail p.

Given their interdefinability, either relation can be used in the formulation and treatment of the projection problem. Following Karttunen (1974), we approach

403

the problem in terms of the "admit" relation: How do the admittance conditions of a complex sentence derive from the admittance conditions of its parts? E.g., we want to predict that for a context c to admit (3), c has to entail that there is a king, but needn't entail that the king has a son. (10) in conjunction with (11) tells us that c will admit (3) just in case (i) c admits (1), and (ii) c + (1) admits (2). Given that we already know the admittance conditions for (1) and (2), this amounts to the following: (i) c has to entail that there is a king, and (ii) c conjoined with the proposition that the king has a son has to entail that there is a king and he has a son. Requirement (ii) will hold automatically whenever (i) does, so the admittance condition for sentence (3) is merely (i). We have now shown that (10) together with (11) can do the job of the previous stipulation (4).

2.2 Context Change Potentials

The general principle (11) need not worry us any further, but (10) is still a stipulation specifically about "if" and is apparently independent of that item's content and presupposition properties. G.'s objection, as reported in 1.1 above, therefore still applies. Next I will show that (10) is actually nothing but an incomplete specification of what I call the "context change potential" (henceforth CCP) of "if. " I will suggest that, while the CCP of "if' cannot be derived from its other properties, one *can* derive the content property from the CCP. More generally, the truthconditional aspect of the meaning of any expression is predictable on the basis of its CCP. Since the CCP also determines the heritage property, I can then answer G.'s objection: A two-fold lexical specification of each item, in terms of CCP and presupposition property, can replace the three-fold specification that appeared to be needed in the K.&P.-theory.

What are CCPs? Intuitively, they are instructions specifying certain operations of context change. The CCP of "It is raining," for instance, is the instruction to conjoin the current context with the proposition that it is raining. (If we construe propositions as sets of possible worlds, as we will here, "conjoin" means "intersect.") The CCPs of complex sentences can be given compositionally on the basis of the CCPs of their constituents. We will illustrate this shortly. We will always write "c + S" to designate the result of executing the CCP of sentence S on context c.

There is an intimate connection between the CCP of a sentence and its truthconditional content:

(13) Suppose c is true (in w) and c admits S. Then S is true (in w) with respect to c iff c + S is true (in w).

(Informally: To be a true sentence is to keep the context true.) Something like (13) has occasionally been used to define CCP in terms of truthconditional content (see e.g., Stalnaker (1979)). I want to exploit it for the opposite purpose: to give an — albeit only partial — definition of truth of a sentence in terms of the CCP of that sentence. The partiality results from the fact that (13) says nothing about the truth of S when c is false. I believe, without offering justification here,[4] that (13) is nevertheless good enough as a truth-definition for sentences. If this is so, then a compositional assignment of CCPs to the sentences of a language can fully replace a compositional assignment of truthconditions of the sort normally envisaged by semanticists, without any loss of empirical coverage.

I indicated that, by specifying the CCP of an expression, the need for a separate specification of its heritage property is obviated. Suppose, e.g., the CCP of "if" is as described in (14).

(14) c + If A, B = c\(c + A\c + A + B)

("M\N" stands for the intersection of M with the complement of N, as usual.) Suppose further, as seems natural, that admittance conditions are conditions on the definedness of the CCP, i.e., that c + S is defined iff c admits S. It is apparent from (14) that c + If A, B is only defined when both c + A and c + A + B are. Under our assumptions, this means that c admits "If A, B" only if c admits A and c + A admits B. In this way, the heritage property of "if" falls out from its CCP (14).

To give another example: If (15) describes the CCP of "not," we can read off immediately that c will admit "Not S" only if it admits S.

(15) c + Not S = c\c + S

In other words, (15) determines that negation is a "hole" in the sense of Karttunen (1973).

Of course, (14) and (15) are motivated independently of the heritage properties of "if" and "not." They are just the CCPs that one would be led to assume if one's only goal were to arrive via (13) at the standard truthconditions for "if"- and "not"-sentences. (The reader should convince herself of this.) So it is fair to say that we have reduced two seemingly independent semantic properties, the content and the heritage property, to just one, the CCP. The current theory no longer implies that content and heritage properties will vary independently across lexical items, or that they need be learned separately, and it is hence no less explanatory than G.'s.

2.3 Accommodation

Suppose S is uttered in a context c which doesn't admit it. We have said that this makes c + S undefined. What does that mean in practice? Does it mean that context change simply comes to a halt at this point and communication breaks down? That would be an unrealistic assumption. In real-life conversations, people deal with this kind of situation effortlessly: They simply amend the context c to a slightly richer context c', one which admits S and is otherwise like c, and then proceed to compute c' + S instead of c + S. Following Lewis (1979), I call this adjustment "accommodation." Accommodation accounts for the common observation that utterances can convey their presuppositions as new information.

The informal characterization of accommodation that I just gave contains a hidden ambiguity, which comes to light when we look at an example: Suppose S presupposes p, and "Not S" is uttered in a context c which fails to entail p, hence doesn't admit "Not S." Some sort of accommodation is called for. One can imagine two quite different ways in which it might occur: (A) The "global" option: Amend c to c & p and, instead of c + Not S, calculate c & p + Not S. Following (15), you will end up with c & p\c & p + S. (B) The "local" option: Amend c to c & p so that you can calculate c & p + S instead of c + S. Then substitute the result of this calculation in the place of "c + S" in (15), so that you end up with c\c & p + S. A is more like pretending that c & p obtained instead of c all along (hence the word "global"). B is rather like adjusting the context only for the immediate purpose of evaluating the constituent sentence S (hence "local"). The results are obviously different, so which way do people proceed in real life? I suggest that the global option is strongly preferred, but the local option is also available in certain circumstances that make it unavoidable. Consider a concrete example.

(16) The king of France didn't come,

uttered in a context which is compatible with France having no king. By the global option, we end up with a context that entails that France has a king; this is presumably how we tend to read (16) in isolation. Under the local option, the resulting context will only entail that either France has no king or he didn't come. We will read (16) this way if we are for some reason discouraged from assuming France to have a king, e.g., if the speaker continues (16) with "because France doesn't have a king." Note that by stipulating a *ceteris paribus* preference for global over local accommodation, we recapture the effect of G.'s assumption that presupposition cancellation occurs only under the threat of inconsistency.[5]

I am here stopping far short of a general and precise formulation of the laws governing accommodation and their interaction with the instructions contained in the CCPs.

3. THE INTERPRETATION OF VARIABLES

While the theory I have sketched builds in many ways on that of K.&P., it also shares a problematic feature with G.'s: It treats presupposition projection as a side-effect of the rules governing context change. It is therefore not straightforwardly applicable below the level of complete sentences (cf. 1.3). Like G., I am faced with the difficulty of assigning CCPs to constituent sentences with variables free in them, i.e., to expressions that don't express propositions.

3.1 Contexts as Sets of Sequence-World-Pairs

We can solve our problem if we abandon the identification of contexts with propositions. The information accumulated in a context need not all be propositional; much of it is rather like information as one finds it represented in a card file, i.e., a collection of cards with a (more or less informative) description [on] each card. Depending on the facts, such a file may be true or false: true if there is at least one collection of individuals that can be lined up with the cards so that each individual fits the description on the corresponding card; false

407

otherwise. If contexts are like files, then context changes in response to utterances are like updating operations: additions of further cards and/or additions of further entries on already established cards. This metaphor is naturally applicable to utterances containing variables: The context change induced by, say, "x_7 is a nation" consists of writing the entry "is a nation" onto card number 7, where this card is either created on the occasion or found among the already established cards, as the case may be.[6]

Technically, files and, I suggest, contexts can be identified with properties of sequences of individuals, i.e., with sets of pairs $<g, w>$, where g is a sequence of individuals (a function from the set of natural numbers into the domain of individuals), and w is a world. Since each such set of pairs determines uniquely a proposition:

(17) Let c be a set of sequence-world-pairs. Then the proposition determined by c is {w: for some g, $<g,w> \in c$}.

we don't give up any of the advantages of identifying contexts with propositions when we identify them with properties of sequences instead. In particular, we can still evaluate contexts in terms of truth and falsity, as shown in (18), and can retain the truth definition for sentence (13) which relies on that.

(18) c is true in w iff for some g, $<g, w> \in c$.

We can now assign CCPs to sentences with free variables, e.g., to sentence (9):

(19) c + (9) = c $\cap$ {$<g, w>$: g(i) has a king in w}

(As for the CCPs for "if" and "not" that I formulated earlier, (14) and (15) carry over just as they stand into the new framework.) We can also formulate admittance conditions for sentences with free variables. E.g., in order to admit (20):

(20) x_i cherishes x_i's king,

a context must, informally speaking, "entail that x_i has a king." By this I mean that it has to be a context c such that, for every $\langle g, w \rangle \in c$, $g(i)$ has a king in w.

3.2 Presuppositions of Quantified Sentences

So how are we going to predict the presuppositions of a sentence like (7)? We have almost everything we need, except for the CCP of "every." Considering the truthconditions to be captured, the following formulation suggests itself.

(21) $c + \text{Every } x_i, A, B = \{\langle g, w \rangle \in c$ for every a, if $\langle g^i/a, w \rangle \in c + A$, then $(g^i/a, w) \in c + A + B\}$

("g^i/a" stands for the sequence that is like g, except that $g^i/a(i) = a$.) We need a further stipulation to ensure that (21) always yields adequate truthconditions: x_i must somehow be required to be a "new" variable at the time when "every x_i" is uttered. In terms of the file metaphor, we want to require that the file which obtains prior to the utterance doesn't yet contain a card number i, so that a fresh card will be set up when x_i is encountered in the evaluation of A. More technically, the stipulation we need is this:

(22) For any two sequences g and g' that differ at most in their i-th member, and for any world w: $\langle g, w \rangle \in c$ iff $\langle g', w \rangle \in c$.

Given (22), (21) will derive the intended truthconditions for a sentence like (7), but not without (22). (The reader should verify this for himself by computing c + (8) for a choice of c that violates (22), e.g., c = $\{\langle g, w \rangle$: g(i) = France$\}$.) For our present purposes, we take (22) to be a lexical property of "every," i.e., part of its presupposition property. In other words, we stipulate that no context that violates (22) will admit a sentence of the form "Every x_i, A, B."[7]

Back to the issue of presupposition projection in "every"-sentences. (21) determines that c + "Every x_i, A, B" can only be defined if c + A and c + A + B are. Applied to (8), this means that c will not admit (8) unless (i) c admits "x_i is a nation," and (ii) c + "x_i is a nation" admits (20). We suppose (i) to be trivially satisfied. As for (ii), we determined in the previous section that c + "x_i is a nation" = c $\cap$ $\{\langle g, w \rangle$: g(i) is a nation in w$\}$, and furthermore that this will admit (20) just in case the following entailment holds:

(ii)   For every <g, w> $\in$ c $\cap$ {<g, w>: g(i) is a nation in w}, g(i) has a king in w.

Now suppose that in every world in which c is true, every nation has a king. This is clearly a sufficient condition for (ii) to hold. It turns out that it is also a necessary condition; one can prove this by exploiting (22). We therefore conclude that a context that is to admit (8) must entail that every nation has a king. In other words: (7) presupposes that every nation has a king. The reasoning by which we arrived at this prediction may strike you as somewhat complicated. But bear in mind that all the machinery we had to invoke (in particular (21) and (22)) was needed independently to predict the truthconditions.

For the type of example discussed so far, i.e., universally quantified sentences with the presupposition-inducing element (here: a definite description) in the "consequent" (i.e., in the B-part of "Every x_i A, B"), our predictions coincide with those of Karttunen and Peters (1979): If B presupposes X, "Every x_i, A, B" presupposes "Every x_i, A, X." But when the presupposition-inducing element is in the "antecedent," i.e., in A, as in (23), my claims differ from theirs.

(23) Everyone who serves his king will be rewarded.

According to K.&P. (1979), (23) presupposes nothing. I am committed, by the assumptions I have introduced so far, to the claim that (23) — normally, at any rate — presupposes that everyone has a king. I say "normally," because the prediction stands only to the extent that there is no local accommodation. As we observed in connection with (16), local accommodation may produce what looks like presupposition cancellation. Limitations of space prevent me from exploring the implications this might have for cases like (23). I can only hope the reader will agree with my impression that a theory which assigns a universal presupposition to (23) as the unmarked case is tolerably close to the actual facts, or at least as close as K.&P.'s analysis or any other simple generalization that comes to mind.

What about quantifiers other than universal? Concerning "no," we find conflicting factual claims in the literature. According to Cooper (1983), (24) should presuppose that every nation (in the relevant domain of discourse) has a king; for Lerner & Zimmermann (1981), it presupposes merely that some nation does.

(24) No nation cherishes its king.

Here as elsewhere, the theory I am advocating gives me no choice: Once I have assigned "no" a CCP that will take care of its truthconditional content, it turns out that I have to side with Cooper. But again, this applies only for the "ordinary" cases which don't involve any local accommodation. When the latter is brought into play, the universal presupposition will appear to be weakened in various ways or even cancelled.

3.3 Indefinites

Karttunen and Peters (1979) point out a difficulty with sentences like (25).

(25) A fat man was pushing his bicycle.

Their rules assign to (25) a presupposition that they admit is too weak: that some fat man had a bicycle. On the other hand, a universal presupposition that every fat man had a bicycle would be too strong. What one would like to predict is, vaguely speaking, a presupposition to the effect that the same fat man that verifies the content of (25) had a bicycle. But it is neither clear what exactly that means nor how it could be worked into K.&P.'s theory.[8]

I have argued elsewhere[9] that indefinites are not quantifying. The logical form of (25) thus lacks the part corresponding to "every x_i" in (8):

(26) x_i (was a) fat man, x_i was pushing x_i's bicycle

(26) is just a sequence of two open sentences with free occurrences of x_i, which are interpreted as though conjoined by "and." The CCP of (26) is simply:

(27) $c + (26) = (c + x_i$ was a fat man$) + x_i$ was pushing x_i's bike

This gives adequate truthconditions — provided that x_i is a new variable. We therefore stipulate that a context must conform to (22) if it is to admit a sentence containing an indefinite indexed i.

Now what about presupposition projection? (27) shows that for c to

411

admit (26), c + "x_i was a fat man" must entail that x_i had a bicycle. It turns out that, due to (22), this entailment will hold just in case every fat man in any world compatible with c had a bicycle. So we are prima facie committed to an unintuitively strong universal presupposition for (25).

I suggest that our actual intuitions are accounted for by the ready availability of a certain kind of accommodation in the evaluation of indefinite sentences. In the case of (25), when c fails to entail that every fat man had a bicycle, the following appears to happen: First, c + "x_i is a fat man" is computed, call the result of this c'. Then c' is found not to admit "x_i was pushing x_i's bicycle." So it is amended to c", which presumably is c' & x_i has a bicycle. From there, c" + "x_i was pushing x_i's bicycle" is calculated. The net result is a context which entails that x_i was a fat man, had a bicycle, and was pushing it, but entails nothing about fat men having bicycles in general.

This sort of accommodation seems to happen with the ease typical of global, rather than local, accommodation. In fact, it *is* global accommodation if we take the defining feature of globality to be that the accommodated piece of information (here that x_i had a bicycle) remains in the context *for good*. (Notice that this criterion distinguishes appropriately between the global and local accommodation options as exemplified above for example (16).) In other words, I speculate that the relative ease with which a missing presupposition is accommodated in the midst of evaluating an indefinite sentence can be subsumed under the general observation that global accommodation is more common than local accommodation. Incidentally, this speculation relies crucially on the non-quantificational analysis of indefinites: only because x_i remains free in (26) does the information that x_i had a bicycle end up being entailed by the context ever after.

4. FINAL REMARK

Many non-trivial aspects of presupposition projection could not even be alluded in this paper, e.g., the heritage properties of "or," modal operators, and propositional attitude verbs. As for the latter two, I expect that the present approach will make reasonable predictions when combined with a treatment of modality in terms of quantification over possible worlds.[10] But I don't expect my readers to take this on faith.

ACKNOWLEDGMENTS

This work is supported by the Center for Cognitive Science of M.I.T. under a grant from the Sloan Foundation's particular program in Cognitive Science. I thank Stanley Peters, Lauri Karttunen, Robin Cooper, and Thomas "Ede" Zimmermann for illuminating conversations on the material.

Notes

1 I don't believe that, but it doesn't matter here.
2 G.'s point is not affected by the fact that Karttunen and Peters (1979) use a "heritage function" which assigns heritage properties to pairs consisting of the content and presupposition properties. For notice that this function is defined point by point, not as a general procedure.
3 Peters, personal communication. G.'s problem with (6) is also pointed out by Soames (1982), whose proposal, however, continues to be affected by the problem with (5).
4 I discuss this point somewhat further in Heim (1982).
5 The examples mentioned at the end of section 1.2 may also be amenable to a treatment in terms of local accommodation.
6 For a more explicit motivation of the file metaphor and the corresponding technical concepts see Heim (1983).
7 This stipulation is derived from the indefiniteness of quantifying NPs in Heim (1982) and (1983).
8 A solution very different from the one sketched below is developed in Cooper (1983).
9 See Heim (1982) and (1983) for details.
10 E.g. along the lines of Kratzer (1981).

References

Cooper, R. (1983), *Quantification and Syntactic Theory*. Dordrecht: Reidel.
Heim, I. (1982). "The Semantics of Definite and Indefinite Noun Phrases." Ph.D. diss., University of Massachusetts.
Heim, I. (1983). "File Change Semantics and the Familiarity Theory of

Definiteness." In A. von Stechow, R. Bauerle, and C. Schwarze (eds.), *Meaning, Use and Interpretation*. Berlin: W. de Gruyter.

Karttunen, L. (1973). "Presuppositions of Compound Sentences." *Linguistic Inquiry* 4:169–193.

Karttunen, L. (1974). "Presupposition and Linguistic Context." *Theoretical Linguistics* 1:181–194. [Reprinted in this volume. Chapter 24]

Karttunen, L., and S. Peters (1979). "Conventional Implicature." In Ch.-K. Oh and D. Dinneen (eds.), *Syntax and Semantics*. Vol. 11: *Presupposition*. New York: Academic Press.

Kratzer, A. (1981). "The Notional Category of Modality." In H. Riesser and J. Eikmeyer (eds.), *Words, Worlds and Contexts*. Berlin: W. de Gruyter.

Lewis. D. (1979). "Scorekeeping in a Language Game." In R. Bauerle, V. Egli, and A. von Stechow (eds.), *Semantics from Different Points of View*. Berlin: Springer-Verlag. [Reprinted in the volume, Chapter 25]

Lerner, J., and T. Zimmermann (1981). "Mehrdimensionale Semantik: Die Prasupposition and die Kontex-tabhangigkeit von 'nur.'" Working paper 50, SFB 99.

Soames, S. (1982). "How Presuppositions Are Inherited: A Solution to the Projection Problem." *Linguistic Inquiry* 13: 483–545.

Stalnaker, R. (1979). "Assertion." In P. Cole (ed.), *Syntax and Semantics*. Vol. 9: *Pragmatics*. New York: Academic Press. [Reprinted in this volume. Chapter 17]

外
教
社
学
术
阅
读
文
库
——
语
义
学
经
典
论
文
选
读

第四部分：
认知语义学

导 读

认知语义学以体验哲学为基础，主要探讨语言与身体经验、认知模式、知识结构等方面的关系。原型理论、隐喻和转喻理论、框架语义学理论以及以用法为基础的理论模型都是认知语义研究的主要组成部分。下面介绍的五篇文章在上述理论的发展中均起到了重要作用。

海拉茨（D. Geeraerts）的《原型理论的前景与问题》（Prospects and Problems of Prototype Theory）一文在对原型理论的背景进行介绍的基础上，主要致力于阐明两个问题：1）"原型性"本身就是原型概念；2）"原型理论"也是原型概念。文末作者还指出学者们在未来对范畴结构的原型性研究中应更多关注其认识性（epistemological）和哲学性（philosophical）的方面。本文的内容主要分为以下三部分：

1）语言学领域内的原型理论研究

本节首先介绍了原型理论产生的背景。该理论起源于20世纪70年代中期，是由美国加州大学伯克利分校心理学家罗施（Rosch）在对范畴的内部结构进行实验研究后提出的。该理论经提出后朝两个方向发展：一是信息处理心理学领域的研究，为概念的储存和运作提供形式模型；二是20世纪80年代早期语言学领域的研究，本文主要对后者进行探讨。

原型理论的主要观点和研究方法同在转换生成语法中风行的语义成分分析模型是对立的。然而原型理论反对的并不是成分分析这种方法。因为不借助某种形式的成分分解法就无法实现语义描述。成分分析法作为词义的描述和对比工具，仍旧是有价值的。原型理论之所以反对成分分析模型，原因有二：1）同经典理论一样，成分分析模型中的词汇概念也是通过一系列特定的属性（attributes）集合来界定的，而原型理论则认为这些充分必要条件并没有存在的必要；2）新结构主义成分分析模型认为自然语言有自主的语义结构，独立于人类其他认知能力，并不考虑百科知识的影响；而原型理论则认为这种自主的语义结构在自然语言中是不存在的，意义的研究不能与个体具有的百科知识分开。由于预设了纯语言的语义结构的存在，结构主义和新结构主义语义学区分了语义知识和百科知识。原型理论主张将此区分最小化，理由是：语言的范畴化属于人类认知能力的一种，因此应该将它与其他认知能力联系起来。至此可看出，原型理论与成分分析法的主要区别在于，前者认为范畴结构不应由充分必要条件来定义，而且应采用跨领域研究方法（interdisciplinary methodology）以借鉴其他认知科学的相关成果。

随后，本节从对语义理论的需求和原型理论自身的优势两方面分析了该理论发展为理想的语义理论的原因：1）需求背景：20世纪80年代，生成语法研究的发展使语义研究的兴趣高涨起来，然而对语义的研究并不充分——生成语法更倾向于句法自治，语义所起的作用相当微弱；而蒙太古语法的形式语义研究仅局限于句子意义层面，无法满足自然语言范畴的内部结构的研究需求。2）原型理论自身的优势。理想的语言理论具有四大重要特性：描写充分性、解释深入性、能产性和形式化。原型理论除了在形式化方面稍逊成分分析模型外，在其他三个方面均具有很强的优势，这表现在：a.该理论解决了很多被结构语义学忽视的问题，如词语范畴边界的模糊性、范畴成员典型性等级的存在、词义的灵活性和动态性以及词义变化中所涉及的隐喻和转喻等。此外，原型理论还促进了词语多义性模式的建立，并使得我们关于等级性（gradedness）、模糊性（fuzziness）、灵活性和词义的聚合性（clustering of senses）的直觉得到了关注；b.原型理论具有很强的扩展性：该理论关于词类结构的观点不仅可以扩展到词汇研究的其他方面，而且可以扩展到语言研究的其他层面如语音学、形态学、句法学、历史语言学、标记理论和理论词典学。这些扩展使原型理论成为认知语言学的基础理论之一，以解释语言结构各层面上语言同其他认知能力的互动；c.原型理论的解释较为深入，这表现在其概括性的特点和跨学科的性质。该理论将语言学与其他学科的研究成果紧密结合在起，这一点在认知科学横跨心理学、神经科学和人工智能等学科的背景下更为重要。

2）原型理论存在的问题一："原型性"本身也是原型概念

然而，原型理论本身也存在着不少问题。首先是对"原型性"的认识问题。作者借用了波斯纳冉（Posner）（1986）的话，声明"原型性"本身就是一个原型概念。这一点是通过对原型性的四个特征的分析表现出来的。这四个特征包括：
1）原型范畴不能通过一系列的充分必要条件来界定；
2）范畴成员之间具有互相重叠的属性组合，即各成员都享有部分共同属性，形成家族相似性；
3）成员之间的地位不是平等的，成员资格和代表性都具有程度之分；
4）原型范畴的边界是模糊的。

针对上述四种特征，作者指出：

1）除上述特征外，还存在着界定原型性的其他特征，包括：a. 与概念对应的世界有关的认识性特征（epistemological features），由于原型理论本质上是"体验性"的，因此原型概念除了具备结构特征外，还应具备知识性特征；b. 可以由上述四类特征来进行解释的特征，因而没有单列出来，如原型范畴的灵活性。

2）上述四类特征系统性地在外延和内涵（extensionally and intensionally）两个层面上相互关联：成员在结构分量上的不平等性在外延层面上体现为代表性（representativeness）程度的不同，在内涵层面上体现为包含较多重叠意义的含义更具有中心性；成员的灵活性和模糊性在外延层面上体现为范畴间不存在明确的界限，在内涵层面上体现为不存在范畴界定的充分必要条件。

3）上述四个特征之间虽然具有循环性关联（circular links），但它们在某范畴中并不一定会同时共现。这一点是本节论述中最重要的部分。作者通过对bird, red, odd number, vers这四个范畴的分析，对这一特点进行了说明：bird范畴只具备前三项特征，即非充要条件界定、意义重合和典型性程度特征；vers只具备后三项特征，即意义重合、典型性程度和边界模糊性特征；red只具备后两项特征，即典型性程度和边界模糊性特征；而odd number只具备第三项特征，即典型性程度特征。通过这几类范畴特征的比较可看出，他们之间也存在着"原型性"和"家族相似性"特点。因此，原型性不仅存在于范畴内的各成员之间，还存在于各范畴之间，这说明"原型概念"本身也具有边界模糊性。

由此，在对原型性的真正含义的探索上，作者提出"原型"这一概念具有很强的灵活性。这表现在：1）"原型"概念适用的范围很广，通过转喻和相似性相连的一系列现象都可以囊括进来，包括概念的结构性特征、概念本身甚至原型范畴的典型实例。2）在"原型性"这一概念的探索中并不存在最根本、最重要的视角，由于各研究的目的不同，受到关注的原型性特征也有所不同，例如在语言习得的研究中成员的代表性特征备受关注，而对多义词的研究则将注意力移向意义重叠的特征。

因此作者认为，对原型性真正含义的探索可转化为各类原型性研究对所关注特征的探索。就此作者指出了原型理论将来研究的方向：对原型性的原型特征进一步地深入研究。

3）原型理论存在的问题二："原型理论"也是原型概念

本节指出不仅"原型性"是原型概念，就连"原型理论"也是一个原型概念。也即是说，在研究原型的各种理论中也有中心性理论和边缘性理论的区分。这一区分主要是为了阐明某些"半经典半原型"（semi-classic & semi-prototypical）的混合理论给"原型性"这一概念的理解造成的混乱。

本节特别分析了韦日比茨卡（Wierzbicka, 1985）和普特南（Putnam, 1975）的"混合"理论。两者的共同特点是都将经典理论的研究方法融入了各自的"原型理论"。其中韦日比茨卡的做法是用经典理论中的充要条件界定法来对范畴内的典型成员进行分析，其直接后果是使范畴的边缘成员受到忽略。然而作者认为，范畴的边缘成员的地位同典型的核心成员一样重要，其存在使得自然语言范畴具备了灵活多义的特性，对不同范畴之间的界定也起着重要作用，因而韦日比茨卡的做法是不可取的。另一混合理论是普特南的"语言层次的切分"（division of linguistic labor）理论。该理论认为，语言知识应划分为两个层面：专家层面和语言使用者层面。前者对自然世界具有充分的了解，所形成的概念可以由经典理论中的充要条件来界定；而后者仅关注事物的显著特征，因而形成的概念具有原型性。然而，普特南的理论也存在很多问题。首先是该理论很难解释除自然事物外的其他概念；其次，自然语言的范畴化不仅由科学研究的状态决定，还由语言社会自身的交际和认知需求决定。

最后作者指出，韦日比茨卡的研究体现了柏拉图式的理想主义，认为人类的头脑是清晰的而外部世界是模糊的，我们应将界限清晰的心理范畴运用于组织混乱的外部世界；而普特南的研究则体现了经验性的客观主义，认为科学是清晰的而日常语言是模糊的，现实的客观结构最好由科学语言来描述。就此作者认为，认知语言学的研究应避开理想主义（idealist）和现实主义（objectivist），学者们在未来对范畴结构的原型性研究中应更多关注其认识性和哲学性的方面。

第二篇为莱考夫的《当代隐喻理论》（The Contemporary Theory of Metaphor）。在本文中，莱考夫对当代隐喻理论作了全面的介绍，指出隐喻是在诗歌语言和常规语言中都有所体现的普遍认知机制。

由于当代隐喻理论认为隐喻涉及了更深层的概念系统（conceptual system），即隐喻现象不单单存在于语言中，也存在于我们的思想和行动里，因此本文中"隐喻"指的是"一种概念系统里的跨域映射"（a cross-domain mapping in the conceptual system）；"隐喻性表达"（metaphorical expressions）则指作为这种跨域映射表层实现（surface realization）的语言表达如词语、短语、句子等。由此看出，"隐喻性表达"所指称的对象，即相当于古典理论里"隐喻"一词所指称的对象。

莱考夫通过日常语言中的许多代表性范例，对当代隐喻理论就词语多义现象、推理模式和新创隐喻的制约规则进行了详述。比如英文中广泛存在着关于隐喻LOVE IS A JOURNEY的表达式，如：

看看我们已走了多远（Look how far we've come.）；
那是一条漫长而颠簸的道路（It's been a long, bumpy road.）；
我们不能走回头路（We can't turn back now.）；
我们身处十字路口（We're at a crossroads.）；
我们或许必须分道而行（We may have to go our separate ways.）等。

在这些表达中，我们实际上是用"旅程"域的内容来思考"爱情"域的内容，这两个概念域之间存在着一种本体对应（ontological correspondences）：情人对应旅人，爱情关系对应交通工具，情人们的共同目标对应旅人们的目的地，爱情里所遭遇的问题对应旅程中所遭遇的困难等。

上述映射是规约性的（conventional），属于我们概念系统中固定的组成部分，在此理解下隐喻不仅仅是语言的事物，更是思想和推理的事物；语言是次要的，映射才是首要的。关于这一主张，莱考夫给出了一个反面论证：如果隐喻仅仅只是语言表达，那么不同的表达式应该是不同的隐喻；这样，前面提到的以旅程的方式来谈论爱情的不同表述，每一项都应涉及不同的隐喻。可是，在上述分析中，我们可以发现这些表达式都是以旅程来概念化爱情的概念隐喻（conceptual metaphor）的实现方式。

此外，莱考夫还指出，每个常规隐喻都是一种映射，是跨概念域的概念对应（conceptual correspondence）的固定类型。它不应该被视为以源域为输入域，目标域为输出域的演算过程；但它在跨域的推理类型之中，确实蕴含了许多潜在的对应。我们可以用源域里新奇的知识结构，来特征化目标域里相对应的知识结构，使得常规隐喻产生新奇的延伸（novel extensions），如歌词中的句子："我们正行驶在爱情高速公路的快车道上"（We're driving in the fast lane on the freeway of love.）。

这里显然使用了"爱情是旅程"的隐喻，但是这个句子并不属于我们的日常语言。由于"爱情是旅程"这样的常规隐喻是我们概念系统的一部分，所以我们很容易便能理解由此延伸出的新奇表述。

除了前面涉及的感情概念外，许多其它基本概念也具有隐喻性，如时间、数量、状态、变化、致使、目的、方式、情态甚至范畴概念。在这些概念的理解中，源域的意象图式被映射到目标域中，这便引出了"恒定原则"（The Invariance Principle），即隐喻映射保留了源域中同目标域的内在结构相一致的意象图式结构。这一原则可保证两域中各成分间的映射具有对应性，从而确保了目标域中的意象图式结构不会被违反。目标域的内在结构能自动地限制映射的可能性。也就是说，在隐喻中，"恒定原则"自动地限制了什么可以被映射，什么不可以。此外，作者还就体现位置/物体相对位移的不同感知模式的隐喻提出了"二元性"（duality）特征。这一特征在"同时映射"（simultaneous mapping）中较为突出：同一表达式如"在将来的几周内"（within coming weeks）涉及两个隐喻，突出了目标域的不同方面。虽然映射作为整体是不合适的，但映射的部分却在目标域中得到叠加。

莱考夫在解释常规隐喻之余，还介绍了两类新奇隐喻（novel metaphors）：意象隐喻（image metaphors）和类层级隐喻（generic-level metaphors）。常规隐喻总是同时映射许多概念到其对应概念上面；意象隐喻则仅仅只映射一个常规心智意象到另一个心理意象上面，它是"一次性"隐喻（"one-shot" metaphor）。例如句子"我妻子的腰是个沙漏"（My wife's waist is an hourglass.）所使用的隐喻并不是常规性的，此句只是将沙漏的心理意象映射到一位女人身材的心理意象上面，离开这个句子，此意象隐喻也不复存在，这也是称其为一次性隐喻的缘故。

"类层级隐喻"则是莱考夫与特纳（Mark Turner）在1989年所提出的新主张。他们在处理拟人化和谚语这两项主题时，发现涉及这两者的隐喻有着一个共同的特征：它们的源域及目标域共享类层级的概念结构，也即是说，源域和目标域的知识结构中可以抽象出称为"类层级图式"（generic-level schema）的一般知识图式（general knowledge schema）。此图式使这类隐喻得以产生，并规范了所映射的特定知识结构的内容。他们同时也从语言实例分析中发现，如果"恒定原则"是正确的，那么获得某一知识结构的类层级图式的方法，就是抽象出它的意象图式结构。

在隐喻理解的机制方面，作者通过对事件结构隐喻的分析，指出隐喻性映射并不总是单独出现，而是经常组成等级结构（hierarchical structure），这些结构通常具有继承性：较低等级的映射会继承（inherit）

较高等级映射的结构。在同一继承等级（inheritance hierarchy）里，通常位置较高的隐喻更具一般性，在人类社会中传播得更广泛；位置较低的隐喻更具特定性，在人类社会中传播得比较有限。当代隐喻理论认为，那些处于最高等级的隐喻，以及少数独立出现的隐喻，都是以我们的直接经验为基础的。事实上，整个概念系统都是以直接经验为基础的：继承等级较低位置的隐喻性映射，可以直接从较高位置的隐喻性映射中继承经验基础。于是，所有概念系统中的概念，以及隐喻所实现的隐喻性表达，都落实在经验世界中。

最后，莱考夫分析了当代隐喻理论同语言哲学的冲突，并由此引出了该理论同形式语义学、管辖约束理论、欧洲哲学、人工智能及信息处理心理学之间的冲突与差异，从而说明了该理论的研究不仅有利于其学科本身的发展，而且若研究结果得以接受，则将对上述各个领域的假设都产生根本性的影响。

克劳夫特（W. Croft）的《 "域" 在隐喻和转喻解读中的作用》（The Role of Domains in the Interpretation of Metaphors and Metonymies）一文研究的主要问题包括：1）利用兰艾克的理论模型将转喻解释为意义延伸过程；2）对莱考夫和约翰逊（Lakoff and Johnson, 1980）的隐喻和转喻区分进行了更为细致的分析，认为隐喻是 "不属于同一矩阵域的两域之间的映射"，而转喻是在 "同一矩阵域中的映射"。值得说明的是，本文从百科语义[1]的视角出发，指出 "域"（domain）在对词义进行隐喻或转喻解读的过程中起到了核心作用：词语所在的构式为词语解读的 "域" 提供了线索，从而决定了其解读方式。本文所指的 "域" 同 "框架"、 "心理空间"、 "脚本" 有相通之处[2]。

文章以句子Denmark shot down the Maastricht Treaty的隐喻和转喻意义构建为切入点提出了 "语义组合性" 观点所遇到的难题：此句中词语的含义似乎在某种程度上是由整句的含义决定的。作者将这种现象称为 "域的概念统一性"（conceptual unity of domain），即在某句法单位中的所有元素都必须在同一域内进行解读。因此 "域" 的界定对词义的解读至关重要。作者认为， "域" 的概念必须通过侧面—基底关系（profile-base relation）来理解。同中心—边缘关系不同，基底指的是在侧面的概念化过程中所预设的那部分知识，而不是附加的、非核心的知识。侧面和基底在概念上具有依存性：不通过基底提供的背景知识就无法理解侧面，而基底也只有作为与侧面相关的认知上具有统一性和限定性的知识集合而存在。鉴于同一知识集可作为多个侧面的基底，作者将

"域"定义为：可以作为至少一个概念侧面的基底的语义结构。

在确立了"域"的明确定义后，作者又提出了"矩阵域"的概念（domain matrix）。由于同一概念可以预设多个不同的域，作者采用"矩阵域"来指由某一概念同时预设的域的集合，并以"字母t"为例说明了概念所预设的矩阵域的复杂性。如下图所示：

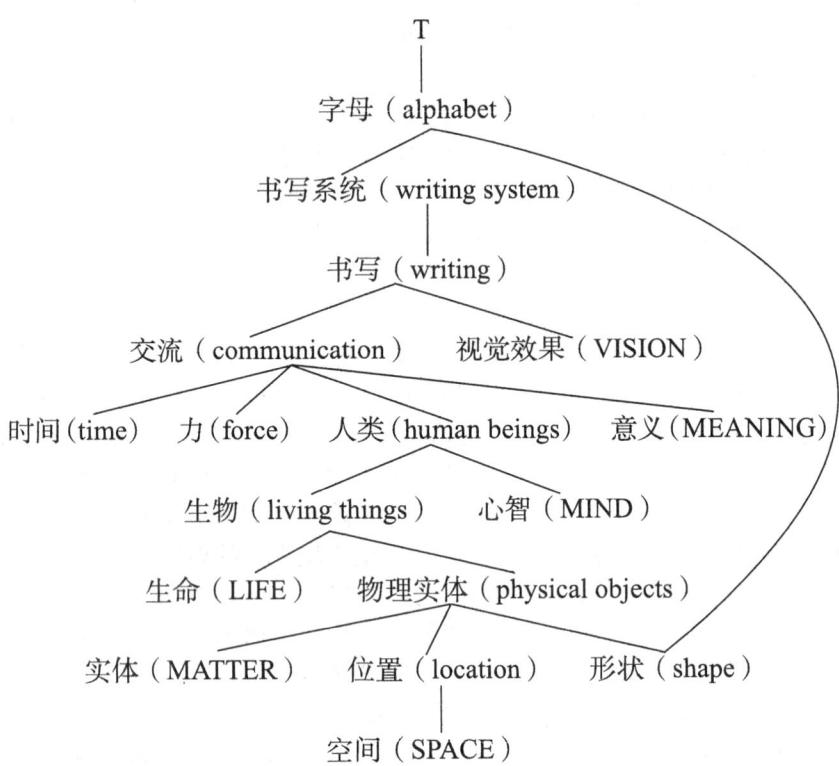

兰艾克（1987:163）指出，矩阵域中的各个域的激活程度不一样：在概念的定义中域的作用越间接，概念激活时该域的激活强度就越弱。"矩阵域"概念的提出为后文阐明"跨域映射"与"域内突显"的区别奠定了基础。

词语隐喻和转喻的解读是"矩阵域"中域之间不同的作用机制的结果，隐喻涉及"跨域映射"（domain mapping）而转喻涉及"域内突显"（domain highlighting）。就此，作者对这两种机制进行了解释。隐喻方面，我们对比下列两句

1) She's in the living room.
2) She's in a good mood.

即可发现，例2）中的隐喻是通过一个独立的"域"中的结构来对另一"域"进行概念化（conceptualization）的过程，即隐喻的产生是两域之间映射的结果。就该句而言，in不能同时表征源域"空间关系"与目标域"情绪关系"，因此源域与目标域并不是同一"矩阵域"中的组成部分。所以，隐喻涉及的是"跨域映射"机制。

与隐喻一样，转喻也涉及映射，但映射发生的范围只局限于同一"矩阵域"中。例如在下列两句中：

3) Proust spent most of his time in bed.
4) Proust is tough to read.

例3）采用了字面义，例4）则采用了转喻的手法通过Proust本人来指代他的作品。而"Proust的作品"还是处于"Proust"这一概念的"矩阵域"中。

需要指出的是，这两种机制与隐喻和转喻的关系并不相同："跨域映射"对隐喻具有界定性；而"域内突显"只是转喻的必要非充分条件，因为概念不同方面（facet）的突显也涉及"域内突显"，它与转喻之间形成一种连续体（continuum）。作者利用转喻的这种百科知识观解决了农贝格（Nunberg）的"语义表征"问题。此外，这两种机制在语言表达式中起作用的条件也不相同："跨域映射"取决于依存性谓语，而"域内突显"取决于自主性谓语。在自主和依存性谓语的语法组合中，依存性谓语可以引起自主性谓语的域内突显，自主性谓语可以引起依存性谓语的跨域映射。

最后，文章论述了三个"概念统一性"——域的概念统一性、心理空间的统一性和选择的统一性（unity of selection）——在话语获得语义连贯性中的重要的作用。兰艾克（1991:33）认为名词和动词短语都涉及三个组织层次：1）概念类型，由光杆名词和动词词干来表示；2）概念类型的语境化的实例（grounded instance），由搭配限定词和从句的完整名词词组来体现；3）概念类型的中间层次的实例（intermediate level of an instance），如带量词的语法结构。其中域的概念统一性属于概念类型层次，心理空间的统一性属于概念类型的语境化的实例的层次，而选择统一性则处于第三层次，涉及个体化与量化问题。在理解话语的过程中，听者以这三个统一性为前提对句子进行解读，必要时采用隐喻、转喻、粗细度（granularity）和对应关系以及其他的焦点调整手段。上述调整也解释了成分的解读如何受到整体意义的影响。

《框架语义学》（Frame Semantics）是菲尔莫尔（Fillmore）倡导的语义学理论模式，它来源于实证语义学（empirical semantics），是认知语言学范式的一部分。本文《框架语义学》原发表在韩国语言学会编的*Linguistics in the Morning Calm*中。在这篇文章里，菲尔莫尔提出了著名的框架理论，认为框架是一种"能与典型情景相联系的语言系统"。框架语义学由格语法发展而来，但摆脱了格语法中难以确定的问题，开创性地将视角（Perspective）和典型（Prototype）概念引入框架中。本文通过系统的介绍，说明了该理论以框架为手段来表述语言同经验和知识结构之间关系的特点。同时本文还揭示了词语和范畴，以及范畴和背景之间关系的性质。

本文共分为四部分，分别界定了"框架"的概念、介绍了"框架语义学"的个人研究历史（即理论的发展历史），以框架语义学的方式来分析各种语义现象，并说明了传统语义学分析方法的不足和框架语义学研究的优势。下面简要就这几部分的内容进行说明。

首先解释"框架"的定义。"框架"在本文中指的是由概念组成的各种系统。这些系统的特点是，要理解其中的一个概念则必须理解它所在的整个结构。当此结构中的一个成分被引入语篇或对话中时，结构中的所有其它部分也被激活。"框架"在本文中是对"图式"（schema）、"脚本"（script）、"情境"（scenario）、"观念框架"（ideational scaffolding）、"认知模式"（cognitive model）、"民俗理论"（folk theory）等概念的统称。框架语义学与形式语义学最大的不同在于它强调的是语言与经验之间的连贯性而非分离性。在Fillmore看来，词语代表了经验的分类（范畴化），这些范畴中的每一个，都是以依赖知识和经验背景的激活情境为基础的。

"框架语义学"理论的建立经历了几个发展阶段：20世纪50年代使用词语串或词类串作为"框架"（frame）来发现英语词语的分布类；60年代初根据动词可接受的表层句法框架和动词的语法"行为"为英语动词分类的研究；60年代末"格语法"的建立，该理论中每一个格框架都被视为刻画一个小的抽象的"情景"（scene）或"境况"（situation）。由于"格语法"语义描写的局限性，菲尔莫尔通过对"判决动词"和"商业事件"域的说明提出了关于"框架"的初步构想；70年代通过语用研究推动该领域的发展，并采用了原型概念来描写词语意义。该时期通过对orphan和breakfast的分析表明，词语提供给我们可以用于多种不同语境的范畴，这些语境是由该范畴典型用法的不同方面决定的，即所谓典型用法是指背景情境或多或少比较准确地跟定义的原型相匹配。

从上述讨论中发展出来的描写框架中的词语和其他语言形式以及范畴，都被看作是具有索引作用的语义或认知范畴。这些范畴自身要在某种更大的概念结构中被认识。要理解这个框架的全部，就要了解相关的语境的知识，言语社区需要倚之使得言语参与者理解这些范畴；了解这些语境产生的经验与实践背景；了解通过"原型"理解的范畴、语境与背景本身。由理论背景可看出，"框架"作为在对语言意义的描写中起作用的概念，是跟一些激活性语境（motivating context）相一致的一个结构化的范畴系统。一些词语的存在，就是为了将这些框架知识提供给交际中的参与者，同时完成对框架的范畴化。背景语境是理解范畴的基础。如果不理解背景，词语的意义不可能真正被理解。人们对一些事物或事情的特别关注，为范畴的存在提供了理由。例如词语"weekend"（周末）之所以能够表达它所表达的意思，是因为日历7天一周，加上生活中有一种特别的经验，即一周内有一个大块连续时间是公众工作时间，又有连续的两天是私人生活时间。如果我们只有一个"休息日"，就可能不需要"weekend"这个词。作者还通过"land"和"ground"、"shore"和"coast"之间的对比说明词语与特殊的认知框架相连，表达出对世界不同的图式化。此外，我们还可以借助认知框架对语言文本进行解释。

在对该理论进行了全面描述后，作者考察了许多关于词语意义或文本解释的观察材料，并认为这些材料可以用框架语义学的概念进行公式化表达。这些语义现象包括：

1) 同一词项的可替换性框架造成的多义性，即同一语词可与两种不同的认知框架相容。如angle既可以视为两条线在某点相交，也可视为是同一条线围绕着某点旋转的结果。

2) 同一场景的可替换框架，即对于同一语言事实，由于采用的框架不同可造成不同的评价，如在特定场景下某人不愿花钱的特征既可被视为stingy（与generous相对），也可被视为thrifty（与wasteful相对）。

3) "框架内的对比"与"框架间的对比"，即同一场景由于采用的框架不同，"否定"或"反对"的方式也不同。如上面的场景，可说He's not stingy — he's really generous，这属于"框架内的对比"；也可说He's not stingy — he's thrifty，这属于"框架间的对比"。

4）由框架借用（frame borrowing）而产生的词义，例如借用人类社会中的bachelor的概念来指称"交配季节无配偶的雄性海豹"。

5）对词汇集合的框架重构（reframing），如在英语用法中，由boy转型为man的年龄通常比girl转型为woman的年龄要早，为了改正此偏见，在翻译时，人们往往有意识地将两者年龄的界定统一起来。

6）在原框架中进行重新词汇化（relexicalizing），例如由于某些社会因素，原来被称之为"犯人"（culprit）的人现在通常称作"嫌疑人"（suspect）。

7）框架冲突造成的交际错误（miscommunication），例如日常用语与法律用语中对"无辜"（innocent）和"有罪"（guilty）的定义有所差别，因而在文献阅读时会有误解现象的产生。

8）专业语言中的阐述更新（reformulation），例如在法律用语中，针对A本来意图要杀B却误杀了C的情况，可添加"意图转移"条例同样判定A的谋杀罪（murder）。

9）用于评价的框架，即由于评价的框架不同，同一词语可获得不同的含义，如a good pencil, a good mother, good coffee 中的 good 的含义是有所差异的。

10）脚本激发（script evocation），即提及框架的一部分会引发整个框架，如文本 "He pushed against the door. The room was empty." 其实包含了 "He pushed against the door. *The door opened. He looked inside. He saw that* the room was empty."。

11）文本中的框架，如特定文化中语言使用的传统在交际目的不同的文本中发展的方式有所差异。

综上所述，"框架语义学"理论从一个新的视角为上述语义现象提供了灵活、自然的分析。

在《基于用法建构的语言习得理论初探》（First Steps toward a Usage-based Theory of Language Acquisition）一文中，汤姆瑟勒（M. Tomasello）采用了功能学派的立场，在结合认知语言学的一些观点的基础上，提出了以使用为基础的语言习得研究模式，确认了儿童语言习得和发展所涉及的认知领域的一般性，对乔姆斯基的语言特殊区域的观点提出了挑战。本文将话语作为最基本的心理语言单位，对儿童语言习得过程中的实际语言使用进行了考察，主要从"语言的产生"和"语法的出现"这两个方面对语言习得中使用的心理语言单位和习得规律进行了说明。

语言最初产生于成人、婴儿和客体交际三角中：从不足一岁时起，婴儿就开始密切关注成人指向外界物体的主观意图，在理解一般交际意图后在与成人的交际中建立共同注意框架（joint attentional formats），参与共同注意的活动，进一步理解特定情景下（usage event）的交际意图。可以说，对交际意图的解读是语言产生的基础。具备了意图解读的能力，儿童就开始在交际过程中产出话语。这最初发出的话语（utterance）并不等同于成人语言中的"词"，而是在特定情境下表达完整交际功能意义的"单词句"（holophrase）。这种"句子"是固化的短语（frozen phrase），在随后的发展中可被进一步分解。随着生活的丰富，儿童的语言产出由单词句发展至早期的词语组合。这种组合通常表现为具有空位（slot）的话语结构，如where's X?、Put X here等。

在语言习得初期，儿童的话语类型（pattern）并未经过任何抽象（abstraction），基本以具体用法为基础（item-based）。汤姆瑟勒认为，儿童早期语法是以动词为中心的话语图式（utterance schema），即"动词岛"（verb island）构式。在此时期，儿童通常模仿成人在具体场景下产出的具有特定功能的话语，从而建构并习得作为交际工具的语言符号的意义，这种现象称为"模仿学习"（imitative learning）或"文化学习"。在这种具体语言用法习得的过程中，儿童不断进行图式化和类推来构建新的用法，但若其成功使用某话语若干次后，便会对其他话语方式产生抵触，出现"语言固化"（entrenchment）的学习困难。在进一步的语言发展中，儿童可以突破对成人语言的模仿，产出创造性的话语。这一过程是在"词符频率"（token frequency）和"词形频率"（type frequency）的基础上完成的：前者使表达式获得"固化"，而后者则通过表达式中的元素变化使其产生创造性。总体来说，儿童在习得语法的过程中，通过对具体语言单位的功能分析，将言语中具有相同交际功能的表达法和建构的用法划分到同一范畴之中，并在"词符频率"和"词形频率"的影响下习得句法的生成性。儿童对语言单位的类型建构（pattern-finding）以意图识别为基础，将语言形式和交际功能并重。

与形式研究中的意义组合性（compositionality）相反，本文中汤姆瑟勒采取的是自上而下（top-down）的语义研究方向，其分析以构式为基础并采用了语言结构依赖于用法的观点。用法建构理论认为，语言认知能力具有一般性，语言获得过程与语言加工过程是统一的。该理论"从社会认知和文化学习入手，揭示了儿童通过社会认知和一般信息加工技能，主动建构最终获得具体语言的过程及其规律"，将语言学理论与发展心理学联系起来。但是该理论不得不承认语言符号系统加工的内在规律，即语言的"模块性"问题，而且对于语法和语用的关系问题以及某些构式不可能合语法的原因并未进行充分的说明，因此用法建构理论还有待改进和调整。

1　Dirven (1993) 也从百科语义的角度对隐喻和转喻进行研究，但两者的观点有一定的差异。

2　见Peeters B. (ed.) 2000. *The lexicon-encyclopedia interface.* U.K.: Elsevier Science.

Prospects and Problems of Prototype Theory

Dirk Geeraerts

1. Prototype theory within linguistics

The starting-point of the prototypical conception of categorial structure is summarized in the statement that

> when describing categories analytically, most traditions of thought have treated category membership as a digital, all-or-none phenomenon. That is, much work in philosophy, psychology, linguistics, and anthropology assumes that categories are logical bounded entities, membership in which is defined by an item's possession of a simple set of criterial features, in which all instances possessing the criterial attributes have a full and equal degree of membership. In contrast, it has recently been argued ... that some natural categories are analog and must be represented logically in a manner which reflects their analog structure (Rosch and Mervis 1975: 573–574).

As we shall see in section 2, the exact definition of the concept of prototypicality as used in linguistics is not without problems. The major part of this introduction to the prototypicality-based studies collected here will, in fact, consist of an attempt at clarification of some of the problematic aspects of the way in which the notion of prototype has been used in linguistics. To begin with, however, we shall be concerned with a brief overview of the state of the art in linguistic prototype theory.[1]

The theory originated in the mid 1970s with Eleanor Rosch's research into

431

the internal structure of categories. (Overviews may be found in Rosch 1978, 1988, and Mervis and Rosch 1981; the basic research is reported on mainly in Heider 1972; Rosch 1973, 1975, 1977; Rosch and Mervis 1975; Rosch, Simpson and Miller 1976; Rosch et al. 1976.) From its psycholinguistic origins, prototype theory has moved mainly[2] in two directions. On the one hand, Rosch's findings and proposals were taken up by formal psycholexicology (and more generally, information-processing psychology), which tries to devise formal models for human conceptual memory and its operation, and which so, obviously, borders on Artificial Intelligence. Excellent overviews of the representational and experimental issues at stake here are Smith and Medin (1981), and Medin and Smith (1984); an interesting sample of current research may be found in Neisser (1987). On the other hand, prototype theory has had a steadily growing success in linguistics since the early 1980s, as witnessed by a number of recent monographs and collective volumes in which prototype theory and its cognitive extensions play a major role (Wierzbicka 1985; Lakoff 1987; Langacker 1987; Craig 1986; Holland and Quinn 1987; Rudzka-Ostyn 1988; Lehmann 1988a; Hüllen and Schulze 1988; Tsohatzidis 1989; Taylor 1989). It is with the latter development that we shall be concerned with here.

Against the background of the development of linguistic semantics, prototype theory may be defined primarily in contrast with the componential model of semantic analysis that was current in transformational grammar and that is stereotypically associated with Katz and Fodor's analysis of *bachelor* (Katz and Fodor 1963); in an early defense of a prototypical approach, Fillmore (1975) called this the 'checklist theory' of meaning. The prototypists' reaction against this featural approach had, however, the negative side-effect of creating the impression that prototypical theories rejected any kind of componential analysis. This is a misconception for the simple reason that there can be no semantic description without some sort of decompositional analysis. As a heuristic tool for the description and comparison of lexical meanings, a componential analysis retains its value (a value that, incidentally, it did not acquire with the advent of componential analysis as an explicit semantic theory, but which had been obvious to lexicographers from time immemorial). Rather, the difficulties with the neostructuralist kind of feature analysis that grew out of structuralist field theory lie elsewhere; it is not the use of decomposition as a descriptive instrument that causes concern, but the status attributed to the featural analysis. Two important points have to be mentioned.

In the first place, as suggested by the quotation at the beginning of this introduction, featural definitions are classically thought of as criterial, i.e. as listing attributes that are each indispensable for the definition of the concept in question, and that taken together suffice to delimit that concept from all others. In contrast, prototype theory claims that there need not be a single set of defining attributes that conform to the necessity-cum-sufficiency requirement.[3]

In the second place, prototype theory is reluctant to accept the idea that there is an autonomous semantic structure in natural languages which can be studied in its own right, in isolation from the other cognitive capacities of man. In particular, meaning phenomena in natural languages cannot be studied in isolation from the encyclopedic knowledge individuals possess; it is precisely the presupposition that there exists a purely linguistic structure of semantic oppositions that enables structuralist and neostructuralist semantics to posit the existence of a distinction between semantic and encyclopedic knowledge. Prototype theory tends to minimize the distinction primarily for methodological reasons: because linguistic categorization is a cognitive phenomenon just like the other cognitive capacities of man, it is important to study it in its relationship to these other capacities. More specific arguments have also been formulated to show that the distinction between an encyclopedic and a semantic level of categorial structure is untenable.[4] For instance, given that the flexible extendibility of prototypical concepts is a synchronic characteristic of linguistic structure, and given the fact that these extensions may be based indiscriminately on allegedly encyclopedic or on allegedly semantic features, the distinction between both kinds of information loses its synchronic relevance. Take the case of metaphor: before *lion* acquires the meaning 'brave man', the feature 'brave' is not structurally distinctive within the semasiological structure of *lion*, and hence, it has to be considered encyclopedic according to structuralist theories. But if it can be accepted (and this is of course the crucial point) that the metaphorical extension of *lion* towards the concept 'brave man' is not just a question of diachronic change, but is merely an effect of the synchronic flexibility of lexical items, the feature clearly acquires semantic status. If, furthermore, the argument can be repeated in the sense that such synchronic metaphorical extensions may be based on any allegedly encyclopedic attribute, the distinction between semantic and encyclopedic concepts as a whole falls.[5]

The matter need not, to be sure, be settled here. What is important for our introductory purposes is rather to see what exactly prototype theory objects to in componential theories of the Katzian type. First, the suggestion that lexical concepts are criterial in the classical sense, and second, the suggestion that there exists a purely linguistic level of conceptual structuring that is neatly separated from other, 'encyclopedic' forms of conceptual information, and that may thus be studied autonomously, in methodological isolation from other kinds of cognitive research. As against these points of view, prototype theory defends a non-criterial conception of categorial structure, and an interdisciplinary methodological perspective that takes into account relevant research from the other cognitive sciences. (The very transposition of the prototypical approach from experimental psychology to linguistics derives from this attitude.)

But this historical positioning of prototype theory with regard to its immediate predecessors within the field of lexical semantics clearly does not explain why it has turned out to be such a successful alternative. Why did (and does) the prototypical approach appeal to a sizeable part of the linguistic community? On the one hand, the historical development of generative grammar had raised a considerable amount of interest in semantic matters. It should not be forgotten, in fact, that it was only after the incorporation of a semantic component into the transformational framework that Chomskyanism became internationally popular; the universal appeal of the generative Standard Theory was at least partly due to the promises held by its Katzian semantic component. On the other hand, the promises were not fulfilled. Within the generative paradigm, Generative Semantics (which most strongly embodied the semantic approach) withered in favor of Autonomous Syntax, in which semantics hardly played a role worthy of note. Outside the generative approach, formal semantics of the Montagovian kind was too narrowly restricted to sentential meaning to be able to hold the attention of those who were interested primarily in the internal structure of natural language categories (and not primarily in the way these categories combine into larger unities).[6] In short, as far as semantics was concerned, there was a gap in the linguistic market of the early 1980s that was not filled by the major approaches of the day.[7]

But again, recognizing that there was an interest in the semantics of natural language categories to which prototype theory could appeal does not tell the whole story. Why didn't people simply stick to the componential theory

popularized by Katz, or to the rival axiomatic method of representation —
even if these gradually moved out of the centre of the linguistic attention as
Autonomous Syntax and Formal Semantics took over? In general, there are a
number of methodological requirements people nowadays expect of linguistic
theories: descriptive adequacy (mainly in the form of a broad empirical scope),
explanatory depth, productivity, and formalization. Although prototype theory
rates much lower on the formalization scale than either the axiomatic or the
featural approach, its assets with regard to the other three points are considerable.

In the first place, it tackles a number of semantic phenomena that had
been swept under the rug by the more structurally minded approaches. The
fuzzy boundaries of lexical categories, the existence of typicality scales for the
members of a category, the flexible and dynamic nature of word meanings, the
importance of metaphor and metonymy as the basis of that flexibility — these
are all intuitively obvious elements of the subject matter of semantics that were
largely neglected by structural semantics. It is true that they were occasionally
pointed at as an indispensable aspect of any full-fledged semantic theory: think,
for instance, of Weinreich's remark (1966: 471) that a semantic theory should
be able to deal with 'interpretable deviance', or Uhlenbeck's plea (1967) for a
dynamic conception of word meaning.[8] These remarks did not, however, have
much effect as far as theory formation was concerned. In particular, it is only
with the advent of prototype theory that contemporary linguistics developed
a valid model for the polysemy of lexical items. This is perhaps the single most
appealing characteristic of prototype theory: here at last is a descriptive approach
to lexical meaning in which our pretheoretical intuitions about gradedness,
fuzziness, flexibility, clustering of senses etc. receive due attention.

In the second place, prototype theory appears to be a productive theory not
just in the sense that its insights into the structure of lexical categories can be
easily applied in various fields of the lexicon, but also in the sense that it may
be extended towards other aspects of linguistics. Whereas prototype theory
started with being descriptively fruitful in lexical semantics, it soon became
theoretically fruitful in the sense that other areas of linguistics were taken into
consideration. A few recent examples of such extensions may suffice: phonology
(Nathan 1986), morphology (Bybee and Moder 1983; Post 1986), syntax (Van
Oosten 1986; Ross 1987), historical linguistics (Winters 1987; Aijmer 1985),
markedness theory (Van Langendonck 1986), theoretical lexicography (Geeraerts

1985c). Through these and similar extensions,[9] prototype theory has become one of the cornerstones of Cognitive Linguistics, which tries to account for the interaction between language and cognition on all levels of linguistic structure: one need only have a look at the prominent place attributed to a prototypical conception of categorial structure in Langacker (1987) (one of the basic works of the Cognitive Linguistic approach) to appreciate its importance.[10] In this sense, the development of prototype theory into Cognitive Linguistics contains exciting promises of a unified cognitive theory of linguistic categorization.

In the third place, the explanatory depth of prototype theory resides partly in its generalizable character, but also in its interdisciplinary nature. The importance of its genetic link with psycholinguistics can only be fully appreciated against the background of the Chomskyan requirements with regard to theories of grammar. Chomsky's methodology is, in fact, in the awkward position of declaring linguistics a cognitive science, but refusing to deal directly with the findings of the other sciences of the mind. Roughly stated, Chomskyan linguistics claims to reveal something about the mind, but imperviously prefers a strictly autonomist methodology over the open dialogue with psychology that would seem to be implied by such a claim. Prototype theory's linguistic application of psycholinguistic findings, on the other hand, takes the Chomskyan ideal of cognitive explanatory depth to its natural consequences, viz. of giving up the methodological autonomy of linguistics in favor of an interdisciplinary dialogue with the other cognitive sciences.[11] Prototype theory takes the cognitive claims of Chomskyanism methodologically seriously by its interdisciplinary openness. This is all the more important at a moment when Cognitive Science is emerging as an interdisciplinary cluster of psychology, neuroscience, Artificial Intelligence, and philosophy. It is probably one of the reasons for the appeal of prototype theory that its interdisciplinary connections hold the promise of linking linguistics to the most important development that the human sciences are currently witnessing.

2. Definitional problems, first series: 'Prototype' as a prototypical notion

The appeal of prototype theory should not, however, obscure the fact that the exact definition of prototypicality is not without problems. The purpose of this section (and the following) is to analyze the sources of the confusion by making clear that prototypicality is itself, in the words of Posner (1986), a prototypical concept. As a first step, we shall have a look at four characteristics that are frequently mentioned (in various combinations) as typical of prototypicality. In each case, a quotation from early prototype studies is added to illustrate the point.

(i) Prototypical categories cannot be defined by means of a single set of criterial (necessary and sufficient) attributes:

We have argued that many words ... have as their meanings not a list of necessary and sufficient conditions that a thing or event must satisfy to count as a member of the category denoted by the word, but rather a psychological object or process which we have called a prototype (Coleman and Kay 1981: 43).

(ii) Prototypical categories exhibit a family resemblance structure, or more generally, their semantic structure takes the form of a radial set of clustered and overlapping meanings:[12]

The purpose of the present research was to explore one of the major structural principles which, we believe, may govern the formation of the prototype structure of semantic categories. This principle was first suggested in philosophy; Wittgenstein (1953) argued that the referents of a word need not have common elements to be understood and used in the normal functioning of language. He suggested that, rather, a family resemblance might be what linked the various referents of a word. A family resemblance relationship takes the form AB, BC, CD, DE. That is, each item has at least one, and probably several, elements in common with one or more items, but no, or few, elements are common to all items (Rosch and Mervis 1975: 574-575).

(iii) Prototypical categories exhibit degrees of category membership; not every member is equally representative for a category:

By prototypes of categories we have generally meant the clearest cases of category membership defined operationally by people's judgments of goodness of membership in the category ... we can judge how clear a case something is and deal with categories on the basis of clear cases in the total absence of information about boundaries (Rosch 1978: 36).

(iv) Prototypical categories are blurred at the edges:

New trends in categorization research have brought into investigation and debate some of the major issues in conception and learning whose solution had been unquestioned in earlier approaches. Empirical findings have established that ... category boundaries are not necessarily definite (Mervis and Rosch 1981: 109).

As a first remark with regard to these characteristics, it should be noted that they are not the only ones that may be used in attempts to define the prototypical conception of categorization. Two classes of such additional features should be mentioned.

On the one hand, there are characteristics that do not pertain (as the four mentioned above) to the structure of categories, but that rather pertain to the epistemological features of so-called non-Aristotelian categories.[13] For instance, the view that prototypical categories are not 'objectivist' but 'experiential' in nature (Lakoff 1987) envisages the epistemological relationship between concepts and the world rather than the structural characteristics of those concepts. In particular, it contrasts the allegedly classical view that 'categories of mind ... are simply reflections of categories that supposedly exist objectively in the world, independent of all beings', with the view that 'both categories of mind and human reason depend upon experiential aspects of human psychology' (Lakoff 1982: 99). Such an epistemological rather than structural characterization of natural concepts also has a methodological aspect to it; it entails that prototypical categories should not be studied in isolation from their experiential context. While such an epistemological or methodological conception of prototypical categorization is extremely valuable, we shall take a structural point of view in the following pages; we shall try to determine whether it is possible to give a coherent, structurally intrinsic characterization of prototypical categories.

On the other hand, there are structural characteristics of prototypical concepts that can be reduced to the four basic structural features mentioned above. For instance, in my own work on prototypical categorization, I have repeatedly stressed the flexibility of prototypical concepts (1983, 1985a), together with the fact that a distinction between semantic and encyclopedic components of lexical concepts cannot be maintained in the case of prototypical concepts (1985b). But the flexibility of prototypical categories is linked in a straightforward manner with the fourth characteristic: uncertainties with regard to the denotational boundaries of a category imply that it need not be used in a rigidly fixed manner. Similarly, the absence of a clear dividing line between encyclopedic and purely semantic information follows from this very flexibility together with the first and second characteristic. As illustrated in the previous section, the possibility of incorporating members into the category that do not correspond in every definitional respect with the existing members entails that features that are encyclopedic (non-definitional) with regard to a given set of category members may turn into definitional features with regard to a flexibly incorporated peripheral category member. The resemblance between central and peripheral cases may be based on allegedly encyclopedic just as well as on allegedly 'semantic' features. In short, features of prototypicality that are not included among the ones mentioned in (i)–(iv) may often be reduced to those four, and this in turn justifies a preliminary restriction of the discussion to the latter.

A second remark with regard to the four characteristics is concerned with the fact that they are systematically related along two dimensions. On the one hand, the third and the fourth characteristic take into account the referential, extensional structure of a category. In particular, they have a look at the members of a category; they observe, respectively, that not all referents of a category are equal in representativeness for that category, and that the denotational boundaries of a category are not always determinate. On the other hand, these two aspects (centrality and non-rigidity) recur on the intensional level, where the definitional rather than the referential structure of a category is envisaged. For one thing, non-rigidity shows up in the fact that there is no single necessary and sufficient definition for a prototypical concept. For another, family resemblances imply overlapping of the subsets of a category. To take up the formulation used in the quotation under (ii) above, if there is no definition adequately describing A, B, C, D, and E, each of the subsets AB, BC, CD, and DE can be defined separately, but obviously, the 'meanings' that are so distinguished overlap. Consequently, meanings exhibiting a greater degree of overlapping (in the example: the senses corresponding with BC and CD) will have more structural weight than meanings that cover peripheral members of the category only. In short, the clustering of meanings that is typical of family resemblances implies that not every meaning is structurally equally important (and a similar observation can be made with regard to the components into which those meanings may be analyzed). The systematic links between the characteristics mentioned at the beginning are schematically summarized in Table 1.

As a third remark, it should be noted that the four characteristics are often thought to be co-extensive, in spite of incidental but clear warnings such as Rosch and Mervis's remark that a family resemblance structure need not be the only source of prototypicality (1975: 599). Admittedly, it is easy to consider them to be equivalent; already in the quotations given above, partial reasons for their mutual interdependence can be found. More systematically, the following links between the four characteristics might be responsible for the idea that prototypicality necessarily entails the joint presence of all four.

Table 1. Characteristics of prototypicality

	NON-EQUALITY differences in structural weight	NON-RIGIDITY flexibility and vagueness
EXTENSIONALLY	degrees of representativity	absence of clear boundaries
INTENSIONALLY	clusters of overlapping senses	absence of classical definition

First, linking the first to the second characteristic is the argument mentioned above: if there is no single definition adequately describing the extension of an item as a whole, different subsets may be defined, but since the members of a category can usually be grouped together along different dimensions, these subsets are likely to overlap, i.e., to form clusters of related meanings.

Second, linking the second to the third characteristic is the idea that members of a category that are found in an area of overlapping between two senses carry more structural weight than instances that are covered by only one meaning. Representative members of a category (i.e., instances with a high degree of representativity) are to be found in maximally overlapping areas of the extension of a category. (In the example, A and E are less typical members that B,

C, and D, which each belong to two different subsets.)

Third, linking the third to the fourth characteristic is the idea that differences in degree of membership may diminish to a point where it becomes unclear whether something still belongs to the category or not. Categories have referentially blurred edges because of the dubious categorial status of items with extremely low membership degrees.

And fourth, linking the fourth to the first characteristic is the idea that the flexibility that is inherent in the absence of clear boundaries prevents the formulation of an essence that is common to all the members of the category. Because peripheral members may not be identical with central cases but may only share some characteristics with them, it is difficult to define a set of attributes that is common to all members of a category and that is sufficient to distinguish that category from all others.

These circular links between the four characteristics are, however, misleading. A closer look at some (familiar and less familiar) examples of prototypicality reveals that they need not co-occur.

BIRD

The concept *bird* (one of Rosch's original examples of prototypicality) shows that natural categories may have clear-cut boundaries. At least with regard to our own, real world, the denotation of *bird* is determinate; educated speakers of English know very well where birds end and non-birds begin. They know, for instance, that a bat is not a bird but that a penguin is. Of course, the principled indeterminacy described by Waismann (1952) as 'open texture' remains: when confronted with an SF creature (a post-World War III mutant) that looks like a bird but talks like a man, we would not be sure whether it should be called a bird or not. A boundary problem that is typical for a prototypical organization of the lexicon would then arise. As it functions now, however, in present-day English, *bird* is denotationally clearly bounded, the archaeopteryx notwithstanding.[14] As has been remarked elsewhere (Lakoff 1987), the existence of prototypicality effects in clearly bounded concepts such as *bird* implies that a strict distinction has to be made between degree of membership and degree of representativity. Membership in the category *bird* is discrete; something is or is not a bird. But some birds may be birdier than others: the swallow does remain a more typical bird than the ostrich.

RED

Color terms such as *red* constituted the starting-point for prototypical research; drawing on the views developed in Berlin and Kay (1969), Rosch's earliest work is an experimental demonstration of the fact that the borderline between different colors is fuzzy (there is no single line in the spectrum where red stops and orange begins), and of the fact that each color term is psychologically represented by focal colors (some hues are experienced as better reds than others) (Heider 1972; Heider and Olivier 1972). These prototypical characteristics on the extensional level are not matched on the definitional level. If *red* can be analytically defined at all (i.e., if it does not simply receive an ostensive definition consisting of an enumeration of hues with their degree of focality), its definition might be 'having a color that is more like that of blood than like that of an unclouded sky, that of grass, that of the sun, that of ... (etc., listing a typical exemplar for each of the other main colors)'. Such a definition (cp. Wierzbicka 1985: 342) does not correspond with either the first or the second characteristic mentioned above.

ODD NUMBER

Armstrong, Gleitman and Gleitman (1983) have shown experimentally that even a mathematical concept such as *odd number* exhibits psychological representativity effects. This might seem remarkable, since *odd number* is a classical concept in all other respects: it receives a clear definition, does not exhibit a family resemblance structure or a radial set of clustered meanings, does not have blurred edges. However, Lakoff (1982) has made clear that degrees of representativity among odd numbers are not surprising if the experiential nature of concepts is taken into account. For instance, because the even or uneven character of a large number can be determined easily by looking at the final number, it is no wonder that uneven numbers below 10 carry more psychological weight: they are procedurally of primary importance.

VERS

As I have tried to show elsewhere (1988a), the first characteristic mentioned above is not sufficient to distinguish prototypical from classical categories, since, within the classical approach, the absence of a single definition characterized by necessity-cum-sufficiency might simply be an indication of polysemy. This means that it has to be shown on independent grounds that the allegedly prototypical concepts are not polysemous, or rather, it means that prototypical lexical concepts will be polysemous according to a definitional analysis in terms of necessary and sufficient conditions (the classical definition of polysemy), but univocal according to certain other criteria. These criteria may be found, for instance, in native speakers' intuitions about the lexical items involved, intuitions that may be revealed by tests such as Quine's (1960) or Zwicky and Sadock's (1975). In this sense, the first characteristic has to be restated: prototypical categories will exhibit intuitive univocality coupled with analytical (definitional) polysemy, and not just the absence of a necessary-and-sufficient definition.

Once this revision of the first characteristic is accepted, it can be demonstrated that the first and the second criterion need not co-occur. Lexical items that show clustered overlapping of senses may either conform or not conform to the revised first characteristic. An example of the first situation is the literal meaning of *bird*, an example of the second situation the Dutch adjective *vers*, which corresponds roughly with English *fresh* (except for the fact that the Dutch word does not carry the meaning 'cool'). Details of the comparison between both categories may be found in the paper mentioned above; by way of summary, Figures 1 and 2 represent the definitional analysis of both items. The distinction in intuitive status between *vers* and *bird* can be demonstrated by means of the Quinean test (roughly, a lexical item is ambiguous if it can be simultaneously predicated and negated of something in a particular context). Thus, taking an example based on the corresponding ambiguity in the English counterpart of *vers*, it would be quite normal to state that the news meant in the sentence *there was no fresh news from the fighting*[15] is fresh in one sense ('recent, new') but not in another ('in optimal condition'): it makes sense to say that the news is at the same time fresh and not fresh. By contrast, it would be intuitively paradoxical to state that a penguin is at the same time a bird and not a bird (disregarding figurative extensions of the semantic range of *bird*). Nevertheless, the definitional analyses in Figures 1 and 2 make clear that both concepts exhibit prototypical clustering. In both cases, too, the structural position of the instances just discussed (news, penguin) is not in the central area with maximal overlapping. In short, then, the revised version of the first characteristic need not coincide with the second characteristic.

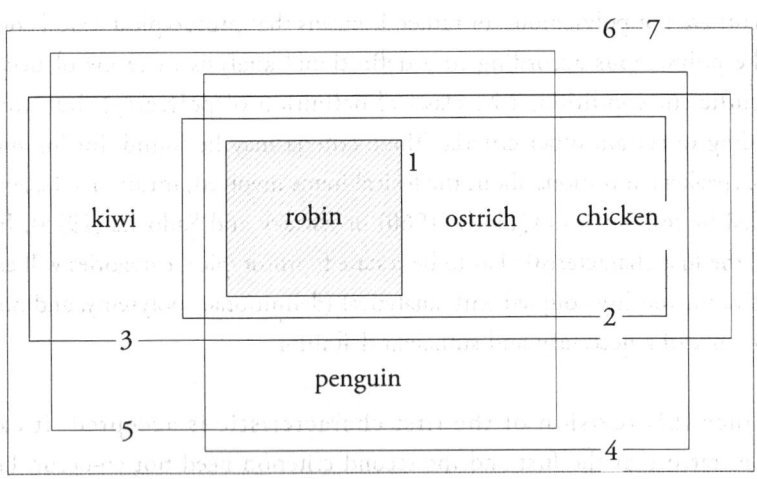

1 being able to fly   2 having feathers   3 being S-shaped
4 having wings   5 not domesticated   6 being born from eggs
7 having a beak or bill

Figure 1. A definitional analysis of *bird*

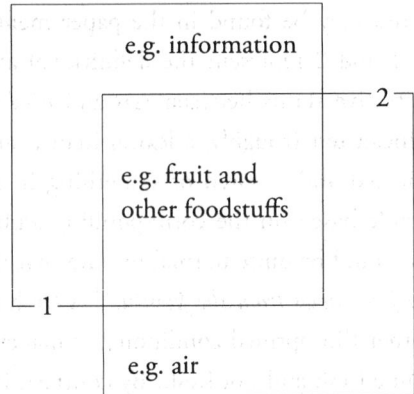

1 new, novel, recent

2 in an optimal condition, pure, untainted

Figure 2. A definitional analysis of *vers*

The insight derived from a closer look at the four examples just described may be summarized as in Table 2. It is now easy to see to what extent 'prototypicality' is itself a prototypical notion. There is no single set of attributes that is common to all of the examples discussed here. Rather, they exhibit a family resemblance structure based on partial similarities. In this sense, the set of prototypical concepts characterized by clustering of senses overlaps with the subset characterized by fuzzy boundaries (because of *vers*), and so on. At the same time, some concepts are more typically prototypical than others. *(Bird* and *vers* are more prototypical than *red.)* Notice, in particular, that the category *fruit* makes a good candidate for prototypical prototypicality, in the sense that it seems to combine all four characteristics. It shares the prototypical characteristics of *bird*, but in addition, things such as coconuts and, perhaps, tomatoes, seem to point out that the denotational boundary of *fruit* is less clear-cut than that of *bird*.

However, although the examples considered above do not have a set of attributes in common, they do share a single feature, viz. degrees of membership representativity. It is highly dubious, though, whether this feature alone suffices to distinguish prototypical concepts from classical concepts. If the possibility of a single necessary-and-sufficient definition is one of the features par excellence with which the classical conception has been identified, it might justifiably be claimed that degrees of representativity are entirely compatible with the classical conception of categorization. It is, in fact, in that sense that Armstrong, Gleitman and Gleitman (1983) deal with a category such as *odd number.* The experiments used by Rosch to measure degrees of representativity are not, they claim, indicative of prototypicality since they occur with classical, rigidly definable concepts such as *odd number.* To say the least, representativity effects are only a peripheral prototypical attribute according to Table 2 (cp. Lakoff 1986). But at the same time, the debate over the status of *odd number* shows that the concept 'prototypical concept' has no clear boundaries: it is not immediately clear whether a concept such as *odd number* should be included in the set of prototypical concepts or not.

Table 2. The prototypicality of 'prototypicality'

	BIRD	VERS	RED	ODD NUMBER
absence of classical definition	+	-	-	-
clusters of overlapping senses	+	+	-	-
degrees of representativity	+	+	+	+
absence of clear boundaries	-	+	+	-

Of course, contrary to the situation in everyday speech, such a boundary conflict should not be maintained in scientific speech. A discipline such as linguistics should try to define its concepts as clearly as possible, and the purpose of this section is precisely to show that what has intuitively been classified together as instances of prototypical categories consists of distinct phenomena that have to be kept theoretically apart. In line with prototype theory itself, however, such an attempt at clear definition should not imply an attempt to define the 'true nature' or the 'very essence' of prototypicality. Determining an 'only true kind' of prototypicality is infinitely less important than seeing what the phenomena are and how they are related to each other by contrast or similarity.

Still, there might seem to be one way in which decent sense could be made of the question what the true meaning of prototypicality would be. To begin with, let us note that the prototypical character attributed to the concept of prototypicality also shows up in the fact that the notion 'prototype' is an extremely flexible one. This can be illustrated in two ways. First, the lexical item *prototypical* is spontaneously used to name a number of phenomena that are linked by metonymy, next to the phenomena linked by similarity that are brought together in Table 2. The lexical item does not only characterize structural features of concepts, and the concepts exhibiting those features themselves, but sometimes even particular (viz., highly representative) instances of the categories in question (the robin as a prototypical bird). Second, context may stress one feature of prototypical organization rather than another (cp. the priming effects in Rosch 1975). The general purpose of one's investigations may lead one to devote more attention to one aspect of the prototypical cluster than to another. To name a few examples: degrees of representativity are important for language development studies (if it is taken into account that most concepts in early language development are acquired via their exemplars), while clustered overlapping of senses will come to the fore in linguistic or lexicographical studies into the structure of polysemy. And a cognitive interest into the epistemological principles underlying natural language will attach more weight to the decoupling of intuitive univocality and analytical, definitional polysemy.[16]

In this respect, the question with regard to the true nature of prototypicality might be transformed into the question what might be the most interesting (or perhaps even the most important) perspective for studying and defining prototypicality. But here again, the 'ultimate essence fallacy' exposed by prototype theory itself lurks round the corner: there will be different preferences for one perspective rather than another, but there will be no single ultimately and eternally most important conception of prototypicality.

In short, the foregoing analysis corroborates Wierzbicka's remark that there are 'many senses' to the notion *prototype,* and that 'the notion prototype has been used in recent literature as a catch-all notion' (1985: 343). However, a more systematic analysis than Wierzbicka's reveals that this very multiplicity of usage also supports Cognitive Semantics, in the sense that it shows that the same categorization principles may guide common sense and scientific thinking. This is, then, a further indication of the metatheoretical relevance of a cognitive conception of linguistic categorization, which I have explored at length elsewhere (1985b). At the same time, it has become clear that one of the major tasks for the further development of prototype theory is the closer investigation of the prototypically clustered characteristics of prototypicality. A major reference in this respect is Lakoff's attempt (1987: chapter 4–8) to determine which different kinds of conceptual models may lie at the basis of prototypicality effects.

3. Definitional problems, second series: 'Prototype theory' as a prototypical notion

Whereas the previous section made clear that prototypicality as used in linguistic semantics is a prototypically structured concept, it should now be noted that the prototype-theoretical movement as well is a prototypically structured approach to semantics. There are, in other words, central as well as more peripheral examples of prototypical theories. In particular, there exist a number of theories that combine aspects of the classical approach to semantic structure with aspects of the prototypical conception. In this section, two approaches will be considered that are to some extent semi-classical as well as semi-prototypical; each of both embodies a strategy for reinstating particular aspects of the classical view against the background of an overall cognitive point of view.

To begin with, some of the clarity and neatness of the classical approach may be recovered by concentrating on the prototypical centre of a category. If the non-classical indeterminacy of lexical concepts stems primarily from the flexible extendibility of concepts, discreteness may be reinstalled by avoiding the problems of clustered polysemy, i.e., by restricting the definitional analysis to the prototypical centre of the category. This approach is vigorously carried through by Wierzbicka (1985), who explicitly defends the discreteness of semantics by introspectively considering only the clear, salient centre of lexical categories. In a discussion of Labov's experimental investigation into the non-classical characteristics of everyday concepts (1973), she notes:[17]

> To state the meaning of a word, it is not sufficient to study its applicability to things; what one must do above all is to study the structure of the concept which underlies and explains that applicability. In the case of words describing natural kinds or kinds of human artefacts, to understand the structure of the concept means to describe fully and accurately the *idea* (not just the visual image) of a typical representative of the kind: the prototype. And to describe it fully and accurately we have to discover the internal logic of the concept. This is best done not through interviews, not through laboratory experiments, and not through reports of casual, superficial impressions or intuitions ... but through methodical introspection and thinking (1985: 19).

It should be noted immediately that Wierzbicka's reinstatement of discreteness does not imply that her definitions do in fact always consist of necessary-and-sufficient conditions, and she acknowledges as much (1985: 60). In this respect, Wierzbicka's approach is only partly a departure from the hard core of prototype-theoretical studies: the absence of necessary-and-sufficient conditions for the definition of certain core concepts is accepted, but the avoidance of the clustered polysemy problem 'tidies up' the semantic description and reinstates some of the classical neatness. Neither does Wierzbicka's approach imply that lexical items are always univocal; in her dictionary of English speech act verbs (1987), several items receive multiple definitions. Each of the definitions does, however, constitute a highly salient meaning, and again, by disregarding peripheral kinds of usage, the clustered or radial structure of the polysemy of lexical items does not enter the picture. The question to be asked, then, is whether Wierzbicka's restriction of the description to the salient meanings of a category is useful and adequate from a cognitive point of view.

From a methodological point of view, the periphery of natural, non-uniquely definable categories is as interesting as their salient centre(s), because it is precisely the relationship between both that typically characterizes natural categories. Cognitive Linguistics is not only interested in what constitutes the centre of a category, but also in how this centre can be extended towards peripheral cases, and how far this extension can go. The mechanisms for incorporating marginal cases into a category at the same time restrict the flexibility of that concept; it is only by studying peripheral cases, for instance, that an answer may be found with regard to the question how dissimilar things can be before they are no longer recognized as basically the same. If, in other words, flexible polysemization is indeed one of the major characteristics of natural language categories, a deliberate restriction of the description to the salient meanings of a category is methodologically less propitious, as it may lead to a neglect of this basic feature.[18]

A second strategy for salvaging aspects of the classical approach is to invoke sociolinguistic mechanisms such as Putnam's 'division of linguistic labor' (1975). According to Putnam, ordinary language users possess no more than 'stereotypical' knowledge about natural kinds, that is to say, they are aware of a number of salient characteristics, such as the fact that water is a transparent, thirst-quenching, tasteless liquid. The technical definition of *water* as H_2O, on the other hand, is to be located primarily with scientific experts. It is the experts' knowledge that ultimately determines how natural kind terms are to be used. On the one hand, a 'division of linguistic labor' ensures that there are societal experts who know that water is H_2O, that there is a distinction between elms and beech, how to recognize gold from pyrites, and so on. On the other hand, laymen attune their own linguistic usage to that of the expert scientists, technicians, etc.. The members of the non-specialized group are not required to have expert knowledge, but if they wish to be considered full-fledged members of the linguistic community, they are supposed to know the 'stereotype' connected with a category. A stereotype is, thus, a socially determined minimum set of data with regard to the extension of a category. Given the similarity between Putnam's stereotypes and the prototypes of Cognitive Linguistics (both consist roughly of the most salient information connected with a category), the division of linguistic labor might be used to rescue the classical view of concepts.[19] Expert definitions being classical (they specify an essentialist 'hidden structure' for natural kinds), the stereotypical concepts of everyday language users might now be seen as hardly more than a sloppy derivative of those classically defined expert categories. 'True' (expert) definitions would be classical, and stereotypical/prototypical concepts might be dismissed as sociolinguistically secondary phenomena.

It should be remarked immediately that such a reinstatement of the

449

classical view is not as obvious for other words than the natural kind terms for which Putnam's theory is in fact intended (what is the expert definition of the preposition *for*?). Moreover, as a sociolinguistic theory about the social factors that determine how lexical items may be used, the 'division of linguistic labor' theory is incomplete to say the least. The primacy of expert definitions would seem to imply that natural language follows the developments and discoveries of science in a strict fashion. In actual fact, however, natural language categorization is not only determined by the state of affairs in the sciences, but also by the communicative and cognitive requirements of the linguistic community in its own right. One of Putnam's own examples may serve as an illustration. Although science has discovered that *jade* refers to two kinds of materials (one with the 'hidden structure' of a silicate of calcium and magnesium, the other being a silicate of sodium and aluminium), ordinary usage continues to refer to both substances indiscriminately as *jade*. That is to say, categorization in everyday language is not entirely dependent upon scientific research, but seems to be determined at least in part by independent criteria: if the classificatory exigencies of everyday communicative interaction do not call for a distinction between the two kinds of jade, the scientific splitting of the category is largely ignored. This implies that an investigation into everyday language categorization as an independent cognitive system is justified. More generally, if Putnam's view is seen as a theory about the sociolinguistic structure of semantic norms, his hierarchical model (with experts at one end and laymen at the other) is only one among a number of alternatives, some of which (such as the one described by Bartsch 1985) link up closely with a prototypical conception of categorial structure. At the same time, however, it should be admitted that the relationship between classical scientific categorization and prototypical common-sense categorization may be explored in more depth than is yet the case.[20]

To summarize: the confusion associated with the notion of prototypicality is further increased by the fact that more straightforwardly prototypical approaches are surrounded by hybrid theories that contain particular strategies for combining classical discreteness with typically prototypical phenomena. We have discussed two such approaches (one in which the strategy in question is methodological, and another one in which it is sociolinguistic), but this does not mean that these are the only ones that might be mentioned.[21] The two approaches mentioned here are, however, particularly revealing, as they link up with two important currents in the history of Western thought. The first one simplifyingly boils down to the view that the mind is neat (if you look hard enough into it), but that the world is fuzzy: the non-discreteness that Cognitive Linguistics is concerned with arises from the fact that we have to apply clear-cut mental categories to an external reality that is so to say less well organized. The conception that the world of mental entities is somehow better organized than the outside world is obviously an idealistic one (though it does not constitute the only possible kind of idealism); Wierzbicka herself stresses the Platonist character of her approach. On the other hand, Putnam's view that science is neat whereas everyday language is fuzzy, links up with the empiricist objectivism of the Ideal Language branch of analytical philosophy: the objective structure of reality is best described by the language of science, and everyday language is at best a weak derivative of scientific categorization, at worst a conceptual muddle teeming with philosophical pseudo-problems. As the previous discussion suggests that hard-core Cognitive Linguistics steers clear of both the idealist and the objectivist option, we have here one more indication[22] for the necessity of a further investigation into the epistemological, philosophical background of the prototypical conception of categorial structure.

Notes

1   The discussion in section 2 will make clear that the term *prototype theory* should be used with care, since the theoretical uniformity that it suggests tends to obliterate the actual distinctions between the diverse forms of prototypicality discussed in the literature. The term is used here as a convenient reference mark only, to indicate a number of related theoretical conceptions of categorial structure that share an insistence on any or more of the various kinds of prototypicality effects discussed in section 2.

2   Though not exclusively: see Rosch (1988: 386).

3   Notice that this claim applies just as well to the axiomatic, postulate-based form of description that developed as the major representational alternative for Katzian componential analysis. The notion of criteriality is just as much part and parcel of the classical versions of the axiomatic alternative as it is of Katzian feature analysis.

4   See, among others, Haiman (1980) and Geeraerts (1985b).

5   The distinction between semantic and encyclopedic concepts against which Cognitive Semantics reacts is often misconstrued. In particular, in the statement that there is no principled distinction between semantic and encyclopedic information, the words *semantic* and *encyclopedic* are not used (as implied by Lehmann 1988b) in the senses 'as may be found in dictionaries' and 'as may be found in encyclopedias', respectively. Rather, the rejected distinction refers to an alleged distinction within an individual language user's conceptual memory; it involves the presupposition that there is an independent level of semantic information that belongs to the language and that is distinct from the individual's world knowledge. The kind of information that is typically found in encyclopedias involves scientific information of the kind 'ovulation triggered by copulation' for the item *cat* (the example is Lehmann's); but while the distinction between scientific and laymen's knowledge is primarily a social one, this kind of 'encyclopedic' information is only relevant for the psychological perspective of Cognitive Semantics if the individual lexicon to be described is that of someone with a certain amount of scientific knowledge of cats (or if, through sociolinguistic idealization, the average language user's lexicon may be supposed to contain that piece of scientific information).

6   There are, of course, exceptions such as Dowty (1979) to confirm the rule. The historical sketch of the advent of prototype theory given here is treated more thoroughly in Geeraerts (1988b).

7   As the semantic interests of the former audience of Generative Semantics were so to say no longer envisaged by the leading theories of the day, it does not come as a total surprise, from this point of view, to find George Lakoff, one of the leading Generative Semanticists, again as one of the leading cognitivists.

8   These antecedents are not the only ones that might be mentioned. I have elsewhere (1988c) drawn the attention to the similarities between the prestructuralist, historical tradition of semantic research and present-day Cognitive Semantics, but there are other (admittedly non-mainstream) traditions of semantic research with which Cognitive Semantics is methodologically related: think, e.g., of the anthropological research of Malinowski, Firth, and the London School in general. Even a structuralist such as Reichling has held views about the structure of polysemy that come

close to the point of view of prototype theory: his influential work on the word as the fundamental unit of linguistics (1935) contains an analysis of the Dutch word spel that is awkwardly similar to Wittgenstein's remarks about the German equivalent Spiel. The point to be stressed is this: as a theory about the (radial, clustered, dynamically flexible) structure of polysemy, prototype theory is to a considerable extent a rediscovery of views that were paramount during the prestructuralist era of the development of lexical semantics, and that lingered on below the surface in the structuralist and transformationalist periods.

9   Because of their large scope, the functionalist approach of Seiler (1986) and the naturalist approach of Dressler (1985) are particularly interesting for the use of prototypicality with regard to various aspects of the formal organization of language.

10   A bibliography of work in Cognitive Linguistics is to be found in Dirven (1988). It is worth mentioning that Cognitive Linguistics is currently in a stage of organization: a first international conference of Cognitive Linguistics was held in Duisburg in March 1989, and a new journal entitled Cognitive Linguistics, published by Mouton, is scheduled to start appearing in the beginning of 1990.

11   Next to the link with psycholinguistics, there is a connection with Artificial Intelligence research, through the correspondences between the notion of prototypicality and that of frame; see Fillmore (1977). It needs to be stressed, though, that the link is relatively weak; specifically, the correspondence just mentioned is to a certain extent counterbalanced by Lakoff's criticism (1987) of the objectivist assumptions of mainstream Artificial Intelligence research (but then again, one of Lakoff's current research projects involves a connectionist approach to the formal modeling of Cognitive Semantic notions such as metaphorical image schemata). In general, sorting out the relationship between Cognitive Semantics and Artificial Intelligence-oriented Cognitive Science will be one of the major tasks for the further development of Cognitive Semantics.

12   See Lakoff (1987: chapter 6) for the notion of a radial set, and compare Givon (1986) for a comparison between the views of Wittgenstein and those of prototype theory. The stress Givon places on the distinctions between both is slightly exaggerated, as it tends to obscure their mutual

rejection of the so-called classical theory. See also the next footnote.

13 The 'so-called' is added to stress, first, that the views of Aristotle also contain features that correspond rather with a cognitive than with a 'classical' approach, and second (more generally), that the philosophical position of prototype theory is in need of further elucidation. The present situation is rather muddled: while the classical Roschian position is to characterize prototype theory as non-Aristotelian and Wittgensteinian, Givon (1986) has argued that prototype theory is non-Wittgensteinian (see the previous note), but whereas Givon also describes prototype theory as non-Platonic, Wierzbicka (to whom we shall come back in section 3) precisely presents an explicitly Platonic version of prototype theory. More generally, the philosophical position of prototype theory has so far been discussed mainly against the background of classical philosophy (Aristotle and Plato), and against the background of contemporary analytical philosophy (see Lakoff 1987). This means that a large part of the history of Western philosophy passes unmentioned; this is to be regretted, as the post-Cartesian period in the history of philosophy is concerned with epistemological questions that are of immediate interest to Cognitive Semantics. In particular, if it can be accepted that one of the major epistemological aspects of a prototypical conception of categorial structure resides in the fact that categories are interpretive schemata that are used flexibly and dynamically in our encounters with reality, a major philosophical reference point for prototype theory will lie with those philosophical theories that recognize the constitutive role of existing knowledge with regard to new experiences. As I have argued elsewhere (1985b), the Husserlian phenomenological movement (as represented, specifically, by Maurice Merleau-Ponty) provides a good starting-point for a further confrontation with philosophy.

14 The archaeopteryx is probably regarded as a species separate from either bird or reptile.

15 The example is taken from the *Longman Dictionary of Contemporary English.*

16 Considered from this point of view, Lakoff's radial sets as such are not particularly unclassical: structured polysemy as such is entirely compatible with the classical view. Kleiber (1988) offers an insightful discussion of the theoretical consequences of the growing importance of the structure of polysemy in prototype-theoretical research.

17   For a more extended discussion of Wierzbicka's views, see Geeraerts (1988d).

18   Notice that the restriction to the prototypical centre of categories correlates with Wierzbicka's Platonic, introspective methodology: it seems probable that the applications of a category that can be accessed introspectively are only the more salient ones; peripheral cases probably do not always pass the threshold of conscious attention. What is interesting from a cognitive point of view, however, is the way people spontaneously categorize and classify things, not the way in which they introspectively reflect upon their own conceptualizations. Any attempt to describe the peripheral instances of a category together with its prototypical centre can therefore not be restricted to an introspective methodology.

19   This is not say that Putnam actually intended his stereotypical theory as such an attempted rescue: his problems lay with the notion of reference rather than with those of polysemy and categorial structure. My remarks about Putnam are an investigation into some of the possible consequences of the notion of division of linguistic labor, not an attempt to give an account of Putnam's view in its original setting. Further, it has to be mentioned that some of Putnam's later philosophical views open up entirely different perspectives for a confrontation with Cognitive Semantics; in particular, see Lakoff (1987) on Putnam and anti-objectivism.

20   An interesting contribution to such an exploration is found in Lakoff (1987: chapter 12), where it is claimed that scientific categories are far from being as classical as is usually assumed.

21   Again, see Lakoff (1987: chapter 9) for some more examples; they are situated within formal psycholexicology rather than within linguistics.

22   Next, that is, to the remarks made in footnote 13.

References

Aijmer, Karen
    1985   The semantic development of *will*. In *Historical Semantics — Historical Word-Formation,* Jacek Fisiak (ed.), 11–21. Berlin/New York: Mouton de Gruyter.
Armstrong, Sharon L., Lila R. Gleitman, and Henry Gleitman
    1983   What some concepts might not be. *Cognition* 13: 263–308.

Bartsch, Renate

1985 *Sprachnormen: Theorie und Praxis*. Tübingen: Niemeyer Verlag.

Berlin, Brent and Paul Kay

1969 *Basic Color Terms*. Berkeley: University of California Press.

Bybee, Joan and Carol L. Moder

1983 Morphological classes as natural categories. *Language* 59: 251–270.

Craig, Colette (ed.)

1986 *Noun Classes and Categorization*. Amsterdam/Philadelphia: John Benjamins.

Dirven, René

1988 Bibliography of Cognitive Linguistics. Duisburg: Linguistic Agency of the University of Duisburg.

Dowty, David

1979 *Word Meaning and Montague Grammar*. Dordrecht: Reidel.

Dressler, Wolfgang

1985 *Morphophonology*. Ann Arbor: Karoma.

Fillmore, Charles J.

1975 An alternative to checklist theories of meaning. In *Proceedings of the First Annual Meeting of the Berkeley Linguistics Society*, Cathy Cogen, Henry Thompson, and James Wright (eds.), 123–131. Berkeley: Berkeley Linguistics Society.

1977 Scenes-and-frames semantics. In *Linguistic Structures Processing*, Antonio Zampolli (ed.), 55–81. Amsterdam: North Holland Publishing Company.

Geeraerts, Dirk

1983 Prototype theory and diachronic semantics: A case study. *Indogermanische Forschungen* 88: 1–32.

1985a *Paradigm and Paradox. Explorations into a Paradigmatic Theory of Meaning and its Epistemological Background*. Leuven: Universitaire Pers.

1985b Les données stéréotypiques, prototypiques et encyclopédiques dans le dictionnaire. *Cahiers de Lexicologie* 46: 27–43.

1985c Cognitive restrictions on the structure of semantic change. In *Historical Semantics — Historical Word Formation*, Jacek Fisiak (ed.), 127–153. Berlin/New York: Mouton de Gruyter.

1988a On necessary and sufficient conditions. *Journal of Semantics* 5: 275–291.

1988b Katz revisited: aspects of the history of lexical semantics. In *Understanding the Lexicon*, Werner Hüllen and Rainer Schulze (eds.), 23–35. Tübingen: Max Niemeyer Verlag.

1988c Cognitive Grammar and the history of lexical semantics. In *Topics in Cognitive Linguistics*, Brygida Rudzka-Ostyn (ed.), 647–677. Amsterdam/Philadelphia: John Benjamins.

1988d Review of Anna Wierzbicka, Lexicography and Conceptual Analysis. *Language in Society* 17: 449–455.

Givon, Talmy

1986 Prototypes: between Plato and Wittgenstein. In *Noun Classes and Categorization*, Colette Craig (ed.), 78–102. Amsterdam/Philadelphia: John Benjamins.

John Haiman

1980 Dictionaries and encylopedias. *Lingua* 50: 329–357.

Heider, Eleanor R.

1972 Universals in color naming and memory. *Journal of Experimental Psychology* 93: 10–20.

Heider, Eleanor R. and Olivier, D.C.

1972 The structure of color space in naming and memory for two languages. *Cognitive Psychology* 3: 337–354.

Holland, Dorothy and Naomi Quinn (eds.)

1987 *Cultural Models in Language and Thought*. Cambridge: Cambridge University Press.

Hüllen, Werner and Rainer Schulze (eds.)

1988 *Understanding the Lexicon. Meaning, Sense, and World Knowledge in Lexical Semantics*. Tübingen: Niemeyer.

Katz, Jerrold J. and Jerry A. Fodor

1963 The structure of a semantic theory. *Language* 39, 170–210.

Kleiber, Georges

1988 Prototype, stéréotype: un air de famille? *DRLAV. Revue de Linguistique* 38: 1–61.

Labov, William

1973 The boundaries of words and their meanings. In *New Ways of Analysing Variation in English*, Charles J. Bailey and Roger Shuy (eds.), 340–373. Washington: Georgetown University Press.

Lakoff, George

1982 Categories and cognitive models. Trier: Linguistic Agency of the University of Trier. Also as: *Berkeley Cognitive Science Report* no. 2. Berkeley: Institute for Human Learning.

1986 Classifiers as a reflection of mind. In *Noun Classes and Categorization,* Colette Craig (ed.), 13–51. Amsterdam/Philadelphia: John Benjamins.

1987 *Women, Fire,* and *Dangerous Things. What Categories Reveal about the Mind.* Chicago: The University of Chicago Press.

Langacker Ronald W.

1987 *Foundations of Cognitive Grammar I.* Stanford: Stanford University Press.

Lehmann, Winfred P. (ed.)

1988a *Prototypes in Language and Cognition.* Ann Arbor: Karoma.

Lehmann Winfred P.

1988b Review of R. Langacker, Foundations of Cognitive Grammar. *General Linguistics* 28: 122–30.

Medin, Doug L. and Edward E. Smith

1984 Concepts and concept formation. *Annual Review of Psychology* 35: 113–138.

Mervis, Carolyn B. and Eleanor Rosch

1981 Categorization of natural objects. *Annual Review of Psychology* 32: 89–115.

Nathan, Geoffrey S.

1986 Phonemes as mental categories. In *Proceedings of the Twelfth Annual Meeting of the Berkeley Linguistics Society,* Vassiliki Nikiforidou, Mary VanClay, Mary Niepokuj, Deborah Feder (eds.), 212–224. Berkeley: Berkeley Linguistics Society.

Neisser, Ulrich

1987 *Concepts and Conceptual Development. Ecological and Intellectual Factors in Categorization.* Cambridge: Cambridge University Press.

Posner, Michael

1986 Empirical studies of prototypes. *Noun classes and categorization,* Colette Craig (ed.), 53–61. Amsterdam/Philadelphia: John Benjamins.

Post, Michael

1986 A prototype approach to denominal adjectives. In *Linguistics across Historical and Geographical Boundaries,* Dieter Kastovsky and Aleksander

Szwedek (eds.), II: 1003–1013. Berlin/New York: Mouton De Gruyter.

Putnam, Hilary

1975   The meaning of Meaning. In *Mind, Language, and Reality. Philosophical Papers II*, Hilary Putnam, 215–271. Cambridge: Cambridge University Press.

Quine, Willard V.O.

1960   *Word and Object*. Cambridge, Mass.: MIT Press.

Reichling, Anton

1935   *Het Woord*. Zwolle: Tjeenk Willink.

Rosch, Eleanor

1973   On the internal structure of perceptual and semantic categories. In *Cognitive Development and the Acquisition of Language,* Timothy E. Moore (ed.), 111–144. New York: Academic Press.

1975   Cognitive representations of semantic categories. *Journal of Experimental Psychology: General* 104: 192–233.

1977   Human categorization. In *Studies in Cross-cultural Psychology I,* Warren, Neil (ed.), 1–49. New York: Academic Press.

1978   Principles of categorization. In *Cognition and Categorization,* Eleanor Rosch and Barbara B. Lloyd (eds.), 27–48. Hillsdale, NJ: Lawrence Erlbaum.

1988   Coherences and categorization: A historical view. In *The Development of Language and Language Researchers. Essays in Honor of Roger Brown,* Frank Kessel (ed.), 373–392. Hillsdale, NJ: Lawrence Erlbaum.

Rosch, Eleanor and Carolyn B. Mervis

1975   Family resemblances: Studies in the internal structure of categories. *Cognitive Psychology* 7: 573–605.

Rosch, Eleanor, Carolyn B. Mervis, Wayne D. Gray, David Johnson, and Penny Boyes-Braem

1976   Basic objects in natural categories. *Cognitive Psychology* 8: 382–439.

Rosch, Eleanor, Carol Simpson, and Scott R. Miller

1976   Structural bases of typicality effects. *Journal of Experimental Psychology: Human Perception and Peformance* 2: 491–502.

Ross, John R.

1987   Islands and syntactic prototypes. In *Papers from the 23rd Annual Meeting of the Chicago Linguistic Society,* Barbara Need, Eric Schiller, and Anna Bosch (eds.), 309–320. Chicago: Chicago Linguistic Society.

Rudzka-Ostyn, Brygida

1988   Semantic extensions into the domain of verbal communication. In *Topics in Cognitive Linguistics,* Brygida Rudzka-Ostyn (ed.), 507–553. Amsterdam/Philadelphia: John Benjamins.

Smith, Edward E. and Doug Medin

1981   *Categories and Concepts.* Cambridge, MA: Harvard University Press.

Taylor, John

1989   *Linguistic Categorization. Prototypes in Linguistic Theory.* Oxford: Clarendon Press.

Tsohatzidis, Savas L. (ed.)

1989   *Meanings and Prototypes. Studies on Linguistic Categorization.* London: Routledge and Kegan Paul.

Uhlenbeck, Eugenius M.

1967   The dynamic nature of word meaning. *Actes du Xe Congrès International des Linguistes* II, 679–685. Bucarest: Editions de l'Academie.

Van Langendonck, Willy

1986   Markedness, prototypes, and language acquisition. *Cahiers de l'Institut de Linguistique de Louvain* 12: 39–76.

Van Oosten, Jeanne

1986   The nature of subjects, topics, and agents: a cognitive explanation. Bloomington: Indiana University Linguistics Club.

Waismann, Friedrich

1952   Verifiability. In *Logic and Language (First Series),* Anthony Flew (ed.), 117–144. Oxford: Basil Blackwell.

Weinreich, Uriel

1966   Explorations in semantic theory. *Current Trends in Linguistics* III: 395–479.

Wierzbicka, Anna

1985   *Lexicography and Conceptual Analysis.* Ann Arbor: Karoma.

1987   *English Speech Act Verbs: A Semantic Dictionary.* Sydney: Academic Press.

Winters, Margaret

1987   Syntactic and semantic space: the development of the French subjunctive. In *Papers from the Seventh International Conference on Historical Linguistics,* Anna G. Ramat, Onofrio Carruba, and Giulano Bernini (eds.), 607–618. Amsterdam/Philadelphia: John Benjamins.

Wittgenstein, Ludwig
    1953   *Philosophische Untersuchungen. Philosophical Investigations.* Oxford:
    Basil Blackwell.
Zwicky, Arnold and Jerry Sadock
    1975   Ambiguity tests and how to fail them. In *Syntax and Semantics 4,* John
    Kimball (ed.), 1–36. New York: Academic Press.

The Contemporary Theory of Metaphor

George Lakoff

Do not go gentle into that good night.
Dylan Thomas
Death is the mother of beauty.
Wallace Stevens, "Sunday Morning"

1. Introduction

These famous lines by Thomas and Stevens are examples of what classical theorists, at least since Aristotle, have referred to as metaphor: instances of novel poetic language in which words like "mother," "go," and "night" are not used in their normal everyday sense. In classical theories of language, metaphor was seen as a matter of language, not thought. Metaphorical expressions were assumed to be mutually exclusive with the realm of ordinary everyday language: everyday language had no metaphor, and metaphor used mechanisms outside the realm of everyday conventional language.

The classical theory was taken so much for granted over the centuries that many people didn't realize that it was just a theory. The theory was not merely taken to be true, but came to be taken as definitional. The word "metaphor" was defined as a novel or poetic linguistic expression where one or more words for a concept are used outside of their normal conventional meaning to express a "similar" concept.

But such issues are not matters for definitions; they are empirical questions. As a cognitive scientist and a linguist, one asks: what are the generalizations governing the linguistic expressions referred to classically as "poetic metaphors"? When this question is answered rigorously, the classical theory turns out to be false. The generalizations governing poetic metaphorical expressions are not in language, but in thought: they are general mappings across conceptual domains. Moreover, these general principles which take the form of conceptual mappings, apply not just to novel poetic expressions, but to much of ordinary everyday language.

In short, the locus of metaphor is not in language at all, but in the way we conceptualize one mental domain in terms of another. The general theory of metaphor is given by characterizing such cross-domain mappings. And in the process, everyday abstract concepts like time, states, change, causation, and purpose also turn out to be metaphorical.

The result is that metaphor (that is, cross-domain mapping) is absolutely central to ordinary natural language semantics, and that the study of literary metaphor is an extension of the study of everyday metaphor. Everyday metaphor is characterized by a huge system of thousands of cross-domain mappings, and this system is made use of in novel metaphor.

Because of these empirical results, the word "metaphor" has come to be used differently in contemporary metaphor research. It has come to mean "a crossdomain mapping in the conceptual system." The term "metaphorical expression" refers to a linguistic expression (a word, phrase, or sentence) that is the surface realization of such a cross-domain mapping (this is what the word "metaphor" referred to in the old theory). I will adopt the contemporary usage throughout this chapter.

Experimental results demonstrating the cognitive reality of the extensive system of metaphorical mappings are discussed by Gibbs (1993). Mark Turner's 1987 book *Death Is the Mother of Beauty*, whose title comes from Stevens' great line, demonstrates in detail how that line uses the ordinary system of everyday mappings. For further examples of how literary metaphor makes use of the ordinary metaphor system, see *More Than Cool Reason: A Field Guide to Poetic Metaphor* by Lakoff and Turner (1989) and *Reading Minds: The Study of English in the Age of Cognitive Science* by Turner (1991).

Since the everyday metaphor system is central to the understanding of poetic metaphor, we will begin with the everyday system and then turn to poetic examples.

1.1 Homage to Ready

The contemporary theory that metaphor is primarily conceptual, conventional, and part of the ordinary system of thought and language can be traced to

463

Michael Reddy's (1993) now classic essay, "The Conduit Metaphor," which first appeared in the first edition of Ortony (1993[1979]). Reddy did far more in that essay than he modestly suggested. With a single, thoroughly analyzed example, he allowed us to see, albeit in a restricted domain, that ordinary everyday English is largely metaphorical, dispelling once and for all the traditional view that metaphor is primarily in the realm of poetic or "figurative" language. Reddy showed, for a single, very significant case, that the locus of metaphor is thought, not language, that metaphor is a major and indispensable part of our ordinary, conventional way of conceptualizing the world, and that our everyday behavior reflects our metaphorical understanding of experience. Though other theorists had noticed some of these characteristics of metaphor, Reddy was the first to demonstrate them by rigorous linguistic analysis, stating generalizations over voluminous examples.

Reddy's chapter on how we conceptualize the concept of communication by metaphor gave us a tiny glimpse of an enormous system of conceptual metaphor. Since its appearance, an entire branch of linguistics and cognitive science has developed to study systems of metaphorical thought that we use to reason and base our actions on, and that underlie a great deal of the structure of language.

The bulk of the chapters in Ortony (1993[1979]), in which the present article appeared originally, were written before the development of the contemporary field of metaphor research. My chapter therefore contradicts much that appears in the other chapters of Ortony (1993[1979]), many of which make certain assumptions that were widely taken for granted in 1977. A major assumption that is challenged by contemporary research is the traditional division between literal and figurative language, with metaphor as a kind of figurative language. This entails, by definition, that: what is literal is not metaphorical. In fact, the word "literal" has traditionally been used with one or more of a set of assumptions that have since proved to be false:

1.2 Traditional false assumptions

– All everyday conventional language is literal, and none is metaphorical.
– All subject matter can be comprehended literally, without metaphor.
– Only literal language can be contingently true or false.
– All definitions given in the lexicon of a language are literal, not metaphorical.

—The concepts used in the grammar of a language are all literal; none are metaphorical.

The big difference between the contemporary theory and views of metaphor prior to Reddy's work lies in this set of assumptions. The reason for the difference is that, in the intervening years, a huge system of everyday, conventional, conceptual metaphors has been discovered. It is a system of metaphor that structures our everyday conceptual system, including most abstract concepts, and that lies behind much of everyday language. The discovery of this enormous metaphor system has destroyed the traditional literal-figurative distinction, since the term "literal," as used in defining the traditional distinction, carries with it all those false assumptions.

A major difference between the contemporary theory and the classical one is based on the old literal-figurative distinction. Given that distinction, one might think that one "arrives at" a metaphorical interpretation of a sentence by "starting" with the literal meaning and applying some algorithmic process to it (see Searle 1993). Though there do exist cases where something like this happens, this is not in general how metaphor works, as we shall see shortly.

1.3   What is not metaphorical

Although the old literal-metaphorical distinction was based on assumptions that have proved to be false, one can make a different sort of literal-metaphorical distinction: those concepts that are not comprehended via conceptual metaphor might be called "literal." Thus, although I will argue that a great many common concepts like causation and purpose are metaphorical, there is nonetheless an extensive range of non-metaphorical concepts. A sentence like *the balloon went up* is not metaphorical, nor is the old philosopher's favorite *the cat is on the mat*. But as soon as one gets away from concrete physical experience and starts talking about abstractions or emotions, metaphorical understanding is the norm.

2. The contemporary theory: Some examples

Let us now turn to some examples that are illustrative of contemporary metaphor research. They will mostly come from the domain of everyday conventional metaphor, since that has been the main focus of the research. I will turn to the discussion of poetic metaphor only after I have discussed the conventional system, since knowledge of the conventional system is needed to make sense of most of the poetic cases.

The evidence for the existence of a system of conventional conceptual metaphors is of five types:

– Generalizations governing polysemy, that is, the use of words with a number of related meanings
– Generalizations governing inference patterns, that is, cases where a pattern of inferences from one conceptual domain is used in another domain
– Generalizations governing novel metaphorical language (see Lakoff and Turner 1989)
– Generalizations governing patterns of semantic change (see Sweetser 1990)
– Psycholinguistic experiments (see Gibbs 1990)

We will be discussing primarily the first three of these sources of evidence, since they are the most robust.

2.1 Conceptual metaphor

Imagine a love relationship described as follows:

Our relationship has hit a *dead-end street.*

Here love is being conceptualized as a journey, with the implication that the relationship is *stalled,* that the lovers cannot *keep going the way they've been going,* that they must *turn back,* or abandon the relationship altogether. This is not an isolated case. English has many everyday expressions that are based on a conceptualization of love as a journey, and they are used not just for talking about love, but for reasoning about it as well. Some are necessarily about love; others can be understood that way:

Look *how far we've come.*
It's been *a long, bumpy road.*

We can't *turn back* now.
We're at a *crossroads*.
We may have to *go our separate ways*.
The relationship isn't *going anywhere*.
We're *spinning our wheels*.
Our relationship is *off the track*.
The marriage is *on the rocks*.
We may have to *bail out* of this relationship.

These are ordinary, everyday English expressions. They are not poetic, nor are they necessarily used for special rhetorical effect. Those like *look how far we've come,* which aren't necessarily about love, can readily be understood as being about love.

As a linguist and a cognitive scientist, I ask two commonplace questions:

– Is there a general principle governing how these linguistic expressions about journeys are used to characterize love?
– Is there a general principle governing how our patterns of inference about journeys are used to reason about love when expressions such as these are used?

The answer to both is yes. Indeed, there is a single general principle that answers both questions, but it is a general principle that is neither part of the grammar of English, nor the English lexicon. Rather, it is part of the conceptual system underlying English. It is a principle for understanding the domain of love in terms of the domain of journeys.

The principle can be stated informally as a metaphorical scenario:

The lovers are travelers on a journey together, with their common life goals seen as destinations to be reached. The relationship is their vehicle, and it allows them to pursue those common goals together. The relationship is seen as fulfilling its purpose as long as it allows them to make progress toward their common goals. The journey isn't easy. There are impediments, and there are places (crossroads) where a decision has to be made about which direction to go in and whether to keep traveling together.

The metaphor involves understanding one domain of experience, love, in terms of a very different domain of experience, journeys. More technically, the metaphor can be understood as a mapping (in the mathematical sense) from a source domain (in this case, journeys) to a target domain (in this case, love). The mapping is tightly structured. There are ontological correspondences, according to which entities in the domain of love (e.g., the lovers, their common goals, their difficulties, the love relationship, etc.) correspond systematically to entities in the domain of a journey (the travelers, the vehicle, destinations, etc.).

To make it easier to remember what mappings there are in the conceptual system, Johnson and I (Lakoff and Johnson 1980) adopted a strategy for naming such mappings, using mnemonics which suggest the mapping. Mnemonic names typically (though not always) have the form: TARGET-DOMAIN IS SOURCE-DOMAIN, or alternatively, TARGET-DOMAIN AS SOURCE-DOMAIN. In this case, the name of the mapping is LOVE IS A JOURNEY. When I speak of the LOVE IS A JOURNEY metaphor, I am using a mnemonic for a set of ontological correspondences that characterize a mapping, namely:

THE LOVE-AS-JOURNEY MAPPING
– The lovers correspond to travelers.
– The love relationship corresponds to the vehicle.
– The lovers' common goals correspond to their common destinations on the journey.

Difficulties in the relationship correspond to impediments to travel. It is a common mistake to confuse the name of the mapping, LOVE IS A JOURNEY, for the mapping itself. The mapping is the set of correspondences, Thus, whenever I refer to a metaphor by a mnemonic like LOVE IS A JOURNEY, I will be referring to such a set of correspondences.

If mappings are confused with names of mappings, another misunderstanding can arise. Names of mappings commonly have a propositional form, for example, LOVE IS A JOURNEY. But the mappings themselves are not propositions. If mappings are confused with names for mappings, one might mistakenly think that, in this theory, metaphors are propositional. They are anything but that: metaphors are mappings, that is, sets of conceptual correspondences.

The LOVE-AS-JOURNEY mapping is a set of ontological correspondences that characterize epistemic correspondences by mapping knowledge about journeys onto knowledge about love. Such correspondences permit us to reason about love using the knowledge we use to reason about journeys. Let us take an example. Consider the expression, *we're stuck,* said by one lover to another about their relationship. How is this expression about travel to be understood as being about their relationship?

We're stuck can be used of travel, and when it is, it evokes knowledge about travel. The exact knowledge may vary from person to person, but here is a typical example of the kind of knowledge evoked. The capitalized expressions represent entities in the ontology of travel, that is, in the source domain of the LOVE-IS-A-JOURNEY mapping given above.

TWO TRAVELERS are in a VEHICLE, TRAVELING WITH COMMON DESTINATIONS. The VEHICLE encounters some IMPEDIMENT and gets stuck, that is, becomes nonfunctional. If the travelers do nothing, they will not REACH THEIR DESTINATIONS. There are a limited number of alternatives for action: They can try to get the vehicle moving again, either by fixing it or getting it past the IMPEDIMENT that stopped it.

They can remain in the nonfunctional VEHICLE and give up on REACHING THEIR DESTINATIONS.

They can abandon the VEHICLE.

The alternative of remaining in the nonfunctional VEHICLE takes the least effort, but does not satisfy the desire to REACH THEIR DESTINATIONS.

The ontological correspondences that constitute the LOVE IS A JOURNEY metaphor map the ontology of travel onto the ontology of love. In doing so, they map this scenario about travel onto a corresponding love scenario in which the corresponding alternatives for action are seen. Here is the corresponding love scenario that results from applying the correspondences to this knowledge structure. The target domain entities that are mapped by the correspondences are capitalized:

TWO LOVERS are in a LOVE RELATIONSHIP, PURSUING COMMON LIFE GOALS. The RELATIONSHIP encounters some DIFFICULTY, which makes it nonfunctional. If they do nothing, they will not be able to ACHIEVE THEIR

LIFE GOALS. There are a limited number of alternatives for action:
They can try to get it moving again, either by fixing it or getting it past the DIFFICULTY.
They can remain in the nonfunctional RELATIONSHIP, and give up on ACHIEVING THEIR LIFE GOALS.
They can abandon the RELATIONSHIP.
The alternative of remaining in the nonfunctional RELATIONSHIP takes the least effort, but does not satisfy the desire to ACHIEVE LIFE GOALS.

This is an example of an inference pattern that is mapped from one domain to another. It is via such mappings that we apply knowledge about travel to love relationships.

2.2 Metaphors are not mere words

What constitutes the LOVE AS JOURNEY metaphor is not any particular word or expression. It is the ontological mapping across conceptual domains, from the source domain of journeys to the target domain of love. The metaphor is not just a matter of language, but of thought and reason. The language is secondary. The mapping is primary, in that it sanctions the use of source domain language and inference patterns for target domain concepts. The mapping is conventional, that is, it is a fixed part of our conceptual system, one of our conventional ways of conceptualizing love relationships.

This view of metaphor is thoroughly at odds with the view that metaphors are just linguistic expressions. If metaphors were merely linguistic expressions, we would expect different linguistic expressions to be different metaphors. Thus, *We've hit a dead-end street* would constitute one metaphor. *We can't turn back now* would constitute another, entirely different metaphor. *Their marriage is on the rocks* would involve still a different metaphor. And so on for dozens of examples. Yet we don't seem to have dozens of different metaphors here. We have one metaphor, in which love is conceptualized as a journey. The mapping tells us precisely how love is being conceptualized as a journey. And this unified way of *conceptualizing* love metaphorically is realized in many different *linguistic* expressions.

It should be noted that contemporary metaphor theorists commonly use the term "metaphor" to refer to the conceptual mapping, and the term "metaphorical expression" to refer to an individual linguistic expression (like *dead-end street*) that is sanctioned by a mapping. We have adopted this terminology for the following reason: Metaphor, as a phenomenon, involves both conceptual mappings and individual linguistic expressions. It is important to keep them distinct. Since it is the mappings that are primary and that state the generalizations that are our principal concern, we have reserved the term "metaphor" for the mappings, rather than for the linguistic expressions.

In the literature of the field, small capitals like LOVE IS A JOURNEY are used as mnemonics to name mappings. Thus, when we refer to the LOVE IS A JOURNEY metaphor, we are referring to the set of correspondences discussed above. The English sentence *love is a journey,* on the other hand, is a metaphorical expression that is understood via that set of correspondences.

2.3 Generalizations

The LOVE IS A JOURNEY metaphor is a conceptual mapping that characterizes a generalization of two kinds:

- Polysemy generalization: a generalization over related senses of linguistic expressions, for example, *dead-end street, crossroads, stuck, spinning one's wheels, not going anywhere,* and so on.
- Inferential generalization: a generalization over inferences across different conceptual domains.

That is, the existence of the mapping provides a general answer to two questions:

- Why are words for travel used to describe love relationships?
- Why are inference patterns used to reason about travel also used to reason about love relationships?

Correspondingly, from the perspective of the linguistic analyst, the existence of such cross-domain pairings of words and of inference patterns provides evidence for the existence of such mappings.

2.4 Novel extensions of conventional metaphors

The fact that the LOVE-IS-A-JOURNEY mapping is a fixed part of our conceptual system explains why new and imaginative uses of the mapping can be understood instantly, given the ontological correspondences and other knowledge about journeys. Take the song lyric, *We're driving in the fast lane on the freeway of love.* The traveling knowledge called upon is this: when you drive in the fast lane, you go a long way in a short time and it can be exciting and dangerous. The general metaphorical mapping maps this knowledge about driving into knowledge about love relationships. The danger may be to the vehicle (the relationship may not last) or the passengers (the lovers may be hurt emotionally). The excitement of the love journey is sexual. Our understanding of the song lyric is a consequence of the preexisting metaphorical correspondences of the LOVE IS A JOURNEY metaphor.

The song lyric is instantly comprehensible to speakers of English because those metaphorical correspondences are already part of our conceptual system.

The LOVE IS A JOURNEY metaphor and Reddy's Conduit Metaphor were the two examples that first convinced me that metaphor was not a figure of speech, but a mode of thought, defined by a systematic mapping from a source to a target domain. What convinced me were the three characteristics of metaphor that I have just discussed:

1. The systematicity in the linguistic correspondences.
2. The use of metaphor to govern reasoning and behavior based on that reasoning.
3. The possibility for understanding novel extensions in terms of the conventional correspondences.

2.5 Motivation

Each conventional metaphor, that is, each mapping, is a fixed pattern of conceptual correspondence across conceptual domains. As such, each mapping defines an open-ended class of potential correspondences across inference patterns. When activated, a mapping may apply to a novel source domain knowledge structure and characterize a corresponding target domain knowledge structure.

Mappings should not be thought of as processes, or as algorithms that mechanically take source domain inputs and produce target domain outputs. Each mapping should be seen instead as a fixed pattern of ontological correspondences across domains that may, or may not, be applied to a source domain knowledge structure or a source domain lexical item. Thus, lexical items that are conventional in the source domain are not always conventional in the target domain. Instead, each source domain lexical item may or may not make use of the static mapping pattern. If it does, it has an extended lexicalized sense in the target domain, where that sense is characterized by the mapping. If not, the source domain lexical item will not have a conventional sense in the target domain, but may still be actively mapped in the case of novel metaphor. Thus, the words *freeway* and *fast lane* are not conventionally used of love, but the knowledge structures associated with them are mapped by the LOVE IS A JOURNEY metaphor in the case of *We're driving in the fast lane on the freeway of love.*

2.6 Imageable idioms

Many of the metaphorical expressions discussed in the literature on conventional metaphor are idioms. On classical views, idioms have arbitrary meanings, but within cognitive linguistics, the possibility exists that they are not arbitrary, but rather motivated. That is, they do not arise automatically by productive rules, but they fit one or more patterns present in the conceptual system. Let us look a little more closely at idioms.

An idiom like *spinning one's wheels* comes with a conventional mental image, that of the wheels of a car stuck in some substance — mud, sand, snow, or on ice — so that the car cannot move when the motor is engaged and the wheels turn. Part of our knowledge about that image is that a lot of energy is being used up (in spinning the wheels) without any progress being made, that the situation will not readily change of its own accord, that it will take a lot of effort on the part of the occupants to get the vehicle moving again — and that may not even be possible.

The LOVE IS A JOURNEY metaphor applies to this knowledge about the image. It maps this knowledge onto knowledge about love relationships: a lot of energy is being spent without any progress toward fulfilling common goals, the situation will not change of its own accord, it will take a lot of effort on the part of the

473

lovers to make more progress, and so on. In short, when idioms have associated conventional images, it is common for an independently motivated conceptual metaphor to map that knowledge from the source to the target domain. For a survey of experiments verifying the existence of such images and such mappings, see Gibbs (1990).

2.7 Mappings are at the superordinate level

In the LOVE-IS-A-JOURNEY mapping, a love relationship corresponds to a vehicle. A vehicle is a superordinate category that includes such basic level categories as car, train, boat, and plane. The examples of vehicles are typically drawn from this range of basic level categories: car (*long bumpy road, spinning our wheels*), train (*off the track*), boat (*on the rocks, foundering*), plane (*just taking off, bailing out*). This is not an accident: in general, we have found that mappings are at the superordinate rather than the basic level. Thus, we do not find fully general submappings like A LOVE RELATIONSHIP IS A CAR; when we find a love relationship conceptualized as a car, we also tend to find it conceptualized as a boat, a train, a plane, and so forth. It is the superordinate category VEHICLE not the basic level category CAR that is in the general mapping.

It should be no surprise that the generalization is at the superordinate level, while the special cases are at the basic level. After all, the basic level is the level of rich mental images and rich knowledge structure. (For a discussion of the properties of basic level categories, see Lakoff 1987: 31–50.) A mapping at the superordinate level maximizes the possibilities for mapping rich conceptual structures in the source domain onto the target domain, since it permits many basic level instances, each of which is information rich.

Thus, a prediction is made about conventional mappings: the categories mapped will tend to be at the superordinate rather than the basic level. One tends not to find mappings like A LOVE RELATIONSHIP IS A CAR OR A LOVE RELATIONSHIP IS A BOAT. Instead, one tends to find both basic level cases (e.g., both cars and boats), which indicates that the generalization is one level higher, at the superordinate level of the vehicle. In the hundreds of cases of conventional mappings studied so far, this prediction has been borne out: it is superordinate categories that are used in mappings.

3. Basic semantic concepts that are metaphorical

Most people are not too surprised to discover that emotional concepts like love and anger are understood metaphorically. What is more interesting, and I think more exciting, is the realization that many of the most basic concepts in our conceptual systems are also normally comprehended via metaphor — concepts like time, quantity, state, change, action, cause, purpose, means, modality, and even the concept of a category. These are concepts that enter normally into the grammars of languages, and if they are indeed metaphorical in nature, then metaphor becomes central to grammar.

I would like to suggest that the same kinds of considerations that lead to our acceptance of the LOVE IS A JOURNEY metaphor lead inevitably to the conclusion that such basic concepts are often, and perhaps always, understood via metaphor.

3.1 Categories

Classical categories are understood metaphorically in terms of bounded regions, or "containers." Thus, something can be *in* or *out* of a category, it can be *put into* a category or *removed from* a category. The logic of classical categories is the logic of containers (see Figure 1).

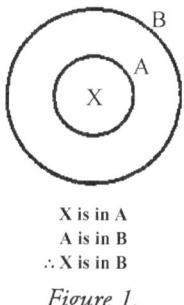

X is in A
A is in B
∴ X is in B

Figure 1.

If X is in container A and container A is in container B, then X is in container B.

This is true not by virtue of any logical deduction, but by virtue of the topological properties of containers. Under the CLASSICAL CATEGORIES ARE CONTAINERS metaphor, the logical properties of categories are inherited from the logical properties of containers. One of the principal logical properties of classical categories is that the classical syllogism holds for them. The classical syllogism,

> Socrates is a man.
> All men are mortal.
> Therefore, Socrates is mortal.

is of the form:

> If X is in category A and category A is in category B, then X is in category B.

Thus, the logical properties of classical categories can be seen as following from the topological properties of containers plus the metaphorical mapping from containers to categories. As long as the topological properties of containers are preserved by the mapping, this result will be true.

In other words, there is a generalization to be stated here. The language of containers applies to classical categories and the logic of containers is true of classical categories. A single metaphorical mapping ought to characterize both the linguistic and logical generalizations at once. This can be done provided that the topological properties of containers are preserved in the mapping.

The joint linguistic-and-inferential relation between containers and classical categories is not an isolated case. Let us take another example.

3.2 Quantity and linear scales

The concept of quantities involves at least two metaphors. The first is the well-known MORE IS UP, LESS IS DOWN metaphor as shown by a myriad of expressions like *prices rose, stocks skyrocketed, the market plummeted,* and so on. A second is that LINEAR SCALES ARE PATHS. We can see this in expressions like:

> John is *far* more intelligent than Bill.
> John's intelligence *goes way beyond* Bill's.
> John is *way ahead of* Bill in intelligence.

The metaphor maps the starting point of the path onto the bottom of the scale and maps distance traveled onto quantity in general.

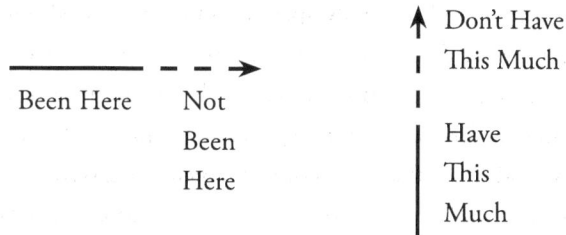

Figure 2.

What is particularly interesting is that the logic of paths maps onto the logic of linear scale (see Figure 2).

> Path inference: if you are going from A to C, and you are now at an intermediate point B, then you have been at all points between A and B and not at any points between B and C.

Example: If you are going from San Francisco to New York along Route 80, and you are now at Chicago, then you have been to Denver but not to Pittsburgh.

> Linear scale inference: if you have exactly $50 in your bank account, then you have $40, $30, and so on, but not $60, $70, or any larger amount.

The form of these inferences is the same. The path inference is a consequence of the cognitive topology of paths. It will be true of any path image-schema. Again, there is a linguistic-and-inferential generalization to be stated. It would be stated by the metaphor LINEAR SCALES ARE PATHS, provided that metaphors in general preserve the cognitive topology (that is, the image-schematic structure) of the source domain.

Looking at the inferential structure alone, one might suggest a non-metaphorical alternative in which both linear scales and paths are instances of a more general abstract schema. But when *both* the inferential and lexical data are considered, it becomes clear that a metaphorical solution is required. An expression like *ahead of* is from the spatial domain, not the linear scale domain: *ahead* in its core sense is defined with respect to one's head — it refers to the direction in which one is facing. To say that there is no metaphorical mapping from paths to scales is to say that *ahead of* is not fundamentally spatial and characterized with respect to heads; it is to claim rather that *ahead* is very abstract, neutral between space and linear scales, and has nothing to do with heads. This would be a bizarre analysis. Similarly, for sentences like *John's intelligence goes beyond Bill's,* the nonmetaphorical analysis would claim that *go* is not fundamentally a verb of motion at all, but is somehow neutral between motion and a linear relation. This would also be bizarre. In short, if one grants that *ahead of* and *go* are fundamentally spatial, then the fact that they can also be used of linear scales suggests a metaphor solution. There could be no such neutral sense of *go* for these cases, since *go beyond* in the spatial sense involves motion, while in the linear scale sense, there is no motion or change, but just a point on a scale. Here the neutral case solution is not even available.

3.3 *The Invariance Principle*

In the examples we have just considered, the image-schemas characterizing the source domains (containers, paths) are mapped onto the target domains (categories, linear scales). This observation leads to the following hypothesis, called "The Invariance Principle":

> Metaphorical mappings preserve the cognitive topology (that is, the image-schema structure) of the source domain, in a way consistent with the inherent structure of the target domain.

What the Invariance Principle does is guarantee that, for container schemas, interiors will be mapped onto interiors, exteriors onto exteriors, and boundaries onto boundaries; for path-schemas, sources will be mapped onto sources, goals onto goals, trajectories onto trajectories, and so on.

To understand the Invariance Principle properly, it is important not to think of mappings as algorithmic processes that "start" with source domain structure and wind up with target domain structure. Such a mistaken understanding of mappings would lead to a mistaken understanding of the Invariance Principle, namely, that one first picks all the image-schematic structure of the source domain, then one copies it onto the target domain unless the target domain interferes.

One should instead think of the Invariance Principle in terms of constraints on fixed correspondences: if one looks at the existing correspondences, one will see that the Invariance Principle holds: source domain interiors correspond to target domain interiors; source domain exteriors correspond to target domain exteriors, and so forth. As a consequence it will turn out that the image-schematic structure of the target domain cannot be violated: One cannot find cases where a source domain interior is mapped onto a target domain exterior, or where a source domain exterior is mapped onto a target domain path. This simply does not happen.

3.4 *Target domain overrides*

A corollary of the Invariance Principle is that image-schema structure inherent in the target domain cannot be violated, and that inherent target domain structure limits the possibilities for mappings automatically. This general principle explains a large number of previously mysterious limitations on metaphorical mappings. For example, it explains why you can give someone a kick, even if that person doesn't have it afterward, and why you can give someone information, even if you don't lose it. This is a consequence of the fact that inherent target domain structure automatically limits what can be mapped. For example, consider that part of your inherent knowledge of actions that says that actions do not continue to exist after they occur. Now consider the ACTIONS ARE TRANSFERS metaphor, in which actions are conceptualized as objects transferred from an agent to a patient, as when one gives someone a kick or a punch. We know (as part of target domain knowledge) that an action does not exist after it occurs. In the source domain, where there is a giving, the recipient possesses the object given after the giving. But this cannot be mapped onto the target domain since the inherent structure of the target domain says that no such object exists after the action is over. The target domain override in the Invariance Principle explains why you can give someone a kick without his having it afterward.

3.5 *Abstract inferences as metaphorical spatial inferences*

Spatial inferences are characterized by the topological structure of image schemas. We have seen cases such as CATEGORIES ARE CONTAINERS and LINEAR SCALES ARE

PATHS where image-schema structure is preserved by metaphor and where abstract inferences about categories and linear scales are metaphorical versions of spatial inferences about containers and paths. The Invariance Principle hypothesizes that image-schema structure is always preserved by metaphor.

The Invariance Principle raises the possibility that a great many, if not all, abstract inferences are actually metaphorical versions of spatial inferences that are inherent in the topological structure of image-schemas. I will now turn to other cases of basic, but abstract, concepts to see what evidence there is for the claim that such concepts are fundamentally characterized by metaphor.

3.6 Time

It has often been noted that time in English is conceptualized in terms of space. The details are rather interesting.

Ontology: Time is understood in terms of things (that is, entities and locations) and motion.

Background condition: The present time is at the same location as a canonical observer.

Mapping:

Times are things.

The passing of time is motion.

Future times are in front of the observer; past times are behind the observer.

One thing is moving, the other is stationary; the stationary entity is the deictic center.

Entailment:

Since motion is continuous and one-dimensional, the passage of time is continuous and one-dimensional.

Special case 1:

The observer is fixed; times are entities moving with respect to the observer.

Times are oriented with their fronts in their direction of motion.

Entailments:

If time 2 follows time 1, then time 2 is in the future relative to time 1.

The time passing the observer is the present time.

Time has a velocity relative to the observer.

Special case 2:

Times are fixed locations; the observer is moving with respect to time.

Entailment:

Time has extension, and can be measured.

An extended time, like a spatial area, may be conceived of as a bounded region.

This metaphor, TIME PASSING IS MOTION, with its two special cases, embodies a generalization that accounts for a wide range of cases where a spatial expression can also be used for time. Special case 1, TIME PASSING IS MOTION OF AN OBJECT, accounts for both the linguistic form and the semantic entailments of expressions like:

The time will come when ... The time has long since gone when ... The time for action has arrived. That time is here. In the weeks following next Tuesday ... On the preceding day ... I'm looking ahead to Christmas.

Thanksgiving is coming up on us. Let's put all that behind us. I can't face the future. Time is flying by. The time has passed when ...

Thus, special case 1 characterizes the general principle behind the temporal use of words like *come, go, here, follow, precede, ahead, behind, fly, pass,* accounting not only for why they are used for both space and time, but why they mean what they mean.

Special case 2, TIME PASSING IS MOTION OVER A LANDSCAPE, accounts for a different range of cases, expressions like:

There's going to be trouble down the road. He stayed there for ten years. He stayed there a long time. His stay in Russia extended over many years. He passed the time happily. He arrived on time. We're coming up on Christmas. We're getting close to Christmas. He'll have his degree within two years. I'll be there in a minute.

Special case 2 maps location expressions like *down the road, for* + location, *long, over, come, close to, within, in, pass*, onto corresponding temporal expressions with their corresponding meanings. Again, special case 2 states a general principle relating spatial terms and inference patterns to temporal terms and inference patterns.

The details of the two special cases are rather different; indeed, they are inconsistent with one another. The existence of such special cases has an especially interesting theoretical consequence: words mapped by both special cases will have inconsistent readings. Take, for example, the *come* of *Christmas is coming* (special case 1) and *We're coming up on Christmas* (special case 2). Both instances of *come* are temporal, but one takes a moving time as first argument and the other takes a moving observer as first argument. The same is true of *pass* in *The time has passed* (special case 1) and in *He passed the time* (special case 2).

These differences in the details of the mappings show that one cannot just say blithely that spatial expressions can be used to speak of time, without specifying details, as though there were only one correspondence between time and space. When we are explicit about stating the mappings, we discover that there are two different — and inconsistent — subcases.

The fact that time is understood metaphorically in terms of motion, entities, and locations accords with our biological knowledge. In our visual systems, we have detectors for motion and detectors for objects/locations. We do not have detectors for time (whatever that could mean). Thus, it makes good biological sense that time should be understood in terms of things and motion.

3.7 Duality

The two special cases (location and object) of the TIME PASSING IS MOTION metaphor are not merely an accidental feature of our understanding of time. As we shall see below, there are other metaphors that come in such location/object pairs. Such pairs are called "duals," and the general phenomenon in which metaphors come in location/object pairs is referred to as "duality."

3.8 Simultaneous mappings

It is important to recall that metaphorical mappings are fixed correspondences that can be activated, rather than algorithmic processes that take inputs and give outputs. Thus, it is *not* the case that sentences containing conventional metaphors are the products of a real-time process of conversion from literal to metaphorical readings. A sentence like *The time for action has arrived* is not understood by first trying to give a literal reading to *arrive,* and then, on failing, trying to give it a temporal reading. Instead, the metaphor TIME PASSING IS MOTION is a fixed structure of existing correspondences between the space and time domains, and *arrive* has a conventional extended meaning that makes use of that fixed structure of correspondences.

Thus, it is possible for two different parts of a sentence to make use of two distinct metaphorical mappings at once. Consider a phrase like, *within the coming weeks.* Here, *within* makes use of the metaphor of time as a stationary landscape which has extension and bounded regions, whereas *coming* makes use of the metaphor of times as moving objects. This is possible because the two metaphors for time pick out different aspects of the target domain. *The coming weeks* conceptualizes those weeks as a whole, in motion relative to the observer. *Within* looks inside that whole, conceptualizing it as a bounded region with an interior. Each mapping is used partially. Thus, although the mappings — as wholes — are inconsistent, there are cases where parts of the mappings may be consistently superimposed. The Invariance Principle allows such parts of the mappings to be picked out and used to characterize reasoning about different aspects of the target domain.

Simultaneous mappings are very common in poetry. Take, for example, the Dylan Thomas line "Do not go gentle into that good night." Here *go* reflects DEATH IS DEPARTURE, *gentle* reflects LIFE IS A STRUGGLE, with death as defeat. *Night* reflects A LIFETIME IS A DAY, with death as night. This one line has three different metaphors for death, each mapped onto different parts of the sentence. This is possible since mappings are fixed correspondences.

There is an important lesson to be learned from this example. In mathematics, mappings are static correspondences. In computer science, it is common to represent mathematical mappings by algorithmic processes that take place in real time. Researchers in information processing psychology and cognitive science also commonly represent mappings as real-time algorithmic procedures. Some researchers from these fields have mistakenly supposed that the metaphorical mappings we are discussing should also be represented as real-time, sequential algorithmic procedures, where the input to each metaphor is a literal meaning. Any attempt to do this will fail for the simultaneous mapping cases just discussed.

4. Event structure

I now want to turn to some research by myself and some of my students (especially Sharon Fischler, Karin Myhre, and Jane Espenson) on the metaphorical understanding of event structure in English. What we have found is that various aspects of event structure, including notions like states, changes, processes, actions, causes, purposes, and means, are characterized cognitively via metaphor in terms of space, motion, and force.

The general mapping we have found goes as follows:

The event structure metaphor
– States are locations (bounded regions in space).
– Changes are movements (into or out of bounded regions).
– Causes are forces.
– Actions are self-propelled movements.
– Purposes are destinations.
– Means are paths (to destinations).
– Difficulties are impediments to motion.
– Expected progress is a travel schedule; a schedule is a virtual traveler, who reaches prearranged destinations at prearranged times.
– External events are large, moving objects.
– Long term, purposeful activities are journeys.

This mapping generalizes over an extremely wide range of expressions for one or more aspects of event structure. For example, take states and changes. We speak of being *in* or *out* of a state, *of going into* or *out of* it, of *entering* or *leaving* it, of getting *to* a state or emerging *from* it.

This is a rich and complex metaphor whose parts interact in complex ways. To get an idea of how it works, consider the submapping "Difficulties are impediments to motion." In the metaphor, purposive action is self-propelled motion toward a destination. A difficulty is something that impedes motion to such a destination. Metaphorical difficulties of this sort come in five types:

blockages;

features of the terrain; burdens; counter-forces; lack of an energy source. Here are examples of each:

Blockages:

He got over his divorce. He's trying to get around the regulations.
He went through the trial. We ran into a brick wall. We've got him boxed into a corner.

Features of the terrain:

He's between a rock and a hard place. It's been uphill all the way. We've been bogged down. We've been hacking our way through a jungle of regulations.

Burdens:

He's carrying quite a load. He's weighed down by a lot of assignments.
He's been trying to shoulder all the responsibility. Get off my back!

Counterforces:

Quit pushing me around. She's leading him around by the nose. She's holding him back.

Lack of an energy source:

I'm out of gas. We're running out of steam.

To see just how rich the event structure metaphor is, consider some of its basic entailments:

– Manner of action is manner of motion.
– A different means for achieving a purpose is a different path.
– Forces affecting action are forces affecting motion.
– The inability to act is the inability to move.
– Progress made is distance traveled or distance from goal.

We will consider examples of each of these one by one, including a number of special cases.

Aids to action are aids to motion:

It is smooth sailing from here on in. It's all downhill from here. There's nothing in our way.

A different means of achieving a result is a different path:

> Do it this way. She did it the other way. Do it any way you can. However you want to go about it is fine with me.

Manner of action is manner of motion:

> We are moving/running/skipping right along. We slogged through it. He is flailing around. He is falling all over himself. We are leaping over hurdles. He is out of step. He is in step.

Careful action is careful motion:

> I'm walking on eggshells. He is treading on thin ice. He is walking a fine line.

Speed of action is speed of movement:

> He flew through his work. He is running around. It is going swimmingly. Keep things moving at a good clip. Things have slowed to a crawl. She is going by leaps and bounds. I am moving at a snail's pace.

Purposeful action is self-propelled motion to a destination; this has the following special cases:

Making progress is forward movement:

> We are moving ahead. Let's forge ahead. Let's keep moving forward. We made lots of forward movement.

Amount of progress is distance moved:

> We've come a long way. We've covered lots of ground. We've made it this far.

Undoing progress is backward movement:

> We are sliding backward. We are backsliding. We need to backtrack. It is time to turn around and retrace our steps.

Expected progress is a travel schedule; a schedule is a virtual traveler, who reaches prearranged destinations at prearranged times:

> We're behind schedule on the project. We got a head start on the project. I'm trying to catch up. I finally got a little ahead.

Starting an action is starting out on a path:

> We are just starting out. We have taken the first step.

Success is reaching the end of the path:

> We've reached the end. We are seeing the light at the end of the tunnel. We only have a short way to go. The end is in sight. The end is a long

way off.

Lack of purpose is lack of direction:

> He is just floating around. He is drifting aimlessly. He needs some direction.

Lack of progress is lack of movement:

> We are at a standstill. We aren't getting any place. We aren't going anywhere. We are going nowhere with this.

External events are large moving objects:

Special case 1: Things

> How're things going? Things are going fine with me. Things are going against me these days. Things took a turn for the worse. Things are going my way.

Special case 2: Fluids

> You gotta go with the flow. I'm just trying to keep my head above water. The tide of events ... The winds of change.... The flow of history ... I'm trying to get my bearings. He's up a creek without a paddle. We're all in the same boat.

Special case 3: Horses

> Try to keep a tight rein on the situation. Keep a grip on the situation. Don't let things get out of hand. Wild horses couldn't make me go. "Whoa!" (said when things start to get out of hand).

Such examples provide overwhelming empirical support for the existence of the event structure metaphor. And the existence of that metaphor shows that the most common abstract concepts — TIME, STATE, CHANGE, CAUSATION, ACTION, PURPOSE and MEANS — are conceptualized via metaphor. Since such concepts are at the very center of our conceptual systems, the fact that they are conceptualized metaphorically shows that metaphor is central to ordinary abstract thought.

4.1 Inheritance hierarchies

Metaphorical mappings do not occur isolated from one another. They are sometimes organized in hierarchical structures, in which "lower" mappings in the hierarchy inherit the structures of the "higher" mappings. Let us consider an example of a hierarchy with three levels:

Level 1: *The event structure metaphor*

Level 2: A PURPOSEFUL LIFE IS A JOURNEY

Level 3: LOVE IS A JOURNEY; A CAREER IS A JOURNEY

To refresh your memory, recall:

The event structure metaphor

– Target domain: Events   Source domain: Space

– States are locations (bounded regions in space).

– Changes are movements (into or out of bounded regions).

– Causes are forces.

– Actions are self-propelled movements.

– Purposes are destinations.

– Means are paths to destinations.

– Difficulties are impediments to motion.

– Expected progress is a travel schedule; a schedule is a virtual traveler, who reaches prearranged destinations at prearranged times.

– External events are large, moving objects.

– Long-term, purposeful activities are journeys.

In our culture, life is assumed to be purposeful, that is, we are expected to have goals in life. In the event structure metaphor, purposes are destinations and purposeful action is self-propelled motion toward a destination. A purposeful life is a long-term, purposeful activity, and hence a journey. Goals in life are destinations on the journey. The actions one takes in life are self-propelled movements, and the totality of one's actions form a path one moves along. Choosing a means to achieve a goal is choosing a path to a destination. Difficulties in life are impediments to motion. External events are large moving objects that can impede motion toward one's life goals. One's expected progress through life is charted in terms of a life schedule, which is conceptualized as a virtual traveler that one is expected to keep up with.

In short, the metaphor A PURPOSEFUL LIFE IS A JOURNEY makes use of all the structure of the event structure metaphor, since events in a life conceptualized as purposeful are subcases of events in general.

A PURPOSEFUL LIFE IS A JOURNEY
– Target domain: Life   Source domain: Space
– The person leading a life is a traveler.
– Inherits event structure metaphor, with:
Events = significant life events
Purposes = life goals

Thus we have expressions like:

> He got a head start in life. He's without direction in his life. I'm where I want to be in life. I'm at a crossroads in my life. He'll go places in life. He's never let anyone get in his way. He's gone through a lot in life.

Just as significant life events are special cases of events, so events in a love relationship are special cases of life events. Thus, the LOVE IS A JOURNEY metaphor inherits the structure of the LIFE IS A JOURNEY metaphor. What is special about the LOVE IS A JOURNEY metaphor is that there are two lovers who are travelers and that the love relationship is a vehicle. The rest of the mapping is a consequence of inheriting the LIFE IS A JOURNEY metaphor. Because the lovers are in the same vehicle, they have common destinations, that is, common life goals. Relationship difficulties are impediments to travel.

LOVE IS A JOURNEY
– Target domain: Love   Source domain: Space
– The lovers are travelers.
– The love relationship is a vehicle.
– Inherits the LIFE IS A JOURNEY metaphor.

A career is another aspect of life that can be conceptualized as a journey. Here, because STATUS IS UP, a career is actually a journey upward. Career goals are special cases of life goals.

A CAREER IS A JOURNEY
– Target domain: Career   Source domain: Space
– A careerist is a traveler.

– Status is up.

– Inherits LIFE IS A JOURNEY, with life goals = career goals. Ideal: to go as high, far, and fast as possible.

Examples include:

> He clawed his way to the top. He's over the hill. She's on the fast track. He's climbing the corporate ladder. She's moving up in the ranks quickly.

This inheritance hierarchy accounts for a range of generalizations. First, there are generalizations about lexical items. Take the word *crossroads*. Its central meaning is in the domain of space, but it can be used in a metaphorical sense to speak of any extended activity, of one's life, of a love relationship, or of a career.

> I'm at a crossroads on this project. I'm at a crossroads in life. We're at a crossroads in our relationship. I'm at a crossroads in my career.

The hierarchy allows one to state a general principle: *crossroads* is extended lexically via the submetaphor of the event structure metaphor that LONG-TERM PURPOSEFUL ACTIVITIES ARE JOURNEYS. All its other uses are automatically generated via the inheritance hierarchy. Thus, separate senses for each level of the hierarchy are not needed.

The second generalization is inferential in character. Thus the understanding of difficulties as impediments to travel occurs not only in events in general, but also in a purposeful life, in a love relationship, and in a career. The inheritance hierarchy guarantees that this understanding of difficulties in life, love, and careers is a consequence of such an understanding of difficulties in events in general.

The hierarchy also allows us to characterize lexical items whose meanings are more restricted: Thus, *climbing the ladder* refers only to careers, not to love relationships or to life in general.

Such hierarchical organization is a very prominent feature of the metaphor system of English and other languages. So far we have found that the metaphors higher up in the hierarchy tend to be more widespread than those mappings at lower levels. Thus, the event structure metaphor is very widespread (and may even be universal), while the metaphors for life, love, and careers are much more restricted culturally.

4.2 Duality in the event structure system

In our discussion of time metaphors, we noted the existence of an object/location duality. There were two related time metaphors. In both, the passage of time was understood in terms of relative motion between an observer and a time. In the object-dual, the observer is fixed and times are moving objects. In the location-dual, the opposite is true. The observer moves and times are fixed locations in a landscape.

The event structure system that we have seen so far is based wholly on location. But there is another event structure system that is the dual of the one we have just discussed — a system based on objects rather than locations. In both systems, CHANGE IS MOTION and CAUSES ARE FORCES that control motion. The difference is this:

- In the location system, change is the motion of the thing-changing to a new location or from an old one.
- In the object system, the thing-changing doesn't necessarily move. Change is instead the motion of an object to, or away from, the thing-changing.

In addition, the object in motion is conceptualized as a possession and the thing-changing as a possessor. Change is thus seen as the acquisition or loss of an object. Causation is seen as giving or taking. Here are some examples:

> I have a headache. (The headache is a possession)
> I got a headache. (Change is acquisition — motion to)
> My headache went away. (Change is loss — motion from)
> The noise gave me a headache. (Causation is giving — motion to)
> The aspirin took away my headache. (Causation is taking — motion from)

We can see the duality somewhat more clearly with a word like "trouble":

> I'm in trouble. (Trouble is a location)

I have trouble. (Trouble is an object that is possessed)

In both cases, trouble is being attributed to me, and in both cases, trouble is metaphorically conceptualized as being in the same place as me (co-location) — in one case, because I possess the trouble-object and in the other case, because I am in the trouble-location. That is, attribution in both cases is conceptualized metaphorically as co-location. In *I'm in trouble,* trouble is a state. A state is an attribute conceptualized as a location. Attributes (or properties) are like states, except that they are conceptualized as possessible objects.

Thus, STATES ARE LOCATIONS and ATTRIBUTES ARE POSSESSIONS are duals, since possession and location are special cases of the same thing — co-location — and since states and attributes are also special cases of the same thing — what can be attributed to someone.

Given this, we can see that there is an object-version of the event structure metaphor:

– Attributes are possessions.
– Changes are movements (of possessions, namely, acquisitions or losses).
– Causes are forces (controlling the movement of possessions, namely, giving or taking away).

These are the duals of:

– States are locations.
– Changes are movements (to or from locations).
– Causes are forces (controlling movement to or from locations).

Similarly, ACTIONS ARE SELF-PROPELLED MOVEMENTS (to or from locations) has as its object-dual ACTIONS ARE SELF-CONTROLLED ACQUISITIONS OR LOSSES. Thus, there is a reason why one can "take" certain actions — one can take a shower, or take a shot at someone, or take a chance.

The submapping PURPOSES ARE DESTINATIONS also has a dual. Destinations are desired locations and so the submapping can be rephrased as PURPOSES ARE DESIRED LOCATIONS, and ACHIEVING A PURPOSE IS REACHING A DESIRED LOCATION. Replacing "location" by "object," we get the dual PURPOSES ARE

DESIRED OBJECTS, and ACHIEVING A PURPOSE IS ACQUIRING A DESIRED OBJECT (or ridding oneself of an undesirable one).

Here are some examples:

ACHIEVING A PURPOSE IS ACQUIRING A DESIRED OBJECT
They just handed him the job. It's within my grasp. It eluded me. Go for it. It escaped me. It slipped through my hands. He is pursuing a goal. Reach for/ grab all the gusto you can get. Latch onto a good job. Seize the opportunity. He found success.

There is also a hierarchical structure in the object-version of the event structure metaphor. A special case of getting an object is getting an object to eat. Hence:

ACHIEVING A PURPOSE IS GETTING SOMETHING TO EAT
He savored the victory. All the good jobs have been gobbled up. He's hungry for success. The opportunity has me drooling. This is a mouth-watering opportunity.

Traditional methods of getting things to eat are hunting, fishing, and agriculture. Each of these special cases can be used metaphorically to conceptualize achieving (or attempting to achieve) a purpose.

TRYING TO ACHIEVE A PURPOSE IS HUNTING
I'm hunting for a job. I bagged a promotion. The pennant is in the bag.

The typical way to hunt is to use projectiles (bullets, arrows, etc.)

I'm shooting for a promotion. I'm aiming for a career in the movies. I'm afraid I missed my chance.

TRYING TO ACHIEVE A PURPOSE IS FISHING
He's fishing for compliments. I landed a promotion. She netted a good job. I've got a line out on a good used car. It's time to fish or cut bait.

TRYING TO ACHIEVE A PURPOSE IS AGRICULTURE
It's time I reaped some rewards. That job is a plum. Those are the fruits of his

labor. The contract is ripe for the picking.

I will not try to survey all the dualities in the English metaphor system, but it is worth mentioning a few to see how subtle and persuasive dualities are. Take, for example, the LIFE IS A JOURNEY metaphor, in which goals in life are destinations, that is, desired locations to be reached. Since the dual of PURPOSES ARE DESTINATIONS is PURPOSES ARE DESIRED OBJECTS, the dual of LIFE IS A JOURNEY is a metaphor in which life is an activity through which one acquires desired objects. In this culture, the principal activity of this sort is business, and hence, LIFE IS A BUSINESS is the dual of LIFE IS A JOURNEY.

A PURPOSEFUL LIFE IS A BUSINESS
He has a rich life. It's an enriching experience. I want to get a lot out of life. He's going about the business of everyday life. It's time to take stock of my life.

Recall that LOVE IS A JOURNEY is an extension of A PURPOSEFUL LIFE IS A JOURNEY. It happens that LOVE IS A JOURNEY has a dual that is an extension of the dual of A PURPOSEFUL LIFE IS A JOURNEY, which is A PURPOSEFUL LIFE IS A BUSINESS. The dual of LOVE IS A JOURNEY is LOVE IS A PARTNERSHIP, that is, a two-person business. Thus, we speak of lovers as "partners," there are marriage contracts, and in a long-term love relationship the partners are expected to do their jobs and to share in both responsibilities (what they contribute to the relationship) and benefits (what they get out of it). Long-term love relationships fail under the same conditions as businesses fail — when what the partners get out of the relationship is not worth what they put into it.

Duality is a newly discovered phenomenon. The person who first discovered it in the event structure system was Jane Espenson, a graduate student at Berkeley who stumbled upon it in the course of her research on causation metaphors. Since Espenson's discovery, other extensive dualities have been found in the English metaphor system. It is not known at present, however, just how extensive dualities are in English, or even whether they are all of the location/object type.

At this point, I will leave off discussing the metaphor system of English, although hundreds of other mappings have been described to date. The major point to take away from this discussion is that metaphor resides for the most part in this huge, highly structured, fixed system, a system anything but "dead." Because it is conventional, it is used constantly and automatically, with neither effort nor awareness. Novel metaphor uses this system, and builds on it, but only rarely occurs independently of it. It is most interesting that this system of metaphor seems to give rise to abstract reasoning, which appears to be based on spatial reasoning.

4.3 Invariance again

The metaphors I have discussed primarily map three kinds of image schemas: containers, paths, and force-images. Because of the complexity of the subcases and interactions, the details are intricate, to say the least. However, the Invariance Principle does make claims in each case as to what image-schemas get mapped onto target domains. I will not go through most of the details here, but so far as I can see, the claims made about inferential structure are reasonable ones.

For example, the logic of force-dynamics does seem to map, via the submapping CAUSES ARE FORCES, onto the logic of causation. The following are inferences from the logic of forces inherent in force dynamics:

– A stationary object will move only when force is applied to it; without force, it will not move.
– The application of force requires contact; thus, the applier of the force must be in spatial contiguity with the thing it moves.
– The application of force temporarily precedes motion, since inertia must be overcome before motion can take place.

These are among the classic inferential conditions on causation: spatial contiguity, temporal precedence, and that A caused B only if B wouldn't have happened without A.

At this point, I would like to take up the question of what else the Invariance Principle would buy us. I will consider two cases that arose while Mark Turner and I were writing *More Than Cool Reason* (Lakoff and Turner 1989). The first concerns image-metaphors and the second, generic-level metaphors. But before I move on to those topics, I should mention an important consequence of invariance.

Johnson and I argued in *Metaphors We Live By* (Lakoff and Johnson 1980) that a complex propositional structure could be mapped by metaphor onto another domain. The main example we gave was ARGUMENT IS WAR. Kövecses and I, in our analysis of anger metaphors (Lakoff 1987: case study 1; Kövecses 1990), also argued that metaphors could map complex propositional structures. The Invariance Principle does not deny this, but it puts those claims in a very different light. Complex propositional structures involve concepts like time, states, changes, causes, purposes, quantity scales, and categories. If all these abstract concepts are characterized metaphorically, then the Invariance Principle claims that what we had called propositional structure is really image-schematic structure. In other words:

– So-called propositional inferences arise from the inherent topological structure of the image-schemas mapped by metaphor onto concepts like time, states, changes, actions, causes, purposes, means, quantity, and categories.

I have taken the trouble to discuss these abstract concepts to demonstrate this consequence of the Invariance Principle: what have been seen in the past as propositional inferences are really image-based inferences. If the Invariance Principle is correct, it has a remarkable consequence:

– Abstract reasoning is a special case of image-based reasoning.

Image-based reasoning is fundamental and abstract reasoning is image-based reasoning under metaphorical projections to abstract domains.

To look for independent confirmation of the Invariance Principle, let us turn to image metaphors.

5. Novel metaphors

5.1 Image metaphors

There are kinds of metaphors that function to map one conventional mental image onto another. These contrast with the metaphors I have discussed so far, each of which maps one conceptual domain onto another, often with many concepts in the source domain mapped onto many corresponding concepts in the target domain. Image metaphors, by contrast, are "one-shot" metaphors: they map only one image onto one other image.

Consider, for example, this poem from the Indian tradition:

Now women-rivers
belted with silver fish
move unhurried as women in love
at dawn after a night with their lovers
(Merwin and Masson 1981: 71)

Here the image of the slow, sinuous walk of an Indian woman is mapped onto the image of the slow, sinuous, shimmering flow of a river. The shimmering of a school of fish is imagined as the shimmering of the belt.

Metaphoric image mappings work in the same way as all other metaphoric mappings: by mapping the structure of one domain onto the structure of another. But here, the domains are conventional mental images. Take, for example, this line from Andre Breton:

My wife ... whose waist is an hourglass.

This is a superimposition of the image of an hourglass onto the image of a woman's waist by virtue of their common shape. As before, the metaphor is conceptual; it is not in the words themselves, but in the mental images. Here, we have a mental image of an hourglass and of a woman, and we map the middle of the hourglass onto the waist of the woman. Note that the words do not tell us which part of the hourglass to map onto the waist, or even that only part of the hourglass shape corresponds to the waist. The words are prompts for us to map from one conventional image to another. Similarly, consider:

His toes were like the keyboard of a spinet.
(Rabelais *The Descriptions of King Lent,* trans. J. M. Cohen)

Here, too, the words do not tell us that an individual toe corresponds to an individual key on the keyboard. The words are prompts for us to perform a conceptual mapping between conventional mental images. In particular, we map aspects of the part-whole structure of one image onto aspects of the part-whole structure of another. Just as individual keys are parts of the whole keyboard, so individual toes are parts of the whole foot.

Image mapping can involve more than mapping physical part-whole relationships. For example, the water line of a river may drop slowly and that slowness is part of a dynamic image, which may be mapped onto the slow removal of clothing:

> Slowly slowly rivers in autumn show
> sand banks
> bashful in first love woman
> showing thighs
> (Merwin and Masson 1981: 69)

Other attributes are also mapped: the color of the sand bank onto the color of flesh, the quality of light on a wet sand bank onto the reflectiveness of skin, the light grazing of the water's touch receding down the bank onto the light grazing of the clothing along the skin. Notice that the words do not tell us that any clothing is involved. We get that from a conventional mental image. Part-whole structure is also mapped in this example. The water covers the hidden part of the bank just as the clothing covers the hidden part of the body. The proliferation of detail in the images limits image mappings to highly specific cases. That is what makes them one-shot mappings.

Such mappings of one image onto another can lead us to map knowledge about the first image onto knowledge about the second. Consider the following example from the Navaho:

> My horse with a mane made of short rainbows.
> (*War God's Horse Song I*, words by Tall Kia ahni, interpreted by Louis Watchman)

The structure of a rainbow, its band of curved lines for example, is mapped onto an arc of curved hair, and many rainbows onto many such arcs on the horse's mane. Such image mapping allows us to map our evaluation of the source domain onto the target. We know that rainbows are beautiful, special, inspiring, larger than life, almost mystic, and that seeing them makes us happy and inspires us with awe. This knowledge is mapped onto what we know of the horse: it too is awe-inspiring, beautiful, larger than life, almost mystic. This line comes from a poem containing a series of such image mappings:

> My horse with a hoof like a striped agate,
> with his fetlock like a fine eagle plume:
> my horse whose legs are like quick lightning
> whose body is an eagle-plumed arrow:
> my horse whose tail is like a trailing black cloud.

Image metaphors raise two major issues for the general theory of metaphor:

– How do they work? What constrains the mappings? What kinds of internal structures do mental images have that permit some mappings to work readily, others only with effort, and others not at all?
– What is the general theory of metaphor that unifies image metaphors with all the conventional metaphors that map the propositional structure of one domain onto the propositional structure of another domain?

Turner and I (Lakoff and Turner 1989) have suggested that the Invariance Principle could be an answer to both questions. We suggest that conventional mental images are structured by image-schemas and that image metaphors preserve image-schematic structure, mapping parts onto parts and wholes onto wholes, containers onto containers, paths onto paths, and so on. The generalization would be that all metaphors are invariant with respect to their cognitive topology, that is, each metaphorical mapping preserves image-schema structure.

5.2 Generic-level metaphors

When Turner and I were writing *More Than Cool Reason,* we hypothesized the existence of what we called "generic-level metaphors" to deal with two problems we faced — first, the problem of personification and second, the problem of proverbs, which requires an understanding of analogy. I shall discuss each in turn.

5.2.1 Personification

In studying a wide variety of poems about death in English, we found that, in poem after poem, death was personified in a relatively small number of ways: drivers, coachmen, footmen; reapers, devourers and destroyers, or opponents in a struggle or game (say, a knight or a chess opponent). The question we asked was: why these? Why isn't death personified as a teacher or a carpenter or an ice cream salesman? Somehow, the ones that occur repeatedly seem appropriate. Why?

In studying personifications in general, we found that the overwhelming number seem to fit a single pattern: events (like death) are understood in terms of actions by some agent (like reaping). It is that agent that is personified. We thus hypothesized a very general metaphor, EVENTS ARE ACTIONS, which combines with other, independently existing metaphors for life and death. Consider, for example, the DEATH IS DEPARTURE metaphor. Departure is an event. If we understand this event as an action on the part of some causal agent — someone who brings about, or helps to bring about, departure — then we can account for figures like drivers, coachmen, footmen, and so forth. Take the PEOPLE ARE PLANTS metaphor. In the natural course of things, plants wither and die. If we see that event as a causal action on the part of some agent, that agent is a reaper. So far, so good. But why destroyers and devourers? And what about the impossible cases?

Destroying and devouring are actions in which an entity ceases to exist. The same is true of death. The overall shape of the event of death is similar in this respect to the overall shapes of the events of destroying and devouring. Moreover, there is a causal aspect to death: the passage of time will eventually result in death. Thus, the overall shape of the event of death has an entity that over time ceases to exist as the result of some cause. Devouring and destroying have the same overall event shape. That is, it is the same with respect to causal structure and the persistence of entities over time.

Turner (1987) had noticed a similar case in *Death Is the Mother of Beauty*, his classic work on kinship metaphor. In expressions like *necessity is the mother of invention*, or *Edward Teller was the father of the H-bomb*, causation is understood in terms of giving birth or fathering, what Turner called the CAUSATION IS PROGENERATION metaphor. But, as he observed (Turner 1987: 145–148), this metaphor could not be used for just any instance of causation. It could only be used for cases that had the overall event shape of progeneration: something must be created out of nothing, and the thing created must persist for a long time (as if it had a life).

Thus, for example, we can speak of Saussure as the father of modern synchronic linguistics, or of New Orleans as giving birth to jazz. But we cannot use this metaphor for a single causal action with a short-lived effect. We could not speak of Jose Canseco as the father of the home run he just hit, or of that home run as giving birth to the Oakland As' victory in the game. We could, however, speak of Babe Ruth as the father of modern home-run hitting, and of home runs giving birth to the era of baseball players as superstars. The overall event shape of the target domain limits the applicability of the metaphor.

Recalling Turner's observation about CAUSATION IS PROGENERATION, we therefore hypothesized that EVENTS ARE ACTIONS is constrained in the following way: the action must have the same overall event shape as the event. What is preserved across the mapping is the causal structure, the aspectual structure, and the persistence of entities. We referred to this as "generic-level structure."

The preservation of generic-level structure explained why death is not metaphorized in terms of teaching, or filling the bathtub, or sitting on the sofa. These actions do not have the same causal and overall event structure, they do not share "generic-level structure."

5.2.2. Proverbs

In Asian figures — proverbs in the form of short poems — the question arises as to what the limitations are on the interpretation of a proverb. Some interpretations are natural; others seem impossible. Why?

Consider the following example from *Asian Figures*, translated by William Merwin.

> Blind
> blames the ditch

To get some sense of the possible range of interpretations, consider the following application of the proverb:

Suppose a presidential candidate knowingly commits some personal impropriety (though not illegal and not related to political issues) and his candidacy is destroyed by the press's reporting of the impropriety. He blames the press for reporting it, rather than himself for committing it. We think he should have recognized the realities of political press coverage when he chose to commit the impropriety. We express our judgment by saying, "Blind/blames the ditch."

Turner and I (1989) observed that the knowledge structure used in comprehending the case of the candidate's impropriety shared certain things with knowledge structure used in comprehending the literal interpretation of "Blind/blames the ditch." That knowledge structure is the following:

- There is a person with an incapacity, namely, blindness.
- He encounters a situation, namely a ditch, in which his incapacity, namely his inability to see the ditch, results in a negative consequence, namely, his falling into the ditch.
- He blames the situation, rather than his own incapacity.
- He should have held himself responsible, not the situation.

This specific knowledge schema about the blind man and the ditch is an instance of a general knowledge schema, in which specific information about the blindness and ditch are absent. Let us refer to it as the "generic-level schema" that structures our knowledge of the proverb. That generic level knowledge schema is:

- There is a person with an incapacity.
- He encounters a situation in which his incapacity results in a negative consequence.
- He blames the situation rather than his own incapacity.
- He should have held himself responsible, not the situation.

This is a very general schema characterizing an open-ended category of situations. We can think of it as a variable template that can be filled in many ways. As it happened, Turner and I were studying this at the time of the Gary Hart scandal. Hart, a presidential candidate, committed certain sexual improprieties during a campaign, had his candidacy dashed, and then blamed the press for his downfall.

"Blind/blames the ditch" fits this situation. Here's how:

- The person is the presidential candidate.
- His incapacity is his inability to understand the consequences of his personal improprieties.
- The context he encounters is his knowingly committing an impropriety and the press's reporting it.
- The consequence is having his candidacy dashed.
- He blames the press.
- We judge him as being foolish for blaming the press instead of himself.

If we view the generic-level schema as mediating between the proverb "Blind/ blames the ditch" and the story of the candidate's impropriety, we get the following correspondence:

- The blind person corresponds to the presidential candidate.
- His blindness corresponds to his inability to understand the consequences of his personal improprieties.
- Falling into the ditch corresponds to his committing the impropriety and having it reported.
- Being in the ditch corresponds to being out of the running as a candidate.
- Blaming the ditch corresponds to blaming the press coverage.
- Judging the blind man as foolish for blaming the ditch corresponds to judging the candidate as foolish for blaming the press coverage.

This correspondence defines the metaphorical interpretation of the proverb as applied to the candidate's impropriety. Moreover, the class of possible ways of filling in the generic-level schema of the proverb corresponds to the class of possible interpretations of the proverb. Thus, we can explain why "Blind/blames the ditch" does not mean *I took a bath* or *My aunt is sitting on the sofa* or any of the myriad things the proverb cannot mean.

All the proverbs that Turner and I studied turned out to involve this sort of generic-level schema, and the kinds of things that turned up in such schemata seemed to be pretty much the same in case after case. They include:

503

– Causal structure

– Temporal structure

– Event shape; that is, instantaneous or repeated, completed or open-ended, single or repeating, having fixed stages or not, preserving the existence of entities or not, and so on

– Purpose structure

– Modal structure

– Linear scales

This is not an exhaustive list, but it includes most of the major elements of generic-level structure we discovered. What is striking to us about this list is that everything on it is, under the Invariance Principle, an aspect of image-schematic structure. In short, if the Invariance Principle is correct, the way to arrive at a generic-level schema for some knowledge structure is to extract its image-schematic structure.

The metaphoric interpretation of such discourse forms as proverbs, fables, allegories, and so on seems to depend on our ability to extract generic-level structure. Turner and I have called the relation between a specific knowledge structure and its generic-level structure the GENERIC IS SPECIFIC metaphor. It is an extremely common mechanism for comprehending the general in terms of the specific.

If the Invariance Principle is correct, then the GENERIC IS SPECIFIC metaphor is a minimal metaphor that maps what the Invariance Principle requires it to and nothing more. Should it turn out that generic-level structure is exactly image-schematic structure, then the Invariance Principle would have enormous explanatory value. It would obviate the need for a separate characterization of generic-level structure. Instead, it would itself characterize generic-level structure, explaining possible personifications and the possible interpretations for proverbs.

5.3 Analogy

The GENERIC IS SPECIFIC metaphor is used for more than just the interpretation of proverbs. Turner (1991) has suggested that it is also the general mechanism at work in analogic reasoning and that the Invariance Principle characterizes the class of possible analogies. We can see how this works with the Gary Hart example cited above. We can convert that example into an analogy with the following sentence: *Gary Hart was like a blind man who fell into a ditch and blamed the ditch.* The mechanism for understanding this analogy makes use of:

– A knowledge schema for the blind man and the ditch
– A knowledge schema concerning Gary Hart
– The GENERIC IS SPECIFIC metaphor

The GENERIC IS SPECIFIC metaphor maps the knowledge schema for the blind man and the ditch into its generic-level schema. The generic-level schema defines an open-ended category of knowledge schemata. The Gary Hart schema is a member of that category, since it fits the generic-level schema given the correspondences stated above.

It appears at present that such analogies use this metaphorical mechanism. But it is common for analogies to use other metaphorical mechanisms as well, for instance, the Great Chain Metaphor and the full range of conventional mappings in the conceptual system. Sentences like *John is a wolf* or *Harry is a pig* use the Great Chain metaphor (see Lakoff and Turner 1989: Chapter 4).

A good example of how the rest of the metaphor system interacts with GENERIC IS SPECIFIC is the well-known example of Glucksberg and Keysar (1993), *my job is a jail.* First, the knowledge schema for a jail includes the knowledge that a jail imposes extreme physical constraints on a prisoner's movements. The GENERIC IS SPECIFIC metaphor preserves the image-schematic structure of the knowledge schema, factoring out the specific details of the prisoner and the jail: X imposes extreme physical constraints on Y's movements. But now two additional conventional metaphors apply to this generic-level schema: The event structure metaphor, with the submetaphor ACTIONS ARE SELF-PROPELLED MOVEMENTS, and PSYCHOLOGICAL FORCE IS PHYSICAL FORCE. These metaphors map "X imposes extreme physical constraints on Y's movements" into "X imposes extreme psychological constraints on Y's actions." The statement *my job is a jail* imposes an interpretation in which X = my job and Y = me, and hence yields the knowledge that "my job imposes extreme psychological constraints on my actions." Thus, the mechanism for understanding *my job is a jail* uses very common, independently existing metaphors: GENERIC IS SPECIFIC, PSYCHOLOGICAL FORCE IS PHYSICAL FORCE, and the Event Structure Metaphor.

5.4 The Glucksberg-Keysar Claim

I mention this example because of the claim by Glucksberg and Keysar (1993) that metaphor is simply a matter of categorization. In personal correspondence, however, Glucksberg has written, "We assume that people can judge and can also infer that certain basic level entities, such as 'jails,' typify or are emblematic of a metaphoric attributive category such as 'situations that are confining, unpleasant, etc.'" Glucksberg and Keysar give no theory of how it is possible to have such a "metaphoric attributive category" — that is, how it is possible for one kind of thing (a general situation) to be metaphorically categorized in terms of a fundamentally spatial notion like "confining." Since Glucksberg is not in the business of describing the nature of conceptual systems, he does not see it as his job to give such an account. I have argued in this essay that the general principle governing such cases is the Event Structure Metaphor. If such a metaphor exists in our conceptual system, then the Glucksberg-Keysar "jail" example is accounted for automatically and their categorization theory is not needed. Indeed, the category he needs — "situations that are confining, unpleasant, etc." — is a "metaphoric attributive category." That is, to get the appropriate categories in their categorization theory of metaphor he needs an account of metaphor. But given such an account of metaphor, the metaphor-as-categorization theory becomes unnecessary.

Even worse for the Glucksberg-Keysar theory, it cannot account for either everyday conceptual metaphor of the sort we have been discussing or for really rich poetic metaphor, such as one finds in the works of, say, Dylan Thomas, or for image metaphor of the sort common in the examples cited above from the Sanskrit, Navaho, and surrealist traditions. Since it does not even attempt to deal with most of the data covered by the contemporary theory of metaphor, it cannot account for "how metaphor works."

5.5 More on novel metaphor

At the time most of the chapters in Ortony (1993 [1979]) were written (the late 1970s), "metaphor" was taken to mean "novel metaphor," since the huge system of conventional metaphor had barely been noticed. The authors therefore never took up the question of how the system of conventional metaphor functions in the interpretation of novel metaphor. We have just seen one such example. Let us consider some others.

As common as novel metaphor is, its occurrence is rare by comparison with conventional metaphor, which occurs in most of the sentences we utter. Our everyday metaphor system, which we use to understand concepts as commonplace as TIME, STATE, CHANGE, CAUSATION, PURPOSE, and so forth is constantly active, and is used maximally in interpreting novel metaphorical uses of language. The problem with all the older research on novel metaphor is that it completely missed the major contribution played by the conventional system.

As Turner and I discussed in detail (Lakoff and Turner 1989), there are three basic mechanisms for interpreting linguistic expressions as novel metaphors: extensions of conventional metaphors, generic-level metaphors, and image metaphors. Most interesting poetic metaphor uses all these superimposed on one another. Let us begin with examples of extensions of conventional metaphors. Dante begins the *Divine Comedy*:

> In the middle of life's road
> I found myself in a dark wood.

"Life's road" evokes the domain of life and the domain of travel, and hence the conventional LIFE IS A JOURNEY metaphor that links them. "I found myself in a dark wood" evokes the knowledge that if it's dark you cannot see which way to go. This evokes the domain of seeing, and thus the conventional metaphor that KNOWING IS SEEING, as in *I see what you're getting at, his claims aren't clear, the passage is opaque,* and so forth. This entails that the speaker doesn't know which way to go. Since the LIFE IS A JOURNEY metaphor specifies destinations are life goals, the speaker must not know what life goals to pursue, that is, he is without direction in his life. All this uses nothing but the system of conventional metaphor, ordinary knowledge structure evoked by the conventional meaning of the sentence, and metaphorical inferences based on that knowledge structure.

Another equally simple case of the use of the conventional system is Robert Frost's

> Two roads diverged in a wood, and I —
> I took the one less traveled by,

And that has made all the difference.

Since Frost's language often does not overtly signal that the poem is to be taken metaphorically, incompetent English teachers occasionally teach Frost as if he were a nature poet, simply describing scenes. (I have actually had students whose high school teachers taught them that!) Thus, this passage could be read non-metaphorically as being just about a trip on which one encounters a crossroads. There is nothing in the sentence itself that forces one to a metaphorical interpretation. But, since it is about travel and encountering crossroads, it evokes a knowledge of journeys. This activates the system of conventional metaphor we have just discussed, in which long-term, purposeful activities are understood as journeys, and further, how life and careers can also be understood as one-person journeys (love relationships, involving two travelers, are ruled out here). The poem is typically taken as being about life and a choice of life goals, though it might also be interpreted as being about careers and career paths, or about some long-term, purposeful activity. All that is needed to get the requisite range of interpretations is the structure of conventional metaphors discussed above, and the knowledge structure evoked by the poem. The conventional mapping will apply to the knowledge structure yielding the appropriate inferences. No special mechanisms are needed.

5.6 Searle's theory

I will not pursue discussion of other more complex poetic examples, since they require lengthy treatment which can be found in Lakoff and Turner (1989), Turner (1987), and Turner (1991). Instead, I will confine myself to discussing three examples from John Searle (1993). Consider first Disraeli's remark, "I have climbed to the top of the greasy pole."

This could be taken nonmetaphorically, but its most likely metaphorical interpretation is via the CAREER IS A JOURNEY metaphor. This metaphor is evoked jointly by source domain knowledge about pole climbing, which is effortful, selfpropelled, destination-oriented motion upward, and knowledge that the metaphor involves effortful, self-propelled, destination-oriented motion upward. Part of the knowledge evoked is that the speaker is as high as he can get on that particular pole, that the pole was difficult to climb, that the climb probably involved backward motion, that it is difficult for someone to stay at the top of a greasy pole, and that he will most likely slide down again. The CAREER IS A JOURNEY metaphor maps this knowledge onto corresponding knowledge about the speaker's career: he has as much status as he can get in that particular career, it was difficult to get to that point in the career, it probably involved some temporary loss of status along the way, it will be difficult to maintain this position, and he will probably lose status before long. All this follows with nothing more than the conventional CAREER-AS-JOURNEY mapping, which we all share as part of our metaphorical systems, plus knowledge about climbing greasy poles.

The second example of Searle's I will consider is *Sally is a block of ice.* Here there is a conventional metaphor that AFFECTION IS WARMTH, as in ordinary sentences like *she's a warm person, he was cool to me,* and so forth. *A block of ice* evokes the domain of temperature and, since it is predicated of a person, it also evokes knowledge of what a person can be. Jointly, both kinds of knowledge activate AFFECTION IS WARMTH. Since *a block of ice* is something very cold and not warmed quickly or easily, this knowledge is mapped onto Sally as being very unaffectionate and not able to become affectionate quickly or easily. Again, common knowledge and a conventional metaphor we all have is all that is needed.

Finally, Searle discusses *the hours crept by as we waited for the plane.* Here we have a verb of motion predicated of a time expression; the former activates the knowledge about motion through space and the latter activates the time domain. Jointly, they activate the TIME-AS-MOVING-OBJECT mapping. Again the meaning of the sentence follows only from everyday knowledge and the everyday system of metaphorical mappings.

Searle accounts for such cases by his Principle 4, which says that "we just do perceive a connection" which is the basis of the interpretation. This is vague and doesn't say what the perceived connection is or why we "just do" perceive it. When we spell out the details of all such "perceived connections," they turn out to be the system of conceptual metaphors I have been describing. But given that system, Searle's theory and his principles become unnecessary.

In addition, Searle's account of literal meaning makes most of the usual false assumptions that accompany that term. Searle assumes that all everyday, conventional language is literal and not metaphorical. He would thus rule out every example of conventional metaphor described not only in this chapter, but in the whole literature of the field.

The study of the metaphorical subsystem of our conceptual system is a central part of synchronic linguistics because much of our semantic system, that is, our system of concepts, is metaphorical, as we saw above. Because this huge system went unnoticed prior to 1980, authors like Searle, Sadock, and Morgan could claim, incorrectly as it turns out, that metaphor was outside of synchronic linguistics and in the domain of principles of language use.

6. The experiential basis of metaphor

The conceptual system underlying a language contains thousands of conceptual metaphors — conventional mappings from one domain to another, such as the Event Structure Metaphor. The novel metaphors of a language are, except for image metaphors, extensions of this large conventional system.

Perhaps the deepest question that any theory of metaphor must answer is this: why do we have the conventional metaphors that we have? Or alternatively: is there any reason why conceptual systems contain one set of metaphorical mappings rather than another? There do appear to be answers to these questions for many of the mappings found so far, though they are in the realm of plausible accounts, rather than in the realm of scientific results.

Take a simple case: the MORE IS UP metaphor, as seen in expressions like prices rose; his income went down; unemployment is up; exports are down; the number of homeless people is very high.

There are other languages in which MORE IS UP and LESS IS DOWN, but none in which the reverse is true, where MORE IS DOWN and LESS IS UP. Why not? Contemporary theory postulates that the MORE IS UP metaphor is *grounded in experience* — in the common experiences of pouring more fluid into a container and seeing the level go up, or adding more things to a pile and seeing the pile get higher. These are thoroughly pervasive experiences; we encounter them every day of our lives. They have structure — a correspondence between the conceptual domain of quantity and the conceptual domain of verticality: MORE corresponds in such experiences to up and LESS corresponds to DOWN. These correspondences in real experience form the basis for the correspondences in the metaphorical cases, which go beyond real experience: *in prices rose* there is no correspondence in real experience between quantity and verticality, but understanding quantity in terms of verticality makes sense because of a regular correspondence in so many other cases.

Consider another case. What is the basis of the widespread KNOWING IS SEEING metaphor, as in expressions like I see what you're saying; his answer was clear; this paragraph is murky; he was so blinded by ambition that he never noticed his limitations? The experiential basis in this case is the fact that most of what we know comes through vision, and in the overwhelming majority of cases, if we see something, then we know it is true.

Consider still another case. Why, in the Event Structure Metaphor, is achieving a purpose understood as reaching a destination (in the location subsystem) and as acquiring a desired object (in the object subsystem)? The answer again seems to be correspondences in everyday experience. To achieve most of our everyday purposes, we either have to move to some destination or acquire some object. If you want a drink of water, you've got to go to the water fountain. If you want to be in the sunshine, you have to move to where the sunshine is. And if you want to write down a note, you have to get a pen or pencil. The correspondences between achieving purposes and either reaching destinations or acquiring objects is so utterly common in our everyday existence, that the resulting metaphor is completely natural.

But what about the experiential basis of A PURPOSEFUL LIFE IS A JOURNEY? Recall that the mapping is in an inheritance hierarchy, where life goals are special cases of purposes, which are destinations in the event structure metaphor. Thus, A PURPOSEFUL LIFE IS A JOURNEY inherits the experiential basis of PURPOSES ARE DESTINATIONS. Thus, inheritance hierarchies provide *indirect experiential bases*, in that a metaphorical mapping lower in a hierarchy can inherit its experiential basis indirectly from a mapping higher in the hierarchy.

Experiential bases motivate metaphors, they do not predict them. Thus, not every language has a MORE IS UP metaphor, though all human beings experience a correspondence between MORE and UP. What this experiential basis does predict is that no language will have the opposite metaphor LESS IS UP. It also predicts that a speaker of a language without that metaphor will be able to learn it much more easily than its reverse.

6.1 Realizations of metaphor

Consider objects like thermometers and stock market graphs, where increases in temperature and prices are represented as being up and decreases as being down. These are objects created by humans to accord with the MORE IS UP metaphor. They exhibit a correlation between MORE and up and are much easier to read and understand than if they contradicted the metaphor, if, say, increases were represented as down and decreases as up.

Such objects are ways in which metaphors impose a structure on real life, through the creation of new correspondences in experience. And once created in one generation, they serve as an experiential basis for that metaphor in the next generation.

There are a great many ways in which conventional metaphors can be made real. They can be realized in obvious imaginative products such as cartoons, literary works, dreams, visions, and myths, but they can be made real in less obvious ways as well, in physical symptoms, social institutions, social practices, laws, and even foreign policy and forms of discourse and history.

Let us consider some examples.

6.1.1 Cartoons

Conventional metaphors are made real in cartoons. A common example is the realization of the ANGER IS A HOT FLUID IN A CONTAINER metaphor, in which one can be *boiling mad* or *letting off steam*. In cartoons, anger is commonly depicted by steam coming out of the character's ears. Social clumsiness is indicated by having a cartoon character *fall on his face*.

6.1.2 Literary works

It is common for the plot of a novel to be a realization of the PURPOSEFUL LIFE IS A JOURNEY metaphor, where the course of a life takes the form of an actual journey. *Pilgrim's Progress* is a classic example.

6.1.3 Rituals

Consider the cultural ritual in which a newborn baby is carried upstairs to ensure his or her success. The metaphor realized in this ritual IS STATUS IS UP, as in: he clawed his way to the top; *he climbed the ladder of success; you'll rise in the world.*

6.1.4 *Dream interpretation*

Conceptual metaphors constitute the vocabulary of dream interpretation. The collection of our everyday conceptual metaphors makes dream interpretation possible. Consider one of the most celebrated of all examples, Joseph's interpretation of Pharaoh's dream from Genesis. In Pharaoh's dream, he is standing on the river bank when seven fat cows come out of the river, followed by seven lean cows that eat the seven fat ones and still remain lean. Pharaoh dreams again. This time he sees seven "full and good" ears of corn growing and then seven withered ears growing after them. The withered ears devour the good ears. Joseph interprets the two dreams as a single dream. The seven fat cows and full ears are good years and the seven lean cows and withered ears are famine years that follow the good years. The famine years devour what the good years produce. This interpretation makes sense to us because of a collection of conceptual metaphors in our conceptual system — metaphors that have been with us since biblical times. The first metaphor is TIMES ARE MOVING ENTITIES. A river is a common metaphor for the flow of time; the cows are individual entities (years) emerging from the flow of time and moving past the observer; the ears of corn are also entities that come into the scene. The second metaphor is ACHIEVING A PURPOSE IS EATING, where being fat indicates success, being lean indicates failure. This metaphor is combined with the most common of metonymies, A PART STANDS FOR THE WHOLE. Since cows and corn were typical of meat and grain eaten, each single cow stands for all the cows raised in a year and each ear of corn for all the corn grown in a year. The final metaphor is RESOURCES ARE FOOD, where using up resources is eating food. The devouring of the good years by the famine years is interpreted as indicating that all the surplus resources of the good years will be used up by the famine years. The interpretation of the whole dream is thus a composition of three conventional metaphors and one metonymy. The metaphoric and metonymic sources are combined to form the reality of the dream.

6.1.5 *Myths*

In the event structure metaphor, there is a submapping EXTERNAL EVENTS ARE LARGE MOVING OBJECTS that can exert a force on you and thereby affect whether you achieve your goals. In English the special cases of such objects are "things," fluids, and horses. Pamela Morgan (in unpublished work) has observed that in

Greek mythology, Poseidon is the god of the sea, earthquakes, horses, and bulls. The list might seem arbitrary, but Morgan observes that these are all large moving objects that can exert a force on you. Poseidon, she surmises, should really be seen as the god of external events.

6.1.6 Physical symptoms

The unconscious mind makes use of our unconscious system of conventional metaphor, sometimes to express psychological states in terms of physical symptoms. For example, in the event structure metaphor, there is a submapping DIFFICULTIES ARE IMPEDIMENTS TO MOTION which has, as a special case, DIFFICULTIES ARE BURDENS. It is fairly common for someone encountering difficulties to walk with his shoulders stooped, as if *carrying a heavy weight* that is *burdening* him.

6.1.7 Social institutions

We have a TIME IS MONEY metaphor, shown by expressions like *he's wasting time; I have to budget my time; this will save you time; I've invested a lot of time in that; he doesn't use his time profitably.* This metaphor came into English use about the time of the industrial revolution, when people started to be paid for work by the amount of time they put in. Thus, the factory led to the institutional pairing of periods of time with amounts of money, which formed the experiential basis of this metaphor. Since then, the metaphor has been realized in many other ways. The budgeting of time has spread throughout American culture.

6.1.8 Social practices

There is a conceptual metaphor that SEEING IS TOUCHING, where the eyes are limbs and vision is achieved when the object seen is "touched." Examples are: *my eyes picked out every detail of the pattern; he ran his eyes over the walls; he couldn't take his eyes off of her; their eyes met; his eyes are glued to the TV.* The metaphor is made real in the social practice of avoiding eye "contact" on the street, and in the social prohibition against "undressing someone with your eyes."

6.1.9. Laws

Law is a major area where metaphor is made real. For example, CORPORATIONS ARE PERSONS is a tenet of American law, which not only enables corporations to be *harmed* or assigned *responsibility* so they can be sued when liable, but also gives them certain First Amendment rights.

6.1.10 *Foreign policy*

A STATE IS A PERSON is one of the major metaphors underlying foreign policy concepts. Thus, there are *friendly* states, *hostile* states, and so forth. Health for a state is economic health and strength is military strength. A threat to economic *health* can be seen as a death threat, as when Iraq was seen to have a *stranglehold* on the *economic lifeline* of the United States. Strong states are seen as male and weak states as female, so that an attack by a strong state on a weak one can be seen as a *rape*, as in the rape of Kuwait by Iraq. A *just war* is conceptualized as a fairy tale with villain, victim, and hero, where the villain attacks the victim and the hero rescues the victim. Thus, the United States and allies in the Gulf War were portrayed as having *rescued* Kuwait. As President Bush said in his address to Congress, "The issues couldn't have been clearer: Iraq was the villain and Kuwait, the victim."

6.1.11 *Forms of discourse*

Common metaphors are often made real in discourse forms. Consider three common academic discourse forms: the guided tour, the heroic battle, and the heroic quest. The guided tour is based on the metaphor that THOUGHT IS MOTION, where ideas are locations and one reasons *step-by-step, reaches conclusions,* or fails to reach a conclusion if engaged in *circular reasoning.* Communication in this metaphor is giving someone a guided tour of some rational argument or of some *intellectual terrain.* This essay is an example of such a guided tour, where I, the author, am the tour guide who is assumed to be thoroughly familiar with the terrain and the terrain surveyed is taken as objectively real. The discourse form of the heroic battle is based on the metaphor that ARGUMENT IS WAR. The author's theory is the hero, the opposing theory is the villain, and words are weapons. The battle is in the form of an argument defending the hero's position and demolishing that of the villain. The heroic quest discourse form is based on the metaphor that knowledge is a valuable but elusive object that can be *discovered* if one perseveres. The scientist is the hero on a quest for knowledge, and the discourse form is an account of his difficult journey of discovery. What is *discovered* is a real entity.

What makes all these cases realizations of metaphors is that in each case something real is structured by conventional metaphor, and thereby made comprehensible, or even natural. What is real differs in each case: an object like a thermometer or graph, an experience like a dream, an action like a ritual, a form of discourse, and so forth. These examples reveal that much of what is real in a society or in the experience of an individual is structured and made sense of via conventional metaphor.

Experiential bases and realizations of metaphors are two sides of the same coin: they are both correlations in real experience that have the same structure as the correlations in metaphors. The difference is that experiential bases precede, ground, and make sense of conventional metaphorical mappings, whereas realizations follow, and are made sense of, via the conventional metaphors. And as we noted above, one generation's realizations of a metaphor can become part of the next generation's experiential basis for that metaphor.

7. Summary of results

As we have seen, the contemporary theory of metaphor is revolutionary in many respects. To give you some idea of how revolutionary, here is a list of the basic results that differ from most previous accounts.

7.1 *The nature of metaphor*

– Metaphor is the main mechanism through which we comprehend abstract concepts and perform abstract reasoning.
– Much subject matter, from the most mundane to the most abstruse scientific theories, can only be comprehended via metaphor. Metaphor is fundamentally conceptual, not linguistic, in nature.
– Metaphorical language is a surface manifestation of conceptual metaphor.
– Though much of our conceptual system is metaphorical, a significant part of it is nonmetaphorical. Metaphorical understanding is grounded in non-metaphorical understanding.
– Metaphor allows us to understand a relatively abstract or inherently unstructured subject matter in terms of a more concrete, or at least more highly structured subject matter.

7.2 *The structure of metaphor*

– Metaphors are mappings across conceptual domains.

- Such mappings are asymmetric and partial.
- Each mapping is a fixed set of ontological correspondences between entities in a source domain and entities in a target domain.
- When those fixed correspondences are activated, mappings can project source domain inference patterns onto target domain inference patterns.
- Metaphorical mappings obey the Invariance Principle: The image-schema structure of the source domain is projected onto the target domain in a way that is consistent with inherent target domain structure.
- Mappings are not arbitrary, but grounded in the body and in everyday experience and knowledge.
- A conceptual system contains thousands of conventional metaphorical mappings which form a highly structured subsystem of the conceptual system.
- There are two types of mappings: conceptual mappings and image mappings; both obey the Invariance Principle.

7.3 Some aspects of metaphor

- The system of conventional conceptual metaphor is mostly unconscious, automatic, and used with no noticeable effort, just like our linguistic system and the rest of our conceptual system.
- Our system of conventional metaphor is "alive" in the same sense that our system of grammatical and phonological rules is alive; namely, it is constantly in use, automatically, and below the level of consciousness.
- Our metaphor system is central to our understanding of experience and to the way we act on that understanding.
- Conventional mappings are static correspondences, and are not, in themselves, algorithmic in nature. However, this by no means rules out the possibility that such static correspondences might be used in language processing that involves sequential steps.
- Metaphor is mostly based on correspondences in our experiences, rather than on similarity.
- The metaphor system plays a major role in both the grammar and lexicon of a language.
- Metaphorical mappings vary in universality; some seem to be universal, others are widespread, and some seem to be culture specific.

– Poetic metaphor is, for the most part, an extension of our everyday, conventional system of metaphorical thought.

These are the conclusions that best fit the empirical studies of metaphor conducted over the past decade or so. Though many of them are inconsistent with traditional views, they are by no means all new, and some ideas — for example, that abstract concepts are comprehended in terms of concrete concepts — have a long history.

8. Concluding remarks

The evidence supporting the contemporary theory of metaphor is voluminous and grows larger each year as research in the field continues. The evidence, as we saw above, comes from five domains:

– Generalizations over polysemy
– Generalizations over inference patterns
– Generalizations over extensions to poetic cases
– Generalizations over semantic change
– Psycholinguistic experiments

I have discussed only a handful of examples of the first three of these, enough, I hope, to make the reader curious about the field.

Evidence is convincing, however, only if it can count as evidence. When does evidence fail to be evidence? Unfortunately, all too often. It is commonly the case that certain fields of inquiry are defined by assumptions that rule out the possibility of counterevidence. When a defining assumption of a field comes up against evidence, the evidence usually loses: the practitioners of the field must ignore the evidence if they want to keep the assumptions that define the field they are committed to.

Part of what makes the contemporary theory of metaphor so interesting is that the evidence for it contradicts the defining assumptions of so many academic disciplines. In my opinion, this should make one doubt the defining assumptions of all those disciplines. The reason is this: the defining assumptions of the contemporary theory of metaphor are minimal. There are only two.

1. The generalization commitment: To seek generalizations in all areas of language, including polysemy, patterns of inference, novel metaphor, and semantic change.
2. The cognitive commitment: To take experimental evidence seriously.

But these are nothing more than commitments to the scientific study of language and the mind. No initial commitment is made as to the form of an answer to the question of what is metaphor.

The defining assumptions of other fields do, however, often entail a commitment about the form of an answer to that question. It is useful, in an interdisciplinary volume of this sort, to spell out exactly what those defining assumptions are, since they will often explain why different authors reach such different conclusions about the nature of metaphor.

8.1   Literal meaning commitments

I started this chapter with a list of the false assumptions about literal meaning that are commonly made. These assumptions are "false" only relative to the kinds of evidence that support the contemporary theory of metaphor. If one ignores all such evidence, the assumptions can be maintained without contradiction.

Assumptions about literality are the locus of many of the contradictions between the contemporary theory of metaphor and various academic disciplines. Let us review those assumptions. In the discussion of literal meaning given above, I observed that it is taken as definitional that what is literal is not metaphorical. The "false assumptions and conclusions" that usually accompany the word "literal" are:

– All everyday conventional language is literal, and none is metaphorical.
– All subject matter can be comprehended literally, without metaphor.
– Only literal language can be contingently true or false.
– All definitions given in the lexicon of a language are literal, not metaphorical.
– The concepts used in the grammar of a language are all literal; none is metaphorical.

We will begin with the philosophy of language. The generalization commitment and the cognitive commitment are *not* definitional to the philosophy of language. Most philosophers of language would feel no need to abide by them, for a very good reason. The philosophy of language is typically not seen as an empirical discipline, constrained by empirical results, such as those that arise from the application of the generalization and cognitive commitments. Instead, the philosophy of language is usually seen as an a priori discipline, which can be pursued using the tools of philosophical analysis alone, rather than the tools of empirical research. Therefore, all the evidence that has been brought forth for the contemporary theory of metaphor simply will not matter for most philosophers of language.

In addition, the philosophy of language comes with its own set of defining assumptions, which entail many of the false assumptions usually associated with the word "literal." Most practitioners of the philosophy of language usually make one or more of the following assumptions.

– The correspondence theory of truth.
– Meaning is defined in terms of reference and truth.
– Natural language semantics is characterized by the mechanisms of mathematical logic, including model theory.

The very field of philosophy of language thus comes with defining assumptions that contradict the main conclusions of the contemporary theory of metaphor. Consequently, we can see why most philosophers of language have the range of views on metaphor that they have: they accept the traditional literal-figurative distinction. They may, like M. Johnson (1981), say that there is no metaphorical meaning, and that most metaphorical utterances are either trivially true or trivially false. Or, like Grice (1989: 34) and Searle (1993), they will assume that metaphor is in the realm of pragmatics, that is, that a metaphorical meaning is no more than the literal meaning of some other sentence which can be arrived at by some pragmatic principle. This is required, since the only real meaning for them is literal meaning, and pragmatic principles are those principles that allow one to say one thing (with a literal meaning) and mean something else (with a different, but nonetheless literal, meaning).

Much of generative linguistics accepts one or more of these assumptions from the philosophy of language. The field of formal semantics accepts them all, and thus formal semantics, by its defining assumptions, is at odds with the contemporary theory of metaphor. Formal semantics simply does not see it as its job to account for the generalizations discussed in this chapter. From the perspective of formal semantics, the phenomena that the contemporary theory of metaphor is concerned with are either nonexistent or uninteresting, since they lie outside the purview of the discipline. Thus Jerrold Sadock (1993) claims that metaphor lies outside of synchronic linguistics. Since he accepts mathematical logic as the correct approach to natural language semantics, Sadock must see metaphor as being outside of semantics proper. He must, therefore, also reject the enterprise of the contemporary theory of metaphor. And Morgan (1993), also accepting those defining assumptions of the philosophy of language, agrees with Grice and Searle that metaphor is a matter of pragmatics.

Chomsky's (1981) theory of government and binding also accepts crucial assumptions from the philosophy of language that are inconsistent with the contemporary theory of metaphor. Government and binding, following my early theory of generative semantics, assumes that semantics is to be represented in terms of logical form. Government and binding, like generative semantics, thus rules out the very possibility that metaphor might be part of natural language semantics as it enters into grammar. Because of this defining assumption, I would not expect government and binding theorists to become concerned with the phenomena covered by the contemporary theory of metaphor.

It is interesting that much of continental philosophy and deconstructionism is also characterized by defining assumptions at odds with the contemporary theory of metaphor. Nietzsche (see Johnson 1981) held that all language is metaphorical, a theory at odds with those results indicating that a significant amount of everyday language is not metaphorical (see subsection, "What is not metaphorical"). Much of continental philosophy, observing that conceptual systems change through time, assumes that conceptual systems are purely historically contingent, that there are no conceptual universals. Though conceptual systems do change through time, there do, however, appear to be universal, or at least very widespread, conceptual metaphors. The event structure metaphor is my present candidate for a metaphorical universal.

Continental philosophy also comes with a distinction between the study of the physical world, which can be scientific, and the study of human beings, which it says cannot be scientific. This is very much at odds with the conceptual theory of metaphor, which is very much a scientific enterprise.

Finally, the contemporary theory of metaphor is at odds with certain traditions in symbolic artificial intelligence and information processing psychology. Those fields assume that thought is a matter of algorithmic symbol manipulation, of the sort done by a traditional computer program. This defining assumption is inconsistent with the contemporary theory of metaphor in two respects.

First, the contemporary theory has an image-schematic basis. The Invariance Principle both applies to image metaphors and characterizes constraints on novel metaphor. Since symbol manipulation systems cannot handle image-schemas, they cannot deal with image metaphors or imageable idioms.

Second, those traditions must characterize metaphorical mapping as an algorithmic process, which typically takes literal meanings as input and gives a metaphorical reading as output. This runs counter to cases where there are multiple, overlapping metaphors in a single sentence, and which require the simultaneous activation of a number of metaphorical mappings.

The contemporary theory of metaphor is thus not only interesting for its own sake. It is especially interesting for the challenge it presents to other disciplines. If the results of the contemporary theory are accepted, the defining assumptions of whole disciplines are brought into question.

Note

① This research was supported in part by grants from the Sloan Foundation and the National Science Foundation (IRI-8703202) to the University of California at Berkeley. The following colleagues and students helped with this essay in a variety of ways, from useful comments to allowing me to cite their research: Ken Baldwin, Claudia Brugman, Jane Espenson, Sharon Fischler, Ray Gibbs, Adele Goldberg, Mark Johnson, Karin Myhre, Eve Sweetser, and Mark Turner.

References

Chomsky, Noam
  1981 *Lectures on Government and Binding.* Dordrecht: Foris Publications.
Gibbs, Raymond W., Jr.

1990   Psycholinguistic studies on the conceptual basis of idiomaticity. *Cognitive Linguistics* 1: 417–462.

1993   Process and products in making sense of tropes. In *Metaphor and Thought*, Andrew Ortony (ed.), 252–276. Cambridge: Cambridge University Press.

Glucksberg, Sam and Boaz Keysar

1993   How metaphors work. In *Metaphor and Thought*, Andrew Ortony (ed.), 401–424. Cambridge: Cambridge University Press.

Grice, Paul

1989   *Studies in the Way of Words.* Cambridge, MA: Harvard University Press.

Johnson, M.

1981   *Philosophical Perspectives on Metaphor.* Minneapolis: University of Minnesota Press.

Köovecses, Zoltan

1990   *Emotion Concepts.* New York: Springer-Verlag.

Lakoff, George

1987   *Women, Fire, and Dangerous Things: What Categories Reveal about the Mind.* Chicago: University of Chicago Press.

Lakoff, George and Mark Johnson

1980   *Metaphors We Live By.* Chicago: University of Chicago Press.

Lakoff, George and Mark Turner

1989   *More Than Cool Reason: A Field Guide to Poetic Metaphor.* Chicago: University of Chicago Press.

Merwin, William S.

1973   *Asian Figures.* New York: Atheneum.

Merwin, William S. and Masson, J. Moussaieff (trans.)

1981   *The Peacock's Egg.* San Francisco: North Point Press.

Morgan, Pamela

1993   In *Metaphor and Thought,* Andrew Ortony (ed.). Cambridge: Cambridge University Press.

Ortony, Andrew (ed.)

1993   *Metaphor and Thought.* Cambridge: Cambridge University Press. (First edition published in 1979.)

Reddy, Michael

1993   The conduit metaphor. A case of frame conflict in our language about language. In *Metaphor and Thought*, Andrew Ortony (ed.), 164–201. Cambridge: Cambridge University Press.

Sadock, Jerrold

1993 Figurative speech and linguistics. In *Metaphor and Thought*, Andrew Ortony (ed.), 42–57. Cambridge: Cambridge University Press.

Searle, John R.

1993 Metaphor. In *Metaphor and Thought*, Andrew Ortony (ed.), 83–111. Cambridge: Cambridge University Press.

Sweetser, Eve

1990 *From Etymology to Pragmatics: The Mind-as-Body Metaphor in Semantic Structure and Semantic Change.* Cambridge: Cambridge University Press.

Turner, Mark

1987 *Death Is the Mother of Beauty: Mind, Metaphor, Criticism.* Chicago: University of Chicago Press.

1991 *Reading Minds: The Study of English in the Age of Cognitive Science.* Princeton: Princeton University Press.

The Role of Domains in the Interpretation of Metaphors and Metonymies

William Croft

1. Introduction

Consider the following sentence:

(1)　*Denmark shot down the Maastricht treaty,*

This sentence is generally taken to involve both metonymy and metaphor: the subject proper noun *Denmark is* a metonymy for 'the voters of Denmark', while the predicate *shot down is* a metaphor for 'cause to fail'. After the fact this is all quite straightforward. But how does the listener know that this sentence is not about a military act, or a particular piece of territory in Europe? The question this paper will address, though not fully answer, is: how are such "figurative" meanings constructed in a particular utterance? What leads speakers to not employ the basic or literal meanings of those words, or, if they do, to shift to the appropriate meaning?

This is a problem of semantic composition, that is, of the relation of the meaning of the whole to the meaning of the parts. Unlike the typical problems of semantic composition discussed in the formal semantic literature, where the meaning of the whole is at least in part determined by the meanings of the parts, the meaning of the parts here seems to be determined in part by the meaning of the whole. I will argue here that the "meaning of the whole" that affects the meanings of the parts is what I call the *conceptual unity of domain:* all of the elements in a syntactic unit must be interpreted in a single domain. In example 1, for instance, the domain is political activity.

Moreover, a large part (though not all) of what is going on in metaphorical

525

and metonymic interpretation is adjustment of the domains of the component elements, and hence their meanings, to satisfy the conceptual unity of domain. I use the word "adjustment" here because the adjustment of domains is related to the conceptualization phenomena that Langacker calls *focal adjustments* (Langacker 1987: Chapter 3). In Section 2, I will describe a theory of word meaning and the role of domains in word meaning, taken largely from Langacker's model of cognitive grammar (Langacker 1987, 1991). In Section 3, I will describe the role of domains in metaphor and metonymy, and argue that metonymy as traditionally conceived usually involves a more general phenomenon of polysemy that critically involves domains. In Section 4, I discuss the relationship between metaphor and metonymy and semantic composition in cognitive grammar, arguing that metaphor applies to dependent predications and metonymy to autonomous predications (Langacker 1987: 8.3). Finally, in Section 5, I argue that the scope of the conceptual unity of domain is a dependent predication and the autonomous predications that it is dependent on, and that a listener's cognitive processing in "solving" the conceptual unity of domain requires reference to context.

2. Word meaning and domains in cognitive grammar

One of the central tenets of cognitive semantics is that the meaning of words is encyclopedic: everything you know about the concept is part of its meaning (Haiman 1980; Langacker 1987: 4.2.1). From this it follows that there is no essential difference between (linguistic) semantic representation and (general) knowledge representation; the study of linguistic semantics is the study of commonsense human experience. Thus, that aspect of "pragmatics" which involves the employment of "world knowledge" or "commonsense knowledge", and even contextual knowledge (since the speech act context is part of our world knowledge, albeit a very specific piece of knowledge), becomes part of semantics.

Not surprisingly, taking seriously the encyclopedic view of semantics rather drastically alters our view of most of the outstanding problems of semantics (without necessarily solving them, however; but at least they look much more natural). Although in theory all knowledge about an entity is accessible — that is, the whole knowledge network is accessible — some knowledge is more central (Langacker 1987: 4.2.2), and the pattern of centrality and peripherality is a major part of what distinguishes the meaning of one word from that of another. Langacker identifies four criteria for centrality: the extent to which knowledge of the concept applies to all entities categorized by the concept (*generic*), the extent to which knowledge of the concept applies to only those entities (*characteristic;* these two criteria together define cue validity, see Rosch 1978); the extent to which the knowledge is general knowledge in the speech community (*conventional*), and the degree to which the knowledge applies to the object itself as opposed to external entities (*intrinsic*).[1]

Understanding the meaning of a word in the encyclopedic view means entering the knowledge network at a certain point — more precisely, activating the network by activating it at a certain point or points:

> The entity designated by a symbolic unit can therefore be thought of as a *point of access* to a network. The semantic value of a symbolic unit is given by the openended set of relations ... in which this *access node* participates. Each of these relations is a cognitive routine, and because they share at least one component the activation of one routine facilitates (but does not always necessitate) the activation of another. (Langacker 1987: 163)

Thus, semantic space is the whole network of an individual's — and a community's — knowledge. This knowledge as a whole is not unstructured. Encyclopedic knowledge appears to be organized into experiential *domains* (Langacker 1987: 4.1; Lakoff 1987, among many others). The notion of a domain is central to the understanding of metaphor and metonymy. In particular, it is critical to identify when one is dealing with a single domain or different domains. Despite its centrality, the notion of domain has not been delineated in detail. It is related to the notion of a semantic field, as in the field theories of Trier and others. This work has come under considerable criticism, not least because the notion of semantic field is left undefined: "What is lacking so far, as most field-theorists would probably admit, is a more explicit formulation of the criteria which define a lexical field than has yet been provided" (Lyons 1977: 267).

The most carefully worked-out description of domains is found in Langacker (1987), some of which is based on Lakoff and Johnson (1980); the description that follows makes explicit some assumptions that are implicit in those works. But to understand the notion of a domain, we must begin by describing a central aspect of a concept symbolized by a word, its division into a profile and base. (What I am calling a "concept" is a semantic structure symbolized by a word; Langacker calls this a *predication,* and I will use these terms interchangeably. While there are concepts that do not — yet — have words that symbolize them, the notion of a concept is sufficiently difficult to identify independently of language that we will restrict ourselves to those that are already symbolized and therefore have a definite existence consecrated by the conventions of a language.)[2]

We will begin with Langacker's example of an arc of a circle (1987: 183–184). A concept, such as that of an arc, presupposes other concepts, in this case that of a circle. An arc is defined only relative to a circle; otherwise it would be merely a curved line segment. What we intuitively think of as the arc itself is the *profile;* the notion of a circle which it presupposes is its *base.* This idea is not totally new; one of its better-known manifestations is as a "frame" in artificial intelligence and linguistics. The concept of [ARC] is not just the profile but also the base; the concept is definable only relative to what it presupposes. (Searle 1979 also argues for the necessary inclusion of background assumptions in the definition of a word.) A circle itself is defined relative to two-dimensional space. The concept [CIRCLE] profiles that shape configuration, and has (two-dimensional) space as its base. (To be precise, it has shape as its base, and the concept of shape — not "a shape", but "shape" — is profiled in two-dimensional space. I return to this issue below.) In other words, a concept can function either as a profile or as a base for another concept profile.

The profile-base relation is not the same as the central-peripheral relation discussed above with respect to the encyclopedic definition of word meaning. The base is that aspect of knowledge which is necessarily presupposed in conceptualizing the profile. Peripheral knowledge is knowledge associated with a concept that is not as generic, characteristic, conventional, and intrinsic as more central knowledge. Peripheral knowledge is not presupposed knowledge, but additional, less central asserted knowledge. Of course, peripheral knowledge as well as central knowledge is organized in a profile-base fashion. This will be illustrated later.

Profile and base are conceptually interdependent. On the one hand, profiled concepts cannot be understood except against the background knowledge provided by the base. On the other hand, the base exists as a cognitively unified and delimited "chunk" of knowledge only by virtue of the concept or concepts defined with respect to it.

A particular base is almost always the base for several concept profiles. For example, a circle is the base not only for [ARC], but also [DIAMETER], [RADIUS], [CHORD], etc. This is what makes the base a domain, in the intuitive sense: several different concept profiles have it as a base. We can now define a domain as *a semantic structure that functions as the base for at least one concept profile* (typically, many profiles). As Taylor (1989: 84) notes, "In principle, any conceptualization or knowledge configuration, no matter how simple or complex, can serve as the cognitive domain for the characterization of meanings." We can say that the domain of a circle includes the concepts of an arc, a diameter, a radius, chord, etc. A circle itself is in the domain of two-dimensional space (actually, shape). This demonstrates that a particular semantic structure can be a concept in a domain (when it is profiled), or a domain itself (when it is functioning as the base to other concept profiles). We return to this point below.

Space itself does not appear to be profiled in a domain that serves as its base. Instead, it emerges directly from experience (cf. Lakoff and Johnson 1980: Chapter 12). Langacker calls space a *basic domain*. Basic domains are concepts that do not appear to be definable relative to other, more basic concepts, at least in the commonsense or folk model of experience. There are a substantial number of such basic domains; in fact, a good idea of the basic domains there are can be found by examining the higher divisions of a good thesaurus.

Langacker calls a nonbasic domain an *abstract domain*. The notion of a circle, functioning as a base, is an example of an abstract domain. An abstract domain itself is a concept that presupposes another domain. The other domain need not be a basic one. I noted above that shape is more precisely the base for [CIRCLE]; the concept of [SHAPE] is in turn profiled in two-dimensional space. (The other major concept profiled in space is [LOCATION].) One can have an arbitrarily deep nesting of abstract domains before reaching a basic domain. However, the base is usually taken to be just the domain immediately presupposed by the profiled concept. We will call this domain the *base domain* (or simply the base; this is also what Langacker calls the *scope of predication;* recall that a predication is a concept). Langacker (1987: 493) notes that the scope of predication/base "may sometimes constitute only a limited portion of relevant domains" (the involvement of multiple domains in the definition of a concept will be discussed below).

529

The relation between an abstract domain and the basic domain it presupposes is not a taxonomic relation (or, as Langacker calls such relations, a schematic one). It is a relationship of concept to background assumption or presupposition. This distinction is sometimes obscured by the English language. The word *shape* stands for the domain as a mass noun, but as a count noun (*a shape*) it is a more general or schematic concept subsuming [CIRCLE], [SQUARE], [TRIANGLE], etc. A more general or schematic concept is not the domain for the particular concept; in fact, it is itself profiled in the same domain as its particular concept. As will be seen below, it is not always easy to distinguish a taxonomic relation from an abstract-basic domain relation.

Langacker argues that some domains involve more than one *dimension* (1987: 150–151). An obvious case is space, which involves three dimensions (some concepts, such as [CIRCLE], need only two dimensions for their definition; others need only one). Many physical qualities that are grounded in the experience of sensory perception, such as temperature and pitch, are one-dimensional. Others, such as color, can be divided into hue, brightness and saturation. Generally, dimensions of a domain are all simultaneously presupposed by concepts profiled in that domain. This is the critical point: a concept may presuppose several different dimensions at once.

In fact, a concept may presuppose several different domains. For example, a human being must be defined relative to the domains of physical objects, living things, and volitional agents (and several other domains, e.g. emotion). The combination of domains simultaneously presupposed by a concept such as [HUMAN BEING] is called a *domain matrix*. Langacker (1987: 152) makes the important point that there is in principle only a difference of degree between dimensions of a domain and domains in a matrix. In practice, we are more likely to call a semantic structure a domain if there are a substantial number of concepts profiled relative to that structure. If there are few, if any, concepts profiled relative to that structure alone, but instead there are concepts profiled relative to that structure and another one, then those structures are likely to be called two dimensions of a single domain. The term "domain" implies a degree of cognitive independence not found in a dimension.

The domain structure presupposed by a concept can be extremely complex. We can begin by considering the domain of physical objects, commonly invoked as a basic domain. The physical object domain is in fact not a basic domain, but a domain matrix. It consists of the domains of matter (an object is made of matter), shape (since objects have a shape; even substances have a shape, although it is not fixed), and location (embodying the principle that two objects cannot occupy the same location). Matter is a basic domain but, as we noted above, shape and location are abstract domains based on space, which is a basic domain.

Physical objects are themselves very general. Let us now consider how one would define what seems to be a kind of physical object, the letter T. It is directly defined as a letter of the alphabet; its base (domain) is hence the alphabet. The alphabet is itself an abstract domain presupposing the notion of a writing system — it is not just an instance of a writing system, since the latter involves not just a set of symbols such as an alphabet but also the means of putting them together, including the order on a page, spaces for words, etc. The domain of writing systems in turn presupposes the activity of writing. The activity of writing must be defined in terms of human communication, which presupposes the notion of meaning — perhaps a basic domain, since the symbolic relation appears not to be reducible to some other relation — and of the visual sensations, since writing is communication via usually perceived inscriptions, rather than auditorily or through gestures. And since writing is an activity, the domains of time and force or causation (both basic domains; force is a generalization of causation, see Talmy 1988) are also involved in the domain matrix of writing, since the letter T is the product of an activity. Since it is a human activity, it presupposes the involvement of human beings. Human beings are living things with mental abilities, such as volition, intention and cognition (themselves dimensions of the mental domain or, better, domains in the matrix of the domain of the mind). Living things in turn are physical objects endowed with life. A diagram exhibiting all of the basic-abstract domain relations presupposed in defining the concept of the letter T is shown in Figure 1 (the basic domains are given in small capitals). From this, it can be seen that it is incorrect to describe the concept of the letter T simply as belonging to the domain of writing, as a typical informal theory of domains would most likely have it. The vast majority of concepts belong to abstract domains which are themselves profiled in complex domain matrices, often also abstract, and so ultimately presuppose a large array of basic domains, which I will call a *domain structure*.

It is not easy to distinguish profile-base relations from taxonomic ones (that is, type vs. instance). For example, is writing an instance of human communication, or is writing an instance of an activity that can only be understood in terms of the goals of human communication? I believe the latter is a more accurate description, and have described it as such. Likewise, since writing is an instance of human activity, human activity does not appear as a domain, but the various domains that it presupposes — time, change, force, volition — do appear, because anything presupposed by a human activity will be presupposed by any instance of it (cf. the discussion of the base of a circle and a shape above).

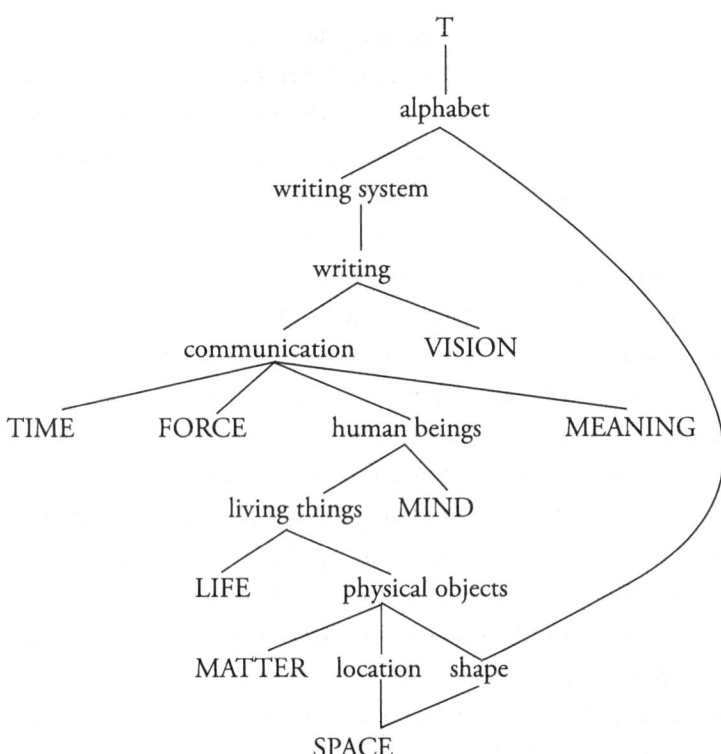

Figure 1. Domain structure underlying the concept of the letter T

It is also difficult to determine direct vs. indirect reference to a domain. Recall that Langacker argues that the definition of an arc does not directly presuppose two-dimensional space, but rather it presupposes a circle which in turn presupposes two-dimensional space. Thus, an arc is not directly a two-dimensional object per se, but only such by virtue of being a part of a circle. Likewise, the letter T is not directly a shape, but only such by virtue of being a letter of the alphabet. But in fact, is the letter T a shape by virtue of being a letter of the alphabet, or by virtue of being the physical product of the activity of writing? I believe it is best described as the former, since the set of symbols is a set of shapes.

Another similar problem in this example is the location of the domain of mental ability. The activity of writing is a volitional, intentional activity, so it presupposes the domain of mental ability. But mental ability is presupposed by writing because writing presupposes human involvement, and the human involvement involves volition and intention.[3] Determining the exact structure of the array of domains upon which a profiled concept is based requires a careful working out of the definitions of concepts, not unlike that carried out by Wierzbicka in her semantic analyses (see, e.g., Wierzbicka 1987, 1988).

It is not clear from Langacker 1987 whether Langacker considers the domain matrix of a concept to include only the base domains against which a concept is directly profiled or the entire domain structure underlying the concept profile. The example of the letter T demonstrates that for many concepts, the domain structure can be quite deep. There is some evidence that the notion of a domain matrix must include all of the domains in question. Consider the concepts [PERSON] and [BODY], [PERSON] is profiled against the abstract domain of human beings. As the diagram above indicates, human beings are living things with certain mental abilities (recall the classic definition of man as a rational animal). Living things in turn are physical objects endowed with life. The concept [BODY] represents a person's physical reality (alive or dead). Its base is nevertheless still the abstract domain of human beings (or, more precisely, animals), but it profiles the physical object domain in the domain structure underlying human beings. Contrast [BODY] with [SOUL], which profiles a nonphysical domain of a human being; or with [CORPSE], which profiles the physical object domain but also profiles a particular region in the life domain, namely [DEAD]. Another example is [KNEEL]. Only things with knees, or something resembling knees, can kneel; hence its base domain is (higher) animals — more precisely the base domain matrix includes animals as well as time and force, since kneeling is a process (see the matrix under "communication" in Figure 1). However, it primarily profiles a particular posture, which is a spatial configuration of the object, and the domain of spatial configuration (shape) is quite deeply nested in the domain structure underlying [KNEEL].

This is still not the end of the matter of describing the domain structure underlying a concept. Recall that meaning is encyclopedic. We have focused our attention only on the most central fact about the letter T, that it is a letter of the alphabet. Langacker calls the alphabet domain the *primary domain* of the concept, since it is the domain in which the most central facts about the concept are defined. However, there are other things we know about the letter T that are also quite central. It is the twentieth letter of the alphabet, which brings in the domain of a scale (ordering; a basic domain) and measurement, which in turn presupposes numbers, which in turn presupposes the notion of a unit of an entity. The letter T also corresponds to a linguistic sound, specifically a consonant, which brings in the domain of sound sensation (another basic domain), vocal articulation (a very abstract domain), and (again) language or communication. And there is much more specific knowledge that is quite peripheral to its meaning, for example that it is the initial of my wife's last name, which presupposes a whole host of abstract domains based on other abstract domains and ultimately a wide range of basic domains.

Whether these other domains form part of the matrix of the concept of the letter T depends on whether the concept of the letter T profiles such things as the fact that it is the twentieth letter of the alphabet, the initial of my wife's last name, etc. Langacker does not precisely answer this question. In the passage quoted above (1987: 163), Langacker states that activation of a concept (presumably, its profile) "facilitates (but does not always necessitate)" the activation of more peripheral knowledge about that concept. He later says that some routines (that is, pieces of knowledge) are sufficiently central to be activated almost every time (1987: 163). This implies that the central-peripheral relation is defined in terms of necessitation vs. facilitation of activation; facilitation can perhaps be thought of as a priming effect. Other factors, such as contextual priming, presumably can convert "facilitation" of activation of peripheral knowledge to actual activation of that knowledge in particular speech events where that peripheral knowledge is relevant.

The activation of the base domain of a profiled concept, on the other hand, is presumably necessary, since the definition of a base domain is the semantic structure presupposed by the profiled concept. This implies that the whole structure given in the diagram is going to be activated. Langacker does not explicitly state this, but he does suggest that the profile-base relation is a matter of attention, in a generalized model of attention which includes multiple loci of attention, which in turn could be modelled in terms of intensity of activation (1987: 188). One could extrapolate that the less direct the involvement of the domain in the definition of the concept, the less intense its activation will be when the concept is activated.

All of the above cognitive semantic structures — encyclopedic definitions, central vs. peripheral knowledge, profile and base, basic and abstract domains — are necessary for the definition of a single meaning of a word (Langacker 1987: 164, fn. 12). There is no apparatus given above for describing multiple meanings of a word. In a later chapter (1987: Chapter 10), Langacker argues for a "schematic network" (cf. Lakoff's 1987 notion of a radial category) for describing different uses of a word which combines both classical and prototype notions. All uses of a single word are related through various types of extensions from an original meaning ("original" in the ontogenetic sense); in addition, a more schematic meaning subsuming many or all of the specific uses can arise and fit into the network. Metaphor and metonymy are two types of extensions of word meaning; they represent different uses of a particular word. We now turn to the role of domains in licensing these semantic extensions.

3. Domains, metaphor and metonymy

The term "metaphor" has been used for many different kinds of figurative language, depending in part on the theory of metaphor subscribed to by the analyst. I will examine the types of metaphors that are central to Lakoff and Johnson's (1980) theory of metaphor. Lakoff and Johnson's theory can be illustrated by the contrast in the following two sentences:[4]

(2) *She's in the living room.*
(3) *She's in a good mood.*

Lakoff and Johnson employ a cognitive semantic model and analyze this type of metaphor as a conceptualization of one domain in terms of the structure of another independent domain, that is, a mapping across domains. The two domains, the source domain and the target domain, do not form a domain matrix for the concepts involved. In this example, the use of *in* in (3) for the relation between a person and her emotional state does not mean that the speaker has constructed a profile for metaphorical *in* simultaneously encoding a spatial relation and an emotional relation. Only the emotional domain is profiled in (3); however, the emotional domain is conceptualized as having the same or similar structure to space by the use of the predicate *in*.

As we saw in Section 2, if one accepts Lakoff and Johnson's theory of metaphor, as I do, one must be more specific as to what domain or domains are involved in a metaphor. I argue that the two domains being compared are base domains, that is, the bases of the profiled predication. In this case, the two domains are, as indicated in the informal description in the preceding paragraph, location and emotion, the base domains of the two uses of *in* in (2) and (3). (Actually, *in* involves containment, so more than location is involved in the source domain.)

In order to get an accurate description of a metaphor, the description of the metaphor has to be formulated in such a way that the two base domains are equated. For example, Lakoff and Johnson (1980: 73) describe the following example as an instance of a metaphor they describe as AN OBJECT COMES OUT OF A SUBSTANCE:

(4)　*I made a statue out of clay.*

The metaphorical expression is *out of.* Its base domain in the metaphorical usage is creation (that is the meaning of *make* selected in this sentence); the literal meaning has motion as its base domain, so the metaphor can be phrased as CREATION IS MOTION. Of course, both of these abstract domains, creation and motion, have multiple domains in their base matrices; for example, motion involves time, change and location.

Likewise, one must be careful to define the metaphor in terms of the base domain of the words in question. This is not always easy. Consider the metaphor described by Lakoff and Johnson (1980: 49) as LOVE IS A PATIENT; the following examples are theirs:

(5)　*This is a* sick *relationship.*
(6)　*They have a* strong, healthy *marriage.*
(7)　*The marriage is* dead — *it can't be* revived.

(8)   *Their marriage is* on the mend.

(9)   *We're getting* back on our feet.

(10) *Their relationship is* in really good shape.

(11) *They've got a* listless *marriage.*

(12) *Their marriage is* on its last legs.

(13) *It's a* tired *affair.*

First, the metaphor is probably best described as LOVE IS A BODILY STATE. The words *sick, strong, healthy, listless* and *tired* all have a bodily state as the base. The phrases *back on our feet, in really good shape,* and *on its last legs* are themselves metaphors whose target domain is also bodily states. However, the words *dead* and *revived* are arguably profiled in the domain of life, which is one of the domains underlying the domain of living things which in turn underlies the domain of bodily states (see the domains underlying "human beings" in Figure 1).[5] They are part of another metaphor, LOVE IS LIFE, which can generate metaphorical expressions using words profiled in the domain of living things:

(14) *Their letters kept their love* alive.

(15) *Her selfishness* killed *the relationship.*

(16) *His effort to understand her* breathed new life into *their marriage.*

Of course, LOVE IS A BODILY STATE and LOVE IS LIFE are metaphors coherent with each other, since bodily states presuppose the notion of life. However, the metaphors cannot be lumped together under something like "love is a living thing", since there are many other aspects of living things that are not metaphors for love, specifically those associated with the body (bodily activities, such as spitting, sweating; or the body itself, e.g. its parts; etc.).

The role of domains in metaphor is quite central to the definition of that concept in Lakoff and Johnson's model. However, to be more precise about the phenomenon that I am examining, I will use the term *domain mapping* to describe metaphor (though since in the Lakoff-Johnson model, the two terms are virtually synonymous, I will continue to use the term "metaphor"). The role of domains in metonymy, on the other hand, is not direct, although it is more pervasive than has generally been noted, once a careful examination of the domain structure underlying a concept is undertaken.

The traditional definition of metonymy is a shift of a word-meaning from the entity it stands for to a "contiguous" entity (Ullmann 1957: 232; cf. Lakoff and Johnson 1980: 35 and Taylor 1989: 122). Entities are contiguous because they are associated in experience (Lakoff and Johnson 1980: 39–40). Lakoff and Turner argue that metonymy, unlike metaphor, "involves only one conceptual domain. A metonymic mapping occurs within a single domain, not across domains" (Lakoff and Turner 1989: 103). However, as we have seen above, a concept is profiled against an often very complex domain structure or matrix, even if there is only one abstract domain as the base. In fact, in the next sentence, Lakoff and Turner switch to describing metonymy as a mapping within a schema; the term "schema" is more amenable to describing a complex domain structure (cf. Taylor 1989: 87). And Lakoff (1987: 288) describes a metonymic mapping as occurring "within a single conceptual domain, which is structured by an ICM [idealized cognitive model]" — which Langacker equates with an abstract domain. Thus, the generalization should be rephrased as "a metonymic mapping occurs within a single domain matrix, not across domains (or domain matrices)". Of course, the domain matrix possesses a unity that is created by experience — the real point of Lakoff's position.[6]

This is indeed the critical difference between metaphor and metonymy. Metaphor is a mapping between two domains that are not part of the same matrix; if you say *She's feeling down*, there is no spatial orientation domain in the matrix of the metaphorical concept of emotion being expressed; HAPPY IS UP involves two different concepts with their own domain structures underlying them. In metonymy, on the other hand, the mapping occurs only within a domain matrix. However, it is possible for metonymy, as well as for other lexical ambiguities, to occur across domains within a domain matrix. In this way, domains do play a significant role in the interpretation of metonymy.[7] I will now illustrate some examples of this role.

Consider the following typical examples of metonymy:

(17) *Proust spent most of his time in bed.*
(18) *Proust is tough to read.*
(19) Time *magazine is pretty vapid.*
(20) Time *took over* Sunset *magazine, and it's gone downhill ever since.*

Sentence (17) and (19) are considered "literal", (18) and (20) "metonymic". However, in the encyclopedic view of semantics, the works of Proust and the company that produces *Time* magazines are part of the concepts of [PROUST] and [TIME-MAGAZINE] respectively. However, they are less central than the fact that Proust was a person and *Time* is a magazine, not least because they are quite extrinsic to the central concepts. The domain matrix of an encyclopedic characterization of [PROUST] will include the domain of creative activity. Since Proust's claim to fame is that he is a writer, and the work produced is a salient element in the domain of creative activity, the metonymic shift is quite natural (and, in fact, is quite productive). Nevertheless, the metonymic shift also involves a shift of domains within the domain matrix (schema, frame, script) for *Proust*. A similar argument applies to *Time magazine:* a secondary domain for magazines is that of the process of publication, in which the publishing company is a salient entity. The metonymy that shifts reference from the magazine to the company also shifts domains from the magazine as an object with semantic content to the domain of publication. We will call this conceptual effect *domain highlighting* (cf. Cruse 1986: 53), since the metonymy makes primary a domain that is secondary in the literal meaning.

Domain highlighting appears to be a necessary though not sufficient condition for metonymy, which also involves shift of reference, at least in the most typical occurrences thereof. Thus, the relation between domain highlighting and metonymy differs from that between domain mapping and metaphor, since domain mapping does appear to be definitional for metaphor. While domain highlighting appears to be a consequence of many if not all instances of metonymy, it also occurs in other types of lexical ambiguity that have not always been considered metonymy. Consider the following sentences:

(21) *This book is heavy.*
(22) *This book is a history of Iraq.*

The concept [BOOK] is profiled in (at least) two primary domains, the domain of physical objects and the domain of meaning or semantic content. In (21), the physical object domain of *book* is highlighted by virtue of the requirements of the predicate *heavy.* In (22), on the other hand, the semantic content domain of *book* is highlighted, again due to the requirements of the predicate *be a history of*

Iraq. (There is another reading of (21) which does refer to the semantic content domain, which I will discuss below.)

It is not clear that there are in fact two different entities being referred to in (21) and (22). From a conceptual point of view, however, the concept symbolized by *this book* is different in (21) and (22). It is not an example of metonymy in the usual sense of that term because the elements profiled in each domain are highly intrinsic; no reference is made to external entities. For both of these reasons, the word *book* is not always treated as metonymic, or even ambiguous, in these sentences.

Another oft-cited example illustrates the distinctness of the domains of space and physical material in characterizing physical objects (see, for example, Cruse 1986: 65; Taylor 1989: 124):

(23) *I broke the window.*
(24) *She came in through the bathroom window.*

These two uses of *window* are usually analyzed as an ambiguity; in the encyclopedic semantic view, they highlight the physical object and shape or topological domains of the concept [WINDOW] respectively. The interpretation of [WINDOW] as an opening in the shape domain is somewhat extrinsic because it makes crucial reference to what is around it — contrast the use of *window* to describe a physical object in a hardware store showroom — though it appears to be less extrinsic to the concept [WINDOW] than the publishing company and writings in examples (18) and (20) above. The existence of examples such as *window* in (23) and (24) suggests that there is a continuum between the clear cases of metonymy and the highlighting of highly intrinsic facets of a concept as in (21) and (22). The existence of this continuum suggests that domain highlighting plays a role in lexical ambiguities other than metonymy (assuming that one does not want to extend the term "metonymy" to the book and window examples).

It may not be the case that domain highlighting within the domain matrix of a word is involved in all cases of metonymy. In some cases, the shift of prominence of domains in the matrix is quite subtle, and sensitive to the semantics of the associated words. For example, consider the following examples of synecdoche, a phenomenon usually subsumed under metonymy (Ullmann

1957: 232; Lakoff and Johnson 1980: 36; examples from Lakoff and Johnson 1980: 36–37):

(25) *We need a couple of strong bodies for our team.*
(26) *There are a lot of good heads in the university.*
(27) *We need some new faces around here.*

Since a part has the whole as its base domain, it appears that no domain selection is involved in these examples. But in fact in an encyclopedic characterization of *body, head,* and *face* the domain matrix of each part is different, since each body part is associated with different human qualities and behaviors. The selection of *bodies* in (25) is sanctioned by the need to highlight the physical strength/ ability domain underlying the domain of human beings; *heads* in (26) by the need to highlight the domain of human intelligence; while *faces* in (27) is a cross-linguistically widespread synecdoche for persons as a whole, the presence or absence thereof being what is the topic of (27) (cf. Lakoff and Johnson 1980: 36–37). The synecdoche is in fact highlighting precisely the domain that is relevant to the predication. Compare (25)–(27) to (28)–(30), in which the choice of parts-for-whole is different:

(28) ??*We need a couple of strong faces for our team.*
(29) ??*There are a lot of good bodies in the university.*
(30) ??*We need some new heads around here.*

While a sentence such as (29) is interpretable, it does not mean the same thing as (26).

Another example of metonymy which involves a subtle shift in domain prominence is

(31) *I filled up the car.*

In (31), it is understood that it is the gas tank that is filled, not the main body of the car. This interpretation is possible only because the phrase [fill up VEHICLE], without the substance indicated, is conventionally interpreted as "fill up with fuel"; only by explicitly indicating the substance can it be interpreted as "the interior of the car", and only by explicitly indicating the gas tank can it be interpreted as "fill the gas tank" with some substance other than fuel:

(32) *I filled up the car with gasoline and set it on fire.* [gas tank or interior of car]

(33) *I filled up the car with sand.* [interior of car only]

(34) *I filled up the gas tank with sand.*

The two meanings of *fill up* are profiled in two different domains: the more general meaning in the domain matrix of substances and containers (shape), and the more specific meaning in the more abstract domain of fuelling, which is based on the substances/containers domain as well as a domain of fuel-requiring mechanical objects. The interpretation of *car* as "gas tank of car" involves the highlighting of the domain of fuelling in the domain matrix of [CAR] as well as a shift to the relevant part of the car; in fact, it is the highlighting of that domain by the predicate *fill up* that sanctions the shift of reference (at least when the conventional expression was first coined).

The analysis of metonymy in an encyclopedic theory of meaning, whether or not a secondary domain is highlighted in the process, casts a different light on a problem in semantic representation raised by Nunberg (1979). Nunberg presents an analysis of metonymy arguing from a non-encyclopedic view of semantics. Nunberg argues that there should be one "basic" denotation of a polysemous term, e.g. for *Proust*, *Time magazine*, and *window*. Metonymic uses are to be derived by a set of pragmatic functions that shift the meaning to the appropriate referent. Nunberg argues that the basic meaning is ultimately undecidable because any word (or at least, any noun) can be used to refer to the type of entity, a token of the type, and also the name for the entity, and a token of the name (the latter two are expressed orthographically with quotation marks, but are not phonologically distinct):

(35) *A cat is a mammal.*

(36) *His cat is called Metathesis.*

(37) *"Cat" has three letters.*

(38) *"Cat" here has a VOT of 40 ms.* [referring to a spectrograph of an occurrence of the word]

In the encyclopedic approach, there is no "basic" meaning; all metonymic meanings are present in the encyclopedic semantic representation. This is also true for the meanings which Nunberg finds ultimately undecidable. Any symbolized concept will have as part of its encyclopedic definition the phonological entity that symbolizes it, and instantiations of the concept (more precisely, concepts of instantiations of the concept type).

This last question leads us to another problem of metonymy: where to locate it in the interaction of words and phrases in semantic composition, or, to put it more generally, conceptual combination. The standard view is that metonymy represents an ambiguity (or pragmatic extension) of the noun, so that in (17)–(31) and (35)–(38), it is a question of the meaning of the noun phrase being shifted from its "basic" or "normal" meaning. Langacker (1984, 1987: 7.3.4) argues for the opposite point of view: the ambiguity is in the predicate (in traditional terms), not the noun phrase (argument). Consider the following examples:

(39) *We all heard the [trumpet].* (Langacker 1987: 271, ex. (24a))
(40) *This is a striped [apple].*

The traditional analysis is that the bracketed nouns symbolize "sound of the trumpet" and "surface of the apple" respectively, and *trumpet* and *apple* are ambiguous. Langacker argues that we should treat the noun phrases as really symbolizing the entities they appear to be symbolizing, namely the trumpet and the apple, and that the reference to the sound/surface is a characteristic of the predicate, so that *hear* can profile "hear the sound of [noisemaking object] " and *striped* can profile "striped surface of [three-dimensional opaque object]". Langacker takes this position for (39) and (40) in order to avoid any syntactic derivational or transformational relation that would "delete" the *sound of [the trumpet] and surface of [the apple].* Although Langacker does not discuss metonymy by name, (39) and (40) are closely related to prototypical instances of metonymy, and an active zone analysis for metonymy is in the spirit of the cognitive grammar view that there is a direct symbolic relation between word and meaning.

Langacker's argument in favor of this position notes the idiosyncrasy and conventionality of the ability of particular predicates to allow "metonymic" noun phrase arguments. For example, *hear* can also take an NP that symbolizes the sound itself:

(41) *We all heard the sound of the trumpet.*

Langacker describes the "metonymized" referent as the *active zone* of the entity symbolized by the argument NP. Thus, the sound produced by the trumpet, and the surface of the apple, are the active zones of the profiled entity, but do not match the profile of the entity itself.

While Langacker's alternative analysis seems reasonable for a number of examples such as those with perception verbs, there are other examples in which the traditional analysis seems more appropriate, and this suggests that a different approach to the question should be taken. For example, predicates describing the actions of national governments virtually always allow the country itself to be the agent of the action:

(42) *Germany pushed for greater quality control in beer production.*
(43) *The United States banned tuna from countries using drift nets.*
(44) *Myanmar executed twenty Muslim activists.*

Also, many of the same predicates allow the seat of government or the head of state to function as the agent; although some significant semantic differences are found so that interchangeability is not possible in all contexts, it is possible to use all three when it is actually the government (rather than the head of state alone) that makes the decision:

(45) *France/Paris/Mitterrand will hold a referendum on the Maastricht treaty.*

It would seem odd to consider every action verb attributable to an act of government to be ambiguous between "act of [a government] ", "act of the government located in and ruling [a country]", "act of the government seated in [a capital city]", and "act of the government led by [a head of state]".[8]

In other cases, the metonymic extension is an idiosyncrasy of the noun, not of the predicate:

(46) *I ate roast chicken for dinner.*

(47) *I ate roast cow for dinner.

One cannot argue that there is an ambiguity in *eat* so that it can mean "eat the flesh of [an animal]", since (47) is unacceptable.[9] The word *chicken* must clearly be taken to stand for "the meat thereof". Nevertheless, there is a clear metonymic relation between chicken flesh and chicken "on the hoof" (to borrow a collocation from Nunberg), which is productive with less commonly eaten animals:

(48) *I ate grilled rattlesnake for dinner.*
(49) *I ate roast tapir for dinner.*
(50) *I ate pan-fried armadillo for dinner.*

If it were not for the existence of examples such as (47), one might have argued that the metonymy resides in the predicate rather than in the noun.

To some extent, the issue of whether the metonymy can be localized in the predicate or in the noun is a red herring: the metonymy occurs by virtue of the collocation of the predicate and the noun, that is, the semantic composition of the two. The encyclopedic view of meaning supports this approach. One of Langacker's motivations for his analysis is to treat the surface object of *hear, the trumpet,* as the "real" object of the verb, without some syntactic transformation that claims that the underlying object of *hear* is the noun phrase "the sound of the trumpet".[10] But in the encyclopedic view of the meaning of *trumpet,* the sound it produces is a quite salient (albeit somewhat extrinsic) aspect of the profiled concept. Conversely, part of the encyclopedic characterization of *hear* is that objects produce sounds that people hear. Thus, one can have one's semantic cake and eat it too: (part of) the profile of *trumpet* is the object of *hear,* and (part of) the profile of what is heard is the object producing the sound.[11] The same is true of the act-of-government examples: a salient part of the profile of a country, a capital city, and a head of state in the encyclopedic definition of those concepts is the government that rules the country, is seated in the capital city, and is headed by the head of state, respectively. Of course, as I describe in more detail in the following section, it is the semantics of the predicate that highlights the relevant aspect of the encyclopedic profile of the concept symbolized by the noun; the metonymic interpretation arises only in the combination of noun and predicate.

4. Differences between domain mapping and domain highlighting

In the preceding section, Lakoff and Johnson's analysis of metaphor as domain mapping was adopted and it was argued that the source and target domains are the base domains of the "literal" and "figurative" concepts symbolized by the word. It was also argued that an essential part of metonymy is the highlighting of an aspect of a concept's profile in a domain somewhere in the entire domain matrix or domain structure underlying the profiled concept. Those analyses imply that a central aspect of figurative language is the manipulation of experiential domains in understanding and communication. In the case of metonymy, the manipulation of domains plays a significant role, but metonymy cannot be reduced to domain highlighting, and domain highlighting is found in other types of lexical ambiguity for which the term "metonymy" may not be appropriate. I will henceforth use the terms "domain mapping" and "domain highlighting" to describe the semantic phenomena that are under examination in this paper. I will now explore under what circumstances one would expect to find domain mapping and domain highlighting in linguistic expressions.

Consider the following examples from Chapter 6 of Lakoff and Johnson (1980), on one type of metaphor, and the subsequent examples from Chapter 8, on metonymy; the figure of speech is italicized as in the original:

(51) He's *in* love.

(52) We're *out* of trouble now.

(53) He's *coming out of* the coma.

(54) I'm *slowly getting into* shape.

(55) He *entered* a state of euphoria.

(56) He *fell into* a depression. (Lakoff and Johnson 1980: 32)

(57) He likes to read the *Marquis de Sade*.

(58) He's in *dance*.

(59) *Acrylic* has taken over the art world.

(60) The *Times* hasn't arrived at the press conference yet.

(61) Mrs. Grundy frowns on *blue jeans*.

(62) *New windshield wipers* will satisfy him. (Lakoff and Johnson 1980: 45)

A glance at these examples and many others suggests that metaphor is associated with predicates (not just verbs, but also prepositions and adjectives), and metonymy with nouns (hence the focus of Nunberg's paper on nominal metonymy). However, this initial hypothesis is simply incorrect. Examples (63)–(66) below involve domain mapping with nouns, and examples (67)–(70) involve domain highlighting with verbs:

(63) *mouth of a person, an animal, a bottle, a cave, a river* (Cruse 1986: 72)
(64) *handle of a door, suitcase, umbrella, sword, spoon* (Cruse 1986: 74)
(65) *tree, phrase structure tree, family tree, clothes tree*
(66) *cup* [for drinking], *acorn cup, resin cup, cup* [for capstan], *cup* [golf hole], *bra cup* (Dirven 1985)
(67) *She swore foully.*
(68) *She swore loudly.*
(69) *The vase fell quickly.*
(70) *The vase fell far.*

In examples (63)–(66), the different uses of *mouth, handle, tree* and *cup* are undoubtedly profiled in different domains, as the explicit or implicit nominal or genitive modifiers suggest. There is a resemblance in shape and function in all of the examples, resemblances which appear to be of the image-schematic kind characteristic of metaphors. These are generally agreed to be nominal metaphors, or at least a figurative phenomenon closely akin to metaphor which involves domain mapping in essentially the same way.

In examples (67)–(70), a verb which has more than one primary domain associated with it has one or the other domain highlighted by virtue of the adverb associated with it. In (67), the content of the imprecation is highlighted, while in (68) it is the sound volume that is highlighted. In (69), the time and change domains in the matrix underlying motion are highlighted, while in (70) it is the location/distance domain.

Although domain mapping and domain highlighting can occur with a word of any lexical category, there is a generalization underlying the distribution of these two cognitive semantic phenomena. In (63)–(66), domain mapping is induced by the nominal/genitive dependents on the noun that is figuratively interpreted. In (67)–(70), domain highlighting is induced by the adverbial modifier to the verbal predicate. In order to formulate the distribution of domain mapping and domain highlighting, we must examine the cognitive grammar description of syntactic/semantic composition.

One of the criteria for the centrality of knowledge to a particular concept is its intrinsicness: the extent to which it refers to (or rather, does not refer to) entities external to that concept. Some concepts, however, inherently involve extrinsic entities; these are called *relational concepts*. The external entities that relational concepts "include" correspond roughly to the arguments of a predicate in formal semantics; examples include [EAT] , which inherently makes reference to an eater, an item eaten, and to a lesser extent to the implement used by the eater in eating.[12] A relational concept contains only a schematic representation of the extrinsic entities associated with it, in our example the eater, the thing eaten, etc. *Things* (a technical term in cognitive grammar) are nonrelational concepts, however (Langacker 1987: 6.1.1). Relational concepts are divided into *atemporal relations* and *processes*, which correspond roughly to those relational concepts that are construed as static (i.e., construed atemporally) and those that are construed as unfolding over time (for the purposes of this paper it is not necessary to describe this distinction in detail). Things are the semantic structures symbolized by nouns, while relations are symbolized by verbs, adjectives, adverbs, and prepositions.

Syntactic/semantic composition, that is, symbolic composition in cognitive grammar, involves two aspects: what the semantic type of the resulting complex expression is, and how the component expressions are fitted together. The phrase *the fat book* and the sentence *The book is fat* symbolize two different semantic sorts: the phrase symbolizes a thing, while the sentence symbolizes a "state of affairs" (in cognitive grammar terms, in *imperfective process*). The two constructions differ (among other things) in their *profile determinant*, that is, the component element that determines the semantic type of the whole. In the phrase, *book* is the profile determinant, since it is also a thing (we are ignoring the semantic contribution of *the*). In the sentence, *book* is not the profile determinant; if we ignore the contribution of *be*, one could say that *(being) fat* is the profile determinant.[13] As can be seen by the different status of *book* and *fat* in the phrase and in the sentence, profile determinacy is a function of the construction into which words enter.

This leaves the matter of how words are combined semantically. Relationality may appear to underlie semantic composition in cognitive grammar, but this is not precisely correct. In the canonical case of a main verb and the subject and object dependent on it, as in *Mara sings*, this appears to be the case: the subject is nonrelational, and the predicate is relational; the subject referent "fills the slot" for the singer in the relational semantic structure for *sing*. But what about *Mara sings beautifully*? Here *beautiful(ly)* is a relational structure with a "slot" for a process, and *sings* "fills that slot". The fact that *sings* is inherently relational is irrelevant to the combination of *sings* and *beautifully*. Thus, in one and the same sentence, *sings* is both an entity with "slots" to be filled, and a "filler" for another entity's "slot".

In one of Langacker's most insightful analyses of the relation between syntax and semantics, he argues that it is not relationality that governs symbolic combinations, but an independent phenomenon which he calls autonomy and dependence. In most grammatical combinations, one predication can be identified as the autonomous one and the other as the dependent one using the following definition: "One structure, D, is dependent on the other, A, to the extent that A constitutes an elaboration of a salient substructure within D" (Langacker 1987: 300). Let us examine our example *Mara sings beautifully* with respect to this definition. *Mara* (that is, the semantic structure symbolized by *Mara)* does indeed elaborate a salient substructure of *sings*, namely the schematic singer in its semantic representation that makes it a relational predication (concept). Having compared *Mara* to *sings,* we must reverse this process and compare *sings* to *Mara*: does *sings* elaborate a salient substructure of *Mara?* The answer is "no", but it is not a categorical answer; after all, the semantic representation of *Mara* is encyclopedic, and part of the encyclopedic knowledge about Mara is that the speaker knows that Mara sings. But this is a very nonsalient substructure of *Mara*. Hence, we can say that *sings* is dependent and *Mara* is autonomous, relative to each other.

Now let us compare *sings* and *beautifully*. *Sings* elaborates a salient substructure of *beautifully*, namely the schematic process that makes it a relational predication. But *beautifully* does not elaborate a salient substructure of *sings*, even though *sings* is relational. At best, *sings* has a not very salient substructure representing the manner in which the process is executed, and *beautifully* elaborates that; but that substructure is not nearly as salient in the semantic representation for *beautifully* as the substructure of *beautifully* that is elaborated by *sings*. So on

549

balance *beautifully* is the dependent predication and *sings* is autonomous. Note that, by this analysis, *sings* is dependent relative to *Mara,* but autonomous relative to *beautifully.* Autonomy and dependence are relative notions, and that is exactly what is needed to describe this aspect of semantic composition.

We may now characterize the conditions under which domain mapping and domain highlighting occurs: domain mapping occurs with dependent predications, and domain highlighting occurs with autonomous predications. As the preceding discussion of *sings beautifully* demonstrates, "dependent" does not necessarily correspond with "relational" (verbs, adjectives, etc.), and "autonomous" does not necessarily correspond with "nonrelational" (nouns). Thus, there is no connection between metaphor/domain mapping and relational predications, or between metonymy (more precisely, domain highlighting) and nonrelational predications. This will account for the cases in (63)–(70). But let us begin with the "typical" cases, (51)–(62).

In (51)–(56), the metaphorical expressions are dependent on the subject and object (more precisely, the object of the preposition in all but [55]); hence they are the ones subject to domain mapping. But in particular it is the autonomous expressions on which they are dependent that induce the domain mapping: *love, trouble, the coma, shape, euphoria* and *depression* are all profiled as states (physical or emotional) of a human being, and those expressions require the metaphorical interpretation of the container-based directional prepositions and verbs.

In contrast, in (57)–(62), the expressions that manifest domain highlighting are all autonomous relative to the main verbs which are dependent on them. And, conversely, the domain highlighting is induced by the dependent expressions in relation to which the italicized expressions are autonomous. For example, in (57) *read* requires that the object be understood as a text; in (60) *arrive* requires that the subject be interpreted as a person (or at least as an animal, but no animal is salient in the domain matrix of *Times*);[14] and in 62, *satisfy* requires that the subject be some completed event.[15] These examples all illustrate the principle to be discussed in Section 5: that in the grammatical combination of an autonomous and a dependent predication, the dependent predication can induce domain highlighting in the autonomous one, and the autonomous predication can induce domain mapping in the dependent one. Now let us turn to the other cases.

Examples (67)–(70) are straightforward: it is clear that the verb is autonomous relative to the adverb, and it is the adverb that induces the domain highlighting. Again, it is important to note that the word in question be autonomous relative to the word that is inducing the domain highlighting.

Examples (63)–(66) are more difficult, because an argument must be made that the nouns *mouth, handle, tree*, and *cup* are dependent on their nominal/genitive modifiers, and can be so construed even when no such modifiers are present. This latter question will be discussed in Section 5. *Mouth* and *handle* are what are called "relational nouns", since they represent parts of wholes; it is those wholes which make up the genitive modifiers. Langacker argues (1987: 185) that relational nouns such as part nouns do not profile the thing (in this case, the whole) that they are related to (what he calls a *landmark*); otherwise they would no longer be nouns/things. Instead, the landmark is a very salient substructure in the base. Of course, the structures in the base are part of the semantic structure of the concept (see Section 2 above). On the other hand, the part elaborated by the head noun is not as salient a substructure of the whole symbolized by the genitive as the whole is for the part. Thus, in the expression *the mouth of the river* (or *the river's mouth*, or *the river mouth*), *mouth* is on balance more dependent on *river*, and *river* is more autonomous relative to *mouth*. And it is *river* that induces the domain mapping for *mouth*.

The same argument can be applied to *handle* and other relational nouns; can it also be applied to *tree, cup*, and other nonrelational nouns that have metaphorical interpretations? In the cases illustrated, the answer is "yes". In some of the examples, e.g. *bra cup*, the word is functioning as a relational noun (part/whole). In the examples *phrase-structure tree* and *family tree*, the modifying nouns essentially name the base domain of the head noun's profile. As such, they are in a relation very much like a part-whole relation: the base domain taken as a whole is a quite salient substructure of the profiled concept, while the profiled concept is not a very salient substructure of the base domain (on average, no more so than any other concept in the domain). In *clothes tree*, *clothes* elaborates a much more salient substructure of *tree* — the tree is made expressly for the purpose of hanging clothes — than *tree* does in *clothes*. An example like *acorn cup* is a closer call: the cup is "for" the acorn and so *acorn* elaborates a salient substructure for *cup*; but the acorn is often conceived of sans cup, and so *cup* elaborates a less salient substructure of *acorn*. While there appears to be no general principle by means of which we can say that the metaphorically interpreted noun is the dependent member, partly because the semantics of noun-noun compounding seems to be so open-ended (Downing 1977), it seems to be a not unreasonable hypothesis given the examples just discussed, and should be investigated further.

5. The unity of domain revisited

In the last section, I argued that domain mapping can occur to a dependent predication when the autonomous predication it is dependent on induces it; and domain highlighting can occur to an autonomous predication when the predication dependent on it induces it. The reason for this is that the grammatical combination of a dependent predication and the autonomous predication(s) it is dependent on must be interpreted in a single domain (or domain matrix). Consider again a simple example of metaphor and metonymy:

(71) *She's in a good mood.* (=(3))
(72) *Proust is tough to read.* (=(18))

In (71), the relational predication *(be) in* is interpreted metaphorically in the target domain of emotion. This renders the sentence semantically coherent because the subject of *be* and the complement of *in* are in the domain of emotion. In (72), Proust is interpreted metonymically because the complex predicate *be tough to read* requires an entity in the domain of semantic content and the metonymic interpretation provides just such an entity in that domain.

In both of these cases, and in all such cases in general, there is an attempt to "match" the domain of the dependent predication and of the autonomous predications that elaborate it. Sentences such as (71) and (72) that do not match domains in the "literal" interpretations of the elements are not rejected as semantically incoherent. Instead, the listener attempts to interpret one or more elements figuratively, using metaphor or metonymy (or other cognitive processes that we have not discussed here). In other words, there is a background assumption on the part of the listener that sentences are semantically coherent. These background assumptions I call the "conceptual unities". The conceptual unity discussed in this paper is the unity of domain.

This account leaves two questions as yet unanswered: the scope of the semantic unit that requires conceptual unity, and the source of the required conceptual unity. We now take up these questions in turn.

It should be clear from our description of conceptual adjustments of domains that the scope of the unity of domain is the dependent predication and the autonomous predications it is dependent on, but no more. That means that if a word enters into grammatical relations with more than one other word — for example, *sings* compared to *Mara* and *sings* compared to *beautifully* — it is possible that it will be interpreted in different domains for each of the grammatical relations it contracts.

The first example of this is illustrated by another problem that Nunberg (1979) found with this analysis of a basic and derived meanings for nouns that allow metonymy. In some examples, the basic and a derived meaning must be simultaneously attributed to a single occurrence of the word:

(73) *Cædmon, who was the first Anglo-Saxon poet, fills only a couple of pages in this book of poetry.*

(Nunberg 1979: 167, ex. 29)

The single occurrence of the word *Cædmon* is used to refer both to the person and to his works. This problem disappears in the encyclopedic view of metonymy. Both domains are present in the domain matrix of the complex. For the word *Cædmon,* more than one part of its domain matrix can be highlighted simultaneously. However, the triggers are found in different grammatical relations: *Cædmon* with respect to the non-restrictive relative clause *who was the first Anglo-Saxon poet,* and with respect to the main clause *fills only a couple of pages in this book of poetry. Cædmon* is the autonomous predication in both cases, but relative to different dependent predications.[16]

The same is true of the following example, in which the main predicate highlights the physical object domain of the object NP, but its PP modifier highlights the semantic content domain:

(74) *I cut out this article on the environment.*

Example (20), repeated below as (75), provides an example of the same phenomenon involving anaphora, with *Sunset magazine* referring to the company and anaphoric *it* referring to the magazine's content:

(75) Time *took over* Sunset *magazine, and it's been downhill ever since.* (=(20))

In fact, different modifiers (adjuncts) in a single phrase can highlight different domains of the head:

(76) *a thin, dog-eared monograph on hallucinogenic mushrooms of the Pacific Northwest*

In (76), the two adjectival modifiers highlight the physical object domain of *monograph* and the prepositional phrase postmodifier highlights the semantic content domain. Here also, the predication *monograph* enters into two different grammatical relations with two different predications which are dependent on it.

If a predication is dependent on more than one autonomous predication, then the whole combination must obey the conceptual unity of domain:

(77) *I won't buy that idea.*

Not only must *buy* be mapped into the domain of mental activity, but the subject *I* also has the domain of the mind highlighted (the person as a being with mental capacities, not a physical object, for instance). *Idea,* of course, has mental activity as its (primary) base domain.

We now turn to the second question, whether or not one can predict what the domain of the combination of a dependent predication and the autonomous predication(s) it is dependent on will be. It turns out that this is not decidable, because, not surprisingly, unexpressed contextual knowledge can enter into the semantic determination of the domain in which an utterance is interpreted.

Either the autonomous or dependent predication in a grammatical unit can have its domain adjusted, via domain mapping or domain highlighting. In the simplest cases, such as (71) and (72), either the autonomous or the dependent predication is interpreted "literally" — that is, as the most intrinsic entity profiled in the concept's primary domain(s) — and the other element of the sentence has its domain adjusted. As (71) and (72) demonstrate, there is no a priori directionality, requiring either the autonomous or the dependent predication to be interpreted literally. In fact, both may be interpreted figuratively, as in (1), repeated here as (78), or (79):

(78) *Denmark shot down the Maastricht treaty.* (=(1))

(79) *Sales rose to $5m last year.*

In (78), the domain of political force is highlighted in the subject NP, and there is a domain mapping in the main verb from weaponry to political action. In (79), the value (price) domain rather than the object, service, etc. domain is highlighted in the subject NP, while there is a domain mapping in the verb from vertical motion to increase in quantity, specifically monetary quantity.

One could identify the object NPs *Maastricht treaty* and *$5m* in (78) and (79) as the source of the figurative interpretations of the subject and the verb, since they "literally" refer to the political activity and monetary value domains, respectively. However, it is not always possible to attribute the figurative interpretations of the parts of a construction to some "literally" interpreted element in the clause. In some examples, only contextual properties can provide the "source" of the figurative interpretations. Consider again the following example:

(80) *This book is heavy.* (=(21))

The profile of the concept symbolized by the word *book* inhabits two domains, physical objects and meaning (semantic content). However, the predicate *heavy* can be interpreted "literally" in the physical object domain, or it can be shifted metaphorically to the meaning domain. Thus, there are interpretations of both subject and predicate in both the physical object and meaning domains, and in fact this sentence is ambiguous out of context for precisely that reason. Another example of this is the following sentence:

(81) *The newspaper went under.*

One interpretation of this sentence has both subject and predicate interpreted figuratively. Metonymy and metaphor interact to produce the interpretation. "The company producing the newspaper went bankrupt". However, there is also another interpretation, "The physical paper went under the surface of the water"; cf. *The boat went under.* Since one of the domains in the matrix of [NEWSPAPER] is that of physical objects, which undergo motion, which is the "literal" domain of

[GO UNDER], this other interpretation is possible as well.

These examples demonstrate that the correct literal or figurative interpretations of the elements of sentences is not decidable from the elements of the sentence by themselves. The domain in which a predication is interpreted can be determined by context. This is possible because the autonomy-dependence relation is a relationship between semantic structures, which need not be overtly expressed in an utterance. A semantic structure symbolized by a word in a sentence can contract an autonomy-dependence relation with a semantic structure left unexpressed in the context. This is why the nominal metaphors in (63)–(66) can be interpreted metaphorically without the nominal modifiers upon which they are dependent being present in the utterance. For example, *cup* [for drinking, for a golf hole, for a capstan] is interpreted in whatever domain is prominent in the context of the speech event. In fact, an interpretation in any domain is possible, short of semantic incompatibility (and conventional limitations on the figurative interpretations of particular words and phrases). This is not surprising, considering that this is generally the case in semantic interpretation.

6. Conclusion

In this paper, I have argued that particular grammatical constructions, those that combine a dependent grammatical element with the autonomous elements it is dependent on, must be interpreted in a single domain (the unity of domain). This is a necessary part of the interpretation of such constructions, which include almost all of the common grammatical constructions, for example predicate-argument, head-modifier, noun-genitive, verb-adverb. In order to achieve the semantic coherence specified by the unity of domain, there must often occur an adjustment of the domains of the individual words in the construction. Domain adjustment is also a major factor, if not the major factor, in a significant portion of what are usually called "metaphors" and "metonymies". In order to focus on this aspect of the interpretation of words, I have more precisely characterized the conceptual semantic phenomena that I have described as "domain mapping" and "domain highlighting" respectively. In the case of metonymy, it is particularly appropriate to choose a different term to describe the domain adjustment involved.

The conceptual unity of domain is one of at least three conceptual unities.

The second is the unity of mental space, including "physical" space and time. A mental space is a conceptual construct that is used to describe the ontological status of entities and situations — e.g. a belief, a desire, a counterfactual hypothesis, or even reality at a particular location in time or space (Fauconnier 1985). Fauconnier (1985) describes in detail the types of conceptual mappings that are required in interpreting sentences in which predicates and arguments originate in different mental spaces, namely the variety of counterpart relations. Consider for example, example (82), which builds a belief mental space M for Margaret's belief:

(82) *Margaret believes that her sister bought a car.*

In (82), assume that Margaret has a sister in "reality" (R; that is, mutually believed space). The complement of *believes* must be interpreted in Mary's belief space M, so the phrase *her sister* must designate individuals in M, which the listener normally takes to be the counterparts of Margaret and her sister in M. Likewise, *a car* must be interpreted as designating an individual in M, whether or not there is a counterpart in R. The crucial point for us here is that all of the entities in the complement are interpreted in M, and if the "normal" interpretation of a linguistic expression is to an entity in a mental space other than M, e.g. Margaret in (82), it must be interpreted as referring to a counterpart in M to be coherent.

The third is the unity of selection (cf. the minor propositional act of selection in Croft 1990), in which predicate and argument must match in individuation, quantification or number (Talmy's 1985 "plexity") and genericness (generic vs. specific, or type vs. token). These construals have been called granularity coercions (Hobbs 1985; Croft in prep.). The necessity of the unity of selection is illustrated in the following examples:

(83) *She is resembling her mother more and more every year.* [stative predicate construed as an inchoative process]
(84) *"Fresh walnut meats"* [substance construed as a set of individuated objects]
(85) *Cats have whiskers.* [bare plural construed as reference to a kind with generic predicate]
(86) *Cats were lounging on the patio.* [bare plural construed as reference to a set

of cats with specific predicate]

The latter unity has been the topic of a considerable amount of work in formal semantics, but no satisfactory unified account has been presented as yet (though see Croft in prep.).

There is some reason to believe that these three conceptual unities are the most important ones in imposing semantic coherence on an utterance. Langacker (1991: 33) argues that both nominal and verbal structure involves three levels of organization: the level of a concept type, manifested in a bare noun or bare verb stem; the level of a grounded instance of the type, manifested in a full nominal with determiner and a full finite clause; and an intermediate level of an instance of the type, corresponding to the grammatical unit at which quantification occurs. The conceptual unity of domain is at the level of the type: a concept type is defined against its base domain. The unity of mental space is at the level of a grounded instance of a type: grounding involves situating the instance with respect to speaker/hearer knowledge (Langacker 1987: 126–127), which is modelled by mental spaces (1991: 97). Finally, the unity of selection is at the level of the instance, since it is at that level that individuation and quantification occur. The conceptual unities represent the reqirement that dependent verbal predications must be semantically coherent with respect to the autonomous nominal predications that they are dependent on.[17]

In comprehending an utterance, the listener assumes the unities of domain, mental space, and selection, and attempts to interpret the sentence as conforming to those unities, employing metaphor, metonymy, granularity, counterpart relations, and other *focal adjustments* (Langacker 1987: 3.3) where necessary. The listener is under a strong Gricean convention that the speaker is being semantically coherent, particularly at the lower levels of semantic composition, such as predicate-argument and head-modifier constructions. For that reason, the listener will generally try as much as possible to adjust the meanings of the parts to yield a coherent interpretation of the whole. The conceptual unities of domain, mental space, and selection are a significant part of what it means for an utterance to be coherent. This adjustment is how the interpretation of the parts is influenced by the meaning of the whole, as described in the introduction. If such focal adjustments do not yield sensible interpretations, or are conventionally prohibited due to the constructions and inflections involved, the listener may assume the sentence is incoherent. A better understanding of the specific types of coherence (the unities) will cast much more light on the "irregularities" of the process of semantic composition. Nevertheless, the process can never be made fully algorithmic. As we observed for the unity of domain, elements of an utterance interact with context, that is, conceptual structures already activated to various levels at the time of the speech event. This will be true for the other unities as well. But this fact is not surprising, and in fact should be of some comfort for those of us who believe that the expressiveness and flexibility of language is essentially open-ended.

Notes

①　An earlier version of this paper was presented at the second International Cognitive Linguistics conference in Santa Cruz, California, in 1991. I am grateful to members of that audience, particularly George Lakoff and Eve Sweetser, for their comments, and to my semantics students, especially Tim Clausner, for many discussions of the ideas contained herein; and to Dirk Geeraerts, René Dirven and an anonymous reviewer for extensive and detailed comments that greatly improved the content of this paper. None of these people bear any responsibility for the content as presented, of course.

1　Centrality is clearly closely related to prototypicality, in the sense of prototypical properties rather than prototypical instances of a category, as the reference to Rosch's analysis of prototypes suggests. However, centrality pertains to the organization of knowledge in the mind, not the categorization of individuals which both gave rise to that knowledge structure and employs that structure.

2　Grammatical morphemes are also predications, of course; however, I will not be discussing them in this paper.

3　There are actions that involve human beings but do not require mental ability, for example seeing a person. But seeing something does not require that something to be a person, only activities inherently referring to mental abilities do.

It is also possible for other entities to write, e.g. for an animal to be taught to produce writing. This is a deviation from the idealized cognitive model (Lakoff 1987) of writing. An abstract domain is a conceptual structure, and

Lakoff convincingly argues in his book (and elsewhere) that conceptual structures involve idealization. Langacker observes that an abstract schema is essentially an idealized cognitive model (1987: 150, fn. 4), which is in turn analogous to the notion of a frame. At any rate, the domain structure represents the presuppositions of the ideal case.

4 Lakoff and Johnson describe a large class of phenomena as metaphors, some of which are probably better accounted for by other cognitive processes. For example, they describe a metaphor MORE OF FORM IS MORE OF CONTENT (1980: 127), illustrated by the intensification represented in *He ran and ran and ran*; this is more likely to be an example of iconic motivation (Haiman 1983, 1985).

5 One could argue that "alive" and "dead" are bodily states also, but they are clearly of a different kind from "listless" or "healthy".

6 Rene Dirven suggests that this characterization will not distinguish between *Tea was a large meal for the Wicksteeds* (metonymy) and *Drinking Kriek-Lambiek is not just drinking, it is eating and drinking together* (metaphor). The first case is clearly metonymy, since the whole meal is profiled in a domain matrix that includes tea. However, drinking Kriek-Lambiek is profiled in a domain consisting of drinking and not eating; this is its source domain, and the target domain is the matrix of both drinking and eating.

7 In some cases, domain mapping occurs between two domains, one of which happens to be in the matrix of the other. This appears to be what is going on with what Goossens (1990) calls "metaphor from metonymy", illustrated below:

(i) *"Oh dear", she giggled, "I'd quite forgotten".* (Goossens 1990: 328)

(ii) *"Get out of here! " he thundered.*

In these cases the usual interpretation is that the act of speaking takes on metaphorical properties of giggling and thundering. As Goossens observes, the metaphor applies to the message (as intended by the speaker) as well as the medium. I would analyze this as a domain mapping, but the source domain (sound) is one of the domains in the matrix of the target (speaking) — hence the appearance of being "metonymy". Goossens' examples of "metonymy within metaphor", on the other hand, appear to be exactly that:

(iii) *She caught the minister's ear and persuaded him to accept her plan.* (Goossens

1990: 334)

Ear is a metonymy for "attention", and that metonymy is itself embedded in a metaphorical use of *catch*.

8   The last interpretation, with the head of state, often is ambiguous, but that is because the predicates describing acts of governments can also describe acts of individuals, so that *Bush lobbied against the biodiversity treaty* can mean the US government, but can also mean (and is more likely to mean) Bush the individual.

9   The unacceptability is due to the historical idiosyncrasy that English speakers appropriated Norman French words to symbolize "the meat thereof" for cows, pigs and sheep (*beef, pork, mutton*). However, this does not make the synchronic situation any less idiosyncratic.

10   This is quite clear in Langacker (1984), in which he uses the same analysis to argue against a "Tough-movement" analysis as in *Hondas are easy to fix*. In the Tough-movement examples, easiness is being attributed to some inherent property of the surface subject, e.g. the make of automobile, and that property is described as "easy to fix".

11   This is true of any sound produced by any sound-producing object, not just the intended sound of objects like trumpets whose purpose is to produce sound. The collocation of a noun symbolizing an object with *hear* will result in the highlighting of any salient sound associated with the object: *I hear the boats on the canal* can refer to any sound produced by the boats — the horn, their splashing, gliding through the water, the people talking on them, etc.

12   In this respect the notion of a relational concept is richer than that of a predicate: less centrally involved extrinsic entities are part of the concept. In fact, one can add manner and other more peripherally involved entities to the entities inherently involved in the act of eating.

13   Cognitive grammar accommodates the fact that some expressions may have no profile determinant, or even more than one profile determinant (Langacker 1987: 291–292).

14   There is another interpretation of *arrive,* as in *The Times arrived at my doorstep,* in which case the physical-object interpretation is possible. In fact, both interpretations are possible in both contexts (see examples 80–81 below), but the adjuncts favor one reading over the other.

15 The other examples involve not just domain highlighting of the autonomous predications but also domain mapping (metaphor) in the dependent predications; this will be discussed in Section 5.

16 If one reverses the two clauses, the sentence is less acceptable (thanks again to René Dirven for pointing this out to me):

(iv) ?*Cædmon, who fills only a couple of pages in this anthology, was the first Anglo-Saxon poet.*

This is due to the fact that although both metonymic interpretations can be accessed from a single occurrence, one meaning is more established than the other (Cruse 1986: 68–71). Nevertheless, an analysis of metonymy must still account for the fact that it is possible for the same linguistic expression to simultaneously highlight two aspects of the concept symbolized by that expression.

17 The notion of conceptual unity is very similar to the notion of "isotopie" (Greimas 1966; Rastier 1987). However, I am using "conceptual unity" to refer only to the three levels of organization of a clause or phrase, whereas isotopie is used for a much wider range of phenomena of semantic coherence.

References

Croft, William
1990   A conceptual framework for grammatical categories (or, a taxonomy of prepo-sitional acts). *Journal of Semantics* 7: 245–279.
in prep. Aspect, countability and the unity of selection.

Cruse, D. Alan
1986   *Lexical Semantics.* Cambridge: Cambridge University Press.

Dirven, René
1985   Metaphor as a means for extending the lexicon. In *The Ubiquity of Metaphor: Metaphor in Language and Thought,* Paprotté, W. and R. Dirven, (eds.), 85–119. Amsterdam/Philadelphia: John Benjamins.

Downing, Pamela
1977   On the creation and use of English compound nouns. *Language* 53: 810–842.

Fauconnier, Gilles

1985   *Mental Spaces.* Cambridge, MA: MIT Press.

Gibbs, Raymond W. Jr.

1990   Psycholinguistic studies on the conceptual basis of idiomaticity. *Cognitive Linguistics* 1: 417–451.

Goossens, Louis

1990   Metaphtonymy: The interaction of metaphor and metonymy in expressions for linguistic action. *Cognitive Linguistics* 1: 323–340.

Greimas, Algirdas-Julien

1966   *Sémantique structurale: recherche de méthode.* Paris: Librairie Larousse.

Haiman, John

1980   Dictionaries and encyclopedias. *Lingua* 50: 329–357.

1983   Iconic and economic motivation. *Language* 59: 781–819.

1985   *Natural Syntax.* Cambridge: Cambridge University Press.

Hobbs, Jerry

1985   Granularity. *Proceedings of the Ninth International Joint Conference on Artificial Intelligence*, 432–435. Tokyo: International Joint Conference.

Lakoff, George

1987   *Women, Fire and Dangerous Things: What Categories Reveal about the Mind.* Chicago: University of Chicago Press.

1990   Invariance Hypothesis: Is abstract reason based on image-schemas? *Cognitive Linguistics* 1: 39–74.

Lakoff, George and Mark Johnson

1980   *Metaphors We Live By.* Chicago: University of Chicago Press.

Lakoff, George and Mark Turner

1989   *More than Cool Reason: A Field Guide to Poetic Metaphor.* Chicago: University of Chicago Press.

Langacker, Ronald W.

1984   Active zones. In *Proceedings of the Tenth Annual Meeting of the Berkeley Linguistics Society,* Brugman, Claudia et al. (eds.), 172–188. Berkeley: Berkeley Linguistics Society.

1987   *Foundations of Cognitive Grammar.* Vol. I: *Theoretical Prerequisites.* Stanford: Stanford University Press.

1991   *Foundations of Cognitive Grammar.* Vol. II: *Descriptive Application.* Stanford: Stanford University Press.

Lyons, John

1977   *Semantics*. 2 vols. Cambridge: Cambridge University Press.

Nunberg, Geoffrey

1979   Nonuniqueness of semantic solutions: Polysemy. *Linguistics and Philosophy* 3:143–184.

Rastier, François

1987   *Sémantique interprétative*. Paris: Presses Universitaires de France.

Rosch, Eleanor

1978   Principles of categorization. In *Cognition and Categorization,* Eleanor Rosch and Barbara Lloyd (eds.), 27–48. Hillsdale, NJ: Lawrence Erlbaum.

Searle, John

1979   Literal meaning. In *Expression and Meaning*. John Searle, 117–136. Cambridge: Cambridge University Press.

Talmy, Leonard

1985   Lexicalization patterns: Semantic structure in lexical forms. In *Language Typology and Syntactic Description,* Vol. 3: *Grammatical Categories and the Lexicon,* Timothy Shopen (ed.), 57–179. Cambridge: Cambridge University Press.

1988   Force dynamics in language and cognition. *Cognitive Science* 12: 49–100.

Taylor, John R.

1989   *Linguistic Categorization: Prototypes in Linguistic Theory*. Oxford: Oxford University Press.

Turner, Mark

1990   Aspects of the Invariance Hypothesis. *Cognitive Linguistics* 1: 247–55.

Ullmann, Stephen

1957   *The Principles of Semantics*. 2nd ed. New York: Barnes and Noble.

Wierzbicka, Anna

1987   *English Speech Act Verbs*. New York: Academic Press.

1988   *The Semantics of Grammar*. Amsterdam/Philadelphia: John Benjamins.

Frame Semantics

Charles J. Fillmore

1. Introduction

With the term 'frame semantics' I have in mind a research program in empirical semantics and a descriptive framework for presenting the results of such research. Frame semantics offers a particular way of looking at word meanings, as well as a way of characterizing principles for creating new words and phrases, for adding new meanings to words, and for assembling the meanings of elements in a text into the total meaning of the text. By the term 'frame' I have in mind any system of concepts related in such a way that to understand any one of them you have to understand the whole structure in which it fits; when one of the things in such a structure is introduced into a text, or into a conversation, all of the others are automatically made available. I intend the word 'frame' as used here to be a general cover term for the set of concepts variously known, in the literature on natural language understanding, as 'schema', 'script', 'scenario', 'ideational scaffolding', 'cognitive model', or 'folk theory'.[1]

Frame semantics comes out of traditions of empirical semantics rather than formal semantics. It is most akin to ethnographic semantics, the work of the anthropologist who moves into an alien culture and asks such questions as, 'What categories of experience are encoded by the members of this speech community through the linguistic choices that they make when they talk?' A frame semantics outlook is not (or is not necessarily) incompatible with work and results in formal semantics; but it differs importantly from formal semantics in emphasizing the continuities, rather than the discontinuities, between language

565

and experience. The ideas I will be presenting in this paper represent not so much a genuine theory of empirical semantics as a set of warnings about the kinds of problems such a theory will have to deal with. If we wish, we can think of the remarks I make as 'pre-formal' rather than 'non-formalist'; I claim to be listing, and as well as I can to be describing, phenomena which must be well understood and carefully described before serious formal theorizing about them can become possible.

In the view I am presenting, words represent categorizations of experience, and each of these categories is underlain by a motivating situation occurring against a background of knowledge and experience. With respect to word meanings, frame semantic research can be thought of as the effort to understand what reason a speech community might have found for creating the category represented by the word, and to explain the word's meaning by presenting and clarifying that reason.

An analogy that I find helpful in distinguishing the operation and the goals of frame semantics from those of standard views of compositional semantics is between a grammar and a set of tools — tools like hammers and knives, but also like clocks and shoes and pencils. To know about tools is to know what they look like and what they are made of — the phonology and morphology, so to speak — but it is also to know what people use them for, why people are interested in doing the things that they use them for, and maybe even what kinds of people use them. In this analogy, it is possible to think of a linguistic text, not as a record of 'small meanings' which give the interpreter the job of assembling these into a 'big meaning' (the meaning of the containing text), but rather as a record of the tools that somebody used in carrying out a particular activity. The job of interpreting a text, then, is analogous to the job of figuring out what activity the people had to be engaged in who used these tools in this order.

2. A private history of the concept 'frame'

I trace my own interest in semantic frames through my career-long interest in lexical structure and lexical semantics. As a graduate student (at the University of Michigan in the late fifties) I spent a lot of time exploring the co-occurrence privileges of words, and I tried to develop distribution classes of English words using strings of words or strings of word classes as the 'frames' within which

I could discover appropriate classes of mutually substitutable elements. This way of working, standard for a long time in phonological and morphological investigations, had been developed with particular rigor for purposes of syntactic description by Charles Fries (Fries 1952) and played an important role in the development of 'tagmemic formulas' in the work of Kenneth Pike (Pike 1967), the scholars who most directly influenced my thinking during this period. Substitutability within the same 'slot' in such a 'frame' was subject to certain (poorly articulated) conditions of meaning-preservation or structure-preservation, or sometimes merely meaningfulness-preservation. In this conception, the 'frame' (with its single open 'slot') was considered capable of leading to the discovery of important functioning word classes or grammatical categories. As an example of the workings of such a procedure, we can take the frame consisting of two complete clauses and a gap between them, as in *John is Mary's husband — he doesn't live with her.* The substitution in this frame of *but* and *yet* suggests that these two words have (by this diagnostic at least) very similar functions; insertion of *moreover* or *however* suggest the existence of conjunctions functioning semantically similarly to *but* and *yet* but requiring sentence boundaries. The conjunctions AND and OR can meaningfully be inserted into the frame, but in each case (and in each case with different effect) the logical or rhetorical 'point' of the whole utterance differs importantly from that brought about by *but* or *yet*. In each of these cases, what one came to know about these words was the kind of structures with which they could occur and what function they had within those structures.

In the early sixties, together with William S.-Y. Wang and eventually D. Terence Langendoen and a number of other colleagues, I was associated with the Project on Linguistic Analysis at the Ohio State University. My work on that project was largely devoted to the classification of English verbs, but now not only according to the surface-syntactic frames which were hospitable to them, but also according to their grammatical 'behavior', thought of in terms of the sensitivity of structures containing them to particular grammatical 'transformations.' This project was whole-heartedly transformationalist, basing its operations at first on the earliest work on English transformational grammar by Chomsky (1957) and Lees (1961), and in its later stages on advances within the theory suggested by the work of Peter Rosenbaum (Rosenbaum 1967) and the book which established the standard working paradigm for transformationalist studies of English, Chomsky (1965). What animated this work was the belief that discoveries in the 'behavior' of particular classes of words led to discoveries in the structure of the grammar of English. This was so because it was believed that the distributional properties of individual words discovered by this research could only be accommodated if the grammar of the language operated under particular working principles. My own work from this period included a small monograph on indirect object verbs (Fillmore 1961) and a paper which pointed to the eventual recognition of the transformational cycle as an operating principle in a formal grammar of English (Fillmore 1963).

The project's work on verbs was at first completely syntactic, in the sense that what was sought was, for each verb, a full account (expressed in terms of subcategorization features) of the deep structure syntactic frames which were hospitable to it, and a full account (expressed in terms of rule features) of the various paths or 'transformational histories' by which sentences containing them could be transformed into surface sentences. The kind of work I have in mind was carried on with much greater thoroughness by Fred Householder and his colleagues at Indiana University (Householder et al 1964), and with extreme care and sophistication by Maurice Gross and his team in Paris on the verbs and adjectives of French (Gross 1975).

In the late sixties I began to believe that certain kinds of groupings of verbs and classifications of clause types could be stated more meaningfully if the structures with which verbs were initially associated were described in terms of the semantic roles of their associated arguments. I had become aware of certain American and European work on dependency grammar and valence theory, and it seemed clear to me that what was really important about a verb was its 'semantic valence' (as one might call it), a description of the semantic role of its arguments. Valence theory and dependency grammar did not assign the same classificatory role to the 'predicate' (or 'VP') that one found in transformationalist work (see, e.g., Tesnière 1959); the kind of semantic classifications that I needed could be made more complete and sensible, I believed, if, instead of relying on theoretically separate kinds of distributional statements such as 'strict subcategorization features' and 'selectional features,' one could take into account the semantic roles of all arguments of a predication, that of the 'subject' being simply one of them. Questioning, ultimately, the relevance of the assumed basic immediate-constituency cut between subject and predicate, I proposed that verbs could be seen as basically having two kinds of features relevant to their distribution in sentences: the first a deep-structure valence description expressed in terms of what I called 'case frames', the second a description in terms of rule features. What I called 'case frames' amounted to descriptions of predicating words that communicated such information as the following: 'Such-and-such a verb occurs in expressions containing three nominals, one designating an actor who performs the act designated by the verb, one designating an object on which the actor's act has a state-changing influence, and one designating an object through the manipulation of which the actor brings about the mentioned state change.' In symbols this statement could be represented as [— A P I], the letters standing for 'Agent', 'Patient' and 'Instrument'. Actually, the kind of description I sought distinguished 'case frames' as the structures in actual individual sentences in which the verbs could appear from 'case frame features' as representations of the class of 'case frames' into which particular verbs could be inserted. In the description of 'case frame features' it was possible to notice which of the 'cases' were obligatory, which were optional, what selectional dependencies obtained among them, and so on (see Fillmore 1968).

We were developing a kind of mixed syntactic-semantic valence description of verbs, and we noticed that the separate valence patterns seemed to characterize semantic types of verbs, such as verbs of perception, causation, movement, etc. Within these syntactic valence types, however, it seemed that some semantic generalizations were lost. There seemed to be important differences between *give it to john* and *send it to Chicago* that could not be illuminated merely by showing what syntactic rules separate *give* from *send,* just as there seemed to be semantic commonalities between *rob* and *steal, buy* and *sell, enjoy* and *amuse,* etc., which were lost in the syntactic class separation of these verbs.

My ultimate goal in this work in 'case grammar' (as the framework came to be called) was the development of a 'valence dictionary' which was to differ importantly from the kinds of valence dictionaries appearing in Europe (e.g., Helbig and Schenkel 1973) by having its semantic valence taken as basic and by having as much as possible of its syntactic valence accounted for by general rules. (Thus, it was not thought to be necessary to explain, in individual lexical entries, which of the arguments in a [V A P I] predication of the type described above was to be the subject and which was to be the object, since such matters were automatically predicted by the grammar with reference to a set of general principles concerning the mapping from configurations of semantic cases into configurations of grammatical relations.)

Although the concept of 'frame' in various fields within cognitive psychology appears to have origins quite independent of linguistics, its use in case grammar was continuous, in my own thinking, with the use to which I have put it in 'frame semantics'. In particular, I thought of each case frame as characterizing a small abstract 'scene' or 'situation', so that to understand the semantic structure of the verb it was necessary to understand the properties of such schematized scenes.

The scene schemata definable by the system of semantic cases (a system of semantic role notions which I held to be maximally general and defining a minimal and possibly universal repertory) was sufficient, I believed, for understanding those aspects of the semantic structure of a verb which were linked to the verb's basic syntactic properties and to an understanding of the ways in which different languages differently shaped their minimal clauses, but they were clearly not adequate for describing with any completeness the semantic structure of the clauses containing individual verbs.

This theory of semantic roles fell short of providing the detail needed for semantic description; it came more and more to seem that another independent level of role structure was needed for the semantic description of verbs in particular limited domains. One possible way of devising a fuller account of lexical semantics is to associate some mechanism for deriving sets of truth conditions for a clause from semantic information individually attached to given predicates; but it seemed to me more profitable to believe that there are larger cognitive structures capable of providing a new layer of semantic role notions in terms of which whole domains of vocabulary could be semantically characterized.

My first attempt to describe one such cognitive structure was in a paper on 'Verbs of judging' (Fillmore 1971) — verbs like *blame, accuse, criticize* — for which I needed to be able to imagine a kind of 'scene schematization' that was essentially different from the sort associated with 'case frames'. In devising a framework for describing the elements in this class of verbs, I found it useful to distinguish a person who formed or expressed some sort of judgment on the worth or behavior of some situation or individual (and I called such a person the Judge); a person concerning whose behavior or character it was relevant for the Judge to make a judgment (I called this person the Defendant); and some situation concerning which it seemed relevant for the Judge to be making a

Judgment (and this I called simply the Situation). In terms of this framework, then, I chose to describe *accuse* as a verb usable for asserting that the Judge, presupposing the badness of the Situation, claimed that the Defendant was responsible for the Situation; I described *criticize* as usable for asserting that the Judge, presupposing the Defendant's responsibility for the Situation, presented arguments for believing that the Situation was in some way blameworthy. The details of my description have been 'criticized' (see esp. McCawley 1975), but the point remains that we have here not just a group of individual words, but a 'domain' of vocabulary whose elements somehow presuppose a schematization of human judgment and behavior involving notions of worth, responsibility, judgment, etc., such that one would want to say that nobody can really understand the meanings of the words in that domain who does not understand the social institutions or the structures of experience which they presuppose.

A second domain in which I attempted to characterize a cognitive 'scene' with the same function was that of the 'commercial event' (see Fillmore 1977b). In particular, I tried to show that a large and important set of English verbs could be seen as semantically related to each other by virtue of the different ways in which they 'indexed' or 'evoked' the same general 'scene'. The elements of this schematic scene included a person interested in exchanging money for goods (the Buyer), a person interested in exchanging goods for money (the Seller), the goods which the Buyer did or could acquire (the Goods), and the money acquired (or sought) by the seller (the Money). Using the terms of this framework, it was then possible to say that the verb *buy* focuses on the actions of the Buyer with respect to the Goods, backgrounding the Seller and the Money; that the verb *sell* focuses on the actions of the Seller with respect to the Goods, backgrounding the Buyer and the Money; that the verb *pay* focuses on the actions of the Buyer with respect to both the Money and the Seller, backgrounding the Goods, and so on, with such verbs as *spend, cost, charge,* and a number of others somewhat more peripheral to these. Again, the point of the description was to argue that nobody could be said to know the meanings of these verbs who did not know the details of the kind of scene which provided the background and motivation for the categories which these words represent. Using the word 'frame' for the structured way in which the scene is presented or remembered, we can say that the frame structures the word-meanings, and that the word 'evokes' the frame.

The structures I have mentioned so far can be thought of as motivating the categories speakers wish to bring into play when describing situations that might be independent of the actual speech situation, the conversational context. A second and equally important kind of framing is the framing of the actual communication situation. When we understand a piece of language, we bring to the task both our ability to assign schematizations of the phases or components of the 'world' that the text somehow characterizes, and our ability to schematize the situation in which this piece of language is being produced. We have both 'cognitive frames' and 'interactional frames', the latter having to do with how we conceptualize what is going on between the speaker and the hearer, or between the author and the reader. By the early seventies I had become influenced by work on speech acts, performativity, and pragmatics in general, and had begun contributing to this field in the form of a number of writings on presuppositions and deixis (see, e.g., Fillmore 1975). Knowledge of deictic categories requires an understanding of the ways in which tenses, person marking morphemes, demonstrative categories, etc., schematize the communicating situation; knowledge of illocutionary points, principles of conversational cooperation, and routinized speech events, contribute to the full understanding of most conversational exchanges. Further, knowing that a text is, say, an obituary, a proposal of marriage, a business contract, or a folktale, provides knowledge about how to interpret particular passages in it, how to expect the text to develop, and how to know when it is finished. It is frequently the case that such expectations combine with the actual material of the text to lead to the text's correct interpretation. And once again this is accomplished by having in mind an abstract structure of expectations which brings with it roles, purposes, natural or conventionalized sequences of event types, and all the rest of the apparatus that we wish to associate with the notion of 'frame'.

In the mid-seventies I came into contact with the work of Eleanor Rosch (Rosch 1973) and that of Brent Berlin and Paul Kay (Berlin and Kay 1969) and began to see the importance of the notion of 'prototype' in understanding the nature of human categorization. Through the work of Karl Zimmer (Zimmer 1971) and Pamela Downing (Downing 1977) on the relevance of categorizing contexts to principles of word-formation and, in work that reflects fruitful collaboration with Paul Kay and George Lakoff, I began to propose descriptions of word meanings that made use of the prototype notion. One generalization that seemed valid was that very often the frame or background against which the meaning of a word is defined and understood is a fairly large slice of the surrounding culture, and this background understanding is best understood as a 'prototype' rather than as a genuine body of assumptions about what the world is like. It is frequently useful, when trying to state truth conditions for the appropriateness of predicating the word of something, to construct a simple definition of the word, allowing the complexity of fit between uses of the word and real world situations to be attributed to the details of the prototype background frame rather than to the details of the word's meaning. Thus we could define an *orphan* as a child whose parents are no longer living, and then understand the category as motivated against a background of a particular kind: in this assumed background world, children depend on their parents for care and guidance and parents accept the responsibility of providing this care and guidance without question; a person without parents has a special status, for society, only up to a particular age, because during this period a society needs to provide some special way of providing care and instruction. The category *orphan* does not have 'built into it' any specification of the age after which it is no longer relevant to speak of somebody as an orphan, because that understanding is a part of the background prototype; a boy in his twenties is generally regarded as being able to take care of himself and to have passed the age where the main guidance is expected to come from his family. It is that background information which determines the fact that the word *orphan* would not be appropriately used of such a boy, rather than information that is to be separately built into a description of the word's meaning. In the prototype situation, an orphan is seen as somebody deserving of pity and concern; hence the point of the joke about the young man on trial for the murder of his parents who asked the court for mercy on the grounds that he was an orphan: the prototype scene against which society has a reason to categorize some children as orphans does not take into account the case in which a child orphans himself.

As a second example of a category that has to be fitted onto a background of institutions and practices we can consider the word *breakfast*. To understand this word is to understand the practice in our culture of having three meals a day, at more or less conventionally established times of the day, and for one of these meals to be the one which is eaten early in the day, after a period of sleep, and for it to consist of a somewhat unique menu (the details of which can vary from community to community). What is interesting about the word *breakfast* is that each of the three conditions most typically associated with it can be independently absent still allowing native speakers to use the word. The fact that someone can work through the night without sleep, and then at sun-up have a meal of eggs, toast, coffee and orange juice, and call that meal breakfast, shows clearly that the 'post-sleep' character of the category is not criterial; the fact that someone can sleep through the morning, wake up at three o'clock in the afternoon, and sit down to a meal of eggs, toast, coffee and orange juice, and call that meal *breakfast*, shows that the 'early morning' character of the category is also not criterial; and lastly, the fact that a person can sleep through the night, wake up in the morning, have cabbage soup and chocolate pie 'for breakfast', shows that the 'breakfast menu' character of the concept is also not criterial. (This in spite of the fact that an American restaurant that advertises its willingness to serve breakfast at any time is referring precisely to the stereotyped breakfast ingredients.) What we want to say, when we observe usage phenomena like that, is not that we have so far failed to capture the true core of the word's meaning, but rather that the word gives us a category which can be used in many different contexts, this range of contexts determined by the multiple aspects of its prototypic use — the use it has when the conditions of the background situation more or less exactly match the defining prototype.

The descriptive framework which is in the process of evolving out of all of the above considerations is one in which words and other linguistic forms and categories are seen as indexing semantic or cognitive categories which are themselves recognized as participating in larger conceptual structures of some sort, all of this made intelligible by knowing something about the kinds of settings or contexts in which a community found a need to make such categories available to its participants, the background of experiences and practices within which such contexts could arise, the categories, the contexts, and the backgrounds themselves all understood in terms of prototypes.

3. Further illustrations and some terminological proposals

A 'frame', as the notion plays a role in the description of linguistic meanings, is a system of categories structured in accordance with some motivating context. Some words exist in order to provide access to knowledge of such frames to the participants in the communication process, and simultaneously serve to perform a categorization which takes such framing for granted.

The motivating context is some body of understandings, some pattern of practices, or some history of social institutions, against which we find intelligible the creation of a particular category in the history of the language community. The word *week-end* conveys what it conveys both because of the calendric seven-day cycle and because of a particular practice of devoting a relatively larger continuous block of days within such a cycle to public work and two continuous days to one's private life. If we had only one 'day of rest' there would be no need for the word *week-end;* one could simply use the name of that day. If we had three days of work and four days of rest, then too it seems unlikely that the name for the period devoted to one's private life would have been given that name. (If the work week is gradually shortened, the word *week-end* might stay; but it is unlikely that the category could have developed naturally if from the start the number of days devoted to work were shorter than the number of the remaining days. An acquaintance of mine who works only on Wednesdays, pleased at being able to enjoy 'a long week-end', recognizes that the word is here being used facetiously.)

The word *vegetarian* means what it means, when used of people in our culture, because the category of 'someone who eats only vegetables' is a relevant and interesting category only against the background of a community many or most of whose members regularly eat meat. Notice that the word designates, not just someone who eats plant food, but someone who eats only plant food. Furthermore, it is used most appropriately for situations in which the individual so designated avoids meat deliberately and for a purpose. The purpose might be one of beliefs about nutrition, or it may be one of concerns for animal life; but the word is not used (in a sentence like *John is a vegetarian.*) to describe people whose diet does not include meat because they are unable to find any, or because they cannot afford to buy it.

Occasionally one comes upon a term whose motivating context is very specific. One such is the compound *flip strength,* used, I am told, in the pornographic literature business. Some publishers of pornographic novels instruct their authors to include a certain quota of high interest words on every page, so that a potential customer, in a bookstore, while 'flipping' the pages of the book, will, no matter where he opens the book, find evidence that the book is filled with wonderful and exciting goings-on. A book which has a high ratio of nasty words per page has high flip strength; a book which has these words more widely distributed has low flip strength. As I understand the word, an editor of such a publication venture might reject a manuscript, requesting that it be returned only after its flip strength has been raised.

With this last example, it is extremely clear that the background context is absolutely essential to understanding the category. It is not that the conditions for using the word cannot be stated without this background understanding (relative flip strength of novels could easily be determined by a computer), but that the word's meaning cannot be truly understood by someone who is unaware of those human concerns and problems which provide the reason for the category's existence.

We can say that, in the process of using a language, a speaker 'applies' a frame to a situation, and shows that he intends this frame to be applied by using words recognized as grounded in such a frame. What is going on here seems to correspond, within the ordinary vocabulary of a language, to lexical material in scientific discourse that is describable as 'theory laden': the word *phlogiston* is 'theoryladen'; the reason it is no longer used in serious discourse is that nobody accepts the theory within which it is a concept. That is, nobody schematizes the physical world in a way that would give a reason to speak of part of it as *phlogiston*.

To illustrate the point with items from everyday language, we can consider the words *land* and *ground* (which I have described elsewhere but cannot forego mentioning here). The difference between these two words appears to be best expressed by saying that *land* designates the dry surface of the earth as it is distinct from the *sea*, whereas *ground* designates the dry surface of the earth as it is distinct from the *air* above it. The words *land* and *ground,* then, differ not so much in what it is that they can be used to identify, but in how they situate that thing in a larger frame. It is by our recognition of this frame contrast that we are able to understand that a bird that 'spends its life on the land' is being described negatively as a bird that does not spend any time in water; a bird that 'spends its life on the ground' is being described negatively as a bird that does not fly.

Though the details are a bit tricky, the two English words *shore* and *coast* (not differently translatable in many languages) seem to differ from each other in that while the *shore* is the boundary between land and water from the water's point of view, the *coast* is the boundary between land and water from the land's point of view. A trip that took four hours 'from shore to shore' is a trip across a body of water; a trip that took four hours 'from coast to coast' is a trip across a land mass. "We will soon reach the coast" is a natural way to say something about a journey on land; "we will soon reach the shore" is a natural way to say something about a sea journey. Our perception of these nuances derives from our recognition of the different ways in which the two words schematize the world.

The Japanese adjective *nurui* is another example of a framing word. Although not all Japanese-speaking informants support this judgment, enough do to make the example worth giving. In the usage that supports my point, *nurui,* used to describe the temperature of a liquid means 'at room temperature', but it is said mainly of liquids that are ideally hot. *Kono ocha ga nurui* (this tea is lukewarm) is an acceptable sentence in the idiolects that support my point, but *kono biiru ga nurui* (this beer is lukewarm) is not. It will be noticed that the English word *lukewarm* does not 'frame' its object in the same way. A cold liquid and a hot liquid can both become lukewarm when left standing long enough; but only the liquid that was supposed to be hot can be described as 'nurui'.

A large number of framing words appear only in highly specialized contexts, such as the term *flip strength* discussed earlier. The legal term *decedent* gives us another example of such context specialization. According to my legal informants (and my available law dictionaries) the word *decedent* is used to identify a dead person in the context of a discussion of the inheritance of that person's property. (The word *deceased*, as in the phrase 'the deceased', is also limited to legal or journalistic contexts, but it is not limited to any particular subdomain within the law.) Another example is *mufti*. Mufti, in the sense it once had in the military service, refers to ordinary clothing when worn by somebody who regularly wears a military uniform. If we see two men wearing identical suits, we can, referring to their clothing, say that one of them is 'in mufti' if that one is a military officer. The property of being 'in mufti' is obviously a property that has relevance only in the context of a military community.

Given all these examples of clear cases of terms linked to highly specific cognitive frames, we can see that the process of understanding a text involves retrieving or perceiving the frames evoked by the text's lexical content and assembling this kind of schematic knowledge (in some way which cannot be easily formalized) into some sort of 'envisionment' of the 'world' of the text. If I tell you (to be somewhat ridiculous) that the decedent while on land and in mufti last weekend ate a typical breakfast and read a novel high in flip strength, you know that I am talking about a now-dead naval officer who during the period including last Saturday and Sunday read a pornographic novel; and you know a few other things about the man, about how he spent his time, and about the setting in which this report of his activities is given. The sentence did not give you this information directly; you had to 'compute' some of it by constructing, in your imagination, a complex context within which each of the lexically signaled framings was motivated. We see in this way that there is a very tight connection between lexical semantics and text semantics, or, to speak more carefully, between lexical semantics and the process of text comprehension. The framing words in a text reveal the multiple ways in which the speaker or author schematizes the situation and induce the hearer to construct that envisionment of the text world which would motivate or explain the categorization acts expressed by the lexical choices observed in the text.

The interpreter's envisionment of the text world assigns that world both a perspective and a history. A report of somebody buying something evokes the frame of the commercial event, but sees that event, for the moment at least, from the point of view of one of its participants. Describing somebody as being *on land* locates the scene in the history of a sea voyage, by noticing that it is relevant to describe the location in this way only if this period is seen as an interruption of a period of sea travel. Saying that somebody is *at bat* locates an event as one part of a particular baseball game. Describing coffee, in Japanese, as *nurui* recognizes that it was once hot and has been allowed to 'cool'. One knows that the coffee is currently at room temperature, but also that it did not get that way by starting out as iced coffee.

Sometimes the perspective which a word assigns is not a perspective on the current scene — something that might be visible in a pictorial representation of the scene — but is that of a much larger framework. Thus, the description of someone as a *heretic* presupposes an established religion, or a religious community which has a well-defined notion of doctrinal correctness. In a community lacking such beliefs or practices, the word has no purpose. Sometimes a word situates an event in a history wider than the history of the ongoing narrative. In speaking of locations within North America, the expressions *out west* and *back east* are frequently used. The terms have the form they do because for a large portion of American families the settlement history of the country traced its way from the east coast to the west coast. European immigrants first landed on the east coast; some of them, or some of their descendants, gradually migrated westward. The eastern part of the country, where these immigrants or their ancestors once were, was *back east*; the western part of the country, not yet reached, was *out west*. The expressions are used today by people whose families did not share in this general westward movement themselves, but the terms recall the historical basis of their creation.

Earlier I spoke of the notion of deep cases as offering an account of the semantic aspects of single-clause predications which figured in the basic grammatical structure of clauses. A broader view of the semantics of grammar, one which owes a great deal to the work of Leonard Talmy (see Talmy 1980) and Ronald Langacker (Langacker 1987), sees lexical framing providing the 'content' upon which grammatical structure performs a 'configuring' function. Thinking in this way, we can see that any grammatical category or pattern imposes its own 'frame' on the material it structures. For example, the English pluperfect can be described as having as its role, in structuring the 'history' of the text world, that of characterizing the situation at a particular time (the narrative time) as being partly explained by the occurrence of an event or situation that occurred or existed earlier on. The progressive aspect, in its turn, schematizes a situation as one which is continuing or iterating across a span of time. Thus, a sentence in a narrative of the form *She had been running,* a form which combines the progressive and the pluperfect forms, can have the function of explaining why, at the narrative time point, "she" was panting, or sweating, or tired. Thus we see that the cognitive frames which inform and shape our understanding of language can differ greatly in respect to their generality or specificity: a lexical verb like *run* can give us a specific kind of physical activity image, while the pluperfect and the progressive combine, each in a general and abstract way, to shape the image of running in a way that fits the current situation and to situate the event of running both temporally and in 'relevance' into the ongoing history of the text world.

It is necessary to distinguish two importantly different ways in which the cognitive frames we call on to help us interpret linguistic texts get introduced into the interpretation process. On the one hand, we have cases in which the lexical and grammatical material observable in the text 'evokes' the relevant frames in the mind of the interpreter by virtue of the fact that these lexical forms or these grammatical structures or categories exist as indices of these frames; on the other hand, we have cases in which the interpreter assigns coherence to a text by 'invoking' a particular interpretive frame. An extremely important difference between frames that are evoked by material in the text and frames that are invoked by the interpreter is that in the latter case an 'outsider' has no reason to suspect, beyond a general sense of irrelevance or pointlessness in the text, that anything is missing. To repeat an example that I have used elsewhere, a Japanese personal letter in the traditional style is supposed to begin with a comment on the current season. Somebody who knows this tradition is able to sense the relevance of an opening sentence in a letter which speaks of the garden floor covered with leaves. The kind of understanding which allows such an interpretation comes from outside of the text itself.

Invoked frames can come from general knowledge, knowledge that exists independently of the text at hand, or from the ongoing text itself.

4. Frame-semantic formulations of empirical semantic observations

In this section I examine a number of observations about lexical meaning or text interpretation which permit formulations in terms of notions from frame semantics. In the following section I examine a number of traditional topics in standard semantic theorizing and raise questions about the importance they would be given in an account of linguistic meaning of the sort we have been exploring.

4.1 Polysemy arising from alternative framings of the same lexical item

For many instances of polysemy it is possible to say that a given lexical item properly fits either of two different cognitive frames. One possibility is that a word has a general use in the everyday language but has been given a separate use in technical language. For example, we might wish to say that the English word *angle* is understood in connection with a perceptual frame as a figure made by two lines joined at a point in a way suggested by a bent stick. Presented in terms of a competing procedural frame, an angle is thought of in terms of the rotation of a line about a point, the angle itself visually represented as the line before and after its rotation. In the procedural frame the notion of a 180 degree angle is intelligible, as is the notion of a 360 degree angle. Within the perceptual frame such notions do not fit. (The example is from Arnheim 1969: 182f.)

4.2 Alternate framings of a single situation

From a frame semantics point of view, it is frequently possible to show that the same 'facts' can be presented within different framings, framings which make them out as different 'facts'. Somebody who shows an unwillingness to give out money in a particular situation might be described by one person as *stingy* (in which case the behavior is contrasted with being *generous),* and by another as *thrifty* (in which case a contrast is made with being *wasteful).* The speaker who applies the *stingy: generous* contrast to a way of behaving assumes that it is to be evaluated with respect to the behaver's treatment of fellow humans; whereas the speaker who evaluates the behavior by applying to it a *thrifty: wasteful* contrast assumes that what is most important is a measure of the skill or wisdom displayed in the use of money or other resources.

4.3 'Contrast within frames' versus 'contrast across frames'

The fact that a single situation can be 'framed' in contrasting ways makes possible two ways of presenting a negation or an opposition. Using the contrasts introduced in the last paragraph, if I say of somebody, *He's not stingy — he's really generous,* I have accepted the scale by which you choose to measure him, and I inform you that in my opinion your application of this scale was in error. If on the other hand I say *He's not stingy — he's thrifty,* what I am doing is proposing that the behavior in question is not to be evaluated along the *stingy: generous* dimension but along the *thrifty: wasteful* dimension. In the first case I have argued for a particular standard in the application of an accepted scale; in the second case my utterance argues for the irrelevance of one scale and the appropriateness of another.

4.4 Word sense creation by frame borrowing

When a speaker wishes to talk about something for which an appropriate cognitive frame has not been established, or for which he wishes to introduce a novel schematization, he can sometimes accomplish this by transferring the linguistic material associated with a frame which makes the distinctions he's interested in onto the new situation, relying on the interpreter to see the appropriateness of the transfer. Certain new senses of words can be best understood as having originated in this way; we might expect that such was the case in the importation of the term *bachelor* into the terminology appropriate to fur seal society, to use the example made common in lexical semantics discussion from the reminder, in Katz and Fodor (1963), of the use of the word *bachelor* to designate 'a male fur seal without a mate during the mating season'. Lakoff and Johnson (1980) have made us aware of the value of metaphor in conceptualization and communication, making the persuasive case that in a great many domains of experience metaphors provide us with the only way of communicating about those experiences.

4.5   Reframing a lexical set

Various kinds of semantic change can be illuminated by considering the phenomena in frame semantic terms. One important type of change consists in reconstituting the motivating circumstances while preserving the lexical item and its basic fit with the associated scene. People observing certain usages of English with an eye to feminist concerns have noticed tendencies on the part of many speakers to have certain asymmetries in the sets of conditions for using the words in the proportion *boy: man :: girl: woman*. In particular, in the usage pattern that I have in mind, males appeared to be classified as *men* at an earlier age than that at which females are classified as *woman*. A number of people, sensing that this usage pattern revealed attitudes toward females (or a history of attitudes toward females reflected in current conventional usage possibly in independence of the user's own attitudes) which ought to be corrected. A number of speakers have succeeded in modifying their usage in a way which established the age boundary between the *boy* to *man* transition at the same place as that between the *girl* to *woman* transition. The semantic change in this case is a real one, which needs to be explained. But it would not be satisfying to see the explanation solely in changes of the meaning of the words *girl* and *woman;* the full explanation must assign the change to the underlying schematization on the part of the language user. The realities (of people of both sexes getting older) have not changed, nor have the available choices of linguistic material; what has changed (in some speakers) is the underlying schematization, the circumstances motivating the category contrasts.

4.6 Relexicalizing unchanged frames

A second kind of semantic change, which oddly can be illustrated with the same words, is one in which the links between words and their frames are changed, but the underlying schematization remains unchanged. The effort to respond to society's new sensitivity to the connections between language and attitudes is perhaps easiest to manage in the short run if it does not require something as deeply cognitive as a reschematization of the domain. A superficial rule-of-thumb for bringing about the appearance of a raised consciousness in the realm of language and sexism is a mechanical principle like "Where I am inclined to say *girl* I should instead say *woman* ". A person who adopts this rule may find that in most cases it performs very well; but one sometimes finds oneself trapped — as in the experience of an acquaintance of mine — when talking about very young females; my friend found himself, several times, using the word *woman* when talking about an eight-year-old girl. The fact that this friend would never accidentally use the word *man* when talking about an eight-year-old boy shows that the change in question is not of the reschematization type discussed in the previous paragraph. An equally clear example of the same phenomenon (as I have discussed elsewhere — Fillmore 1972) is in the use of the word *suspect* where the speaker or writer might have been inclined to use such a word as *burglar, murderer, arsonist,* or more generally, *culprit.* Conscious of the legal doctrine that a person is to be considered innocent until proven guilty, and conscious too of the danger of committing libel, journalists and police officers have learned to identify persons accused of crimes but not (yet) legally held to be guilty of them as *suspects*. A change in usage which would clearly reflect the adoption of the legal doctrine mentioned above about guilt and innocence as the underlying cognitive frame would not result in some of the frequent mistakes people make in the use of the word *suspect.* The word *suspect* is supposed to be used of a person who is suspected of committing the crime in question; for it to be used appropriately, there has to be some specific person of whom it can be said that that person is suspected by someone of committing the crime. The current journalistic use of *suspect* even when nobody has been accused of the crime shows that the change is of the superficial kind, following the application of a rule of thumb that says, "Wherever I am inclined to say *culprit* (etc.), I should instead say *suspect.*" I have in mind such usages as can be found in reports like "Police investigating the murder have found no clues as to the identity of the suspect."

4.7 Miscommunication by frame conflict

The law provides many contexts in which specific new framings need to be constructed for familiar words. The notion *innocent* mentioned above is an example. In both everyday language and legal language there is a contradictory opposition between *innocent* and *guilty*. In everyday language, the difference depends on whether the individual in question did or did not commit the crime in question. In legal language, by contrast, the difference depends on whether the individual in question has or has not been declared guilty by the court as a result of legal action within the criminal justice system. This disparity of schematization is responsible for frequent misunderstandings in the use of these words. An example of such misunderstandings (which I have discussed in Fillmore 1978) was in a conversation between a prospective juror and lawyers in a voir dire hearing in a municipal court in Berkeley. The attorney for the defense asked the prospective juror "Do you accept the American legal doctrine that a man is innocent until proven guilty?" The citizen answered that a person should be treated as innocent until proven guilty, but that it would be strange to say that he was actually innocent. The attorney asked again, saying, "I'm talking about the doctrine that a man *is* innocent until proven guilty. Do you or do you not accept that doctrine?" The citizen answered that if the man *is* innocent, then there is no need for a trial. (This rude answer excused the man from jury duty.) This little bit of miscommu-nicating could easily have been avoided. The citizen was not really being asked whether or not he accepted a particular legal doctrine, but whether or not he was willing to adopt for the purpose of discussion in the trial which was about to start the framing of the words *innocent* and *guilty* provided by the criminal justice institutions in place of the everyday use of these same words.

外教社学术阅读文库 ——语义学经典论文选读

4.8 Reformulations in technical language

Legal contexts give us further ways of seeing changes between general and special-purpose framings of words. In many cases this is because the everyday sense of a word does not cover all cases in which it should be appropriate to use the word. In the prototype case of events fitting the word *murder,* one person (A), intending to kill a second person (B), acts in such a way as to cause that person to die. This prototype does not cover a case in which A, intending to kill B, aims his gun at B, and kills C (who is standing next to B) instead. Some of the properties of *murder* relate A and B; others relate A to C. The question somebody needs to answer, of course, is whether, for the purposes of the law, it is proper to say that A murdered C. The law does this, not by modifying the definition of *murder* so that it will cover this 'wrong-target' case, but by adding to the system of legal semantics a statutory interpretation principle called 'Transfer of Intent' according to which A's intent to kill B is fictitiously transferred to C so that the definition of *murder* can fully fit what A did to C. With respect to judgments of reprehensibility and legal provisions for punishment, A's killing of C should be treated in the same way as A's successful killing of B would have been. The Transfer of Intent principle makes it possible for the non-prototypic case to fall under the same definition.

Other such reinterpretations in the law are equally founded on intentions associated with the prototypical case. The concept of *forcible entry* involves one person gaining entry to another person's property by overcoming the resistance of persons trying to prevent that person's entry. The usual definition of *forcible entry*, however, includes not only the situation in which the intruder physically overpowers the other, but also the situation in which, as it is usually put, "resistance would be unavailing". If you, being twice my size and strength, insist on being admitted to my apartment, and I meekly let you enter (on the reasonable grounds that if we had a fight, I would lose), then too you can be charged with *forcible entry*. A third example is *oral agreement*. Basically an *oral agreement* is a contract or agreement which two parties entered into orally, that is, without putting the agreement in a written form and without signing our names to it. The importance of the notion *oral agreement* in the law is that the conditions of its authenticity and its bindingness distinguish it from agreements that are fully written out and signed. The critical difference, for the given legal purposes, is the presence or absence of the signatures of the principals. The important part of the contrast, then, is that between being signed and not being signed. Accordingly, provisions made in the law for *oral agreements* also apply to written agreements which happen not to be signed. The prototype background in which the notion *oral agreement* is motivated, is one in which agreements are either made by word of mouth or by means of documents which are written and signed. In situations which depart from the prototype the law has needed to determine which aspect of the prototype contrast is legally the most salient (the presence or absence of the signatures supporting a written document) and let that be the criterion which specifies the contrast.

4.9　Frames for evaluation

One important area in which semantic interpretation depends crucially on lexical framing is that of attributions of value. Evaluative adjectives can contain in their meanings reference to the dimensions, scales, or standards according to which something is evaluated, as with adjectives like *fragrant, tasty, efficient, intelligent,* etc. In many cases, however, an adjective is abstractly evaluative (as with the English words *good* and *bad)* and interpretations of their attributive use depend on knowledge of the ideational frames to which they are indexed. The fact that speakers of English are able to interpret such phrases as *a good pencil, good coffee, a good mother, a good pilot,* etc., shows that they are able to call into their consciousness for this purpose the fact that a pencil is used for writing and can be evaluated for how easy or efficient it is to write with it, or how clearly its traces appear on the paper, the fact that coffee is a drink and can be evaluated for its taste, its contribution to the drinker's alertness, etc., that mothers and pilots do what they professionally and conventionally do and can be evaluated for how easily, how effectively, and how efficiently they do it. The point was made earlier that cognitive frames called on to assist in text interpretation may derive from general background knowledge or may be brought into play by the textual context. This is particularly true in the case of the interpretation of evaluative adjectives, since some nouns have frames associated with them whose evaluative dimensions are provided in advance, while others designate things that could be evaluated only if the context provided some basis for the evaluation. When we come across the phrase *a good stick* we expect to find in the context some explanation of a situation within which one stick could function better than another (for propping a window open, for repelling a raccoon, for skewering marshmallows, etc.). A general concept of 'framing' involves contextualizing or situating events in the broadest sense possible; within linguistic semantics proper the concern is with patterns of framing that are already established and which are specifically associated with given lexical items or grammatical categories.

4.10   Script evocation

I said earlier about cognitive frames that to speak of one of its elements is to speak of the others at the same time. More carefully put, to speak of one part of a frame is to bring to consciousness, or to raise into question, its other components. This effect is particularly striking in connection with the kinds of frames known as 'scripts', frames whose elements are sequenced types of events. Text understanding that makes use of scriptal knowledge (on which see Schank and Abelson 1977) involves the activation of whole-scale scripting of events on the presentation of an event that can be seen to part of such a script. Thus, in a textlet like "He pushed against the door. The room was empty." we make the two sentences cohere by assuming that the goal somebody might have in pushing against a door is to get that door open, and that if one succeeded in getting the door open by such an act, one could then be in a position to notice whether the room was empty. Reading between the lines, we expand the text to mean: "He pushed against the door. *the door opened. he looked inside. he saw that* The room was empty."

4.11   Frames for texts

Discussion of text structure on the part of Robert Longacre and others shows that languages or cultures can differ with respect to the ways in which texts with particular communicative goals can have particular conventionalized forms. Recipes in English make consistent use of imperatives. In Hungarian recipes, first person plural descriptions are the norm. And Longacre has described (in conversation) a language lacking in procedural discourse uses narrative form for such purposes. Here it would be difficult to believe that languages differ from each other in the presence of material usable for particular kinds of discourse, it seems rather to be the case that traditions of language use within the culture develop in different ways in texts with different communicative goals.

5. Frame-semantic formulations of issues in technical semantics

In this section I examine a small number of topics that one traditionally finds in standard treatises on technical semantics: proportionality, paradigms, taxonomies, syncategorematicity, the supposed contrast between 'dictionary' and 'encyclopedia', the goal of descriptive simplicity and redundancy elimination, and, lastly, the troubled notion of 'lexical presupposition'.

5.1 Proportionality

One of the most frequently used heuristic devices for discovering and demonstrating the existence of semantic features in the vocabulary of a language is that of setting up a proportionality involving four words and asking for intuitive agreement about the identity of pairwise differences among them. Believing that man is to woman as boy is to girl, we set up the ratio *man: woman :: boy: girl*. Others frequently used are *come: go :: bring: take, look: see :: glance: glimpse, inhale: exhale :: sniff: snort,* and *man: woman :: bachelor: spinster.* The approach which sees the basic semantic relations as holding among words taken in isolation fails to help us become aware of the possibly quite separate ways in which individual members of these proportions are fitted onto, or frame, their reality. I have already pointed out that in many people's speech the differentiating criterion for *boy* vs. *man* might be importantly different from that for *girl* vs. *woman; bring* is separate enough in its semantics from *come* for it to have acquired quite separate patterns of dialect variation; and the motivation for the categories *bachelor* and *spinster* appear to be considerably different, in spite of one's inclination, as a systematizer, to put the two words together. One might wish to propose that the abstract structural patterns underlying these word groups are simple and straightforward, in the ways suggested by the proportions, even though certain facts about the world make the domain look less orderly. I think such a proposal is not helpful, because it is not one which asks the analyst to look for the background and motivating situations which separately give reasons for the existence of the individual categories, one by one.

5.2 Paradigms

A prime example of semantic structure among lexical items is the 'paradigm'; and the best example of a lexical-semantic paradigm is the kind of display of livestock terms represented by Table 1.

Table 1.

cattle	sheep	horse	swine
cow	ewe	mare	sow
bull	ram	stallion	boar
steer	wether	gelding	barrow

Here the proposal that we have a closed system of terms tied together by such features as General, Female, Male, and Neuter, cross-cut by features identifying species (Bovine, Ovine, Equine, Porcine), seems very attractive. Unfortunately the display disguises many facts about both these words and the domain which they appear to cover. *cattle* and *swine* are plurals; *sheep* and *horse* are not. The words *wether* and *barrow* are known only to specialists. In the case of *cattle, cow* and *bull* appear to have the status of 'basic level objects' (in the sense of Rosch 1973), whereas the general terms have that function in the case of *sheep* and *horse*. In the case of *swine,* a word not in the table, namely *pig,* is the best candidate for 'basic level object' status.

In short, the regularities apparent in the paradigm (and this set of terms — together with terms for young, newborn, etc. — make up what is generally accepted as the best example of a semantic paradigm) are misleading. To which we ought to add the Neuter category of the words in the bottom row is not just a 'neutral' category operating in the same line of business as the categories Female and Male. The category is differently motivated in the different species, which is another way of saying that one has different reasons for castrating a bull and a horse, one might do it at different (relative) ages, etc,

5.3 Taxonomies

The next most common kind of lexical semantic formal structure is the 'semantic taxonomy', a semantic network founded on the relation 'is a kind of'. Scientific taxonomies have obvious uses in scientific discourse, and research that has led to the uncovering of folk taxonomies has been among the most important empirical semantic research yet done. But there are two aspects of taxonomic structures that argue against regarding them as representing merely a formal system of relationships founded on a single clear semantic relation. The first is that at different levels in a taxonomy the community might have had different reasons for introducing the categories; the second is that the usual tree-form display of the elements of a taxonomy does not show how it is that particular elements in the taxonomy are 'cognitively privileged categories' in important ways. Both of these points can be illustrated with a 'path' in a taxonomy of zoological terms in English, namely

animal
　vertebrate
　　mammal
　　　dog
　　　　retriever

Of this set of words, *dog* and *animal* seem to be the cognitively privileged categories, privileged in the sense that they are the words that would most ordinarily be used when in everyday natural talk one is describing one's experiences. *vertebrate* and *mammal* are terms whose employment fits a particular kind of interactional or contextual schema (that of scientific discourse), while *retriever* as a category occurs most naturally as an answer to a question about what kind of a dog one has. Suppose that you, hearing a splash in my back yard, were to ask me what that noise was, and suppose the fact is that my pet retriever fell in the family swimming pool. As a way of explaining the source of the noise, it would be natural for me to say "An animal fell in the pool" or "A dog fell in the pool", but it would be very unnatural for me to say "A vertebrate fell in the pool" or "A mammal fell in the pool", and unnatural in a different way for me to say "A retriever fell in the pool". The latter three terms seem to appear more natural in utterances used in acts of classifying, but seem unnatural when used in acts of referring. This functional difference is not revealed within the logic of a standard taxonomic tree.

5.4 Syncategorematic terms

It has frequently been discussed (e.g., Austin 1964, Lecture VII) that a word like *imitation* does not semantically modify a word it grammatically modifies in the standard 'set intersection' way. Rather, it combines with the meaning of its partner to form a fairly complex concept. Something correctly described as *imitation coffee* looks like coffee and tastes like coffee, and it looks and tastes like coffee not by accident, but because somebody manufactured it so that it would have these properties; but, whatever it is, it is not made of coffee beans. Understanding the category, in fact, requires understanding the role of coffee in our lives and (perhaps) the reasons someone might have for making a coffee substitute.

By contrast a word like *real* appears to contribute nothing at all to the noun to which it is attached as a modifier. To describe something as *real coffee* is to do nothing more than to assert that something is coffee, against the background of (the possibility of) somebody's suspicion that it is imitation coffee. As with *imitation,* a part of a full understanding of an expression with *real* is knowing the reasons one might have for providing substitutes for the thing in question. The notion *real coffee* makes sense to us because we know that in some settings coffee is scarce, and we know that some people find coffee damaging to their health or held offensive by their religion. We can understand a category like *real gold* or *real diamond* because we can imagine a reason why somebody might choose to produce fake gold or fake diamonds, and we can imagine why someone might have doubts about the authenticity of particular samples. By contrast, a notion like *real pants* is unintelligible, because it is impossible to imagine something looking like pants and functioning like pants which do not, by virtue of those properties alone, count as being genuine pants.

5.5 Redundancy elimination

A common goal in structural semantics is the elimination or minimization of redundant information in the semantic description of lexical items. Frequently a semantic theorist will declare that the goal of a 'semantic dictionary' is that of saying just enough about each word in the language to guarantee that it is semantically in contrast with each other word in the language (Bendix 1966).

It is a goal which presupposes the analyst's ability to have an overview of the entire lexical repertory of the language. Such a goal is completely antithetical to the goals of frame semantics, since frame semantics aims at discovering what categorizing functions the word serves in the contexts in which its use is motivated. This kind of knowledge is in principle attainable independently of knowledge about other words in the language, except for those relatively few cases in which the 'mosaic' image is appropriate, the image by which the meaning given to any one word is dependent on the meanings of its neighboring words (as in Trier 1931).

5.6 Dictionary vs. encyclopedia

The various structuralist approaches that find a goal of redundancy elimination relevant, also find it intelligible to draw a clear distinction between 'dictionaries' and 'encyclopedias'. In particular, certain scholars insist on a distinction between purely semantic information about words and encyclopedic information about the designata of words. Somebody holding this view might expect to be able to justify certain characteristics of carpenters (or the concept *carpenter)* as belonging to the semantic category of the noun, other distinct characteristics of carpenters as simply being true of the individuals who satisfy the criteria associated with the category. A frame-semantic approach would rather say that communities of men contain individuals who by trade make things out of wood, using particular kinds of tools, etc., etc., and would note that these people are called *carpenters.* The possibility of separating some features of a full description of what carpenters do as related to the concept and others as related to the people does not seem important. There is a distinction to be made between knowledge about words and knowledge about things, but it is not to be made in a way that serves the interests of the semanticists I have just been describing. True 'encyclopedic' information about carpenters as people might say something about wages, union affiliations, job related diseases, etc.; such information is not a matter of dispute.

5.7 Simplicity of description

While in respect to redundancy elimination it has appeared that standard approaches value simplicity and frame-semantic approaches do not, there is another sense in which simplicity of description is enhanced by the frame semantics approach. A recent lively discussion between Paul Kay and Linda Coleman on the one hand (Coleman and Kay 1981) and Eve Sweetser on the other hand (Sweetser 1981) concerns the possibility of a prototype background of assumptions (or, as Sweetser calls it, a 'folk theory') as providing the grounding for a simplified definition of the noun *lie*. On the Kay/Coleman account, a *lie* is something which is (1) false in fact, (2) believed by the speaker to be false, and (3) said in order to deceive.

Sweetser's suggestion is that if we can characterize a folk theory of human communication involving cooperation, expressing what one believes, etc., then it is possible to describe a *lie* as simply a 'false statement', those other understandings we have about the concept falling out through an understanding of why one would bother to produce a false statement.

5.8 *Presupposition*

Claims about 'presuppositional' information being associated with individual lexical items have not received a good press. I find that within frame semantics, the concept of lexical presupposition does not seem unjustified. Consider the case of a verb like English *chase*, a verb for which a lexical presuppositionist might be inclined to say that when it is used of two beings moving in the same course, the movement of the one in front is presupposed, independently of whether the movement of the individual designated by the subject of the verb is asserted, denied, questioned, or supposed. In a setting in which one person is running, especially where it is understood that that person is fleeing, it is relevant to consider whether some other person is or is not going to try to prevent that first person from getting away. (My illustration is with people, but that's not an important condition.) The verb *chase* exists as a category by recognition of such relevance. If I ask, "Did anybody chase him?", or if I say "We didn't chase him", our reason for understanding that 'he' was running (fleeing) is that we know the kind of situation against which the category *chase* has a reason for being. It is in that sense, it seems to me, that one can talk about lexical presuppostions.

6. Concluding remarks

In this paper I have argued for a view of the description of meaning-bearing elements in a language according to which words (etc.) come into being only for a reason, that reason being anchored in human experiences and human institutions. In this view, the only way in which people can truly be said to understand the use to which these meaning-bearing elements are being put in actual utterances is to understand those experiences and institutions and to know why such experiences and institutions gave people reasons to create the categories expressed by the words. The semanticist's job is to tease out the precise nature of the relationship between the word and the category, and the precise nature of the relationships between the category and the background. I believe that some of the examples I have offered have shown the advantages of looking at language in this way.

Note

1   For a recent attempt to differentiate these terms, see Beaugrande 1981: 303.

References

Arnheim, Rudolf
  1969   *Visual Thinking.* Berkeley: University of California Press.
Austin, John L.
  1964   *Sense and Sensibilia.* (Reconstructed from manuscript notes by Geoffrey J. Warnock.) Oxford University Press.
Beaugrande, Robert de
  1981   Design criteria for process models of reading. *Reading Research Quarterly* 16(2): 261–315.
Bendix, Edward H.
  1966   *Componential Analysis of General Vocabulary: The Semantic Structure of a Set of Verbs in English, Hindi and Japanese.* Bloomington: Indiana University Press.
Berlin, Brent and Paul Kay
  1969   *Basic Color Terms.* Berkeley: University of California Press.

Chomsky, Noam A.

1957   *Syntactic Structures.* The Hague: Mouton

1965   *Aspects of the Theory of Syntax.* Cambridge, MA: M.I.T. Press

Coleman, Linda and Paul Kay

1981   Prototype semantics. *Language* 57: 26–44.

Downing, Pamela

1977   On the creation and use of English compound nouns. *Language* 53: 810–842.

Fillmore, Charles J.

1961   *Indirect Object Constructions in English and the Ordering of Transformations.* The Hague: Mouton.

1963   The position of embedding transformations in a grammar. *Word* 19: 208–301.

1968   The case for case. In *Universals in Linguistic Theory,* Emmon Bach and Richard Harms (eds.), 1–90. New York: Holt, Rinehart & Winston.

1971   Verbs of judging: An exercise in semantic description. In *Studies in Linguistic Semantics,* Charles J. Fillmore and D. Terrence Langendoen (eds.), 272–289. New York: Holt, Rinehart and Winston.

1972   On generativity. In *The Goals of Linguistic Theory,* Stanley Peters (ed.), 1–19. Englewood Cliffs: Prentice Hall.

1975   *Santa Cruz Lectures on Deixis.* Bloomington: Indiana University Linguistics Club.

1977a   The case for case reopened. In *Syntax and Semantics 8: Grammatical Relations,* Peter Cole and Jerry Sadock, (eds.), 59–82. New York: Academic Press.

1977b   Topics in lexical semantics. In *Current Issues in Linguistic Theory,* Roger W. Cole (ed.), 76–138. Bloomington: Indiana University Press.

1978   On the organization of semantic information in the lexicon. In *Papers from the Parasession on the Lexicon,* 1–11. Chicago: The Chicago Linguistic Society.

Fries, Charles C.

1952   *The Structure of English.* New York: Harcourt, Brace & World.

Gross, Maurice

1975   *Méthodes en syntaxe.* Paris: Hermann.

Helbig, Gerhard and Wolfgang Schenkel

1973   *Wörterbuch zur Valenz und Distribution deutscher Verben.* Leipzig: VEB Verlag Enzyklopädie.

Householder, Fred W., et al.

1964   *Linguistic Analysis of English,* Final Report on NSF Grant No. GS-108.

Katz, Jerrold J. and Jerry A. Fodor

1963   The structure of a semantic theory. *Language* 39: 170–210.

Lakoff, George and Mark Johnson

1980   *Metaphors We Live By.* Chicago: University of Chicago Press.

Langacker, Ronald W.

1987   Foundations of Cognitive Grammar. vol. 1: *Theoretical Prerequisites.* Stanford: Stanford University Press.

Lees, Robert B.

1960   *The Grammar of English Nominalizations.* The Hague: Mouton

McCawley, James D.

1975   Verbs of bitching. In *Contemporary Research in Philosophical Logic and Linguistic Semantics,* David Hockney et al. (eds.), 313–332. Dordrecht: Reidel.

Pike, Kenneth L.

1967   *Language in Relation to a Unified Theory of the Structure of Human Behavior.* The Hague: Mouton.

Rosch, Eleanor H.

1973   On the internal structure of perceptual and semantic categories. In *Cognitive Development and the Acquisition of Language,* Timothy E. Moore (ed.), 111–144. New York: Academic Press.

Rosenbaum, Peter S.

1967   *The Grammar of English Predicate Complement Constructions.* Cambridge, MA: MIT Press

Schank, Roger C. and Robert P. Abelson

1977   *Scripts, Plans, Goals and Understanding: An Inquiry into Human Knowledge Structures.* Hillsdale, N.J.: Lawrence Erlbaum.

Sweetser, Eve E.

1981   The definition of *lie:* An examination of the folk theories underlying a semantic prototype. Unpublished ms.

Talmy, Leonard

1980   Grammar and cognition. Unpublished ms. University of California at San Diego, Cognitive Science Program.

Tesnière, Lucien

1959 *Elements de syntaxe structurale.* Paris: Klingksieck.

Trier, Jost

1931 *Der deutsche Wortschatz im Sinnbezirk des Verstandes.* Heidelberg.

Wilson, Deirdre

1975 *Presuppositions and Non-Truth-Conditional Semantics.* London: Academic Press.

Zimmer, Karl E.

1971 Some general observations about nominal compounds. In *Working Papers on Language Universals* 5: 1–24. Stanford: Stanford University Press. (Reprinted in 1981 in *Wortbildung,* Leonard Lipka and Hartmut Günther (eds.), 233–257. Darmstadt: Wissenschaftliche Buchgesellschaft Darmstadt.)

First Steps toward a Usage-based Theory of Language Acquisition

Michael Tomasello

外教社学术阅读文库 — 语义学经典论文选读

In usage-based models of language — for example, those of Langacker (1987, 1988, 2000), Bybee (1985, 1995), and Croft (2000) — all things flow from the actual usage events in which people communicate linguistically with one another. The linguistic skills that a person possesses at any given moment in time — in the form of a "structured inventory of symbolic units" — result from her accumulated experience with language across the totality of usage events in her life. This accumulated linguistic experience undergoes processes of entrenchment, due to repeated uses of particular expressions across usage events, and abstraction, due to type variation in constituents of particular expressions across usage events. Given this focus on usage events and the processes of language learning that occur within these events, a crucial item on the research agenda of usage-based models of language is, or should be, the study of how human beings build up the most basic aspects of their linguistic competence during childhood.

From the point of view of research in child language acquisition, perhaps the most attractive feature of usage-based models is their openness on the question of what are the linguistic units with which people operate. For example, usage-based theories explicitly recognize that human beings learn and use many relatively fixed, item-based linguistic expressions such as *How-ya-doin?, Could you please ...*, *I'm simply amazed,* and *You keep out of this* — which, even when they are potentially decomposable into elements, are stored and produced as single units (see Bybee and Scheibman 1999 for psycholinguistic evidence focused on *I dunno*). On the other hand, people also operate with some highly abstract linguistic constructions such as, in English, the ditransitive construction, the resultative construction, and the caused motion construction — based on commonalities in the forms and functions of a whole host of different specific expressions (Goldberg 1995). Finally, people also control many "mixed" constructions that revolve around concrete and particular linguistic items but are partly abstract as well, for example, the "What's X doing Y" construction, as in *What's that fly doing my soup?* (Kay and Fillmore 1999) — which has its own distinctive linguistic form and communicative function (see Michaelis and Lambrecht 1996 and Fillmore et al. 1988 for other mixed constructions).

The important methodological point is that the psycholinguistic units with which people operate are identified through observation of their language use. Since it is obvious to all empirically oriented students of language acquisition that children operate with different psycholinguistic units than adults (Tomasello 2000), this theoretical freedom to identify these units on the basis of actual language use, rather than adult-based linguistic theory, is truly liberating. My procedure in this article, therefore, will be to examine children's early use of language in an effort to identify what are the psycholinguistic units — in terms of both complexity and abstractness — with which the process of language acquisition begins. I will also seek to identify some of the developmental processes by means of which children's use of language becomes more adult-like over time.

1. The emergence of language

Following the general strictures of cognitive linguistics, to identify the fundamental units of language use we must begin with basic processes of human cognition and communication. Following the general lead of many functionally oriented theorists, my candidate for the most fundamental psycholinguistic unit is the utterance (see especially Croft 2000). An utterance is a linguistic act in which one person expresses towards another, within a single intonation contour, a relatively coherent communicative intention in a communicative context.

1.1 *Understanding communicative intentions*

For current purposes, a communicative intention may be defined as one person expressing an intention that another person share attention with her to some third entity (Tomasello 1998a). This is not a trivial cognitive achievement, and indeed the expression and comprehension of communicative intentions is a species-unique characteristic of *Homo sapiens* (Tomasello 1999). It is thus interesting to note that there are currently no observations indicating that nonhuman primates use any vocalization to direct the attention of groupmates to any external entity such as a predator or food. (Vervet monkeys make different alarm calls for different predators, but a close inspection of the way they use these calls leads to the conclusion that "monkeys cannot communicate with the intent to modify the mental states of others because ... they do not recognize that such mental states exist", Cheney and Seyfarth 1990: 310). Nor are there any observations indicating that nonhuman primates use any facial or manual gesture to direct the attention of groupmates to an external entity; they do not point, hold up objects to show them to others, or even offer objects to others (chimpanzees raised by humans sometimes learn to point or use "symbols", but only for imperative, not declarative, purposes — which suggests that they may be attempting to direct the behavior, not the attention, of others; Tomasello and Camaioni 1997). The simple fact is that nonhuman primates do not as a matter of course in their natural environment "express an intention that another share attention with them to some third entity" — perhaps because they do not understand that others have attention (Tomasello and Call 1997).

Prelinguistic human infants are able to discriminate sounds and associate particular experiences with them (Haith and Benson 1997), but they do not comprehend and produce linguistic symbols until about their first birthdays. They do not do this quite simply because they do not yet understand communicative intentions. From about their first birthdays, however, infants begin to understand that when other persons are making funny noises at them they are trying to manipulate their attention with respect to some external entity. This understanding is one manifestation of a momentous shift in the way human infants understand other persons — which occurs at around nine to twelve months of age, as indicated by the near simultaneous emergence of a wide array of joint attentional skills involving outside objects. This includes such things as following into the gaze direction and pointing gestures of others, imitating the actions of others on objects, and manipulating the attention of others by pointing or holding up objects to "show" them to others declaratively.

The first language emerges on the heels of these non-linguistic triadic behaviors (involving you, me, and it) and is highly correlated with them — in the sense that children with earlier emerging skills of nonlinguistic joint attention begin to acquire linguistic skills at an earlier age as well (Carpenter, Nagell, and Tomasello 1998). Similarly, children with autism have problems with joint attention and language in a correlated fashion, that is, those who have the poorest nonlinguistic joint attentional skills are those who have the poorest language skills (Sigman and Capps 1997). When children begin to understand the actions of others as intentional in general, they also begin to understand the communicative actions of others as intentional in the sense that they are aimed at directing attention.

Even given the ability to understand communicative intentions in general, it is still far from straightforward to determine a specific communicative intention in a specific usage event. Wittgenstein (1953) in particular analyzed the many problems involved (e.g., he pointed out the fundamental indeterminacy of ostensive definitions; see also Quine 1960) and concluded that communicative intentions can only be comprehended if they are experienced within the context of some already familiar "form of life" that serves as their functional grounding. In language acquisition, these are what Bruner (1983) called joint attentional "formats" — mutually understood social interactions between child and adult that constitute the shared presuppositions and joint attentional framework of the usage event (see also Tomasello, in press). It is easy to see that over ontogenetic time the forms of life that structure early language acquisition turn into the wider knowledge bases that a number of cognitive-functional linguists have pointed to as crucial in the proper characterization of linguistic meaning. The frames, scripts, and other larger entities within which specific linguistic forms gain their communicative significance — as specified, for example, in Fillmore's (1988) frame semantics and Langacker's (1987) base-profile distinction — have their ontogenetic roots in the nonlinguistically learned and experienced joint attentional formats of child language acquisition. Within these larger intersubjectively shared wholes, children come to understand utterances as attempts to manipulate or "window" the attention of other persons with respect to particular aspects of these interaction-encompassing background frames (Talmy 1996).

And so, if we take the understanding of communicative intentions as primary in the child's initiation into linguistic communication, our fundamental unit of analysis must be the most complete and coherent communicative act, the utterance — which is most reliably identified by its simultaneous functional and prosodic coherence. Children come to understand utterances as they come to understand the intentional actions, including communicative actions, of others. They do this within the context of intersubjectively shared forms of life — joint attentional formats — which constitute the medium within which skills of linguistic communication function and grow. Thus, in the current view, utterances are the primary units of linguistic communication since they are used to express complete and coherent communicative intentions, and other smaller units of language are communicatively significant only by virtue of the role they play in utterances.

1.2 Holophrases and early word combinations

Children naturally want to understand all of what an adult is trying to communicate to them in an utterance, and so when they attempt to communicate with other people they attempt to produce (i.e., to reproduce) the entire utterance — even though they often succeed in (re)producing only one linguistic element out of the adult's whole utterance. This kind of expression has often been called a "holophrase" since it is a single linguistic symbol functioning as a whole utterance, for example, *That!* meaning "I want that" or *Ball?* meaning "Where's the ball?" (Barrett 1982). The child's attempt is thus not to reproduce one component of the goal-directed communicative act but rather the entire goal-directed act, even though she may only succeed in producing one element. This element is often the one designating the "new" aspect of the situation (Greenfield and Smith 1986), and so it is possible to think of holophrases as kind of primitive predications, with joint attentional formats serving as a kind of topical ground (although young children are clearly not adult-like in explicitly establishing shared topics with an interlocutor and then predicating something about the topic that is new for *her*, the interlocutor).

Holophrases come in many forms; they do not just correspond to single adult words. Thus, most children also have in their early language some so-called frozen phrases that are learned as holophrases but will at some point be broken down into their constituent elements, for example, *Lemme-see, Gimme-that, I-wanna-do-it, My-turn,* and many others (Lieven et al. 1992). This is of course especially true of children learning languages less isolating than English (e.g., Inuktitut; Allen 1996). And so what the holophrastic child needs to do to become a syntactically competent language user is to be able to move in both directions — from part to whole and from whole to part. She must be able either to "break down" or to "fill out" her holophrases so that she can express her communicative intentions in the more linguistically articulated way of adult speakers. Learning how to do this depends on the child's ability to comprehend not only the adult utterance as a whole, but also the functional role being played by the different linguistic elements in that whole. This is the beginnings of grammar.[1]

One could imagine that children learn holophrases, or perhaps even words disembodied from any particular speech act function, and then combine these in situations in which they both are relevant — with both words having roughly equivalent status. For example, a child has learned to name a ball and a table and then spies a ball on a table and says, "Ball table". There may be some initial linguistic productions that are like this for some children, including both "successive single-word utterances" (Bloom 1973) and some word combinations. But in fact most of children's early multiword speech shows a functional asymmetry between constituents, that is, there is one word or phrase that seems to structure the utterance in the sense that it determines the speech act function of the utterance as a whole (often with help from an intonational contour), with the other linguistic item(s) simply filling in variable slot(s). This kind of organization is responsible for what has been called the "pivot look" of early child language, which is characteristic of most children learning most of the languages of the world (Braine 1976; Brown 1973). Early multi-word productions are thus things like: *Where's the X?, I wanna X, More X, It's a X, I'm X-ing it, Put X here, Mommy's X-ing it, Let's X it, Throw X, X gone, I X-ed it, Sit on the X, Open X, X here, There's a X, X broken,* and so on and so forth.

These early word combinations serve the same kinds of functions as early holophrases (indeed many begin their life in one way or another as a holophrase); they simply have a bit more grammatical structure in the sense that they have constant linguistic material that (i) has some internal complexity in some cases (in adult eyes and perhaps the child's as well), and (ii) they have at least one open slot in which many different lexical items and phrases may be placed. Because of this wholistic, utterance-level organization along with open slots, we may call

603

these utterance schemas (see Wray and Perkins 2000 for a similar proposal).

2. The emergence of grammar

Because young children are learning a particular natural language, their early utterances will for the most part be describable with the traditional, adult-based structural categories of that language. But from a psycho-linguistic point of view, it is not at all clear that children are actually operating with adult-like categories. Thus, when the child says something like "Wanna play horsie", it is possible that she understands infinitival clauses in general; it is possible that she understands something like *Wanna + activity wanted;* and it is possible that this is an undifferentiated holophrase. The only way to begin to resolve the issue is to look at this particular child's usage of the word *want* or *wanna,* her use of the word *horsie* and related terms, and her use of other apparent complement clause constructions with other words. In syntactic analyses based on generative grammar and its offshoots this is never done — the child's utterance is simply treated as if it were an adult utterance — and in more functionally based analyses it is often not done with enough critical rigor (e.g., with attention to issues of data sampling).

The issue at stake here is the nature of children's underlying linguistic representations. Do they consist primarily of concrete, item-based utterance schemas and other constructions, or do they consist of more abstract linguistic "rules" (plus a lexicon to fill out the rules with semantic content)? Methodologically, the key issue is children's productivity or creativity with language. To the extent that they are operating with concrete words, phrases, and utterance schemas, children's productivity will be tied to this specific linguistic material (e.g., filling in slots in item-based utterance schemas). To the extent that they are working with highly abstract syntactic rules they should be much more productive, while still being canonical, with all structures of their language. Choosing between these alternatives is, or should be, an empirical matter based on distributional analyses (and experiments) of the language use of particular children during particular developmental periods — just as the structures of particular languages are, or should be, determined through distributional analyses (and experiments) of their speakers' actual language use (Croft 2000; Dryer 1997).

2.1 Verb islands and other item-based constructions

Early work in developmental psycholinguistics, such as that of Braine (1976) and Bowerman (1976), found many highly concrete, highly local, item-based patterns in corpora of many different children learning many different languages. The conclusion was thus that child language was not fully adult-like. But these researchers seemingly could not believe their own eyes and so maintained that whereas children learned some item-based formulae early on (some children more than others), most children also possessed a number of more abstract linguistic representations from early on as well. Other researchers at this time spent some effort trying to discover whether there were other kinds of abstract schemas underlying children's early utterances, such as nonlinguistic sensory-motor cognition (e.g., Brown 1973).

Recent research suggests, however, that most of young children's early language is not based on abstractions of any kind, linguistic or otherwise — with the exception that they control from early on some item-based structures with highly constrained "slots".[2] For example, in a detailed diary study Tomasello (1992) found that most of his English-speaking daughter's early multi-word speech revolved around specific verbs and other predicative terms. That is to say, at any given developmental period each verb was used in its own unique set of utterance-level schemas, and across developmental time each verb began to be used in new utterance-level schemas (and with different TAM morphology) on its own developmental timetable irrespective of what other verbs were doing during that same time period. There was thus no evidence that once the child mastered the use of, for example, a locative construction with one verb that she could then automatically use that same locative construction with other semantically appropriate verbs. Generalizing this pattern, Tomasello (1992) hypothesized that children's early grammars could be characterized as an inventory of verb-island constructions (utterance schemas revolving around verbs), which then defined the first syntactic categories as lexically based things such as "hitter", "thing hit", and "thing hit with" (as opposed to subject/agent, object/patient, and instrument; see also Tomasello and Brooks 1999). Lieven, Pine, and Baldwin (1997; see also Pine et al. 1998) found some very similar results in a sample of 12 English-speaking children, namely, they found that 92 percent of their children's earliest multi-word utterances emanated from one of their first 25 lexically-based patterns, which were different for each child (see also Pine and Lieven 1997).

A number of systematic studies of children learning languages other than English have also found basically item-based organization. For example, in a study of young Italian-speaking children Pizzuto and Caselli (1992, 1994) found that of the six possible person-number forms for each verb in the present tense, about half of all verbs were used in one form only, and an additional 40 percent were used with two or three forms. Of the ten percent of verbs that appeared in four or more forms, approximately half were highly frequent, highly irregular forms that could only have been learned by rote — not by application of an abstract rule. In a similar study of one child learning to speak Brazilian Portugese, Rubino and Pine (1998) found adult-like subject-verb agreement patterns only for the parts of the verb paradigm that appeared with high frequency in adult language (e.g., first-person singular), not for low frequency parts of the paradigm (e.g., third-person plural). The clear implication of these findings is that Romance-speaking children do not master the whole verb paradigm for all their verbs at once, but rather they only master some endings with some verbs — and often different ones with different verbs. (For additional findings of this same type, see Serrat 1997 for Catalan; Behrens 1998 for Dutch; Allen 1996 for Inuktitut; Gathercole et al. 1999 for Spanish; Stoll 1998 for Russian; and Berman and Armon-Lotem 1995 for Hebrew.) It should also be noted that syntactic overgeneralization errors such as *Don't fall me down* — which might be seen as evidence of more general and categorical syntactic knowledge — are almost never produced before about two-and-a-half to three years of age (see Pinker 1989).

Finally, experiments using novel verbs have also found that young children's early productivity with syntactic constructions is highly limited. For example, Tomasello and Brooks (1998) exposed two- to three-year-old children to a novel verb used to refer to a highly transitive and novel action in which an agent was doing something to a patient. In the key condition the novel verb was used in an intransitive sentence frame such as *The sock is tamming* (to refer to a situation in which, for example, a bear was doing something that caused a sock to "tam" — similar to the verb *roll* or *spin)*. Then, with novel characters performing the target action, the adult asked children the question: *What is the doggie doing?* (when the dog was causing some new character to tam). Agent questions of this type encourage a transitive reply such as *He's tamming the car* — which would be creative since the child has heard this verb only in an intransitive sentence frame. The outcome was that very few children produced a transitive utterance with the novel verb, and in another study they were quite poor at two tests of comprehension as well (Akhtar and Tomasello 1997). As a control, children also heard another novel verb introduced in a transitive sentence frame, and in this case virtually all of them produced a transitive utterance — demonstrating that they can use novel verbs in the transitive construction when they have heard them used in that way. Moreover, four- to five-year-old children are quite good at using novel verbs in transitive utterances creatively, demonstrating that once they have indeed acquired more abstract linguistic skills children are perfectly competent in these tasks (Pinker et al. 1987; Maratsos et al. 1987; see Tomasello 2000 for a review). Finally, Akhtar (1999) found that if 2.5- to 3.5-year-old children heard such things as *The bird the bus meeked,* when given new toys they quite often repeated the pattern and said such things as *The bear the cow meeked —* only consistently correcting to canonical English word order at 4.5 years of age. This behavior is consistent with the view that when two-to-three-year-olds are learning about *meeking* they are just learning about *meeking;* they do not assimilate this newly learned verb to some more abstract, verb-general linguistic category or construction that would license a canonical English transitive utterance.

The general conclusion is clear. In the early stages, children mostly use language the way they have heard adults using it. This leads to an inventory of item-based utterance schemas, with perhaps some slots in them built up through observed type variation in that utterance position. The reason that children do not operate with more abstract linguistic categories and schemas is quite simply because they have not yet had sufficient linguistic experience in particular usage events to construct these adult-like linguistic abstractions.

2.2 *Imitative learning, entrenchment, and abstraction*

If children are acquiring mainly item-based constructions early in development — and children acquiring different languages acquire different item-based constructions — an important part of the process must be some form of imitative learning. Imitation has been almost banished from the study of child language because it is most often defined as the child repeating verbatim what an adult has just said without understanding its meaning, and indeed this process very likely does not play a central role in language acquisition. But, there are forms of social learning called cultural learning in which the learner understands the purpose or function of the behavior she is reproducing (Tomasello et al. 1993). Thus, Meltzoff (1995) found that 18-month-old infants attempted to reproduce the intentional action they saw an adult attempting to perform, even when that action was not carried through to completion, Carpenter, Akhtar, and Tomasello (1998) found that 16-month-old infants attempted to reproduce an adult's intentional, goal-directed actions, but not her accidental actions. In the case of language, if they are to use a piece of language in an adult-like way, children must understand and reproduce both its surface linguistic form and its underlying communicative function — in the sense of using it in connection with the same communicative intention (Tomasello 1998a, 1999).

Cultural learning of this type works simultaneously on multiple hierarchical levels, and indeed it must work in this way if the child is to become creative with conventional, culturally based skills. As a nonlinguistic example, a child may see an adult use a stapler and understand that his goal is to staple together two pieces of paper. In some cases, the child may understand also that the goal/function of placing the papers inside the stapler's jaws is to align them with the stapling mechanism inside the stapler, and that the goal/function of pressing down on the stapler is to eject the staple through the two papers — with both of these sub-actions being in the service of the overall goal/function of attaching the two sheets of paper. To the extent that the child does not understand the sub-functions, she will be lost when she encounters some new stapler, for example, one whose stapling mechanism works differently (e.g., does not require pressing down). Only to the extent that the child understands the relevant subfunctions, will she be able to adapt to this new situation creatively (e.g., adjusting her behavior to effect the same outcome with the new stapling mechanism). The comparable linguistic example is that the child hears an adult say "I stapled your papers" and comprehends not only the utterance and its overall communicative intention, but also, for example, the word *stapled* and its communicative subfunction in the utterance (the contribution it is making to the utterance as a whole), along with the phrase *your papers* and its communicative subfunction in the utterance — with *your* serving a sub-function within that phrase. Again, only if the child performs some "functionally based distributional analysis" of this type will she be able in the future to use these linguistic elements creatively in novel utterances.

Reconceptualized in this way to include intention reading, my claim is that cultural (imitative) learning is more important in language development, especially in the early stages, than has traditionally been recognized. This is clear in the data reviewed in the foregoing, which revealed that before their third birthdays children use individual verbs and syntactic constructions in just the way they have heard and understood them being used — with only very limited abilities to go beyond what they have heard. Interestingly, there are two phenomena of child language acquisition that are often taken to be evidence against imitative learning, but which are actually evidence for it — if we look at exactly what children do and do not hear. First, many young children say things like "Her open it", an accusative subject which they supposedly have not heard from adults. But children hear things like "Let her open it" or "Help her open it" all the time, and so it is possible that when they say these things they are simply reproducing the end part of the utterances they have heard. Very telling is the fact that children almost never make the complementary error "Mary hit I" or "Jim kissed she" — the reason being that they never hear anything like this anywhere. A similar account can be given for some of the findings going under the general rubric of optional infinitives (Rice 1998). Children hear a very large number of nonfinite verbs right after nominative nouns, especially in questions such as "Should he open it?" and "Does she eat grapes?" The child might then later say, in partially imitative fashion: "He open it" and "She eat grapes".

It is also important that children seem to have special difficulties in going beyond what they have heard when they have heard it multiple times, that is, it is entrenched. Thus, Brooks, Tomasello, Lewis, and Dodson (1999) modeled the use of a number of fixed-transitivity English verbs for children from 3;5 to 8;0 years — verbs such as *disappear* that are exclusively intransitive and verbs such as *hit* that are exclusively transitive. There were four pairs of verbs, one member of each pair typically learned early by children and used often by adults (and so presumably more entrenched) and one member of each pair typically learned later by children and used less frequently by adults (less entrenched). The four pairs were: *come-arrive, take-remove, hit-strike, disappear-vanish* (the first member of each pair being more entrenched). The finding was that, in the face of adult questions attempting to induce them to overgeneralize, children of all ages were less likely to over-generalize the strongly entrenched verbs than the weakly entrenched verbs; that is, they were more likely to produce *I arrived it* than *I comed it*. This finding suggests not only that children say what they hear, but that the more they hear it the more it seems to them that this is the only way it can be said.

The imitative learning and entrenchment of particular linguistic forms cannot be the whole story of language acquisition, however, since children do at some point go beyond what they hear from adults and create novel yet canonical utterances. As noted above, they do this first by creating "slots" in otherwise item-based schemas (Tomasello et al. 1997). It is not known precisely how they create these slots, but one possibility is that they observe in adult speech variation in that utterance position and so induce the slot on the basis of "type frequency". In general, in usage-based models the token frequency of an expression in the language learner's experience tends to entrench an expression — enabling the user to access and fluently use the expression as a whole (Langacker 1988; Krug 1998; Bybee and Scheibman 1999) — whereas the type frequency of an expression (i.e., the number of different forms in which the language learner experiences the expression or some element of the expression) determines the creative possibilities, or productivity, of the construction (Bybee 1985, 1995). Together, these two types of frequency — along with the corresponding child learning processes — may explain the ways in which young children acquire the use of specific linguistic expressions in specific communicative contexts and then generalize these expressions to new contexts based on various kinds of type variations they hear — including everything from type variation in a single slot to type variation in all of the constituents of a construction. The extent of type variation needed for different kinds of productivity is not known at this time, and indeed after a certain point in development it may be that type variation in the slots of constructions becomes less important as these slots come to be more precisely defined functionally.

Another possibility — not mutually exclusive but rather complementary to the foregoing — is that abstract constructions are created by a relational mapping across different verb-island constructions (Gentner and Markman 1997). For example, in English the several verb-island constructions that children have with the verbs *give, tell, show, send,* and so forth, all share a "transfer" meaning and they all appear in a structure: NP+V+NP+NP (identified by the appropriate morphology on NPs and VPs). The specific hypothesis is thus that children make constructional analogies based on similarities of both form and function: two utterances or constructions are analogous if a "good" structure mapping is found both on the level of linguistic form and on the level of communicative function. Precisely how this might be done is not known at this time, but there are some proposals that a key element in the process might be some kind of "critical mass" of exemplars, to give children sufficient raw material from which to construct their abstractions (Marchman and Bates 1994).

In either case, the main point is that young children begin by imitatively learning specific pieces of language in order to express their communicative intentions, for example, in holophrases and other fixed expressions. As they attempt to comprehend and reproduce the utterances produced by mature speakers — along with the internal constituents of those utterances — they come to discern certain patterns of language use (including patterns of token and type frequency), and these patterns lead them to construct a number of different kinds of (at first very local) linguistic categories and schemas. As with all kinds of categories and schemas in cognitive development, the conceptual "glue" that holds them together is function; children categorize together things that do the same thing (Mandler 1997). In this case, children understand as instances of the same kind of linguistic units those that serve "the same" or "similar" communicative functions in utterances.

2.3. Usage-based syntactic operations

Given that children are acquiring linguistic constructions of various shapes and sizes and degrees of abstraction throughout early development (i.e., building their linguistic inventories), we may now ask about their ability to put these constructions together creatively in order to adapt to the exigencies of particular usage events. Tomasello, Lieven, Behrens, and Forwergk (to appear) addressed this issue in a naturalistic study of one two-year-old child learning English. The novelty was that this child's language was recorded using extremely dense taping intervals. Specifically, the child was recorded in linguistic interaction with her mother for one hour per day, five days per week, for six weeks — making the taped data roughly five to ten times denser than most existing databases of child language, and accounting for approximately eight to ten percent of all of the child's utterances during this six-week period. In order to investigate this child's syntactic creativity, all of her 500+ utterances produced during the last one-hour taping session at the end of the six-week period were designated as target utterances. Then, for each target utterance, there was a search for "similar" utterances produced by the child (not the mother) in the previous six weeks of taping. Was it an utterance she had said before exactly? Was it an utterance based on some highly frequent schema from before but with a new linguistic item in the slot? Was it an utterance pieced together from previously mastered language in some more creative way? Or did the target utterance have no previous precedents in the child's productive language at all?

The main goal was thus to determine for each utterance recorded on the final day of the study what kinds of syntactic operations were necessary for its production, that is to say, in what ways did the child have to modify things she had previously said (her "stored linguistic experience") to produce the thing she was now saying. We may call these operations "usage-based syntactic operations" since they explicitly take into account that the child does not put together each of her utterances from scratch, morpheme by morpheme, but rather, she puts together her utterances from a motley assortment of different kinds of pre-existing psycholinguistic units. And so, following the usage-based models of Bybee (1995), Langacker (2000), and Croft (2000), the question was how this child was able to "cut and paste" together her previously mastered linguistic constructions in order to create a novel utterance in a specific usage event. What was found by this procedure was:

– Of the 455 intelligible utterances produced, 78 percent were utterances that this child had said before during the previous six weeks of sampling — in exactly this same form as whole utterances. Many of these were utterance routines like *Thank-you, There-you-go,* etc., but many were simply frequently used multi-word utterances such as *Where's Daddy?*

– Another 18 percent of the target utterances were things the child had said before but with one minor change, that is, they consisted of an established utterance schema plus other linguistic material "filled in" or "added on". For example, the child had said many scores of times previously *Where's X,* but on the target tape she said *Where's the butter?,* which was new *(butter* having been said on five occasions previously in other linguistic contexts). As another example, the child said *I got one here,* which was new. But she had said *I got one* seven times previously, and she had added *here* onto the end of utterances many scores of times previously.

– Only four percent of this child's target utterances were different from things she had said before in more than one way. These mostly involved the combination of "filling in" and "adding on" to an established utterance schema. For example, the child said creatively *I want tissue lounge,* which seemingly derived from the utterance schema *I want object* (which she had said over 50 times previously), with a slotting in of the word *tissue* (which she had said nine times previously in other contexts), and adding on of the word *lounge* (which she had said three times previously in other contexts).

– There were exactly three utterances (less than one-half of one per cent) that could not be accounted for in a relatively straightforward application of this procedure, and two of these were heavily scaffolded by the immediate discourse context (i.e., the child took some other utterance not from her stored linguistic experience but rather from her mother's immediately preceding speech).

It is thus clear that in the vast majority of cases, this child's creative utterances were based directly on things she had said before many times previously. Moreover, in the vast majority of cases, one of the pieces of language on which the child's creative utterance was based was what we called an utterance schema. Utterance schemas were things the child had said before as full utterances with some variation in one (or, infrequently, more than one) slot — such things as *Where's the X?, I wanna X, More X, It's a X, I'm X-ing it, Put X here, Mommy's X-ing it, Let's X it,* and so forth. Importantly, these utterance schemas were things that the child had said before, on average, an estimated 150 times during the previous six weeks, and the other language used in these creative utterances (e.g., to fill the slot) had been said before, on average in one or another context, an estimated 70 times during the previous six weeks (these estimations are aimed at reflecting the child's total experience as projected from our ten-percent sample). Further evidence for the psychological reality of these utterance schemas derives from the fact that there were virtually no insertions of linguistic material into previously invariant sequential strings within the schemas (e.g., the child never put adverbs or other modifiers into the middle of an established utterance schema) or substitutions of linguistic material into places that did not already have established slots. It is also important that there was almost perfect functional consistency across different uses of these utterance schemas; the child filled the slot with the same kind of linguistic item or phrase (e.g., an object word or a locative phrase) across the six-week period of study.

The usage-based approach is also quite revealing in the case of more complex constructions. For example, Diessel and Tomasello (in press) looked at seven children's earliest utterances with sentential complements and found that virtually all of them were composed of a simple sentence schema that the child had already mastered combined with one of a delimited set of matrix verbs (see also Bloom 1992). These matrix verbs were of two types. First were epistemic verbs such as *think* and *know*. In almost all cases children used *I think* to indicate their own uncertainty about something, and they basically never used the verb *think* in anything but this first-person, present tense form; that is, there were virtually no examples of *He thinks ...*, *She thinks ...*, etc., virtually no examples of *I don't think ...*, *I can't think ...*, etc., and virtually no examples of *I thought ...*, *I didn't think ...*, etc. And there were almost no uses with a complementizer (virtually no examples of *I think that ...*). It thus appears that for many young children *I think* is a relatively fixed phrase meaning something like *Maybe*. The child then pieces together this fixed phrase with a full sentence as a sort of evidential marker, but not as a "sentence embedding" as it is typically portrayed in more formal analyses. The second kind of matrix verbs are attention-getting verbs like *Look* and *See* in conjunction with full finite clauses. In this case, children use these "matrix" verbs almost exclusively in imperative form (again almost no negations, no nonpresent tenses, no complementizers), once more suggesting an item-based approach not involving syntactic embedding. Thus, when examined closely, children's earliest complex sentences look much less like adult sentential complements (which are used most often in written discourse) and much more like various kinds of "pastiches" of various kinds of established item-based constructions.

The findings of both of these studies are best explained by a usage-based model in which children's early linguistic competence is organized as an inventory of item-based constructions, many of which are best characterized as utterance schemas since they structure whole utterances. Fluency with a construction is a function of its token frequency in the child's experience (entrenchment); creativity with a construction emanates from the child's experience of type variation in one or more of its constituents (abstraction). In this way, children build up in their linguistic inventories a very diverse set of constructions — concrete, abstract, and mixed — to call upon as needed in particular usage events. Putting together a creative utterance then involves usage-based syntactic operations in which the child in some way integrates already mastered constructions and elements of various shapes, sizes, and degrees of abstraction in some way that is functionally appropriate for the usage event at hand.

3. Conclusion

The study of language acquisition has always tagged along behind models from linguistics — because to study how children acquire something we should first know what that something is. The new usage-based models of cognitive and functional linguistics offer some exciting new perspectives for developmentalists because they are concerned with the actual psychological processes by means of which individuals comprehend and produce utterances. But cognitive and functional linguists have something to learn from developmental psycholinguists as well. If we are interested in people's "stored linguistic experience", and how they use that experience in acts of linguistic communication, it would seem relevant to investigate systematically the processes by which linguistic experience is built up and used in human ontogeny.

The general picture that emerges from my application of the usage-based view to problems of child language acquisition is this: When young children have something they want to say, they sometimes have a set expression readily available and so they simply retrieve that expression from their stored linguistic experience. When they have no set expression readily available, they retrieve linguistic schemas and items that they have previously mastered (either in their own production or in their comprehension of other speakers) and then "cut and paste" them together as necessary for the communicative situation at hand — what I have called "usage-based syntactic operations". Perhaps the first choice in this creative process is an utterance schema which can be used to structure the communicative act as a whole, with other items being filled in or added on to this foundation. It is important that in doing their cutting and pasting, children coordinate not just the linguistic forms involved but also the conventional communicative functions of these forms — as otherwise they would be speaking creative nonsense. It is also important that the linguistic structures being cut and pasted in these acts of linguistic communication are a variegated lot, including everything from single words to abstract categories to partially abstract utterance or phrasal schemas.

Irrespective of the accuracy of the current proposals, there can be no doubt that it is time for cognitive functional linguistics and the study of child language acquisition to come together (Tomasello 1998b). The view I am espousing here is that the most promising theoretical frameworks in which this might be done are the new usage-based models in which (i) the units of language with which people operate are not presupposed or prejudged, (ii) there is an explicit concern with processes of communication in usage events, and (iii) the primary research questions are how human linguistic competence has evolved historically and how today it develops ontogenetically.

Notes

① Thanks to Holger Diessel and Elena Lieven for comments on a previous version of the manuscript.

1 One could argue that holophrases are already in a sense grammatical since in many instances the child seems to control an intonational contour and to combine it productively with some phonologically expressed linguistic symbol. But it is in fact unknown the degree to which young children productively combine intonation and phonology, and indeed it is just as likely that in the beginning children use each linguistic symbol in the same way as adults (although in some cases the adult, and so the child, uses it in more than one way, e.g., both *Ball!* and *Ball?).

2 It could be argued that repeated tokens of *I'm sorry* represent an abstraction of a single utterance type, with the same reasoning also applying to the constant segment of formulae such as *Wanna* _____. However, I am focusing, as is common, on possible abstractions across utterance types, not tokens.

References

Akhtar, Nameera

1999 Acquiring basic word order: Evidence for data-driven learning of syntactic structure. *Journal of Child Language* 26: 339–356.

Akhtar, Nameera and Michael Tomasello

1999 Young children's productivity with word order and verb morphology. *Developmental Psychology* 33: 952–965.

Allen, Shanley

1996 *Aspects of Argument Structure Acquisition in Inuktitut.* Amsterdam/ Philadelphia: John Benjamins.

Barrett, Martin

1982 The holophrastic hypothesis: Conceptual and empirical issues. *Cognition* 11: 47–76.

Behrens, Heike

1988 Where does the information go? Paper presented at MPI workshop on argument structure, Nijmegen.

Berman, Ruth and S. Annon-Lotem

1995 How grammatical are early verbs? Paper presented at the *Colloque International de Besancon sur l'Acquisition de la Syntaxe.* November, Besancon, France.

Bloom, Lois

1973 *One Word at a Time.* The Hague: Mouton.

1992 *Language Development from Two to Three.* Cambridge: Cambridge University Press.

Bowerman, Melissa

1976 Semantic factors in the acquisition of rules for word use and sentence construction. In *Normal and Deficient Child Language,* D. Morehead and A. Morehead (eds.), Baltimore: University Park Press.

Braine, Martyn

1976 Children's first word combinations. Monographs of the Society for Research in Child Development 41(1).

Brooks, Patricia, Michael Tomasello, Lawrence Lewis, and Kelly Dodson

1999 Children's overgeneralization of fixed transitivity verbs: The entrenchment hypothesis. *Child Development* 70: 1325–1337. Brown, Roger *A First Language: The Early Stages.* Cambridge, MA: Harvard University Press.

Bruner, Jerome

1983 *Child's Talk.* New York: Norton.

Bybee, Joan

1985 *Morphology.* Amsterdam/Philadelphia: John Benjamins.

Regular morphology and the lexicon. *Language and Cognitive Processes* 10: 425–455.

Bybee, Joan and Joanne Scheibmann

1985   The effect of usage on degrees of constituency: The reduction of *don't* in English. *Linguistics* 37: 575–596.

Carpenter, Malinda, Nameera Akhtar, and Michael Tomasello

1998   14- through 18-month-old infants differentially imitate intentional and accidental actions. *Infant Behavior and Development* 21: 315–330.

Carpenter, Malinda, Katherine Nagell, and Michael Tomasello

1998   Social cognition, joint attention, and communicative competence from 9 to 15 months of age. Monographs of the Society for Research in Child Development 255.

Cheney, Dorothy and Robert Seyfarth

1990   *How Monkeys See the World.* University of Chicago Press.

Croft, William

2000   *Explaining Language Change: An Evolutionary Approach.* London: Longman.

Diessel, Holger and Michael Tomasello

in press Why complement clauses do not have a *that*-complementizer in early child language. *Proceedings of Berkeley Linguistic Society.*

Dryer, Mathew

1997   Are grammatical relations universal? In *Essays on Language Function and Language Type,* Joan Bybee, John Haiman and Sandra Thompson (eds.), 115–143. Amsterdam: John Benjamins.

Fillmore, Charles

1988   Toward a frame-based lexicon. In *Frames, Fields, and Contrast,* A. Lehrer and E. Kittay (eds.), 75–102. Hillsdale, NJ: Erlbaum. Fillmore, Charles, Paul Kaye, and Mary O'Connor

1988   Regularity and idiomaticity in grammatical constructions: The case of *let alone. Language* 64: 501–538.

Gathercole, Virginia, Eugenia Sebastian, and Pilar Soto

1999   The early acquisition of Spanish verbal morphology: Across-the-board or piecemeal knowledge? *International Journal of Bilingualism* 3: 133–182.

Gentner, Dedre, and Arthur Markman

1997   Structure mapping in analogy and similarity. *American Psychologist* 52:

45–56.

Goldberg, Adele

1995 *Constructions: A Construction Grammar Approach to Argument Structure.* University of Chicago Press.

Greenfield, Patricia and Joshua Smith

1986 *Structure of Communication m Early Language Development.* New York: Academic Press.

Haith, Marshall and Janet Benson

1997 Infant cognition. In *Handbook of Child Psychology*, vol. 2, D. Kuhn, D. and R. Siegler (eds.) New York: Wiley.

Kay, Paul and Charles Fillmore

1999 Grammatical constructions and linguistic generalizations. *Language* 75: 1–33.

Krug, Manfred

1998 String frequency: A cognitive motivating factor in coalescence, language processing, and language change. *Journal of English Linguistics* 26: 286–320.

Langacker, Ronald W.

1987 *Foundations of Cognitive Grammar*, vol. 1. Stanford University Press.

1988 A usage-based model. In *Topics in Cognitive Linguistics*, B. Rudzka-Ostyn (ed.), 127–161. Amsterdam: John Benjamins.

2000 A dynamic usage-based model. In *Usage-Based Models of Language,* M. Barlow and S. Kemmer (eds.). Stanford: SLI Publications.

Lieven, Elena, Julian Pine, and Helen Dresner Barnes

1992 Individual differences in early vocabulary development. *Journal of Child Language* 19: 287–310.

Lieven, Elena, Julian Pine, and Gillian Baldwin

1997 Lexically-based learning and early grammatical development. *Journal of Child Language* 24: 187–220.

Mandler, Jean

1997 Representation. In *Cognition, Perception, and Language,* vol. 2: *Handbook of Child Psychology,* D. Kuhn, D. and R. Siegler (eds.). New York: Wiley.

Maratsos, Michael, Ronald Gudeman, Patricia Gerard-Ngo, and Ganie DeHart

1987 A study in novel word learning: The productivity of the causative. In *Mechanisms of Language Acquisition,* B. Mac Whinney (ed.). Hillsdale, NJ:

Erlbaum.

Marchman, Virginia and Elizabeth Bates

    1994   Continuity in lexical and morphological development: A test of the critical mass hypothesis. *Journal of Child Language* 21: 339–366.

Meltzoff, Andrew

    1995   Understanding the intentions of others: Re-enactment of intended acts by 18-month-old children. *Developmental Psychology* 31: 838–850.

Michaelis, Laura and Knud Lambrecht

    1996   Toward a construction-based theory of language function: The case of nominal extraposition. *Language* 72: 215–247.

Pine, Julian, and Elena Lieven

    1997   Slot and frame patterns in the development of the determiner category. *Applied Psycholinguistics* 18: 123–138.

Pine, Julian, Elena Lieven, and Carolyn Rowland

    1998   Comparing different models of the development of the English verb category. *Linguistics* 36: 4–40.

Pinker, Steven

    1989   *Learnability and Cognition: The Acquisition of Verb-Argument Structure.* Cambridge MA: Harvard University Press.

Pinker, Steven, David Lebeaux, and Laura Frost

    1987   Productivity and constraints in the acquisition of the passive. *Cognition* 26:195–267.

Pizutto, Elena and Christina Caselli

    1992   The acquisition of Italian morphology. *Journal of Child Language* 19: 491–557.

    1994   The acquisition of Italian verb morphology in a cross-linguistic perspective. In *Other Children, Other Languages,* Y. Levy (ed.). Hillsdale, NJ: Erlbaum.

Quine, Willard

    1960   *Word and Object.* Cambridge, MA: MIT Press.

Rice, Mabel (ed.)

    1998   *Toward a Genetics of Language.* Mahwah, NJ: Erlbaum.

Rubino, Rafael and Julian Pine

    1998   Subject-verb agreement in Brazilian Portugese: What low error rates hide. *Journal of Child Language* 25: 35–60.

Serrat, Elissabet

1997 Acquisition of verb category in Catalan. Unpublished dissertation.

Sigman, Marian and Lisa Capps

1997 *Children with Autism: A Developmental Perspective.* Cambridge: Harvard University Press.

Stoll, Sabine

1998 The acquisition of Russian aspect. *First Language* 18: 351–378.

Talmy, Leonard

1996 The windowing of attention in language. In *Grammatical Constructions: Their Form and Meaning,* M. Shibatani and S. Thompson (eds.). Oxford: Oxford University Press.

Tomasello, Michael

1992 *First Verbs: A Case Study of Early Grammatical Development.* Cambridge University Press.

1998a Reference: Intending that others jointly attend. *Pragmatics and Cognition* 6: 219–234.

1998b The return of constructions. *Journal of Child Language* 75: 431–447.

1999 *The Cultural Origins of Human Cognition.* Cambridge, MA: Harvard University Press.

2000 Do young children have adult syntactic competence? *Cognition* 74: 209–253.

in press Perceiving intentions and learning words in the second year of life. In *Language Acquisition and Conceptual Development,* Melissa Bowerman and Steven Levinson (eds.). Cambridge University Press.

Tomasello, Michael, Nameera Akhtar, Kelly Dodson, and Laura Rekau

1997 Differential productivity in young children's use of nouns and verbs. *Journal of Child Language* 24: 373–387.

Tomasello, Michael and Patricia Brooks

1998 Young children's earliest transitive and intransitive constructions. *Cognitive Linguistics* 9: 379–395.

1999 Early syntactic development: A Construction Grammar approach. In *The Development of Language,* M. Barrett (ed.). Psychology Press.

Tomasello, Michael and Josep Call

1997 *Primate Cognition.* Oxford University Press.

Tomasello, Michael and Luigia Camaioni

1997   A comparison of the gestural communication of apes and human infants. *Human Development* 40: 7–24.

Tomasello, Michael, Ann Kruger, and Hiliary Ratner

1993   Cultural learning. *Behavioral and Brain Sciences* 16: 495–552.

Tomasello, Michael, Elena Lieven, Heike Behrens, and Heike Forwergk

to appear Early syntactic creativity: A usage based approach. Submitted for publication.

Wittgenstein, Ludwig

1953   *Philosophical Investigations.* New York: MacMillan.

Wray, Alison and Michael Perkins

2000   The functions of formulaic language: An integrated model. *Language and Communication* 20: 1–28.

外教社学术阅读文库 | 语义学经典论文选读